Augsburger Rechtsstudien

Herausgegeben im Auftrag der
Juristischen Fakultät der Universität Augsburg von

Professor Dr. Arnd Koch
Professor Dr. Thomas M.J. Möllers
Professor Dr. Matthias Rossi

Band 89

Charl Hugo | Thomas M. J. Möllers (eds.)

Legal Certainty and Fundamental Rights

A Cross-Disciplinary Approach to Constitutional Principles in German and South African Law

Nomos

JUTA

Onlineversion
Nomos eLibrary

The Deutsche Nationalbibliothek lists this publication in the Deutsche Nationalbibliografie; detailed bibliographic data are available on the Internet at http://dnb.d-nb.de

ISBN: HB (Nomos) 978-3-8487-6521-8
ePDF (Nomos) 978-3-7489-0606-3

British Library Cataloguing-in-Publication Data
A catalogue record for this book is available from the British Library.

ISBN: HB (Juta) 978-1-4851-3775-7

Library of Congress Cataloging-in-Publication Data
Hugo, Charl / Möllers, Thomas M. J.
Legal Certainty and Fundamental Rights
A Cross-Disciplinary Approach to Constitutional Principles in German and South African Law
Charl Hugo / Thomas M. J. Möllers (eds.)
442 pp.
Includes bibliographic references.

ISBN 978-1-4851-3775-7 (hardcover Juta)

1st Edition 2020

Preface

Collaboration and academic friendship between colleagues of the law faculties of the University of Johannesburg and the University of Augsburg, which now spans almost two decades, forms the personal background to this publication, *Legal Certainty and Fundamental Rights: A Cross-Disciplinary Approach to Constitutional Principles in German and South African Law*. It is the third book that has arisen from this context, the first two being *Transnational Impacts on Law: Perspectives from South Africa and Germany (2017)*, and *Legality and Limitation of Powers: Values, Principles and Regulations in Civil Law, Criminal Law and Public Law (2019)*.

The present volume comprises the results of our research meeting, which took place from the 6th to the 9th of June 2019 on the island *Frauenchiemsee*. Surrounded by the impressive backdrop of the "Bavarian Sea" (as Lake Chiemsee is also known) and the Chiemgau Alps, the participating researchers had the opportunity to examine current issues in various fields of law in a comparative legal setting with regard to the basic theme of "legal certainty and fundamental rights".

The book shares two characteristics with the previous volumes referred to above. In the first place, the editors have strived successfully to encourage younger researchers to participate in the project, either alone, or by involving a more experienced colleague. We have done so in the belief that this way of working contributes to the building of both research capacity and research networks – and is a valuable investment in the future. Secondly, the book is again jointly published by *Nomos* in Germany and *Juta* in South Africa.

Legal Certainty and Fundamental Rights takes the form of contributions by South African authors, with responses by their German counterparts. To meet the requirements of the Department of Higher Education in South Africa for governmental subsidisation of research, all the South African contributions to the book were subjected to a double-blind peer review. The papers together with the comments of the peer reviewers were returned to the authors who improved their contributions by taking into account the comments of the peer reviewers.

The financing of the research meeting, and its organisation and realisation was generously and competently provided by the *Augsburg Center for Global Economic Law and Regulation (ACELR)*. Amongst its staff we would like to single out the academic assistants *Michael Biesinger*, *Tristan*

Eickholt and *Tobias Wolf*, for their tireless efforts. We would also like to acknowledge with appreciation the fact that the University of Johannesburg and the University of Augsburg funded the travelling expenses of the participants.

A special word of thanks is also due to the *Frauenwörth Abbey*, that kindly made its conference facilities available to us for our research meeting.

Freely adapted from the words of the former German national football coach, *Sepp Herberger*, "after the conference is before the conference". In this sense we are looking forward to further deepening our cooperation in the coming years through further research visits and meetings, and collaborative publications. In the meantime, we wish you, dear reader, a pleasant reading of this volume.

The editors

Thomas M.J. Möllers (Augsburg)
Charl Hugo (Johannesburg)

August 2020

Content

Introduction

I

As emerges from our preface above, this is the third volume arising from research collaboration between the law faculties of the University of Johannesburg and the Universität Augsburg. More on this, what we would term "proud", history is related in the introductions to the previous two volumes, and we leave it there, except for reflecting briefly on the final paragraph of our first joint publication, *Transnational Impacts on Law: Perspectives from South Africa and Germany (2017),* in which we expressed the hope that "we will one day be able to look back on a series". Now, in the third publication arising from our collaboration, and with the fourth already being conceptualised, it is perhaps not inappropriate to celebrate the existence of our *Augsburger-Johannesburger-Schriftenreihe,* a *Reihe* which not only provides the opportunity for collaboration between established legal scholars from South Africa and Germany, but also actively encourages the participation of younger researchers.

II

Commenting on one of the South African contributions *Aqilah Sandhu,* one such younger researcher, refers to the "lively tension" identified by the legal philosopher, *Gustav Radbruch,* between justice and legal certainty stating as follows (p. 137 et seq., footnotes omitted):

> "He [*Radbruch*] stated … that 'legal certainty is not the only value that law must effectuate, nor is it the decisive value. Alongside legal certainty, there are two other values: purposiveness [the German *Zweckmäßigkeit*] and justice'. He suggested resolving the conflict between justice and legal certainty using the famous formula that came to be known as the '*Radbruch* formula': 'The positive law, secured by legislation and power, takes precedence even when its content is unjust and fails to benefit people, unless the conflict between statute and justice reaches such an intolerable degree that the statute, as "flawed law", must yield to justice.' A law, that does not even attempt to serve justice, that deliberately betrays 'equality, the core value of justice' is,

> according to *Radbruch*, 'not merely "flawed law", it lacks completely the very nature of law' (i.e. 'statutory *Unrecht*')."

In constitutional states such as Germany and South Africa, this statement must of course be filtered by fundamental rights. Law violating fundamental human rights is, in principle, intolerable. This, perhaps, is the closest one can get to a general proposition running through the wide ranging and multi-disciplinary contributions contained in this book. Legal certainty is important, but fundamental rights and justice cannot be sacrificed on the altar of legal certainty.

III

The first contribution emerges from the highly publicised phenomenon of state capture in South Africa. *Hennie Strydom* and *Martha Bradley* paint a dismal picture of the future in their contribution "The Rise of the Neo-Patrimonial State in South Africa: From the Rule of Law to the Rule of Persons" (p. 19 et seq.). They relate how, especially the Zuma administration, established patrimonial networks in key state-owned enterprises and governmental institutions for personal gain in South Africa, which are largely still intact and unaccountable. Chillingly, in conclusion, they identify factors that may render efforts at dismantling this neo-patrimonial state ineffective. This has amounted to a shift from the rule of law to the rule of persons characterised, as *Stefan Lorenzmeier* puts it in his response (p. 43 et seq.), "by the co-existence and interaction between the formal, rule-based institutions of a modern state and the informal practices of governance encountered in patrimonial forms of authority" (p. 43). Since this type of shift from impersonal to personal power is not for the moment discernible in Germany or the EU, Lorenzmeier's response focuses more generally on the rule of law in Germany and the EU. A "stark contrast" emerges regarding "the way in which the rule of law is dealt with in the different legal systems" (p. 49) – a contrast that lies not so much in relation to legal rules than their application. Readers are confronted by the harsh reality that justice and fundamental rights may be threatened not only by over-emphasising legal certainty, but also by persons in power circumventing the rule of law for personal gain.

The next three contributions have an international-law focus. In the first of these, "Legal Certainty in terms of Head of State Immunity: The Article 27(2) Conundrum" (p. 53 et seq.), *Roxan Venter* and *Martha Bradley* plead the case for legal certainty regarding the accountability, before the International Criminal Court, of heads of state who have committed international crimes. The *factual background* of their contribution is the failure of Jordan to arrest President Al-Bashir when he visited the Hashemite Kingdom in 2017 and the ensuing proceedings before the International Criminal Court. The disregard of arrest warrants issued against Al-Bashir by member states to the Rome Statute, including by South Africa,[1] has strengthened the call for legal certainty in this regard. The *legal background* is what *Thilo Rensmann*, who responded to their contribution (p. 85 et seq.), terms the "Babelesque confusion regarding the proper foundations and limits of head of state immunity before international criminal tribunals" (p. 88). In this respect Venter and Bradley argue for the horizontal application of Article 27(2) of the Rome Statute, a view subsequently endorsed by the Appeals Chamber of the ICC in the Jordan matter on 6 May 2019. However, the hope of the authors that this decision would bring certainty to the interpretation of the treaty was dashed by the insistence of the Appeals Chamber to base its decision on customary international law, without evidence of either usus or opinio juris – the basic tenets of customary international law (an issue that is also explored by Roux and Hassen in their contribution discussed immediately below). Rensmann points out that this approach by the Appeals Chamber attracted much uncomfortable scholarly criticism of the ICC – criticism to which the Venter/Bradley/ Rensmann cluster in this book now contributes meaningfully.

The focus remains on legal certainty and international crimes in the next contribution (p. 103 et seq.). Pointing to the fact that international tribunals have the difficult task of "maintaining a balance between the preservation of justice and fairness towards the accused and taking into account the preservation of world order" (p. 130, footnote omitted) *Mispa Roux* and *Sabreen Hassen* examine core international crimes recognised in the Rome Statute and the Malabo Protocol with reference to the nulla poena and nullum crimen principles, as well as the basic requirements of customary international law – usus and opinio juris. In her comment on this contribution (p. 135 et seq.) *Aqilah Sandhu* explores the tension between legal certainty and fundamental rights (or legal certainty and the retroactive punishment of international crimes), the nulla poena and nulla

1 On South Africa's own shameful failure to arrest Al-Bashir when he visited the country in 2015, see *Hennie Strydom*, "Treaty-making and select foreign policy matters under constitutional and judicial scrutiny in South Africa" in Charl Hugo & Thomas M.J. Möllers (eds.), Transnational Impacts on Law: Perspectives from South Africa and Germany, (Nomos and Juta, 2017), (the first book in the Augsburger-Johannesburger-Schriftenreihe).

crimen principles in the European legal order, and, finally, the impact of supranational human rights bodies on domestic criminal law.

This domestic focus of Sandhu's comment focuses on the German twin-track system of sanctions which differentiates between penalties or punishments ("*Strafen*") and measures of correction and prevention ("*Maßregeln der Besserung und Sicherung*"). Although not the primary objective of her comments, they tie in neatly with another contribution in the book, namely that of *Murdoch Watney*, "Preventive Justice and the Dangerous Offender: Seeking Solutions to Protect Society" (p. 189 et seq.). Watney scrutinizes preventive justice measures internationally with reference to the law of England and Wales, Canada and Germany stressing the important call that such measures must be subject to universally accepted fundamental human rights.

Mispa Roux is also the author of the final international-law contribution, "The Significance of the *Erga Omnes* Obligation to Prosecute Genocide for Legal Certainty in International Criminal Law" (p. 157 et seq.). She makes the point that the domestication of international criminal law is important but that the erga omnes nature of gross human rights violations, such as genocide, may never be disregarded. The contribution shows the way in which the international community can comply with the erga omnes obligation to prosecute genocide and thereby ensure legal certainty in international criminal law.

The next contribution investigates fundamental rights and legal certainty in a very different context – the use of cannabis. As explained by *Kgomotso Mokoena* in her contribution, "The Legislative Possibilities and Challenges Relating to the Private Possession and Use of Cannabis in South Africa" (p. 221 et seq.), the possession, use and cultivation of cannabis for private purposes has recently been decriminalised by the constitutional court in South Africa. The court took the view that the prohibition constituted an unjustifiable limitation of the fundamental right to privacy. While supporting the judgment in principle she makes the point that it has raised a number of unanswered questions, and, specifically, the implications of privacy in this context. The impact of the judgment on the rights of employers to discipline employees as a result of positive drug tests of employees is a particular focus of her contribution. *Johannes Kaspar*, in his response (p. 239 et seq.), points out that in Germany it is not the use of, but the possession of and dealing in, cannabis that is criminalised (the purpose being the protection of society). Hence, the right to privacy does not feature. Exemption from criminal liability in Germany for small quantities arises on a procedural level, but, since the concept of "small quantity" is not defined, it has led to marked differences from state to state, which is problematic in the context of the constitutional principle of equality. This leads him to the conclusion that further steps towards decriminalisation should be considered in Germany.

The focus moves to environmental law in the contribution of *Jenny Hall*, "Sustainable Development, Bureaucratic Implementation and the Need for Jurisprudential Certainty" (p. 257 et seq.). She argues that whilst sustainable development is the dominant approach to address environmental problems, environmental legislation does not provide, and is unlikely ever to be capable of providing, a level of detailed guidance on how it should be applied in the context of a particular decision with its own particular set of facts – i.e. on how to balance the three different facets of sustainable development, the social, economic and environmental. Against this background she explores the important potential role of South African courts to guide decision-making by the multitude of officials involved in environmental decisions and identifies some strengths and shortcomings in this regard. In response *Matthias Rossi* (p. 289 et seq.), deals with the statutory development of sustainable development in German and European environmental law, after expressing scepticism as to whether a clear line can be achieved in case law, since each case is based on its own factual circumstances and the decision is influenced by the submissions made by the parties. In his view, therefore, one should not expect to derive "abstract-general-legal principles from court rulings that might, beyond the concrete dispute, even clarify or avoid all other future issues of dispute" (p. 290). In his conclusion, co-titled "disillusion", Rossi cautions against overstating the value of the concept and warns against it being used as a "meta-argument that prevents the discussion of the concrete factual arguments" (p. 298).

The next cluster deals with fundamental rights in the context of labour law. The fundamental rights of vulnerable workers in the informal economy are considered by *Elmarie Fourie* and *Marius van Staden* in their contribution, "Labour Law, Vulnerable Workers and the Human Rights Paradigm" (p. 301 et seq.). They explore the role of judicial interpretation of statutes to extend key human rights to vulnerable workers (such as informal street vendors) – with specific emphasis on the fundamental right to human dignity. Their arguments lead to the conclusion that laudable developments in labour law have been achieved not only by "traditional labour law instruments", but also by "other legal regimes" (p. 330); hence they call for an interdisciplinary approach which will lead to labour law not functioning in isolation but in conjunction with administrative law, social security law, corporate law, family law and human rights. *Martina Benecke*, in turn (p. 335 et seq.), focuses on the right against discrimination. Her discussion centres on the *Allgemeines Gleichbehandlungsgesetz (AGG)* which had implemented the European Directives against discrimination, the prosecution of discrimination and the available sanctions, the potential claimants and defendants in discrimination cases, the prohibited grounds of discrimination and their significance, legal institutions against discrimination, and the abuse of anti-discrimination laws.

In the penultimate contribution, "Equality, Legal Certainty and Insolvency" (p. 353 et seq.), *Kathleen van der Linde* and *Juanitta Calitz* investigate whether there is a link between the fundamental or constitutional right to equality and the equal treatment of creditors in insolvency law. Their argument leads them to the conclusion that any correlation in this respect is superficial; the paritas creditorum principle, even in its eroded form pertaining only to concurrent creditors, represents formal equality as opposed to the substantive or transformative equality guaranteed by the constitution. They put forward the point, however, that it may be possible through judicial development of the common law or by legislative intervention, to design a set of general rules to counter the disparate effect of insolvency on vulnerable creditors. In his response (p. 383 et seq.) *Michael Kort* points out that there is no general principle in German civil or commercial law that debtors must treat their creditors equally, and that even in insolvency law the principle of equal treatment of creditors is not adhered to strictly. Creditors are instead divided into groups, some of which are privileged over others, and equal treatment of creditors applies only within a group. He considers various specific issues relating to the winding-up process of a German company, including some legal policy considerations, and concludes in summary that liquidators must focus solely on the purpose of the winding up, and not on any additional requirement of treating creditors equally.

The final contribution deals with the regulation of financial institutions in South Africa. The background is the decision to move from the silo model (in terms of which different types of financial institutions are regulated in all respects by different regulators) to the twin peaks model which differentiates between prudential and market conduct regulation. The Prudential Authority now has the responsibility for the prudential regulation of all financial institutions, and the Financial Sector Conduct Authority the responsibility for the market conduct of all financial institutions. This development is described by *Daleen Millard* and *Choene Jacqueline Maholo* in their contribution, "Market Conduct Regulation in Perspective: Triumphs and Tribulations post Twin Peaks" (p. 393 et seq.). As is evident from the title the focus is on the proposed market conduct regulation as envisaged by the Conduct of Financial Institutions Bill (the legislation governing this aspect of the Twin Peaks model not yet having been implemented). They identify positive aspects but also warn that this new dispensation is likely to bring about an expensive bureaucracy that may not be conducive to promote the important cause of financial inclusion in South Africa. In response (p. 423 et seq.) *Thomas M.J. Möllers* shows that Germany also has such a two-tier system. Nevertheless, the Wirecard balance sheet scandal in the summer of 2020 demonstrates loopholes in the law governing the capital market. The German Federal Financial Supervisory Authority (BaFin) only works in public interest; cases involving potential criminal offences are handed over to the local public prosecutor's offices which may have little expertise in this particular field. In addition, there is no corporate criminal liability in Germany. De lege ferenda, it would be preferable to give jurisdiction over such cases to an Attorney General's Office. Alternatively, the BaFin should be given the power to impose regulatory sanctions on corporations rather than handing over the cases to the public prosecutor's office. On the European level, Möllers pleads for a significant expansion of the European Securities and Markets Authority's (ESMA) power.

IV

In paragraph II, we identified the golden thread binding together the wide-ranging and diverse contributions described above. We conclude by revisiting one *observation* and one *image*. The observation comes from the Fourie/Van Staden paper in which the authors plead that labour law should not be functioning (or studied) in isolation but in conjunction with administrative law, social security law, corporate law, family law and human rights. We believe that both sides of this sentence can be extended. This observation should not be restricted to labour law, and the list of conjuncts should similarly be extended. Different fields of law enrich one another, and good legal scholars need to venture out of their comfort zones to become great legal scholars.

The observation, however, must be extended further, as has been done in all clusters of this book, to include not only different aspects of the law of a particular jurisdiction, but also the law of other jurisdictions. Different jurisdictions can enrich one another. We believe this to be true also for Germany and South Africa.

This brings us to the image – the silo referred to in the Millard/Maholo paper. The point we wish to underscore with this image is essentially the same: law is not to be sought in silos – neither in silos representing specific fields of law, nor in silos representing a specific jurisdiction.

We trust that *Legal Certainty and Fundamental Rights: A Cross-Disciplinary Approach to Constitutional Principles in German and South African Law* will assist all who read it to appreciate these fundamental truths.

Charl Hugo
Thomas M.J. Möllers

August 2020

The Rise of the Neo-Patrimonial State in South Africa: From the Rule of Law to the Rule of Persons

Hennie Strydom[*] / *Martha M. Bradley*[**]

Abstract: This chapter deals with the state capture phenomenon in South Africa after 1994 which has enabled members of the ruling elite, and their families and business partners, to gain control over key government institutions for personal gain as part of a well-orchestrated strategy which became public knowledge through various publications only in the latter half of former President Jacob Zuma's ignominious reign which ended in 2018, leaving the patrimonial networks established before and during his reign still largely intact and unaccountable by the end of 2019. The chapter commences with situating these developments within the broader context of the neo-patrimonial state in Africa which epitomises the co-existence of a rule-based bureaucratic order within a constitutional state and one that is based on client-patron relationships facilitating the rule by persons as opposed to the rule by law. The chapter then juxtaposes this phenomenon with the values and principles of the post-1994 constitutional disposition and concludes with the factors that may render efforts at dismantling the neo-patrimonial state ineffective.

* Hennie Strydom, *B. Iuris, LL.B., LL.M. (University of the Free State), LL.D. (UNISA)*, Professor of International Law, Incumbent South African Research Chair for International Law, University of Johannesburg.

** Martha M. Bradley, *LL.B., LL.M., LL.D. (University of Pretoria), LL.M. (University of Cape Town)*, Research Associate, South African Research Chair in International Law, University of Johannesburg. The work is based on research supported by the National Research Foundation of South Africa (Grant Number 85104).

I. Introduction

With the adoption of the new constitutional dispensation after 1994, South Africa has radically moved away from the Westminster concept of government and its underlying constitutional law principles. The new edifice on which the post-apartheid South African Republic was to be built was inspired by post-World War II constitutionalism that claimed explicit adherence to governance under the rule of law, human rights guarantees, judicial powers of review, and accountable government. The way in which these foundational principles were entrenched in the 1996 Constitution provided a solid foundation for rule-based and responsible governance, strengthened in the course of time by a corpus of jurisprudence that won acclaim from many parts of the world.

Some 25 years later this edifice has been undermined by a rotten and corrupt political culture within the ruling party to the extent that governance in several key areas has become dysfunctional.[1] In this sense, and contrary to popular belief, South Africa has followed the same pattern for which post-colonial states in Africa have become so notorious.[2] Twenty years into democracy the newly-formed, decolonised states, with all the formal trappings of modern statehood, started to unravel. It is unlikely that South Africa will implode in the same way as many other African countries have done, but there are common political factors that explain the current crisis in South Africa which has become synonymous with the phenomenon of state capture[3] and a plethora of other corrupt activities for personal gain by key figures in the ruling party, their families and business associates. This has been extensively covered in the Public Protector's 2016 report on state capture[4] and in numerous other reports and publications over the last few years.[5] Further evidence is currently emerging in testimony before the Zondo Commission of Inquiry into allegations of state capture.[6]

---

1 See also *Adetiba* and *Asuelime*, Journal of African Foreign Affairs 2018, 107.

2 See also *Gumede*, Politikon 2017 vol 44, no 1, 27.

3 In general, on the origin and definition of state capture, see *Dassah*, Journal of Transdisciplinary Research in Southern Africa 2018, 1.

4 Available at http://saflii.org/images/329756472-State-of-Capture.pdf (last visited 28 Nov 2019).

5 See n. 53 below.

6 Available at https://www.sastatecapture.org.za (last visited 28 Nov 2019). See also *Adetiba* and *Asuelime* (n. 1), 120, 121.

The scope and depth of the malfeasance that has culminated under the administration of former President Jacob Zuma, who survived several impeachment attempts, point to the implementation over time of a well-planned strategy to gain control over key organs of state and government institutions that facilitated the looting of state assets on a grand scale and protected the President and his accomplices.[7] Involved in this network were key figures in state security, the revenue service, the police, the prosecuting authority and some in several state-owned enterprises, in particular Eskom, the national electricity provider.

However, what should be emphasised is the fact that several of the factors instrumental in making it possible for this shadow state of fraud and corruption to emerge were already in place prior to the ascendancy of the Zuma kleptocracy.[8] These factors point to the pervasive influence of the neo-patrimonial state in African politics and governance on which volumes of literature exists.[9] We aim to address in this chapter this phenomenon and its implications for the rule of law and human rights guarantees.

The chapter is structured as follows: Part II explains what is meant by a neo-patrimonial state and how it relates to the rule-based constitutional state; Part III provides a brief account of the main ingredients of the South African constitutional dispensation to ensure accountable government, with the aim of making clear the contrast between this historical moment and the rise of the neo-patrimonial state in South Africa, which is the subject of Part IV. Part V contains the conclusions.

7 See *Pauw*, The President's Keepers (2017). This book played a seminal role in publicising the extent of corruption and state capture during the Zuma presidency.

8 Between 1994 and 2008, R185 billion left South Africa in the form of illegal outflows alone as a result of corruption. In 2011, three years after Zuma's ascendancy to the Presidency, Willie Hofmeyer, the then head of the Special Investigation Unit informed Parliament that annually between R25 billion and R30 billion of the government's procurement budget alone was lost as a result of corruption, incompetence and negligence. See https://www.corruptionwatch.org.za/whats-the-real-cost-of-corruption-part-one/, (last visited 20 June 2020).

9 See inter alia the bibliographical information in *Eisenstadt* and *Lemarchand* (eds.), Political Clientalism, Patronage and Development (1981), 297 et seqq; *Gumede* (n. 2).

II. Key features of a neo-patrimonial state

Patrimonialism is a form of political rule in which the elite rules through personal and arbitrary control over a bureaucracy. According to the German sociologist, Max Weber, the ruler in a patrimonial system extends personal graces and favours at the expense of traditional limitations on the exercise of authority. In such systems of authority, the rational-legal state and bureaucracy characterised by impersonal rule are absent.[10] Consequently, in systems of patrimonial rule obedience is owed to the person who occupies the position of authority instead of to the enacted rules.

Neo-patrimonialism, on the other hand, is a concept that dates back to African studies undertaken in the 1970s and revived in the 1990s after a decline in the 1980s, to explain the phenomenon of the post-colonial state in Africa, Asia, the Middle East and even in post-Communist Europe, which is characterised by the co-existence and interaction between the formal, rule-based institutions of a modern state and informal practices of governance of the type encountered in patrimonial forms of authority.[11] Even so, the literature on this phenomenon remains closely related to the writings of Max Weber (1864–1920), in particular his *Economy and Society* referred to earlier, and published post-humously in 1922.

Given the co-existence of customs and patterns of traditional patrimonialism with rational-legal institutions in certain political transitions, Erdmann and Engel[12] have proposed that neopatrimonialism

> "is a mixture of two, partly interwoven, types of domination that co-exist: namely, patrimonial and legal-rational bureaucratic domination. Under patrimonialism, all power relations between ruler and ruled, political as well as administrative relations, are personal relations; there is no differentiation between the private and the public realm. However, under neo-patrimonialism the distinction between the private and the public, at least formally, exists and is accepted, and public reference can be made to this distinction (it is a different matter whether this is observed or not). Neo-patrimonial rule takes place within the framework of, and with the claim to, legal-rational bureaucracy or modern 'stateness'. Formal structures and rules do

10 *Weber*, Economy and Society (1922).

11 *Erdmann*, in: Cheeseman, Anderson and Scheibler (eds.), Routledge Handbook of African Politics (2013), 61.

12 *Erdmann* and *Engel*, Neo-Patrimonialism Revisited – Beyond a Catch-All Concept, Working Paper No. 16, German Institute of Global and Area Studies (2006), 18.

> exist, although in practice, the separation of the private and the public sphere is not always observed. In other words, two systems exist next to each other, the patrimonial of the personal relations, and the legal-rational of the bureaucracy. Naturally these spheres are not isolated from each other; quite to the contrary, they permeate each other; or more precisely, the patrimonial penetrates the legal- rational system and twists its logic, functions, and effects. That is, informal politics invade formal institutions."

A similar understanding of neo-patrimonialism is put forward by Bratton and Van de Walle in one of their oft-quoted contributions. They also argue that while aspects of neo-patrimonial practices can be found in all political systems, it is a core feature of politics in Africa and in states such as Haiti, the Philippines and Indonesia.[13] A comparative analysis of this kind falls outside the scope of this contribution. Instead, our focus is on select salient aspects of neo-patrimonialism and the application of this concept to contemporary developments in South Africa in respect of the state capture phenomenon.

We begin by examining the salient aspects. First, it is not in dispute that practices of neo-patrimonialism are responsible for fiscal crises and stagnation in economic growth.[14] Maintaining, in such circumstances, networks of personal loyalty that grant undue favours to select persons and groups is likely to create discontent among those excluded from the spoils, which increases the risk of social and political unrest.[15] Second, the struggle over spoils often leads to fracturing, that is, the emergence of political factions whose positions are determined by whether they are insiders or outsiders in relation to the patronage system.[16] Third, neo-patrimonial systems are characterised by struggles over rules. Compare in this instance the many disputes in Africa over the application of constitutions (especially as regards the tenure of the President's office) and electoral laws

13 *Bratton* and *Van de Walle*, World Politics 1994, 453, 458, 459; see also *Erdmann* and *Engel* (n. 12), 9; *Tsheola*, African Journal of Public Affairs 2017, 1, 9: "Given the predominance of patrimonialism in post-colonial Africa, though, constructions of governance of the party-state-society interactionism could assume a deliberate preference for informality that serves distributive regimes and patronage on behalf of the elite and private commercial interests." See also *Duthie*, Africa Insight 2015, 104, 111.

14 *Sandbrook* with *Barker*, The Politics of Africa's Economic Stagnation (1985).

15 *Bratton* and *Van de Walle* (n. 13), 460.

16 Ibid., 463.

in times of contested elections.[17] Fourth, political power or office in a neo-patrimonial state, while formally a public matter, is often perceived as personal power with the result that the distinction between the public office and the incumbent is blurred.[18]

As Erdmann and Engel have pointed out, a political system that is neo-patrimonial in its make-up is characterised by insecurity concerning the behaviour and role of state institutions. This insecurity manifests itself in the fact that actions of state institutions or by government officials are not calculable – all actors strive to safeguard their personal interests and positions through the use or abuse of the formal and informal elements of the state; formal state institutions cannot fulfil their public calling and therefore struggle to instil confidence in their output legitimacy since politics and policies are determined by particularistic interests and orientations; and the affairs of the state are conducted under a separate political culture characterised by institutionalised informality.[19]

III. The South African version of the rational-legal state

The rule of law as a constitutional value has been developed through the case law of the Constitutional Court and is often used to counter the abuse of power by state organs.[20] De Vos and Freedman highlight the fact that the rule of law is a foundational concept in South African constitutional law and that "[i]ts prominence is evidenced by the manner in which the courts have invoked the rule of law as mechanism aimed to limit, regulate as well as give more precise meaning to how government power is exercised".[21] The Constitutional Court is the custodian of this value, relying on the rule of law to redress the abuse of power by state organs.[22] On a number of occasions the rule of law has been employed as a test of whether government action complies with this value.[23] For example, the

17 Ibid., 466.

18 *Erdmann* and *Engel* (n. 12), 18.

19 Ibid., 19.

20 *De Vos* and *Freedman* (eds.), South African Constitutional Law in Context (2014), 81.

21 Ibid.

22 Ibid., 81–84.

23 For a discussion of these occasions, see *De Vos* and *Freedman* (n. 20), 82–84 and *Rautenbach* and *Venter*, Rautenbach-Malherbe Constitutional Law (7th ed. 2018), 9–10.

legality of the actions of Ministers[24], the South African Police Service[25] and the President[26] have been tested against this value.

This part is not intended to give a comprehensive account of South Africa's post-1994 constitutional dispensation. For purposes of this chapter, a brief overview of its salient aspects will suffice. After all, the idea merely is to juxtapose the rational-legal state with its neo-patrimonial counterpart. We first highlight the main elements of the constitutional framework aimed at ensuring a law-based and accountable government and public administration, which we then supplement with select case-law citations.

The founding provisions of the Constitution make it clear that the Republic of South Africa is founded, inter alia, upon the supremacy of the Constitution and the rule of law.[27] Constitutionally this means that law or conduct inconsistent with the Constitution will be invalid, and that obligations imposed by the Constitution must be fulfilled.[28] The founding provisions further declare that the state will comprise a multi-party system of government to ensure accountability, responsiveness and openness.[29]

The Bill of Rights, in Chapter 2 of the Constitution, is the "cornerstone of democracy in South Africa" and the "state must respect, protect, promote, and fulfil the rights in the Bill of Rights",[30] which "applies to all

---

24 *Carmichele v Minister of Safety and Security* (CCT 48/00) [2001] ZACC 22, 2001 4 SA 938 (CC), 2001 10 BCLR 995 (CC) (16 Aug 2001); *Affordable Medicines Trust and Others v Minister of Health and Another* 2006 3 SA 247 (CC) (11 Mar 2005); *South African Diamond Producers Organisation v Minister of Minerals and Energy NO and Others* (CCT234/16) [2017] ZACC 26, 2017 10 BCLR 1303 (CC), 2017 6 SA 331 (CC) (24 Jul 2017).

25 *Carmichele* (n. 24); *National Commissioner of the South African Police Service v Southern African Human Rights Litigation Centre and Another* [2014] ZACC 30; *Glenister v President of the Republic of South Africa and Others* (CCT 41/08) [2008] ZACC 19, 2009 1 SA 287 (CC), 2009 2 BCLR 136 (CC) (22 Oct 2008).

26 *President of the Republic of South Africa and Others v South African Rugby Football Union and Others* (CCT16/98) [1999] ZACC 11, 2000 1 SA 1, 1999 10 BCLR 1059 (10 Sep 1999); *Pharmaceutical Manufacturers Association of South Africa, In Re Ex Parte President of the RSA* 2003 3 BCLR 241 (CC); *Kaunda and Others v President of the Republic of South Africa* (CCT 23/04) [2004] ZACC 5, 2005 4 SA 235 (CC), 2004 10 BCLR 1009 (CC) (4 Aug 2004); *President of the Republic of South Africa and Another v Modderklip Boerdery (Pty) Ltd* (CCT20/04) [2005] ZACC 5, 2005 5 SA 3 (CC), 2005 8 BCLR 786 (CC) (13 May 2005).

27 Constitution of the Republic of South Africa, 1996, Section 1(c).

28 Ibid., Section 2.

29 Ibid., Section 1(d).

30 Ibid., Sections 7(1) and (2).

law and binds the legislature, the executive, the judiciary and all organs of state".[31] Uniquely, the right to administrative action that is lawful, reasonable and procedurally fair is an integral part of the Bill of Rights[32] and has been given effect to by the Promotion of Administrative Justice Act No. 3 of 2000, which expands on the requirements for the legality, reasonableness and procedural fairness of government decisions, their reviewability by the courts and the remedies available to a person whose rights have been affected.

Turning to the legislative power (parliament), the following constitutional provisions are of relevance. First, when exercising its legislative function, parliament is bound only by the Constitution and must act in accordance with and within the limits of the Constitution;[33] second, prior to commencing their duties in parliament, members of the legislature must take an oath confirming their faithfulness to the Republic and obedience to the Constitution;[3] and, third, the legislature must maintain oversight of the exercise of the national executive authority to ensure that all executive organs are accountable to it.[34] By the same token, the Constitution ordains that members of the cabinet are individually and collectively accountable to parliament for the exercise of their functions,[35] must act in accordance with the Constitution[36] and must swear or affirm faithfulness to the Republic and obedience to the Constitution.[37]

As far as law enforcement is concerned, the Constitution instructs the prosecuting authority to exercise its functions without fear, favour or prejudice,[38] and the security services, which include the police service, are to act in accordance with the Constitution and the law[39] and not perform their functions in a manner that will, in a partisan manner, further any interest of a political party.[40]

Finally, the public administration is constitutionally governed by the democratic values and principles enshrined in the Constitution, which include, in more specific terms, a high standard of professional ethics; the

31 Ibid., Section 8(1).
32 Ibid., Section 33.
33 Ibid., Section 44(4).
34 Ibid., Section 55(2).
35 Ibid., Section 92(2).
36 Ibid., Section 92(3).
37 Ibid., Section 95.
38 Ibid., Section 179(4).
39 Ibid., Section 199(5).
40 Ibid., Section 199(7).

efficient, economic and effective use of resources; the provision of services in an impartial, fair, equitable and bias-free manner; and accountability and transparency.[41]

The above constitutional framework will now be further explicated with reference to select case law. Since the rule of law has assumed such an important foundational value in South African constitutional law, it must be pointed out that the principle of legality has become firmly entrenched as an incidence of the rule of law.[42] This is further confirmed in the following dictum of Ngcobo J in the *Affordable Medicines Trust* case:[43]

> "The exercise of public power must therefore comply with the Constitution, which is the supreme law, and the doctrine of legality, which is part of that law. The doctrine of legality, which is an incident of the rule of law, is one of the constitutional controls through which the exercise of public power is regulated by the Constitution ... In this sense the Constitution entrenches the principle of legality and provides the foundation for the control of public power."

The courts have on occasion also used the rule of law to find against arbitrary decision making by public officials and to call for the exercise of public powers in a rational manner, meaning that the power must be exercised for the purpose for which it was given.[44] Rationality has also been held as an entry-level requirement for any exercise of public power,[45] and when a decision is challenged on this ground courts are obliged to examine the means selected to determine whether they are rationally related to the objective provided for in law.[46]

Directly relevant for the subject matter of this contribution is the ruling of the Constitutional Court in *Glenister v President of the Republic of South Africa*,[47] arguably one of the most significant decisions on government accountability under the 1996 Constitution. The case involves a constitutional challenge to the disbandment, by legislative amendments,

41 Ibid., Section 195.

42 See, inter alia, *Fedsure Life Assurance Ltd and Others v Greater Johannesburg Transitional Metropolitan Council and Others* 1998 12 BCLR 1458; *Pharmaceutical Manufacturers Association of South Africa* (n. 26); *Democratic Alliance v President of South Africa and Others* 2012 12 BCLR 1297 (CC).

43 *Affordable Medicines Trust* (n. 24), para. 49.

44 *Lesapo v North West Agricultural Bank and Another* 2000 1 SA 409 (CC).

45 *Kaunda* (n. 26), paras. 79, 80.

46 *Albutt v Centre for the Study of Violence and Reconciliation* 2010 3 SA 293 (CC), para. 51.

47 2011 3 SA 347 (CC).

of the Directorate of Special Operations, an elite corruption-fighting unit located within the structure of the National Prosecuting Authority (NPA), known as the "Scorpions", and its replacement with the Directorate for Priority Crime Investigation located within the structure of the South African Police Service (SAPS), known as the "Hawks". This step was taken shortly after the notorious Polokwane conference of the African National Congress (ANC) in 2007, which led to the ousting of Thabo Mbeki as President of the ANC and, as a result, of the country, and his replacement by Jacob Zuma. Following a decision by the ANC at the conference for the dissolution of the Scorpions, Jacob Zuma signed this into law soon after his assumption of power as President of South Africa. While certain political actors among the ruling elite claimed that the use of the Scorpions by political factions to pursue selective investigations against rivals was the reason for their dissolution, it was also known that as an independent crime-fighting unit it was successful in the investigation and prosecution of high-profile politicians.[48] It is also public knowledge that some of these investigations involved prominent members of the ANC.

The constitutional challenge to the legislative amendment centered on the independence of the Hawks, that is, whether, as an integral part of the South African Police Service, it was sufficiently insulated from political influence in its structure and functioning. It must also be pointed out that when these developments took place, South Africa already was a signatory to the United Nations Convention Against Corruption (2003) which requires in its Article 6(2) that a state party must provide a body with the task of preventing corruption with the necessary independence to enable it to carry out its functions free from undue influence. It had also adopted implementation legislation in the form of the Prevention and Combating of Corrupt Activities Act No. 12 of 2004, which in its Preamble, assented to by parliament, lists the corrosive effects of corruption, namely: that it undermines the Bill of Rights and the values and institutions of democracy; endangers the stability and security of societies; jeopardises the rule of law and the credibility of government; and provides a breeding ground for organised crime.

In *Glenister* the majority (five to four) commenced their ruling on the constitutional validity of the impugned amendments by stating that corruption[49]

48 See *Cameron*, Duke Journal of Comparative and International Law 2013, 389, 391–393.

49 *Glenister* (n. 47), para. 166.

> "blatantly undermines the democratic ethos, the institutions of democracy, the rule of law and the foundational values of our nascent constitutional project. It fuels maladministration and public fraudulence and imperils the capacity of the state to fulfil its obligations to respect, protect, promote and fulfil all the rights enshrined in the Bill of Rights."

The Court then linked the obligation to establish an independent body to combat corruption and organised crime to the Constitution itself and in particular to Section 7(2) of the Bill of Rights, which, as indicated earlier, obliges the state to respect, protect, promote and fulfil the rights in the Bill of Rights.[50] The Court construed this provision as an obligation imposed on government which also implicitly requires that, in fulfilling this obligation, government is constitutionally required to create an anti-corruption entity with the necessary independence, since corruption is corrosive of the very rights the Bill of Rights sets out to protect.[51]

On the issue of independence, the majority compared the organisational and functional independence of the disbanded Scorpions with that of the Hawks and came to the conclusion that the Hawks were markedly less independent than the Scorpions and that the level of independence the Hawks enjoyed under the legislative amendments fell below the standard required by the Constitution. According to the Court, this manifested itself in the following: insecurity of tenure which undermines employment security for members serving in the Hawks; direct political oversight by the executive, which is incompatible with adequate independence; the absence of statutorily-secured remuneration; and the coordination of the Hawks' activities by a ministerial committee (as opposed to a multi-party parliamentary committee), which caused the exercise of functions to be subject to the policy guidelines of the committee.[52]

Barely five years after this judgment was handed down, instructing the government to take remedial action on the independence issue, the first reports on state capture and grant corruption (see the next part) entered the public domain. Among the many casualties were the Hawks and the NPA, rendered dysfunctional by political interference and manipulation. The lesson to be learned is that no matter how good a country's constitution is, its effectiveness as an instrument preventing the abuse of power will always be precarious if it is not also embedded in a broad-based

50 Ibid., paras. 194, 195.
51 Ibid., paras. 197, 200.
52 Ibid., paras. 210–248.

political culture that takes its values and principles seriously as normative imperatives for the exercise of governmental power.

IV. The South African version of the neo-patrimonial state

In this part we do not intend to deal with the extent and depth of corruption and the looting of state resources in the democratic era. This has been extensively covered in a range of publications over the last decade or more.[53] Instead, and given the constraints of time and space, we will focus on the main elements of the neo-patrimonial state in South Africa and the main drivers that facilitated this type of political rule to invade and undermine the basic principles and values of the democratic constitutional order explained in the previous part.

In one of his bi-annual reports for the *South African Monitor*, Matthee has alerted the South African public and foreign governments and investors of a new political and symbolic order under the presidency of Jacob Zuma that has replaced the liberal democratic constitutional order. This paradigm shift, Matthee argues, has created a hybrid regime in which the locus of politics has shifted from accountable democratic institutions to a political arena where weak democratic institutions and non-democratic institutions interact.[54] To compensate for a fragmented and weakened state authority and power, and inefficient service delivery by a growing number of dysfunctional institutions, the political order is re-shaped along the lines of a network of local deals and relationships dependent upon links and mutual obligations and patron-client relationships.

According to Croucamp and Malan, state capture in this sense constitutes a methodical regime preference, which, from a theoretical perspective, means that state capture is a "defined means of social order and con-

53 See for instance *Holden*, The Arms Deal in Your Pocket (2008); *Holden* and *Plaut*, Who Rules South Africa? (2012); *Holden* and *Van Vuuren*, The Devil in the Detail: How the Arms Deal Changed Everything (2011); *Boraine*, What's Gone Wrong? On the Brink of a Failed State (2014); *Olver*, How to Steal a City (2017); State Capacity Research Project, Betrayal of the Promise: How South Africa is being Stolen (2017); Organisation Undoing Tax Abuse, No Room to Hide: A President Caught in the Act (2017), https://cisp.cachefly.net/assets/articles/attachments/69697_2.-report.pdf (last visited 28 Nov 2019); *Pauw* (n. 7); *Myburgh*, Gangster State: Unravelling Ace Magashule's Web of Capture (2019); *Shaw,* in: Alum & Gilmour (eds.), Handbook of Organized Crime and Politics (2019), 321.

54 *Matthee*, South African Monitor, Political Turbulence and Business Risks in the ANC's Hybrid Regime, Report No. 7 (2016), 10.

trol".[55] Even so, the question remains whether legitimate organs of state are not deliberately kept dysfunctional to rationalise their replacement with a patron-client regime. As Matthee has argued, the new personalised political regime has also given a new meaning to rights and entitlements and what the South African state stands for in the sense that it is no longer seen as rooted first and foremost in responsible citizenship, impartial service delivery and loyalty to other citizens, but as a source of self-gratification and enrichment of the inner circle of patrons, their business associates, friends and families.[56] Even more to the point is the following assessment by Tsheola:[57]

> "the predominance of informality of governance is a virtual preference of the governing party because it consolidates a weak state through which the Public Service Sector, including Chapter 9 institutions, is undermined in favour of 'relational patronage'."

Drawing on the vast and well-developed literature on neo-patrimonialism, others have referred to the emergence under the Zuma presidency of the symbiotic relationship between the constitutional state and the shadow state. While the former refers to the formalised constitutional, legislative and jurisprudential framework of rules determining the conduct of government officials and the legality of their decisions, the latter refers to

> "the networks of relationships that cross-cut and bind together a specific group of people who need to act together for whatever reason in secretive ways so that they can either effectively hide, actively deny or consciously 'not know' that which contradicts their formal roles in the constitutional state."[58]

Writing on neo-patrimonial politics in the ANC, Lodge has identified the following indicators of neo-patrimonialism in the ruling party, among others:[59] First, while formal distinctions between the public and the private are widely recognised, in practice officials use their public powers for

---

55 *Croucamp* and *Malan*, African Journal of Public Affairs 2018, 86, 88.

56 Matthee (n. 54). For further confirmation of this trend, see also Organisation Undoing Tax Abuse (n. 53); *Matthee* (n. 50). See also *Haywood*, "Coup by the Connected and Corrupt", Mail & Guardian (31 Aug 2012); State Capacity Research Project (n. 53), 6.

57 *Tsheola* (n. 13), 20.

58 State Capacity Research Project (n. 53), 6.

59 *Lodge*, African Affairs 2014, 1, 2. See also *Masenya*, African Journal of Public Affairs 2017, 146.

personal gain; second, the rise of factionalism as a result of the emergence of internal rival groups formed on the basis of personal loyalty rather than a shared political ideology; third, the revival and appeal to an Africanist racial solidarity and nostalgic memories of a patriarchal social order, ostensibly for legitimation reasons, rather than on the quality of government performance; fourth, the acquisition of business interests by leading politicians and their families; and, fifth, the control exercised over local governments and their fiscal assets by informal networks aligned to the ANC. It is now also an indisputable fact that the majority of local governments under ANC control are failing or failed institutions with their capacity so eroded by corruption, maladministration and cadre deployment that no efficient service delivery can realistically be expected.[60]

Although the establishment by stealth of the patron-client political order is associated with the Zuma era, much deeper social forces and processes predating Zuma's accession to the presidency were instrumental in the sharp rise of the patrimonial order during his reign. For instance, Von Holdt[61] has pointed out that one defining moment of such social process in post-apartheid South Africa is the formation of a new, black, economically-powerful elite which was to come about through the policy of black economic empowerment,[62] employment equity, land redistribution and radical economic transformation. However, since the formal economic sectors were dominated by established business entities constricted by economic realities, competition, and an underperforming national economy, the state as a provider of employment, tenders and licensing became an obvious means in the formation of the new elite. However, greed and ur-

60 See https://www.polity.org.za/article/good-governance-africa-2019-government-performance-index-2019-04-29 (last visited 28 Nov 2019). See also Business Tech Report (last visited 18 Apr 2019), https://businesstech.co.za/news/government/312104/these-are-the-best-and-worst-runmunicipalities-in-south-africa/ (last visited 28 Nov 2019). See also *Masuku*, African Journal of Democracy and Governance 2019, 117; *Croucamp* and *Malan* (n. 55), 94, 95: "Informal networks of social control literally captured institutions and extractive regimes at the municipal level on the basis of justified systemic patronage, but not necessarily with the aim of serving the interests of the greater good. …The aim of cadre deployment is to consolidate the relational tissue of systemic patronage".

61 *Von Holdt*, The Political Economy of Corruption: Elite-Formation, Factions and Violence, Working Paper No. 10, Society, Work and Politics Institute (February 2019), 3.

62 See also *Tsheola* (n. 13), 19: "Hence, the logic of the Broad-based Black Economic Empowerment (BEE) is drawn from the liberationalist connections between the governing party and the state".

gency caused this objective to be pursued not by lawful means but, as Von Holdt explains, by an informal and pervasive political-economic system shaped by the intersection of patronage and factionalism in order to gain control over strategic positions and state resources.[63] It is this system "in which Zuma and his networks were able to locate themselves, and which also provided the basis for the emergence of the formal discourse of radical economic transformation within the ANC".[64] Moreover, by allowing loyal party barons to conduct their own operations by means of the informal political-economic system, while at the same time disobeying the laws and rules of the formal constitutional political system, the pace of the looting of state resources during the Zuma era was accelerated.[65]

In a joint submission to the Zondo Commission of Inquiry into State Capture by Corruption Watch and the Institute of Security Studies in April 2019[66] the two organisations highlighted the role played by the manipulation of the criminal justice system in facilitating the entrenchment of corruption and state capture at the highest levels of government by summarising their detailed submission as follows:[67]

> "Manipulation of criminal justice agencies by the Executive has been an endemic feature of the Zuma era, and has played an important role in enabling the state capture project. This is firstly because the viability of state capture in South Africa hinged on the control of the ANC by Jacob Zuma and his allies. Apart from explicitly protecting Zuma himself and his family from prosecution, the manipulation of criminal justice agencies has primarily functioned to secure control of the ANC for the 'Zuma-centred power elite'."

In a public lecture delivered on 25 July 2019,[68] the newly-appointed Director of Public Prosecutions, Advocate Shamila Batohi, has given an unsettling account of how the manipulation of the criminal justice system has eroded the state's law enforcement capability and rendered the prosecuting authority dysfunctional and seriously lacking in public trust.

---

63 *Von Holdt* (n. 61), 3.

64 Ibid., 9.

65 Ibid., 14.

66 Available at https://issafrica.s3.amazonaws.com/site/uploads/2019-06-20-other-zondocommission-submission.pdf (last visited 28 Nov 2019).

67 Ibid., 9.

68 Available at https://www.youtube.com/watch?v=A3B0SgZygwEid 9 (last visited 28 Nov 2019).

Some commentators have even submitted that the ruling party not only is subversive of the constitutional order but that it has all the hallmarks of a criminal enterprise.[69] At a broader level, the highly-respected international commentator on South African affairs, RW Johnson, has detailed what he calls the "culture of theft" that has become an intrinsic interest of the new functionaries of the state, the bureaucratic bourgeoisie, to "enrich themselves by all and every means", a phenomenon that applies to the whole of post-colonial independent African states.[70]

V. Conclusion

The remaining question is whether the ANC, as the ruling party, can dismantle the neo-patrimonial state, or, put differently, whether it has the political will to do so. Following the publication of the state capture and grand-scale looting of state assets perpetrated by Zuma and his allies within and outside the ANC, the party has publicly announced that it will embark on a process of rejuvenating the party and to return to its moral high ground. Undertakings of this kind are easily swallowed by the politically naive and largely uneducated electorate whose survival of whatever kind is intrinsically dependent on the largesse the party can dispense in exchange for loyalty and votes in election years. By contrast, a sober outlook suggests that the bureaucratic, rule-based, constitutional state and its patrimonial counterpart will continue to co-exist in a symbiotic relationship. Constitutional, ideological and socio-political reasons, briefly addressed below, make this unavoidable.

While the constitution entrenches the rule of law and the principle of legality as foundational to all government conduct, through its interpretation and application by legal scholars and the judiciary,[71] the constitution has also become the source of a racially-based redistributive regime enforced by a vast statutory and administrative regulatory framework in

69 *Hoffman*, "ANC of Today has All the Hallmarks of a Criminal Enterprise", Business Maverick (16 Jul 2019).

70 *Johnson*, How Long Will South Africa Survive? The Looming Crisis (2015), 105 et seqq.

71 See for instance *Klare*, South African Journal of Human Rights 1998, 146; *Moseneke*, South African Journal of Human Rights 2002, 309; *Helen Suzman Foundation v President of the Republic of South Africa* 2015 (1) BCLR 1 (CC). For a more comprehensive and iconoclastic account of this development and its supporting literature see *Malan*, There Is No Supreme Constitution (2019), ch. 7.

almost every sphere of economic activity. This formally paved the way for the patronage regime to systemically become integrated with the formal, legal-bureaucratic redistributive regime of the constitutional state. Beneficial for this process is the concurrence between the rational objective of the "master narrative" (the constitutional/legal regime) and the redistributive morality of the liberationist narrative of the incumbents of power. As a contending regime within the state, systemic patronage, according to Croucamp and Malan,[72] is not interested in managing the state[73] as an open democracy, but as an institution to be occupied and controlled. When this occurs as a compromise between economic elites and corrupt political elites, the relationships "are extremely hard to dismantle as it becomes a feature of the anatomy of governance".

Arguably the most dominant ideological factor is the obsession of the ANC with the national democratic revolution (NDR) as a political strategy for the re-making of the South African state with socialism as the end goal.[74] Based on a Soviet model for the advancement of developing countries towards socialism through incremental reforms, ANC thinking has remained ideologically consumed by the NDR, despite the fact that it followed the USSR into oblivion.[75]

Of interest for purposes of this chapter is that part of the NDR which sees the process of political and economic transformation as strategically dependent upon the ruling party, as the "vanguard of the NDR", taking control of all levers of powers in all organs of state, the economy, educa-

---

72 *Croucamp* and *Malan* (n. 55), 101, 102.

73 This also explains why building a capable state is not a priority for the ruling party, nor is it in its interest. Instead, building the party and ensuring unity within the party and among the tri-partite alliance, correlate more perfectly with the objective of controlling the redistributive machinery of the state.

74 On this see https://irr.org.za/reports/research-policy-brief/research-and-policy-brief-the-nationaldemocratic-revolution-ndr-its-origins-and-implications-31st-may-2012 (last visited 28 Nov 2019); ANC, The Second Transition: Building a National Democratic Society and the Balance of Forces in 2012, http://pmg-assets.s3-website-eu-west-1.amazonaws.com/docs/120306ancdoc.pdf (last visited 28 Nov 2019); Strategy and Tactics of the African National Congress, Discussion Document adopted at the 5th National Policy Conference (Jun/Jul 2017), https://www.sahistory.org.za/sites/default/files/file%20uploads%20/national_policy_conference_2017_stratey_and_tactics.pdf (last visited 28 Nov 2019). For an historical account of the development of the ANC's National Democratic Revolution and its Marxist-Leninist origins and links with the North Vietnamese Viet Cong and its strategies for the revolutionary war against the South, see *Jeffrey*, People's War: New Light on the Struggle for South Africa (2019).

75 *Johnson*, Fighting for a Dream (2019), 107; *Jeffrey* (n. 74), 202 et seqq.

tion and mass organisations. This has, and is still, taking place through what is commonly known as "cadre deployment" in all centres of power with the party acting as the integrative forum for its cadres in these centres.[76] Not only has this strategy eroded the separation between state and party but it has undermined, across the whole spectrum of state functions, effective service delivery by government departments and state-owned enterprises as a result of the high levels of functional illiteracy amongst the ANC's cadre constituency, rampant corruption and mismanagement of state resources. The irony is that it is precisely this strategy of the ANC that has provided dazzling opportunities for self-enrichment by its cohorts once they were deployed in positions of power and gained access to huge budgets.[77] It becomes even more ironic when one reads in the party's 2017 Strategy and Tactics document that "the constitutional provisions for a law-governed process of social change and the dispersal of authority across the various arms of government was a matter of principled choice, inspired by the objective to prevent a recurrence of the abuse of power from whichever quarter".[78] However, as the party itself has observed, there is a "difference between the ideals provided for in the basic law of the land and the capacity and will to pursue them".[79]

As socio-political reasons two examples can be mentioned. The one is the ANC's links with the criminal underworld before, during and after the exile years. This is a matter of public knowledge,[80] and, as Johnson explains, a gangster elite was part of the ANC's constituency from the start, and during the struggle recruiting from this violent underworld was par for the course so that "by the time of the Zuma era gangster enforcement (including death threats and assassinations) was part and parcel of the system". While this is equally destructive of good governance, Johnson

76 See for instance Strategy and Tactics (n. 74), paras. 140, 142, 143. Also note the following comment by *Croucamp* and *Malan* (n. 55), 101: "Cadres are deployed to state owned enterprises or the bureaucracy to enforce the authority of the state through the occupation (capture) of the institution, not to affirm historical, reciprocal relations between state and society.... Cadres, therefore, act as the point of merger-of-interests between economic strongmen in the formal economy and the distributive regime of the state".

77 See also *Boraine* (n. 53), 100.

78 Strategy and Tactics (n. 74), para. 34.

79 Ibid., para. 33.

80 See for instance *Bayart, Ellis* and *Hibou*, The Criminalisation of the State in Africa (1999); *Ellis*, External Mission: The ANC in Exile (2012), 253 et seqq.; *Boraine* (n. 53), 100, 101.

points out that "good governance was by then not the name of the game anyway. Government was a spoils system, pure and simple".[81]

Given the current levels of dysfunctionality and corruption in the law enforcement agencies, there is no realistic hope that this patronage-crime nexus can be effectively dismantled. However, even if law enforcement capabilities are restored and prosecutions actively pursued, as the government has promised, there is the danger of growing factionalism in the party between those who want to preserve their spoils and avoid prosecution and those who want to see the triumph of legal accountability. Consequently, if the political price associated with greater disunity in the party becomes too high for the ruling elite to stomach, a few select prosecutions for symbolic effect are likely to be the chosen strategy. Existing networks will then remain intact and emboldened to pursue their criminal activities with impunity. It may also be noted that despite available prima facie evidence and years of police and other investigations in some cases, none of the main beneficiaries of state capture and grand corruption have been brought to justice.

The other is the practice of re-deploying party apparatchiks who were involved in corrupt activities, fraud, the abuse of power or serious maladministration of their portfolios, which is an integral part of the strategy to maintain the systemic patronage system. Through this reshuffling of the deck chairs, party loyalists are retained within the system and its patrimonial networks. The party's golden mantra justifying such action in cases where the dysfunctional law enforcement system has failed, deliberately or otherwise, to pursue criminal prosecution of the incumbent, often is that a person is innocent until proven guilty. This is a perversion of a criminal law notion in a constitutional setting. The principles and values of the Constitution on accountability and good governance are separate and independent standards for measuring the conduct of officials and must be honoured as such.

Finally, it is rather revealing that in an open letter to Nelson Mandela, written in 1994 by the award-winning South African author and poet, Breyten Breytenbach, who was imprisoned for activities against the apartheid state, we find the following prophetic words:[82]

> "We have to produce successes which can be measured morally. If we were to go down the Algerian road of a liberation movement bringing

81 *Johnson* (n. 75), 115.

82 Open letter reproduced in *Breytenbach*, The Memory of Birds in Times of Revolution (1996), 82, 85.

> to power a largely exiled leadership which then sets about looting the state in a prolonged orgy of corruption … we shall surely reap the same whirlwind: In due time a generation of fundamentalists will rise up to vomit the very ideals transported by national liberation …"

Bibliography

Toyin C. Adetiba and *Lucky E. Asuelime*, "ANC Accountability and Control of the South African Parliament: In Whose Interest: The State or the Party?", Journal of African Foreign Affairs, 2018, 107.

ANC, The Second Transition: Building a National Democratic Society and the Balance of Forces in 2012, http://pmg-assets.s3-website-eu-west-1.amazonaws.com/docs/120306ancdoc.pdf (last visited 28 Nov 2019).

Jean-Francois Bayart, Stephen Ellis and *Beatrice Hibou*, The Criminalisation of the State in Africa (Indiana University Press, Oxford 1999).

Alex Boraine, What's Gone Wrong? On the Brink of a Failed State (Jonathan Ball Publishers, Johannesburg and Cape Town 2014).

Michael Bratton and *Nicolas Van de Walle*, "Neo-Patrimonial Regimes and Political Transitions in Africa", World Politics 1994, 453.

Business Tech Report (18 Apr 2019), https://businesstech.co.za/news/government/312104/these-are-the-best-and-worst-runmunicipalities-in-south-africa/ (last visited 28 Nov 2019).

Edwin Cameron, "Constitutionalism, Rights, and International Law: The *Glenister* Decision", Duke Journal of Comparative and International Law 2013, 389.

Commission of Inquiry into State Capture, "The Judicial Commission of Inquiry into Allegations of State Capture, Corruption and Fraud in the Public Sector including Organs of state" (2019), https://www.sastatecapture.org.za/ (last visited 28 Nov 2019).

Corruption Watch and The Institute for Security Studies, State Capture and the Political Manipulation of Criminal Justice Agencies: A Joint Submission to the Judicial Commission of Inquiry into Allegations of State Capture (April 2019), https://issafrica.s3.amazonaws.com/site/uploads/2019-06-20-other-zondo-commission-submission.pdf (last visited 28 Nov 2019).

Piet A. Croucamp and *L Malan*, "The Theory of Systemic Patronage and State Capture", African Journal of Public Affairs 2018, 86.

Maurice Oscar Dassah, "Theoretical Analysis of State Capture as a Governance Problem in South Africa", Journal of Transdisciplinary Research in Southern Africa 2018, 1.

Pierre de Vos and *Warren Freedman* (eds.), South African Constitutional Law in Context (Oxford University Press, South Africa 2014).

Shawn Robert Duthie, "Beyond the Rhetoric: A Theoretical Analysis of the Effects of Neopatrimonialism on the Integration Process in Africa", (2015) Africa Insight 2015, 104.

Shmuel Noah Eisenstadt and *René Lemarchand* (eds.), Political Clientelism, Patronage and Development (Sage Publications, Beverly Hills 1981).

Stephen Ellis, External Mission: The ANC in Exile (Oxford University Press, United Kingdom 2012).

Gero Erdmann, "Neo-Patrimonialism and Political Regimes", in: Nic Cheeseman, David Anderson and Andrea Scheibler (eds.), Routledge Handbook of African Politics (Routledge, USA and Canada 2013).

Gero Erdmann and *Ulf Engel*, Neo-Patrimonialism Revisited – Beyond a Catch-All Concept, Working Paper No. 16, German Institute of Global and Area Studies (2006).

William Gumede, "The Democracy Deficit of Africa's Liberation Movements Turned Governments", Politikon 2017, 27.

Mark Heywood, "Coup by the Connected and Corrupt", Mail & Guardian (31 Aug 2012).

Paul Hoffman, "ANC of Today has All the Hallmarks of a Criminal Enterprise", Business Maverick (16 Jul 2019).

Paul Holden, The Arms Deal in Your Pocket (Jonathan Ball Publishers SA, Johannesburg 2008).

Paul Holden and *Martin Plaut*, Who Rules South Africa? (Bite Back Publishing, South Africa 2012).

Paul Holden and *Hennie van Vuuren*, The Devil in the Detail: How the Arms Deal Changed Everything (Jonathan Ball Publishers SA, Johannesburg 2011).

Anthea Jeffery, People's War: New Light on the Struggle for South Africa (Jonathan Ball Publishers, Johannesburg and Cape Town 2019).

Robert Wood Johnson, How Long Will South Africa Survive? The Looming Crisis (C Hurst & Co Publishers Ltd, United Kingdom 2015).

Robert Wood Johnson, Fighting for a Dream (Jonathan Ball Publishers, Johannesburg and Cape Town 2019).

Karl Klare, "Legal Culture and Transformative Constitutionalism" South African Journal of Human Rights 1998, 146.

Tom Lodge, "Neo-Patrimonial Politics in the ANC", African Affairs 2014, 1.

Lorraine Louw, What's the real cost of corruption – part one (4 July 2013), https://www.corruptionwatch.org.za/whats-the-real-cost-of-corruption-part-one/, (last visited 20 June 2020).

Koos Malan, There Is No Supreme Constitution: A Critique of Statist-individualist Constitutionalism (African Sun Media, South Africa 2019).

Malesela Jim Masenya, "Neo-Patrimonialism, Corruption and Governance in South Africa", African Journal of Public Affairs 2017, 146.

Mandla Mfundo Masuku, "Effective Governance in South Africa: reality or myth", African Journal of Democracy and Governance 2019, 117.

Heinrich Matthee, South African Monitor, Political Turbulence and Business Risks in the ANC's Hybrid Regime, Report No. 7 (2016).

Dikgang Moseneke, "Fourth Bram Fischer Memorial Lecture: Transformative Adjudication" South African Journal of Human Rights 2002, 309.

Pieter-Louis Myburgh, Gangster State: Unravelling Ace Magashule's Web of Capture (Penguin Random House South Africa, South Africa 2019).

Crispian Olver, How to Steal a City (Jonathan Ball Publishers, Johannesburg and Cape Town 2017).

Organisation Undoing Tax Abuse (OUTA), No Room to Hide: A President Caught in the Act (2017), https://cisp.cachefly.net/assets/articles/attachments/69697_2.-report.pdf (last visited 28 Nov 2019).

Jacques Pauw, The President's Keepers: Those Keeping Zuma In and Out of Prison (Tafelberg Publishers, South Africa 2017).

Public Protector, Report State of Capture (14 Oct 2016), http://saflii.org/images/329756472-State-of-Capture.pdf (last visited 28 Nov 2019).

Ignatius Rautenbach and *Roxan Venter*, Rautenbach-Malherbe Constitutional Law (Lexis Nexis, 7th ed., South Africa 2018).

SABC Digital News, "Adv. Shamila Batohi delivers Kadar Asmal Memorial Lecture", https://www.youtube.com/watch?v=A3B0SgZygwEid 9 (last visited 28 Nov 2019).

Strategy and Tactics of the African National Congress, Discussion Document adopted at the 5th National Policy Conference (Jun/Jul 2017), https://www.sahistory.org.za/sites/default/files/file%20uploads%20/national_policy_conference_2017_stratey_and_tactics.pdf (last visited 28 Nov 2019).

Richard Sandbrook with *Judith Barker*, The Politics of Africa's Economic Stagnation (Cambridge University Press, Cambridgeshire 1985).

Mark Shaw, "South Africa: the origins of the mafia state – political transition, organized crime and the impact on democracy" in Felia Alum & Stan Gilmour (eds.) Handbook of Organized Crime and Politics (Edward Elgar 2019) 321.

State Capacity Research Project, Mark Swilling (Convenor), Betrayal of the Promise: How South Africa is Being Stolen (2017), http://47zhcvti0ul2ftip9rxo9fj9.wpengine.netdna-cdn.com/wp-content/uploads/2017/05/Betrayal-of-the-Promise-25052017.pdf (last visited 28 Nov 2019).

Johannes P. Tsheola, "Governance of the Party, State and Society Triad in a Democratic South Africa", African Journal of Public Affairs 2017, 1.

Karl von Holdt, The Political Economy of Corruption: Elite-Formation, Factions and Violence, Working Paper No. 10, Society, Work and Politics Institute (Feb 2019).

Max Weber, Economy and Society (University California Press, Berkeley 1922).

Register of cases

Affordable Medicines Trust and Others v Minister of Health and Another 2006 3 SA 247 (CC).

Albutt v Centre for the Study of Violence and Reconciliation 2010 3 SA 293 (CC).

Carmichele v Minister of Safety and Security (CCT 48/00) [2001] ZACC 22, 2001 4 SA 938 (CC), 2001 10 BCLR 995 (CC) (16 Aug 2001).

Democratic Alliance v President of South Africa and Others 2012 12 BCLR 1297 (CC).

Fedsure Life Assurance Ltd and Others v Greater Johannesburg Transitional Metropolitan Council and Others 1998 12 BCLR 1458.

Glenister v President of the Republic of South Africa 2011 3 SA 347 (CC).

Glenister v President of the Republic of South Africa and Others (CCT 41/08) [2008] ZACC 19, 2009 1 SA 287 (CC), 2009 2 BCLR 136 (CC) (22 Oct 2008).

Helen Suzman Foundation v President of the Republic of South Africa 2015 (1) BCLR 1 (CC).

Kaunda v President of the Republic of South Africa 2005 4 SA 235 (CC).

Lesapo v North West Agricultural Bank and Another 2000 1 SA 409 (CC).

Pharmaceutical Manufacturers Association of South Africa, In Re Ex Parte President of the RSA 2003 3 BCLR 241 (CC).

President of the Republic of South Africa and Others v South African Rugby Football Union and Others (CCT16/98) [1999] ZACC 11, 2000 1 SA 1, 1999 10 BCLR 1059 (10 Sep 1999).

President of the Republic of South Africa and Another v Modderklip Boerdery (Pty) Ltd (CCT20/04) [2005] ZACC 5, 2005 5 SA 3 (CC), 2005 8 BCLR 786 (CC) (13 May 2005).

South African Diamond Producers Organisation v Minister of Minerals and Energy NO and Others (CCT234/16) [2017] ZACC 26, 2017 10 BCLR 1303 (CC), 2017 6 SA 331 (CC) (24 Jul 2017).

Comment: Rule of Law under German and European Constitutional Law – Comments on the Rise of the Neo-Patrimonial State in South Africa: From the Rule of Law to the Rule of Persons

Stefan Lorenzmeier[*]

I. Introduction

In their joint contribution, *Strydom* and *Bradley* assess the value of the rule of law in the South African Constitution, especially in light of identified neo-patrimonial tendencies in South Africa.[1] They describe a shift from the rule of law to the rule of persons in their country and use the sociological concept of neo-patrimonialism to explain this shift. In their understanding, neo-patrimonialism is characterized by the co-existence and interaction between the formal, rule-based institutions of a modern state and the informal practices of governance encountered in patrimonial forms of authority.[2] The concept of patrimonialism was expounded by

* Stefan Lorenzmeier, *Dr. iur.*, *LL.M.*; senior research and teaching position, University of Augsburg, Faculty of Law.

1 *Strydom* and *Bradley*, in this book, 19.

2 *Erdmann*, in: Cheeseman, Anderson and Scheibler (eds.), Routledge Handbook on African Politics (2013), 61.

Max Weber and basically means that the ruler in a patrimonial system bestows personal grace and favors at the expense of traditional limitations on the exercise of authority,[3] a trend that can be seen not only in African countries, but also in all states with weak enforcement of the rule of law in which the impersonal rule is replaced by a personal one. *Strydom* and *Bradley* provide us with ample examples of how this concept has been applied in post-colonial Africa and especially in South Africa.

In Germany and the European Union (EU), the shift from impersonal to personal power can, at least for the moment, not be detected. Therefore, the aim of this Comment is to say a few words about the rule of law in Germany and the EU, which is rightly seen by *Strydom* and *Bradley* as the juxtaposition to the rule of neo-patrimonialism in a society.[4] However, the concept of the rule of law is not a fixed one; different readings of it endure in common- and civil-law countries. Thus, this Comment will first deal with two different approaches to the rule of law (the "thin" and "thick" theories, as they have been labelled by *Strydom* and *Bradley* in an earlier draft of their contribution) and will then go on to describe the system of the rule of law under the German and EU Constitutions.

II. The rule of law – "thin" or "thick"?

Since the early 20th Century, German and Austrian constitutional lawyers have discussed extensively the concept of the rule of law as a limit on the power of the relevant monarch. On the one hand, it is a concept of depersonalized and public power, and on the other, of limiting the arbitrary use of that power by providing clear rules for its exercise. In essence, the rule of law must create an expectation of legal certainty and consistency. At least in continental Europe, the concept is closely connected with the principle of positivism.[5]

At the heart of the dispute between the "thick" and "thin" theories is the issue of whether moral values form part of the concept of legal positivism and the rule of law.[6] According to proponents of the "thin" theory, the basic norm of a positive legal order created by the rule of law

3 *Weber*, Economy and Society (1922).

4 *Strydom* and *Bradley* (n. 1), 25.

5 *Kelsen*, General Theory of Law and State (1945), 113.

6 *Kelsen* was one of the fervent supporter of the non-application of any moral values in a legal system based on the rule of law because this would be a step back to a legal system based upon natural law, see ibid., 114.

is nothing more than the fundamental rule according to which the various norms of the order are to be created.[7] In principle, if a norm has been lawfully created in accordance with higher norms, it is valid and has to be respected.[8]

In Germany, this approach gave rise to problems during the Nazi dictatorship. The Weimar Constitution was in force until 1945 and was used by the dictator to enact rules, barring any moral standard, in a manner formally in accordance with the rules of the Weimar Constitution. After the Second World War, this led to the pressing question of whether the rule of law, in combination with pure legal positivism, should be the applicable standard for a normative legal system, or whether moral values should also be applied. In a famous post-war essay, *Radbruch* stated that positive law, secured by legislation and power, took precedence even when its content was unjust and failed to benefit people, unless the conflict between statute and justice reached such an intolerable degree that the statute, as a flawed law, had to yield to justice.[9] According to *Radbruch*, this was, for instance, the case for some (if not most) laws enacted during the Third Reich. Moreover, it is worth pointing out that, for *Radbruch*, there was a need for statutes in a positivist legal order, and that the *Rechtsstaat* served the ideas of both justice and legal certainty as well as possible.[10]

Most notably, *Radbruch's* ideas were put forward and adapted by *Alexy*. He stressed the intrinsic connection between the principles of legal certainty and positivism as embodied in the rule of law.[11] He even considered that legal certainty was the idea underlying positivism and that exceptions to the principle of legal certainty also always shook the foundations of legal positivism.[12]

Thus, the principle of the rule of law, the *Rechtsstaat*, in modern German legal culture is not understood as being limited to pure legal positivism, but entails an element of "justice" as well. This precludes the abhorrent, unjust results of applying pure legal positivism and is an application of the "thick" theory in the sense of a substantive or material concept of the rule of law.[13]

---

7 Ibid., 114.
8 Ibid., 115.
9 *Radbruch*, 26 Oxf. J. Leg. Stud. 2006, 1, 7; *Sandhu,* in this book, 138.
10 *Radbruch* (n. 9), 11; *Sandhu* (n. 9), 138.
11 *Alexy*, 28 Ratio Juris 2015, 441, 443; *Sandhu* (n. 9), 138.
12 *Alexy* (n. 11), 444; *Sandhu* (n. 9), 138.
13 *Strydom* and *Bradley* (n. 1), 22.

III. The rule of law in the German Constitution

In this part of the Comment it will be shown, by way of a brief analysis, which theoretical concept of the rule of law was embodied in the German Constitution, the Basic Law (*Grundgesetz* – GG), after 1949. The main constitutional principles are enshrined in Article 20 GG, and the rule of law particularly in the norm's third paragraph.

Article 20(3) GG states:

> "The legislature shall be bound by the constitutional order, the executive and the judiciary by law and justice."

The provision is accompanied by other constitutional norms, especially Article 1(3) GG, which reads:

> "The following basic rights shall bind the legislature, the executive and the judiciary as directly applicable law."

And Article 79(3) GG, which provides:

> "Amendments to this Basic Law affecting [...] the principles laid down in Articles 1 and 20 shall be inadmissible."

Even from the norms quoted above, it can clearly be seen that the rule of law is one of the basic, fundamental principles of the German Constitution. However, there is widespread academic discussion regarding whether Article 20(3) GG entirely covers the principle of the rule of law given that other provisions in the Constitution, like Article 1(3) GG, also contain elements of the principle. However, Article 20(3) GG is still regarded as the main guarantor of the rule of law. In this context, it has to be stressed that Article 20(3) GG, as crucially pointed out by Article 79(3) GG, is one of the cornerstones of the German Constitution, which cannot be amended under the existing legal system.

Given the experience of the Weimar Constitution,[14] the drafters of the *Grundgesetz* were of the view that a constitution must be able to defend itself against forces which intend to overturn the existing legal order, and provided for certain principles with a special status, which cannot be changed by the legislature. Other provisions of the German Constitution

14 It had already been mentioned that the Weimar Constitution was in force until 1945 but that some fundamental principles of the constitution had been undermined by the dictatorial law-makers.

can be altered or amended by a two-thirds majority; this is not the case for the rule of law, as Article 79(3) GG expressly points out.

In addition, the principle of the rule of law (in accordance with Article 20(3) GG and other provisions of the German Constitution) is constituted by a wide array of elements. Significant elements which the German Constitutional Court (*Bundesverfassungsgericht* – BVerfG) and scholarly writings recognize are:

- The guarantee of individual freedoms, namely basic rights.
- The separation of powers.
- The administration must act in accordance with legal norms.
- The individual right of access to court.
- The State must act in a predictable way
- The principles of proportionality and legality.[15]

The listed components of the rule of law clearly show that the relationship between the State and its citizens is governed by legal and personal aspects. The State cannot exercise personal or arbitral control over a bureaucracy. There is a clear distinction between the private and public realms, the latter being governed by clear and objective rules. The disentanglement of the private from the public, the State from persons acting, can be identified from German history after the Second World War. This process was rather successful and no serious intrusions occurred.

IV. The rule of law in the EU

The principle of the rule of law is not only embedded in, and protected by, the national constitutions of EU Member States, but it is also protected by the EU's primary law, especially the Treaty on the European Union (TEU).[16] Although the EU treaties do not enjoy the formal status of a constitution, they can rightly be regarded as a constitution in substance. During the last couple of years, the content of the principle at EU level had to be clarified by the European Court of Justice (ECJ) in a number

15 For the sake of brevity only a few sources will be named: *Sachs*, in: Sachs (ed.), Grundgesetz – Kommentar (8th ed. 2018), Article 20, paras. 1 et seqq.; *Grzeszick*, in: Maunz and Dürig (eds.), Grundgesetz (87th ed. 2019), Article 20, paras. 1 et seqq.; *Stern*, *Sachs* and *Dietlein*, in: Stern (ed.), Das Staatsrecht der Bundesrepublik Deutschland, Die einzelnen Grundrechte, vol. IV/2 (2011), chapter 6, § 123.

16 OJ 2008 C 115/13 et seq.

of rulings concerning certain EU Member States, amongst others Hungary and Poland.

The rule of law is explicitly named in Article 2 TEU,[17] which is contained in Title I of the Treaty, on "Common Provisions". According to ECJ jurisprudence (and which is not really contested in academic writing or by the Member States), the EU treaties are considered to be of "constitutional character"[18] and contain the fundamental rules for the relationship between the EU, its Member States and their natural and legal persons. They do not constitute a constitution in a formal sense, but rather in a substantive sense, because the treaties reflect the fundamental values of the organization and its members.

Despite its very general wording, Article 2 TEU is subject to judicial consideration and has been interpreted by the ECJ in many instances. Recently, the ECJ emphasized the rule of law and its content in light of the problem with the judicial systems of certain Member States.[19] Due to different concepts of the rule of law in Member States, the meaning of the term "rule of law" in Article 2 TEU is anything but self-explanatory. Thus, it is important to note that the term is, as is usual in the EU treaties, an autonomous term of EU law, which must be interpreted independently of the Member States' legal systems.[20]

However, the core of the principle is common to all Member States and the EU, and the separation between the individual and public institutions is (even in the absence of an ECJ ruling in this respect) certainly part of it. Any kind of patrimonialism would constitute a breach of the rule of law protected by Article 2 TEU. This is illustrated by the Santer Commission's

---

17 The provision reads: "The Union is founded on the values of respect for human dignity, freedom, democracy, equality, the rule of law and respect for human rights, including the rights of persons belonging to minorities. These values are common to the Member States in a society in which pluralism, non-discrimination, tolerance, justice, solidarity and equality between women and men prevail.".

18 ECJ, Judgment of 23 Apr 1986, C-294/83, ECLI:EU:C:1986:166, para. 23 – Les Verts; ECJ, Opinion 2/13 of 8 Dec 2014, ECLI:EU:C:2014:2454, para. 163 – Accession to the ECHR.

19 ECJ, Judgment of 27 Feb 2018, C-64/16, ECLI:EU:C:2018:117 – Associao Sindical dos Juizes Portugueses; ECJ, Judgment of 24 Jun 2019, C-619/18, ECLI:EU:C:2019:531 – Independence of the Polish Supreme Court.

20 On interpretation see: ECJ, Judgment of 17 Apr 2018, C-414/16, ECLI:EU:C:2018:257, para. 44 – Egenberger.

resignation on March 15, 1999.[21] The collective commission of the European Communities (at that time) resigned on that date due to accusations of fraud, nepotism and mismanagement of aid funds by the European Parliament. This incident led to a much-improved budget-control system within the EU and has so far been the only instance in which systemic violations of the rule of law by an EU organ were at issue.

To summarize, the EU is also bound by the principle of the rule of law although its content is different from that under the German Constitution. Yet, as a rule-based organization with special supranational powers, it is of the utmost importance that the EU itself also be bound by the fundamental rules of a legal system accepted in its Member States.[22] The example of the Santer Commission clearly indicated the need for disentangling the rule from the ruler, even for the EU.

V. Conclusion

This brief Comment has endeavored to illustrate the application of the rule of law in Germany and the EU in contrast to the situation in South Africa as described by *Strydom* and *Bradley*. It has highlighted the stark contrast in the way in which the rule of law is dealt with in the different legal systems, while it must be stated that in South Africa, it is not the legal rules that seem to be the problem, but rather their application.

In a more theoretical part of this Comment, the development of the "thin" and "thick" theories on the rule of law in Germany were explained. In light of German history, this development was rather different than in other jurisdictions. Due to the events during the Third Reich, Germany turned from a pure, dogmatic approach towards the legality principle, to a slightly watered-down one limited by issues of morality in extreme circumstances. The EU's provisions on the rule of law are derived from the ideas of its Member States, and are largely in line with the German conception of the rule of law, despite the slight modifications necessary in the case of an international organization.

---

21 For a political analysis see e.g. *Ringe*, The Santer Commission Resignation Crisis – Government-Opposition Dynamics in Executive-Legislative relations of the EU (2003), http://aei.pitt.edu/2919/1/156.pdf (last visited 28 Jan 2020).

22 In this respect see e.g. the Lisbon-ruling of the German Constitutional Court on the integration of the Federal Republic into the European Union: BVerfG, Judgment of 30 Jun 2009, 2 BvE 2/08 et al., BVerfGE 123, 267 et seqq. – Lisbon.

In summary, both the German and EU legal orders are aimed at establishing an objective system disconnected from the person in charge, which seems to be the preferred way of applying the rule of law, especially in light of the situation in South Africa and the accompanying problems which *Strydom* and *Bradley* describe in their book.

Bibliography

Robert Alexy, "Legal Certainty and Correctness", 28 Ratio Juris 2015, 441.

Gero Erdmann, "Neo-Patrimonialism and Political Regimes", in: Nic Cheeseman, David Anderson and Andrea Scheibler (eds.), Routledge Handbook of African Politics, (Routledge, USA and Canada 2013), 61.

*Hans Kelse*n, General Theory of Law and State (Harvard University Press, Cambridge 1945).

Theodor Maunz and *Günter Dürig* (eds.), Grundgesetz, looseleaf (C.H. Beck, 87th ed., Munich 2019).

Gustav Radbruch, "Gesetzliches Unrecht und übergesetzliches Recht" ("Statutory Lawlessness and Supra-Statutory Law"), translated by Bonnie Litschewski Paulson and Stanley L Paulson, 26 Oxford Journal of legal Studies (Oxf. J. Leg. Stud.) 2006, 1.

Nils F. Ringe, "The Santer Commission Resignation Crisis – Government-Opposition Dynamics in Executive-Legislative relations of the EU" (2003), http://aei.pitt.edu/2919/1/156.pdf (last visited 28 Jan 2020).

Michael Sachs (ed.), Grundgesetz – Kommentar (C.H. Beck, 8th ed., Munich 2018).

Aqilah Sandhu, "Comment: Legal Certainty and Human Rights in the European Legal Order – the case of preventive detention between the Federal Constitutional Court and the European Court of Human Rights", in: Thomas M.J. Möllers and Charl Hugo (eds.), Legal Certainty and Fundamental Rights, this book (Nomos, Baden-Baden 2020), 135.

Klaus Stern (ed.), Das Staatsrecht der Bundesrepublik Deutschland, Die einzelnen Grundrechte, vol. IV/2, (C.H. Beck, Munich 2011).

Hennie Strydom and *Martie Bradley*, "The Rise of the Neo-Patrimonial State in South Africa: From the Rule of Law to the Rule of Persons", in: Thomas M.J. Möllers and Charl Hugo (eds.), Legal Certainty and Fundamental Rights, this book (Nomos, Baden-Baden 2020), 19.

Max Weber, Economy and Society (University California Press, Berkeley 1922).

Register of cases

ECJ, Judgment of 23 Apr 1986, C-294/83, ECLI:EU:C:1986:166 – Les Verts.

ECJ, Judgment of 27 Feb 2018, C-64/16, ECLI:EU:C:2018:117 – Associao Sindical dos Juizes Portugueses.

ECJ, Judgment of 17 Apr 2018, C-414/16, ECLI:EU:C:2018:257 – Egenberger.

ECJ, Judgment of 24 Jun 2019, C-619/18, ECLI:EU:C:2019:531 – Independence of the Polish Supreme Court.

ECJ, Opinion 2/13 of 8 Dec 2014, ECLI:EU:C:2014:2454 – Accession to the ECHR.

BVerfG, Judgment of 30 Jun 2009, 2 BvE 2/08 et al., BVerfGE 123, 267 et seqq. – Lisbon.

Legal Certainty in Terms of Head-of-State Immunity from an African and an International Perspective: The Article 27(2) Conundrum*

*Roxan Venter*** / *Martha M. Bradley****

* This contribution was written prior to the Appeals Decision being handed down on 6 May 2019: ICC Appeals Chamber, Situation in Darfur, Sudan, In the Case of *The Prosecutor v Omar Hassan Ahmad Al-Bashir*, Judgment in the Jordan Referral re Al-Bashir Appeal, ICC-02/05–01/-09 (6 May 2019). Therefore, the chapter is restricted to reflections on the diverse positions of international organisations and of professors in international law as per the submissions. The Appeals Decision confirmed the conclusion drawn by the authors in this contribution that Article 27(2) of the Rome Statute applies horizontally. See specifically para. 149: "In sum, Resolution 1593 gives the Court power to exercise its jurisdiction over the situation in Darfur, Sudan, which it must exercise 'in accordance with [the] Statute'. This includes Article 27(2), which provides that immunities are not a bar to the exercise of jurisdiction. As Sudan is obliged to 'cooperate fully' with the Court, *the effect of Article 27(2) arises also in the horizontal relationship* – Sudan cannot invoke Head of State immunity if a State Party is requested to arrest and surrender Mr Al-Bashir. Therefore, there was no Head of State immunity that Sudan could invoke in relation to Jordan, had the latter arrested Mr Al-Bashir on the basis of an arrest warrant issued by the Court…" [Emphasis added]. This contribution nevertheless remains valuable since the Appeals Decision did not discuss these issues in detail. The Appeals Chamber does state that Article 27(2) has horizontal effect but it does not provide an interrogation of the provision in order to justify this conclusion. See Appeals Chamber, Situation in Darfur, Sudan, In the Case of *The Prosecutor v Omar Hassan Ahmad Al-Bashir*, Judgment in the Jordan Referral re Al-Bashir Appeal, ICC-02/05–01/-09 (6 May 2019) at paras. 127 – 132. Therefore this contribution, specifically, and the debate relating to Article 27, in general, remain relevant. The authors wish to thank our correspondent, Prof. Dr. Thilo Rensmann, for his generous and insightful feedback. We would also like to thank Prof. Hennie Strydom and Prof. Charl Hugo for commenting on this chapter.

** Roxan Venter, *B.Com., LL.B., LL.M., LL.D. (University of Johannesburg)*, Senior Lecturer in Constitutional Law and Human Rights Law, Faculty of Law, University of Johannesburg.

*** Martha M. Bradley, *LL.B., LL.M., LL.D. (University of Pretoria), LL.M. (University of Cape Town)*, Research Associate, South African Research Chair in International Law, University of Johannesburg. The work is based on research supported by the National Research Foundation of South Africa (Grant Number 85104).

Roxan Venter / Martha M. Bradley

Abstract: The ongoing debate concerning the nature of head-of-state immunity regarding the prosecution of heads of state by international criminal tribunals, specifically the International Criminal Court, for the commission of international crimes is entwined with the fight against impunity – especially in relation to holding heads of state criminally responsible for such violations. The non-arrest of President Al-Bashir on various occasions has fuelled this debate, especially on the African continent, and has prompted an inquiry into the meaning of Articles 27 and 98 of the Rome Statute. State parties to the Rome Statute attribute their hesitance in arresting President Al-Bashir to the so-called "strained relationship" between Articles 27 and 98 of the Rome Statute and the effect of the wording of Security Council Resolution 1593. The debate was reignited when Jordan, a member state to the International Criminal Court, in March 2017, failed to arrest President Al-Bashir when he visited the Hashemite Kingdom. These events emphasise the need for legal certainty regarding the accountability of heads of state for the commission of international crimes. This chapter addresses this problem by highlighting the opposing views concerning the horizontal application and interpretation of Article 27(2) of the Rome Statute (the immunity provision). Additionally, the chapter considers the decision on the request for leave to reply and further processes in the appeal by the Hashemite Kingdom of Jordan against the "Decision under Article 87(7) of the Rome Statute on Non-Compliance by Jordan with the Request by the Court for the Arrest and Surrender [of] Omar Al-Bashir" of 11 December 2017.

I. Introduction

This chapter considers whether Article 27(2) of the Rome Statute has a horizontal dimension and is applicable between states.[1] This interpreta-

1 Rome Statute of the International Criminal Court of 17 Jul 1998, entered into force 1 Jul 2002, 2187 UNTS 90.

tive conundrum has been used by various states, most recently by the Hashemite Kingdom of Jordan, to justify its failure to arrest President Al-Bashir pursuant to an arrest warrant issued by the International Criminal Court (ICC).[2] States have offered various legal justifications for their failure to arrest President Al-Bashir, ranging from arguments related to the content and scope of the immunity provisions of the Rome Statute; the question of whether Security Council Resolution 1593 (2005) waives the immunity of non-state officials; the legal effect of a referral in terms of Articles 27 and 98 of the Rome Statute on customary international law; and, finally, the content of the doctrine of head-of-state immunity under customary international law.[3] The *Order on the Conduct of the Hearing before the Appeals Chamber in the Jordan Referral re the Al-Bashir Appeal* outlined specific issues and questions relating to head-of-state immunity and invited parties and *amici curiae* to address these during its public hearings.[4]

---

2 ICC Pre-Trial Chamber II, Situation in Darfur, Sudan, In the Case of *The Prosecutor v Omar Hassan Ahmad Al-Bashir*, Decision under Article 87(7) of the Rome Statute on the Non-Compliance by Jordan with the Request by the Court for the Arrest and Surrender of Omar Al-Bashir, ICC-02/05–01/-09 (11 Dec 2017), paras. 7, 33–44; ICC Pre-Trial Chamber I, Situation in Darfur, Sudan, In the Case of *The Prosecutor v Omar Hassan Ahmad Al-Bashir*, Warrant of Arrest for Omar Hassan Ahmad Al-Bashir, ICC-02/05–01/-09 (4 Mar 2009); ICC Pre-Trial Chamber I, Situation in Darfur, Sudan, In the Case of *The Prosecutor v Omar Hassan Ahmad Al-Bashir*, Second Warrant of Arrest for Omar Hassan Ahmad Al-Bashir, ICC-02/05–01/-09 (12 Jul 2010).

3 Compare Jordan Decision (n. 2); ICC Pre-Trial Chamber I, Situation in Darfur, Sudan, In the Case of *The Prosecutor v Omar Hassan Ahmad Al-Bashir*, Decision Pursuant to Article 87(7) of the Rome Statute on the Failure by the Republic of Malawi to Comply with the Cooperation Requests Issued by the Court with Respect to the Arrest and Surrender of Omar Hassan Ahmad Al-Bashir, ICC-02/05–01/09 (12 Dec 2011); ICC Pre-Trial Chamber I, Situation in Darfur, Sudan, In the Case of *The Prosecutor v Omar Hassan Ahmad Al-Bashir*, Decision Pursuant to Article 87(7) of the Rome Statute on the Refusal of the Republic of Chad to Comply with the Cooperation Requests Issued by the Court with Respect to the Arrest and Surrender of Omar Hassan Ahmad Al-Bashir, ICC-02/05–01/09 (13 Dec 2011); ICC Pre-Trial Chamber II, Situation in Darfur, Sudan, In the Case of *The Prosecutor v Omar Hassan Ahmad Al-Bashir*, Decision under Article 87(7) of the Rome Statute on the Non-Compliance by South Africa with the Request by the Court for the Arrest and Surrender of Omar Al-Bashir, ICC-02/05–01/09 (6 Jul 2017).

4 ICC Appeals Chamber, Situation in Darfur, Sudan, In the Case of *The Prosecutor v Omar Hassan Ahmad Al-Bashir*, Order on the Conduct of the Hearing Before the Appeals Chamber in the Jordan Referral re Al-Bashir, ICC-02/05–01/09 OA2 (27 Aug 2018), paras. 4–9.

These issues highlight the need for legal certainty.[5] Prior to the *Al-Bashir* cases, the horizontal effect of Article 27(2) of the Rome Statute had not received much attention. The provision, however, is now enjoying more attention, especially on the part of the Kingdom of Jordan, the African Union and the League of Arab States.[6] The African Union, in its Supplementary Submission of 28 September 2018 following the oral hearings in Jordan's appeal against a finding of non-cooperation, deemed that the outcome of the appeal would turn on two issues.[7] The first concerns the meaning of Article 27(2), while the other relates to whether the provision applies horizontally between states.[8] In light of these determinations, the authors examine the horizontal application of Article 27(2), paying particular attention to the submissions made in terms of the *Order Inviting Submissions: In the Case of The Prosecutor v Omar Hassan Ahmad Al-Bashir* issued on 25 May 2018.[9] This chapter highlights the fact that legal uncer-

5 Ibid.

6 ICC Appeals Chamber, Situation in Darfur, Sudan, In the Case of *The Prosecutor v Omar Hassan Ahmad Al-Bashir*, The League of Arab States' Observations on the Hashemite Kingdom of Jordan's Appeal Against the Decision under Article 87(7) of the Rome Statute on the Non-Compliance by Jordan with the Request by the Court for the Arrest and Surrender [of] Omar Al-Bashir, ICC-02/05–01/09 (16 Jul 2018), paras. 24–28; ICC Appeals Chamber, Situation in Darfur, Sudan, In the Case of *The Prosecutor v Omar Hassan Ahmad Al-Bashir*, The Hashemite Kingdom of Jordan's Response to the Observations Submitted by the African Union and the League of Arab States, ICC-02/05–01/09 (14 Aug 2018), paras. 6 and 7; ICC Appeals Chamber, Situation in Darfur, Sudan, In the Case of *The Prosecutor v Omar Hassan Ahmad Al-Bashir*, The African Union's Submission in the Hashemite Kingdom of Jordan's Appeal Against the Decision under Article 87(7) of the Rome Statute on the Non-Compliance by Jordan with the Request by the Court for the Arrest and Surrender [of] Omar Al-Bashir, ICC-02/05–01/09 OA2 (16 Jul 2018), paras. 11–26; ICC Appeals Chamber, Situation in Darfur, Sudan, *In the Case of The Prosecutor v Omar Hassan Ahmad Al-Bashir*, Supplementary African Union Submission in the Hashemite Kingdom of Jordan's Appeal Against the Decision under Article 87(7) of the Rome Statute on the Non-Compliance by Jordan with the Request by the Court for the Arrest and Surrender [of] Omar-Al-Bashir with Annex 1, Annex 2, Annex 3, Annex 4 and Annex 5, ICC-02/05–01/09 (28 Sep 2018), paras. 5–13.

7 Supplementary African Union Submission (n. 6), para. 2.

8 Ibid.

9 Order on the conduct of the hearing (n. 4); The following submissions addressed the interpretation of Article 27(2): ICC Appeals Chamber, Situation in Darfur, Sudan, In the Case of *The Prosecutor v Omar Hassan Ahmad Al-Bashir*, Request by Professor Nicholas and Dr Michail Vagias for Leave to Submit Observations on the Merits of the Legal Questions Presented in the Hashemite Kingdom of Jordan's Appeal Against the Decision Under Article 87(7) of the Rome Statute on the Non-

tainty surrounding the meaning of Article 27(2) is a hindrance in the fight against impunity.

The purpose of Article 27 of the Rome Statute is to remove the juridical bar afforded by the doctrine of head-of-state immunity that *may* protect heads of state, and others holding a similar office, from prosecution in the

---

Compliance by Jordan with the Request by the Court for the Arrest and Surrender of Omar Al-Bashir of 12 Mar 2018, ICC-02/05–01/09 OA2 (29 Apr 2018); ICC Appeals Chamber, Situation in Darfur, Sudan, In the Case of *The Prosecutor v Omar Hassan Ahmad Al-Bashir*, Amicus Curiae Observations Submitted by Prof Flavia Lattanzi Pursuant to Rule 103 of the Rules of Procedure and Evidence on the Merits of the Legal Questions Presented in the Hashemite Kingdom of Jordan's Appeal Against the Decision Under Article 87(7) of the Rome Statute on the Non-Compliance by Jordan with the Request by the Court for the Arrest and Surrender [of] Omar Al-Bashir of 12 March 2018, ICC-02/05–01/09 OA2 (18 Jun 2018); ICC Appeals Chamber, Situation in Darfur, Sudan, In the Case of *The Prosecutor v Omar Hassan Ahmad Al-Bashir*, Request for Leave to Submit Amicus Curiae Observations Pursuant to Rule 103 of the Rules of Procedure and Evidence, Source: Professor Annalisa Ciampi, ICC-02/05–01/09 OA2 (30 Apr 2018); ICC Apeals Chamber, Situation in Darfur, Sudan, In the Case of *The Prosecutor v Omar Hassan Ahmad Al-Bashir*, Request by Professors Robinson, Cryer, deGuzman, Lafontaine, Oosterveld, Stahn and Vasiliev for Leave to Submit Observations, ICC-02/05–01/09 OA2 (26 Apr 2018); ICC Appeals Chamber, Situation in Darfur, Sudan, In the Case of *The Prosecutor v Omar Hassan Ahmad Al-Bashir*, Request by Professor Claus Kress with the assistance of Erin Pobjie for Leave to Submit Observations on the Merits of the Legal Questions Presented in the Hashemite Kingdom of Jordan's Appeal Against the Decision Under Article 87(7) of the Rome Statute on the Non-Compliance by Jordan With the Request by the Court for the Arrest and Surrender [of] Omar Al-Bashir of 12 March 2018, ICC-02/05–01/09 OA2 (25 Apr 2019); ICC Appeals Chamber, Situation in Darfur, Sudan, In the Case of *The Prosecutor v Omar Hassan Ahmad Al-Bashir*, Final Observations by Professor Roger O'Keefe Pursuant to Rule 103 of the Rules of Procedure and Evidence and the President's Oral Direction of 14 Sep 2018, on the Merits of the Legal Questions Presented in the Hashemite Kingdom of Jordan's Appeal Against the Decision Under Article 87(7) of the Rome Statute on the Non-Compliance by Jordan with the Request by the Court for the Arrest and Surrender [of] Omar Al-Bashir of 12 March 2018, ICC-02/05–01/09 (18 Jun 2018); The League of Arab States' Observations (n. 6); Supplementary African Union Submission (n. 6); ICC Pre-Trial Chamber II, Situation in Darfur, Sudan, In the Case of *The Prosecutor v Omar Hassan Ahmad Al-Bashir*, Prosecution's Response to the Hashemite Kingdom of Jordan's Notice of Appeal Against the Article 87(7) Decision, or in the Alternative, Application for Leave to Appeal the Decision Under Article 82(1)(d), ICC-02/05–01/09 (21 Dec 2017); ICC Appeals Chamber, Situation in Darfur, Sudan, In the Case of *The Prosecutor v Omar Hassan Ahmad*

International Criminal Court.[10] The authors emphasise the term "may", as this vague term confounds a clear determination of the content of the doctrine of head-of-state immunity under customary international law.[11] The wording of Article 27, which had been deemed clear and aligned to the object and purpose of the Rome Statute, was challenged during the appeals phase of the proceedings against Jordan.[12] Now the generally accepted interpretation of Article 27 is being challenged.[13] Put simply, the general understanding has been that states, by ratifying the Rome Statute, consent that Article 27 waives head-of-state immunity and the im-

---

Al-Bashir, The Hashemite Kingdom of Jordan's Response to the Observations Submitted by Professors of International Law Pursuant to Rule 103 of the Rules of Procedure and Evidence, ICC-02/05–01/09 (16 Jul 2018); ICC Appeals Chamber, Situation in Darfur, Sudan, In the Case of *The Prosecutor v Omar Hassan Ahmad Al-Bashir*, Prosecution Response to the Observations of the African Union and the League of Arab States, ICC-02/05–01/09 (14 Aug 2018); Jordan's Response to the Observations Submitted by the African Union and the League of Arab States (n. 6); The African Union's Submission (n. 6).

10 Rome Statute (n. 1).

11 It is not clear whether head-of-state immunity applies to the extent of barring the prosecution of heads of state for the commission of international crimes before an international criminal tribunal such as the International Criminal Court, or whether it is limited to barring the prosecution of heads of state in foreign courts. For scholarly discussion of this issue, see *Akande* and *Shah*, 21 European Journal of International Law 2010, 815–852. For a contrary opinion, see *Orakshelashvili*, 22 European Journal of International Law 2011, 849–855 and *Kiyani*, 12 Chinese Journal of International Law 2013, 486–490.

12 ICC Pre-Trial Chamber II, Situation in Darfur, Sudan, In the Case of *The Prosecutor v Omar Hassan Ahmad Al-Bashir*, The Hashemite Kingdom of Jordan's Notice of Appeal of the Decision Under Article 87(7) of the Rome Statute on the Non-Compliance by Jordan with the Request by the Court for the Arrest and Surrender of Omar Al-Bashir, ICC-02/05/01/09–312 (18 Dec 2017), paras. 33–45; or, in the Alternative, ICC Pre-Trial Chamber II, Leave to Seek an Appeal of the Decision Under Article 87(7) of the Rome Statute on the Non-Compliance by Jordan with the Request by the Court for the Arrest and Surrender of Omar Al-Bashir, ICC-02/05–01/09 (18 Dec 2017), para. 4(b); Prosecution's Response to the Hashemite Kingdom of Jordan's Notice of Appeal (n. 9), para. 5; ICC Pre-Trial Chamber II, Situation in Darfur, Sudan, In the Case of *The Prosecutor v Omar Hassan Ahmad Al-Bashir*, Decision on Jordan's Request for Leave to Appeal, ICC-02/05–01/09 (21 Feb 2018), para. 11.

13 *Triffterer* and *Burchard*, in: Triffterer and Ambos (eds.), Rome Statute of the International Criminal Court: A Commentary (2016), 1037–1055. See Article 31 of the Vienna Convention on the Law of Treaties of 23 May 1969, entered into force 27 Jan 1980, 1155 UNTS 331 (VCLT).

munity of other members of government in terms of the Rome Statute.[14] Furthermore, it was commonly understood that Article 27(2) of the Rome Statute, therefore, enabled member states to arrest the visiting head of state of another member state if so requested by the International Criminal Court.[15]

In the Jordan proceedings it was not disputed that Article 27(1) of the Rome Statute lifted the immunity of a signatory's head of state should the Court request the arrest and surrender for prosecution.[16] Pre-Trial Chamber II refers to this understanding of the terminology as being the vertical effect of Article 27.[17] The non-arrest of President Al-Bashir, however, sparked a debate regarding the true meaning of Article 27(2) of the Rome Statute, and whether it has horizontal application.[18] The effect of horizontal application of Article 27 means that signatories to the Rome Statute cannot rely on immunity in order to prevent arrest or prosecution by the International Criminal Court at the request of other member states.[19] If Article 27(2) operates on a horizontal level, all immunity is waived between all member states, and a member state may arrest a head of state or a diplomat of another member state if requested to do so by the International Criminal Court.[20]

Seemingly, the interpretation that Article 27 has a horizontal application is a logical deduction, as it is aligned with the fact that the function and success of the International Criminal Court depends on co-operation by member states.[21] The African Union consistently argues that Article 27 of the Rome Statute "does not affect the horizontal application of immunities between states which remain intact under Article 98 of the

---

14 See n. 9 for a summary of the submissions addressing the interpretation of para. 27. This is discussed in part 5 of this submission.

15 *Triffterer* and *Burchard* (n. 13), 1037–1049.

16 See *Triffterer* and *Burchard* (n. 13), 1040, who explain the vertical dimension of Article 27(1) of the Rome Statute as follows: "Article 27 deals with the vertical, top-down relationship between the Court and the state granting an immunity *ratione materiae* to *personae* to the accused.".

17 South African Decision (n. 3), para. 77. The Trial Chamber describes the vertical dimension as follows: "[T]he … – vertical – line, any immunity belonging to a state party, including that of its head of state, is irrelevant and cannot be raised as a ground for refusing the arrest and surrender of a person sought by the Court.".

18 See n. 9.

19 For an elaboration on the horizontal theory, see part 3 of this contribution.

20 See *Triffterer* and *Burchard* (n. 13), 1040–1041; South African Decision (n. 3), para. 76.

21 *Triffterer* and *Burchard* (n. 13), 1041; South African Decision (n. 3), para. 79.

Rome Statute".[22] Thus, the African Union is of the opinion that Article 27 of the Rome Statute does not remove the immunity of heads of state of non-state parties from foreign criminal jurisdiction as there is no horizontal application of Article 27(2) of the Rome Statute.[23] Even though the Arab League and Jordan agree with this interpretation, this is a contested view which does not enjoy scholarly support.[24]

The chapter's methodology entails using traditional sources of international law, listed in Article 38(1) of the International Court of Justice Statute.[25] In determining the content and implications of Article 27(2) of the Rome Statute, the law of treaty interpretation, as set out in Articles 31 to 33 of the Vienna Convention on the Law of Treaties, is employed to facilitate the interpretation of Article 27.[26]

The chapter navigates the debate central to the "probable" horizontal application of Article 27(2) of the Rome Statute and highlights the international and regional perspectives on this issue. Part I, the introduction, explains the research problem. Part II provides an overview of the proceedings involving the Hashemite Kingdom of Jordan as a result of its failure to arrest President Al-Bashir. Part III employs Articles 31 to 33 of the Vienna Convention on the Law of Treaties in order to determine whether Article 27(2) indeed applies horizontally. Part IV gives an overview of the debate and views fuelled by the Jordan proceedings.[27] Part V offers the perspective of the international community concerning head-of-state immunity in relation to Article 27 of the Rome Statute, more generally, and specifically in relation to Jordan's failure to arrest President Al-Bashir. Special attention is paid to the African Union's perspective and that of African states. Finally, a conclusion is presented.

22 African Union's Submission (n. 6), para. 18.

23 Ibid., paras. 22–26.

24 See part V of this contribution.

25 Statute of the International Court of Justice of 26 Jun 1945, entered into force 24 Oct 1945, TS No. 993 (ICJ Statute).

26 Vienna Convention on the Law of Treaties (n. 13).

27 When the authors refer to the Jordan Proceedings, we refer to all the legal proceedings before the ICC resulting from Jordan's non-arrest of president Al-Bashir.

II. Events leading to the "Jordan Appeal"

On 31 March 2005 the United Nations (UN) Security Council adopted Resolution 1593 of 2005 under its Chapter VII powers.[28] Resolution 1593 referred the ongoing situation in Darfur, Sudan, to the International Criminal Court.[29] The referral was necessary as Sudan is not a signatory to the Rome Statute.[30] As a result, the Prosecutor of the International Criminal Court conducted an investigation, and Pre-Trial Chamber I issued two arrest warrants against Omar Al-Bashir, President of Sudan, for the alleged commission of international crimes committed in Darfur between July 2008 and March 2013.[31] President Al-Bashir remains at large as several member states to the International Criminal Court have failed to exercise the warrant and arrest of President Al-Bashir during his visits to these member states.[32]

President Al-Bashir travelled to Jordan and attended the 28th Arab League Summit and afterwards returned to Sudan without an attempt by Jordan to arrest him.[33] Jordan is a member state to the Rome Statute.[34] Jordan's failure to give effect to the arrest warrant issued by the International Criminal Court prompted the Court to lodge proceedings pursuant to Article 87(7) of the Rome Statute and in line with regulation 109 of the Regulations of the Court against Jordan.[35] On 11 December 2017 Pre-Trial Chamber II rendered its decision under Article 87(7) of the Rome Statute and determined that Jordan had failed to comply with its obligations as a party to the Rome Statute by not adhering to the arrest warrant issued against President Al-Bashir.[36] Pre-Trial Chamber II referred the matter to

---

28 SC Res 1593 (2005) on Violations of International Humanitarian Law and Human Rights Law in Darfur, Sudan, S/RES/1593 (2005) (31 Mar 2005).

29 Ibid. For a discussion of the legal nature of Security Council referrals to the ICC, see *Akande*, 7 JICJ 2009, 333–352 and *De Wet*, 112 AJIL Unbound 2018, 33–37. Charter of the United Nations of 24 Oct 1945, 1 UNTS XVI.

30 For an up-to-date list of the ICC member states, see https://asp.icc-cpi.int/en_menus/asp/states%20parties/Pages/the%20states%20parties%20to%20the%20rome%20statute.aspx (last visited 4 Dec 2019).

31 Jordan Decision (n. 2), para. 2.

32 Jordan Decision (n. 2), para. 4. These states include Chad, Malawi and South Africa.

33 Jordan Decision (n. 2), para. 8.

34 See https://asp.icc-cpi.int/en_menus/asp/states%20parties/Pages/the%20states%20parties%20to%20the%20rome%20statute.aspx (last visited 27 Jan 2020).

35 Jordan Decision (n. 2), para. 8.

36 Jordan Decision (n. 2), para. 21.

the Assembly of State Parties of the Rome Statute as well as the United Nations Security Council.[37] In response to this ruling, Jordan lodged an application for leave to appeal against the ruling of Pre-Trial Chamber II in the *Decision Under Article 87(7) of the Rome Statute on the Non-Compliance by Jordan with the Request by the Court for the Arrest and Surrender of Omar Al-Bashir* on 18 December 2017 (Jordan decision).[38]

Among other grounds, Jordan disputed the fact that Article 27(2) had a horizontal effect.[39] On 21 December 2017 the Prosecutor of the International Criminal Court responded that it did not object to Jordan's request for leave to appeal.[40] On 21 February 2018 Pre-Trial Chamber II granted the leave to appeal against the *Decision Under Article 87(7) of the Rome Statute on the Non-Compliance by Jordan with the Request by the Court for the Arrest and Surrender of Omar Al-Bashir*, and included questions regarding the horizontal application of Article 27(2) of the Rome Statute (the immunity provision) as well as the customary nature of Al-Bashir's head-of-state immunity and the nature of Security Council Resolution 1593 (2005).[41] As permitted by the *Decision on the Requests for Leave to File Observations Pursuant to Rule 103 of the Rules of Procedure and Evidence, the Request for Leave to Reply and Further Processes in the Appeal,*[42] the Appeal Chamber invited international organisations, states and international law scholars to submit observations regarding the various legal arguments and questions, most of which related to concerns regarding head-of-state immunity as raised in the *Order on the Conduct of the Hearing Before the Appeals Chamber in the Jordan Referral Re Al-Bashir Appeal.*[43] These observations included questions about the horizontal application of Articles 27 and 98 of the Rome Statute, to the effect of Security Council Resolution 1593 (2005), as well as the nature of customary international law regulating head-of-state

---

37 Ibid.

38 Jordan's Notice of Appeal (n. 12).

39 Jordan's Notice of Appeal (n. 12), para. 4(b).

40 Prosecution's Response to the Hashemite Kingdom of Jordan's Notice (n. 9).

41 ICC Pre-Trial Chamber II, Situation in Darfur, Sudan, In the Case of *The Prosecutor v Omar Hassan Ahmad Al-Bashir*, Decision on Jordan's Request for Leave to Appeal, ICC-12/05–01/09 (21 Feb 2018).

42 ICC Appeals Chamber, Situation in Darfur, Sudan, In the Case of *The Prosecutor v Omar Hassan Ahmad Al-Bashir*, Decision on the Request for Leave to File Observations Pursuant to Rule 103 of the Rules of Procedure and Evidence, the Request for Leave to Reply and Further Processes in the Appeal of 21 May 2018, ICC-02/05–01/09–309 (25 May 2018).

43 Order on the Conduct of the Hearing (n. 4).

immunity.[44] The League of Arab States, the African Union and several scholars of international law submitted valuable observations and participated in the oral proceedings which took place between 10 and 14 September 2018.[45] These proceedings and submissions, in particular, inform the analysis conducted in this discussion.

III. Interpreting Article 27(2) in accordance with the Vienna conventions

This part employs Articles 31 to 33 of the Vienna Convention on the Law of Treaties to determine whether Article 27(2) regulates immunities on an inter-state level and, therefore, demonstrates a horizontal dimension.[46] The horizontal effect of Article 27 refers to the relationship between the requested state and the state granting immunity or, rather, to inter-state relationships between state parties to the Rome Statute.[47] It is argued that the horizontal effect of Article 27(2) renders immunities irrelevant.[48] In summary, Pre-Trial Chamber II has indicated that the result of the horizontal application of Article 27(2) is that a state party cannot refuse to comply with an arrest and surrender request by the International Criminal Court, even in respect of a head of state of another state party, as any possible immunities that bar the Court from exercising jurisdiction are rendered redundant by Article 27 of the Rome Statute.[49] Pre-Trial Chamber II contends that this regime applies to state parties alone, while arrest and surrender requests in relation to non-state parties are regulated by Article 98(1) of the Rome Statute.[50] Furthermore, the view of Pre-Trial Chamber II, and the majority of scholars, is that the effect of United Nations Securi-

44 Order on the Conduct of the Hearing (n. 4), paras. 4–6.

45 For a complete list of states' representatives, see ICC Appeals Chamber, Situation in Darfur, Sudan, In the Case of *The Prosecutor v Omar Hassan Ahmad Al-Bashir*, Prosecution Notice of Further Reference List for Certain Oral Submissions, ICC-02/05–01/09 (12 Sep 2018), para. 2.

46 For a discussion on the general rules of treaty interpretation, see *Linderfalk*, On the Interpretation of Treaties: The Modern International Law as Expressed in the 1969 Vienna Convention of the Law of Treaties (1st ed. 2001); *Linderfalk*, On the Interpretation of Treaties: The Modern International Law as Expressed in the 1969 Vienna Convention on the Law of Treaties (2nd ed. 2007).

47 See *Triffterer* and *Burchard* (n. 13), 1040–1041; South African Decision (n. 3), para. 76.

48 See *Triffterer* and *Burchard* (n. 13), 1040–1041.

49 South African Decision (n. 3), para. 80.

50 South African Decision (n. 3), paras. 71–83, 94, 107–108.

ty Council Resolution 1593 is that Article 27 applies to Sudan as though it were a member state, and that the Security Council Resolution transforms the Sudan *sui generis* into a member state.[51] Consequently, from a practical perspective this horizontal approach to Article 27(2) means that Jordan (and the other member states that had the opportunity but failed to do so) had to arrest President Al-Bashir. However, if the opposite interpretation, which is supported by the African Union, the League of Arab States and Jordan, is followed, it would mean that Jordan's non-arrest of President Al-Bashir is not an infraction of Article 27 of the Rome Statute.[52]

Articles 27(1) and 27(2) of the Rome Statute makes no direct reference to either a "vertical" or a "horizontal" dimension. Furthermore, neither provision refers to the possessive pronoun nor any terminology which indicates the relationship between the member state and the official whose immunity is waived. For instance, Article 27 does not refer to a member state's "own" official.[53] However, reliance on the wording of the Article is not sufficient.[54]

Article 31(1) of the Vienna Convention determines that words should not be studied in isolation, but that a provision should be interpreted in good faith by examining the wording in light of the context and taking cognisance of the object and purpose of the relevant treaty. Article 31(2) of the Vienna Convention lists various tools which may be employed to determine context, including the treaty's Preamble. The Preamble is particularly helpful as a means of establishing context.[55] The Rome Statute's Preamble emphasises that the overall purpose of the International Criminal Court is to punish those individuals who are most responsible for serious crimes of international concern in order to combat impunity from prosecution.[56] The core international crimes included in Article 5

51 South African Decision (n. 3), paras. 91 and 94.

52 See Jordan's Response to the Observations Submitted by the African Union and the League of Arab States (n. 6), paras. 6 and 7; The League of Arab States' Observations (n. 6), paras. 24–28; Supplementary African Union Submission (n. 6), paras. 5–13.

53 Compare Rome Statute (n. 1), Article 27.

54 Vienna Convention on the Law of Treaties (n. 13), Article 31(1).

55 Vienna Convention on the Law of Treaties (n. 13), Article 31(2).

56 Rome Statute (n. 1). The authors cite a portion of the Preamble in support of their deductions: "Affirming that the most serious crimes of concern to the international community as a whole must not go unpunished and that their effective prosecution must be ensured by taking measures at the national level and by enhancing international cooperation; Determined to put an end to impunity for the perpetrators of these crimes and thus to contribute to the prevention of

of the Rome Statute are of such a nature that governmental authorities, including heads of state, often play a role in the commission of these crimes as, by their nature and scale, they necessitate the involvement of state machinery – for instance, systematic crimes such as genocide, as well as war crimes. The purpose of the International Criminal Court is not to prosecute low-ranking officials, but rather high-ranking officials such as military leaders, as well as the most senior government officials such as heads of state.[57] This aim is not feasible if Article 27 does not have horizontal application.[58]

Article 32(2) of the Vienna Convention asserts that the relevant subsequent agreements between the parties to the treaty, coherent subsequent practice of states party to the treaty regarding its interpretation,[59] as well as the relevant rules of international law applicable in relations between the parties, form part of the context.[60] There are no relevant subsequent treaties to aid this interpretation. This section now considers whether sufficient subsequent state practice exists which may be helpful.[61] The notion of "subsequent practice", as included in Article 31(3)(b) of the Vienna Convention, refers to the application of the treaty provisions by its state parties.[62] In order for subsequent practice to be used as an interpretative tool, the conduct of state parties must be uniform and understood in the same way by all the signatories to the relevant treaty.[63]

The International Law Commission Study Group on subsequent agreements and subsequent practice in relation to the interpretation of treaties reads Article 31(3)(b) to necessitate that subsequent practice is sufficient to aid treaty interpretation only when the relevant evidence exists which

---

such crimes; Recalling that it is the duty of every state to exercise its criminal jurisdiction over those responsible for international crimes ... Determined to these ends and for the sake of present and future generations, to establish an independent permanent International Criminal Court in relationship with the United Nations system, with jurisdiction over the most serious crimes of concern to the international community as a whole.".

57 Rome Statute (n. 1), Article 1.

58 Request by Professor Claus Kress (n. 9), para. 7.

59 For a comprehensive discussion of the law of subsequent treaty practice, see *Nolte* (ed.), Treaties and Subsequent Practice (2013).

60 Vienna Convention on the Law of Treaties (n. 13), Article 31(3).

61 Vienna Convention on the Law of Treaties (n. 13), Article 31(3)(b).

62 *Nolte* (n. 59), 309: "'Subsequent practice' covers any application of the treaty. It can also take various forms and may consist of action or inaction.".

63 *Gardiner*, Treaty Interpretation (2008), 227.

proves that such conduct is "concordant", "consistent" and "common".[64] Subsequent practice, therefore, requires a much higher threshold of uniformity in state practice than customary international law, in that it demands complete uniformity.[65] As the meaning of Article 27(2) is contentious and states are divided as to its horizontal application, this interpretive tool is not helpful. Customary international law concerning the doctrine of head-of-state immunity may be consulted as per Article 31(3)(c) of the Vienna Convention. However, its relevance is highly disputed, and it is unlikely that any rules of customary international law regulate head-of-state immunity before international criminal tribunals.[66] It is doubtful that sufficient state practice and *opinio juris* exist to establish a customary international law rule which determines that heads of state enjoy immunity from prosecution by international criminal tribunals. Heads of state in fact do not enjoy immunity for the commission of international crimes or *jus cogens* crimes or lose immunity from prosecution by international criminal tribunals as this example is a manifestation of a customary exception to the rule that heads of states have absolute immunity under international law.[67] There are no treaties regulating head-of-state immunity, only regarding the immunities of diplomats and consular officials. Therefore Article 31(3)(c) also is not helpful.[68]

Article 32 of the Vienna Convention offers supplementary means of interpretation, which include the preparatory work of a treaty.[69] This section examines key contributions made during the negotiation of the

64 Ibid.

65 *Nolte* (n. 59), 17.

66 In *The Minister of Justice and Constitutional Development v The Southern African Litigation Centre* 2016 3 SA 317 (SCA); for a definition of the concept "foreign court", see *Cassese* et al., International Criminal Law: Cases and Commentary (2011), 76. For a discussion of immunity of heads of state before foreign courts, Compare *Hood* and *Cormier*, 13 Melbourne Journal of International Law 2012, 236–264; *Akande* and *Shah* (n. 11), 815–852. For a contrary opinion, see *Orakshelashvili* (n. 11), 849–855.

67 Ibid. See also the plethora of questions raised in this regard in Order Inviting Submissions (n. 4), 4–6.

68 Vienna Convention on Diplomatic Relations of 18 Apr 1961, 23 UST 3227, TIAS No. 7502, 500 UNTS 95; Vienna Convention on Consular Relations of 24 Apr 1963, 21 UST 77, TIAS No. 6820, 596 UNTS 261.

69 See Vienna Convention on the Law of Treaties (n. 13), 32, which recognises the drafting history of a treaty as a supplementary source of treaty interpretation. For an in-depth discussion of Article 32 itself, see *Le Bouthillier*, in: Corten and Klein (eds.), The Vienna Conventions on the Law of Treaties: A Commentary, vol. 1 (2011), 841–863.

Rome Statute as a supplementary means of interpretation in order to establish whether the drafting history provides any insight into the possible horizontal application of Article 27(2) of the Rome Statute.[70] The relevant sections of the drafting history support a view that the drafters had no intention of allowing heads of state or other officials to be entitled to any form of official immunity.[71] The proposal which Australia submitted regarding the immunity provision reads as follows: "In the course of investigations or procedures performed by, or at the request of the Court, no person may make a plea of immunity from jurisdiction irrespective of whether on the basis of international or national law."[72] The drafting history refers to Article 7(2) of the Statute of the International Criminal Tribunal for the Former Yugoslavia (ICTY), which states: "(2) The official position of any accused person, whether as head of state or government or as a responsible government official, shall not relieve such person of criminal responsibility nor mitigate punishment."[73] The Siracusa draft echoes the Australian submission's approach as well as Article 7(2) of the ICTY Statute, but emphasises that heads of state in particular are not entitled to immunity.[74]

Although the wording of Article 27(2) of the Rome Statute, as well as the minutes capturing its drafting history, did not have an explicit reference to a horizontal dimension, in light of the context of this treaty, the authors submit that Article 27(2) has a horizontal dimension. In our view this is the only logical conclusion. A clause which aims to lift the immunity of officials so as to enable an International Criminal Court, established to prosecute serious crimes committed by those most responsi-

70 The drafting history is published in United Nations Diplomatic Conference of Plenipotentiaries on the Establishment of an International Criminal Court, 15 Jun–17 Jul 1998, vol. II, Summary Records of the Plenary Meetings and of the Meetings of the Committee of the Whole (2002), http://legal.un.org/diplomatic-conferences/1998_icc/vol2.shtml (last visited 4 Dec 2019).

71 *Jun Yoshida* (Rapporteur), Summary of the Proceedings of the Preparatory Committee on the Establishment of an International Criminal Court, 25 Mar–12 Apr 1996, A/AC.249/1 (7 May 1996), para. 90.

72 Ibid., para. 77.

73 Statute of the International Criminal Tribunal for the Former Yugoslavia of 25 May 1993, S/25704.

74 Summary of the Proceedings (n. 71), para. 78. The Siracusa draft determined: "2. The official position of an individual who commits a crime under this Statute *and particularly the fact that he acts as head of state* or government or as a responsible government official *does not relieve him of criminal responsibility* nor mitigate punishment" (emphasis added).

ble, including high-ranking officials, and which depends on co-operation by member states, requires horizontality. The submissions of Jordan, the African Union and the League of Arab States do not correspond with this argument, and will be discussed in part V below.

IV. An overview of the debate as highlighted by the Jordan Referral

As discussed above, in the Jordan Decision, Pre-Trial Chamber II relied on its earlier decision in *The Decision under Article 87(7) of the Rome Statute on the Non-Compliance by South Africa with the Request by the Court for the Arrest and Surrender of Omar Al-Bashir* with regard to the interpretation of Article 27(2) of the Rome Statute.[75] Pre-Trial Chamber II confirmed that Article 27(2) had horizontal application and that in the event of a United Nations Security Council referral (such as in the case of Security Council Resolution 1593 (2005)) the referred state should be treated as if it were a member state.[76] Pre-Trial Chamber II furthermore determined that Article 98 was not applicable in the assessment of Jordan's failure to arrest President Al-Bashir, owing to the horizontal nature of Article 27(2).[77] Jordan, therefore, cannot take refuge in President Al-Bashir's immunity as such immunity is lifted by Article 27 of the Rome Statute.[78] The following ruling by Pre-Trial Chamber II is one of the grounds appealed by Jordan and has ignited a great deal of discussion in the subsequent submissions:

> "The Chamber finds, by majority, that because the rights and obligations as provided for in the Statute, including Article 27(2), are applicable to Sudan (by imposition of the Security Council acting under Chapter VII of the UN Charter), the immunities of Omar Al-Bashir as head of state, under customary international law, do not bar state parties to the Rome Statute from executing the Court's request of his arrest and surrender for crimes under the jurisdiction of the Court allegedly committed in Darfur within the parameters of the Security Council referral. While it has not been established before the Chamber that the 1953 Convention is in force between Sudan and Jordan, the same conclusion would hold also with respect to any immunity of Omar Al-Bashir under Article 11 of the said convention. Article 98(1)

75 Jordan Decision (n. 2), para. 33; South African Decision (n. 3), para. 76–80.
76 Jordan Decision (n. 2), para. 33.
77 Jordan Decision (n. 2), paras. 32 and 33.
78 Jordan Decision (n. 2), paras. 38 and 39.

> of the Statute is not applicable to the situation of Omar Al-Bashir, and state parties to the Rome Statute, including Jordan, are under the duty to execute the warrants of arrest issued by the Court, and to implement the Court's request for the arrest of Omar Al-Bashir and his surrender to the Court."[79]

In its leave to appeal, Jordan asserted that Pre-Trial Chamber II incorrectly determined that Article 27(2) of the Rome Statute had the above-mentioned effect in that Jordan argued that Article 27 did not apply horizontally and that Article 98 was the appropriate provision to address the resolution of the dispute.[80] During the submissions phase, all but a single professor in international law, who elected to address the application of Article 27(2), agreed that Pre-Trial Chamber II had interpreted and applied Article 27(2) correctly in the Jordan Decision.[81] The African Union and the League of Arab States sided with Jordan in maintaining that Article 27(2) did not have horizontal application.[82] The League of Arab States and Jordan supported the arguments submitted by the African Union.[83]

The discussion now turns to the African Union's submissions.[84] The African Union made two submissions – the first on 13 July 2018 prior to the oral proceedings which took place during the appeals phase, and the second on 28 September 2018 after the appeals phase. Both submissions pertained to the African Union's view on the interpretation and scope of application of Article 27 of the Rome Statute.[85]

The African Union's Submission in the Hashemite Kingdom of Jordan's Appeal Against the Decision under Article 87(7) of the Rome Statute on the Non-Compliance by Jordan with the Request by the Court for the Arrest and Surrender [of] Omar Al-Bashir reveals that the African Union disagrees with the reading of Article 27 of the Rome Statute by Pre-Trial Chamber II.[86]

---

79 Jordan Decision (n. 2), para. 44.

80 Jordan Referral or Leave to Appeal (n. 12), para. 4(B).

81 O'Keefe (n. 9), paras. 8–11.

82 Jordan's Reply to African Union's Submission (n. 6), para. 26; African Union's Submission (n. 6), paras. 11–26; The League of Arab States' Observations (n. 6), paras. 24–28.

83 Jordan's Response to the Observations Submitted by the African Union and the League of Arab States (n. 6), paras. 6 and 7; The League of Arab States' Observations (n. 6), para. 27.

84 African Union's Submission (n. 6); African Union Supplementary Submission (n. 6).

85 Ibid.

86 African Union's Submission (n. 6), paras. 11–26.

The African Union interprets Article 27 of the Rome Statute to operate vertically only.[87] According to the African Union, Article 27 lifts the immunity of the accused belonging to a member state only in respect of that member state.[88] This interpretation means, for example, that if a warrant is issued to arrest the President of South Africa, then South Africa alone can arrest its head of state without a breach of relevant obligations under the law of head-of-state immunity.[89] Another member state, for instance Jordan, cannot arrest the President of South Africa, as Article 27 does not have horizontal application.[90] The African Union believes that the horizontal relationship and, therefore, also co-operation between states in relation to the immunities of an official of another state, are regulated by Article 98 of the Rome Statute.[91]

The African Union relied on the rules of treaty interpretation to support its reading of Article 27(2), but emphasised that, in light of Article 31, the context of a treaty provision should be taken into account when it is interpreted.[92] The African Union, however, stressed that the context should derive from the parts of the treaty in which the provisions are located.[93] For instance, Article 27 is situated in Part 3 of the Rome Statute, which is concerned with the rules that the International Criminal Court uses in order to determine the guilt or innocence of an accused.[94] All the rules under Part 3 of this treaty concern the relationship between the Court and the accused, namely, a vertical relationship.[95] Part 3 is not relevant to member state cooperation with the Court or with the obligations of states party to the Rome Statute.[96] In the view of the African Union, Article 98 of the Rome Statute has horizontal application and regulates the waiver of immunity under international law *vis-à-vis* member states and third states.[97] The African Union asserts that this interpretation is supported by the context as well as by the fact that Article 98 is in Part 9 of the

87 Ibid, para. 14.
88 Ibid.
89 Ibid, paras. 14 and 17.
90 Ibid, para. 16.
91 Ibid, paras. 17 and 18.
92 Ibid, paras. 30–31.
93 Ibid, para. 31.
94 Ibid.
95 Ibid.
96 Ibid, paras. 31–32.
97 Ibid.

Rome Statute indicates the obligations of state parties to the International Criminal Court as well as those of other states.[98]

The African Union reiterated this interpretation in its additional submission, once again arguing that Article 27 must be understood in the context of Part 3 and not of Part 9 of the Rome Statute.[99] This argument has merit in that context may be derived from the part of the treaty in which a provision is situated, but it is overrated. In the opinion of the authors, the "geographical placement" of a provision is not the only relevant context. The overall object and purpose of a treaty in its entirety cannot be disregarded and, contrary to the opinion of the African Union, the overall object and purpose of the Rome Statute supports the horizontal application of Article 27(2).[100]

The African Union offered an additional argument in its supplementary submission which supported the interpretation that Article 27(2) does not apply horizontally.[101] This argument reflects on Article 31(3)(c) of the Vienna Convention which states that, together with context, any relevant rules of international law applicable in the relations between the parties must be taken into account in the interpretation of a treaty.[102] The African Union maintains that Article 27(2) should be interpreted in line with custom and that customary international law does not permit exceptions in granting head-of-state immunity.[103] The authors at this point part ways with the statement by the African Union that "[i]t is trite that customary international law knows no exception to immunity of heads of state".[104] The only settled rule of customary international law that relates to head-of-state immunity is that heads of state enjoy absolute immunity before foreign jurisdictions.[105] The International Criminal Court is not a foreign court but an international court.[106] There simply is not sufficient state

98 Ibid, para. 31.

99 African Union Supplementary Submission (n. 6), para. 9.

100 See discussion in part 4 of this contribution.

101 African Union Supplementary Submission (n. 6), para. 5.

102 Ibid, para. 11.

103 Ibid.

104 African Union Supplementary Submission (n. 6), para. 11.

105 See *Akande* and *Shah* (n. 11), 815–852. For a contrary opinion, see *Orakshelashvili* (n. 11), 849–855.

106 For a definition of the concept "foreign court", see *Cassese* et al., International Criminal Law: Cases and Commentary (2011), 76. For a discussion on immunity of heads of state before foreign courts, compare *Hood* and *Cormier* (n. 67), 236–264; *Akande* and *Shah* (n. 11), 815–852. For a contrary opinion, see *Orakshelashvili* (n. 11), 849–855.

practice and *opinio juris* to assert that any rule or exceptions exist under customary international law which regulate head-of-state immunity in the context of international criminal tribunals. It is not trite law, and the content of customary international law is a matter of dispute to the extent that in the *Order on the Conduct of the Hearing Before the Appeals Chamber in the Jordan Referral re Al-Bashir Appeal* questions were raised on which views were solicited.[107]

Most submissions by scholars of international law addressing the interpretation and the "disputed" horizontal application of Article 27(2) of the Rome Statute concur with the opinion of the Pre-Trial Chamber as well as that of the Prosecutor.[108] The contributions by Professors Flavia Lattanzi and Nicholas Tsagourias and Doctor M Vagias are significant and nuanced in their challenge to the opinions provided by the African Union, the League of Arab States and Jordan.[109] Professor Tsagourias and Doctor Vagias determine that the Security Council referral renders Sudan a quasi-state party and triggers the horizontal application of Article 27(2) of the Rome Statute, whereas Article 98 of the Rome Statute is rendered inapplicable.[110] They argue that other sources of international law are not an obstacle to the International Criminal Court exercising jurisdiction.[111] Their argument is based on an appraisal of Article 21 of the Rome Statute, which ranks the applicable sources on which the ICC may rely, and conclude that this provision prioritises ICC-specific sources.[112] In the current matter, Article 27 of the Rome Statute is the ICC-specific source on the issue of head-of-state immunity, which clearly declares that immunities were considered but rejected, with the consequence that, as there are no legal *lacunae*, there is no need to consult other sources.[113] Following this line of reasoning, Professor Tsagourias and Doctor Vagias concluded that neither customary international law nor external treaty law can be imposed directly to limit the International Criminal Court's jurisdiction. Specifically, they establish that "customary and treaty law cannot be used indirectly to interpret *contra legem* the Rome Statute under Article 31(3)(c)

107 Order on the Conduct of the Hearing (n. 4), 4–6.

108 Compare O'Keefe (n. 9), paras. 8–11, as he challenges the interpretation of Article 27(2) by the African Union, Jordan and the Office of the Prosecutor.

109 Tsagourias and Vagias Submission (n. 9), 4, 5; Lattanzi Submission (n. 9), para. 3.

110 Tsagourias and Vagias Submission (n. 9), 5.

111 Ibid.

112 Tsagourias and Vagias Submission (n. 9), 4.

113 Ibid.

VCLT, as such approach would be inconsistent with Articles 10, 121 and 122 of the Statute".[114]

In his submission, Professor Flavia Lattanzi reiterates the opinion that Article 27 of the Rome Statute represents a derogation of the immunities enjoyed by officials (and specifically heads of state) under public international law, and this factor is regardless of the legal sources, whether customary international law or treaty law.[115] He argues that Article 27 of the Rome Statute is binding and consequently lifts immunities without exception.[116] Professor Lattanzi applies an argument which relies on this interpretation of Jordan's legal conundrum.[117] Consequently, in his opinion, a horizontal relationship between Jordan and Sudan is regulated by Article 27 of the Rome Statute and inhibits a claim on immunity by President Al-Bashir.[118] He concludes:

> "Conclusively, Jordan was never faced with conflicting obligations *vis-à-vis* Sudan, as both states are bound by Article 27(2) and none of them is entitled to claim immunities pursuant to Article 98(1)."[119]

V. International and African Perspectives

Part V of this contribution provides an overview of the international and regional perspectives on the immunity provision of the Rome Statute. The Jordan submissions enable the authors to present perspectives on Article 27(2) by the African Union, Jordan and the League of Arab States. The responses of states arising from Jordan's failure to arrest President Al-Bashir also offers insight. The positions of the African Union, the League of Arab States and Jordan are similar.[120] The two regional intergovernmental organisations, as well as Jordan, expressed the opinion that heads of state enjoyed absolute immunity under customary international law and that

114 Ibid.

115 Lattanzi Submission (n. 9), para. 3.

116 Ibid.

117 Ibid.

118 Lattanzi Submission (n. 9), para. 5.

119 Ibid.

120 Compare Jordan's Reply to African Union Submission (n. 6), para. 26; The League of Arab States' Observations (n. 6), para. 27; African Union Submission (n. 6), paras. 22–26; Supplementary African Union Submission (n. 6), paras. 5–13.

Article 27(2) has vertical application alone.[121] They averred that if a member state wishes to arrest a president or official entitled to immunity under conventional or customary international law, then the waiver of immunity is regulated by Article 98 of the Rome Statute, and that it is for states, and not the Court, to make such a determination.[122] Therefore, without an explicit waiver of all immunities by the requested state, a member state cannot give effect to the arrest warrant issued by the International Criminal Court for the head of state of another state.[123] This problem is well illustrated by the scenarios discussed below regarding individual instances of states' refusal to give effect to the ICC warrant issued for the arrest of President Al-Bashir.

1. South Africa

For purposes of this discussion it should be noted that South Africa has been a party to the Rome Statute of the International Criminal Court since 1998. According to Section 231(4) of the Constitution of the Republic of South Africa, 1996, an international agreement becomes enforceable law in terms of South African law once it is incorporated into the South African domestic law in terms of an act of parliament. The international obligations contained in the Rome Statute were incorporated into South African law by means of the Implementation of the Rome Statute of the International Criminal Court Act No. 27 of 2002 (Implementation Act). As previously stated in this contribution, the ICC relies heavily on the cooperation of state parties to the agreement.

In the case of South Africa, President Al-Bashir arrived in the country on 13 June 2015 in order to attend a summit of the African Union. On the same day, ICC Pre-Trial Chamber II ordered that the South African authorities should arrest Al-Bashir and surrender him to the ICC to face prosecution. At the same time, a South African non-governmental organi-

---

121 Ibid. For the opinion of Jordan, the League of Arab States and the African Union concerning the extent of head-of-state immunity under customary international law, see Jordan Appeal (n. 6), para. 37; The League of Arab States' Observations (n. 6), para. 22; African Union Submission (n. 6), paras. 10, 23; Supplementary African Union Submission (n. 6), para. 11.

122 Jordan Appeal (n. 6), paras. 3(a), 10–14; The League of Arab States' Observations (n. 6), paras. 31–32; African Union Submission (n. 6), paras. 15–19, 26; Supplementary African Union Submission (n. 6), paras. 8, 13.

123 Ibid.

sation (Southern African Litigation Centre) applied at the North Gauteng High Court for an urgent order compelling the arrest and surrender of Al-Bashir by the South African authorities.[124] Such interim order was granted on 14 June 2015, pending the hearing on 15 June 2015, when the government should have submitted replying affidavits as to why the order should not be made final.[125] After the government had submitted their replying affidavits late on 15 June 2015, without explanation, it transpired that Al-Bashir had already left the country during the course of the hearing.[126] Although the Court had on 15 June 2015 granted an order that the South African government must take all reasonable steps to prepare to arrest Al-Bashir and to take all precautions to prevent Al-Bashir's departure from the country, the Court was informed that Al-Bashir had in fact left the country prior to its handing down of the judgment.[127] Nevertheless, the Court's judgment still considers the merits of the respondent's case with regard to their refusal to arrest and prevent the departure of President Al-Bashir and the relevant international law provisions and principles.

The arguments by the South African authorities were predominantly focused on the view that Al-Bashir enjoyed immunity from arrest while in South Africa and, therefore, that he could not have been arrested or detained. In support of this argument, the South African authorities relied on an AU host state agreement that they had entered into with the AU Commission which determined that privileges and immunities were provided to certain delegates attending the summit. This agreement was incorporated into South African law on 5 June 2015 by means of ministerial notice.[128] For purposes of this contribution, however, we turn to South Africa's approach to its obligation under Article 27(2) to determine whether it accepted the horizontal application of Article 27(2) of the Rome Statute. Regarding President Al-Bashir's supposed immunity, the Court stated that the only two possible grounds for Al-Bashir's immunity were those in terms of the Immunities Act, which provides heads of state with immunity from civil and criminal prosecution, to the extent afforded un-

---

124 *Southern Africa Litigation Centre v Minister of Justice and Constitutional Development & Others* 2015 5 SA 1 (GP); for a thorough discussion of the case, see *De Wet*, 13 JICJ 2015, 1049; also see *Tladi*, 13 JICJ 2015, 1027.

125 *Southern Africa Litigation Centre* case (n. 124), paras. 4–6.

126 *Southern Africa Litigation Centre* case (n. 124), paras. 6–7.

127 *Southern Africa Litigation Centre* case (n. 124), paras. 7–8.

128 Government Gazette 38860, https://archive.opengazettes.org.za/archive/ZA/2015/government-gazette-ZA-vol-600-no-38860-dated-2015-06-05.pdf (last visited 27 Jan 2020); see *Southern Africa Litigation Centre* case (n. 126), paras. 13–16.

der customary international law, or in terms of the AU host agreement.[129] The Rome Statute (which has been incorporated into South African law by the Implementation Act) expressly states that heads of state are not afforded immunity in terms of its provisions (which includes Article 27 of the Rome Statute).[130] The reason for this is obvious. If head-of-state immunity were recognised in terms of the provisions of the Rome Statute, this would leave the ICC powerless to prosecute heads of state that commit international crimes, which would defeat the purpose of the ICC. The Court, therefore, did not dispute the horizontal effect of Article 27(2) of the Rome Statute. The Court also correctly pointed out that the Pre-Trial Chamber of the ICC had already found that, because of the crimes committed by Al-Bashir, his immunity as head of state had been waived by the UN Security Council.[131] The South African authorities, therefore, could not have relied on this ground of immunity when refusing to arrest and surrender President Al-Bashir. It therefore follows that there were no grounds on the basis of which immunity could be afforded to President Al-Bashir, and that the South African authorities had no grounds for their refusal to arrest and surrender Al-Bashir.

De Wet correctly points out that the South African government's clear circumvention of its international law obligations is indicative of a clear trend of resentment among African countries toward the ICC Prosecutor regarding what these countries perceive as the "targeting of African leaders".[132] Be that as it may, these international obligations remain part of South African law until they are repealed. The South African authorities, therefore, remain bound by these obligations.

However, this was not the end of the matter. The Minister of Justice and Constitutional Development appealed against the decision of the High Court in the Supreme Court of Appeal.[133] For the sake of brevity, the authors will only discuss arguments relevant to the debate on whether or not Article 27 of the Rome Statute applies horizontally. On appeal, the argument of the South African authorities differed from the arguments submitted before the High Court. The government now based its argument on Section 4(1) of the Immunities Act and principles of customary international law in order to show that President Al-Bashir in fact enjoyed head-of-state immunity and that the South African government, therefore,

129 *Southern Africa Litigation Centre* case (n. 124), para. 28.

130 Ibid.

131 Ibid.

132 *De Wet* (n. 124), 1070; see, for example, *Van der Wilt*, 9 JICJ 2011, 1043.

133 *Southern Africa Litigation Centre* (SCA) (n. 66).

could not have arrested him during his stay in South Africa.[134] The Southern African Litigation Centre argued that the provisions of the Implementation Act, in Sections 4(2) and 10(9) respectively, affirmed the South African authorities' obligation to arrest Al-Bashir in terms of the Rome Statute.[135] The Supreme Court found that Section 4(1) in fact did confer immunity on heads of state, and that Section 4(2) of the Implementation Act did not remove this immunity. Sections 4(2) and 10(9), however, preclude a person from raising the defence of immunity in circumstances of the prosecution for international crimes.[136] Therefore the interpretation by the Supreme Court supported the horizontal application of the immunity provision.

2. Democratic Republic of the Congo

In another case concerning the non-arrest of President Al-Bashir, this time by the Democratic Republic of the Congo (DRC), Pre-Trial Chamber II of the ICC came to a conclusion which was similar to its later decision regarding the non-arrest of Al-Bashir after his visit to South Africa, a case referred to elsewhere in this contribution.[137] The DRC argued that President Al-Bashir enjoyed head-of-state immunity and that the request to arrest and surrender Al-Bashir was against its obligations to respect these immunities.[138] The Pre-Trial Chamber held that according to Article 27(2), including Security Council Resolution 1593 (2005), immunities did not bar the Court's jurisdiction, while also confirming that member states of the UN have a duty to carry out the decisions of the Security

---

134 *Southern Africa Litigation Centre* (SCA) (n. 66), para. 14.

135 *Southern Africa Litigation Centre* (SCA) (n. 66), para. 16; Section 10(9) of the Implementation Act states that a request for arrest and surrender by the ICC cannot be refused on the ground of the person in question being a head of state.

136 *Southern Africa Litigation Centre* (SCA) (n. 66), paras. 49–51.

137 ICC Pre-Trial Chamber II, Situation in Darfur, Sudan, In the Case of *The Prosecutor v Omar Hassan Ahmad Al-Bashir*, Decision on the Cooperation of the Democratic Republic of the Congo Regarding Omar Al-Bashir's Arrest and Surrender to the Court, ICC-02/05–01/09 (9 Apr 2014); see ICC Pre-Trial Chamber II, Situation in Darfur, Sudan, In the Case of *The Prosecutor v Omar Hassan Ahmad Al-Bashir*, Decision Under Article 87(7) of the Rome Statute on the Non-Compliance by South Africa With the Request by the Court for the Arrest and Surrender of Omar Al-Bashir, ICC-02/05–01/09 (11 Dec 2017).

138 Decision on the Cooperation of the Democratic Republic of the Congo (n. 137), para. 19; also see *Southern Africa Litigation Centre* case (n. 124), para. 31.

Council.[139] In cases that entail state and non-state parties to the Statute, the combined effect of the horizontal application of Article 27(2) and any UN Security Council resolutions would, therefore, be decisive in overriding head-of-state immunity and ensuring successful prosecutions of those who commit international crimes.

This interpretation of the authority of an international criminal court, which makes it completely dependent on the co-operation of member states, is not in the interests of ending impunity from prosecution. The position of the African Union corresponds with Article 46*bis* of its Malabo Protocol and the various statements published by the African Union since the arrest warrant for President Al-Bashir was issued.[140] The African Union at the same time maintains that it is engaged in the fight against impunity, but alleges that it also respects the balance of the norms of immunity, criminal justice and sovereignty of states.[141] This obviously does not promote legal certainty with regard to keeping heads of state responsible before international courts and tribunals.

VI. *Conclusion*

This chapter has illuminated the uncertainty surrounding head-of-state immunity in the context of the immunity provision (Article 27) of the Rome Statute, and emphasised how this situation of legal uncertainty hinders attempts to establish head-of-state responsibility and hampers the fight against impunity under customary international law. The legal proceedings instituted against Jordan, and specifically the written submissions made prior to the hearing before the Appeals Chamber in the *Jordan Referral re Al-Bashir Appeal* in relation to *Hashemite Kingdom of Jordan's Appeal Against the Decision under Article 87(7) of the Rome Statute on the*

139 See the entire argument of the Court in the Decision on the Cooperation of the Democratic Republic of the Congo (n. 137), paras. 25–34; also see *Southern Africa Litigation Centre* case (n. 124), para. 32.

140 Protocol on Amendments to The Protocol on The Statute of The African Court of Justice and Human Rights (Malabo Protocol) of 27 Jun 2014; African Union, Decision on the Meeting of African States Parties to the Rome Statute of the International Criminal Court (3 Jul 2009), Assembly/AU/13(XIII), https://au.int/sites/default/files/treaties/36398-treaty-0045_-_protocol_on_amendments_to_the_protocol_on_the_statute_of_the_african_court_of_justice_and_human_rights_e.pdf (last visited 27 Jan 2020).

141 African Union's Submission (n. 6), para. 4.

Non-Compliance by Jordan with the Request by the Court for the Arrest and Surrender [of] Omar Al-Bashir, highlights the way in which legal uncertainty contributes to state parties disregarding an arrest warrant issued against President Al-Bashir.

In the third part of this contribution the authors examined the wording of the immunity provision of the Rome Statute, Article 27(2), in accordance with the interpretation provisions encapsulated in the Vienna Convention on the Law of Treaties. The ordinary means of interpretation did not offer legal certainty as to whether or not Article 27(2) of the Rome Statute has horizontal application. In light of the overall object and purpose of the Rome Statute, which essentially aims to end impunity in the commission of international crimes by punishing those who bear the greatest responsibility for serious crimes of international concern, the authors support that interpretation. The individuals most responsible include high-ranking military officers or state officials, as well as heads of state. Enforcing their prosecution depends on waiving immunity and through co-operation by member states, making the horizontal effect of Article 27(2) the favoured interpretation.

The authors examined the debate relating to the "possible" horizontal effect of Article 27 of the Rome Statute in light of the oral submissions before the Appeals Chamber in the *Jordan Referral re Al-Bashir Appeal.* A survey of the *amicus curiae* submissions before the Appeals Chamber in the *Jordan Referral re Al-Bashir Appeal,* as well as scholarly writings, reveals that the majority view (in line with the *Decision under Article 87(7) of the Rome Statute on the Non-Compliance by South Africa with the Request by the Court for the Arrest and Surrender of Omar Al-Bashir*) is that Article 27(2) does have horizontal application and that, as a consequence, Jordan had a duty to arrest President Al-Bashir.

In conclusion, the chapter revealed that the mistaken exclusively "vertically applicable" nature of the immunity provisions of the Rome Statute inhibits the ability of the International Criminal Court to carry out its functions. Absolute head-of-state immunity alongside an interpretation of Article 27(2) as being restricted to vertical application is against the interests of ending impunity. It is submitted that the Appeals Chamber decision has now put to rest some of the legal questions raised during the Jordan Appeals proceedings and greatly enhances legal certainty on these contentious issues.

Bibliography

African Union, Decision on the Meeting of African States Parties to the Rome Statute of the International Criminal Court (3 Jul 2009), Assembly/AU/13(XIII), https://au.int/sites/default/files/treaties/36398-treaty-0045_-_protocol_on_amendments_to_the_protocol_on_the_statute_of_the_african_court_of_justice_and_human_rights_e.pdf (last visited 27 Jan 2020).

Dapo Akande, "The Legal Nature of Security Council Referrals to the ICC and its Impact on Al-Bashir's Immunities", 7 JICJ 2009, 333.

Dapo Akande and *Sangeeta Shah*, "Immunities of State Officials, International Crimes, and Foreign Domestic Courts", 21 European Journal of International Law 2010, 815.

Antonio Cassese et al., International Criminal Law: Cases and Commentary (Oxford University Press, New York 2011).

Erika de Wet, "Referrals to the International Criminal Court under Chapter VII of the United Nations Charter and the Immunity of Foreign State Officials", 112 AJIL Unbound 2018, 33.

Erika de Wet, "The Implications of President Al-Bashir's Visit to South Africa for International and Domestic Law", 13 JICJ 2015, 1049.

Anna Hood and *Monique Cormier*, "Prosecuting International Crimes in Australia: The Case of the Sri Lankan President", 13 Melbourne Journal of International Law 2012, 236.

Asad D. Kiyani, "Al-Bashir and the ICC: The Problem of Head of State Immunity", Chinese Journal of International Law 2013, 486.

Yves Le Bouthillier, in: Oliver Corten and Pierre Klein (eds.), The Vienna Conventions on the Law of Treaties: A Commentary, vol. 1 (Oxford University Press, Oxford 2011), 841.

Ulf Linderfalk, On the Interpretation of Treaties: The Modern International Law as Expressed in the 1969 Vienna Convention of the Law of Treaties (Springer, 1st ed., New York 2001).

Ulf Linderfalk, On the Interpretation of Treaties: The Modern International Law as Expressed in the 1969 Vienna Convention on the Law of Treaties (Springer, 2nd ed., Dordrecht 2007).

Georg Nolte, Treaties and Subsequent Practice (Oxford University Press, Oxford 2013).

Alexander Orakhelashvili, "Immunities of State Officials, International Crimes, and Foreign Domestic Courts: A Reply to Dapo Akande and Sangeeta Shah", 22 European Journal of International Law 2011, 849.

Dire Tladi, "The Duty on South Africa to Arrest and Surrender President Al-Bashir Under South African and International Law", 2015 JICJ 1027.

Otto Triffterer and *Christoph Burchard*, Article 27: Irrelevance of Official Capacity, in: Otto Triffterer and Kai Ambos (eds.), Rome Statute of the International Criminal Court: A Commentary (C.H. Beck, Munich 2016), 1037.

United Nations Diplomatic Conference of Plenipotentiaries on the Establishment of an International Criminal Court, 15 Jun–17 Jul 1998, vol. II, Summary Records of the Plenary Meetings and of the Meetings of the Committee of the Whole (2002), http://legal.un.org/diplomaticconferences/1998_icc/vol2.shtml (last visited 4 Dec 2019).

Harmen van der Wilt, "Universal Jurisdiction Under Attack. An Assessment of African Misgivings Towards International Criminal Justice as Administered by Western States", 9 JICJ 2011, 1043.

Jun Yoshida (Rapporteur), Summary of the Proceedings of the Preparatory Committee on the Establishment of an International Criminal Court, 25 Mar–12 Apr 1996, A/AC.249/1 (7 May 1996).

Register of cases

South Africa

The Minister of Justice and Constitutional Development v The Southern African Litigation Centre 2016 3 SA 317 (SCA).

Southern Africa Litigation Centre v Minister of Justice and Constitutional Development & Others 2015 5 SA 1 (GP).

ICC Cases

ICC Pre-Trial Chamber II, Situation in Darfur, Sudan, In the Case of *The Prosecutor v Omar Hassan Ahmad Al-Bashir*, Decision under Article 87(7) of the Rome Statute on the Non-Compliance by Jordan with the Request by the Court for the Arrest and Surrender of Omar Al-Bashir, ICC-02/05–01/-09 (11 Dec 2017).

ICC Pre-Trial Chamber I, Situation in Darfur, Sudan, In the Case of *The Prosecutor v Omar Hassan Ahmad Al-Bashir*, Warrant of Arrest for Omar Hassan Ahmad Al-Bashir, ICC-02/05–01/-09 (4 Mar 2009).

ICC Pre-Trial Chamber I, Situation in Darfur, Sudan, In the Case of *The Prosecutor v Omar Hassan Ahmad Al-Bashir*, Second Warrant of Arrest for Omar Hassan Ahmad Al-Bashir, ICC-02/05–01/-09 (12 Jul 2010).

ICC Pre-Trial Chamber I, Situation in Darfur, Sudan, In the Case of *The Prosecutor v Omar Hassan Ahmad Al-Bashir*, Decision Pursuant to Article 87(7) of the Rome Statute on the Failure by the Republic of Malawi to Comply with the Cooperation Requests Issued by the Court with Respect to the Arrest and Surrender of Omar Hassan Ahmad Al-Bashir, ICC-02/05–01/09 (12 Dec 2011).

ICC Pre-Trial Chamber I, Situation in Darfur, Sudan, In the Case of *The Prosecutor v Omar Hassan Ahmad Al-Bashir*, Decision Pursuant to Article 87(7) of the Rome Statute on the Refusal of the Republic of Chad to Comply with the Cooperation Requests Issued by the Court with Respect to the Arrest and Surrender of Omar Hassan Ahmad Al-Bashir, ICC-02/05–01/09 (13 Dec 2011).

ICC Pre-Trial Chamber II, Situation in Darfur, Sudan, In the Case of *The Prosecutor v Omar Hassan Ahmad Al-Bashir*, Decision under Article 87(7) of the Rome Statute on the Non-Compliance by South Africa with the Request by the Court for the Arrest and Surrender of Omar Al-Bashir, ICC-02/05–01/09 (6 Jul 2017).

ICC Appeals Chamber, Situation in Darfur, Sudan, In the Case of *The Prosecutor v Omar Hassan Ahmad Al-Bashir*, Order on the Conduct of the Hearing Before the Appeals Chamber in the Jordan Referral re Al-Bashir, ICC-02/05–01/09 OA2 (27 Aug 2018).

ICC Appeals Chamber, Situation in Darfur, Sudan, In the Case of *The Prosecutor v Omar Hassan Ahmad Al-Bashir*, The League of Arab States' Observations on the Hashemite Kingdom of Jordan's Appeal Against the Decision under Article 87(7) of the Rome Statute on the Non-Compliance by Jordan with the Request by the Court for the Arrest and Surrender [of] Omar Al-Bashir, ICC-02/05–01/09 (16 Jul 2018).

ICC Appeals Chamber, Situation in Darfur, Sudan, In the Case of *The Prosecutor v Omar Hassan Ahmad Al-Bashir*, The Hashemite Kingdom of Jordan's Response to the Observations Submitted by the African Union and the League of Arab States, ICC-02/05–01/09 (14 Aug 2018).

ICC Appeals Chamber, Situation in Darfur, Sudan, *In the Case of The Prosecutor v Omar Hassan Ahmad Al-Bashir*, Supplementary African Union Submission in the Hashemite Kingdom of Jordan's Appeal Against the Decision under Article 87(7) of the Rome Statute on the Non-Compliance by Jordan with the Request by the Court for the Arrest and Surrender [of] Omar-Al-Bashir with Annex 1, Annex 2, Annex 3, Annex 4 and Annex 5, ICC-02/05–01/09 (28 Sep 2018).

ICC Appeals Chamber, Situation in Darfur, Sudan, In the Case of *The Prosecutor v Omar Hassan Ahmad Al-Bashir*, The African Union's Submission in the Hashemite Kingdom of Jordan's Appeal Against the Decision under Article 87(7) of the Rome Statute on the Non-Compliance by Jordan with the Request by the Court for the Arrest and Surrender [of] Omar Al-Bashir, (ICC-02/05–01/09) (16 Jul 2018).

ICC Appeals Chamber, Situation in Darfur, Sudan, In the Case of *The Prosecutor v Omar Hassan Ahmad Al-Bashir*, Request by Professor Nicholas and Dr Michail Vagias for Leave to Submit Observations on the Merits of the Legal Questions Presented in the Hashemite Kingdom of Jordan's Appeal Against the Decision Under Article 87(7) of the Rome Statute on the Non-Compliance by Jordan with the Request by the Court for the Arrest and Surrender of Omar Al-Bashir of 12 Mar 2018, ICC-02/05–01/09 OA2 (29 Apr 2018).

ICC Appeals Chamber, Situation in Darfur, Sudan, In the Case of *The Prosecutor v Omar Hassan Ahmad Al-Bashir*, Amicus Curiae Observations Submitted by Prof Flavia Lattanzi Pursuant to Rule 103 of the Rules of Procedure and Evidence on the Merits of the Legal Questions Presented in the Hashemite Kingdom of Jordan's Appeal Against the Decision Under Article 87(7) of the Rome Statute on the Non-Compliance by Jordan with the Request by the Court for the Arrest and Surrender [of] Omar Al-Bashir of 12 March 2018, ICC-02/05–01/09 OA2 (18 Jun 2018).

ICC Appeals Chamber, Situation in Darfur, Sudan, In the Case of *The Prosecutor v Omar Hassan Ahmad Al-Bashir*, Request for Leave to Submit Amicus Curiae Observations Pursuant to Rule 103 of the Rules of Procedure and Evidence, Source: Professor Annalisa Ciampi, ICC-02/05–01/09 OA2 (30 Apr 2018).

ICC Apeals Chamber, Situation in Darfur, Sudan, In the Case of *The Prosecutor v Omar Hassan Ahmad Al-Bashir*, Request by Professors Robinson, Cryer, deGuzman, Lafontaine, Oosterveld, Stahn and Vasiliev for Leave to Submit Observations, ICC-02/05–01/09 OA2 (26 Apr 2018).

ICC Appeals Chamber, Situation in Darfur, Sudan, In the Case of *The Prosecutor v Omar Hassan Ahmad Al-Bashir*, Request by Professor Claus Kress with the assistance of Erin Pobjie for Leave to Submit Observations on the Merits of the Legal Questions Presented in the Hashemite Kingdom of Jordan's Appeal Against the Decision Under Article 87(7) of the Rome Statute on the Non-Compliance by Jordan With the Request by the Court for the Arrest and Surrender [of] Omar Al-Bashir of 12 March 2018, ICC-02/05–01/09–326, ICC-02/05–01/09 OA2 (25 Apr 2019).

ICC Appeals Chamber, Situation in Darfur, Sudan, In the Case of *The Prosecutor v Omar Hassan Ahmad Al-Bashir*, Final Observations by Professor Roger O'Keefe Pursuant to Rule 103 of the Rules of Procedure and Evidence and the President's Oral Direction of 14 Sep 2018, on the Merits of the Legal Questions Presented in the Hashemite Kingdom of Jordan's Appeal Against the Decision Under Article 87(7) of the Rome Statute on the Non-Compliance by Jordan with the Request by the Court for the Arrest and Surrender [of] Omar Al-Bashir of 12 March 2018, ICC-02/05–01/09–326, ICC-02/05–01/09 OA2 (18 Jun 2018).

ICC Pre-Trial Chamber II, Situation in Darfur, Sudan, In the Case of *The Prosecutor v Omar Hassan Ahmad Al-Bashir*, Prosecution's Response to the Hashemite Kingdom of Jordan's Notice of Appeal Against the Article 87(7) Decision, or in the Alternative, Application for Leave to Appeal the Decision Under Article 82(1)(d), ICC-02/05–01/09 (21 Dec 2017).

ICC Appeals Chamber, Situation in Darfur, Sudan, In the Case of *The Prosecutor v Omar Hassan Ahmad Al-Bashir*, The Hashemite Kingdom of Jordan's Response to the Observations Submitted by Professors of International Law Pursuant to Rule 103 of the Rules of Procedure and Evidence, ICC-02/05–01/09 (16 Jul 2018).

ICC Appeals Chamber, Situation in Darfur, Sudan, In the Case of *The Prosecutor v Omar Hassan Ahmad Al-Bashir*, Prosecution Response to the Observations of the African Union and the League of Arab States, ICC-02/05–01/09 (14 Aug 2018).

ICC Appeals Chamber, Situation in Darfur, Sudan, In the Case of *The Prosecutor v Omar Hassan Ahmad Al-Bashir*, Judgment in the Jordan Referral re Al-Bashir Appeal, ICC-02/05–01/-09 (6 May 2019).

ICC Pre-Trial Chamber II, Situation in Darfur, Sudan, In the Case of *The Prosecutor v Omar Hassan Ahmad Al-Bashir*, The Hashemite Kingdom of Jordan's Notice of Appeal of the Decision Under Article 87(7) of the Rome Statute on the Non-Compliance by Jordan with the Request by the Court for the Arrest and Surrender of Omar Al-Bashir, ICC-02/05/01/09–312 (18 Dec 2017).

ICC Pre-Trial Chamber II, Leave to Seek an Appeal of the Decision Under Article 87(7) of the Rome Statute on the Non-Compliance by Jordan with the Request by the Court for the Arrest and Surrender of Omar Al-Bashir, ICC-02/05–01/09 (18 Dec 2017).

ICC Pre-Trial Chamber II, Situation in Darfur, Sudan, In the Case of *The Prosecutor v Omar Hassan Ahmad Al-Bashir*, Decision on Jordan's Request for Leave to Appeal, ICC-02/05–01/09 (21 Feb 2018).

ICC Pre-Trial Chamber II, Situation in Darfur, Sudan, In the Case of *The Prosecutor v Omar Hassan Ahmad Al-Bashir*, Decision on the Cooperation of the Democratic Republic of the Congo Regarding Omar Al-Bashir's Arrest and Surrender to the Court, ICC-02/05–01/09 (9 Apr 2014).

Comment: Head of State Immunity in Times of Uncertainty for International Law

Thilo Rensmann[*]

I. The ICC Appeals Chamber judgment in the Al-Bashir case and the persisting uncertainty surrounding head of state immunity

Given the deadline set to the authors for submitting the first draft of their chapter, *Roxan Venter* and *Martie Bradley* were certainly put in an unenviable position. In their draft, they were expected to elaborate on an issue which in all likelihood would be authoritatively settled by the Appeals Chamber of the International Criminal Court (ICC) before this volume was even published.

However, when the Appeals Chamber's judgment in the case of the (now) former Sudanese President Omar Al-Bashir was handed down on 6 May 2019,[1] Venter and Bradley must have breathed a sigh of relief. The understandable worry that their chapter would somehow be rendered moot by this judgment proved completely unfounded on two counts:

---

* Thilo Rensmann, *Dr. iur.*; Professor, University of Augsburg Faculty of Law. Chair for Public, International and European Union Law.

1 ICC Appeals Chamber, Judgment in the Jordan Referral re Al-Bashir Appeal, ICC-02/05–01/09OA2 (6 May 2019).

Firstly, the Appeals Chamber based the denial of Al-Bashir's immunity precisely on the argument championed by the authors, namely the "horizontal" application of Article 27 (2) of the Rome Statute[2] and the extension of its reach to a head of state from a non-state party by virtue of a referral by the United Nations Security Council.[3]

Secondly and somewhat paradoxically, the hope expressed by the authors that the Appeals Chamber would settle the issue of head of state immunity once and for all, was nevertheless disappointed. This is due to the fact that the Appeals Chamber insisted on resting its decision on a second leg: the Chamber contended that in arrest proceedings at the request of an international criminal tribunal, the defence of head of state immunity is not only excluded by virtue of the combined effect of the Rome Statute and a Security Council referral but also as a matter of customary international law.[4]

To most observers this bifurcated approach came as quite a surprise,[5] since the customary international law route pursued in the ICC's early Pre-Trial Chamber jurisprudence[6] had given way in later

---

2 Rome Statute of the International Criminal Court of 17 Jul 1998, 2187 United Nations Treaty Series (UNTS) 38544.

3 ICC Appeals Chamber (n. 1), paras. 122–149.

4 ICC Appeals Chamber (n. 1), paras. 100–119.

5 See, e.g., *Akande*, "ICC Appeals Chamber Holds that Heads of State Have No Immunity Under Customary International Law Before International Tribunals", EJIL: Talk! (6 May 2019), https://www.ejiltalk.org (last visited 13 Nov 2019); *Batros*, "A Confusing ICC Appeals Judgment on Head-of-State Immunity", Just Security (7 May 2019), https://www.justsecurity.org/63962/a-confusing-icc-appeals-judgment-on-head-of-state-immunity/ (last visited 13 Nov 2019); *Jacobs*, "You have just entered Narnia: ICC Appeals Chamber adopts the worst possible solution on immunities in the Bashir case", Spreading the Jam (6 May 2019), https://dovjacobs.com (last visited 13 Nov 2019). See, however, *Kress*, Preliminary Observations on the ICC Appeals Chamber's Judgment of 6 May 2019 in the Jordan Referral re Al-Bashir Appeal, TOAEP Occasional Paper Series No. 8 (2019); *Sadat*, "Why the ICC's Judgment in the Al-Bashir Case Wasn't So Surprising", Just Security (12 Jul 2019), https://www.justsecurity.org/64896/why-the-iccs-judgment-in-the-al-bashir-case-wasnt-so-surprising/ (last visited 13 Nov 2019).

6 ICC Pre-Trial Chamber I, Decision Pursuant to Article 87(7) of the Rome Statute on the Failure by the Republic of Malawi to Comply with the Cooperation Requests Issued by the Court with Respect to the Arrest and Surrender of Omar Hassan Ahmad Al-Bashir, ICC-02/05–01/09–139-Corr. (13 Dec 2011), paras. 37–43; Decision Pursuant to Article 87(7) of the Rome Statute on the Refusal of the Republic of Chad to Comply with the Cooperation

decisions[7] to the treaty-based approach advocated by Venter and Bradley. By resuscitating the highly contentious customary international law argument, hopes were dashed that the appeal would finally provide legal certainty on this issue. In fact, even the ICC itself appeared to harbour certain doubts as to the persuasiveness of its reasoning. In response to the scathing criticism of the Appeals Chamber's judgment in initial assessments by highly respected colleagues[8], the ICC, in an unprecedented move, published a press release in which it lashed out at its critics by questioning their scholarly "honesty, integrity and fairness".[9] The insistence that the issue of head of state immunity "has now been settled conclusively"[10] rings hollow in the light of the heavy-handed attempt to rebut uncomfortable scholarly criticism in a "Q&A" document, which in itself raises the question as to the shelf-life of the answers originally provided by the Appeals Chamber.

The quest for legal certainty with regard to head of state immunity before international criminal tribunals thus continues, as does the concomitant legal discourse to which Venter and Bradley have certainly made an important contribution.

Requests Issued by the Court with Respect to the Arrest and Surrender of Omar Hassan Ahmad Al-Bashir, ICC-02/05-01/09 (13 Dec 2011), para. 13.

7 ICC Pre-Trial Chamber II, Decision on the Cooperation of the Democratic Republic of the Congo Regarding Omar Al-Bashir's Arrest and Surrender to the Court, ICC-02/05–01/09 (9 Apr 2014), paras. 23–33; ICC Pre-Trial Chamber II, Decision Under Article 87(7) of the Rome Statute on the Non-Compliance by South Africa with the Request by the Court for the Arrest and Surrender of Omar Al-Bashir, ICC-02/05–01/09–302 (6 July 2017), paras. 68, 71–97; ICC Pre-Trial Chamber II, Decision Under Article 87(7) of the Rome Statute on the Non-Compliance by Jordan with the Request by the Court for the Arrest and Surrender of Omar Al-Bashir, ICC-02/05–01/09–309 (11 Dec 2017), paras. 27, 33–44.

8 Apparently the comments were in particular aimed at *Akande* (n. 5).

9 ICC, Q&A Regarding Appeals Chamber's 6 May 2019 Judgment in the Jordan Referral Re Al-Bashir Appeal (16 May 2019), https://www.icc-cpi.int/itemsDocuments/190515-al-bashir-qa-eng.pdf (last visited 13 Nov 2019).

10 Ibid.

II. *Head of state immunity and the uncertain foundations of current international law*

Given the fact that the ICC issued its first arrest warrant against Omar Al-Bashir ten years ago,[11] it is striking that we still find ourselves in almost Babelesque confusion regarding the proper foundations and limits of head of state immunity before international criminal tribunals and in related proceedings before national courts and prosecuting authorities.

It is submitted that it is not so much the intricacy of the specific legal issues raised by the immunity defence in such proceedings but rather the current uncertainty about the nature of the international legal order as such which lies at the heart of the persistent lack of legal certainty with regard to the extent of the immunities enjoyed by senior state officials charged with the commission of international crimes.

The question as to whether immunity may serve as a valid defence against being prosecuted for international crimes pits the time-honoured principle of *par in parem non habet imperium* against the fledgling normative aspiration of the international community to fight the impunity of perpetrators of serious human rights violations.[12] We are thus faced with a head-on collision between classical state-oriented international law founded on the axiom of state sovereignty on the one hand and a more modern concept of international law based on community interest and human rights values on the other. At the high-water mark of the "humanization" and "constitutionalization" of international law following the collapse of the Soviet empire in the 1990s, it seemed for a moment, as if the Westphalian system of international law was finally giving way to an international legal order in which human rights and multilateralism would trump national assertions of sovereignty. In this vein, some observers at the time perceived the Pinochet judgment of the British House of Lords[13] and Article 27 (2) of the 1998 Rome Statute as harbingers of a general

11 ICC Pre-Trial Chamber I, Decision on the Prosecution's Application for a Warrant of Arrest against Omar Hassan Ahmad Al-Bashir, ICC-02/05–01/09–3 (4 Mar 2009).

12 This point and the following observations build on *Rensmann*, in: Kamminga and Scheinin (eds.), The Impact of International Human Rights Law on General International Law (2009), 151–170.

13 *R v. Bow Street Metropolitan Stipendiary Magistrate, ex parte Pinochet Ugarte* (No. 1), [1998] 3 WRL 1456; *R v. Bow Street Metropolitan Stipendiary Magistrate, ex parte Pinochet Ugarte* (No. 3), [1999] 2 WRL 827.

immunity exception in national and international criminal proceedings for gross and systematic human rights violations.[14]

Twenty years down the road, the liberal optimism of the 1990s has vanished. The ideals of multilateralism and a human rights-based global order are on the retreat and we appear to be gradually moving back towards a more Westphalian paradigm of international law.[15] The resulting uncertainty as to the extent to which the traditional immunities of States and their officials must yield to the interest of giving effect to human rights values is exacerbated by the fact that the underlying conflict between the "old" sovereignty-based and "new" human rights-oriented international law goes hand in hand with a fundamental methodological schism.[16]

Traditionally, rules of international law are established by ascertaining the will of sovereign states with the dowsing rod of Article 38 (1) of the Statute of the International Court of Justice (ICJ)[17]. By contrast, "modern" human rights-based approaches to international law perceive the role of State consent in international law-making to be contingent on the effective realization of the core values of humanity.[18] Thus the will of states, as expressed through traditional sources of international law, must always be tested against fundamental human rights considerations which may, in any given case, result in a partial or complete displacement of state consent.[19]

According to Article 2 of the Charter of the United Nations (UN Charter)[20] state sovereignty still takes pride of place as the first "principle" of our global order and our perception of the sources of international law are still primarily shaped by Article 38 (1) of the ICJ Statute. However, human rights values have made significant inroads into the traditional sovereignty-based structure of international law, ranging from the recognition of

14 See references in *Rensmann* (n. 12), 151–154.

15 See, e.g., *Bruné*, 112 (2018) Proceedings of the ASIL Annual Meeting, 335–339; *Pellet*, Values and Power Relations – The "Disillusionment" of International Law?, KFG Working Paper Series No. 34 (2019).

16 See *Rensmann* (n. 12), 160–169.

17 Statute of the International Court of Justice (26 June 1945), 15 UNCIO 355.

18 See *Rensmann* (n. 12), 163–169.

19 Ibid. and infra Part III.

20 Charter of the United Nations (26 June 1945), 892 UNTS 119.

jus cogens[21] and *erga omnes*-obligations[22] to holding senior state officials individually responsible under international criminal law.

Accordingly, we currently find ourselves somewhere between the old Westphalian and a new "humanized" and "constitutionalized" international legal order. In today's multipolar world it seems more difficult than ever to establish the exact position of international law on its journey from sovereignty-based Westphalia to the sunlit uplands of human rights. It is precisely this lack of a clear theoretical and methodological reference point which accounts for the uncertainty international lawyers face when charting the waters between traditional immunities and the modern aspiration to eradicate impunity for serious human rights violations. The remainder of this brief comment attempts to demonstrate how these observations have played out in the Al-Bashir case.

III. The interplay between immunity and methodology in the Al-Bashir case

Had the Al-Bashir case been a normal instance of mutual criminal assistance between two states, it would have been a fairly clear-cut matter from the perspective of current international law. Assuming that at the time Germany rather than the ICC had requested the extradition of Al-Bashir from Jordan, the then Sudanese president would undoubtedly have enjoyed absolute immunity before German courts and prosecuting authorities. In its 2002 Arrest Warrant judgment the ICJ unequivocally confirmed that under international law as it stands today, there is insufficient state practice to support any human rights-based exception from the immunity of incumbent heads of state, heads of government or foreign ministers, even if core international crimes, such as genocide or crimes against humanity are at issue.[23] More recently this position has been endorsed by the International Law Commission (ILC) in its preliminarily adopted "Draft Articles on Immunity of State Officials from Foreign Criminal Jurisdiction".[24]

---

21 See Articles 53, 64 Vienna Convention on the Law of Treaties (22 May 1969), 1155 UNTS 331.

22 ICJ, *Barcelona Traction, Light and Power Company Ltd (Second Phase) (Belgium v. Spain)*, Judgment of 5 Feb 1970, [1970] ICJ Rep. 3, 32, para. 33.

23 ICJ, *Arrest Warrant of 11 April 2000 (Democratic Republic of the Congo v. Belgium)*, Judgment of 14 Feb 2002, [2002] ICJ Rep. 3.

24 See Articles 3, 4 and 7 of the Draft Articles on Immunity of State Officials from Foreign Criminal Jurisdiction, provisionally adopted, ILC, Report of the

To what extent does the legal situation change, however, if it is not another state but – as in the Al-Bashir case – the ICC which requests the arrest and surrender of a head of state of a non-state party to the Rome Statute? From the perspective of traditional international law it should in principle make no difference that Article 27 (2) of the Rome Statute excludes reliance on head of state immunity in proceedings before the ICC since, in relation to non-state parties, the Rome Statute is *res inter alios acta*.[25] This is, in fact, highlighted by the Rome Statute itself which sets forth in Article 98 (1) that an arrest warrant issued by the ICC may not override the immunities a "third state" would otherwise enjoy in extradition proceedings before the courts and prosecuting authorities of a contracting state.

However, as highlighted by Venter and Bradley, due to the fact that the proceedings against Al-Bashir are based on a referral by the United Nations Security Council[26], the exclusion of the immunity defence can be convincingly argued without transcending the *pacta tertiis*-rule. Given that all member states of the United Nations are bound by Security Council resolutions issued under Chapter VII UN Charter,[27] Sudan – by virtue of the Security Council referral – can be considered to be under an obligation to fully cooperate with the ICC as if it were a state party to the Rome Statute.[28] With regard to the cooperation regime set out in Part 9 of the Rome Statute,[29] Sudan thus ceases to be a "third state". To this extent the magic wand of the Security Council referral may well be viewed as having turned Sudan into an *ad hoc* or – as Venter and Bradley put it – *sui generis* state party to the Rome Statute.

If we assume – as persuasively argued by Venter and Bradley, and now endorsed by the Appeals Chamber[30] – that the exclusion of immunity in Article 27 (2) Rome Statute extends to the "horizontal" situation of a state party enforcing an ICC arrest warrant against the head of state of another state party, Sudan should accordingly not have been able to successfully claim immunity before Jordanian courts for its then head of state Omar Al-Bashir.

International Law Commission on the work of its 69th session, A/72/10 (2017), 175–178.

25 Article 34 Vienna Convention on the Law of Treaties.

26 SC Res 1593 (2005) on the basis of Article 13 (b) Rome Statute.

27 Article 25 UN Charter.

28 ICC Appeals Chamber (n. 1), paras. 141–142.

29 As to this important caveat see ICC Appeals Chamber (n. 1), para. 142.

30 ICC Appeals Chamber (n. 1), paras. 127–133.

But what is the situation with regard to a head of state from a non-state party who has become subject to prosecution by the ICC by virtue of a referral by a state party[31] or a *proprio motu* investigation by the prosecutor[32]? Given the current political constellation in the international community and the unsatisfactory experience with the Al-Bashir prosecution, it is not to be expected that the Security Council will be prepared to refer any third state situation to the ICC for the foreseeable future. Consequently, as recently highlighted by the preliminary proceedings relating to the crimes committed against the Rohingya population in Myanmar[33] and to the conduct of the United States military and the CIA in Afghanistan[34], the immunity issue will in future most likely arise in third state scenarios without Security Council referral.

Against this backdrop it is safe to assume that it was precisely with such genuine third state situations in mind that the Appeals Chamber in the Al-Bashir case resuscitated the customary international law approach.[35] Since in such a case any direct reliance on the immunity exception set forth in Article 27 (2) Rome Statute would be barred by the *pacta tertiis*-rule, customary international law becomes the last resort in attempting to overcome the immunity hurdle in arrest proceedings.[36] The Appeals Chamber accordingly contends that Article 27 (2) Rome Statute – including its "hor-

31 Articles 13 (a), 14 Rome Statute.

32 Articles 13 (c), 15 Rome Statute.

33 ICC Pre-Trial Chamber I, Decision on the Prosecution's Request for a Ruling on Jurisdiction under Article 19(3) of the Statute, ICC-RoC46(3)-01/18 (6 Sep 2018); ICC Pre-Trial Chamber III, Decision Pursuant to Article 15 of the Rome Statute on the Authorisation of an Investigation into the Situation in the People's Republic of Bangladesh/Republic of the Union of Myanmar, ICC-01/19–27 (14 Nov. 2019).

34 ICC Pre-Trial Chamber II, Decision Pursuant to Article 15 of the Rome Statute on the Authorisation of an Investigation into the Situation in the Islamic Republic of Afghanistan, ICC-02/17–33 (12 Apr 2019); ICC Pre-Trial Chamber II, Decision on the Prosecutor and Victims' Requests for Leave to Appeal the Decision Pursuant to Article 15 of the Rome Statute on the Authorisation of an Investigation into the Situation in the Islamic Republic of Afghanistan, ICC-02/17–62 (17 Sep 2019).

35 *Kress* (n. 5), 6. See, however, the disclaimer in the Joint Concurring Opinion of Judges Eboe-Osuji, Morrison, Hofmański and Bossa to the Appeals Chamber judgment in the Jordan Referral re Al-Bashir Appeal (n. 1), ICC-02/05–01/09–397-Anx1-Corr (6 May 2019), paras. 10, 451.

36 See Article 38 Vienna Convention on the Law of Treaties: "Nothing in Articles 34–37 precludes a rule set forth in a treaty from becoming binding upon a third State as a customary rule of international law, recognized as such.".

izontal" dimension – has crystallised into customary international law.[37] By virtue of this metamorphosis, the treaty-based immunity exclusion would suddenly become opposable to non-contracting states and render moot the immunity reservation in Article 98 (1) Rome Statute.

Following traditional international law methodology there is very little support for this bold contention. As is well known, the emergence of customary international law requires state practice and a concomitant *opinio juris*.[38] However, most of the practice the Appeals Chamber points to[39] does not address the specific issue of immunity in domestic arrest proceedings at the request of an international court squarely. The statutes of other international tribunals cited by the Appeals Chamber only deal with substantive criminal responsibility and thus remain silent on the procedural question of immunity. In contrast, the Malabo Protocol which explicitly preserves head of state immunity in criminal proceedings before the future African Court of Justice and Human Rights[40] is not even mentioned in the Appeals Chamber judgment. Apart from a prior Pre-Trial Chamber decision relating to Malawi's refusal to arrest Al-Bashir[41], the Appeals Chamber only refers to a single international precedent in point, the Charles Taylor case before the Special Court for Sierra Leone[42]. However, this case was only concerned with ("vertical") immunity before the Special Court for Sierra Leone itself. The only case mentioned by the Appeals Chamber,[43] which directly touches upon the issue of "horizontal" immunity, is the Al-Bashir judgment of the Supreme Court of Appeal of South Africa[44]. However, in this decision the Supreme Court of Appeal in fact explicitly dismissed the existence of a customary international law exception[45] and

37 ICC Appeals Chamber (n. 1), paras. 100–119; Joint Concurring Opinion (n. 35), paras. 65–180; 413–451.

38 Article 38 (1) (b) ICJ Statute.

39 ICC Appeals Chamber (n. 1), paras. 103–113; Joint Concurring Opinion (n. 35), paras. 65–180.

40 Article 46A Statute of the African Court of Justice and Human Rights, Protocol on Amendments to the Protocol on the Statute of the African Court of Justice and Human Rights, Annex (27 Jun 2014), https://au.int/en/treaties/protocol-amendments-protocol-statute-african-court-justice-and-human-rights (last visited 13 Nov 2019).

41 See supra n. 6.

42 Special Court for Sierra Leone Appeals Chamber, *The Prosecutor v. Charles Ghankay Taylor*, SCSL-03-01-A (26 Sep 2013).

43 ICC Appeals Chamber (n. 1), para. 210.

44 *Minister of Justice and Constitutional Development & Others v Southern Africa Litigation Centre & Others*, 2016 (3) SA 317 (SCA).

45 Supreme Court of Appeal (n. 44), para. 70–84.

relied instead on the argument that the domestic legislation implementing the Rome Statute had overridden customary international law immunities by virtue of the authority under Section 232 of the South African Constitution.[46] In sum, it can therefore hardly be argued that state practice has reached the "critical mass"[47] required for the establishment of customary international law.

The Appeals Chamber was, of course, well aware of the weakness of its customary law argument and conjured up an ingenious idea, namely to simply reverse the onus of establishing customary international law. According to the Appeals Chamber it is not the *exception* to head of state immunity which must be demonstrated but rather the contention that the traditional *rule* of head of state immunity also extends to proceedings before international criminal tribunals and related enforcement proceedings before domestic courts.[48] The logic on which this reversal of onus is based is strikingly simple: international criminal tribunals are not domestic courts.[49] Given the functional link between head of state immunity and state sovereignty,[50] the Appeals Chamber considers the immunity issue moot in relation to the ICC which it perceives as representing not only the contracting states of the Rome Statute but "the international community as a whole".[51]

Whilst at first sight appealing, on closer inspection this argument proves fundamentally flawed. Unless international criminal tribunals are created by the Security Council, as in the case of the International Criminal Tribunal for the former Yugoslavia (ICTY)[52] and the International

46 Supreme Court of Appeal (n. 44), para. 103. In a more recent decision the Kenyan Court of Appeal also contended that Al-Bashir could not claim immunity as a defence against the enforcement of an ICC arrest warrant, see Kenyan Court of Appeal at Nairobi, *Attorney General et al. v. Kenya Section of International Commission of Jurists*, Civil Appeal 105 of 2012 & Criminal Appeal 274 of 2011 (Consolidated) (16 Feb 2018), [2018] eKLR. The Court did not rely on an immunity exception supported by state practice and *opinio juris* but argued instead that the prosecution of *jus cogens* violations would trump traditional immunities; as to the fallacy of the *jus cogens* argument see *Rensmann* (n. 12), 163–167.

47 ICC Pre-Trial Chamber I, Malawi-Decision (n. 6), para. 42; ICC Appeals Chamber (n. 1), paras. 112–113.

48 ICC Appeals Chamber (n. 1), para. 116.

49 ICC Appeals Chamber (n. 1), paras. 115–116.

50 As to the functional foundations going beyond the protection of state sovereignty see infra n. 61.

51 ICC Appeals Chamber (n. 1), para. 115.

52 SC Res 827 (1993).

Criminal Tribunal for Rwanda (ICTR)[53], they remain treaty bodies acting on behalf of the state parties to the constituent treaty of the tribunal in question. This also holds true for the ICC. Apart from the special situation of a Security Council referral, the authority of the ICC rests exclusively on the Rome Statute, a multilateral treaty with currently 122 states parties.[54] Over 70 states – including the United States of America, the Russian Federation and the People's Republic of China – which account for roughly two-thirds of the world population and 70 percent of global military forces[55] have chosen not to ratify the Rome Statute. As it stands today, it can thus hardly be argued that the ICC is a truly international tribunal "representing the international community as a whole".

On the other hand, it must be conceded that in today's international legal order the establishment of customary international law goes beyond a purely empirical exercise of ascertaining the will of states as expressed in their practice. In putting the puzzle pieces of state practice together, *lacunae* will always remain which need to be filled by recourse to first principles. Such reliance on the foundational principles or values of the international community must take into consideration the fact that human rights, despite not being explicitly mentioned in Article 2 UN Charter, have long been recognized as belonging to the core constitutional "principles" underpinning current international law.[56] Therefore it would indeed be inappropriate to rely mechanically on the *Lotus* presumption[57] and resolve any *non liquet* in favour of state sovereignty.

With regard to the immunity of senior state officials accused of international crimes this point has been cogently made by Judges Higgins, Kooijmans, and Buergenthal in their joint separate opinion to the Arrest Warrant case:[58] The traditional perception that immunities constitute the "rule" and any assertion of jurisdiction the "exception" ceases to be unassailable if one views the immunity of states and their officials in the wider

---

53 SC Res 955 (1994).

54 See United Nations Treaty Collection, Ch. XVIII.10, https://treaties.un.org (last visited 13 Nov 2019).

55 See *Thakur*, "The End of the International Criminal Court?", Japan Times (18 May 2019), https://www.japantimes.co.jp (last visited 13 Nov 2019).

56 See *Rensmann*, Wertordnung und Verfassung (2007), 371–388 with further references.

57 PCIJ, *The Case of the S.S. 'Lotus' (France v. Turkey)*, Judgment of 7 Sep 1927, [1927] PCIJ Series A No. 10, 18, para. 44.

58 ICJ, *Arrest Warrant of 11 April 2000 (Democratic Republic of the Congo v. Belgium)*, Judgment of 14 Feb 2002, [2002] ICJ Rep. 3, 63 (Joint sep. op. Higgins, Kooijmans, and Buergenthal).

context of the entire international legal system. From this perspective immunity then mutates into an exception to the rule of jurisdiction.[59]

Since there is thus no pre-established relationship of rule and exception between immunity and jurisdiction, none of the underlying principles or values deserves priority *per se.*[60] In this context it must also be borne in mind that the immunities granted to high state officials play an important role in protecting the proper functioning of the network of mutual inter-state relations.[61] They therefore may not be lightly sacrificed on the altar of *jus cogens*, however noble the humanitarian cause pursued by such peremptory norms may seem.

Accordingly, in determining the ambit of the immunities enjoyed by senior state officials accused of core international crimes, the conflicting values of preserving functioning international relations and avoiding impunity need to be carefully balanced against one another.[62] This does not mean, however, that judges and other decision-makers are endowed with an unfettered mandate to accommodate these values without paying due regard to the traditional sources of international law.[63] In current international law it remains first and foremost the prerogative of states to balance the competing values of the international community by establishing specific rules in state practice and treaties. The judicial function is thus limited to interpreting these rules and to filling potential gaps.

However, in the Al-Bashir case the Appeals Chamber assumes a far more activist role. Quoting Justice Cardozo, the Chamber arrogates the power of lifting rules from the murkiness of "morality" and "justice" and endowing them with "jural quality" by virtue of judicial *imprimatur*.[64] It is precisely this missionary zeal which informs the posited reversal of the rule-exception relationship between immunity and jurisdiction, since the

---

59 Ibid., para. 71.

60 Ibid., para. 79.

61 Ibid., paras. 75, 79.

62 Ibid., paras. 70–85.

63 See ICJ, *Armed Activities on the Territory of the Congo (New Application: 2002) (Democratic Republic of the Congo v. Rwanda)*, Judgment of 3 Feb 2006, [2006] ICJ Rep. 6, 86 (Sep. op. Dugard), para. 12. See also *Jones v. Kingdom of Saudi Arabia*, [2006] UKHL 26, para. 63 (per Lord Hoffmann).

64 ICC Appeals Chamber (n. 1), para. 113 with note 335 citing United States Supreme Court, *New Jersey v Delaware,* 291 U.S. 361, 383 (1934) ("International law, or the law that governs between states, has at times, like the common law within states, a twilight existence during which it is hardly distinguishable from morality or justice, till at length the imprimatur of a court attests its jural quality.").

concomitant shift of onus for establishing customary international law in effect gives *a priori* precedence to the value of fighting impunity. The Chamber consequently largely ignores current state practice pointing to the reluctance of States to countenance any human rights-driven restriction of traditional head of state immunity in domestic criminal proceedings.[65]

Instead, the Chamber succumbs to the temptation of a "moral reading"[66] of customary international law in which human rights values indiscriminately trump the immunities granted to heads of state and other high state officials. Traditional distinctions, such as the difference between substantive criminal responsibility and procedural immunity from criminal jurisdiction,[67] or between the jurisdiction exercised by international tribunals on the one hand, and domestic courts cooperating with such tribunals on the other,[68] are branded as "tedious"[69] "formalism"[70] and simply swept away in the name of higher "morality and justice".[71]

---

65 As to the Malabo Protocol see supra n. 40. The Appeals Chamber also fails to take into consideration the highly contentious discourse within the ILC about the potential restriction of the immunity of senior state officials accused of severe human rights violations. The draft provision limiting immunity *ratione materiae* in such cases met with considerable resistance in the ILC and the Sixth Committee of the UN General Assembly; the ILC could not agree on a unanimous position and – in an unusual move – provisionally adopted the draft provision by a majority vote (21 in favour, 8 against, 1 abstaining), see Report of the ILC on its 69th session (n. 24), para. 74. As to the "heated debate" on this issue in the Sixth Committee see the summary in *Escobar Hernández* (Special Rapporteur), Sixth report on immunity of State officials from foreign criminal jurisdiction, A/CN.4/722 (12 June 2018), paras. 13–21. The Special Rapporteur had also proposed a provision according to which the immunity of senior state officials would be "without prejudice" to the obligation of the forum state to cooperate with an international tribunal, see Report of the ILC on its 69th session (n. 24), para. 71, note 756. The Drafting Committee of the ILC has decided, however, to postpone the issue to a later stage of the deliberations, see ILC, Report of the International Law Commission on the work of its 71st session, A/74/10 (2019), para. 147.

66 This term is borrowed from *Dworkin*, Freedom's Law: The Moral Reading of the American Constitution (1997). As to the non-transferability of *Dworkin's* approach to international law see *Jones v. Kingdom of Saudi Arabia*, [2006] UKHL 26 (2007), para. 63 (per Lord Hoffmann).

67 ICC Appeals Chamber, Joint Concurring Opinion (n. 35), paras. 219–252.

68 ICC Appeals Chamber (n. 1), paras. 114, 127; Joint Concurring Opinion (n. 35), paras. 441–445.

69 ICC Appeals Chamber, Joint Concurring Opinion (n. 35), para. 241.

70 ICC Appeals Chamber, Joint Concurring Opinion (n. 35), para. 238.

71 See supra n. 64.

IV. Conclusion

Si tacuisses. Had the Appeals Chamber simply endorsed the treaty-based approach followed in the decision on appeal and advocated by Venter and Bradley, it would have made a significant contribution to consolidating a limited but important inroad into the immunities traditionally granted to senior state officials before domestic courts. By attempting to establish a far more ambitious immunity exemption under customary international law, however, the Appeals Chamber reignited a debate thought to have been largely settled.

Despite its undoubtedly laudable intentions, the Appeals Chamber's judicial activism plays into the hands of those who have always been wary and sceptical of the ICC.[72] In this context it should be recalled that the African member states of the United Nations have tabled a motion in the General Assembly to request an advisory opinion from the ICJ on the matter of immunities in proceedings before the ICC.[73] The uncertainty and irritation created by the Appeals Chamber's Al-Bashir judgment might in fact prove decisive in garnering the required majority in the General Assembly.[74] Paradoxically, the Appeals Chamber may have thus made an important contribution to the issue being "settled conclusively"[75] after all. It is to be expected, however, that were the ICJ be seized with the matter,

72 See *Akande* (n. 5).

73 See United Nations General Assembly, Agenda of the seventy-fourth session of the General Assembly, A/74/251 (20 Sep 2019), item 87: "Request for an advisory opinion from the International Court of Justice on the consequences of legal obligations of States under different sources of international law with respect to immunities of Heads of State and Government and other senior officials".

74 This is reflected in a recent statement by the Chinese representative to the United Nations, Liu Yuang, at the UN General Assembly. He said "that there have been mounting misgivings at the international level about the Court's authority and credibility. Major concerns of some States parties were not effectively addressed, and the way the Court dealt with the rule on immunity of State officials from foreign criminal jurisdictions sparked controversy, with a good number of States believing that the General Assembly should request an advisory opinion from the International Court of Justice on this matter." United Nations General Assembly, "Meetings Coverage, Plenary Seventy-fourth Session, 25th & 26th Meetings" (4 Nov 2019), https://www.un.org/press/en/2019/ga12210.doc.htm (last visited 13 Nov 2019).

75 See supra n. 10.

it would exercise considerably more judicial self-restraint in translating the moral imperative of human rights into positive international law.[76]

Bibliography

Dapo Akande, "ICC Appeals Chamber Holds that Heads of State Have No Immunity Under Customary International Law Before International Tribunals", EJIL: Talk! (6 May 2019), https://www.ejiltalk.org (last visited 13 Nov 2019).

Ben Batros, "A Confusing ICC Appeals Judgment on Head-of-State Immunity", Just Security (7 May 2019), https://www.justsecurity.org/63962/a-confusing-icc-appeals-judgment-on-head-of-state-immunity/ (last visited 13 Nov 2019).

Jutta Bruné, "Multilateralism in Crisis", 112 (2018) Proceedings of the ASIL Annual Meeting, 335.

Ronald Dworkin, Freedom's Law: The Moral Reading of the American Constitution (1997).

Concepción Escobar Hernández (Special Rapporteur), Sixth report on immunity of State officials from foreign criminal jurisdiction, A/CN.4/722 (12 June 2018).

International Criminal Court, Q&A Regarding Appeals Chamber's 6 May 2019 Judgment in the Jordan Referral Re Al-Bashir Appeal (16 May 2019), https://www.icc-cpi.int/itemsDocuments/190515-al-bashir-qa-eng.pdf (last visited 13 Nov 2019).

International Law Commission, Report of the International Law Commission on the work of its 69th session, A/72/10 (2017).

International Law Commission, Report of the International Law Commission on the work of its 71st session, A/74/10 (2019).

Dov Jacobs, "You have just entered Narnia: ICC Appeals Chamber adopts the worst possible solution on immunities in the Bashir case", Spreading the Jam (6 May 2019), https://dovjacobs.com (last visited 13 Nov 2019).

Claus Kress, Preliminary Observations on the ICC Appeals Chamber's Judgment of 6 May 2019 in the Jordan Referral re Al-Bashir Appeal, TOAEP Occasional Paper Series No. 8 (2019).

---

76 As to the ICJ's cautious approach towards the recognition of a "human rights exception" to the traditional immunities of States and their officials see ICJ, *Arrest Warrant* judgment (n. 23); ICJ, *Jurisdictional Immunities of the State (Germany v. Italy: Greece intervening)*, Judgment of 3 Feb 2012, [2012] ICJ Rep. 99. Note, in particular, that the *obiter dictum* in the *Arrest Warrant* case (n. 23, at para. 61) according to which "an incumbent or former Minister for Foreign Affairs may be subject to criminal proceedings before *certain* international criminal courts" (emphasis provided) does not relate to immunity restrictions under customary international law. When citing the ICC as an example, the ICJ exclusively refers to the treaty-based immunity exception of Article 27 (2) Rome Statute.

Alain Pellet, Values and Power Relations – The "Disillusionment" of International Law?, KFG Working Paper Series No. 34 (2019).

Thilo Rensmann, "Impact [of International Human Rights Law] on the Immunity of States and Their Officials", in: Menno Kamminga and Martin Scheinin (eds.), The Impact of International Human Rights Law on General International Law (Oxford University Press, Oxford 2009), 151.

Thilo Rensmann, Wertordnung und Verfassung (Mohr Siebeck, Tübingen 2007).

Leila Sadat, "Why the ICC's Judgment in the Al-Bashir Case Wasn't So Surprising", Just Security (12 Jul 2019), https://www.justsecurity.org/64896/why-the-iccs-judgment-in-the-al-bashir-case-wasnt-so-surprising/ (last visited 13 Nov 2019).

Ramesh Thakur, "The End of the International Criminal Court?", Japan Times (18 May 2019), https://www.japantimes.co.jp (last visited 13 Nov 2019).

United Nations General Assembly, Agenda of the seventy-fourth session of the General Assembly, A/74/251 (20 Sep 2019).

United Nations General Assembly, "Meetings Coverage, Plenary Seventy-fourth Session, 25th & 26th Meetings" (4 Nov 2019), https://www.un.org/press/en/2019/ga12210.doc.htm (last visited 13 Nov 2019).

Register of cases

International Court of Justice

Armed Activities on the Territory of the Congo (New Application: 2002) (Democratic Republic of the Congo v. Rwanda), Judgment of 3 Feb 2006, [2006] ICJ Rep. 6.

Arrest Warrant of 11 April 2000 (Democratic Republic of the Congo v. Belgium), Judgment of 14 Feb 2002, [2002] ICJ Rep. 3.

Barcelona Traction, Light and Power Company Ltd (Second Phase) (Belgium v. Spain), Judgment of 5 Feb 1970, [1970] ICJ Rep. 3.

Jurisdictional Immunities of the State (Germany v. Italy: Greece intervening), Judgment of 3 Feb 2012, [2012] ICJ Rep. 99.

International Criminal Court

Appeals Chamber, Judgment in the Jordan Referral re Al-Bashir Appeal, ICC-02/05–01/09OA2 (6 May 2019).

Pre-Trial Chamber I, Decision on the Prosecution's Application for a Warrant of Arrest against Omar Hassan Ahmad Al-Bashir, ICC-02/05–01/09–3 (4 Mar 2009).

Pre-Trial Chamber I, Decision Pursuant to Article 87(7) of the Rome Statute on the Failure by the Republic of Malawi to Comply with the Cooperation Requests Issued by the Court with Respect to the Arrest and Surrender of Omar Hassan Ahmad Al-Bashir, ICC-02/05–01/09–139-Corr. (13 Dec 2011).

Pre-Trial Chamber I, Decision Pursuant to Article 87(7) of the Rome Statute on the Refusal of the Republic of Chad to Comply with the Cooperation Requests Issued by the Court with Respect to the Arrest and Surrender of Omar Hassan Ahmad Al-Bashir, ICC-02/05-01/09 (13 Dec 2011).

Pre-Trial Chamber I, Decision on the Prosecution's Request for a Ruling on Jurisdiction under Article 19(3) of the Statute, ICC-RoC46(3)-01/18 (6 Sep 2018).

Pre-Trial Chamber II, Decision on the Cooperation of the Democratic Republic of the Congo Regarding Omar Al-Bashir's Arrest and Surrender to the Court, ICC-02/05–01/09 (9 Apr 2014).

Pre-Trial Chamber II, Decision Under Article 87(7) of the Rome Statute on the Non-Compliance by South Africa with the Request by the Court for the Arrest and Surrender of Omar Al-Bashir, ICC-02/05–01/09–302 (6 July 2017).

Pre-Trial Chamber II, Decision Under Article 87(7) of the Rome Statute on the Non-Compliance by Jordan with the Request by the Court for the Arrest and Surrender of Omar Al-Bashir, ICC-02/05–01/09–309 (11 Dec 2017).

Pre-Trial Chamber II, Decision Pursuant to Article 15 of the Rome Statute on the Authorisation of an Investigation into the Situation in the Islamic Republic of Afghanistan, ICC-02/17–33 (12 Apr 2019).

Pre-Trial Chamber II, Decision on the Prosecutor and Victims' Requests for Leave to Appeal the 'Decision Pursuant to Article 15 of the Rome Statute on the Authorisation of an Investigation into the Situation in the Islamic Republic of Afghanistan, ICC-02/17–62 (17 Sep 2019).

Pre-Trial Chamber III, Decision Pursuant to Article 15 of the Rome Statute on the Authorisation of an Investigation into the Situation in the People's Republic of Bangladesh/Republic of the Union of Myanmar, ICC-01/19–27 (14 Nov 2019).

Permanent Court of International Justice

The Case of the S.S. 'Lotus' (France v. Turkey), Judgment of 7 Sep 1927, [1927] PCIJ Series A No. 10.

Special Court for Sierra Leone

Appeals Chamber, The Prosecutor v. Charles Ghankay Taylor, SCSL-03–01-A (26 Sep 2013).

Kenya

Kenyan Court of Appeal at Nairobi, Attorney General et al. v. Kenya Section of International Commission of Jurists, Civil Appeal 105 of 2012 & Criminal Appeal 274 of 2011 (Consolidated) (16 Feb 2018), [2018] eKLR.

South Africa

Minister of Justice and Constitutional Development & Others v Southern Africa Litigation Centre & Others, 2016 (3) SA 317 (SCA).

United Kingdom of Great Britain and Northern Ireland

Jones v. Kingdom of Saudi Arabia, [2006] UKHL 26.

R v. Bow Street Metropolitan Stipendiary Magistrate, ex parte Pinochet Ugarte (No. 1), [1998] 3 WRL 1456.

R v. Bow Street Metropolitan Stipendiary Magistrate, ex parte Pinochet Ugarte (No. 3), [1999] 2 WRL 827.

United States of America

New Jersey v Delaware, 291 U.S. 361 (1934).

Legal Certainty and International Crimes: A Public International Law Perspective

Sabreen Hassen[*] / *Mispa Roux*[**]

Abstract: International criminal law is the branch of international law that enforces both international human rights and international humanitarian law. Therefore, a discussion about the gross violation of human rights has to include international criminal law. Legal certainty sits at the heart of any criminal defence, and is the main element within the concept of the rule of law. Nulla poena sine lege and nullum crimen sine lege are the foundations upon which legality is built. By examining customary international law and the four core international crimes, in terms of both the Rome Statute and the Malabo Protocol, this contribution seeks to show that in an international setting, legal certainty cannot apply in the same manner as it would in a domestic setting. Customary international law is a primary source of international criminal law and consists of two basic requirements: usus and opinio juris. However, little to no guidance is provided relating to the application of these requirements. Furthermore, international criminal law is ever changing, and by its very nature treaty provisions are broad, even ambiguous. Whether this ambiguity is because it is impossible to define human rights violations comprehensively or to protect state sovereignty is immaterial. Whilst international tribunals have acknowledged that legal certainty does exist within the international law context, it must be noted that the concept must be adapted to apply appropriately to each case.

---

* LLB, LLM; Lecturer in the Department of Practical Business Law, Faculty of Law, University of Johannesburg.

** LLB, LLM, LLD; Senior Lecturer in the Department of Public Law, Faculty of Law, University of Johannesburg; Deputy Director at the South African Institute for Advanced Constitutional, Public, Human Rights, and International Law (SAIFAC), a Centre of the University of Johannesburg.

I. Introduction

"*Rattssakerhet*" (Swedish) and "*rettssikkerhet*" (Norwegian) both mean "rule of law" or "legal certainty".[1] Legal certainty is not only the common element within the different versions of the rule of law, but also its main element.[2]

The principle of legality developed at the same time as the *trias politica* doctrine.[3] Both key doctrines were created in order to limit the abuse of a centralised power.[4] In a system which adheres to the doctrine of *trias politica*, the principle of legality not only curtails the power of, but also places obligations on, all three branches of government.[5] The legislature or law-making branch is compelled to set out clearly the penalty of a particular crime, including its severity.[6] Similarly, the judicial branch is required to comply with the listed sanctions and prohibited to apply the sanctions retroactively.[7]

Legal certainty has been described as an ideal, rather than a descriptive concept.[8] Lei asserts that legal certainty "is not an established fact but a goal which requires lawyers to strive for it".[9] Achieving this goal involves different fields which relate to the law,[10] one of which is the process of creating law. During the drafting process it must be ensured that laws are precisely drafted, and do not create *lacunae*.[11] Once laws have been drafted, it is up to the judiciary to apply the law, and in doing so, develop legal certainty. The application or interpretation of the law by judges is as a

---

1 *Lei*, 5 RCLR 2017, 25, 28.
2 *Lei* (n. 1), 28.
3 *Dana*, 99 JCLC 2009, 857, 862.
4 *Dana* (n. 3), 862.
5 *Dana* (n. 3), 862.
6 *Dana* (n. 3), 862.
7 *Dana* (n. 3), 862.
8 *Lei* (n. 1), 30.
9 *Lei* (n. 1), 30.
10 *Lei* (n. 1), 30.
11 *Lei* (n. 1), 30.

result of two things:[12] firstly the judicial outcome is not based on a judge's personal opinion but on legal rules which have been communicated to the public in advance, and, secondly, as result of this citizens are able to predict what the judicial outcome will be.[13]

There is a possibility that a judicial outcome will not be based on legal rules but rather on what the public expects the outcome to be.[14] This is for instance in cases where "political morality is in conflict with legal norms".[15] Therefore, legal certainty and/or legal predictability "involves the normatively applicative range of general rules, rather than the actually made judicial decisions".[16] If one accepts this, then as long as a judicial decision falls within a general legal norm, it will meet the standard of legal predictability or legal certainty.[17]

In general criminal law, the maxims *nulla poena sine lege* ("*nulla poena*") and *nullum crimen sine lege* ("*nullum crimen*") form the foundation on which the principle of legality is built.[18] Both maxims sit at the heart of any defence to a criminal prosecution,[19] serving multiple purposes:[20] firstly, it ensures that any actions or conduct which is prohibited is clearly and expressly set out;[21] secondly, citizens are thereby made aware of the law and are therefore able to act accordingly to avoid sanction or punishment;[22] and, lastly, it prevents a state from arbitrarily taking action against a citizen under a *lacunae* created by the law.[23]

In their most basic forms, *nulla poena* and *nullum crimen* explain that not only the conduct which is prohibited or criminalised, but also the sanction or punishment attached to such conduct, must be clearly defined before any prosecution of such conduct can take place.[24] This in turn gives rise to the fact that laws which criminalise any conduct must be drafted in line with the principle of specificity, which indicates absolute precision.[25]

---

12 *Lei* (n. 1), 31.
13 *Lei* (n. 1), 31.
14 *Lei* (n. 1), 32.
15 *Lei* (n. 1), 32.
16 *Lei* (n. 1), 32.
17 *Lei* (n. 1), 32.
18 *Dana* (n. 3), 861.
19 *Van Schaak*, 97 GLJ 2008, 119, 121.
20 *Van Schaak* (n. 19), 122.
21 *Van Schaak* (n. 19), 122.
22 *Van Schaak* (n. 19), 122.
23 *Van Schaak* (n. 19), 122.
24 *Van Schaak* (n. 19), 122.
25 *Van Schaak* (n. 19), 122.

These laws must then be carefully interpreted and favour the accused in any instances of ambiguities.[26]

Nulla poena and *nullum crimen* each protect equivalent interests.[27] For example, *nullum crimen* protects citizens from the abuse of power which may ultimately infringe on their right to freedom, whereas *nulla poena* protects the right to freedom by clearly stipulating the length and type of sanction to be codified.[28] Similarly, *nullum crimen* protects the principle of fair notice, which requires that citizens are, at a minimum, made aware of the consequences of participating in a criminal activity.[29] In turn, *nulla poena* achieves the same purpose, but by ensuring that the sanction or punishment is predictable.[30]

One of the defences used by Nazi war criminals charged at the Nuremberg tribunal, was *nullum crimen sine lege, nulla poena sine lege* ("no crime without law, no punishment without law"),[31] which meant that the Tribunal lacked jurisdiction to try the major war criminals, as there was no law prohibiting their acts at the time of commission,[32] specifically with regard to waging a war of aggression.[33] Questions regarding legal certainty were raised around this new development as neither crimes against humanity nor war crimes had been previously defined.[34] The accused argued that the

> "*ex post facto* punishment is abhorrent to the law of all civilised nations, that no sovereign power had made aggressive war a crime at the time that the alleged criminal acts were committed, that no statute had defined aggressive war, that no penalty had been fixed for its commission, and no court had been created to try and punish offenders".[35]

---

26 *Van Schaak* (n. 19), 122.
27 *Dana* (n. 3), 863.
28 *Dana* (n. 3), 863.
29 *Dana* (n. 3), 863.
30 *Dana* (n. 3), 863.
31 Ratner, Abrams, Jason and Bischoff (eds.), Accountability for Human Rights Atrocities in International Law: Beyond the Nuremberg Legacy (2009), 23.
32 *Davidson*, 91 SJLR 2017, 37, 38.
33 International Military Tribunal sitting at Nuremberg, *The Trial of German Major War Criminals*, Judgment of 1 October 1946, 411, 444.; *Ratner* (n. 31), 23–24.
34 *Gallant*, The Principle of Legality in International and Comparative Criminal Law (2009), 67–68, 107–108.
35 The *Nuremberg* case (n. 33) 217.

The Tribunal held that *nullum crimen sine lege, nulla poena sine lege* "has no application to the present facts"[36] and that it would be "unjust" to allow those who violate international treaties "to go unpunished",[37] and that it had been previously condemned.[38]

The heritage of Nuremberg is apparent in Article 22 of the ICC Statute, which provides that a person may be held criminally responsible only for conduct that "constitutes, at the time it takes place, a crime within the jurisdiction of the Court",[39] and that the definition of such crime "shall be interpreted in favour of the person being investigated, prosecuted or convicted".[40] With regard to the maxim *nulla poena sine lege*, Article 23 provides that punishment of a convicted person may only be "in accordance with this Statute".[41] The ICC further confirms its commitment to the principle by not only defining the crimes over which it has jurisdiction in the Rome Statute but also by providing further definitions in a separate document,[42] called "Elements of Crimes".[43] This type of adherence to the principle of *nullum crimen* and its strict interpretation is uncommon in international criminal law,[44] as will be illustrated in the next part.

Most major international criminal and human rights instruments have incorporated the maxims by interpretation, not by explicitly providing for them as was done in the ICC Statute.[45] For example, the Universal Declaration of Human Rights states that:

> "no one shall be held guilty of any penal offence on account of any act or omission which did not constitute a penal offence, under national or international law, at the time when it was committed".[46]

While provisions such as this one are theoretically aimed at all branches of government, practically they only apply to the judicial branch when a

36 The *Nuremburg* case (n. 33) 217.
37 The *Nuremburg* case (n. 33) 217.
38 *Gallant* (n. 34), 67–68, 107–108.
39 Article 22(1) of the Rome Statute.
40 Article 22(2) of the Rome Statute.
41 Article 23 of the Rome Statute.
42 *Davidson* (n. 32), 40.
43 International Criminal Court, Elements of Crimes, ICC-PIDS-LT-03–002/11_Eng (2011).
44 *Davidson* (n. 32), 38.
45 Articles 22 and 23 of the Rome Statute.
46 Article 11(2) of the Universal Declaration of Human Rights.

court is applying legislation retroactively or interpreting existing rules in a different manner.[47]

The *nullum crimen* principle is not explicitly provided for in the Statutes of the International Criminal Tribunal for the Former Yugoslavia (ICTY) and the International Criminal Tribunal for Rwanda (ICTR),[48] but more by interpretation. Other treaties such as the African Charter on Human and Peoples' Rights, Protocol on the African Human Rights Court, Protocol on the Statute of the African Court of Justice and Human Rights, and the Protocol on Amendments to the Protocol on the Statute of the African Court of Justice and Human Rights (Malabo Protocol) all incorporate the maxims by implication, not expressly. In particular, the *nulla poena* principle is alluded to in the Malabo Protocol, which states that "the penalties imposed by the Court shall be limited to prison sentences and/or pecuniary fines".[49]

As mentioned above, neither the ICTY nor the ICTR Statutes explicitly mentioned these maxims,[50] yet one may infer the *ad hoc* tribunals' support of them in principle through their jurisprudence.[51] For example, the ICTY stated:

> "[i]n practice this means 'that penal statutes must be strictly construed' and that the 'paramount duty of the judicial interpreter [is] to read into the language of the legislature, honestly and faithfully, its plain and rational meaning and to promote its object.'"[52]

Notwithstanding this alleged support for the *nullum crimen* principle, both the ICTY and ICTR deliberately avoided strict compliance with it. As an exception to this, the ICTR paid strict adherence to the principle by interpreting the law on genocide in a more lenient fashion.[53] Exceptions in this regard were only made where "the cost of recognizing the principle was low".[54]

---

47 *Van Schaak* (n. 19), 122.
48 *Van Schaak* (n. 19), 123.
49 Article 43A(2) of the Malabo Protocol.
50 *Davidson* (n. 32), 38.
51 *Gallant* (n. 34), 304.
52 International Criminal Tribunal for the Former Yugoslavia, *The Prosecutor v Galic*, Judgment and Opinion of 5 Dec 2003, Case No. IT-98–29-T, para. 93.
53 International Criminal Tribunal for Rwanda, *The Prosecutor v Akayesu*, Judgment of 2 Sep 1998, ICTR-96–4-T.
54 *Davidson* (n. 32), 38.

The ICTY and ICTR judges were uncertain whether a strict construction of the *nullum crimen* principle can be applied at all within international criminal law.[55] Even the judges who believed that a strict construction did apply, limited its application by referring to it as a last resort, a consideration only to be used after all other interpretative tools had been used.[56]

Despite explicit provision for the *nullum crimen sine lege, nulla poena sine lege* principle in international instruments, and support thereof at the various international criminal courts and tribunals, some questions still remain unanswered.[57] The most important question is, how exactly can one strictly interpret *opinio juris* and state practice?[58] The next part will engage with the question of the strict interpretation of the requirements for the establishment of a customary international law rule, namely *opinio juris* and *usus*.

II. Customary international law and the strict interpretation of opinio juris and usus

International customary law is recognised as a source of international law in the Statute of the International Court of Justice (ICJ).[59] Recognition of customary law as a primary source of international law is what distinguishes the international law system from domestic law systems.[60] Customary laws are rules which have not been created by a specialised law making institution – such as a court or the legislature for example – and yet they are legally binding.[61]

In a developing domestic system, customary law is an important source of law until legislative and judicial branches are developed.[62] Once the judicial branch becomes functional, the customary rules are codified into statutes.[63] The problem in the international law context is that there is no

55 *Davidson* (n. 32), 39.
56 *Davidson* (n. 32), 39.
57 *Davidson* (n. 32), 40.
58 *Davidson* (n. 32), 42.
59 Article 38(1)(b) of Statute of the International Court of Justice.
60 *Bennett* and *Strug*, Introduction to International Law (2013), 7.
61 *Bennett* and *Strug* (n. 60), 7.
62 *Dugard*, International Law: A South African Perspective (5th ed. 2018), 30.
63 *Dugard* (n. 62), 30.

legislative branch, therefore customary law retains its importance in this setting.[64]

International law is premised on consent from states. When a state ratifies a treaty, it is essentially giving consent to be bound by the rules set out in that treaty. Similarly, states must consent to being bound by customary international law. While it may be difficult to prove that a state has consented to a customary rule, consent can generally be inferred by their conduct.[65]

The ICJ has identified two requirements in order for a customary rule to be binding as a source of international law: *usus* and *opinio juris*. These requirements have also been confirmed by the International Law Commission (ILC).[66] Customary rules arise from *usus* or state practice.[67] In the *Asylum* case the ICJ stated that there must be "constant and uniform usage practiced by the states in question".[68] The ICJ further explained that in order to qualify as a rule of customary international law, the rule must "receive general or widespread acceptance".[69] The ICJ clarified that universal acceptance is not necessary for a rule to crystallise into customary law.[70]

Dixon believes that it is not possible to define *usus* comprehensively.[71] He explains that state practice could be inferred by an act or omission, statements made, adoption of resolutions, domestic legislation and conduct of international organisations.[72] This list is merely a guideline and not exhaustive.[73] The ILC also recognises that the conduct of states during activities at international organisations may form part of the *usus* require-

---

64 *Dugard* (n. 62), 30.

65 *Dugard* (n. 62), 30.

66 ILC, Michael Wood (Special Rapporteur), Fifth Report on Identification of Customary International Law, 70th Session, A/CN.4/717 (14 March 2018), paras. 106–111 (Draft Conclusions on Identification of International Customary Law) (Do you refer to the fifth report or the draft conclusions? As I understand there are two different documents and "A/CN.4/717" refers to the report.) The fifth report.

67 *Dixon*, Textbook on International Law (7th ed. 2013), 32.

68 ICJ, *Colombia v Peru (Asylum Case)*, Judgment of 20 Nov 1950, ICJ Reports, at 14.

69 ICJ, *Federal Republic of Germany v Iceland (Fisheries Jurisdiction case)*, Judgment of 25 Jul 1974, ICJ Reports 1974, 175, para. 53.

70 ICJ, *Federal Republic of Germany v Netherlands and Denmark (North Sea Continental Shelf cases)*, Judgment of 20 Feb 1969, ICJ Reports 1969, 3, para. 62.

71 *Dixon* (n. 67), 32.

72 *Dixon* (n. 67), 32. See further: Conclusion 5 Draft Conclusions on Identification of International Customary Law, A/CN.4/717 (14 March 2018) (n. 70).

73 *Dixon* (n. 67), 32.

ment, but is of the opinion that it is primarily the practice of States that must be considered.[74]

Furthermore, state practice must be constant. The Permanent Court of International Justice (PCIJ)[75] required that *usus* must be "constant and uniform".[76] The ICJ later confirmed that *usus* should be settled practice.[77] A question then arises as to what degree of consistency is required? The ICJ stated that the degree of consistency will differ on a case by case basis.[78] For example, if there is a state attempting to alter the position of a customary rule which has obtained the status of *jus cogens*, then the *usus* should be universally consistent. States which act contrary to a *jus cogens* norm must be seen as breaching the customary rule as opposed to trying to create a new one.[79] Any conduct which is contrary to customary law will not be condoned by a state merely arguing it was attempting to clarify or change customary law.[80]

In addition to the requirement of *usus*, states must have a sense of obligation to be bound.[81] *Opinio juris* can be either a state's belief that certain conduct is required by law, or that certain conduct should become law.[82] The ICJ has placed emphasis on the requirement of *opinio juris*.[83] The ILC is of the opinion that a practice will be able to qualify as *opinio juris* if it can be differentiated from a habit.[84] Dugard acknowledges that it is difficult to prove *opinio juris*.[85] In a dissenting opinion, Judge Tanaka

---

74 Conclusion 4(1) Draft Conclusions on Identification of International Customary Law A/CN.4/717 (14 March 2018) (n. 70).

75 The PCIJ was the predecessor of the ICJ. The PCIJ was established in 1922 by the League of Nations. Both the PCIJ and the League of Nations were replaced by the ICJ and United Nations respectively.

76 PCIJ, Case of the SS "Lotus", Judgment of 7 Sep 1927, Publications of the PCIJ 1927 Series A No. 10.

77 ICJ, *Germany v Italy: Greece Intervening (Jurisdiction Immunities of the State case)*, Judgment of 3 Feb 2012, ICJ Reports 2012, 99, para. 55.

78 ICJ, *United Kingdom v Norway (Anglo Norwegian Fisheries case)*, Judgment of 18 Dec 1951, ICJ Reports 1951, 116.

79 ICJ, *Nicaragua v United States of America*, Judgment of 27 Jun 1986, ICJ Reports 1986, 14.

80 *Dixon* (n. 67), 33.

81 *Dugard* (n. 62), 36.

82 *Bennett* and *Strug* (n. 60), 19.

83 The *North Sea Continental Shelf* cases (n. 70).

84 Conclusion 9(2) Draft Conclusions on Identification of International Customary Law A/CN.4/717 (14 March 2018) (n. 70).

85 *Dugard* (n. 62), 36.

mentioned that where *usus* exists, one could automatically assume that *opinio juris* also does.[86]

However, the ICJ clearly disagreed with this view,[87] in particular by requiring that the party alleging proof of the customary international law rule's existence must provide concrete proof of *opinio juris*.[88] However, in the *Lotus* case, the PCIJ accepted that *opinio juris* did exist because state practice was consistent.[89] This inference had the effect of requiring the opposing party to prove that *opinio juris* did not exist.[90] Similarly, the ICJ dispensed with the *usus* requirement in the *Nicaragua* case because there was sufficient evidence in relation to *opinio juris*.[91]

In relation to customary international law, the only thing which is certain is that both *usus* and *opinio juris* are recognised as requirements. However, whether both of these requirements must be actually present and from where their existence can be deduced, is completely uncertain and left to be decided on a case-by-case basis.

The inconsistencies within *usus* and *opinio juris* have been referred to as a "sliding scale".[92] Kirgis explains that the requirement which the court will be willing to disregard will depend on the reasonableness of the rule.[93] Koskenniemi notes that both requirements are necessary to offset the effect that they would each have if applied individually.[94] He explains further that, if *usus* is considered on its own, then we would not be able to differentiate between "might and right", nor would international law be based on any standards.[95] Conversely, if *opinio juris* is considered on its own then the entire system of international criminal law would not be based on state's behaviour, but rather on an idealistic notion of morality.[96]

The next part will consider the core international crimes included in the Rome Statute, which are considered to reflect customary international law.

---

86 The *North Sea Continental Shelf* cases (n. 70).
87 The *North Sea Continental Shelf* cases (n. 70) and the *Nicaragua* case (n. 79).
88 The *North Sea Continental Shelf* cases (n. 70).
89 The *Lotus* case (n. 76).
90 *Bennett* and *Strug* (n. 60), 20.
91 The *Nicaragua* case (n. 79).
92 *Kirgis*, 81 AJIL 1987, 146, 149.
93 *Kirgis* (n. 92), 149.
94 *Koskenniemi*, From Apology to Utopia (2005), 388.
95 *Koskenniemi* (n. 94), 388.
96 *Koskenniemi* (n. 94), 388.

III. The core international crimes and the ICC Statute

Gallant believes that it is not necessary to interpret international human rights laws strictly.[97] Sadat further explains that "the Rome Statute's legality provision was the product of the positive law inclinations of many states and states' desire to understand and clearly demarcate the risks to states' own government officials".[98] The Rome Statute requests states to take action, therefore they needed to have clear definitions in order to understand what their obligations would be.[99]

The Rome Statute stipulates that the ICC would have jurisdiction over four core, international crimes, namely genocide,[100] crimes against humanity,[101] war crimes[102] and the crime of aggression.[103] These four crimes are accepted as being "the most serious crimes of concern to the international community as a whole".[104]

1. Genocide

The word 'genocide', as originally coined by Raphael Lemkin, originates from the Greek word *genos*, meaning kind, type or race, and the Latin word *cide*, meaning to kill.[105] Genocide was first recognised as an international crime under customary international law.[106] It was then codified in the Convention on the Prevention and Punishment of the Crime of Genocide (Genocide Convention). The ICJ classified the prohibition of genocide as a *jus cogens* norm,[107] which are "norm[s] from which no

---

97 *Gallant* (n. 34), 359.
98 *Sadat*, The International Criminal Court and Transformation of International Law: Justice for the New Millennium (2002), 182.
99 *Sadat* (n. 98), 182.
100 Article 5(1)(a) of the Rome Statute.
101 Article 5(1)(b) of the Rome Statute.
102 Article 5(1)(c) of the Rome Statute.
103 Article 5(1)(d) of the Rome Statute
104 Article 5(1) of the Rome Statute.
105 *Lemkin*, Axis Rule in Occupied Europe (1944), 79.
106 *Dugard* (n. 62), 228 and ILC Report, Draft Code of Crimes against Peace and Security of Mankind with Commentaries, 48th session, Yearbook of the International Law Commission 1996, vol. II, part two.
107 ICJ, *Belgium v Spain (Barcelona Traction, Light & Power Company Limited case)*, Judgment of 5 Feb 1970, ICJ Reports 1970, para. 34.

derogation is permitted".[108] *Jus cogens* is closely linked to obligations *erga omnes*. *Erga omnes* has been described by the ICJ as "a duty owed towards the international community as a whole".[109]

Genocide was first prosecuted at the Nuremburg Tribunal in 1947. The Nazi leaders were prosecuted for crimes against humanity in terms of the Charter of the International Military Tribunal (Nuremburg Charter).[110] The Nuremburg Charter does not make specific reference to the term genocide, however, the term was used throughout the Nuremburg Trial.[111] Even though the word genocide itself was not mentioned in the judgment, scholars believe that what was described in the judgment amounts to genocide.[112] During the Nuremburg Trials the terms genocide and crimes against humanity were used synonymously.[113] This meant that genocide was linked with an armed conflict.[114] The Nuremburg Tribunal restricted its decision to "war time genocide and did not include peace time genocide".[115]

Subsequent to the Nuremburg judgment, the General Assembly recognised genocide as an international crime of its own[116] and proceeded with the drafting of the Genocide Convention. The Genocide Convention contributed to legal certainty in three respects: firstly, it confirmed genocide as a separate international crime;[117] secondly, it recognised that the crime of genocide could be committed in either a "time of peace or time of war"; and, finally, provided a definition for the crime.[118]

In the Genocide Convention genocide was defined as "any ... act[s] committed with intent to destroy, in whole or in part, a national, ethnical, racial or religious group".[119] The Genocide Convention also contains specific crimes that will amount to genocidal acts.[120] These acts are not

---

108 Article 53 of the Vienna Convention on the Law of Treaties.

109 The *Barcelona Traction, Light & Power Company Limited* case (n. 107) para. 32.

110 The Charter of the International Military Tribunal (Nuremburg Charter) of 1945.

111 *Schabas*, 40 CWRJIL 2008, 35, 37.

112 *Schabas* (n. 111), 42 and *Lemkin*, 41 AJIL 1947, 145, 147.

113 *Schabas* (n. 111), 53.

114 See generally *Schabas* (n. 111).

115 *King, Ferencz* and *Harris*, 40 CWRJIL 2008, 13, 14.

116 GA Res 96 (I), *The Crime of Genocide* (11 Dec 1946).

117 Article 1 of the Genocide Convention.

118 Article 1 of the Genocide Convention.

119 Article 2 of the Genocide Convention.

120 Article 2 of the Genocide Convention mentions the following acts:
Killing members of the group;

only limited but must also be carried out against a protected group of people.[121] These groups were identified in particular because "membership ... would seem to be normally not challengeable by its members, who belong to it automatically, by birth, in a continuous and often irremediable manner".[122]

This definition has been criticised as being "rigid"[123] and "narrow".[124] The courts have "softened" this definition through interpretation.[125] The ICTR has expressed the view that a protected group should not be limited to the four which are mentioned but should also include "any stable and permanent group".[126] Cassese clearly disagrees with this expansion as he believes that the drafters of the Genocide Convention clearly expressed their intention to protect those four groups in particular.[127] The ICTR did, however, go on to provide a definition for each of the protected groups.[128]

The listed acts of genocide were also expanded upon by the ICTY and the ICTR. "Killing"[129] must be intentional killing or "murder".[130] "Causing serious bodily harm"[131] was interpreted to be something which is "beyond temporary unhappiness"[132] but "does not necessarily mean that the harm is permanent and irremediable".[133] "Deliberately inflicting on the group conditions of life calculated to bring about its physical destruction"[134] was interpreted as "the creation of circumstances that would

---

Causing serious bodily or mental harm to members of the group;
Deliberately inflicting on the group conditions of life calculated to bring about its physical destruction in whole or in part;
Imposing measures intended to prevent births within the group;
Forcibly transferring children of the group to another group.

121 Article 2 of the Genocide Convention mentions the following groups: national, ethnical, racial and religious.
122 The *Akayesu* case (n. 53) para. 511.
123 *Cassese*, International Criminal Law (2nd ed. 2008), 110.
124 *Schabas* (n. 111), 46.
125 *Cassese* (n. 123), 110.
126 The *Akayesu* case (n. 53) para. 516.
127 *Cassese* (n. 123), 120.
128 The *Akayesu* case (n. 53), paras. 512–515.
129 Article 2(a) of the Genocide Convention.
130 The *Akayesu* case (n. 53), paras. 500–501.
131 Article 2(b) of the Genocide Convention.
132 International Criminal Tribunal for the Former Yugoslavia, *The Prosecutor v Radislav Krstić*, Judgment of 19 Apr 2004, IT-98–33-A, para. 513.
133 The *Akayesu* case (n. 53), paras. 502–504.
134 Article 2(c) of the Genocide Convention.

lead to a slow death".[135] "Imposing measures intended to prevent births within the group" could include a mental element for example rape.[136] Furthermore the ICTR held that it was possible to commit genocide by performing an act against a single person.[137]

The definition provided in the Genocide Convention was used verbatim in the Statutes of the ICTY,[138] ICTR[139] and the ICC.[140] Whilst these provisions themselves may comply with legal certainty and the rule of law, the continuous expansion through judicial interpretation, as highlighted above, cannot be reconciled with a narrow interpretation on legal certainty.

2. Crimes against humanity

The term "crimes against humanity" was mentioned for the very first time in 1915, when the Armenians were being killed.[141] Jointly, the French, British and Russian governments issued a statement mentioning "crimes against humanity and civilisation".[142]

Crimes against humanity are accepted as being crimes under customary international law.[143] The prohibition of crimes against humanity is also a *jus cogens* norm.[144] Crimes against humanity were first prosecuted at the Nuremburg Tribunal and they were defined in the Nuremburg Charter.[145]

---

135 International Criminal Tribunal for the Former Yugoslavia, *The Prosecutor v Radoslav Brdanin*, Judgment of 1 Sep 2004, IT-99–36-T, para. 691.

136 The *Akayesu* case (n. 53), para. 508.

137 The *Akayesu* case (n. 53), para. 521.

138 Article 4 of the Statute of the International Criminal Tribunal for the Former Yugoslavia (ICTY Statute).

139 Article 2 of the Statute of the International Criminal Tribunal for the Rwanda (ICTR Statute).

140 Article 6 of the Rome Statute.

141 *Dugard* (n. 62), 254 and *Cassese* (n. 123), 84.

142 Author, Papers Relating to the Foreign Relations of the United States (1915), 981.

143 *Bassiouni*, Crimes Against Humanity in International Criminal Law (2nd ed. 1999), 470; *Schabas* (n. 111), 46 and *Cassese* (n. 123), 90.

144 *Dixon* (n. 67), 41.

145 Article 6(c) of the Nuremburg Charter provides "Crimes against humanity: namely, murder, extermination, enslavement, deportation, and other inhumane acts committed against any civilian population, before or during the war, or persecutions on political, racial or religious grounds in execution of or in con-

The definition in the Nuremburg Charter is problematic. It required crimes against humanity to be linked to crimes against peace and war crimes and thereby implied that crimes against humanity could only be committed during a war.[146] Notwithstanding the limitation of the link to "war", the inclusion of this crime was developmental in the field of international criminal law.[147] The inclusion of crimes against humanity meant that the international community was expanding the list of acts or crimes that could be considered as an international concern.[148] Even more importantly, it meant that crimes against humanity could be punished even when they were committed in terms of domestic laws.[149]

Whilst the specific provision on crimes against humanity in the Nuremburg Charter does not expressly mention state policy, it is in the *chapeau* of Article 6 to refer to state policy:[150] "acting in the interests of the European Axis countries, whether as individuals or as members of organizations".[151] Therefore crimes against humanity can be described as a crime of state.[152] Bassiouni explains that the essence of crimes of state is, "harmful conduct committed by state actors who abuse their power as part of state action or in execution of state policy against a civilian population".[153]

Crimes against humanity remained as a crime of state until the establishment of the *ad hoc* tribunals.[154] During the conflict in both Yoguslavia and Rwanda it became apparent that non-state actors were also committing crimes against humanity.[155] This in turn affected the characterisation of a conflict as being international or non-international.[156] As a result the *ad hoc* tribunals opted to use a more practical characteristic to define crimes against humanity.[157]

---

nection with any crime within the jurisdiction of the Tribunal, whether or not in violation of the domestic law of the country where perpetrated.".

146 *Cassese* (n. 123), 86.

147 *Cassese* (n. 123), 87.

148 *Cassese* (n. 123), 87.

149 *Cassese* (n. 123), 87.

150 *Bassiouni* (n. 143), 3.

151 Article 6 of the Nuremburg Charter provides "acting in the interests of the European Axis countries, whether as individuals or as members of organizations".

152 *Bassiouni* (n. 143), 3.

153 *Bassiouni* (n. 143), 3.

154 *Bassiouni* (n. 143), 7.

155 *Bassiouni* (n. 143), 7.

156 *Bassiouni* (n. 143), 7.

157 *Bassiouni* (n. 143), 7.

The definition of crimes against humanity in the statutes of both the ICTY[158] and ICTR,[159] differ from not only the Nuremburg Charter, but from each other as well. Both the Nuremburg and ICTY definition include a link to war. The ICTR definition does not include a link to war, and expressly mentions a "widespread and systematic attack".

The ICTY Appeals chamber read in a further element in the *Tadic* judgment, namely that "crimes against humanity are to be distinguished from war crimes against individuals. In particular, they [crimes against humanity] must be widespread or demonstrate a systematic character."[160] This new element was echoed in other judgments of the ICTY.[161]

The Rome Statute's provision on crimes against humanity is indicative of customary international law.[162] Article 7 of the Rome Statute expressly mentions a "widespread or systematic attack" and does not contain a link to war.[163] Therefore it is accepted that crimes against humanity can be committed in both war or at a time of peace.

---

158 Article 5 provides: "The International Tribunal shall have the power to prosecute persons responsible for the following crimes when committed in armed conflict, whether international or internal in character, and directed against any civilian population: (a) murder; (b) extermination; (c) enslavement; (d) deportation; (e) imprisonment; (f) torture; (g) rape; (h) persecutions on political, racial and religious grounds; (i) other inhumane acts.".

159 Article 3 provides: "The International Tribunal for Rwanda shall have the power to prosecute persons responsible for the following crimes when committed as part of a widespread or systematic attack against any civilian population on national, political, ethnic, racial or religious grounds: (a) Murder; (b) Extermination; (c) Enslavement; (d) Deportation; (e) Imprisonment; (f) Torture; (g) Rape; (h) Persecutions on political, racial and religious grounds; (i) Other inhumane acts.".

160 International Criminal Tribunal for the Former Yugoslavia, *The Prosecutor v Dusko* Tadic, Appeal Judgment of 15 Jul 1999, IT-94–1-A, para. 248.

161 International Criminal Tribunal for the Former Yugoslavia, *Prosecutor v Tihomir Blaškić*, Judgment of 3 Mar 2000, IT-95–14-T, para. 202; International Criminal Tribunal for the Former Yugoslavia, *Prosecutor v Dario Kordić and Mario Cerkez*, Judgment of 26 Feb 2001, IT-95–14/2-T, para. 178 and International Criminal Tribunal for the Former Yugoslavia, *Prosecutor v Dragoljub Kunarac, Radomir Kovac and Zoran Vukovic*, Judgment of 22 Feb 2001, IT-96–23-T and IT-96–23/1-T, paras. 430 and 625.

162 *Cassesse* (n. 123), 90.

163 Article 7 provides: "For the purpose of this Statute, 'crime against humanity' means any of the following acts when committed as part of a widespread or systematic attack directed against any civilian population, with knowledge of the attack:
(a) Murder;
(b) Extermination;

The fact that the Rome Statute includes "other inhumane acts of a similar character intentionally causing great suffering, or serious injury to body or to mental or physical health",[164] cannot, in itself, be reconciled with the principle of legality or the rule of law. How does one "strictly interpret" this category of acts, which is open ended and completely reliant on a subjective interpretation?

The Statute of the Special Court for Sierra Leone (SCSL) also includes "other inhumane acts" as a crime against humanity.[165] The SCSL acknowledges that this category of "other inhumane acts" is recognised under customary international law.[166] The SCSL highlighted that "the crime of other inhumane acts is a residual category for serious acts which are not otherwise enumerated in Article 2".[167]

The SCSL held that the crime of forced marriage was separate to the crimes of rape and sexual slavery.[168] The court held that forced marriage was considered as an inhumane act in terms of crimes against humanity.[169] The SCSL is of the opinion that "the crime of other inhumane acts is

---

(c) Enslavement;
(d) Deportation or forcible transfer of population;
(e) Imprisonment or other severe deprivation of physical liberty in violation of fundamental rules of international law;
(f) Torture;
(g) Rape, sexual slavery, enforced prostitution, forced pregnancy, enforced sterilization, or any other form of sexual violence of comparable gravity;
(h) Persecution against any identifiable group or collectivity on political, racial, national, ethnic, cultural, religious, gender as defined in paragraph 3, or other grounds that are universally recognised as impermissible under international law, in connection with any act referred to in this paragraph or any crime within the jurisdiction of the Court;
(i) Enforced disappearance of persons;
(j) The crime of apartheid;
(k) Other inhumane acts of a similar character intentionally causing great suffering, or serious injury to body or to mental or physical health.".

164 Article 7(1)(k) of the Rome Statute.

165 Article 2(i) of the Statute of Special Court of the Special Court for Sierra Leone.

166 Special Court of Sierra Leone, *The Prosecutor v Alex Tamba Brima, Brima Bazzy Kamara and Santigie Borbor Kanu*, Judgment of 22 Feb. 2008, SCSL-2004–16-A, para. 198.

167 Special Court of Sierra Leone, *The Prosecutor v Issa Hassan Sesay, Morris Kallon and Augustine Gbao*, Judgment of 2 March 2009, SCSL-04–15-T 2, para. 165.

168 The *Sesay* case (n. 167) paras. 2306–2307.

169 The *Sesay* case (n. 167) para. 1473.

designed to be inclusive in nature, intended to avoid unduly restricting the Statute's application to crimes against humanity".[170]

3. War crimes

International humanitarian law has been described as "the law of armed conflict".[171] War crimes are crimes which are committed in terms of international humanitarian law, thereby linking international humanitarian law with international criminal law.[172] The two main sources of international humanitarian law are the law of the Hague and the law of Geneva.[173]

The law of the Hague consists of the series of Hague Conventions signed in 1890, 1907 and 1954.[174] The law of Geneva is comprised of the four Geneva Conventions and the two additional protocols.[175] The Hague Conventions relate to the methods of warfare. The Geneva Conventions on the other hand govern the protection of the victims of war. Additional Protocols I and II merged the law of the Hague and Geneva.[176]

Out of the four core crimes mentioned in the Rome Statute, war crimes were the first type of international crime to be prosecuted.[177] In 1921 German soldiers were tried for "acts in violation of the laws and customs of war".[178] They were prosecuted in terms of the Treaty of Versailles,[179] during the Leipzig trials.

Like genocide and crimes against humanity, the prohibition of committing war crimes also has the status of being a *jus cogens* norm.[180] Similarly war crimes are also part of customary international law.[181] Traditionally

---

170 The *Sesay* case (n. 167) para. 166.
171 *Sassoli*, in: Cassese (ed.), The Oxford Companion to International Criminal Justice (2009), 111, 111.
172 *Sassoli* (n. 165), 111.
173 *Dugard* (n. 62), 258.
174 Hague Conventions I-XII and Hague Convention for the Protection of Cultural Property.
175 Geneva Conventions 1–4; Protocol I and Protocol II.
176 *Sassoli*, *Bouvier* and *Quintin* (eds.), How Does Law Protect in War (2011), 141.
177 *Dugard* (n. 62), 258.
178 *MacCormack*, in: MacCormack and Simpson (eds.), The Law of War Crimes: National and International Approaches (1997), 31, 49.
179 Article 228 of the Treaty of Versailles.
180 *Dixon* (n. 67), 41.
181 *MacCormack* (n. 172), 49.

the perpetrators of war crimes were punished by their own state.[182] This, however, changed with the Nuremburg Charter.

In terms of the Nuremburg Charter war crimes were defined in Article 6(b).[183] At the end of the First World War it was proposed that individuals should be held responsible for their infringement of *jus in bello* (rules of behaviour in war).[184] The *chapeau* of Article 6, mentions "individual responsibility", a concept that had never before been connected with war crimes.[185]

Initially there were only four acts which were considered as war crimes: "violations of recognised norms on waging military operations by servicemen themselves; illegal acts in wartime committed by persons not serving in military forces; espionage and treason; and marauding".[186] Furthermore, war crimes could only be committed during an international armed conflict.[187]

In 1949 new crimes were added as war crimes in the Geneva Conventions and were described as "grave breaches".[188] All four Geneva Conventions as well as the First Additional Protocol classify the following as grave breaches: "wilful killing, torture or inhuman treatment, including biological experiments, wilfully causing great suffering or serious injury to body or health, and extensive destruction and appropriation of property, not justified by military necessity and carried out unlawfully and wantonly".[189] The Geneva Conventions not only confer universal jurisdiction to

182 *Cassese* (n. 123), 64.

183 Article 6(b) provides: "War crimes: namely, violations of the laws or customs of war. Such violations shall include, but not be limited to, murder, ill treatment or deportation to slave labour or for any other purpose of civilian population of, or in occupied territory, murder or ill treatment of prisoners of war or persons on the seas, killing of hostages, plunder of public or private property, wanton destruction of cities, towns or villages, or devastation not justified by military necessity".

184 *Bennett* and *Strug* (n. 60), 385.

185 *Cassese* (n. 123), 64.

186 *Rehetov*, in: Ginsburgs and Kudriavtsev (eds.), Nuremburg Tribunal and International Law (1990), 167, 1677.

187 *Cassese* (n. 123), 71.

188 *Cassese* (n. 123), 65.

189 Article 50 of the Geneva Convention for the Amelioration of the Condition of the Wounded and Sick in Armed Forces in the Field; Article 51 of the Geneva Convention for the Amelioration of the Condition of Wounded, Sick and Shipwrecked Members of Armed Forces at Sea; Article 130 of the Geneva Convention Relative to the Treatment of Prisoners of War; Article 147 of the Geneva Convention Relative to the Protection of Civilian Persons in Time of

states over grave breaches,[190] but also recognise that war crimes may be committed in a non-international armed conflict.[191]

The ICTY Statute does not make reference to either an international or non-international armed conflict. However, through its jurisprudence the ICTY has acknowledged that customary international law had developed to include war crimes committed in a non-international armed conflict.[192] The Statute of the ICTR makes reference to the Geneva Common Article 3 relating to non-international armed conflicts.

The Rome Statute contains an expansive provision on war crimes.[193] The provision in the Rome Statute recognises that war crimes may be committed in both an international and non-international armed conflict.[194] The Rome Statute provision on war crimes has been defined as being "narrower than laid down in customary international law".[195]

This is because the ICC's jurisdiction is limited to war crimes which are "committed as part of a plan or policy or as part of a large-scale commission of such crimes".[196] Furthermore, the additional actions listed in Article 8(2)(b), will only be considered as war crimes if they are accepted as war crimes "within the established framework of international law".[197] There is no explanation within the Rome Statute as to what exactly is the "established framework of international law". Cassese proposes that

---

War; and Article 85 of the Protocol Additional to the Geneva Conventions of 12 August 1949, and Relating to the Protection of Victims of International Armed Conflicts (Protocol I).

190 Article 49 of the Geneva Convention for the Amelioration of the Condition of the Wounded and Sick in Armed Forces in the Field; Article 50 of the Geneva Convention for the Amelioration of the Condition of Wounded, Sick and Shipwrecked Members of Armed Forces at Sea; Article 129 of the Geneva Convention Relative to the Treatment of Prisoners of War; Article 146 of the Geneva Convention Relative to the Protection of Civilian Persons in Time of War.

191 Article 3 of the Geneva Convention for the Amelioration of the Condition of the Wounded and Sick in Armed Forces in the Field; Article 3 of the Geneva Convention for the Amelioration of the Condition of Wounded, Sick and Shipwrecked Members of Armed Forces at Sea; Article 3 of the Geneva Convention Relative to the Treatment of Prisoners of War; Article 3 of the Geneva Convention Relative to the Protection of Civilian Persons in Time of War.

192 The *Tadic* case (n. 160), paras. 97–137.

193 Article 8 of the Rome Statute.

194 Article 8(2)(c) of the Rome Statute.

195 *Cassese* (n. 123), 81.

196 Article 8(1) of the Rome Statute.

197 Article 8(2)(b) of the Rome Statute.

it could mean customary international law.[198] The jurisprudence of the SCSL provides some guidance in this regard, particularly in that both Articles 8(2)(b)(xxvi) and 8(2)(e)(vii) recognise that "conscripting or enlisting children under the age of fifteen years into the national armed forces or using them to participate actively in hostilities" constitutes a war crime.[199] The SCSL is a hybrid tribunal which enjoys temporal jurisdiction over "serious violations of international humanitarian law and Sierra Leonean law committed in the territory of Sierra Leone since 30 November 1996".[200]

In accordance with the above, Sam Hinga Norman was charged with war crimes and crimes against humanity, specifically for the recruitment of child soldiers.[201] The accused argued that the SCSL had no jurisdiction as the recruitment of child soldiers was not considered a customary intenational law crime at the time of his indictment. The SCSL Appeals Chamber, however, found that the recruitment of child soldiers was in fact a customary international law crime before 1996. The court cited the wide ratification of the Geneva Conventions[202] and Additional Protocol 2[203] as an indication of its customary international law status.[204]

With respect to the *nullum crimen* principle, the SCSL quoted the ICTY,[205]

> "In interpreting the principle *nullum crimen sine lege*, it is critical to determine whether the underlying conduct at the time of its commission was punishable. The emphasis is on conduct, rather than on the specific description of the specific offence in substantive criminal law, is of primary relevance……it must only be foreseeable and accessible to a possible perpetrator that his concrete conduct was punishable at the time of commission."[206]

---

198 *Cassese* (n. 123), 80.
199 Article 8(2)(c) of the Rome Statute.
200 Article 1 of the Statute of the Special Court for Sierra Leone.
201 Special Court for Sierra Leone, *The Prosecutor v Sam Hinga Norman*, Judgment of 31 May 2004, SCSL-2004–14-AR72(E).
202 The Geneva Convention Relative to the Protection of Civilian Persons in Time of War.
203 Protocol Additional to the Geneva Conventions Relating to the Protection of Victims of International Armed Conflicts.
204 The *Norman* case (n. 201), para. 18.
205 The *Norman* case (n. 201), para. 25.
206 International Criminal Court, *The Prosecutor v Hadzihasanovic, Alagic and Kubura*, Judgment of 12 Nov 2002, IT-01–47-PT, para. 62.

The SCSL, in dismissing Norman's appeal, concluded that "a norm need not be expressly stated in an international convention for it to crystallise as a crime under customary international law".[207]

To return to the ICC, it recently held that rape, sexual slavery and other sexual crimes were prohibited against the person.[208] The ICC therefore found Ntaganda guilty of committing these sexual crimes against his own child soldiers.[209] The Court explained that "members of the same armed forces are not per se excluded as potential victims of the war crimes ... under Article 8(2)(e)(vi)".[210]

Once again, the development of war crimes is not compatible with a narrow definition of legal certainty. The definition and scope of war crimes have been developed and will continue to develop through judicial interpretation, as will all the other core crimes. Furthermore, the inclusion of the term "established framework of international law" in the Rome Statute has no explanation or definition attached and therefore cannot be reconciled with the *nullum crimen* principle.

4. Crime of aggression

No international court or tribunal has had jurisdiction over the crime of aggression since the Nuremburg Tribunal. The Tribunal was given jurisdiction over aggression via the provision on crimes against peace.[211] In the Nuremburg judgment the Tribunal described aggression as "not only an international crime; it is the supreme international crime differing only from other war crimes in that it contains within itself the accumulated evil of the whole".[212]

The "suppression of acts of aggression" is one of the United Nations main purposes.[213] In 1974, the United Nations (UN) General Assembly adopted a resolution in which it provided a definition for the crime of

207 The *Norman* case (n. 201), para. 38.

208 International Criminal Court, *The Prosecutor v Bosco Ntaganda*, Judgment of 8 Jul 2019, ICC -01/04–02/06, para. 965.

209 The *Ntaganda* case (n.208) para. 968.

210 The *Ntaganda* case (n. 208) para. 965.

211 Article 6(a) provides: "Crimes against peace: namely, planning, preparation, initiation or waging of a war of aggression, or a war in violation of international treaties, agreements or assurances, or participation in a common plan or conspiracy for accomplishment of any of the foregoing.".

212 The *Nuremburg* case (n. 33), 25.

213 Article 1 of the United Nations Charter.

aggression.[214] Aggression was defined as "the use of armed force by a State against the sovereignty, territorial integrity or political independence of another State, or in any other manner inconsistent with the Charter of the United Nations, as set out in this definition".[215]

The crime of aggression was included in the jurisdiction of the ICC in Article 5.[216] However, the ICC would not have immediate jurisdiction over this crime, as it would only acquire jurisdiction once there was a provision "defining the crime and setting out the conditions under which the Court shall exercise jurisdiction with respect to this crime".[217] In terms of the Rome Statute, any amendment needs to be approved by a "two-thirds majority of State Parties",[218] translating into the approval of at least 30 member states.

In 2010 state parties met in Kampala, Uganda, to discuss a definition for the crime of aggression. Aggression was defined as "the planning, preparation, initiation or execution, by a person in a position effectively to exercise control over or to direct the political or military action of a State, of an act of aggression which, by its character, gravity and scale, constitutes a manifest violation of the Charter of the United Nations".[219]

According to the Adoption of Amendments on the Crime of Aggression (Kampala Amendment), the ICC would only be able to exercise its jurisdiction over the crime of aggression after it has received 30 ratifications from state parties.[220] Furthermore, after obtaining the necessary ratifications, the jurisdiction will only be triggered after 1 January 2017.[221] The Kampala amendment confirms that the prosecutor of the ICC will be able to exercise *proprio motu* powers over the crime of aggression, or by

214 GA Res 3314 (XXIX), *Definition of Aggression* (14 Dec 1974).
215 Article 1 of the GA Res 3314 (XXIX) (n. 196).
216 Article 5(1)(d) of the Rome Statute.
217 Article 5(2) of the Rome Statute.
218 Article 121(3) of the Rome Statute.
219 Article 8*bis*, International Criminal Court Resolution RC/Res.6 *The Crime of Aggression* 11 June 2010.
220 Article 15*bis*(2), International Criminal Court Resolution RC/Res.6 *The Crime of Aggression* 11 June 2010.
221 Article 15*bis*(3), International Criminal Court Resolution RC/Res.6 *The Crime of Aggression* 11 June 2010.

way of state referral.[222] The crime of aggression may also come under the jurisdiction of the ICC through a Security Council referral.[223]

At present there are 38 state parties who have ratified the Kampala Amendment.[224] The Assembly of State Parties decided to activate the ICC's jurisdiction over aggression as of 17 July 2018.[225]

IV. International crimes in terms of the Malabo Protocol

As seen above, crimes against humanity, genocide and war crimes were the focus of international tribunals. This is because they were thought to be extreme and deserving of the tribunal's limited resources.[226] As a result this has created a hierarchy in which these crimes are at the fore and other human rights violations recede into the background, irrespective of the gravity.[227]

In 2014 the African Union (AU) adopted the Protocol on Amendments to the Protocol on the Statute of the African Court of Justice and Human Rights (Malabo Protocol). The Malabo Protocol establishes the African Court of Justice and Human and Peoples Rights (ACJHRP). This Court will have jurisdiction over both human rights and international crimes.[228] The Malabo Protocol will enter into force once it has received at least 15 ratifications.[229] At the time of writing only 11 out of the 55 African

222 Article 15*bis*(6), International Criminal Court Resolution RC/Res.6 *The Crime of Aggression* 11 June 2010.

223 Article 15*ter*, International Criminal Court Resolution RC/Res.6 *The Crime of Aggression* 11 June 2010.

224 Andorra, Argentina, Austria, Belgium, Botswana, Chile, Costa Rica, Croatia, Cyprus, Czech Republic, El Salvador, Estonia, Finland, Georgia, Germany, Guyana, Iceland, Ireland, Latvia, Liechtenstein, Lithuania, Luxembourg, Malta, Netherlands, North Macedonia, Panama, Paraguay, Poland, Portugal, Samoa, San Marino, Slovakia, Slovenia, Spain, State of Palestine, Switzerland, Trinidad and Tobago and Uruguay.

225 Assembly of State Parties Resolution ICC-ASP/16/Res, *Activation of the Jurisdiction of the Court Over the Crime of Aggression* (14 Dec 2017).

226 *Dugard* (n. 62), 250.

227 *Authers* and *Charlesworth*, in: Van der Heijden (ed.), Centre for International Governance and Justice Regnet Research Paper (2013), 1, 14.

228 Articles 28 and 28A of the Malabo Protocol.

229 Article 11 of the Malabo Protocol.

Union states have signed the Malabo Protocol,[230] with no ratifications.[231] Therefore the Protocol is not in operation as yet.

The Malabo Protocol goes far beyond the Rome Statute, including not only crisis crimes but also quotidian crimes.[232] Quotidian crimes are crimes which are prevalent on the African continent. The list of crimes in the Malabo Protocol include crimes which are well established and recognised in customary international law, crimes which are recognised in various AU treaties as well as crimes over which international courts traditionally have not had jurisdiction.[233] In total the ACJHPR will have jurisdiction over 14 international crimes, as opposed to the four core international crimes over which the ICC has jurisdiction.[234]

Jalloh refers to these additional crimes as "Rome Statute plus crimes".[235] The Protocol also allows for the introduction of new crimes and does not subject any of the crimes listed to a statute of limitations.[236] The fact that the crimes included in the Malabo Protocol have all been acknowledged as crimes before means that the principle of legality and the rule of law are both complied with in general. However, whilst the principle of *nullum crimen* is adhered to, the question then arises as to whether these crimes are deserving of international law attention?

For the most part the Malabo Protocol defines crimes against humanity, genocide and war crimes in the same manner as the Rome Statute.[237] There are however minor differences which must be highlighted. Regard-

230 Benin, Chad, Congo, Ghana, Guinea-Bissau, Mauritius, Sierra Leone and Sao Tome and Principe.

231 List of Countries which have Signed, Ratified/Acceded to The Protocol on Amendments to the Protocol on the Statute of the African Court of Justice and Human Rights: https://au.int/sites/default/files/treaties/36398-sl-PROTOCOL%20ON%20AMENDMENTS%20TO%20THE%20PROTOCOL%20ON%20THE%20STATUTE%20OF%20THE%20AFRICAN%20COURT%20OF%20JUSTICE%20AND%20HUMAN%20RIGHTS.pdf (last visited 14 Nov 2019).

232 *Sirleaf*, 54 CJTL 2016, 699, 702.

233 Amnesty International, Malabo Protocol: Legal and Institutional Implications of the Merged and Expanded African Court (2016), 15.

234 Article 28A of the Malabo Protocol provides: "Genocide, Crimes Against Humanity, War Crimes, the Crime of Unconstitutional Change of Government, Piracy, Terrorism, Mercenarism, Corruption, Money Laundering, Trafficking in Persons, Trafficking in Drugs, Trafficking in Hazardous Wastes, Illicit Exploitation of Natural Resources and the Crime of Aggression.".

235 *Jalloh*, 1 AJICJ 2014, 3, 5.

236 Article 28A(2) of the Malabo Protocol.

237 *Gevers*, in: William and Woolaver (eds.), Civil Society and International Criminal Justice in Africa Challenges and Opportunities (2016), 95, 113.

ing crimes against humanity the only difference is the inclusion of an "enterprise" as an element.[238] This inclusion is problematic as the Protocol does not define what an "enterprise" is.[239] The definition of genocide in the Protocol also includes "acts of rape or any other form of sexual violence".[240] This is not a factor mentioned in the Rome Statute, but as seen above is commonly accepted as a weapon and method of warfare, as interpreted by the ICTR in the *Akayesu* case.[241] This inclusion is a positive development as it is a more progressive definition.[242] It also complies with a strict interpretation of legal certainty.

Under the Malabo Protocol war crimes consist of 22 acts as opposed to the Rome Statute which only lists 12 acts.[243] Amongst these additional acts are the use of nuclear weapons and weapons of mass destruction.[244] In terms of international criminal law, this is a welcome development as the ICJ could not "conclude definitively whether the threat or use of nuclear weapons would be lawful or unlawful in an extreme circumstance of self-defence, in which the very survival of a State would be at stake".[245] However these additions do not comply with a narrow interpretation of legal certainty. Rather they are reflective of the situation in which the law is as opposed to what the community thinks it should be.

V. *Conclusion*

Gallant explains that in terms of international human rights law, courts are not obliged to interpret crimes in the narrowest possible way because "the current system of international human rights does not require this".[246] Similarly the *nullum crimen* principle does not apply the same way in a domestic law system as it does in an international criminal law system.[247] The ICTY stated "the principles of legality in international criminal law

238 Article 28C(1) of the Malabo Protocol.
239 *Amnesty International* (n. 215), 17.
240 Article 28B(f) of the Malabo Protocol.
241 The *Akayesu* case (n. 53).
242 Amnesty International (n. 215), 16.
243 Article 28D of the Malabo Protocol.
244 Article 28D(g) of the Malabo Protocol.
245 ICJ, *Legality of the Threat or Use of Nuclear Weapons*, Advisory Opinion of 8 Jul 1996, ICJ Reports 1996, 226.
246 *Gallant* (n. 34), 359.
247 *Van Schaak* (n. 19), 134.

are different from their related national legal systems with respect to their application and standards".[248]

Gil argues that not all states understand and apply the *nullum crimen* principle in the same way.[249] Therefore there is no one interpretation of the *nullum crimen* principle that can be applicable to international law.[250] She explains further that international courts are able to adapt the way in which they apply the *nullum crimen* principle because they are not bound to a singular interpretation like domestic courts.[251]

One must also be cognisant of the fact that "the terminology in many international treaties is open textured".[252] Whether this is because the drafters found it impossible to draft an exhaustive list of conduct or if it is designed to protect sovereignty is irrelevant.[253] The fact remains that it is up to international courts and tribunals to expand on these provisions through their judicial interpretation.[254]

Van Schaak highlights that "perfect positivism is impossible where customary international law...remains an integral source of international criminal law]".[255] As seen above, customary international law is determined through *usus* and *opinio juris*, and by their very nature these two concepts cannot be reconciled with a narrow interpretation of legal certainty.

The ICTY echoed the Nuremburg Tribunal's sentiment, that the *nullum crimen* principle is a "principle of justice".[256] It further explained that this principle "does not prevent a court...from determining an issue through a process of interpretation and clarification as to the elements of a particular crime",[257] "nor does it preclude the progressive development of the law by

---

248 International Criminal Tribunal for the Former Yugoslavia, *The Prosecutor v Zdravko Mucic, Hazim Delic, Esad Landzo and Zenjil Delalic*, Judgment of 16 Nov 1998, IT-96–21-T, para. 405.

249 *Gil*, 3 JICJ 2005, 1082, 1087.

250 *Gil* (n. 231), 1087.

251 *Gil* (n. 231), 1087.

252 *Van Schaak* (n. 19), 136.

253 *Van Schaak* (n. 19), 136.

254 *Van Schaak* (n. 19), 136.

255 *Van Schaak* (n. 19), 138.

256 International Criminal Tribunal for the Former Yugoslavia, *The Prosecutor v Milan Milutinovic, Nikola Sainovic and Dragoljub* Ojdanic, Decision of 21 May 2003 on Dragoljub Ojdanic's Motion Challenging Jurisdiction – Joint Criminal Enterprise, IT-99–37-AR72, para. 37.

257 International Criminal Tribunal for the Former Yugoslavia, *The Prosecutor v Zlatko Aleksovski*, Judgment of 24 Mar 2000, IT-95–14/1-A, para. 127.

the court".[258] It does, however, "prevent a court from creating new law or from interpreting existing law beyond the reasonable limits of acceptable clarification".[259]

Cassese explains, that at the Nuremburg Tribunal,

> "the *nullum crimen sine lege* principle could be regarded as a moral maxim destined to yield to superior exigencies whenever it would have been contrary to justice not to hold accountable for appalling atrocities".[260]

International courts are given the difficult task of "maintaining a balance between the preservation of justice and fairness towards the accused and taking into account the preservation of world order".[261]

Whilst tribunals accept that the legal certainty and the *nullum crimen* principle are applicable to international criminal law,[262] it is noted that these principles must be adapted to appropriately apply to every case in which it finds application.[263] Furthermore, because international criminal law jurisdiction is, in its very nature, different to national criminal jurisdiction, the manner in which the *nullum crimen sine lege* principle applies will be different in each context.[264]

Bibliography

Benjamin Authers and *Hilary Charlesworth*, "International Human Rights Law and the Language of Crisis", in: Jeroen van der Heijden (ed.), Centre for International Governance and Justice Regnet Research Paper (Regulatory Institutions Network, Australia 2013), 1.

M. Cherif Bassiouni, Crimes Against Humanity in International Criminal Law (Brill, 2nd ed., Netherlands 1999).

Tom Bennett and *Jonathan Strug*, Introduction to International Law (Juta, South Africa 2013).

---

258 The *Milutinovic* case (n. 238), para. 37.

259 The *Milutinovic* case (n. 238), para. 37.

260 *Cassese*, International Criminal Law (1st ed. 2003), 72.

261 The *Mucic* case (n. 230), para. 405.

262 International Criminal Tribunal for Rwanda, *The Prosecutor v Edouard Karemera, Mathieu Ngirumpatse, Joseph Nzirorera and Andre Rwamakuba*, Decision of 11 May 2004 on Defense's Preliminary Motions Challenging Jurisdiction: Joint Criminal Enterprise, ICTR-98–44-T, para. 39.

263 *Van Schaak* (n. 19), 141.

264 *Van Schaak* (n. 19), 141.

Antonio Cassese, International Criminal Law (Oxford University Press, 2nd ed., New York 2008).

Antonio Cassese, International Criminal Law (Oxford University Press, 1st ed., New York 2003).

Antoinio Cassese, The Oxford Companion to International Criminal Justice (Oxford University Press, 1st ed., New York 2009.

Shahram Dana, "Beyond Retroactivity to Realizing Justice: a Theory on the Principle of Legality in International Criminal Law", 99 The Journal of Criminal Law and Criminology (JCLC) 2009, 857.

Caroline Davidson, "How to Read International Criminal Law: Strict Construction and the Rome Statute of the International Criminal Court", 91 Saint John's Law Review (SJLR) 2017, 37.

Martin Dixon, Textbook on International Law (Oxford University Press, 7th ed., United Kingdom 2013).

John Dugard, International Law: A South African Perspective (Juta, 5th ed., South Africa 2018).

Kenneth Gallant, The Principle of Legality In International and Comparative Criminal Law (Cambridge University Press, United Kingdom 2009).

Cristopher Gevers, "Back to the future? Civil society, the 'Turn to Complementarity' in Africa and Some Critical Concerns", in: Sarah William and Hannah Woolaver (eds.), Civil Society and International Criminal Justice in Africa Challenges and Opportunities (Juta, South Africa 2016), 95.

Alicia Gil, "The Flaws of the Scilingo Judgment", 3 Journal of International Criminal Justice (JICJ) 2005, 1082.

Charles Jalloh, "Editorial", 1 African Journal of International Criminal Justice (AJICJ) 2014, 3.

Frederic Lee Kirgis, "Custom on a Sliding Scale", 81 American Journal of International Law (AJIL) 1987, 146.

Henry King, Benjamin Ferencz and *Whitney Harris*, "Origins of the Genocide Convention", 40 Case Western Reserve Journal of International Law (CWRJIL) 2008, 13.

Martti Koskenniemi, From Apology to Utopia (Cambridge University Press, United Kingdom 2005).

Lei Lei, "Legal Methods, Legal Certainty and the Rule of Law", 5 Renmin Chinese Law Review (RCLR) 2017, 25.

Raphael Lemkin, "Genocide as a Crime under International Law", 41 American Journal of International Law (AJIL) 1947, 145.

Raphael Lemkin, Axis Rule in Occupied Europe (Carnegie Endowment for International Peace, 1st ed., Washington 1944).

Timothy MacCormack, "From Sun Tzu to the Sixth Committee: The Evolution of an International Criminal Law Regime", in: Timothy MacCormack and Gerry Simpson (eds.), The Law of War Crimes: National and International Approaches (Brill, Netherlands 1997), 31.

Leila Nadyja Sadat, The International Criminal Court and Transformation of International Law: Justice for the New Millennium (Martinus Nijhoff, New York 2002).

Steven R. Ratner, Jason S. Abrams and *James L. Bischoff*, Accountability for Human Rights Atrocities in International Law: Beyond the Nuremberg Legacy (Oxford University Press, Oxford, 1st ed., 2009).

Marco Sassoli, Antoine A. Bouvier and Anne Quintin (eds.), How Does Law Protect in War (International Committee of the Red Cross, Geneva, 3rd ed., 2011).

Beth Van Schaak, "Crimen Sine Lege: Judicial Law-making at the Intersection of Law and Morals", 97 The Georgetown Law Journal (GLJ) 2008, 119.

William Schabas, "Origins of the Genocide Convention: From Nuremberg to Paris", 40 Case Western Reserve Journal of International Law (CWRJIL) 2008, 35.

Matiangai V. Sirleaf, "Regionalism, Regime Complexes and Crisis in International Criminal Justice", 54 Columbia Journal of Transnational Law (CJTL) 2016, 699.

Register of cases

International Criminal Court

ICC, *The Prosecutor v Bosco Ntaganda*, Judgment of 8 Jul 2019, ICC-01/04–02/06.

ICC, *The Prosecutor v Hadzihasanovic, Alagic and Kubura*, Judgment of 12 Nov 2002, IT-01–47-PT.

International Court of Justice

ICJ, *Colombia v Peru (Asylum Case)*, Judgment of 20 Nov 1950, ICJ Reports, 14 (ICJ Reports 1950, 266.

ICJ, *Belgium v Spain (Barcelona Traction, Light & Power Company Limited case)*, Judgment of 5 Feb 1970, ICJ Reports 1970, 3.

ICJ, *Federal Republic of Germany v Iceland (Fisheries Jurisdiction case)*, Judgment of 25 Jul 1974, ICJ Reports 1974, 175.

ICJ, *Germany v Italy: Greece Intervening (Jurisdiction Immunities of the State case)*, Judgment of 3 Feb 2012, ICJ Reports 2012, 99.

ICJ, *Legality of the Threat or Use of Nuclear Weapons*, Advisory Opinion of 8 Jul 1996, ICJ Reports 1996, 226.

ICJ, *Nicaragua v United States of America*, Judgment of 27 Jun 1986, ICJ Reports 1986, 14.

ICJ, *Federal Republic of Germany v Netherlands and Denmark (North Sea Continental Shelf cases)*, Judgment of 20 Feb 1969, ICJ Reports 1969, 3.

ICJ, *United Kingdom v Norway (Anglo Norwegian Fisheries case)*, Judgment of 18 Dec 1951, ICJ Reports 1951, 116.

International Criminal Tribunal for Rwanda

ICTR, *The Prosecutor v Akayesu*, Judgment of 2 Sep 1998, ICTR-96–4-T.

ICTR, *The Prosecutor v Edouard Karemera, Mathieu Ngirumpatse, Joseph Nzirorera and Andre Rwamakuba*, Decision of 11 May 2004 on Defense's Preliminary Motions Challenging Jurisdiction: Joint Criminal Enterprise, ICTR-98–44-T.

International Criminal Tribunal for the Former Yugoslavia

ICTY, *The Prosecutor v Dusko Tadic*, Appeal Judgment of 15 Jul 1999, IT-94–1-A.

ICTY, *The Prosecutor v Radislav Krstić*, Judgment of 19 Apr 2004, IT-98–33-A.

ICTY, *The Prosecutor v Radoslav Brdanin*, Judgment of 1 Sep 2004, IT-99–36-T.

ICTY, *The Prosecutor v Zdravko Mucic, Hazim Delic, Esad Landzo and Zenjil Delalic*, Judgment of 16 Nov 1998, IT-96–21-T.

ICTY, *Prosecutor v Dario Kordić and Mario Cerkez*, Judgment of 26 Feb 2001, IT-95–14/2-T.

ICTY, *Prosecutor v Dragoljub Kunarac, Radomir Kovac and Zoran Vukovic*, Judgment of 22 Feb 2001, IT-96–23-T and IT-96–23/1-T.

ICTY, *Prosecutor v Tihomir Blaškić*, Judgment of 3 Mar 2000, IT-95–14-T.

ICTY, *The Prosecutor v Galic*, Judgment and Opinion of 5 Dec 2003, Case No. IT-98–29-T.

ICTY, *The Prosecutor v Milan Milutinovic, Nikola Sainovic and Dragoljub* Ojdanic, Decision of 21 May 2003 on Dragoljub Ojdanic's Motion Challenging Jurisdiction – Joint Criminal Enterprise, IT-99–37-AR72.

ICTY, *The Prosecutor v Zlatko Aleksovski*, Judgment of 24 Mar 2000, IT-95–14/1-A.

International Military Tribunal

International Military Tribunal sitting at Nuremberg, *The Trial of German Major War Criminals*, Judgment of 1 October 1946.

Permanent Court of International Justice

PCIJ, Case of the SS "Lotus", Judgment of 7 Sep 1927, Publications of the PCIJ 1927 Series A No. 10.

Special Court for Sierra Leone

SCSL, The Prosecutor v Alex Tamba Brima, Brima Bazzy Kamara and Santigie Borbor Kanu, Judgment of 22 Feb. 2008, SCSL-2004–16-A.

SCSL, The Prosecutor v Issa Hassan Sesay, Morris Kallon and Augustine Gbao, Judgment of 2 March 2009, SCSL-04–15-T 2.

SCSL, The Prosecutor v Sam Hinga Norman, Judgment of 31 May 2004, SCSL-2004–14-AR72(E).

United Nations Documents

Assembly of State Parties Resolution ICC-ASP/16/Res, Activation of the Jurisdiction of the Court Over the Crime of Aggression (14 Dec 2017).

GA Res 96 (I), The Crime of Genocide (11 Dec 1946).

GA Res 3314 (XXIX), Definition of Aggression (14 Dec 1974).

Internet Sources

List of Countries which have Signed, Ratified/Acceded to The Protocol on Amendments to the Protocol on the Statute of the African Court of Justice and Human Rights: https://au.int/sites/default/files/treaties/36398-sl-PROTOCOL%20ON%20AMENDMENTS%20TO%20THE%20PROTOCOL%20ON%20THE%20STATUTE%20OF%20THE%20AFRICAN%20COURT%20OF%20JUSTICE%20AND%20HUMAN%20RIGHTS.pdf (last visited 14 Nov 2019).

Comment: Legal Certainty and Human Rights in the European Legal Order – The Treatment of Preventive Detention in the German Federal Constitutional Court and the European Court of Human Rights

*Aqilah Sandhu**

* Aqilah Sandhu, Academic Assistant at the Chair for Constitutional Law, Administrative Law, European Union Law and Legislation Theory of Prof. Dr. Matthias Rossi, University of Augsburg.

I. Introduction

In their contribution, *Roux* and *Hassen*[1] set out the foundational principles of what is referred to in Germany as the "*Rechtsstaat*" (the rule of law) with regard to public international law, and focus specifically on the principle of legal certainty and international crimes.

Among the most important guarantees of the rule of law in criminal law is the requirement of legal certainty that all branches of power must ensure: the legislature must draft legal provisions in a sufficiently clear and precise manner, while the judiciary is responsible for applying and interpreting the law within the boundaries set by the legislature. In criminal law, the principle entails the well-known maxims, *nulla poena sine lege* and *nullum crimen sine lege*, meaning that the punishable conduct and any sanction must be explicitly laid down by law before the crime is committed. Referring to the Nuremburg Trials, the authors show that, in international criminal law, exceptions to the principles of *nulla poena* and *nullum crimen* have been made, as neither crimes against humanity nor war crimes were codified as punishable acts at the time the Nazi regime committed them. Apparently, the Judges of the Nuremburg Tribunal did not apply the principle of legal certainty, opining that not punishing the Nazi war criminals for their abhorrent acts would be "unjust". Today, these principles are defined in Articles 22 and 23 of the Statute of the International Criminal Court ("ICC") as "general principles of criminal law". The authors state that, in most major international criminal and human rights instruments, the *nullum crimen* and *nulla poena* maxims are not laid down explicitly, but are rather incorporated implicitly. They further show how international tribunals have developed these principles in their jurisprudence.

Finally, *Roux* and *Hassen* deal with the recently-adopted Malabo Protocol amending the Statute of the African Court on Human and Peoples' Rights ("ACHR") of the African Union ("AU"). According to the Malabo Protocol, the subject-matter jurisdiction of the Court will be extended to international crimes. Consequently, the former ACHR will be renamed the "African Court of Justice and Human and Peoples' Rights" ("ACJHPR"). The Court will have a Human Rights Section, hearing individual human rights cases, and a General Affairs Section with the authority to hear all other cases. However, of the 15 required ratifications (of a total of 55 AU Member States), the Malabo Protocol has not managed even one to date (April 2020). As the ACHR Statute introduces a range of international

---

1 *Roux* and *Hassen*, in this book, 103 et seqq.

crimes that are not included in the ICC Statute and in part defines them differently, the question of legal certainty in international crimes arises.

In the following response to *Roux* and *Hassen*, I would like to focus on two core issues raised in their contribution and illustrate their relevance to the German, and a wider European, context: First, this response will illustrate how the tension between legal certainty and the retroactive punishment of crimes was resolved by courts in the young Federal German Republic that had to deal with the heritage of two "*Unrechtsstaaten*" in the space of only half a century (II.). Secondly, this comment will focus on how a supranational human rights body can shape and influence domestic criminal law (III.). Again, the German example provides valuable insights into the functioning of supranational human rights courts and their relationship to national constitutional courts. Germany is a member state of the Council of Europe and party to its European Convention on Human Rights (the "Convention"), an international convention on the protection of human rights. I will therefore consider the complex relationship between the court that was established by the Convention, the European Court of Human Rights ("ECtHR") and the German Federal Constitutional Court (*Bundesverfassungsgericht* – "BVerfG") to show how it influences domestic criminal law in a positive way and reinforces the constitutional guarantee of *nulla poena* (IV.). In my concluding remarks, I will apply the findings to the newly-established ACJHPR (V.).

II. The "lively tension" between legal certainty and substantive justice

As *Roux* and *Hassen* establish in their contribution, when the Nuremburg Tribunal convicted functionaries of the Nazi regime, it favoured substantive justice over a strict interpretation of the *nullum crimen* maxim. This clash between justice (a substantive principle) and legal certainty (a formal principle) was described by the legal philosopher, *Gustav Radbruch*, as a "lively tension".[2] He stated in his oft-cited essay, that "legal certainty is not the only value that law must effectuate, nor is it the decisive value. Alongside legal certainty, there are two other values: purposiveness [the German *Zweckmäßigkeit*] and justice".[3] He suggested resolving the conflict

2 *Radbruch*, in: Kaufmann (ed.), Gustav Radbruch: Gesamtausgabe, vol. 3 (1990), 39, 50.

3 *Radbruch*, 26 Oxf. J. Leg. Stud. 2006, 1, 6; *Radbruch*, in: Kaufmann (ed.), Gustav Radbruch: Gesamtausgabe, vol. 3 (1990), 83, 89.

between justice and legal certainty using the famous formula that came to be known as the "*Radbruch* formula": "The positive law, secured by legislation and power, takes precedence even when its content is unjust and fails to benefit people, unless the conflict between statute and justice reaches such an intolerable degree that the statute, as 'flawed law', must yield to justice."[4] A law, that does not even attempt to serve justice, that deliberately betrays "equality, the core value of justice" is, according to *Radbruch*, "not merely 'flawed law', it lacks completely the very nature of law" (i.e. "statutory *Unrecht*").[5] He nevertheless did not question the necessity of legal statutes in a *Rechtsstaat*, a form of government "that serves as well as possible the ideas of both justice and legal certainty".[6] A government of law, he concludes, "is like our daily bread, like water to drink and air to breathe."[7] While opposing a strict legal positivism, *Radbruch* at the same time acknowledges the need for legal realism which, however, must always enable individual justice. Following this critical stance towards a rigorous legal positivism, *Robert Alexy* pointed out that there is "an intrinsic connection between the principle of legal certainty and positivity"[8]; legal certainty is even "the ground of positivity".[9] Exceptions to the principle of legal certainty are thus also a statement against the rigorous legal positivism that prevailed in the German Reich at the time the war crimes were committed. According to *Alexy's* concept of the dual nature of law, law comprises not only a factual dimension (i.e. the defined authoritative issuance) but also an ideal dimension that requires the correctness of content.[10] Correctness is understood as "justice" or "moral correctness". This leads to a non-positivistic concept of law.

The term *Unrecht* cannot be fully captured by the English term "injustice"; it constitutes in fact a gross and utter disregard for the most basic common principles of a just society, a system in which "law" no longer deserves to be labelled as such. *Unrecht* is, as one commentator once put it, "the opposite of law".[11] The German Courts applied the *Radbruch* formula in civil- and public-law cases that dealt with National Socialist *Unrecht*,

---

4 *Radbruch*, 26 Oxf. J. Leg. Stud. 2006, 1, 7.
5 Ibid.
6 Ibid., 11.
7 Ibid.
8 *Alexy*, 28 Ratio Juris 2015, 441.
9 Ibid., 444.
10 Ibid.
11 *Steinbeis, "Editorial: Ranks and Titles" (11 May 2019)*, https://verfassungsblog.de/ranks-and-titles/ (last visited 31 May 2019).

especially in the fields of inheritance, family law, civil service and citizenship laws. The BVerfG explicitly referred to the *Radbruch* formula to justify the inapplicability of National Socialist statutes.[12] It differentiated between *Unrecht*, which lacked the very nature of law, and merely unjust National Socialist statutes which, while not amounting to "obvious *Unrecht*", nevertheless had to be considered illegitimate, but legally in force due to their "sociological validity".[13] In its decision on the killing of fugitives at the border between the two former German states, the BVerfG also applied the *Radbruch* formula in a criminal-law context for the first time.[14] The law justifying the killing of fugitives had to be considered non-existent at the time the act was committed because it legalised the intentional killing of other human beings for merely crossing the border inside Germany.[15] Thus, the *nulla poena* guarantee of Article 103, para. 2 of the German Constitution, which is referred to as the Basic Law (*Grundgesetz* – GG), is not absolute if the overriding needs of justice demand that those who commit unjust acts be held accountable. In this situation, the principle of substantive justice, which also encompasses internationally-acknowledged human rights, demands that the protection of legitimate expectations ("*Vertrauensschutz*") guaranteed by Article 103, para. 2 GG yield in favour of substantive justice. However, if there is an applicable criminal statute in place that prescribes certain sanctions, the prohibition of retroactive criminal laws in Article 103, para. 2 GG is absolute.

III. The nulla poena and nullum crimen principles in the European legal order

In Europe, the principles of *nulla poena* and *nullum crimen* are explicitly enshrined in various legal and constitutional documents at multiple levels. There are norms to ensure coherence and consistency in the application of these human rights instruments, as each falls under the jurisdiction of different courts. If the various courts demand that they have the final say, tensions may arise in the application and interpretation of these principles. In this section, I will first outline the various legal foundations in the

12 See e.g. BGH, Judgment of 11 Feb 1953, II ZR 51/52, NJW 1953, 542, 544.

13 BVerfG, Order of 19 Feb 1957, BvR 357/52, BVerfGE 6, 132, 199 – Gestapo.

14 BVerfG, Judgment of 24 Oct 1996, 2 BvR 1851, 1853, 1875, 1852/94, BVerfGE 95, 96 – Mauerschützen; *Alexy*, in: Alexy, Koch, Kuhlen and Rüßmann (eds.), Elemente einer juristischen Begründungslehre (2003), 469.

15 BVerfG, Judgment of 24 Oct 1996, 2 BvR 1851, 1853, 1875, 1852/94, BVerfGE 95, 135, para. 143 – Mauerschützen.

national, supranational and international legal orders (1.). I will then elaborate on the divergent understanding of the BVerfG and the ECtHR as to which sanctions qualify as "*poena*", i.e. penalty or punishment within the meaning of the relevant guarantees (2.). This will lead me to some general remarks on the role of the Convention in the German constitutional order (3.).

1. Legal foundations of the principles

a) The German Constitution

In the German Constitution, the *nulla poena* and *nullum crimen* maxims are equivalent to a fundamental right and are enshrined in Article 103, para. 2, which provides that an "act may be punished only if it was defined by a law as a criminal offence before the act was committed". This prohibits the retroactive application of criminal laws. Not only must a crime be strictly defined at the time of the relevant criminal conduct, but the punishment must also be foreseeably laid down in the statute in advance. This is further concretised in Section 2, para. 1 of the German Criminal Code (*Strafgesetzbuch* – StGB), according to which the "penalty and any ancillary measures shall be determined by the law which is in force at the time of the act." This means that lawful conduct may not be turned into a punishable crime retroactively. The principle is also part of the general rule-of-law guarantee, albeit not laid down there explicitly: from Article 20, para. 3 GG as well as the fundamental rights follows a general prohibition against retrospective legislation as an element of the rule-of-law principle, which is not absolute, but subject to the balancing of interests in each case.[16]

b) The European Convention on Human Rights

This essential rule-of-law principle is also enshrined in the European Convention on Human Rights. According to Article 7, para. 1, sentence 1 of the Convention, "[n]o one shall be held guilty of any criminal offence on account of any act or omission which did not constitute a criminal offence

16 See on the dogmatic foundations in detail *Werndl*, Zweispurigkeit und Vertrauensschutz (2019), 266 et seqq.

under national or international law at the time when it was committed", thus codifying the *nullum crimen* maxim. Article 7, para. 1, sentence 2 of the Convention contains the *nulla poena* maxim, stating: "Nor shall a heavier penalty be imposed than the one that was applicable at the time the criminal offence was committed." "Criminal offence" is understood to include offences under national and international law, ensuring that conduct that was legal under domestic law can be punished retrospectively if it constituted an international crime. Article 7, para. 2 of the Convention is a direct response to the Nuremburg Trials and reads as follows: "This Article shall not prejudice the trial and punishment of any person for any act or omission which, at the time when it was committed, was criminal according to the general principles of law recognised by civilised nations." The Federal Republic of Germany initially made a reservation in respect of this provision when it ratified the Convention to ensure that Article 7, para. 2 of the Convention would only be applied within the boundaries of Article 103, para. 2 GG. This reservation was later withdrawn[17] so that Article 7, para. 2 of the Convention has since been fully applicable in Germany. However, as the ECtHR has made clear, this provision is not of a constitutive nature, but is "only a contextual clarification of the liability limb of that rule, included so as to ensure that there was no doubt about the validity of prosecutions after the Second World War in respect of the crimes committed during that war".[18] The ECtHR also clarified that this did not allow a general exception to the rule of non-retroactivity. Both Article 7, para. 1 and para. 2 of the Convention are, according to the ECtHR, "interlinked and are to be interpreted in a concordant manner".[19] The provision contains the principles of legality and legal certainty, as well as the prohibition against detrimental analogy.[20] The Convention does not allow any exception or derogation from this provision (see Article 15, para. 3 of the Convention), not even in the case of emergency or war.

c) The European Charter of Fundamental Rights

In addition, these principles are secured in the Charter of Fundamental Rights of the European Union (the "Charter"). According to Article 49,

---

17 Federal Law Gazette (BGBl.) of 7 Nov 2003, part II, 1580.
18 ECtHR, Judgment of 18 Jul 2013, 2312/08 and 34179/08, para. 72 – Maktouf and Damjanović v. Bosnia and Herzegovina.
19 Ibid.
20 *Sanz-Caballero*, 28 E. J. I. L. 2017, 787, 789.

para. 1, sentences 1 and 2 of the Charter, "[n]o one shall be held guilty of any criminal offence on account of any act or omission which did not constitute a criminal offence under national law or international law at the time when it was committed. Nor shall a heavier penalty be imposed than that which was applicable at the time the criminal offence was committed". Parallel to Article 7, para. 2 of the Convention, Article 49, para. 2 of the Charter makes an exception for the trial and punishment of acts that were criminal "according to the general principles recognised by the community of nations". The Nuremburg exception has thus been fully incorporated into the European Human Rights Instruments.

d) Difference in scope and content

While at first glance the principles of *nulla poena* and *nullum crimen* are guaranteed almost identically in the various human rights instruments that are binding on Germany, there is room for argument as to the scope and content of the guarantees. There are supranational and various national constitutional courts in Europe that claim to have the final say in human rights issues, so tensions and jurisdictional conflicts are therefore inevitable. As Germany is an EU member state, Article 49, para. 2 of the Charter is not only directly applicable in the domestic legal order, but even takes precedence in its application over conflicting national (including constitutional) law, being part of EU primary law according to Article 6, para. 1 of the Treaty of the European Union (TEU). The European Court of Justice (ECJ), whose judgments are of relevance in the German legal order, is charged with interpreting the Charter. As a Member to the Council of Europe, Germany is also bound by the Convention's guarantees. However, as the EU has not yet acceded to the Convention (which it should according to Article 6, para. 2 of the TEU), the Convention's guarantees do not hold primacy over the law of its Member States, whereas the Charter does enjoy primacy over the national constitutions of the EU Member States. Instead, the Convention only indirectly influences the fundamental-rights provisions of the Basic Law. The complex interplay between the Convention and the Basic Law will be outlined on the basis of the case concerning the legality of the retroactive prolongation of preventive detention. The BVerfG and the ECtHR do not define what kind of penalties are included by Article 7, para. 1 sentence 2 of the Convention and Article, 103 para. 2 GG, both containing the *nulla poena* principle.

2. Legal certainty caught in judicial dialogue

a) The German twin-track system of sanctions

The StGB distinguishes between penalties or punishments ("*Strafen*"), and measures of correction and prevention ("*Maßregeln der Besserung und Sicherung*"). This so-called "twin-track system of sanctions" goes back to the "Law on dealing with dangerous habitual offenders and on measures of correction and prevention" of 1933.[21] Whereas penalties (i.e. prison sentences and fines) are repressive in nature and determined in relation to an offender's guilt, measures of correction and prevention are independent of guilt and preventively aim at rehabilitating the offender or protecting the public from the danger posed by a convicted criminal.[22] Penalties and measures of correction and prevention are not mutually exclusive, but can be imposed simultaneously. This distinction due to the twin-track system of sanctions is upheld as it relates to the question of legal certainty. Whereas a penalty must be determined by the law that is in force at the time of the act, the measure of correction and prevention is based on the law in force at the time of the court's decision (see Article 2 para. 1 and para. 6 StGB). Measures of correction and prevention are laid down in Section 61 et seq. StGB. They include for example confinement in a psychiatric hospital, and placement in custodial addiction treatment or preventive detention. The latter – "the most disputed of all measures"[23] – will be discussed here in more detail.

b) Preventive detention as a measure of correction and prevention

If a convicted person, after having served his or her full prison sentence, is still considered dangerous to the public and likely to commit offences as a result of his or her propensity to reoffend, the sentencing criminal

21 "Gesetz gegen gefährliche Gewohnheitsverbrecher und über Maßregeln der Besserung und Sicherung" of 24 Nov 1933, Law Gazette of the German Reich (RGBl.) of 27 Nov 1933, part I, 995; on the history see *Stisser*, Die Sicherungsverwahrung (2019), 21 et seqq.

22 The landmark judgment of the Federal Constitutional Court on preventive detention begins with this sentence: "Every social order depends on protecting itself from dangerous criminals", Judgment of 5 Feb 2004, 2 BvR 2029/01, BVerfGE 109, 133, 134, para. 2.

23 *Kaspar*, 4 Peking Univ. L. J. 2016, 80, 95.

court can, under certain circumstances laid down in law, order placement in additional preventive detention according to Section 66 StGB to protect society from the offender. Until 1998, the maximum duration of preventive detention was ten years.[24] The law was amended in 1998 by the "Act to Combat Sexual Offences and Other Dangerous Offences",[25] loosening the formal requirements for imposing the measure and allowing for its indefinite prolongation in Section 67d, para. 3 StGB. The newly amended law provided: "(3) If a person has spent ten years in preventive detention, the court shall declare the termination of the measure if there is no danger that the detainee will, due to his criminal tendencies, commit serious offences resulting in considerable psychological or physical harm to the victims. […]". The Introductory Act to the Criminal Code was also amended, so that the newly-altered provision applied without restriction *ratione temporis*, i.e. even retroactively, by stating: "Section 67d of the Criminal Code, as amended by the Act to Combat Sexual Offences and Other Dangerous Offences of 26 January 1998, shall apply without restriction."[26] This meant that the newly amended Section 67d, para. 3 StGB was also applicable to detainees whose preventive detention had been ordered prior to the change in law and who, until then, had had the legitimate expectation of at least being released after ten years in detention. This raised questions about legal certainty and the prohibition against the retroactive application of criminal laws. Due to the twin-track system of sanctions, the prohibition against retroactive application of the law does not apply to the measure of preventive detention. The relevant law reads as follows: "Unless otherwise provided by law, measures of rehabilitation and incapacitation shall be determined according to the law in force at the time of the decision" (Section 2, para. 6 StGB). Thus, the amended provision of 1998 was applicable to prisoners whose preventive detention had been ordered prior to the law's amendment. The rules on preventive detention have been expanded even further with time, for example to

---

24 Section 67d para. 1–3 of the German Criminal Code as in force in 1998 states: "(1) […] the first period of preventive detention may not exceed ten years. […] (3) If the maximum duration has expired, the detainee shall be released […]".

25 "Gesetz zur Bekämpfung von Sexualdelikten und anderen gefährlichen Straftaten", Federal Law Gazette (BGBl.) of 26 Jan 1998, part I, 160; on this see *von Harbou*, Das neue Recht der Sicherungsverwahrung (1999), passim.

26 Article 1a para. 3 of the Introductory Act to the Criminal Code (Einführungsgesetz zum Strafgesetzbuch – EGStGB).

include even juveniles or to enable subsequent preventive detention,[27] all giving rise to the question of validity with a view to the prohibition of retroactivity.[28] Given its limited scope, this contribution will focus on the case concerning the retrospective prolongation of the maximum period of preventive detention.

c) Qualifying preventive detention: the BVerfG's view

A convicted criminal who had been serving his prison sentence since 1986, and was subsequently placed in preventive detention in 1991, was affected by this change in law that had occurred at the time he was in preventive detention. According to the law at the time of his conviction, his preventive detention would have ended in 2001 at the latest. However, according to the amended law in place in 1998, the maximum ten-year period no longer applied. Instead, his detention could be extended retrospectively for an unlimited period as long as he showed the propensity to commit serious criminal acts. The detainee launched a constitutional complaint with the BVerfG, which was dismissed in 2004. He argued that the retroactive abolition of the maximum period of preventive detention in Section 66, para. 3 StGB, read with Article 1a, para. 3 of the Introductory Act to the Criminal Code, violated the prohibition against retroactive punishment under Article 103, para. 2 GG.[29] The BVerfG held that Article 103, para. 2 GG did not cover measures of correction and prevention, but only applied to penalties. Preventive detention however, did not qualify as a penalty or punishable act within the meaning of Article 103, para. 2 GG, as it was not a measure expressing the sovereign censure of illegal and culpable conduct, and was not imposed to compensate for or punish guilt.[30] Article 103, para. 2 GG did not apply to other measures interfering with a person's

27 See BVerfG, Order of 23 Aug 2006, 2 BvR 226/06, NJW 2006, 3483, declaring subsequent detention to be compatible with the Basic Law. In contrast, the ECtHR found it to be in violation of the Convention in the Judgment of 19 Apr 2012, 61272/09 – B. v. Germany; see also ECtHR, Judgment of 12 Jan 2011, 6587/04, NJW 2011, 3423 – Haidn v. Germany and BVerfG, Judgment of 10 Feb 2004, 2 BvR 834/02, BVerfGE 109, 190 (lack of competence) on the retrospective order of preventive detention in Bavarian Law.

28 For a recent concise overview see *Stisser,* Die Sicherungsverwahrung (2019), 31–33.

29 BVerfG, Judgment of 5 Feb 2004, 2 BvR 2029/01, BVerfGE 109, 133, 145 et seq. – Langfristige Sicherungsverwahrung.

30 Ibid., 173, para. 146 et seqq.

rights, in particular not measures of correction and prevention, which differed from penalties under the Criminal Code's twin-track system. According to the BVerfG, preventive detention was a purely preventive measure aimed at protecting the public from a dangerous offender and was therefore not covered by the strict and absolute prohibition against retroactivity in Article 103, para. 2 GG.

The legality test was thus reduced to the general rule-of-law provision in Article 20, para. 3 GG read with the right to liberty under Article 2, para. 2 GG, which requires the balancing of interests.[31] The application of the amended Criminal Code provision to criminals who had been placed in preventive detention prior to its enactment, and who were still serving their sentences, was declared to conform with the principle of *Vertrauensschutz* (protection of legitimate expectations guaranteed in a State governed by the rule of law). Concerning Section 2, para. 6 StGB on measures of correction and prevention, a detainee could from the very outset expect changes in law. The BVerfG found that the legislature's interest in protecting the public against interference with their life, health and sexual integrity outweighed the detainee's right to liberty and reliance on the law not to change.[32]

d) Strasbourg's divergent view on the definition of "penalty"

The detainee, M., finally lodged an individual complaint (under Article 34 of the Convention) against this decision. He argued that continued preventive detention beyond the ten-year period that had been the maximum under the law applicable at the time of his offence and conviction violated Article 5, para. 1 of the Convention and the principle of *nulla poena* in Article 7, para. 1 of the Convention. This was because the retroactive prolongation of his preventive detention after having served the ten-year period amounted to the imposition of a "heavier penalty" than the one that had been applicable at the time the criminal offence was committed.

In its landmark decision, the ECtHR found that Germany had violated these provisions because national criminal law lacked foreseeability in its application, as the detainee could not, at the time of his conviction, have foreseen that his offence would lead to preventive detention for an

31 Ibid., 180, para. 170 et seqq.
32 Ibid., 186, para. 187 et seqq.

unlimited period.[33] The ECtHR noted that there was no uniform approach to preventive detention in the Convention States: whereas some qualified it as an additional penalty, others treated it as a merely preventive measure, like Germany. Referring to the German criminal law, according to which preventive detention is not considered a penalty and thus not protected by the absolute ban on retrospective punishment, the ECtHR stressed that "the concept of 'penalty' in Article 7 is autonomous in scope and it is thus for the Court to determine whether a particular measure should be qualified as a penalty, without being bound by the measure's qualification under domestic law."[34]

The term "penalty", within the meaning of the provision, generally refers to a measure that is imposed following conviction for a criminal offence. The ECtHR further examined the nature and purpose of a measure, its intensity and categorisation under national law.[35] When applying these criteria, the ECtHR did not take a purely formal point of view; instead, it compared preventive detention and prison sentences in practice. It noted that "[m]inor alterations to the detention regime compared to that of an ordinary prisoner serving his sentence, including privileges such as detainees' right to wear their own clothes and to further equip their more comfortable prison cells, cannot mask the fact that there is no substantial difference between the execution of a prison sentence and that of a preventive detention order."[36] Given the fact that preventive detention is ordered by criminal courts, the real circumstances of the individuals affected and the indefinite prolongation of preventive detention, the ECtHR concluded that preventive detention did not merely serve a preventive purpose, but was instead punitive in nature. This was because preventive detention is ordered against individuals who have been found guilty of a grave criminal offence and they are treated like ordinary long-term prisoners who are not provided with special treatment.[37] From the fact that people in preventive detention are not given psychological care and special support within a coherent framework to reduce the risk that they will reoffend, the Court concluded that the measure had to be categorised as a "penalty"

33 ECtHR, Judgment of 17 Dec 2009, 19359/04, NJW 2010, 2495, 2497, para. 104 – M. v. Germany.

34 Ibid., 2498, para. 126.

35 *Sanz-Caballero,* 28 E. J. I. L. 2017, 787, 791.

36 ECtHR, Judgment of 17 Dec 2009, 19359/04, NJW 2010, 2495, 2497, para. 127 – M. v. Germany.

37 Ibid., 2499, para. 128.

for the purposes of Article 7, para. 1 of the Convention.[38] Therefore, the subsequent prolongation of the applicant's preventive detention was considered to be a heavier additional punishment that was imposed retrospectively and thus violated Article 7 of the Convention. The ECtHR did not contest the twin-track system of sanctions as such. However, it did challenge the purely formal approach adopted by the German courts to defining the term "penalty" and indicated that even a preventive measure could amount to a penalty within the meaning of Article 7, para. 1 of the Convention, thus giving rise to the absolute prohibition against the retroactive application of criminal law.[39]

e) The implementation of the ECtHR's judgment in German law

In reaction to the ECtHR's decision, the German legislature adopted the "Act to Reform the Law of Preventive Detention" in December 2010, reducing the number of offences justifying preventive detention, as well as the "Act on Therapeutic Confinement" (*Therapieunterbringungsgesetz* – ThUG).[40] This was to comply with the requirements laid down by the ECtHR and to provide a therapeutically-oriented, special detention for individuals falling under Article 5, para. 1 lit. e of the Convention (persons "of unsound mind"). In particular, Article 1a of the Introductory Act to the Criminal Code, which allowed the unlimited retroactive prolongation of preventive detention, was repealed.

3. The role of the Convention in the German legal order

When, in 2011, the BVerfG was again called to decide (this time on the legality of the retrospective extension as well as on the subsequent imposition of preventive detention) it had to implement the ECtHR's decision.

38 Ibid., paras. 129–133.

39 What followed were subsequent convictions of Germany by the ECtHR in its Judgments of 13 Jan 2011, 17792/07 – Kallweit v. Germany; 20008/07 – Mautes v. Germany and 27360/04, 42225/07 – Schummer v. Germany.

40 "Gesetz zur Neuordnung des Rechts der Sicherungsverwahrung" and "Gesetz zur Therapierung und Unterbringung psychisch gestörter Gewalttäter", Federal Law Gazette (BGBl.) of 22 Dec 2010, part I, 2300. For the constitutionality of the Therapeutic Confinement Act see BVerfG, Order of 11 Jul 2013, 2 BvR 2302/11, 2 BvR 1279/12, NJW 2013, 3151.

From a procedural point of view, judicial review was possible because the judgments of the ECtHR were treated as legally-relevant changes to the factual and legal circumstances.[41] As an agreement under public international law, the Convention had the status of a federal statute when it became German law according to Article 59, para. 2 GG. It thus ranked below the Basic law in the legal hierarchy of norms. The Convention guarantees "are not a direct constitutional standard of review in the German legal system", but they do have "constitutional significance", as "they influence the interpretation of the fundamental rights and rule-of-law principles of the Basic Law".[42] As the BVerfG had earlier established, the Convention and the ECtHR's jurisprudence serve "as guides to interpretation in determining the content and scope of fundamental rights and the constitutional principles of the Basic Law",[43] as long as this does not reduce the level of protection guaranteed under the German Constitution. The openness of the Basic Law to international law requires it not to conflict with international and supranational agreements. Going beyond its *Görgülü* decision, where it only required the indirect consideration of the Convention's provisions, the BVerfG further propagates an active dialogue, concluding that "even the 'last word' of the German Constitution is not opposed to an international and European dialogue between courts, but is the normative basis for this."[44]

Given the contradicting judgment of the ECtHR, the BVerfG therefore had to correct its previous decision on preventive detention. It could have agreed to categorise preventive detention as a "penalty" and thus consider the retroactive extension to be in violation of Article 103, para. 2 GG. However, it chose not to do so. Instead, it showed the limits of international integration when it refused "a schematic parallelisation of individual constitutional concepts" and stressed that the human rights content of international agreements "must be 'reconceived' in an active process (of reception)".[45] The Convention had to be integrated carefully into the "dog-

41 BVerfG, Judgment of 4 May 2011, 2 BvR 2365/09, 740/10, 2333/08, 1152/10, 571/10, BVerfGE 128, 326, 367, para. 82 – EGMR Sicherungsverwahrung.

42 Ibid., para. 88.

43 BVerfG, Order of 14 Oct 2004, 2 BvR 1481/04, BVerfGE 111, 307, 316 et seq., paras. 31–32 – Görgülü.

44 BVerfG, Judgment of 4 May 2011, 2 BvR 2365/09, 740/10, 2333/08, 1152/10, 571/10, BVerfGE 128, 326, 369, para. 89 – EGMR Sicherungsverwahrung.

45 Ibid., 370, para. 91, citing *Häberle*, Europäische Verfassungslehre (7th ed. 2011), 255 et seq.

matically differentiated national legal system".[46] It therefore saw no need to completely adapt to the interpretation of the term "penalty" in Article 7, para. 1 of the Convention, but instead upheld its qualification of preventive detention as a measure of prevention and correction, and not as a punishment within the meaning of Article 103, para. 2 GG due to the formal distinction in the Criminal Code.[47] An independent definition in national law was possible due to the Convention's flexibility and lack of precision that has to take into account the legal, linguistic and cultural variety of the Member States.[48] The BVerfG instead applied Article 2, para. 2 GG (the right to liberty) together with Article 20 para. 3 GG (the rule of law) as "the requirement of the protection of legitimate expectations is closely related and structurally similar to the 'nulla poena' principle".[49] Thus, the guarantees in Articles 5 and 7, para. 1 of the Convention had to be taken into account in relation to the detainee, as they reinforced the weight of the relevant concerns regarding the protection of legitimate expectations. Preventive detention was subject to a strict review of proportionality and could only be justified to protect the highest constitutional interests. This meant that not only the measure as such, but also its practical realisation had to be subjected to a strict proportionality review. While *de jure* preventive detention did not qualify as a penalty, it was *de facto* executed like a criminal sentence.

On the facts, the BVerfG held that the retrospective extension of preventive detention beyond the previous ten year-period constituted a serious encroachment on the affected detainee's reliance and on the fundamental right to liberty.[50] It not only considered the execution, but even the legislation to be deficient and thus unconstitutional.[51] Only if certain criteria were met, could it be ensured that preventive detention would remain fundamentally different from prison sentences. These were, in particular, the distance requirement, imposing preventive detention as a measure of last resort, offering detainees individual treatment, therapy and support, and certain objective parameters of confinement (the separation rule, i.e.

46 Ibid., 371, para. 93.
47 Ibid., 392, para. 141.
48 Ibid., 393, para. 142.
49 Ibid., 392, para. 141.
50 Ibid., 4th guiding sentence.
51 Ibid., 387, para. 128: "lack of an overall statutory concept".

distance from regular imprisonment or the rule of minimization).[52] While the BVerfG did not formally incorporate the ECtHR's interpretation of "penalty", it declared that if preventive detention was not executed with sufficient distance from regular imprisonment, the weight of the affected detainee's reliance amounted to "absolute protection of legitimate expectations"[53], which is in effect similar to the definition in Article 103, para. 2 GG. However, it is considered paradoxical that the BVerfG, while refusing to take Article 103, para. 2 GG as the standard of review, chose to apply the identical guarantee in Article 7, para. 1 of the Convention indirectly to reinforce the detainee's interests, thereby contradicting the fact that, according to its interpretation of the term "penalty", the provision would not be applicable at all.[54]

To circumvent the immediate release of all dangerous individuals from preventive detention, the BVerfG did not declare the provisions null and void immediately, but that they remain in force until the legislature reformed the current law, which had to take place by 31 May 2013 at the latest. The legislature codified the detailed provisions of the BVerfG in the "Act on the Implementation of the Distance-requirement in the Law on Preventive Detention" of December 2012.[55] Only under exceptional circumstances is the retrospective extension beyond the ten-year period now permitted and, even then, only if preventive detention is clearly distinguished from prison sentences.

In follow-up cases, the ECtHR explicitly welcomed the BVerfG's approach to interpreting the Basic Law in the light of the Convention and considered that, through this judgment, Germany had sufficiently implemented the ECtHR's findings in the domestic legal order.[56] In several decisions since 2016, the ECtHR has also not had any general objections

52 Ibid., 378, paras. 109–118; for a brief summary see *Kaspar*, 4 Peking Univ. L. J. 2016, 80, 92 et seqq.; critical with regard to the very detailed judgment leaving no discretion to the legislature: *Vollkmann*, JZ 2011, 835, 841.

53 BVerfG, Judgment of 4 May 2011, 2 BvR 2365/09, 740/10, 2333/08, 1152/10, 571/10, BVerfGE 128, 326, 391, para. 139 – EGMR Sicherungsverwahrung.

54 *Werndl*, Zweispurigkeit und Vertrauensschutz (2019), 374, also with regard to the lack of differentiation between Articles 5 and 7 of the Convention.

55 Federal Law Gazette (BGBl.) of 5 Dec 2012, part I, 2425, the law amended the German Criminal Code, the ThUG and other laws concerning preventive detention.

56 ECtHR, Judgment of 9 June 2011, 30493/04, para. 41 – Schmitz v. Germany; Judgment of 24 Nov 2011, 4646/08, paras. 68 and 118 – O. H. v. Germany, although it found a violation of Article 5 para. 1 and Article 7 para. 1 of the Convention in this case.

to the new legal framework. While it still maintained that preventive detention generally qualified as a penalty under Article 7, para. 1 of the Convention, it did not consider the specific confinement of a complainant under the new Therapeutic Detention Act to amount to a penalty.[57] It thus acknowledged that the German legislature codified the requirements of the BVerfG, and thereby strengthened the preventive and therapeutic aspect of preventive detention to actually reduce the danger posed by offenders.[58]

IV. Reciprocal influences

This Comment does not aim to evaluate the law on preventive detention or the legal requirements under criminal law in detail. Nor does it aspire to cover thoroughly the controversy around preventive detention in Germany. Instead, the relevant cases should serve as an example of how basic rule-of-law principles, like legal certainty and the prohibition against the retroactive application of criminal sanctions, are developed in the dialogue between judges. In an increasingly integrated global order, legal certainty can only be ensured if there is a certain common understanding of key human rights provisions amongst the relevant courts. To avoid open defiance, the BVerfG in this case chose to implement the ECtHR decisions gently into the German legal order, thereby reversing its 2004 judgment without breaking with German legal tradition. However, it reserved its authority to have the final say in constitutional matters in relation to the ECtHR, and thereby left room for legal uncertainty. While the legal framework of preventive detention would never have been reformed had it not been for the stringent judgments of the ECtHR, it must also be recognised that conformity with the Convention was a gradual and long process that left many of the affected detainees in legal limbo.[59] Nevertheless, the influence of the Convention (as interpreted by the ECtHR) on the Basic Law is obvious. As the example of Germany and its relationship with

57 ECtHR, Judgment of 7 Jan 2016, 23279/14, NJW 2017, 1007 – Bergmann v. Germany.

58 ECtHR, Judgment of 7 Jan 2016, 23279/14, NJW 2017, 1007, para. 173 – Bergmann v. Germany.

59 For details see the critique of *Kaspar,* 4 Peking Univ. L. J. 2016, 80, 95 et seqq.; *Vollkmann*, JZ 2011, 835, 838; sceptical with regard to the harmony between the national and supranational human rights frameworks *Michaelsen,* 12 Hum. Rts. L. Rev. 2012, 148, 166, criticizing the "retrospective academic romanticism".

the European Council shows, supranational courts influence the domestic legal order and may even have a considerable impact on areas that fall within the sovereign power of nation states. With criminal law being part of the highly- sensitive "*domaine réservé*" and therefore less open to international influence, changes arise only if a state allows the integration into, and openness towards, the international legal order. International criminal courts are a huge step towards the general acceptance and enforcement of uniform rule-of-law principles. The significance of international courts and human rights bodies can therefore for the most part be seen in their transformative influence on national legal systems. When judging (international) crimes, national courts should not be viewed only as state organs, but beyond that as agents of the international community as a whole charged with safeguarding fundamental human rights and thus taking a "quasi-independent role in the international legal order".[60]

V. Conclusion

Neither the members of the AU nor the European Council form a supranational body comparable to the EU. Instead, the AU is distinguished by the central principle of sovereign equality and interdependence among its Member States (Article 4 lit. a of the Constitutive Act of the African Union), as is the Council of Europe. The challenging question is how to reconcile national sovereignty with integration into an international human rights system. The AU Member States will have to share their sovereignty when they implement the ACJHPR's judgments without at the same time having to compromise their respective legal traditions and maintaining the necessary degree of legitimacy. The flexible approach of the BVerfG could be seen as a model in this respect. However, the vague incorporation of the ECtHR's jurisprudence turns out to be detrimental to legal certainty. Apart from these jurisdictional uncertainties, the ACJHPR could be an opportunity to foster respect for fundamental human rights and the effective prosecution of international crimes within the legal orders of its Member States. It could learn from the example of the ECtHR, which has considerable influence on powerful Member States from vastly different regions across Europe.

The global development of international criminal law is also an important marker of the gradual shift from a state- to an individual-centric

60 *Nollkaemper*, 101 Am. J. Int'l L. 2007, 760, 799.

understanding of international law. As international law increasingly enshrines directly-enforceable individual rights, constitutional courts are caught between obligations deriving from the international legal order on the one hand, and possibly-conflicting national constitutional requirements on the other. While there might be an effective judicial remedy on the international level, there is often a lack of readiness to comply with international court decisions at state level. The controversy around preventive detention discussed in this Comment exemplifies the individual's dilemma in terms of legal protection: while the EU (in a wider sense) has one of the highest densities of regional human rights instruments and complementary effective national constitutions, the enshrined rights must also prove to be effective in practice. If we apply *Alexy*'s concept of the dual nature of law, we might say that, in the European legal order (in the wider sense), the second dimension of law (the factual or real dimension) falls prey to uncertainty, as effective application essentially depends on the readiness of national courts and legislators to comply with the ECtHR's case law, while the ideal dimension is ambitious and aspiring. However, a law that is ideal, but inefficient might soon be perceived as an empty promise, thus losing general acceptance and legitimacy.

Bibliography

Robert Alexy, "Legal Certainty and Correctness", 28 Ratio Juris 2015, 441.

Robert Alexy, "Mauerschützen. Zum Verhältnis von Recht, Moral und Strafbarkeit" (1993), reprinted in: Robert Alexy, Hans-Joachim Koch, Lothar Kuhlen and Helmut Rüßmann (eds.), Elemente einer juristischen Begründungslehre (Nomos, Baden-Baden 2003), 469.

Peter Häberle, Europäische Verfassungslehre (Nomos, 7th ed., Baden-Baden 2011).

Anna von Harbou, Das neue Recht der Sicherungsverwahrung: die Änderungen durch das "Gesetz zur Bekämpfung von Sexualdelikten und anderen gefährlichen Straftaten" (Kiel University, Diss., Kiel 1999).

Johannes Kaspar, "Preventive Detention in German Criminal Law", 4 Peking University Law Journal (Peking Univ. L. J.) 2016, 80.

Christopher Michaelsen, "'From Strasbourg, with Love' – Preventive Detention before the German Federal Constitutional Court and the European Court of Human Rights", 12 Human Rights Law Review (Hum. Rts. L. Rev.) 2012, 148.

André Nollkaemper, "Internationally Wrongful Acts in Domestic Courts", 101 American Journal of International Law (Am. J. Int'l L.) 2007, 760.

Gustav Radbruch, "Der Zweck des Rechts (1937)", in: Arthur Kaufmann (ed.), Gustav Radbruch: Gesamtausgabe, volume 3 Rechtsphilosophie III (C. F. Müller, Heidelberg 1990), 39.

Gustav Radbruch, "Gesetzliches Unrecht und übergesetzliches Recht (1946)", in: Arthur Kaufmann (ed.), Gustav Radbruch: Gesamtausgabe, volume 3 Rechtsphilosophie III (C. F. Müller, Heidelberg 1990), 83.

Gustav Radbruch, "Statutory Lawlessness and Supra-Statutory Law (1946)", translated by Bonnie Litschewski Paulson and Stanley L. Paulson, 26 Oxford Journal of Legal Studies (Oxf. J. Leg. Stud.) 2006, 1.

Susana Sanz-Caballero, "The Principle of Nulla Poena Sine Lege Revisited: The Retrospective Application of Criminal Law in the Eyes of the European Court of Human Rights", 28 European Journal of International Law (E.J.I.L.) 2017, 787.

Maximilian Steinbeis, "Editorial: Ranks and Titles" (11 May 2019), https://verfassungsblog.de/ranks-and-titles/ (last visited 31 May 2019).

Davina Theresa Stisser, Die Sicherungsverwahrung – de lege lata et de lege ferenda (Nomos, Baden-Baden 2019).

Monika Johanna Werndl, Zweispurigkeit und Vertrauensschutz: Das Recht der Sicherungsverwahrung zwischen Sicherheit und rechtsstaatlichem Vertrauensschutzgebot (Nomos, Baden-Baden 2019).

Uwe Vollkmann, "Fremdbestimmung – Selbstbehauptung – Befreiung: Das BVerfG in der Frage der Sicherungsverwahrung", Juristenzeitung (JZ) 2011, 835.

Register of cases

BGH, Judgment of 11 Feb 1953, II ZR 51/52, NJW 1953, 542.

BVerfG, Order of 19 Feb 1957, 1 BvR 357/52, BVerfGE 6, 132 – Gestapo.

BVerfG, Judgment of 24 Oct 1996, 2 BvR 1851, 1853, 1875, 1852/94, BVerfGE 95, 96 – Mauerschützen.

BVerfG, Judgment of 5 Feb 2004, 2 BvR 2029/01, BVerfGE 109, 133 – Langfristige Sicherheitsverwahrung.

BVerfG, Judgment of 10 Feb 2004, 2 BvR 834/02, BVerfGE 109, 190 – Nachträgliche Sicherungsverwahrung.

BVerfG, Order of 14 Oct 2004, 2 BvR 1481/04, BVerfGE 111, 307 – Görgülü.

BVerfG, Order of 23 Aug 2006, 2 BvR 226/06, NJW 2006, 3483.

BVerfG, Judgment of 4 May 2011, 2 BvR 2365/09, 740/10, 2333/08, 1152/10, 571/10, BVerfGE 128, 326 – EGMR Sicherungsverwahrung.

BVerfG, Order of 11 Jul 2013, 2 BvR 2302/11, 2 BvR 1279/12, NJW 2013, 3151 – ThUG.

ECtHR, Judgment of 18 Jul 2013, 2312/08 and 34179/08, para. 72 – Maktouf and Damjanović v. Bosnia and Herzegovina.

ECtHR, Judgment of 17 Dec 2009, 19359/04, NJW 2010, 2495 – M. v. Germany.

ECtHR, Judgment of 12 Jan 2011, 6587/04, NJW 2011, 3423 – Haidn v. Germany.

ECtHR, Judgment of 13 Jan 2011, 17792/07 – Kallweit v. Germany.

ECtHR, Judgment of 13 Jan 2011, 20008/07 – Mautes v. Germany.

ECtHR, Judgment of 13 Jan 2011, 27360/04, 42225/07 – Schummer v. Germany.

ECtHR, Judgment of 9 Jun 2011, 30493/04 – Schmitz v. Germany.

ECtHR, Judgment of 24 Nov 2011, 4646/08 – O. H. v. Germany.

ECtHR, Judgment of 19 Apr 2012, 61272/09 – B. v. Germany.

ECtHR, Judgment of 7 Jan 2016, 23279/14, NJW 2017, 1007 – Bergmann v. Germany.

The Significance of the *Erga Omnes* Obligation to Prosecute Genocide for Legal Certainty in International Criminal Law*

*Mispa Roux***

Abstract: In international criminal law, legal certainty means that criminal conduct and its punishment must be clearly defined. International criminal law treaties require member states to domesticate their provisions, which contributes to the development of the field in general. Although this development is to be encouraged, the result of domestication of these treaties is that there may be lack of continuity in domestic laws, as various adaptions are tailormade to suit states' unique contexts. This is particularly the case for genocide, as the prohibition of the commission of genocide forms part of jus cogens norms, and the obligation imposed upon the international community as a whole to prevent and prosecute this gross human rights violation is erga omnes in nature. This contribution illustrates the way in which the international community can comply with the erga omnes obligation to prosecute genocide, and thereby ensure legal certainty in international criminal law. It does so in three parts: first, by examining events immediately following in the aftermath of violations, in particular the investigation of atrocities and peacebuilding processes. The second part examines three obligations in terms of individual criminal prosecution, namely aut dedere aut judicare, the duty of cooperation, and compliance with the principle of complementarity. The final part briefly examines civilly liability in terms of the principles of state responsibility.

* See in general *Roux*, A Comparative Analysis of the Causes for Breaching the Erga Omnes Obligation to Prevent and Prosecute Gross Human Rights Violations (2012 LL.D. thesis University of Johannesburg), 84–153, 215–237.

** Mispa Roux, *LL.B.*, *LL.M.*, *LL.D.*, Senior Lecturer in the Department of Public Law, University of Johannesburg, Head: Sexual and Gender-Based Violence Unit at the South African Institute for Advanced Constitutional, Public, Human Rights, and International Law (SAIFAC), a Centre of the University of Johannesburg.

I. Prefatory remarks

Legal certainty lies central to the rule of law, and this means that those subjected to the law must know how to regulate their conduct in accordance with the law.[1] In international criminal law, it means that criminal conduct must be clearly defined, and so must any sanction or punishment attached to it. Most international criminal law treaties oblige states to domesticate their provisions, which in turn contributes to the development of international criminal law as states adapt such treaties' provisions to suit their own, unique needs. Although this development is to be encouraged, the result of domestication of these treaties is that there may be lack of continuity in domestic laws, as various adaptions are tailormade to suit states' unique contexts.[2] This was recognised in 2006 by the International Law Commission when it adopted a document drafted by the Study Group on the Fragmentation of International Law, entitled *Difficulties Arising from the Diversification and Expansion of International Law*.[3] It was

1 *Fenwick* and *Wrbka*, in: Fenwick and Wrbka (eds.), Legal Certainty in a Contemporary Context: Private and Criminal Law Perspectives (2016), 1–2; *Cançado Trindade*, in: Gaja and Grote Stoutenburg (eds.), Enhancing the Rule of Law through the International Court of Justice (2014), 1; *Gerkens*, 16 Fundamina 2010, 121.

2 Conclusions of the work of the ILC Study Group on the Fragmentation of International Law: Difficulties arising from the Diversification and Expansion of International Law, 58th session, A/61/10 (2006), para. 251.

3 Ibid.

recognised that a hierarchy of norms exists in international law,[4] and that both *jus cogens* norms[5] and obligations *erga omnes*[6] form part of this. The association between *erga omnes* obligations and *jus cogens* norms was highlighted as follows:

> "It is recognised that while all obligations established by *jus cogens* norms… also have the character of *erga omnes* obligations, the reverse is not necessarily true. Not all *erga omnes* obligations are established by peremptory norms of general international law. This is the case, for example, of certain obligations under 'the principles and rules concerning the basic rights of the human person', as well as of some obligations relating to the global commons."[7]

This is particularly true for genocide,[8] since the prohibition of the commission of this international crime forms part of *jus cogens* norms,[9] and the obligation imposed upon the international community as a whole to prevent and prosecute this gross human rights violation[10] is *erga omnes* in nature.[11] This position, that forms the basis for this chapter, is based on an

---

4 Ibid. para. 31.

5 Ibid. paras. 31–33.

6 Ibid. paras. 37–39.

7 Ibid. paras. 37–38.

8 Articles II and III of the Convention on the Prevention and Punishment of the Crime of Genocide.

9 Article 53 of the Vienna Convention on the Law of Treaties; GA Res 96 (1), The Crime of Genocide (11 Dec 1946); ILC, Dire Tladi (Special Rapporteur), Fourth Report on Peremptory Norms of General International Law (Jus Cogens), 71st session, A/CN.4/727 (31 Jan 2019), paras. 78–90, 116–121; *Lepard*, Customary International Law: A New Theory with Practical Applications (2010), 243–260; *Orakhelashvili*, Peremptory Norms in International Law (2006), 291; *Parker* and *Neylon*, 12 HICLR 1989, 411, 430–431.

10 It must be noted that persecution as a crime against humanity is strongly connected to the crime of genocide: the two crimes belong to the same *genus*. However, the grounds of persecution in terms of crimes against humanity afford more protection to victims than the limited scope of grounds of persecution in terms of genocide. See further in this regard: ICTY, *The Prosecutor v Kupreškić*, Judgment of 14 Jan 2000, Case No. IT-95–16-T, para. 636; ICJ, *Application of the Convention on the Prevention and Punishment of the Crime of Genocide (Bosnia and Herzegovina v Serbia and Montenegro)*, Judgment of 26 Feb 2007, ICJ Reports 2007, 43, paras. 121–122. *Roux*, AYIHL 2012, 98, 100–101.

11 ICJ, *Application of the Convention on the Prevention and Punishment of the Crime of Genocide (Bosnia and Herzegovina v Serbia and Montenegro)*, Preliminary Objections and Judgment of 11 July 1996, ICJ Reports 1996, 595, para. 31 at 616; ICJ, *Barcelona Traction, Light and Power Company, Limited (Belgium v Spain)*, Judgment

interpretation of the view expressed by the International Court of Justice in the 1951 *Reservations to the Convention on Genocide* advisory opinion,[12] that was confirmed in 1996 by the same Court in the *Bosnia Genocide* judgment.[13] In the *Reservations* advisory opinion, the Court stated "that the principles underlying the Convention are principles which are recognized by civilized nations as binding on States, even without any conventional obligation [and] the condemnation of genocide and of the co-operation required 'in order to liberate mankind from such an odious scourge' [is] universa1 (in) character".[14] Then, in 1996, the International Court of Justice confirmed this advisory opinion in the *Bosnia* preliminary objections judgment by deciding that "the rights and obligations enshrined by the Convention are rights and obligations *erga omnes* [and] that the obligation each State thus has to prevent and to punish the crime of genocide is not territorially limited by the Convention".[15]

Prevention and prosecution are therefore clearly inextricably linked. If states were unsuccessful in preventing gross human rights violations, they are still obliged to prosecute their commission, and the prosecution of perpetrators of gross human rights violations can in turn prevent these atrocities from recurring in the future.[16] The deterrent nature of prosecutions is crucial, as "post-mortem justice without a corresponding commitment of military, political, and economic resources significantly dilutes the message of accountability and undermines its long-term viability in preventing crimes".[17]

States in the international community have repeatedly breached the *erga omnes* obligation to prevent gross human rights violations by failing to implement available preventative measures against perpetrator states

---

of 5 Feb. 1970, ICJ Reports 1970, 3, 32; Resolution by the Fifth Commission of the Institut de Droit International, Obligations *Erga Omnes* in International Law, Krakow Session (27 Aug. 2005), http://www.idi-iil.org/app/uploads/2017/06/2005_kra_01_en.pdf (last visited 18 Jul 2019); *Ratner*, *Abrams* and *Bischoff*, Accountability for Human Rights Atrocities in International Law: Beyond the Nuremberg Legacy (2009), 42–44; *Bassiouni*, LCP 1996, 63; *Roux* (n. 10), 102–108.

12 ICJ, *Reservations to the Convention on the Prevention and Punishment of the Crime of Genocide,* Advisory Opinion of 28 May 1951, ICJ Reports 1951, 15, 23.

13 *Bosnia* preliminary objections (n. 11), para. 31 at 616.

14 *Reservations* Advisory Opinion (n. 12), 23.

15 *Bosnia* preliminary objections (n. 11), para. 31 at 616.

16 *Akhavan*, in: Falk, Elver and Hajjar (eds.), Human Rights: Critical Concepts in Political Science, vol. III (2008), 123.

17 Ibid. 153.

when early warning signals[18] appeared, or when states eventually decided to implement some measures, they were in most instances too late, rendering the measures completely ineffective. The international community is extremely hesitant to act pre-emptively by implementing anticipatory preventative measures, and various obstacles have been identified as standing in the way of the successful prevention of gross human rights violations. The effect of these obstacles is that the international community is not truly aware of the full extent of the crimes committed against the targeted victim groups,[19] and it is usually only once arms are laid down, mass graves are discovered and the genocidal or extermination policies are exposed, that the international community truly begins to fathom the abhorrent magnitude of the violations committed against members of the targeted groups. It is in this critical time that the responsible state (where the genocide was committed), third states (states with no jurisdictional link to the genocide), as well as members of the United Nations (UN) and regional organisations should take active steps to comply with the *erga omnes* obligation of prosecuting and punishing the perpetrators of these gross human rights violations to ensure that impunity is avoided.[20]

The purpose of this contribution is to illustrate the way in which the international community can comply with the *erga omnes* obligation to prosecute genocide, and thereby ensure legal certainty in international criminal law. What can states do in the extremely vulnerable time period immediately following the commission of genocide? How can perpetrators of this international crime be held criminally liable? Are there other possibilities for accountability? The contribution will illustrate this in three parts: the first part will examine the events immediately following in the aftermath of violations, when in most instances, a new government is established within the responsible state. The reaction of this new government will be examined: in general, what is the response of the new government to atrocities committed by the previous regime? The various reactions of the international community will also be examined when the reality of these atrocities unfold, as well as whether member states of the United Nations and regional organisations put political pressure on these organisations to establish courts or tribunals to try the alleged perpetrators. The subsequent investigation of the alleged atrocities and establishment of tribunals or courts will also be examined. The most vulnerable persons

18 *Roux*, TSAR 2011, 650.
19 *Roux*, TSAR 2018, 106.
20 *Roux* (n. 10), 110.

after the commission of gross human rights violations are victims and survivors: it is crucial that the new government within the responsible state, third states, as well as member states of regional and international organisations take active steps to recognise and protect victims' rights, and ensure that they have access to effective remedies.[21] The new government and the international community must also set up peacebuilding processes in the state to ensure that lasting peace is achieved.

The second part of this contribution will examine which obligations are imposed upon states in terms of the obligation to prosecute, and whether states have complied with these obligations. Certain obligations arise in terms of the *erga omnes* obligation to prosecute once a decision has been made at an investigative stage to prosecute individual perpetrators either by setting up an *ad hoc* or hybrid criminal court or tribunal, or, as currently may be done, by issuing an arrest warrant by the International Criminal Court (ICC). Three obligations regarding criminal prosecution of individual perpetrators will be discussed in the contribution: the first obligation is in terms of the maxim *aut dedere aut judicare* ("extradite or try"). Flowing from this is the second obligation, namely, to cooperate with international or national courts or tribunals to prosecute perpetrators. The third obligation is that states must comply with the principle of complementarity between national and international courts and tribunals.

The final part of this contribution will examine another option available to states in order to ensure accountability for gross human rights violations, namely, to hold the state where these atrocities were committed civilly liable in accordance with the principles of state responsibility.

II. The time period immediately following the commission of gross human rights violations within the responsible state

The situation in a state or region immediately following gross human rights violations is intensely fragile. The entire state is disrupted and must be rebuilt to function adequately again. The entire state apparatus is usually used to commit gross human rights violations; therefore, the entire society of such states need to be transformed. The horrific events of the near past must be reconciled with the present and future. Within the state itself, a new government is put in place with the difficult task of dealing

21 Victims' rights and access to remedies were discussed more fully in a previous article by the author. See *Roux* (n. 10), 87.

with the crimes of its predecessors. Investigations are initiated and events are probed to decide whether there is enough evidence to charge perpetrators for their crimes. Survivors and victims are acutely traumatised and often displaced. Perpetrators often live alongside their victims and victims' families, and those who were part of the upper ranks of the previous genocidal regimes are in some instances appointed to positions in the new government. Decisions are made to establish criminal tribunals or courts, or to issue warrants of arrest for the perpetrators. All of these events take place in the state that has recently been ravaged by genocide and crimes against humanity, and it all has an influence on the chances of success of the prosecution process.

1. The establishment of a new government

One of the most controversial issues facing a new government in a state where genocide or crimes against humanity were committed is how the crimes of the previous genocidal regime should be dealt with.[22] The new government should also distinguish itself from the previous one by proving to its citizens, as well as to the international community, that it is indeed different and that it strives to transform into a society that conforms with the rule of law.[23] A good method to prove this difference is by ensuring that perpetrators of the gross human rights violations do not enjoy impunity and are held criminally accountable for their crimes.[24] The

22 *Cohen*, in: Falk, Elver and Hajjar (eds.), Human Rights: Critical Concepts in Political Science, vol. III (2008), 174.

23 The Sudan is currently experiencing significant political changes. In April 2019, President Al Bashir was ousted, and the government replaced by a "Transitional Military Council" under Lt. General Ibn Auf. Whether or not individual criminal accountability of Al Bashir and others for international crimes will follow, and if so whether in the International Criminal Court or in the Sudanese courts, remains to be seen. Thus far, Al Bashir has been charged with corruption in a domestic court. See in this regard: Twenty-ninth Report of the Prosecutor of the International Criminal Court to the United Nations Security Council pursuant to UNSCR 1593 (2005) (19 Jun 2019), https://www.icc-cpi.int/itemsDocuments/190619-rep-otp-UNSC-Darfur-Sudan-ENG.pdf (last visited 18 Jul 2019).

24 Ibid. 194. Another method that could be utilised by the new government to differentiate itself from the previous government that committed gross human rights violations is by means of lustration. Lustration is the removal of individuals associated with the previous regime or government from public positions to ensure that they no longer hold any political influence over the new government. The purpose of lustration is to ensure that the new government makes a clean

international community must also indicate their willingness to conduct international relations with the newly established government, and a good indication of whether the newly established government is recognised by other states is to determine the state's representation at the United Nations Security Council, and whether the new government is recognised as the legitimate one by member states of the General Assembly.[25]

2. The investigation of alleged violations and establishment of criminal tribunals and courts

States are obliged to investigate alleged gross human rights violations in order to fulfil the *erga omnes* obligation to prevent or prosecute these violations.[26] The obligation to investigate reports of alleged gross human rights violations is based upon an interpretation of the *erga omnes* obligation

break from the past and gross human rights violations committed by the previous regime. This is considered to be a method that holds individuals accountable for their previous misdeeds without charging them criminally. Lustration was used mainly in Europe, specifically in Germany after the Second World War to "denazify" the state, and states where communism came to an end. It was used most recently in Iraq after Saddam Hussein was overthrown. See in this regard: *Evans*, International Law (2010), 779; *Ratner* et al. (n. 11), 285–287; *Shelton*, Remedies in International Human Rights Law (2005), 393–394.

25 In this regard, the establishment of a new government in Cambodia after the genocide serves as a good example. The United Nations, by allowing the Khmer Rouge to "retain" its seat at the UN by recognising the coalition government as the legitimate one, thereby showed its "tacit approval" of the genocidal regime. Also, Rwanda was a non-permanent member of the Security Council for the entire duration of the genocide in 1994. See further in this regard: GA Res 34 (2), Credentials of Representatives to the Thirty-Fourth Session of the General Assembly (21 Sep 1979); GA Res 35 (4), Credentials of Representatives to the Thirty-Fifth Session of the General Assembly (13 Oct 1980); GA Res 36 (2A), Credentials of Representatives to the Thirty-Sixth Session of the General Assembly (18 Sep 1981); GA Res 37 (5A), Credentials of Representatives to the Thirty-Seventh Session of the General Assembly (26 Oct 1982); GA Res 37 (6), The Situation in Kampuchea (28 Oct 1982); United Nations, "Members of the Security Council in 1994", https://www.un.org/securitycouncil/search/year?field_uw_membership_years_value%5Bvalue%5D%5Byear%5D=1994 (last visited 18 Jul 2019).

26 *Lamont*, International Criminal Justice and the Politics of Compliance (2010), 1–2, 4, 12–13.

to prevent or prosecute these violations.[27] Investigations into reports of alleged mass violations therefore have to be undertaken over a period of time, and in most cases they are initiated during the commission of the atrocities[28] and finalised in the aftermath of the violations. However, it is of paramount importance to establish criminal courts or tribunals as soon after the commission of the atrocities as possible. The reason for this is that evidence is more readily available; witnesses are more effective because events are still vivid memories; and the new government in the state in which atrocities were committed is still proving that it is different from the previous regime by showing a determination to hold perpetrators criminally accountable for their crimes.

There are several purposes in investigating and prosecuting perpetrators of gross human rights violations. Most importantly, this fulfils the *erga omnes* obligation which rests on the international community to prosecute genocide and crimes against humanity, and thereby to avoid bestowing impunity on perpetrators of gross human rights violations.[29] Prosecution and investigation are also important, because revealing the facts could prevent the commission of genocide and crimes against humanity in the future, and prosecution can also therefore be employed as a preven-

27 See further: *Reservations* Advisory Opinion (n. 12), 15, 23; *Bosnia* case (n. 10), paras. 121–122; *Bosnia* preliminary objections (n. 11), para. 31 at 616; *Kupreškić* case (n. 10), para. 636 at 255.

28 The case of international crimes committed during the armed conflict in the Syrian Arab Republic serves as a good example. In August 2011, the UN Human Rights Council established the Independent International Commission of Inquiry on the Syrian Arab Republic with the mandate "to investigate all alleged violations of international human rights law since March 2011 in the Syrian Arab Republic, to establish the facts and circumstances that may amount to such violations and of the crimes perpetrated and, where possible, to identify those responsible with a view to ensuring that perpetrators of violations, including those that may constitute crimes against humanity, are held accountable". The Commission of Inquiry works in close cooperation with the International, Impartial and Independent Mechanism to assist in the Investigation and Prosecution of Persons Responsible for the Most Serious Crimes under International Law committed in the Syrian Arab Republic since March 2011, established in December 2016 by the United Nations General Assembly. See further in this regard: HRC Resolution, Situation of Human Rights in the Syrian Arab Republic, S-17/1 (22 Aug 2011); GA Res 71 (248), International, Impartial and Independent Mechanism to Assist in the Investigation and Prosecution of Persons Responsible for the Most Serious Crimes under International Law Committed in the Syrian Arab Republic since March 2011 (11 Jan 2017).

29 *Paust*, in: Constantinides and Zaikos (eds.), The Diversity of International Law: Essays in Honour of Professor Kalliopi K Koufa (2009), 581.

tative measure.[30] Another purpose of prosecution is to serve as a deterrent.[31] Prosecution and punishment of perpetrators also ensure that these *hostes humanis generalis* are "incapacitated" because of their incarceration: "[T]hey are not playing active roles and undermining extremely fragile peace in the countries they once manhandled."[32]

It is also important to investigate alleged international crimes in order to face the realities and to avoid denying the gross human rights violations. The time when investigation of the genocide and crimes against humanity is initiated can therefore be described as the "truth phase",[33] which is the "recovery or uncovering of the past [, which] is an onslaught on all ... forms of denial – personal and collective, the conscious cover-up and the convenient forgetting, the euphemistic renaming".[34] Facing the truth of the gross human rights violations by investigating them is important on different levels: for victims and survivors of genocides and crimes against humanity, as well as their families, friends and acquaintances, it is crucial because "after generations of denials, lies, cover-ups, and evasions, many people have a powerful, almost obsessive desire to know exactly what happened".[35] Prosecution and punishment can therefore also be seen as a type of reparation that is made to the victims, survivors and their families, as the violation is acknowledged by the international community in the prosecution process.[36] The investigation and prosecution of gross human rights violations are also important to ensure that the state that experienced these atrocities enjoys lasting peace and achieves reconciliation in itself.[37]

To illustrate, individual criminal prosecution of perpetrators of the Holocaust, Cambodian genocide, atrocities committed in the Former Republic of Yugoslavia, and the Rwandan genocide all took place on an *ad*

30 *Roux* (n.), 132–133; *Stolle* and *Singelnstein*, in: Kaleck, Ratner, Singelnstein and Weiss (eds.), International Prosecution of Human Rights Crimes (2007), 37, 39–43.

31 *Cohen* (n. 22), 184; *Power*, in: Falk, Elver and Hajjar (eds.), Human Rights: Critical Concepts in Political Science, vol. III (2008), 274, 279. The problem with deterrence is that it is difficult to ascertain: How do you know whether you stopped an imminent genocide or crime against humanity?

32 *Power* (n. 31), 280.

33 *Cohen* (n. 22), 179–186.

34 Ibid. 181.

35 Ibid. 183; *Power* (n. 31), 280–281.

36 *Stolle* and *Singelnstein* (n. 30), 44–45.

37 *Cohen* (n. 22), 198–200; *Power* (n. 31), 282–283.

hoc basis,[38] whereas criminal prosecution of perpetrators of the genocide in Darfur is currently taking place at the International Criminal Court. The establishment of the ICC means that a goal which was set after the Second World War has been achieved: to create a permanent international criminal court to put an end to impunity of international criminals. The ICC was established to prosecute "the most serious crimes of concern to the international community as a whole",[39] and has jurisdiction over genocide,[40] crimes against humanity,[41] war crimes[42] and crimes of aggression[43] committed by persons "who bear the greatest responsibility".[44] The ICC is a permanent criminal court,[45] but it only has jurisdiction over crimes that were committed after its entry into force; therefore there will be no retrospective jurisdiction.[46] The ICC will be able to exercise jurisdiction over cases referred to the Prosecutor by a member state[47] or by the United Nations Security Council acting in terms of Chapter VII

38 Report of *Robert H. Jackson*, United States Representative to the International Conference on Military Trials, Memorandum of Proposals for the Prosecution and Punishment of Certain War Criminals and Other Offenders (London 30 Apr 1945); London Charter of the International Military Tribunal of 8 Aug 1945; Agreement on a Comprehensive Political Settlement of the Cambodia Conflict, the Agreement Concerning the Sovereignty, Independence, Territorial Integrity and Inviolability, Neutrality and National Unity of Cambodia and the Declaration on Rehabilitation and Reconstruction of Cambodia of 23 Oct 1991; Agreement between the United Nations and the Royal Government of Cambodia Concerning the Prosecution under Cambodian Law of Crimes Committed During the Period of Democratic Kampuchea of 6 Jun 2003; Law on the Establishment of Extraordinary Chambers in the Courts of Cambodia for the Prosecution of Crimes Committed during the Period of Democratic Kampuchea of 27 October 2004; SC Res 827 (1993) of 25 May 1993; SC Res 955 (1994) of 8 Nov 1994; Organic Law No. 08/96 of 30 Aug 1996 on the Organisation of Prosecutions for Offences constituting the Crime of Genocide or Crimes against Humanity Committed since 1 October 1990, https://reparations.qub.ac.uk/assets/uploads/ORGANIC-LAW-No.pdf (last visited 18 Jul 2019).

39 Preamble, Articles 1 and 5 of the ICC Statute.

40 Ibid. Articles 5 and 6.

41 Ibid. Articles 5 and 7.

42 Ibid. Articles 5 and 8.

43 Ibid. Articles 5, 8 *bis*, 15 *bis*, and 15 *ter*.

44 *Ocampo*, Statement at Informal Meeting of Legal Advisors of Ministries of Foreign Affairs (24 Oct 2005), 5.

45 *Ambos*, in: Stahn and Van den Herik (eds.), Future Perspectives on International Criminal Justice (2010), 161, 165.

46 Article 11 of the ICC Statute.

47 Ibid. Articles 13(a) and 14. See also in this regard *Schabas*, 19 CLF 2008, 5, 9–22.

of the UN Charter,[48] or cases arising from the Prosecutor's decision to initiate an investigation into a situation.[49] Factors which the Office of the Prosecutor will take into account when deciding whether to investigate a situation include the crimes falling within the jurisdiction of the court,[50] admissibility,[51] interests of justice, "all the circumstances"[52] surrounding the alleged international crime, "the gravity of the crime, the interests of victims and the age or infirmity of the alleged perpetrator, and his or her role in the alleged crime".[53]

Various practical obligations flow from the obligation to establish criminal courts and tribunals to prosecute perpetrators of gross human rights violations. States with membership affiliations to international criminal courts and tribunals are obliged to contribute financially to their establishment and running.[54] States must also provide highly qualified experts and other staff to be employed at the courts and tribunals to ensure the smooth running of proceedings and successful prosecution of accused persons.

Prosecution at international courts and tribunals focuses mainly on heads of state or government, senior government officials, or persons with the highest level of responsibility for carrying out the genocide or crime against humanity. The prosecution of mid- and lower-level accused is left mainly to national courts.[55]

---

48 Article 13(b) of the ICC Statute.

49 Ibid. Articles 13(c) and 15.

50 Articles 5–8 of the ICC Statute.

51 Ibid. Articles 9–19.

52 Ibid. Article 53(2)(c).

53 Ibid.

54 Article 30 of the London Charter; Article 32 of the ICTY Statute; Article 30 of the ICTR Statute; Article 44 new of the ECCC Law; Articles 113–118 of Part 12 of the ICC Statute.

55 *Bellelli*, in: Bellelli (ed.), International Criminal Justice: Law and Practice from the Rome Statute to its Review (2010), 5, 56; *Clark*, in: Eboe-Osuji (ed.), Protecting Humanity: Essays in International Law and Policy in Honour of Navanethem Pillay (2010), 367, 368; *Del Ponte*, in: Bellelli (ed.), International Criminal Justice: Law and Practice from the Rome Statute to its Review (2010), 125, 126; *Leang* and *Smith*, in: Bellelli (ed.), International Criminal Justice: Law and Practice from the Rome Statute to its Review (2010), 143, 148–151; *Pocar*, in: Bellelli (ed.), International Criminal Justice: Law and Practice from the Rome Statute to its Review (2010), 67, 74; *Møse*, in: Bellelli (ed.), International Criminal Justice: Law and Practice from the Rome Statute to its Review (2010), 80, 89–90, 96–98.

3. Peacebuilding

The disruptive effects of gross human rights violations must be corrected by the new government in the responsible state and the international community in the time period immediately following the commission of genocide and crimes against humanity. One of the ways in which this can be done is by setting up peacebuilding processes in the state. It is very important not to withdraw peacekeeping troops immediately from a state in which the UN has deployed them: these troops should only be withdrawn once it is absolutely certain that lasting peace has been established. A characteristic of genocide and crimes against humanity is that they more often than not take place against the backdrop of armed conflict,[56] and it is crucial that peace agreements between the warring factions are complied with. Yet, such peace agreements can also be misleading and can be entered into prematurely, as was illustrated by the various peace and ceasefire agreements signed in the early 1990s in the Balkan states and in Rwanda.

Examples of peacebuilding measures can be reflected by the establishment of international or national criminal tribunals, referring cases to the International Criminal Court to prosecute alleged perpetrators, or by trying perpetrators at existing national courts. The effect of prosecuting perpetrators is deterrent in nature: it not only ensures that perpetrators do not enjoy impunity, but can also serve as a preventative measure in seeing to it that gross human rights violations are not committed by the state again:

> "[T]he threat of punishment may persuade potential perpetrators to adjust their behaviour. This cost-benefit calculation has implications for preventing conflicts, and also for preventing their resumption. In preconflict scenarios, it may discourage decisions to foment ethnic hatred and violence, since power thus accrued would be undermined by international isolation and accountability. In postconflict scenarios, leaders may be incapacitated outright (by arrests or being forced to flee), and the message conveyed that further incitement and violence will incur at a high political cost. The credible threat of punishment through vigorous arrests and prosecutions removes impediments to stability from the political stage, and provides an incentive for constructive political behaviour."[57]

---

56 *Roux* (n. 18), 652.

57 *Akhavan*, in: Falk, Elver and Hajjar (eds.) (n. 16), 123, 130.

It is therefore crucial to prosecute and punish perpetrators of genocide and crimes against humanity for their deeds in order to ensure that the state in which these atrocities took place can enjoy lasting peace.[58] The proceedings at the International Criminal Tribunal for the former Yugoslavia (ICTY), for instance, contributed to peacebuilding in the period following the gross human rights violations that were committed in the Federal Republic of Yugoslavia.[59] The situation in Rwanda is different, as the intensity of the genocide "severely circumscribes the potential impact of the International Criminal Tribunal for Rwanda (ICTR) on postconflict peacebuilding".[60] However, "some evidence suggests that the ICTR has contributed to discrediting and incapacitating the remnants of the former *génocidaire* government",[61] thereby making "a modest contribution to post-conflict peacebuilding".[62]

III. Erga omnes obligations regarding individual criminal responsibility

Individual criminal responsibility entails that individuals can be held personally responsible for the commission of international crimes. This responsibility of states to hold perpetrators accountable is based upon obligations in international instruments, national legislation and customary international law.[63] Certain obligations are imposed upon the responsible state, third states and member states of the constitutive documents of international courts and tribunals after their establishment. These obligations flow from the *erga omnes* obligation to prosecute and punish the perpetrators of the violations. It is important to note the difference between signatory states and non-signatory states to the international instruments establishing the courts or tribunals: in terms of international law the constitutive documents will impose obligations only upon member or signatory states. However, in terms of the *erga omnes* obligation, violations of such a nature will impose obligations upon all states in the international community, regardless of whether that state is a member or signatory of that instrument. The obligations discussed below are therefore imposed upon the international community as a whole, but mention will be made of

58 Ibid. 138.
59 Ibid. 131–143.
60 Ibid. 143.
61 Ibid.
62 Ibid.
63 Ibid. paras. 3–4 at 1.

specific obligations imposed specifically in constitutive instruments. These obligations have been breached in a number of ways, but compliance has also been satisfactory in some instances.

1. *Aut dedere aut judicare* – the duty to extradite or prosecute

The maxim *aut dedere aut judicare* means that if persons accused of international crimes find themselves within the territory of a state, that state must make the decision either to extradite the accused to the state, tribunal or court that issued a warrant of arrest, or to try the accused before its own national courts by exercising universal jurisdiction.[64] The obligation to extradite or try implies that if a government is aware that an alleged international criminal is within its territory, that state may not harbour or hide that person. The reason for the accused person's presence on the territory of the state is irrelevant, and "an absolute obligation"[65] to extradite or try the person exists and "any state that ignores this duty is in breach of its international obligations".[66]

2. The obligation to cooperate with international or national criminal courts and tribunals

Flowing from the obligation to arrest and extradite or prosecute is the duty to cooperate with international or national courts or tribunals issuing warrants of arrest for alleged perpetrators.[67] If a state decides instead to extradite the accused to the state, court or tribunal which issued the warrant of arrest, that state is at the same time complying with the obligation to cooperate. Cooperation means that third states must give their support to other states, courts or tribunals to arrest and try persons accused of inter-

64 *Steven*, 39 VJIL 1999, 425, 430. See further: *Brownlie*, in: Salerno (ed.), Diritti Dell'Uomo, Estradizione ed Espulsione: Atti del Convegno di Studaio Organizzato dall'Università di Ferrara per Salutare Giovanni Battaglini (29–30 Ottobre 1999) (2003), 3, 3–5.

65 *Steven* (n. 64), 443.

66 Ibid.

67 *Prost*, in: Schabas and Bernaz (eds.), Routledge Handbook of International Criminal Law (2011), 305; *Bellelli* (n. 55), 211.

national crimes.[68] If these international or national courts or tribunals request information or evidence, states must cooperate to make it available.[69] When states fail to cooperate with international courts or tribunals in the investigation or arrest of perpetrators, "the entire international human rights regime" is undermined.[70]

General international law and criminal law in particular are heavily dependent upon the cooperation of states.[71] Article 25 of the United Nations Charter obliges states "to accept and carry out the decision of the Security Council",[72] and Article 103 provides that if there is a conflict between obligations imposed by the UN and those imposed by another treaty, then the obligations in terms of the UN Charter "shall prevail".[73] The most effective way of ensuring that the international community will cooperate with the International Criminal Court is when the Security Council refers a situation for investigation to the Court, as this would impose an obligation in terms of the UN Charter upon UN member states to cooperate:[74] non-member states of the ICC Statute will in such a case "be obliged to cooperate with the ICC on the basis of the Security Council resolution, not the Rome Statute".[75]

---

68 GA Res 3074 (XXVIII), Principles of International Cooperation in the Detection, Arrest, Extradition and Punishment of Persons Guilty of War Crimes and Crimes against Humanity (3 Dec 1973), para. 4 at 2; Articles 89–92 of the ICC Statute.

69 Principles of International Cooperation (n. 68), para. 6 at 2.

70 *Roper* and *Barria*, 21 LJIL 2008, 457, 458.

71 *Ambos* (n. 45), 55.

72 Article 25 of the UN Charter.

73 Ibid. Article 103.

74 *Roper* and *Barria* (n. 70), 458.

75 The referral of the situation in the Sudan by the Security Council illustrates the question on whether such a referral overrides the customary international law obligation to respect the sovereign equality and immunity of other states. Articles 27 and 98 of the ICC Statute has also added to the controversy, and the relationship between these two Articles is still unclear. See further: SC Res 1593 (2005) of 31 Mar 2005; ICC, *The Prosecutor v Omar Hassan Ahmad Al Bashir,* Decision of 27 Aug 2010 informing the United Nations Security Council and the Assembly of the States Parties to the Rome Statute about Omar Al-Bashir's Presence in the Territory of the Republic of Kenya, ICC-02/05–01/09; ICC, *The Prosecutor v Omar Hassan Ahmad Al Bashir,* Decision of 27 Aug. 2010 informing the United Nations Security Council and the Assembly of the States Parties to the Rome Statute about Omar Al-Bashir's Recent Visit to the Republic of Chad, ICC ICC-02/05–01/09; ICC, *The Prosecutor v Omar Hassan Ahmad Al-Bashir*, Decision of 6 July 2017 under Article 87(7) of the Rome Statute on the non-compliance by South Africa with the request by the court for the arrest and surrender of Omar Al-Bashir, ICC-02/05–01/09; *Southern Africa Litigation Centre v Minister of Justice*

Cooperation is extensively provided for in the ICC Statute.[76] Cooperation between the International Criminal Court and third states has been described as a "three-level game" where "bargaining power" is exercised.[77] The first level is perhaps the most complicated: the ICC negotiates with the state where genocide or crimes against humanity were committed, and the ICC is to "attempt to convince the state to cooperate in the implementation of its indictments".[78] The second level involves negotiation between the ICC, third states and international organisations "to bring pressure to bear on the territorial state to arrest a suspect or may, in some situations, consider direct military intervention aimed at securing the arrest of an indictee".[79] Negotiations at the third level would be between the ICC and "domestic actors" in the state where gross human rights violations were committed,[80] which is largely dependent on whether the ICC enjoys support within the state in question.

It is important to take note of these "three levels" at which the ICC negotiates cooperation with the responsible state, third states, and member states of the United Nations and regional organisations, as they make it clear that the ICC is wholly dependent upon the cooperation of states in order to function properly in the prosecution of perpetrators of international crimes within the jurisdiction of the Court. Member states of the ICC Statute undertake to "cooperate fully with the Court in its investigation and prosecution of crimes within the jurisdiction of the Court",[81] and the Court may also "make requests" to member states to cooperate.[82] Member states must also ensure that their municipal laws are brought in line with the ICC Statute[83] in that there must be "procedures available under their national law for all of the forms of cooperation which are specified" in Part 9 of the Statute.[84] If a state fails to cooperate with the ICC after a request to do so has been made, the ICC may "make a finding to that effect and refer the matter to the Assembly of States Parties

---

and Constitutional Development 2015 5 SA 1 (GP); *Minister of Justice and Constitutional Development v Southern Africa Litigation Centre* 2016 3 SA 317 (SCA); *Rastan*, 21 LJIL 2008, 431, 442.

76 Preamble, Article 15(2), Articles 86–102 (Part 9) of the ICC Statute.

77 *Burke-White*, 21 LJIL 2008, 477, 481; *Roper* and *Barria* (n. 70), 463–467.

78 *Burke-White* (n. 77), 481.

79 Ibid.

80 Ibid. 482.

81 Article 86 of the ICC Statute.

82 Ibid. Article 87(1)(a).

83 See below for the discussion on the principle of complementarity.

84 Article 88 of the ICC Statute. See also: *Rastan* (n. 75), 434–435.

or, where the Security Council referred the matter to the Court, to the Security Council".[85]

3. Primacy and the principle of complementarity: the relationship between national and international criminal courts and tribunals

Another duty flowing from the obligation to extradite or try is to comply with the principle of complementarity.[86] States are obliged to establish national legislation which establishes jurisdiction over international crimes, because the principal duty to prosecute gross human rights violations lies first and foremost with national courts.[87] The constitutive documents of international tribunals or courts will determine whether the tribunal or court will enjoy primacy over national prosecution, or whether the international or national courts are to function in accordance with the principle of complementarity, thereby making the international court or tribunal subordinate to national prosecution. This principle flows from the second leg of the duty to extradite or try: if a state on whose territory accused persons find themselves decides to try those persons before their own national courts, then that state is acting in accordance with the principle of complementarity.

It is important to differentiate between states that follow a "monistic" tradition and states that follow a "dualistic" one in respect of its national legislation: for a state following the principle of monism it is unnecessary to adopt separate legislation to incorporate international treaties and conventions, and it automatically forms part of national law, but nothing will prevent these states from still incorporating international law into municipal law by passing legislation in this regard.[88] Several Western European states have incorporated legislation granting their national courts the au-

85 Article 87(7) of the ICC Statute.

86 *Ratner* et al. (n. 11), 254.

87 *Bellelli* (n. 55), 212–214.

88 South Africa follows the dualistic school of thought. Section 39(1)(b) provides that when a court, tribunal or forum is "interpreting the Bill of Rights", international law "must" be considered. International instruments, if ratified by the South African government, are binding on South Africa. For the relationship between South Africa and the International Criminal Court, see: *Roux* (n. 19), 113–115; *Roux*, in: Bilchitz and Correa Henau (eds.), Transitional Justice and Distributive Justice: Comparative Lessons from Colombia and South Africa (forthcoming 2021).

thority to exercise universal jurisdiction over international crimes,[89] and Belgium, especially, has been a significant campaigner against such crimes. The Belgian War Crimes Statute of 1993 conferred universal jurisdiction on Belgium to prosecute all perpetrators of international crimes in Belgian courts. The International Court of Justice (ICJ) found in the *Arrest Warrant* case that the legislation was in fact overreaching, and Belgium subsequently amended it accordingly.[90]

In contrast to this, states following the principle of dualism are obliged to adopt international treaties and conventions as national legislation in order for these to have effect within the state.[91] It is such states in particular that must ensure that national legislation bestows criminal jurisdiction over gross human rights violations on that state's courts in order to comply with the obligation to try such accused persons if found on the territory of that state, or that national legislation recognises the jurisdiction of international courts or tribunals.

It must be noted, however, that Article V of the Genocide Convention provides that signatory states "undertake to enact, in accordance with their respective Constitutions, the *necessary* legislation to give effect to the provisions of the present Convention, and, in particular, to provide effective penalties for persons guilty of genocide or any of the other acts".[92] The principle of complementarity adhered to by the ICC also means that states must bring their national legislation into line with the ICC Statute to criminalise genocide, crimes against humanity and war crimes within their national systems.[93]

It is important to point out that prosecution of international crimes by national courts is primarily based upon the principle of universal jurisdiction, and states wishing to exercise universal jurisdiction should pass national legislation enabling them to do so. States may also base the exercise of jurisdiction over international crimes on the principle of

---

89 *Ryngaert*, 19 CLF 2008, 153, 160–173.

90 ICJ, *Arrest Warrant of 11 April 2000 (Democratic Republic of the Congo v Belgium)*, Judgment of 14 Feb. 2002, ICJ Reports 2002, 3; *McGregor*, in: Kaleck et al. (eds.) (n. 30), 69; *Ratner*, 97 AJIL 2003, 888. Universal jurisdiction has also been conferred on Germany to exercise jurisdiction over genocide, crimes against humanity and war crimes. See in this regard: *Jessberger*, in: Kaleck, Ratner, Singelnstein and Weiss (eds.), International Prosecution of Human Rights Crimes (2007), 213. See also discussion below on universal jurisdiction.

91 European states following a civil law tradition usually adhere to the monistic school of thought.

92 Article V of the Genocide Convention (own emphasis).

93 Article 17 of the ICC Statute; *Chung*, 40 CWRJIL 2008, 227, 228–229.

territoriality, active nationality, passive personality or the principle of the protection of the state.[94] The territoriality principle "allows a state to exercise jurisdiction concerning the status of persons or things within the state's territory, over conduct that occurs, in whole or in part, within the state's territory, and over extraterritorial conduct that has a substantial effect within the state's territory".[95] This principle is an extension of the territorial sovereignty of states.[96] The principle of active nationality allows a state to exercise jurisdiction over its own nationals who committed crimes abroad.[97] The principle of passive personality allows a state to exercise jurisdiction over crimes committed abroad which harmed one of its nationals.[98] The protection of the state principle allows a state to exercise jurisdiction over acts which affect the safety and security of the state.[99]

Municipal legislation granting jurisdiction to national courts over international crimes either enacts legislation in terms of international treaty obligations, such as the obligation to incorporate the ICC Statute into national legislation, or grants national courts universal jurisdiction over international crimes.[100] When a state enacts legislation incorporating an international convention or treaty into municipal law, the state is acting in terms of an international obligation in terms of the treaty, whereas when a state enacts legislation granting the state universal jurisdiction, that state is acting "voluntarily", therefore acting in terms of international principles of a "permissive" nature.[101] It is therefore important to differentiate between, on the one hand, the "option" available to states to exercise universal jurisdiction, and, on the other, the obligation to enact legislation to grant jurisdiction to national courts over international crimes in terms of treaty obligations.

Universal jurisdiction is not an obligation imposed upon states as such, but is an option available to states that wish to hold perpetrators of inter-

---

94 *Brownlie* (n. 64), 300–307. See also in this regard: PCIJ, *Case of the SS "Lotus"*, Judgment of 7 Sep 1927, [1927] PCIJ Series A No. 10; *Dugard*, International Law: A South African Perspective (2011), 148–154; *Ratner* et al. (n. 11), 177–178.

95 *Steven* (n. 64), 432. See further *Brownlie* (n. 64), 301–303.

96 *Brownlie* (n. 64), 301.

97 Ibid. 303–304.

98 Ibid. 304.

99 Ibid. 304–305.

100 *Hays Butler*, in: Macedo (ed.), Universal Jurisdiction: National Courts and the Prosecution of Serious Crimes Under International Law (2006), 67, 67–68.

101 *Gaeta*, in: Gaetano Arangio-Ruiz (ed.), Studi di Diritto Internazionale in Onore di Gaetano Arangio-Ruiz, vol. III (2004), 1923, 1924–1926.

national crimes liable.[102] It is particularly when a state exercises universal jurisdiction that the question of legal certainty arises, as it has an impact on the *nullum crimen sine lege feranda* principle.[103]

The International Law Commission recently decided to recommend that the topic of universal criminal jurisdiction must be included in its long-term programme of work,[104] in particular to provide clarity on its "scope and application".[105] Such a study of the topic would then provide states with much-needed "draft guidelines or draft conclusions",[106] as the exact meaning of this form of jurisdiction is ambiguous:

> "for working purposes, it can be described as *criminal* jurisdiction based solely on the nature of the crime, without regard to the territory where the crime was committed, the nationality of the alleged or convicted perpetrator, the nationality of the victim, or any other connection to the State exercising such jurisdiction. This means that a State may exercise universal jurisdiction regarding a crime committed by a foreign national against another foreign national outside its territory."[107]

It is further agreed that universal jurisdiction is generally exercised over genocide, crimes against humanity and war crimes.[108] In 2005, the *Institut de Droit International* defined the principle of universal jurisdiction as follows:

> "Universal jurisdiction in criminal matters, as an additional ground of jurisdiction, means the competence of a State to prosecute alleged offenders and to punish them if convicted, irrespective of the place of commission of the crime and regardless of any link of active or passive

102 See further: Report of the ILC, 70th session, Supplement No. 10, A/73/10 (2018), Chapter VIII, Annex A; *Akande* and *Shah*, 21 EJIL 2011, 815, 834–838; *Steven* (n. 64), 439–443.

103 *Kebe*, in: Riziki Majinge (ed.), Rule of Law through Human Rights and International Criminal Justice: Essays in Honour of Adama Dieng (2015), 376, 379–386.

104 Report of the ILC, 70th session, Supplement No. 10, A/73/10 (2018), para. 369.

105 GA Res 73 (208), *The Scope and Application of the Principle of Universal Jurisdiction* (14 Jan 2019).

106 2018 ILC Report (n. 104), Chapter VIII, Annex A paras. 14, 19–20, 31.

107 Ibid. para. 1.

108 Ibid. paras. 3–10.

nationality, or other grounds of jurisdiction recognized by international law."[109]

The legality of exercising universal jurisdiction may be unclear.[110] Various problems may arise when states exercise universal jurisdiction. What would happen should a national court and an international criminal tribunal or court that chooses to exercise universal jurisdiction issue a warrant for the arrest of an alleged international criminal?[111] Furthermore, how is one to choose between national and international courts or tribunals which have jurisdiction over international crimes?[112] What should happen in the event that previous regimes have granted amnesty to the perpetrators of gross human rights violations, but another state or international court or tribunal wishes to exercise universal jurisdiction over the alleged perpetrators? These issues are mainly dealt with in the constitutive instruments of *ad hoc* and permanent international criminal courts and tribunals, and depend on whether the jurisdiction of these courts and tribunals is subordinate to, concurrent with, or superior to other jurisdictions. The London Agreement makes it clear that, even though the Nuremberg Tribunal was established to prosecute the "major war criminals"[113] of Nazi Germany, the jurisdiction of "any national or occupation court established or to be established in any allied territory or in Germany for the trial of war criminals" shall not be prejudiced.[114] Therefore the London Agreement expressly recognised that the international community might exercise universal jurisdiction over perpetrators of war crimes and

---

109 Article 1 of the Resolution by the 17th Commission of the Institut de Droit International, Universal criminal jurisdiction with regard to the crime of genocide, crimes against humanity and war crimes, Krakow Session (26 Aug 2005), http://www.idi-iil.org/app/uploads/2017/06/2005_kra_03_en.pdf (last visited 27 Jul 2018).

110 ICJ, *Arrest Warrant of 11 April 2000 (Democratic Republic of the Congo v Belgium)*, Dissenting Opinion of Judge van den Wyngaert to the Judgment of 14 Feb. 2002, ICJ Reports 2002, 137, para. 42 at 164. The ICJ did not furnish clarity on the legality of universal jurisdiction, especially in view of the divergent judgments of the judges in the Case.

111 *Orentlicher*, in: Falk, Elver and Hajjar (eds.), Human Rights: Critical Concepts in Political Science, vol. III (2008), 63, 76.

112 Ibid. 79.

113 Preamble, Articles 1 and 3 of the London Agreement.

114 Ibid. Article 6.

the Holocaust, which has been done on countless occasions in the years following the Second World War.[115]

The International Court of Justice was confronted with the question whether a Belgian national court could exercise universal jurisdiction over an incumbent Minister of Foreign Affairs of the Democratic Republic of the Congo by issuing a warrant for his arrest for the commission of crimes against humanity in the *Arrest Warrant* case.[116] The ICJ did not address the issue as to whether universal jurisdiction may have been used by Belgium in this instance in the majority judgment.[117] However, universal jurisdiction was discussed extensively in separate as well as dissenting opinions by the different judges. Judge President Guillaume stated in a separate opinion that universal jurisdiction was only recognised in cases of piracy by customary international law,[118] and that "international law does not accept universal jurisdiction".[119] In a dissenting opinion Judge Oda recognised the controversial nature of universal jurisdiction, and stated that it was "increasingly recognised in cases of terrorism and genocide".[120] Judge Oda further agreed with the majority in "refraining from taking a definitive stance in this respect as the law is not sufficiently developed and, in fact, the Court is not requested in the present case to take a decision on this point".[121] Judges Higgens, Kooijmans and Buergenthal delivered a joint separate opinion in which they were of the view that it was "undeniable" that "no established practice in which States exercise universal jurisdiction, properly so called" existed, but that that did not "necessarily indicate, ... that such an exercise would be unlawful".[122] In a dissenting opinion Judge van den Wyngaert described the failure of the majority to examine universal jurisdiction as leaving questions unanswered, and a "narrow per-

115 See further: German Control Council Law No. 10 of 1945 on Punishment of Persons Guilty of War Crimes Against Peace and Against Humanity.

116 The *Arrest Warrant* case (n. 90).

117 *Oda*, 51 JYIL 2008, 427, 431.

118 ICJ, *Arrest Warrant of 11 April 2000 (Democratic Republic of the Congo v Belgium)*, Separate Opinion of President Guillame to the Judgment of 14 Feb 2002, ICJ Reports 2002, 35, para. 5 at 37–38, para. 12 at 42.

119 Ibid. para. 16 at 44.

120 ICJ, *Arrest Warrant of 11 April 2000 (Democratic Republic of the Congo v Belgium)*, Dissenting Opinion of Judge Oda to the Judgment of 14 Feb. 2002, ICJ Reports 2002, 46, para. 8 at 49, para. 12 at 51.

121 Ibid. para. 12 at 51.

122 ICJ, *Arrest Warrant of 11 April 2000 (Democratic Republic of the Congo v Belgium)*, Joint Separate Opinion of Judges Higgens, Kooijmans and Buergenthal to the Judgment of 14 Feb. 2002, ICJ Reports 2002, 63, para. 45 at 76.

spective".[123] Van den Wyngaert stated that universal jurisdiction was not prohibited in international law, and that it was clearly recognised in cases of crimes against humanity and war crimes.[124]

Unfortunately granting universal jurisdiction over genocide is not consistently supported: proponents of denying universal jurisdiction for genocide[125] base their argument on the fact that prosecution in terms of the Genocide Convention is limited to either a "competent tribunal of the State in the territory of which the act was committed" or by an "international penal tribunal" with the necessary jurisdiction.[126] It is therefore argued that prosecution by a third state in a domestic court is *not* included in the Convention; therefore it could be interpreted that states may not exercise jurisdiction over genocide based on universal jurisdiction. Proponents of denying universal jurisdiction for genocide further argue that the "trend" of universal jurisdiction "was essentially a post-Cold War discourse and self-feeding hype generated by NGOs, activist lawyers and judges, academic conferences and papers, and mass media".[127]

Despite the many challenges faced by national prosecution of international crimes, there are many factors which make national prosecution favourable. One of the most important of these is "the proximity of the evidence, the knowledge of the accused and the victims, and the better perspective which it has on all circumstances surrounding the crime".[128] The Genocide Convention also provides that a person charged with committing genocide "shall be tried by a competent tribunal of the state in the territory of which the act was committed".[129] This means that the primary responsibility to prosecute international criminals is imposed upon national courts.[130]

A comparison between international and national fora further highlights the advantages of domestic prosecution: international adjudication is extremely expensive, while national courts are "relatively inexpensive".[131]

---

123 *Arrest Warrant* Dissenting Opinion of Judge van den Wyngaert (n. 110), para. 42 at 164.

124 Ibid. para. 46 at 166, paras. 52–62 at 169–175.

125 *Hajjar*, in: Falk, Elver and Hajjar (eds.), Human Rights: Critical Concepts in Political Science, vol. III (2008), 42, 52.

126 Article 6 of the Genocide Convention.

127 *Reydams*, in: Schabas and Bernaz (eds.), Routledge Handbook of International Criminal Law (2011), 337, 350.

128 *Ryngaert* (n. 89), 158–159. See also *Ratner* et al. (n. 11), 176.

129 Article VI of the Genocide Convention.

130 *Ratner* et al. (n. 11), 176.

131 Ibid. 203.

It is also difficult to establish an international court or tribunal, whereas it is "generally easier" to pursue national prosecution.[132] International courts and tribunals "are distant from and inaccessible to the affected populations",[133] whereas justice is "seen to be done" if criminal trials take place in the state where gross human rights violations were committed: "[T]he entire process becomes more deeply connected with the society, providing it with the potential to create a strong psychological effect on the population".[134] If international courts and tribunals are not situated within the state where atrocities took place, it is more difficult to use the prosecution as a reconciliation and peacebuilding tool. The vast numbers of perpetrators involved in the commission of gross human rights violations also make it impossible for international fora to prosecute everyone who played a role in the commission of genocide and crimes against humanity.[135] Therefore, an advantage of domestic courts is that they can deal with greater numbers of accused, and it is suggested that lower-level accused should be charged by national courts, whether within the responsible state or within third states. International courts and tribunals should try only the highest level accused and those involved in the planning of genocide and crimes against humanity.

However, strong arguments can be advanced against national prosecution of international crimes. Although the state with primary jurisdiction over international crimes is the state where the crimes were committed in the first place, the judicial system in states which have recently suffered from gross human rights violations are hardly ever in the position to prosecute such crimes successfully.[136] It is therefore up to other third states, as well as international courts and tribunals, to exercise universal jurisdiction over such crimes in order to avoid impunity.

All the *erga omnes* obligations mentioned thus far, albeit preventative obligations or obligations with regard to prosecution, are imposed upon the responsible state, third states, member states of the United Nations or regional organisations, and member states of applicable international conventions. As illustrated, states repeatedly breach these obligations imposed upon them. An option available in international law, in addition to

---

132 Ibid.
133 Ibid. 252.
134 Ibid. 203.
135 Ibid. 195–196. Ratner states that an estimated 800 000 persons participated in the Rwandan genocide: by 2008 an estimated 10 000 perpetrators had been tried in domestic courts and 70 000 persons had been brought before *gacaca* courts.
136 *Gioia*, 19 LJIL 2006, 1095, 1106–1109; *Orentlicher* (n. 111), 63, 81.

individual criminal responsibility, is for third states to hold states civilly accountable for breaching the obligations to prevent and prosecute *jus cogens* crimes in terms of the principles of state responsibility. It is important to clarify that the option available to states to hold the state where gross human rights violations took place responsible for the atrocities is concerned with civil liability. This is not to hold a state criminally liable, but to ensure that the state is held liable on a civil basis.[137]

IV. Civil accountability in terms of the principles of state responsibility

Article IX of the Genocide Convention makes provision for state responsibility, and states that a "dispute" between member states with regard to "the interpretation, application or fulfilment" of the Convention "including those relating to the responsibility of a State for genocide or of any of the other acts enumerated in Article III" must be referred to the International Court of Justice for adjudication.

State responsibility for the commission of genocide and crimes against humanity has several advantages, especially if the dispute was referred to the International Court of Justice for adjudication. A judgment or advisory opinion by the ICJ could exert strong pressure upon wrongdoing states to comply with their *erga omnes* obligations to prevent and prosecute gross human rights violations.[138] Such a judgment could also provide "an authoritative factual record ... which may provide psychological support to victims and their loved ones".[139] Referral to the ICJ is also much quicker than referring situations to the ICC or other criminal courts or tribunals: the initiation of cases can be done "relatively quickly and inexpensively, and [its] work does not require apprehension of offenders".[140]

V. Conclusion

This contribution examined which measures are available to states seeking to fulfil their *erga omnes* obligation to prosecute gross human rights viola-

137 *Wyler* and *Castellanos-Jankiewicz*, in: Schabas and Bernaz (eds.), Routledge Handbook of International Criminal Law (2011), 385.

138 *Ratner* et al. (n. 11), 257.

139 Ibid.

140 Ibid.

tions, and whether states have actually used all possible means. It is clear that there are numerous measures available to ensure that the commission of genocide and crimes against humanity are prosecuted or adjudicated. The purpose of such measures is to avoid the enjoyment of impunity[141] for the commission of gross human rights violations. Unfortunately, not all of these measures are fully utilised, and therefore states are breaching the *erga omnes* obligation to prosecute genocide and crimes against humanity.

Should all available measures be utilised in order to comply with the *erga omnes* obligation to prosecute genocide and crimes against humanity, legal certainty in international criminal law will hereby be ensured. It will mean that there will be uniformity in state practice, and ultimately that states are complying with the rule of law.

Bibliography

Dapo Akande and *Sangeeta Shah*, "Immunities of State Officials, International Crimes, and Foreign Domestic Courts", 21 European Journal of International Law (EJIL) 2011, 815.

Payam Akhavan, "Beyond Impunity: Can International Criminal Justice Prevent Future Atrocities?", in: Richard Falk, Hilal Elver and Lisa Hajjar (eds.), Human Rights: Critical Concepts in Political Science, volume III (Routledge, United Kingdom 2008), 123.

Kai Ambos, "International Criminal Law at the Crossroads: From *Ad Hoc* Imposition to a Treaty-Based Universal System", in: Carsten Stahn and Larissa van den Herik (eds.), Future Perspectives on International Criminal Justice (TMC Asser Press, The Hague 2010), 161.

M. Cheriff Bassiouni, "International Crimes: *Jus Cogens* and *Obligatio Erga Omnes*", Law and Contemporary Problems (LCP) 1996, 63.

Roberto Bellelli, "The Establishment of the System of International Criminal Justice", in: Roberto Bellelli (ed.), International Criminal Justice: Law and Practice from the Rome Statute to its Review (Ashgate, Great Britain 2010), 5.

Ian Brownlie, "The Obligation to Extradite for the Repression of International Crimes under Customary Law", in: Fransesco Salerno, Diritti Dell'Uomo, Estradizione ed Espulsione: Atti del Convegno di Studaio Organizzato dall'Università di Ferrara per Salutare Giovanni Battaglini (29–30 Ottobre 1999) (Casa Editrice Dott, Antonio Milani, Italy 2003), 3.

William W. Burke-White, "Bargaining for Arrests at the International Criminal Court: A Response to Roper and Barria", 21 Leiden Journal of International Law (LJIL) 2008, 477.

141 *Robertson*, CILJ 2005, 649.

Antônio Augusto Cançado Trindade, "Reflections on a Century of International Justice and Prospects for the Future", in: Giorgio Gaja and Jenny Grote Stoutenburg (eds.), Enhancing the Rule of Law through the International Court of Justice (Koninklijke Brill Nijhoff, Leiden, The Netherlands 2014), 1.

Christine H. Chung, "The Punishment and Prevention of Genocide: The International Criminal Court as a Benchmark of Progress and Need", 40 Case Western Reserve Journal of International Law (CWRJIL) 2008, 227.

Roger S. Clark, "The Development of International Criminal Law", in: Chili Eboe-Osuji (ed.), Protecting Humanity: Essays in International Law and Policy in Honour of Navanethem Pillay (Martinus Nijhoff Publishers, Leiden and Boston 2010), 367.

Stanley Cohen, "State Crimes of Previous Regimes: Knowledge, Accountability, and the Policing of the Past", in: Richard Falk, Hilal Elver and Lisa Hajjar (eds.), Human Rights: Critical Concepts in Political Science, volume III (Routledge, United Kingdom 2008), 174.

Carla Del Ponte, "Reflections Based on the ICTY's Experience", in: Roberto Bellelli (ed.), International Criminal Justice: Law and Practice from the Rome Statute to its Review (Ashgate, Great Britain 2010), 125.

John Dugard, International Law: A South African Perspective (Juta & Co. Ltd, Lansdowne 2011).

Malcolm D. Evans, International Law (Oxford University Press, Oxford 2010).

Mark Fenwick and *Stefan Wrbka*, "The Shifting Meaning of Legal Certainty", in: Mark Fenwick and Stefan Wrbka (eds.), Legal Certainty in a Contemporary Context: Private and Criminal Law Perspectives (Springer, Singapore 2016), 1.

Paola Gaeta, "National Prosecution of International Crimes: International Rules on Grounds of Jurisdiction", in: Gaetano Arangio-Ruiz (ed.), Studi di Diritto Internazionale in Onore di Gaetano Arangio-Ruiz, vol. III (Oxford University Press, Oxford 2004), 1923.

Jean-Francois Gerkens, "Legal Certainty v Legal Precision", 16 Fundamina 2010, 121.

Federica Gioia, "State Sovereignty, Jurisdiction, and 'Modern' International Law: The Principle of Complementarity in the International Criminal Court", 19 Leiden Journal of International Law (LJIL) 2006, 1095.

Lisa Hajjar, "Chaos as Utopia: International Criminal Prosecutions as a Challenge to State Power", in: Richard Falk, Hilal Elver and Lisa Hajjar (eds.), Human Rights: Critical Concepts in Political Science, volume III (Routledge, United Kingdom 2008), 42.

A. Hays Butler, "The Growing Support for Universal Jurisdiction in National Legislation", in: Stephen Macedo (ed.), Universal Jurisdiction: National Courts and the Prosecution of Serious Crimes Under International Law (University of Pennsylvania Press, Philadelphia, Pennsylvania 2006), 67.

Florian Jessberger, "Universality, Complementarity, and the Duty to Prosecute Crimes Under International Law in Germany", in: Wolfgang Kaleck, Michael Ratner, Tobias Singelnstein, and Peter Weiss (eds.), International Prosecution of Human Rights Crimes (Heidelberg, Springer 2007), 213.

Mouhamed Kebe, "State and Universal Jurisdiction: Assessing an Uneasy Relationship", in: Charles Riziki Majinge (ed.), Rule of Law through Human Rights and International Criminal Justice: Essays in Honour of Adama Dieng (Cambridge Scholars Publishing, Newcastle upon Tyne 2015), 376.

Christopher K. Lamont, International Criminal Justice and the Politics of Compliance (Ashgate, Great Britain 2010).

Chea Leang and *William Smith*, "The Early Experience of the Extraordinary Chambers in the Courts of Cambodia", in: Roberto Bellelli (ed.), International Criminal Justice: Law and Practice from the Rome Statute to its Review (Ashgate, Great Britain 2010), 143.

Brian D. Lepard, Customary International Law: A New Theory with Practical Applications (Cambridge University Press, United States of America 2010), 243.

Lorna McGregor, "Addressing the Relationship between State Immunity and *Jus Cogens* Norms: A Comparative Assessment", in: Wolfgang Kaleck, Michael Ratner, Tobias Singelnstein and Peter Weiss (eds.), International Prosecution of Human Rights Crimes (Heidelberg, Springer 2007), 69.

Erik Møse, "The International Criminal Tribunal for Rwanda" in: Roberto Bellelli (ed.), International Criminal Justice: Law and Practice from the Rome Statute to its Review (Ashgate, Great Britain 2010), 80.

Shigeru Oda, "International Court of Justice: Its Myth and Reality", 51 Japanese Yearbook of International Law (JYIL) 2008, 427.

Alexander Orakhelashvili, Peremptory Norms in International Law (Oxford University Press, Oxford 2006).

Diane F. Orentlicher, "The Future of Universal Jurisdiction in the New Architecture of Transnational Justice", in: Richard Falk, Hilal Elver and Lisa Hajjar (eds.), Human Rights: Critical Concepts in Political Science, volume III (Routledge, United Kingdom 2008), 63.

Karen Parker and *Lyn Beth Neylon*, "*Jus Cogens*: Compelling the Law of Human Rights", 12 Hastings International and Comparative Law Review (HICLR) 1989, 411.

Jordan J. Paust, "Restoring the Rule of Law: Ending Official Elite Impunity for International Crimes", in: Aristotle Constantinides and Nikos Zaikos (eds.), The Diversity of International Law: Essays in Honour of Professor Kalliopi K Koufa (Martinus Nijhoff Publishers, Leiden, Boston 2009), 581.

Rod Rastan, "Testing Cooperation: The International Criminal Court and National Authorities", 21 Leiden Journal of International Law (LJIL) 2008, 431.

Steven R. Ratner, "Belgium's War Crimes Statute: A Postmortem", 97 American Journal of International Law (AJIL) 2003, 888.

Steven R. Ratner, *Jason S. Abrams* and *James L. Bischoff*, Accountability for Human Rights Atrocities in International Law: Beyond the Nuremberg Legacy (Oxford University Press, Oxford 2009).

Fausto Pocar, "The International Criminal Tribunal for the Former Yugoslavia", in: Roberto Bellelli (ed.), International Criminal Justice: Law and Practice from the Rome Statute to its Review (Ashgate, Great Britain 2010), 67.

Sarah Power, "Stopping Genocide and Securing 'Justice': Learning by Doing – International Justice, War Crimes, and Terrorism: The US Record", in: Richard Falk, Hilal Elver and Lisa Hajjar (eds.), Human Rights: Critical Concepts in Political Science, volume III (Routledge, United Kingdom 2008), 274.

Kimberley Prost, "State Cooperation and Transfers", in: William A. Schabas and Nadia Bernaz (eds.), Routledge Handbook of International Criminal Law (Routledge Taylor & Frances Group, London and New York 2011), 305.

Luc Reydams, "The Rise and Fall of Universal Jurisdiction", in: William A. Schabas and Nadia Bernaz (eds.), Routledge Handbook of International Criminal Law (Routledge Taylor & Frances Group, London and New York 2011), 337.

Geoffrey Robertson, "Ending Impunity: How International Criminal Law can put Tyrants on Trial", Cornell International Law Journal (CILJ) 2005, 649.

Steven D. Roper and *Lilian A. Barria*, "State Cooperation and International Criminal Court Bargaining Influence in the Arrest and the Surrender of Suspects", 21 Leiden Journal of International Law (LJIL) 2008, 457.

Mispa Roux, "Early Warning of Gross Human Rights Violations: an International Law Perspective", Tydskrif vir die Suid-Afrikaanse Reg (TSAR) 2011, 650.

Mispa Roux, "The *Erga Omnes* Obligation to Prevent and Prosecute Gross Human Rights Violations with Special Emphasis upon Genocide and Persecution as a Crime Against Humanity", African Yearbook on International Humanitarian Law (AYIHL) 2012, 98.

Mispa Roux, "Sexual violence during armed conflict and reparation: paying due regard to a unique trauma", African Yearbook on International Humanitarian Law (AYIHL) 2014, 87.

Mispa Roux, "Obstacles to the Prevention of Gross Human Rights Violations", Tydskrif vir die Suid-Afrikaanse Reg (TSAR) 2018, 106.

Mispa Roux, "Withdrawal from the International Criminal Court: South Africa's legacy of overlooking the *erga omnes* obligation to prosecute international crimes by prioritising peace", in: David Israel Bilchitz and Magdalena Ines Correa Henau (eds.), Transitional Justice and Distributive Justice: Comparative Lessons from Colombia and South Africa (forthcoming 2021).

Cedric Ryngaert, "Applying the Rome Statutes Complementarity Principle: Drawing Lessons from the Prosecution of Core Crimes by States Acting Under the Universality Principle", 19 Criminal Law Forum (CLF) 2008, 153.

William A. Schabas, "Addressing Impunity in Developing Countries: Lessons from Rwanda and Sierra Leone", in: Hélène Dumont and Anne-Marie Boisvert (eds.), The Highway to the International Criminal Court: All Roads Lead to Rome (Les Éditions Thémis Inc., Montréal, Québec 2004).

William A. Schabas, "'Complementarity in Practice': Some Uncomplimentary Thoughts", 19 Criminal Law Forum (CLF) 2008, 5.

Dinah Shelton, Remedies in International Human Rights Law (Oxford University Press, Oxford 2005).

Lee A. Steven, "Genocide and the Duty to Extradite or Prosecute: Why the United States is in Breach of its International Obligations", 39 Virginia Journal of International Law (VJIL) 1999, 425.

Peer Stolle and *Tobias Singelnstein*, "On the Aims and Actual Consequences of International Prosecution of Human Rights Crimes", in: Wolfgang Kaleck, Michael Ratner, Tobias Singelnstein, and Peter Weiss (eds.), International Prosecution of Human Rights Crimes (Heidelberg, Springer 2007), 37.

Eric Wyler and *Léon Arturo Castellanos-Jankiewicz*, "State Responsibility and International Crimes" in: William A Schabas and Nadia Bernaz (eds.), Routledge Handbook of International Criminal Law (Routledge Taylor & Frances Group, London and New York 2011), 385.

Register of cases

Permanent Court of International Justice

PCIJ, *Case of the SS "Lotus"*, Judgment of 7 Sep. 1927, [1927] PCIJ Series A No. 10.

International Court of Justice

ICJ, Reservations to the Convention on the Prevention and Punishment of the Crime of Genocide, Advisory Opinion of 28 May 1951, ICJ Reports 1951, 15.

ICJ, Barcelona Traction, Light and Power Company, Limited (Belgium v Spain), Judgment of 5 Feb. 1970, ICJ Reports 1970, 3.

ICJ, Application of the Convention on the Prevention and Punishment of the Crime of Genocide (Bosnia and Herzegovina v Serbia and Montenegro), Preliminary Objections and Judgment of 11 July 1996, ICJ Reports 1996, 595.

ICJ, Arrest Warrant of 11 April 2000 (Democratic Republic of the Congo v Belgium), Judgment of 14 Feb. 2002, ICJ Reports 2002, 3.

ICJ, Arrest Warrant of 11 April 2000 (Democratic Republic of the Congo v Belgium), Separate Opinion of President Guillame to the Judgment of 14 Feb. 2002, ICJ Reports 2002, 35.

ICJ, Arrest Warrant of 11 April 2000 (Democratic Republic of the Congo v Belgium), Dissenting Opinion of Judge Oda to the Judgment of 14 Feb. 2002, ICJ Reports 2002, 46.

ICJ, Arrest Warrant of 11 April 2000 (Democratic Republic of the Congo v Belgium), Joint Separate Opinion of Judges Higgens, Kooijmans and Buergenthal to the Judgment of 14 Feb. 2002, ICJ Reports 2002, 63.

ICJ, Arrest Warrant of 11 April 2000 (Democratic Republic of the Congo v Belgium), Dissenting Opinion of Judge van den Wyngaert to the Judgment of 14 Feb. 2002, ICJ Reports 2002, 137.

ICJ, Application of the Convention on the Prevention and Punishment of the Crime of Genocide (Bosnia and Herzegovina v Serbia and Montenegro), Judgment of 26 Feb. 2007, ICJ Reports 2007, 43.

International Criminal Court

ICC, *The Prosecutor v Omar Hassan Ahmad Al Bashir,* Decision of 27 Aug. 2010 informing the United Nations Security Council and the Assembly of the States Parties to the Rome Statute about Omar Al-Bashir's Presence in the Territory of the Republic of Kenya, ICC-02/05–01/09.

ICC, *The Prosecutor v Omar Hassan Ahmad Al Bashir,* Decision of 27 Aug. 2010 informing the United Nations Security Council and the Assembly of the States Parties to the Rome Statute about Omar Al-Bashir's Recent Visit to the Republic of Chad, ICC ICC-02/05–01/09.

ICC, *The Prosecutor v Omar Hassan Ahmad Al-Bashir*, Decision of 6 July 2017 under Article 87(7) of the Rome Statute on the non-compliance by South Africa with the request by the court for the arrest and surrender of Omar Al-Bashir, ICC-02/05–01/09.

International Criminal Tribunal for the Former Yugoslavia

ICTY, *The Prosecutor v Kupreškić*, Judgment of 14 Jan. 2000, Case No. IT-95–16-T.

South Africa

Southern Africa Litigation Centre v Minister of Justice and Constitutional Development 2015 5 SA 1 (GP).

Minister of Justice and Constitutional Development v Southern Africa Litigation Centre 2016 3 SA 317 (SCA).

Preventive Justice and the Dangerous Offender: Seeking Solutions to Protect Society

*Murdoch Watney**

Abstract: This contribution investigates the concept of preventive justice and its practical application pertaining to dangerous offenders in South Africa (which has a mixed legal system influenced by both the Roman-Dutch and English criminal law), the common law jurisdictions of England and Wales and Canada as well as the continental legal system of Germany. The duty of the State in a constitutional dispensation to protect the rights of individuals against dangerous offenders is viewed in a serious light as a failure to do so might cause individuals to feel justified in using self-help to protect their rights. Preventive measures pertaining to dangerous offenders take on various forms internationally. Some countries employ indefinite imprisonment with subsequent release dependent on rehabilitation whilst others emphasise monitoring and rehabilitation within the wider community. Other legal systems follow an approach in terms of which preventive detention is imposed after a sentenced offender has already served a period of imprisonment in respect of the initial conviction. This additional period of detention forms part of the concept of preventive justice and is imposed in cases where the offender is deemed to pose a threat to the community even after incarceration. Although various measures are applied internationally in recognition of the duty to protect the public against dangerous offenders, an important call is made to subject these measures to the universally accepted human rights principles applicable to all members of society.

* Murdoch Watney, *B.A. (Law), LL.B., LL.M. (RAU), LL.M. (SA), Dip. E-C Law (TJSL), LL.D. (RAU)*, Professor of Law, Faculty of Law, University of Johannesburg.

I. Introduction

The legal system developed over centuries from the practicing of private vengeance by individuals and groups to punishment by the State of offenders who inflict harm to fellow citizens.[1] The social contract in terms of which private citizens renounce to the State their ancient right to self-governance (and to exact vengeance against those individuals who caused them harm) requires of citizens to obey the law.[2] In return the State owes a duty to those citizens to provide protection and security for their persons and property and thus their safety, which is a prerequisite of freedom.[3]

---

1 *Burchell*, Principles of Criminal Law (3rd ed. 2005), 19; *De Wet*, De Wet en Swanepoel Strafreg (4th ed. 1985), 3–20; *Lintott*, in: Johnston (ed.), The Cambridge Companion to Roman Law (1st ed. 2015), 301–307.

2 *Ashworth* and *Zedner*, Preventive Justice (2014), 7–8; *Harries*, Law and Crime in the Roman World (2007), 1–7.

3 *Ashworth and Zedner* (n. 2), 8. In *S v Makwanyane* 1995 3 SA 391 (CC) the South African Constitutional Court made the following remarks in this regard: "Members of the public are understandably concerned, often frightened, for their life and safety in a society where the incidence of violent crime is high and the rate of apprehension and conviction of the perpetrators low. This is a pressing public concern. However important it undoubtedly is to emphasise the constitutional importance of individual rights, there is a danger that the other leg of the constitutional State compact may not enjoy the recognition it deserves. I refer to the fact that in a constitutional State individuals agree (in principle at least) to abandon their right to self-help in the protection of their rights only because the State, in the constitutional State compact, assumes the obligation to protect these rights. If the State fails to discharge this duty adequately, there is a danger that individuals might feel justified in using self-help to protect their rights. This is not a fanciful possibility in South Africa. 'The need for a strong deterrent to violent crime' is underscored by the President in his judgment, as is the duty of the State, through the criminal justice system, to ensure that offenders will be apprehended

Burchell indicates that this process was completed when the political authority had the power to enforce a system in which private vengeance was no longer tolerated.[4] When the development of this phase reached completion the process of refining the alternative system of public punishment commenced with developments relating to criminal procedure, crime definition, philosophy of punishment and the role of justice in the imposition of public punishment.[5]

Ashworth and Zedner argue in this regard that governmental concern about the prevention of harm served as motivation for the founding of the modern criminal justice system and is as such, a major feature of contemporary social policies in various Western countries.[6] In recognising that crime prevention might be achieved by punishing criminals through incarceration as it would incapacitate and deter specific individuals and others by example from further criminality, Steiker observes that punishment is not the most common or most effective means of crime prevention.[7] The preventive state would also identify and neutralise dangerous individuals before they commit crimes by restricting their liberty through expanding the functions of the institutions involved in the criminal justice system such as the police, prison and the civil commitment process.[8] It is exactly in respect of these preventive measures[9] that the challenge arises: the normal criminal justice safeguards often do not apply as these measures are seen as merely preventive and not punitive and the coercive measures are designed to sit outside and alongside the criminal process.[10]

---

and convicted, for these steps are conditions precedent to punishment" (168). Also see *AK v Minister of Safety and Security* 2019 1 SACR 529 (ECP); *Carmichele v Minister of Safety and Security* 2002 1 SACR 79 (CC) para. 62; *Burchell*, Principles of Criminal Law (5th ed. 2016), 83–84. Even post-conviction and after sentence the State has a legal duty to ensure that the processes relating to release on parole are executed with due care (see *Watney*, TSAR 2017, 704, 730–732; *Naidu v Minister of Correctional Services* 2017 2 SACR 14 (WCC)).

4 *Burchell* (n. 1), 19.

5 *Burchell* (n. 1), 19–20.

6 *Ashworth* and *Zedner* (n. 2), 11, 27–50.

7 *Steiker*, Journal of Criminal Law and Criminology 1998, 771, 774.

8 *Steiker* (n. 7), 774.

9 *Ashworth* and *Zedner* (n. 2), 13 identified preventive endeavours relating to counterterrorist measures, civil preventive orders, immigration laws, policing, criminal procedure and the preventive detention of the dangerous offender which have become prominent in recent years.

10 *Steiker* (n. 7), 778; *Ashworth* and *Zedner* (n. 2), observe that "the politics of the preventive has a strong element of irresistibility built into it, since it generally appears perverse to argue against a preventive measure. Who could be against

Preventive measures pertaining to dangerous offenders take on various forms internationally. Some countries employ indefinite imprisonment with subsequent release dependent on rehabilitation whilst others rely on monitoring and rehabilitation within the community. Other legal systems follow an approach in terms of which preventive detention is imposed after a sentenced offender has served his period of imprisonment in respect of the initial conviction. This additional period of detention forms part of the concept of preventive justice and is imposed in cases where the offender is deemed (still) to pose a threat to the community.[11]

The aim of this contribution is to consider the concept of preventive justice and its practical application pertaining to dangerous offenders in South Africa (which has a mixed legal system influenced by both the Roman-Dutch and English criminal law), the common law jurisdictions of England and Wales and Canada as well as the continental legal system of Germany. The question is asked whether preventive detention is a justifiable solution to the challenge presented to society by dangerous offenders. This contribution does not include a discussion of the legal position of minors in conflict with the law nor of offenders facing mental health challenges of such a nature that they are diverted from the main stream criminal justice process.

II. Preventive detention in various jurisdictions

1. South Africa

Subsequent to the declaration of the death sentence as unconstitutional in the *Makwanyane* case,[12] the three most serious sentencing options that remain available from a preventive detention point of view in terms of

---

the prevention of harm? The political force behind terms such as prevention, security, public protection, and public safety is practically very powerful, not least because the critics of any such measure can be portrayed as courting insecurity and jeopardizing public safety" (13).

11 *Ashworth* and *Zedner* (n. 2), define a coercive preventive measure as such if "it is created in order to avert, or reduce the frequency or impact of, behavior that is believed to present an unacceptable risk of harm. It is coercive if it involves state imposed restrictions on liberty of action, backed by a coercive response, or the threat of a coercive response, to the restricted individual" (20).

12 The *Makwanyane* case (n. 3).

the South African Criminal Procedure Act[13] (the CPA) are declaration of a person as an habitual criminal,[14] declaration of a person as a dangerous criminal[15] and life imprisonment.[16]

a) Declaration as habitual criminal

The declaration of a person as an habitual criminal as sentencing option is primarily a preventive measure aimed at protecting the community against a person who regularly offends and in respect of whom normal sentencing options seemingly have no positive effect.[17] Section 286 read with Section 276(1)(*d*) of the CPA provides that a superior or a regional court which convicts a person of one or more offences may, if it is satisfied that the said person habitually commits offences and that the community should be protected against the offender, declare him an habitual criminal. A person younger than 18 years may not be declared as an habitual criminal[18] and neither may an offender be so declared if the court is of the opinion that the offence(s) in respect of which he is to be sentenced, justifies the imposition of a sentence exceeding 15 years imprisonment.[19] Section 73(6)(*c*) of the Correctional Services Act[20] (CSA 1998) provides that a person who has been declared an habitual criminal may not be released on parole before serving at least seven years imprisonment but may not be detained for a period exceeding 15 years.

Prior to enactment of the CSA 1998, Section 65(4)(*b*)(iv) of the Correctional Services Act 8 of 1959 (CSA 1959) read with Section 286 of the CPA had the effect that a person who had been declared an habitual criminal had to be detained in prison for an indefinite period of time but for a minimum period of 7 years. In the *Niemand* case the Constitutional Court, however, found indefinite detention in respect of habitual criminals to be an unjustifiable infringement of the right to freedom and security of the

13 Act No. 51 of 1977.
14 Sections 276(1)(*d*) and 286 of the CPA.
15 Section 286A of the CPA.
16 Section 276(1)(*b*) of the CPA.
17 *S v Nawaseb* 1980 1 SA 339 (SWA) 346D-F. In *S v Niemand* 2001 2 SACR 654 (CC) the Constitutional Court found that "(t)he crux of the matter is that the law seeks to punish a person who manifests a persistent tendency to commit crime by sentencing him/her to what amounts to preventive detention" (para. 12).
18 Section 286(2)(*a*) of the CPA.
19 Section 286(2)(*c*) of the CPA.
20 Act No. 111 of 1998.

person which includes the right not to be treated in a cruel, inhuman or degrading way in terms of Section 12(1)(*e*) of the Constitution.[21] The basis of the court's finding in this regard was set out as follows:

> "[25] Life imprisonment for crimes such as murder and rape may be proportional to the heinous nature of the crimes. However, the imposition of life imprisonment, in the guise of an indeterminate sentence, for an habitual criminal who is neither violent nor a danger to society as contemplated in s 286A of the CPA is a different matter. The sentence is grossly disproportionate to the length of the imprisonment merited by such offences and as such constitutes a violation of s 12(1)(*e*) of the Constitution. The imposition of such a sentence is clearly grossly disproportionate to the stated purpose for which it is imposed, namely to protect society against repeat offenders. The class of habitual criminal that we are concerned with here does not pose a threat to society that warrants indefinite incarceration.
> [26] The indeterminacy of the sentence also exacerbates the cruel, inhuman or degrading nature of the punishment on the grounds that the maximum period of incarceration remains at all times unknown to the prisoner and the period of his/her incarceration is dependent on the executive. This, no doubt, is the cause of considerable torment. I therefore conclude that to sentence a person to what may potentially constitute a life long imprisonment, infringes the right of such person not to be subjected to cruel, inhuman or degrading treatment or punishment."[22]

The court found the legislative omission to provide for a maximum period of imprisonment when declaring a person as an habitual criminal, to be constitutionally flawed and made an order reading into Section 65(4)(*b*)(iv) that no prisoner declared an habitual criminal shall be detained for a period exceeding 15 years.[23] Sec 73(6)(*c*) of the CSA 1998 came into operation after the judgment in *Niemand* and therefore regulates the position in accordance with the Constitutional Court's judgment.

21 Constitution of the Republic of South Africa, 1996.

22 The *Niemand* case (n. 17) paras. 25–26.

23 *Rautenbach,* Rautenbach-Malherbe Constitutional Law (6th ed. 2012), 347–348; *Kruger,* Hiemstra's Criminal Procedure, 28–48; *Terblanche,* A Guide to Sentencing in South Africa (3rd ed. 2016), 274.

b) Declaration as dangerous criminal

Section 286A of the CPA provides a superior or regional court with the discretion to declare a convicted person as a dangerous criminal if it is satisfied that the said person represents a danger to the physical or mental well-being of other persons or that the community should be protected against him. Depending on the evidence presented during the course of the trial a court will have the discretion to institute an enquiry into the dangerousness of the offender subsequent to conviction.[24] The enquiry will be conducted and reported on by the medical superintendent of a psychiatric hospital designated by the court and a psychiatrist appointed by the accused if he so wishes.[25] The relevant report shall include a description of the nature of the inquiry and a finding as to whether the accused represents a danger to the physical or mental well-being of other persons.[26]

Subsequent to declaring a person as a dangerous criminal, the court shall sentence the convicted person to an indefinite period of imprisonment and direct that he be brought before the court on the expiration of a period determined by the court.[27] This provision provides the courts with a sentencing option to deal with accused persons with anti-social disorders and the aim is to detain the person for as long as he remains a danger.[28] When the person is brought before court after expiration of the stipulated date, the court may reconsider the sentence after consideration of a report by the parole board.[29] The court has a discretion to confirm the sentence of indefinite imprisonment and set a new date when the person has to be brought before court again or convert the sentence into correctional supervision or release the person with or without conditions. If a person released on correctional supervision is subsequently found to be unfit for such sentence, the court may reconsider the release and confirm the sentence of indefinite imprisonment.[30]

---

24 *Terblanche* (n. 23) indicates that a court may declare an offender a dangerous criminal without a full enquiry (277). Section 286A(2)(*b*) of the CPA provides that the court will inform the accused of its intention to conduct such an enquiry.

25 The court has a discretion to refer an accused to a psychiatric hospital for purposes of the enquiry for periods not exceeding 30 days at a time. See Section 286A(3)(*a*)–(*b*) of the CPA.

26 Section 286A(3)(*d*) of the CPA.

27 Section 286B(1) of the CPA.

28 *Terblanche* (n. 23), 277; *Du Toit* et al., Commentary on the Criminal Procedure Act (service 61, 2019), 28–24C.

29 Section 286B(2) and (4) of the CPA.

30 Section 286B(4) and (5) of the CPA.

The Supreme Court of Appeal considered the constitutionality of Sections 286A and 286B in *S v Bull; S v Chavulla*[31] and concluded that provided the principle against gross disproportionality is respected, these provisions are not in conflict with Section 12(1)(*e*) of the Constitution which provides that everyone has the right to freedom and security of the person, which includes the right not to be treated or punished in a cruel, inhuman or degrading way.[32] The court, however, emphasised that the aim with Sections 286A and 286B was not to provide for a more severe sentence than life imprisonment.[33] With this interpretation the Supreme Court of Appeal in effect limited the time period within which the person had to appear before the court again for reconsideration of sentence to a maximum of 25 years. Nothing, however, prohibits the court then to

31 2001 (2) SACR 681 (SCA).

32 The court remarked as follows: "Reverting to the dangerous criminal provisions of the Act, there could, in the first place, be no constitutional objection to an indeterminate sentence, *per se*, since the protection of society is a legitimate purpose of sentencing, provided that the constitutional principle against gross disproportionality is respected ... In recent years the protection of the community and the purpose of prevention of future offences have received greater emphasis by our courts, particularly in cases of violent crime. In the *Makwanyane* case Chaskalson P said the following about the interests of society:
'The level of violent crime in our country has reached alarming proportions. It poses a threat to the transition to democracy, and the creation of development opportunities for all, which are primary goals of the Constitution. The high level of violent crime is a matter of common knowledge ...... It is of fundamental importance to the future of our country that respect for the law should be restored, and that dangerous criminals should be apprehended and dealt with firmly.'
Ackermann J put it thus:
'With the abolition of the death penalty society needs the firm assurance that the unreformed recidivist murderer or rapist will not be released from prison, however long the sentence served by the prisoner may have been, if there is a reasonable possibility that the prisoner will repeat the crime. Society needs to be assured that in such cases the State will see to it that such a recidivist will remain in prison permanently'" (para. 15).

33 The *Bull* case (n. 31) para. 26. The court remarked as follows: "(t)he trial Court further misdirected itself in regarding a sentence in terms of s 286B as the most severe sentence it could impose ... It also misdirected itself in concluding that, in order to achieve its stated purpose of removing the appellants permanently from society, s 286B entitled it to impose non-parole sentences of 50 and 30 years' imprisonment. In so doing the trial Court overlooked the fact that such sentences could keep the appellants in prison even if the justification for the sentences, ie their dangerousness, no longer existed ... Furthermore, the denial of the right to be considered for parole for such long periods was not only improper but also amounted to cruel and inhuman punishment" (para. 43).

confirm the sentence of indefinite imprisonment provided that the person is again brought before court on the expiration of a further period determined by the court.

This is the only sentencing option in South African law which provides a court and not the Correctional Supervision and Parole Board, the National Council for Correctional Services and the Minister of Justice with the final say about the release of a prisoner serving a life sentence. Despite the opportunity it presents a court to exercise supervision over the process and to ensure that a prisoner is only released when he presents no further danger to the community, this sentencing option is seldom used.[34]

c) Life imprisonment

Section 276(1)(*b*) of the CPA provides for life imprisonment as sentencing option. In terms of Section 73(1)(*b*) of the CSA 1998 an offender sentenced to life incarceration has to remain in a correctional centre for the rest of his life. This provision is qualified by Section 73(6)(*iv*) of the CSA 1998 which provides that a person may be considered for release on parole after serving 25 years of the life sentence.[35] After completion of this period a person may be released on parole on a date determined by the minister of justice and correctional services.[36]

Although the constitutionality of life imprisonment as a sentencing option has not yet arisen in a South African court, certain indications were given in the *Makwanyane* case that life imprisonment will in all probability not be unconstitutional. Referring to the decision by the German Federal

---

34 *Kruger* (n. 23), 28–51 opines that this might be due to a reluctance by courts to "venture into uncharted waters" and a lack of initiative by prosecutors to propose declaration as a dangerous criminal as a sentencing option.

35 Section 73(6)(*vi*) provides that a prisoner, excluding a person declared as a dangerous offender, may be released on parole on reaching the age of 65 years provided that he or she has served at least 15 years of such sentence. Due to amended legislation shorter periods of incarceration are applicable to persons sentenced before 1 March 1994 and 1 October 2004. See *Watney,* TSAR 2018, 389, 393–394 for a discussion on the different periods.

36 Section 73(5)(*a*) CSA 1998. After consideration of a report by the correctional supervision and parole board the national council for correctional services may recommend to the minister that a person be released on parole (Section 78). The decisive role fulfilled by the executive authority in the parole process of persons serving life imprisonment (with the exception of dangerous criminals) is a contentious matter (see *Watney*, TSAR 2018, 88, 100–104).

Constitutional Court[37] which found that there is nothing constitutionally objectionable to serving a sentence of life imprisonment in full in cases where the criteria for release on parole are not met, justice Ackermann remarked as follow:

> "The President has rightly pointed out in his judgment that, in considering the deterrent effect of the death sentence, the evaluation is not to be conducted by contrasting the death penalty with no punishment at all, but between the death sentence and 'severe punishment of a long term of imprisonment which, in an appropriate case, could be a sentence of life imprisonment'. I agree with this approach. With the abolition of the death penalty society needs the firm assurance that the unreformed recidivist murderer or rapist will not be released from prison, however long the sentence served by the prisoner may have been, if there is a reasonable possibility that the prisoner will repeat the crime. Society needs to be assured that in such cases the State will see to it that such a recidivist will remain in prison permanently.
> ... I appreciate the concern of not wishing to anticipate the issue as to whether life imprisonment, however executed and administered, is constitutional or not. At the same time I do not believe that the two issues can be kept in watertight separate juristic compartments. If the death penalty is to be abolished, as I believe it must, society is entitled to the assurance that the State will protect it from further harm from the convicted unreformed recidivist killer or rapist. If there is an individual right not to be put to death by the criminal justice system, there is a correlative obligation on the State, through the criminal justice system, to protect society from once again being harmed by the unreformed recidivist killer or rapist. The right and the obligation are inseparably part of the same constitutional state compact."[38]

For purposes of protecting society from an unreformed and recidivist dangerous offender the indication from the Constitutional Court is therefore that preventative detention in the form of life imprisonment (even until

---

37 The *Life Imprisonment* case, BVerfG, Judgment of 21 Jun 1977, 1 BvL 14/76, BVerfGE 45, 187. Also see *Ackermann*, Human Dignity: Lodestar for Equality in South Africa (1st ed. 2012), 126–127; *Currie* and *De Waal*, The Bill of Rights Handbook (6th ed. 2013), 254–255.

38 Paras. 170–171.

death) would in all probability be acceptable from a constitutional point of view.[39]

2. England and Wales

Ashworth points out that several legal systems make special provision to protect the public from persons who are deemed "dangerous offenders."[40] The three preventive measures of life imprisonment, imprisonment for public protection and extended sentences in the law of England and Wales will be considered in this Section.

a) Life imprisonment

Since the abolition of capital punishment in England and Wales in 1965 life imprisonment has become the prime preventive sentencing option. Life imprisonment is the mandatory sentence for all persons aged 21 and over convicted of murder.[41] In addition thereto Section 225 of the Criminal Justice Act 2003 provides that a court must impose a life sentence if the court is *inter alia* of opinion that the offender "poses a significant risk to members of the public of serious harm occasioned by the commission by him of further specified offences".[42] Judges also have a historical discretion

39 *Steytler*, Constitutional Criminal Procedure (1st ed. 1998) indicates that "there is no constitutional objection to the purpose of an indeterminate prison sentence; preventing further offending for the protection of the community is a legitimate purpose of sentencing. The emphasis on the protection of society is in accordance with the general purpose of criminal law and sentencing in particular. The indeterminacy of the imprisonment is thus not *per se* objectionable provided that the constitutional principle against gross disproportionality is respected" (420).

40 *Ashworth*, Sentencing and Criminal Justice (6th ed. 2015), 237.

41 In terms of Section 1(1) of the Murder (Abolition of Death Penalty) Act 1965. See *Appleton* and *Van Zyl Smit*, in: Van Zyl Smit and Appleton (eds.), Life Imprisonment and Human Rights (1st ed. 2016), 219; *Wasik*, A Practical Approach to Sentencing (5th ed. 2014), 121–124. In terms of Section 269(2) of the Criminal Justice Act 2003 the judge in every murder case has to set a minimum term which the offender must serve before being considered for early release. This provision is no doubt aimed to address the criticism aimed at the mandatory nature of sentence in respect of murder where varying degrees of offender culpability will render a life sentence unjust.

42 *Appleton* and *Van Zyl Smit* (n. 41), 220–221. Further conditions are that the offence must be one for which a life sentence is a competent verdict and that

to impose a sentence of life imprisonment in respect of a range of serious offences.[43]

Prisoners sentenced to life imprisonment have neither a guaranteed date of release nor an absolute right to be released from prison.[44] When life imprisonment is imposed the court announces a minimum term that must be served before the prisoner may be considered for release on licence by the parole board. A prisoner so released is subject to a life licence which implies that he may be recalled to prison for the remainder of his life if there are indications that he poses a risk to the public.[45] In respect of exceptionally serious murder cases a judge may impose a whole life order with the result that no minimum period is set for consideration of release.[46]

In *Vinter v United Kingdom*[47] the European Court for Human Rights (ECtHR) held the administration of whole life orders in England to be in conflict with Article 3 of the European Convention for Human Rights (ECHR)[48] due to the absence of a legal procedure creating a prospect of release in the prisoner's lifetime, provided that he no longer presented a threat to the community.[49] The English Court of Appeal, however, rejected this interpretation of English law in *Vinter* and found that Section 30 of the Crime (Sentences) Act, 1997 provided for a dedicated review mechanism which gave the Secretary of State authority to release any prisoner on compassionate grounds when exceptional circumstances existed.[50] In the subsequent decision of *Hutchinson v United Kingdom*[51] the ECtHR accepted the interpretation of the English law provided in the *Newell* case.[52]

the court considers the committed offence serious enough to impose life imprisonment.

43 These include more than 50 offences, amongs others manslaughter, rape, attempted murder and robbery. See *Appleton* and *Van Zyl Smit* (n. 41), 220.

44 *Appleton* and *Van Zyl Smit* (n. 41), 217.

45 *Appleton* and *Van Zyl Smit* (n. 41), 218.

46 *Appleton* and *Van Zyl Smit* (n. 41), 218.

47 (2012) 55 EHRR 34 1003.

48 Article 3 ECHR declares that "(n)o one shall be subjected to torture or to inhuman or degrading treatment or punishment.".

49 *Appleton* and *Van Zyl Smit* (n. 41), 228; *Mavronicola,* Modern Law Review 2014, 292, 296–299.

50 *R v Newell; R v McLoughlin* 2014 EWCA Crim 188.

51 (2015) 61 EHRR 13 393.

52 *Appleton* and *Van Zyl Smit* (n. 41) criticise the *Hutchinson* case (n. 51) on the basis that "[…] for a whole life order to be compliant with Article 3 of the ECHR it must be reviewed after a fixed time, subject to precise published criteria, governed by the standards of procedural fairness and communicated to the prisoner at the

Striving towards the goal to protect the public from dangerous repeat offenders, the Crime (Sentences) Act, 1997 introduced an automatic life sentence which required judges to impose indeterminate life imprisonment on any offender convicted of a second serious violent or sexual offence.[53] The automatic life sentence provision was repealed by the Criminal Justice Act 2003 and replaced with imprisonment for public protection.[54] The life sentence for a second listed offence was, however, re-introduced, albeit no longer as an automatic sentence.[55]

b) Imprisonment for public protection (IPP)

Although the IPP sentencing option was repealed in 2012 the preventive aim as well as the far reaching effect of the measure require closer analysis.[56]

Appleton and Van Zyl Smit point out that the IPP measure was legislated at a stage when the government placed considerable emphasis on public protection and the proportionality requirement in sentencing was less pronounced.[57] An IPP sentence formed part of the "dangerous offenders" provisions of the Criminal Justice Act 2003 and was mandatory in respect of 153 violent or sexual offences listed in the act, provided that the court believed that there was a significant risk to members of the public of serious harm by the offender's commission of specified crimes in future.[58] A rebuttable presumption of dangerousness was created in respect of of-

outset of the sentence" (229). The authors indicate that Section 30 of the 1997 Act does not reflect these requirements. They also correctly raise doubts whether review by a political appointee can be considered sufficiently independent in terms of modern human rights standards (230).

53 *Appleton* and *Van Zyl Smit* (n. 41), 221. The automatic life sentence was mandatory unless exceptional circumstances existed that justified deviation.

54 Sections 224 to 236 of the Criminal Justice Act 2003 provided for imprisonment for public protection.

55 Section 122 of the Legal Aid, Sentencing and Punishment of Offenders Act 2012 created the sentence by inserting Section 224A into the Criminal Justice Act 2003. See *Wasik* (n. 41), 101–102.

56 Repealed by the Legal Aid, Sentencing and Punishment of Offenders Act 2012. See *Ashworth* (n. 40), 238.

57 *Appleton* and *Van Zyl Smit* (n. 41), 231.

58 Section 224 of the Criminal Justice Act defines serious harm as "death or serious personal injury, whether physical or psychological." See *Ashworth* and *Zedner* (n. 1), 158.

fenders who had a previous conviction of any of the specified offences.[59] The IPP sentence was therefore designed as a preventive measure to protect the public from potentially dangerous offenders whose original offence did not justify a life sentence. The IPP sentence involved a sentence of imprisonment followed by indefinite detention until the parole board determined that the risk was reduced to such an extent that detention for public protection was no longer required.[60]

Criticism of the IPP sentencing regime focused mainly on the fact that offenders were sentenced to indefinite periods of imprisonment based on the future risk they may pose, rather than on the offence in respect of which they had been convicted. The release procedures were also criticised as the techniques for assessing dangerousness and predicting risk were deemed questionable.[61] As a result of a massive influx of large numbers of offenders sentenced to short minimum IPP sentences, the prison services faced a challenge to provide appropriate rehabilitative and resettlement programmes before expiry of the minimum terms of imprisonment. IPP prisoners were as a result unable to indicate to the parole board that the risk they posed to the general public had been reduced, which in turn prolonged further detention. As a result the ECtHR[62] held that an additional period spent in detention after expiry of the minimum term of imprisonment due to the absence of rehabilitative treatment, was in breach of Section 5 of the ECHR and therefore unlawful.[63] In a subsequent judgment by the UK Supreme Court it was held that failure to provide rehabilitative courses did not render ongoing detention unlawful, but that it was nevertheless harmful to IPP prisoners who would be prejudiced by the unlawful decrease in their chances of release.[64] Widespread criticism of the IPP sentencing option eventually led to its abolition.[65]

59 *Appleton* and *Van Zyl Smit* (n. 41), 231.

60 *Ashworth* and *Zedner* (n. 1), 158; *Appleton* and *Van Zyl Smit* (n. 41), 231; *Tonry*, Retributivism has a Past. Has it a Future? (1st ed. 2011), 132.

61 *Appleton* and *Van Zyl Smit* (n. 41), 232.

62 *James, Wells and Lee v United Kingdom* (2013) 56 EHRR 399.

63 Section 5 ECHR only allows detention when there is a lawful basis for it.

64 *R (Haney, Kaiyam and Massey) v The Secretary of State for Justice* 2014 UKSC 66.

65 *Appleton* and *Van Zyl Smit* (n. 41) refer to the IPP sentencing option as a "scandal" (236).

c) Extended sentences

An extended sentence may be imposed by a court if (i) the offender is convicted of a specified violent or sexual offence, (ii) the court considers the offender dangerous in the sense that there is a significant risk to members of the public of serious harm caused by the offender committing further specified offences, (iii) life imprisonment is unavailable or not justified, and (iv) the offender has a previous conviction for a listed offence or the current offence justifies imprisonment of at least four years.

The court will impose a sentence of imprisonment in respect of the offence convicted and also fix an extended licence period up to a maximum of eight years. When the offender is released on either parole or expiry of the prison term, he will be subject to licence (parole) under supervision of the national offender management service until expiry of the extended period.[66]

For purposes of dealing with dangerous offenders Lucraft states the preventive detention regime in the law of England and Wales as follow:

> "Both the extended determinate sentence and the life sentence under the CJA 2003 serve a public protection purpose, with Parole Board release mechanisms and licence periods enabling supervision and recall. Both are grounded in proportionality and offence seriousness and therefore the length of the sentence (or minimum as the case may be) are governed by an assessment of culpability and harm in the usual way…The public protection element therefore comes in the release mechanism of each sentence and additionally by way of the licence. Under the extended determinate sentence, offenders are eligible for release at the two-thirds point of the custodial term and entitled to be released at the expiry of the custodial term. Upon release, any remaining period of the custodial term is served on licence in addition to the extended licence period. Under the life sentence, offenders are eligible to be released at the expiry of the minimum term but are not entitled to be released at any point."[67]

Before a court imposes any sentence of discretionary life imprisonment, life imprisonment for a second listed offence or an extended sentence, it

---

66 *Ashworth* (n. 40), 242–243; Sentencing Council, "Extended Sentences" (2019), https://www.sentencingcouncil.org.uk/about-sentencing/types-of-sentence/extended-sentences (last visited 9 Sep 2019).

67 *Lucraft* et al., Archbold Criminal Pleading Evidence & Practice (71st ed. 2019), 797.

is required to make certain predictive findings about the offender. The court firstly has to determine whether there is a significant risk of the offender committing further specified offences and secondly whether there is a significant risk that such offences will cause serious harm to the public.[68] Assessing dangerousness and predicting risk are aspects that will be considered later.

3. Canada

The primary purpose of Canadian sentencing law is the protection of society.[69] Whilst it has rejected the approach of further detention following a determinate sentence, the country has nonetheless made provision for a specialised procedure for sentencing those offenders who pose a serious risk of reoffending. As Canadian preventive detention legislation dates back to 1947 several provisions thereof have been the subject of litigation which in turn provide clarity and certainty especially in respect of the constitutionality of preventive detention measures. For purposes of this discussion the Canadian approach to preventive detention and preventive supervision will be divided into three categories namely provisions relating to dangerous offenders, long-term offenders, and preventive recognizances.

a) Dangerous offenders

The Canadian Criminal Code[70] provides that if, on application by a prosecutor, a court is of the opinion that there are reasonable grounds to believe that an offender who is convicted of a serious personal injury offence[71] might be found to be a dangerous offender, the court shall before sentence

---

68 *Ashworth* (n. 40), 243–244.

69 *Manson* et al., Sentencing and Penal Policy in Canada – Cases, Materials and Commentary (5th ed. 2016), 660.

70 Section 752.1(1) of the Criminal Code.

71 The following offences, *inter alia,* qualify as serious personal injury offences in terms of Section 752 of the Criminal Code: an indictable offence involving the use or attempted use of violence against another person or conduct endangering or likely to endanger the life or safety of another person or inflicting or likely to inflict severe psychological damage to another person and for which the offender may be sentenced to imprisonment for 10 years or more. The offence of sexual assault is also included in this category.

is imposed, remand the offender for a maximum period of 60 days in the custody of a person designated by the court who can perform an assessment for use as evidence in an application for finding that the offender is a dangerous offender. If application is thereafter made on the basis of the requested report the court shall find the offender to be a dangerous offender if it is satisfied that the requirements set out in Section 753(1)(*a*) and (*b*) of the Criminal Code have been met.[72]

The court has three sentencing options after finding an offender to be a dangerous offender: (i) impose a sentence of detention in a penitentiary for an indeterminate period; or (ii) impose a sentence in respect of the offence for which the offender was convicted (which must be a minimum of 2 years imprisonment) and order that the offender be subject to supervision for a period not exceeding 10 years; or (iii) impose a sentence for the offence for which the offender has been convicted.[73] The Criminal Code is clear in its requirement that a court shall impose a sentence of indeterminate detention on a dangerous offender unless it is satisfied by evidence presented that there is a reasonable expectation that the lesser sentences mentioned in (ii) and (iii) will adequately protect the public

72 Section 753(1) requires that the court must be satisfied that the offence for which the offender was convicted is a personal injury offence and that the offender constitutes a threat to the life, safety or physical or mental well-being of other persons on the basis of evidence establishing, in relation to the offence for which he has been convicted: (i) a pattern of repetitive behavior by the offender showing a failure to restrain his behavior and a likelihood of causing death or injury or inflicting severe psychological damage on other persons, through failure in the future to restrain his behavior, or (ii) a pattern of persistent aggressive behavior showing a substantial degree of indifference on his part respecting the reasonably foreseeable consequences to other persons of his behavior, or (iii) any behavior by the offender that is of such a brutal nature as to compel the conclusion that it is in the future unlikely to be inhibited by normal standards of behavioral restraint, or (iv) that the offender has shown a failure to control his sexual impulses and a likelihood of causing injury, pain or other evil to other persons through failure to control his sexual impulses. In addition thereto Section 753(1.1) created a presumption that the requirements of Section 753(1)(*a*) and (*b*) have been met if the offence of which the offender has been convicted is a primary designated offence (including, *inter alia*, specified sexual offences, attempted murder, specified assaults and kidnapping) and that the offender has previously been convicted at least twice of a primary designated offence and sentenced to at least 2 years imprisonment for each of the convictions. Section 753(1.1) was subsequently found to infringe the principle of fundamental justice guaranteed in Section 7 of the Charter (*S v Hill* 2012 ONSC 5050, 291 CCC (3d) 321 para. 82).

73 Section 753(4) of the Criminal Code.

against the commission by the offender of murder or a serious personal injury offence.[74]

When a person was sentenced to detention for an indeterminate period the parole board must as soon as possible after expiry of 7 years from the day the person was taken into custody and not later than 2 years after the previous review, review the condition, history and circumstances of the offender in order to determine whether he should be granted parole and if so, on what conditions.[75]

The constitutionality of the dangerous offender regime was challenged in *R v Lyons:*[76]

> "The broad issues raised ... are whether the dangerous offenders provisions of the Criminal Code ... contravene the rights guaranteed by the Canadian Charter of Rights and Freedoms to 'liberty' and 'not to be deprived thereof except in accordance with the principles of fundamental justice' (s 7), 'not to be arbitrarily detained or imprisoned' (s 9), ... 'not to be subjected to any cruel and unusual treatment or punishment' (s 12), and if so whether they can be justified under s 1 of the Charter as being 'reasonable limits prescribed by law as can be demonstrably justified in a free and democratic society'."[77]

Two of the most important constitutional challenges pertained to the following: the appellant contented that the dangerous offender regime resulted in deprivation of liberty that is not in accordance with the principles of fundamental justice and thus in violation of Section 7 of the Charter in that it allowed a person to be sentenced for crimes which he had not committed or for crimes for which he had already been punished. This contention was rejected by the Canadian Supreme Court as it held that the prescribed punishment flowed from the actual commission of a specific crime which had been proved beyond a reasonable doubt.[78] In addition thereto the court made the following important observation confirming the protection of society as primary aim of Canadian sentencing law:

> "... it cannot be considered a violation of fundamental justice for Parliament to identify those offenders who, in the interests of protecting the public, ought to be sentenced according to considerations which

74 Section 753(4.2) of the Criminal Code.
75 Section 761(1) of the Criminal Code.
76 (1987) 2 SCR 309, 61 CR (3d) 1.
77 The *Lyons* case (n. 76) para. 1.
78 The *Lyons* case (n. 76) para. 25.

> are not entirely reactive or based on a 'just deserts' rationale. The imposition of a sentence which 'is partly punitive but is mainly imposed for the protection of the public' ... seems to me to accord with the fundamental purpose of the criminal law generally, and of sentencing in particular, namely, the protection of society. In a rational system of sentencing, the respective importance of prevention, deterrence, retribution and rehabilitation will vary according to the nature of the crime and the circumstances of the offender ...
> Part XXI merely enables the court to accommodate its sentence to the common sense reality that the *present* condition of the offender is such that he or she is not inhibited by normal standards of behavioural restraint, so that *future* violent acts can quite comfortably be expected of that person. In such circumstances it would be folly not to tailor the sentence accordingly."[79]

A second constitutional challenge raised contended that the dangerous-offender regime violated Section 12 of the Charter in that it "imposes a punishment that is unusually severe and serves no valid penological purpose more effectively than a less severe punishment (e.g. a determinate sentence)."[80] The Supreme Court, however, found that although an indeterminate sentence would in all probability be unconstitutional, in this instance the "parole process saves the legislation from being successfully challenged under s. 12, for it ensures that incarceration is imposed for only as long as the circumstances of the individual case require".[81]

It is therefore clear that the various challenges in Canada aimed at the constitutionality of the preventive detention of offenders based on the assessment of their future dangerousness, have been unsuccessful.

b) Long-term offenders

The Criminal Code provides for preventive detention after a court has found a person to be a long-term offender. In terms of this provision a court may on application, find an offender to be a long-term offender if it is satisfied that (i) it would be appropriate to impose a sentence of 2 years imprisonment or more in respect of the offence for which the offender has been convicted; (ii) there is a substantial risk that the offender will

79 The *Lyons* case (n. 76) paras. 26–27.
80 The *Lyons* case (n. 76) para. 37.
81 The *Lyons* case (n. 76) para. 49.

reoffend; and (iii) there is a reasonable possibility of eventual control of the risk in the community.[82] After finding an offender to be a long-term offender, the court shall sentence the offender in respect of the offence he has been convicted of to a period of at least 2 years imprisonment and order that the offender be subject to long-term community supervision for a period not exceeding 10 years.[83]

According to Manson this sentencing provision is aimed at sexual offenders as well as offenders convicted of serious personal injury offences and was intended to be a middle ground between an indeterminate sentence and an ordinary fixed-term sentence.[84] The aim with this sentencing regime was described in *R v Ipeelee* as protection of the public from the risk of re-offence as well as rehabilitation and reintegration of the offender into the community.[85]

c) Preventive recognizances

The Canadian Criminal Code provides for the situation when concerns arise about perceived dangerousness after completion of a sentence. The code provides for 5 post-sentence preventive mechanisms.[86] Application has to be made to a court to issue the preventive recognizance and may result in a recognizance for a period up to 12 months with specific conditions. This measure operates outside the trial and conviction procedure of a criminal trial and has been used to acquire post-sentence control in the community over individuals with a criminal history.[87]

---

82 Section 753.1(1) of the Criminal Code.

83 Section 753.1(3) of the Criminal Code.

84 *Manson* et al. (n. 69), 727–728, 742. Also see *R v Weasel* 2003 SKCA 131, 181 CCC (3d) 358 para. 52. The National Parole Board of Canada may include any condition in the supervision of the offender that is regarded as reasonable and necessary to protect society and to facilitate the successful reintegration of the offender into society (see *R v Ipeelee* 2012 SCC 13, [2012] 1 SCR 433).

85 N. 84, para. 48.

86 It provides for the scenario where fear exists that a person will commit one of the following offences: a criminal organization offence (Section 810.01); a terrorism offence (Section 810.011); a sexual offence against a child (Section 810.1); a forced marriage of a person under 16 years of age (Section 810.02); and a serious personal injury offence (Section 810.2).

87 *Manson* et al. (n. 69), 660.

4. Germany

Life imprisonment is the most severe punishment available in Germany. In addition thereto post-sentence preventive detention is available as a preventive measure for dangerous offenders. Some authors argue that post-sentence preventive detention is, similar to life imprisonment, the harshest sanction available in German criminal law.[88] This contribution will consider both options but focus more specifically on the underlying philosophy and implementation of preventive detention.

a) Life imprisonment

The German Criminal Code (*Strafgesetzbuch* – StGB) provides for fixed term imprisonment not exceeding 15 years or for life imprisonment which may be imposed in respect of a variety of offences.[89] An offender serving life imprisonment may be released on parole after a minimum period of 15 years.[90] Mandatory life imprisonment is reserved for murder committed under aggravating circumstances.[91]

The German Federal Constitutional Court affirmed that life imprisonment does not violate the fundamental principle of human dignity as contained in the Basic Law.[92] The court, however, reiterated that all life

---

88 See *Dünkel* and *Van Zyl Smit,* 5 German L.J. 2004, 619.

89 Section 38 StGB. See *Dessecker,* in: Van Zyl Smit and Appleton (eds.), Life Imprisonment and Human Rights (1st ed. 2016) 411, 412; *Watney* (n. 35), 402.

90 Section 57a StGB; *Weigend,* in: Heller and Dubber (eds.), The Handbook of Comparative Criminal Law (1st ed. 2011), 252, 275. *Demleitner,* in: Dubber and Hörnle (eds.), The Oxford Handbook of Criminal Law (1st ed. 2014), 941 remarks: "Life sentences in Germany [...] rarely mean a life-long sentence but presumptively end with release upon parole after 15 to 18 years" (952).

91 *Bohlander,* Principles of German Criminal Law (1st ed. 2009), 188–189; Section 211 StGB. Aggravating circumstances include, *inter alia,* a person who kills another for pleasure, for sexual gratification, out of greed, by stealth or cruelly or by means that pose a danger to the public or in order to cover up another offence.

92 BVerfG, Judgment of 21 Jun 1977, 1 BvL 14/76, BVerfGE 45, 187. This principle was also confirmed in BVerfG, Decision of 08 Nov 2006, 2 BvR 578/02, 2 BvR 796/02, BVerfGE 117, 71 in which the Constitutional Court had to consider the position of two offenders convicted of aggravated murder with a sexual element and who have been in custody for more than 30 years due to unfavourable predictions of dangerousness. The court ruled that these long periods of imprisonment violated neither the principle of human dignity nor the right to liberty; *Dessecker* (n. 89), 415, 422.

prisoners have the right that their earlier release be considered according to set procedures and that detention be aimed at rehabilitation and eventual resocialisation in the community.[93] The court with jurisdiction over the execution of sentences (*Strafvollstreckungskammer*) has the final say as to whether an offender may be conditionally released from life imprisonment.[94]

b) Post-sentence preventive detention

The concept of preventive detention in Germany is explained as follows:

> "Every society faces the age-old problem of what to do with prisoners about to complete their jail terms but whose mental state or reputation for lawlessness poses a continuing threat to society … the federal government and several states (Länder) had passed laws extending the confinement of prisoners – sex offenders in particular – who are resistant to rehabilitation and likely to repeat their crimes."[95]

Preventive detention (*Sicherungsverwahrung*) is a measure available in terms of Section 66 StGB intended for the post-sentence secure confinement in prison of an offender who due to the propensity to commit serious offences resulting in serious emotional trauma or physical injury to the victim, poses a danger to the general public.[96] Merkel indicates that the aim of preventive detention "is not the retribution for past offences, but solely the protection of society from future harm".[97] An order for preventive detention may be issued by a court during the sentencing phase (Section 66) or a court may defer the decision whether to issue such an order to no later than 6 months before the date of early conditional release (Section 66a) or the court may make the order before the expiry of the offender's term of imprisonment (Section 66b). A judicial review of the preventive

93 *Van Zyl Smit,* in: Dubber and Hörnle (eds.), The Oxford Handbook of Criminal Law (1st ed. 2014), 1007; *Kommers* and *Miller,* The Constitutional Jurisprudence of the Federal Republic of Germany (3rd ed. 2012), 366.

94 See *Watney* (n. 35), 402; *Dessecker* (n. 89), 418; *Beyens, Snacken* and *Van Zyl Smit,* in: Daems, Van Zyl Smit and Snacken (eds.), European Penology? (1st ed. 2017), 271, 286.

95 *Kommers* and *Miller* (n. 93), 371.

96 *Dessecker* (n. 89), indicates that preventive detention has been imposed most often in respect of sexual and violent offenders (413). *Bohlander,* The German Criminal Code – A Modern English Translation (2008), 61.

97 *Merkel,* 11 German L.J. 2010, 1046, 1048.

detention is undertaken every 2 years and every year in respect of detainees whose preventive detention period exceed 10 years.[98]

Dessecker indicates that although life imprisonment and preventive detention are both potentially indefinite criminal sanctions, their legal foundations are completely different: whereas a life sentence is based on the degree of the offender's guilt, preventive detention forms part of a category of criminal sanctions other than punishment and which is based on the assumption of dangerousness.[99]

The distinction drawn in German law between penalties (*Strafen*) and measures of correction and protection (*Massregeln der Besserung und Sicherung*) which forms the basis of the distinction between life imprisonment and preventive detention, was scrutinised by the ECtHR in *M v Germany.*[100] M was sentenced to 5 years imprisonment on a charge of attempted murder and robbery and to the maximum of 10 years preventive detention in terms of the law at the time. The law was subsequently amended to allow for the imposition of indefinite preventive detention and this was retrospectively imposed on M. The German Constitutional Court held that preventive detention was not a penalty but rather of purely preventative nature as it aimed to protect the public against dangerous offenders and as such the new law could be applied retrospectively to M, resulting in his indefinite detention. The ECtHR however disagreed and ruled that an order for preventive detention was a penalty and as such contrary to Section 7 of the ECHR that provides "7(1) [n]or shall a heavier penalty be imposed than the one that was applicable at the time the criminal offence was committed".[101] The ECtHR concluded that:

> "Furthermore, having regard to the realities of the situation of persons in preventive detention, the Court cannot subscribe to the Government's argument … that preventive detention served a purely preventive, and no punitive, purpose. It notes that, pursuant to Article 66 of the Criminal Code, preventive orders may be made only against persons who have repeatedly been found guilty of criminal offences of a certain gravity. It observes, in particular, that there appear to be no special measures, instruments or institutions in place, other than those available to ordinary long-term prisoners, directed at persons

---

98 *Dessecker* (n. 89), 423.

99 *Dessecker* (n. 89), 413.

100 (2010) 51 EHRR 41 976.

101 *Ashworth* and *Zedner* (n. 1), 166. And as such also a violation of the *nulla poena sine lege* principle (*Dessecker* [n. 89], 424).

> subject to preventive detention and aimed at reducing the danger they present and thus at limiting the duration of their detention to what is strictly necessary in order to prevent them from committing further offences."[102]

As a result the ECtHR found that the offender's Section 7 ECHR rights which prohibit retrospective application of legislation had been infringed.[103]

Subsequent to this finding of the ECtHR, the German Federal Constitutional Court (*Bundesverfassungsgericht* – BVerfG) in its decision of 4 May 2011 attempted to differentiate between imprisonment as a penalty and preventive detention as a measure of rehabilitation and incapacitation in a more sophisticated manner. Recognising that preventive detention presents a serious interference of the right to liberty the court stressed that application of preventive detention must differ substantially from the enforcement of an ordinary prison sentence.[104] The court also provided a set of standards to the legislature in order to develop a comprehensive concept of preventive detention.[105] The legislature was given a 2 year period to introduce a version of preventive detention that would comply with constitutional requirements.[106] One of the practical measures that was implemented resulted in the construction of separate detention facilities on existing prison premises for detainees.[107]

---

102 The *M v Germany* case (n. 100) para. 128.

103 *Vormbaum* and *Bohlander*, A Modern History of German Criminal Law (1st ed. 2014), 253; *Harris, O'Boyle* and *Warbrick*, Law of the European Convention on Human Rights (4th ed. 2014), 497, n. 54; *Merkel* (n. 97), 1052–1053; *Andenas* and *Bjorge*, 105 Am. J. Int'l L. 2011, 768, 769–770. This approach was confirmed by the ECtHR in *Haidn v Germany*, Judgment of 13 Jan 2011, No. 6587/04, ECLI:CE:ECHR:2011:0113JUD000658704. See *Merkel*, 12 German L.J. 2011, 968, 972–973.

104 *Ambos*, European Criminal Law (1st ed. 2018), 132; *Alexander, Graf* and *Janus*, 29 Ariz. J. Int'l & Comp. L. 2012, 605, 620–622.

105 *Dessecker* (n. 89), 425–426. These standards, *inter alia*, include that preventive detention should only be considered as a last resort, it must be aimed at liberty and directed to therapeutic treatment, measures to relax the conditions of detention should be part of the treatment program and enforcement of detention has to be reviewed within one year by a court and thereafter every year.

106 *Dessecker* (n. 89), 426.

107 *Watney* (n. 35), 404.

III. Discussion

The challenge presented by dangerous repeat offenders is a universal phenomenon and the preventative measures taken in respect thereof can be traced back to developments in the criminal justice system of the eighteenth- and nineteen-century.[108] The challenge is, however, treated differently by the traditional legal systems with post-sentence preventive detention preferred in some jurisdictions such as Germany as opposed to the imposition of indeterminate sentences as well as long-term community based supervision orders in other jurisdictions.[109]

The state's duty to protect its citizens against violent crime and other human rights infringements can be derived from either the common-law or constitutional provisions.[110] Ashworth and Zedner indicate, with reference to *Van Colle v United Kingdom*[111] and *Osman v United Kingdom*,[112] that "there will be a breach of the positive obligation if the authorities knew or ought to have known at the time of a real and immediate risk to the life of an identified individual ... from the criminal acts of a third party if they failed to take measures within the scope of their powers which ... might have been expected to avoid that risk".[113] The constitutional duty owed by the police to protect the public in general against an invasion of their fundamental rights by perpetrators of violent crime, was also emphasised in the South African context.[114]

Various human rights instruments protect the right to liberty and security, but set limitations in this regard. Section 12 of the South African constitution for example provides for freedom and security of the person, but subject to the limitations contained in Section 36[115] whilst Article 5 of the ECHR guarantees the right to liberty and security but allows for detention post-conviction when it is reasonably considered necessary to prevent an individual from committing an offence.[116]

---

108 *Ashworth* and *Zedner* (n. 1), 49.
109 *Ambos* (n. 104), 105.
110 *Burchell*, Principles of Criminal Law (5th ed. 2016), 83–84.
111 (2013) 56 EHRR 23.
112 (1998) 29 EHRR 245.
113 *Ashworth and Zednar* (n. 2), 146, 148.
114 The *Carmichele* case (n. 3) para. 62.
115 Section 36 of the constitution allows for limitation of the Section 12 rights, but only in terms of law of general application "to the extent that the limitation is reasonable and justifiable in an open and democratic society based on human dignity, equality and freedom".
116 Article 5.1(c) ECHR; *Ashworth* and *Zedner* (n. 1), 145.

Ashworth points out that although prospects are poor to predict correctly whether a person will re-offend, the imposition of disproportionate sentences remains popular with especially politicians in the hope of protecting society against dangerous offenders.[117] Justification for disproportionate deprivation of liberty could perhaps be found in the following comment by Ashworth on some of the conclusions made by the Floud Committee:[118]

> "The Floud Committee concluded that the question is really a matter of the just redistribution of risk, between a known offender and a potential victim of a predicted offence. It is a moral choice between competing claims: who should bear the risk? Generally, they argued, everyone is presumed to be harmless. But once a person has manifested, by committing a serious crime, the capacity to be harmful to others, that presumption no longer applies. It may therefore be justifiable to redistribute the risk of future harms by protecting the potential victims (who are unlikely to have lost the presumption of harmlessness) and by burdening the known offender (who has lost the benefit of that presumption). Although they proposed various procedural safeguards for defendants before a protective sentence could be imposed, the Committee concluded that the redistribution of risk should favour potential victims."[119]

The risk that arises in this regard is that courts will emphasise the offender's record and downplay the current offence with the result that a disproportionate sentence will be imposed with prevention as main aim.[120] As citizens correctly demand greater protection from dangerous offenders the question arises whether the answer is to be found in preventive detention. The immediate challenge that arises when undue emphasis is placed on preventive measures involve a weakening of the aims and principles of justice and more particularly constitutional principles relating to the freedom and security of the individual. How is balance to be achieved between the rights of individual offenders *vis-à-vis* the rights of the community to

117 *Ashworth* (n. 40), 246. See *Ashworth* and *Zedner* (n. 1), 22, n. 57 who confirms that predictions of serious harm are more frequently wrong than right as well as the authorities they refer to.

118 The Howard League for Penal Reform established a research group on the dangerous offender in 1976 which produced a report *Floud* and *Young*, Dangerousness and Criminal Justice (1981). Also see *Ashworth* and *Zedner* (n. 1), 22–23.

119 *Ashworth* (n. 40), 247.

120 *Ashworth* (n. 40), 248.

live in a free and secure environment? Ashworth and Zedner refer in this regard to the possibility of imposing less invasive, non-custodial sentences that still restrict liberty but which may nonetheless be utilised successfully as an alternative to detention.[121]

In comparing the positions in various jurisdictions it is clear that a one size fits all approach is not feasible. The South African provision of declaring a convicted person as a dangerous criminal appears to be a sentencing option with considerable benefits in that it allows for a court to make the ultimate decision as to the release of the offender. It allows, *inter alia*, a court to monitor the rehabilitation of the offender and to decide whether he is indeed still a danger to society. It is suggested that the courts are in a better position to perform such an assessment. Release on parole after imposition of life imprisonment on the other hand, involves a correctional supervision and parole board, the National Council for Correctional Services and ultimately the Minister of Justice and Correctional Services. Criticism of the competence of the parole boards and involvement of political role players in parole decisions has been expressed elsewhere.[122] From a constitutional point of view the South African courts have placed a clear emphasis on the proportionality of the sentence in relation to the offence committed. This approach was clearly illustrated in the interpretation the courts attached to the applicable legislation in respect of both habitual criminals as well as dangerous criminals. In addition thereto the courts have clearly articulated the duty of the state to protect society from the unreformed recidivist serious offender, if need be with a sentence for life.

In England and Wales the now repealed provisions of imprisonment for public protection serve as an example of the undesirable results that follow when public protection is overemphasised and the importance of proportionality in sentencing understated. The imposition of a whole life order in that jurisdiction presents with the difficulties highlighted in the *Vinter* case which have, despite the subsequent decisions in the *McLoughlin* and *Hutchinson* cases, not been resolved satisfactorily. As such the whole life order provision still remains to a large extent in conflict with Article 3 of the ECHR. The use of extended sentences in England and Wales has the benefit to allow for the offender to rehabilitate in the community but still

121 *Ashworth* and *Zedner* (n. 1), refer, *inter alia,* to curfew orders with electronic monitoring, prohibited activities, residence requirements, mental health, drug and alcohol treatment requirements, supervision requirement and attendance centre requirements (154–155).

122 See *Watney* (n. 36), 100–104 and the authorities cited.

under official supervision. This measure shows strong resemblance to the Canadian long-term offenders' provision.

The dangerous offender provisions in Canadian law have been extensively scrutinised by the courts in that country and are probably the most constitutionally sound of all the systems considered.[123] The relevant legislation pertaining to an indeterminate sentence clearly provides for those aspects pertaining to constitutionality which have evaded the whole life orders regime of England. In addition thereto the Canadian provisions relating to long-term offenders and preventive recognizances are aimed at addressing the challenge of dangerous offenders in the least intrusive manner with emphasis on measures other than detention. Successful application of these provisions would obviously require that an effective and sophisticated system is in place to monitor these type of offenders within the community appropriately.

The German procedures in respect of earlier release and the aims to rehabilitate and reintegrate, ensure that life imprisonment in that jurisdiction is not in violation of the fundamental principle of human dignity and therefore constitutional. Decisions relating to conditional release from life sentences are taken by a specialist court which ensures both a non-political as well as judicial interrogation of the relevant considerations. As a result of the guidance provided by the ECtHR the initially questionable German position relating to post-sentence preventive detention is in the process to be normalised. A clear distinction is now being drawn between an ordinary prison sentence and preventive detention and the practical treatment of offenders subject to preventive measures.

Ashworth and Zedner remark that "[t]he duty to protect the public is always liable to be laid down as a trump card. Preventive justice does not contest this duty, but it does contest its claim to outplay all other values and insists that preventive measures should be subject to restraining principles".[124] Their comment summarises the crux of the preventive detention debate and as communities grapple with this challenge, much can be learnt from the various approaches adopted internationally. It is, however, clear that the universally accepted human rights principles applicable to all members of society should inform this important function of the criminal justice system.

---

123 With exception of the Canadian Parole Board which still forms part of a government ministry and which is therefore under political control. See *Watney* (n. 36), 101–102.

124 *Ashworth* and *Zedner* (n. 1), 266.

Bibliography

Laurie Ackermann, Human Dignity: Lodestar for Equality in South Africa (Juta, Cape Town 2012).

Shawn Alexander, Leah Graf and *Eric Janus*, "M v Germany: The European Court of Human Rights Takes a Critical Look at Preventive Detention", 29 Arizona Journal of International and Comparative Law (Ariz. J. Int'l & Comp. L.) 2012, 605.

Kai Ambos, European Criminal Law (Cambridge University Press, 1st ed., Cambridge 2018).

Mads Andenas and *Eirik Bjorge*, "Preventive Detention", 105 American Journal of International Law (Am. J. Int'l L.) 2011, 768.

Catherine Appleton and *Dirk van Zyl Smit*, "The Paradox of Reform: Life Imprisonment in England and Wales", in: Dirk van Zyl Smit and Catherine Appleton (eds.), Life Imprisonment and Human Rights (Hart Publishing, Oxford and Portland, Oregon 2016), 217.

Andrew Ashworth, Sentencing and Criminal Justice (Cambridge University Press, 6th ed., Cambridge 2015).

Andrew Ashworth and *Lucia Zedner*, Preventive Justice (Oxford University Press, Oxford 2014).

Kristel Beyens, Sonja Snacken and *Dirk van Zyl Smit*, "Truth in (the Implementation of) Sentencing: Belgium and Elsewhere", in: Daems, Van Zyl Smit and Snacken (eds.), European Penology? (Hart Publishing, Oxford and Portland, 1st ed., Oregon 2017), 271.

Michael Bohlander, The German Criminal Code – A Modern English Translation (Hart Publishing, Oxford and Portland, Oregon 2008).

Michael Bohlander, Principles of German Criminal Law (Hart Publishing, Oxford and Portland, 1st ed., Oregon 2009).

Jonathan Burchell, Principles of Criminal Law (Juta, 3rd ed., Cape Town 2005).

Jonathan Burchell, Principles of Criminal Law (Juta, 5th ed., Cape Town 2016).

Iain Currie and *Johan de* Waal, The Bill of Rights Handbook (Juta, 6th ed., Cape Town 2013).

Nora Demleitner, "Types of Punishment", in: Dubber and Hörnle (eds.), The Oxford Handbook of Criminal Law (Oxford University Press, Oxford 2014), 942.

Axel Dessecker, "Constitutional Limits on Life Imprisonment and Post-Sentence Preventive Detention in Germany", in: Dirk van Zyl Smit and Catherine Appleton (eds.), Life Imprisonment and Human Rights (Hart Publishing, Oxford and Portland, Oregon 2016), 411.

Johannes Christiaan de Wet, De Wet en Swanepoel Strafreg (Butterworth, 4th ed., Durban 1985).

Frieder Dünkel and *Dirk van Zyl Smit*, "Preventive Detention of Dangerous Offenders Re-examined: A Comment on two decisions of the German Federal Constitutional Court and the Federal draft Bill on Preventive Detention of 9 March 2004", 5 German Law Journal (German L.J.) 2004, 619.

Etienne du Toit, Frederick de Jager, Andrew Paizes, Andrew St Q Skeen, Steph van der Merwe and *Stephan Terblanche*, Commentary on the Criminal Procedure Act (Juta, service 61, Cape Town 2019).

Jill Harries, Law and Crime in the Roman World (Cambridge University Press, New York 2007).

David Harris, Michael O'Boyle, Ed Bates and *Carla Buckley*, Law of the European Convention on Human Rights (Oxford University Press, 4th ed., Oxford 2018).

Donald Kommers and *Russel Miller*, The Constitutional Jurisprudence of the Federal Republic of Germany (Duke University Press, 3rd ed., Durham and London 2012).

Albert Kruger, Hiemstra's Criminal Procedure (LexisNexis, service 11, Durban 2018).

Andrew Lintott, "Crime and Punishment", in: David Johnston (ed.), The Cambridge Companion to Roman Law (Cambridge University Press, New York 2015), 301.

Mark Lucraft, Gregory Dickinson, Linda Dobbs, Nicholas Hilliard et al., Archbold Criminal Pleading Evidence & Practice (Sweet & Maxwell, 71st ed., London 2019).

Allan Manson, Patrick Healey, Gary Trotter, Julian Roberts and *Dale Ives*, Sentencing and Penal Policy in Canada – Cases, Materials and Commentary (Emond, 3rd ed., Toronto 2016).

Natasa Mavronicola, "Inhuman and Degrading Punishment, Dignity, and the Limits of Retribution", Modern Law Review 2014, 292.

Grischa Merkel, "Incompatible Contrasts – Preventive Detention in Germany and the European Convention on Human Rights", 11 German Law Journal (German L.J.) 2010, 1046.

Grischa Merkel, "Retrospective Preventive Detention in Germany: A Comment on the ECHR Decision Haidn v Germany", 12 German Law Journal (German L.J.) 2011, 968.

Ig Rautenbach, Rautenbach-Malherbe Constitutional Law (LexisNexis, 6th ed., Durban 2012).

Sentencing Council, "Extended Sentences" (2019), https:// www.sentencingcouncil.org.uk/about-sentencing/types-of-sentence/extended-sentences (last visited 9 Sep 2019).

Carol S. Steiker, "The Limits of the Preventive State", Journal of Criminal Law and Criminology 1998, 771.

Nico Steytler, Constitutional Criminal Procedure – A Commentary on the Constitution of the Republic of South Africa, 1996 (LexisNexis, 1st ed., Durban 1998).

Stephan Terblanche, A Guide to Sentencing in South Africa (LexisNexis, 3rd ed., Durban 2016).

Dirk van Zyl Smit, "Prison Law", in: Dubber and Hörnle (eds.), The Oxford Handbook of Criminal Law (Oxford University Press, 1st ed., Oxford 2014), 988.

Thomas Vormbaum and *Michael Bohlander*, A Modern History of German Criminal Law (Springer, 1st ed., Heidelberg, New York, Dordrecht, London 2014).

Martin Wasik, A Practical Approach to Sentencing (Oxford University Press, 5th ed., Oxford 2014).

Murdoch Watney, "Assessment of the South African parole system", Tydskrif vir die Suid-Afrikaanse Reg (TSAR) 2017, 704 and Tydskrif vir die Suid-Afrikaanse Reg (TSAR) 2018, 88.

Murdoch Watney, "Enkele gedagtes oor lewenslange gevangenisstraf en die lot van die verste gevallenes", Tydskrif vir die Suid-Afrikaanse Reg (TSAR) 2018, 389.

Thomas Weigend, "Germany", in: Heller and Dubber (eds.), The Handbook of Comparative Criminal Law (Stanford University Press, Stanford California 2011), 252.*Michael Tonry*, Retributivism has a Past. Has it a Future? (Oxford University Press, Oxford 2011).

Register of cases

South Africa

AK v Minister of Safety and Security 2019 (1) SACR 529 (ECP).

Carmichele v Minister of Safety and Security (Centre for Applied Legal Studies Intervening) 2002 (1) SACR 79 (CC).

Naidu v Minister of Correctional Services 2017 (2) SACR 14 (WCC).

S v Bull; S v Chavulla 2001 2 SACR 681 (SCA).

S v Makwanyane 1995 3 SA 391 (CC).

S v Nawaseb 1980 1 SA 339 (SWA).

S v Niemand 2001 2 SACR 654 (CC).

European Court for Human Rights (ECtHR)

Haidn v Germany, Judgment of 13 Jan 2011, No. 6587/04, ECLI:CE:ECHR:2011:0113JUD000658704.

Hutchinson v United Kingdom (2015) 61 EHRR 13 393.

James, Wells and Lee v United Kingdom (2013) 56 EHRR 399.

M v Germany (2010) 51 EHRR 41 976.

Osman v United Kingdom (1998) 29 EHRR 245.

Van Colle v United Kingdom (2013) 56 EHRR 23.

Vinter v United Kingdom (2012) 55 EHRR 43 1003.

England and Wales

R (Haney, Kaiyam and Massey) v The Secretary of State for Justice 2014 UKSC 66.
R v Newell; R v McLoughlin 2014 EWCA Crim 188.

Canada

S v Hill 2012 ONSC 5050, 291 CCC (3d) 321.
R v Ipeelee 2012 SCC 13, (2012) 1 SCR 433.
R v Lyons (1987) 2 SCR 309, 61 CR (3d) 1.
R v Weasel 2003 SKCA 131, 181 CCC (3d) 358.

Germany

BVerfG, Judgment of 21 Jun 1977, 1 BvL 14/76, BVerfGE 45, 187.
BVerfG, Decision of 08 Nov 2006, 2 BvR 578/02, 2 BvR 796/02, BVerfGE 117, 71.

The Legislative Possibilities and Challenges Relating to the Private Possession and Use of Cannabis in South Africa

Kgomotso Mokoena[*]

Abstract: Even prior to 18 September 2018, cannabis was the most commonly used illicit substance in South Africa, having been prohibited by a suite of legislative provisions, which provided for the criminalization of its use, possession and sale. In South Africa, the National Survey of Youth Risk Behaviour indicated that 12,8 % of South African students in grades 8–10 have used cannabis and 9,2 % of those in the last month. A further study, the South African Stress and Health Study (SASH), surveyed 400 adults and found 8,4 % lifetime use. So it is clear that use of cannabis recreationally is fairly common amongst South Africans. The Constitutional Court, per Zondo ACJ, delivered a judgment which some of have criticised as creating more questions than answers. Although the judgment quite clearly decriminalises the use, cultivation and possession of cannabis for private purposes, the question of what constitutes "private" brings the judgment quite squarely into the terrain of a number of different areas of law.

* Kgomotso Mokoena, *B.A., LL.B., LL.M. (Wits)*, Lecturer, Faculty of Law, University of Johannesburg.

I. Prefatory comments

Prior to 18 September 2018, cannabis was the most commonly used illicit substance in South Africa, having been prohibited by a suite of legislative provisions, which provided for the criminalisation of its use, possession and sale. In South Africa, the National Survey of Youth Risk Behaviour indicated that 12,8 % of South African students in grades 8–10 have used cannabis and 9,2 % of those in the last month.[1] A further study, the South African Stress and Health Study (SASH), surveyed 400 adults and found 8,4 % lifetime use. Therefore, it is clear that use of cannabis recreationally is fairly common amongst South Africans.

The Constitutional Court, per Zondo ACJ, delivered a judgment which some have criticised as creating more questions than answers. Although the judgment quite clearly decriminalises the use, cultivation and possession of cannabis for private purposes, the question of what constitutes "private" brings the judgment quite squarely into the terrain of a number of different areas of law.

This chapter will consider extensively the judgments of both the High Court and the Constitutional Court in light of the right to privacy. Specifically, I will consider the gap left by the Court in relation to how long cannabis stays in the system and how employers may be able to ascertain whether their employees are under the influence of cannabis at work. The central question then is whether a positive test result of an employee can trigger disciplinary action if an employee is able to perform his or her tasks.

II. Introduction

This matter was first heard in the High Court[2] and dealt primarily with the constitutional validity of two key pieces of legislation. The first is the Drugs and Drug Trafficking Act (the Drugs Act),[3] specifically Sections 4(b) and 5(b), and the second is the Medicines and Related Substances Control Act (the Medicines Act),[4] specifically Sections 22A(9)(a)(i) and 22A(10).

---

1 World Health Organization, The health and social effects of nonmedical cannabis use, Report (2016), https://www.who.int/substance_abuse/publications/cannabis_report/en/ (last visited 13 Nov 2019).

2 *Prince v Minister of Justice* [2017] ZAWCHC 30; 2017 4 SA 299 (WCC).

3 Drugs and Drug Trafficking Act No. 140 of 1992.

4 Medicines and Related Substances Control Act No. 101 of 1965.

In essence Section 4(b)[5] of the Drugs Act prohibits the use or possession of any dangerous dependence-producing substance unless one or more

---

5 "No person shall use or have in his possession— ... (b) any dangerous dependence-producing substance or any undesirable dependence-producing substance, unless —

(i) he is a patient who has acquired or bought any such substance—
(aa) from a medical practitioner, dentist or practitioner acting in his professional capacity and in accordance with the requirements of the Medicines Act or any regulation made thereunder; or
(bb) from a pharmacist in terms of an oral instruction or prescription in writing of such medical practitioner, dentist or practitioner,
and uses that substance for medical purposes under the care or treatment of the said medical practitioner, dentist or practitioner;
(ii) he has acquired or brought any substance for medical purposes—
(aa) from a medical practitioner, veterinarian, dentist or practitioner acting in his professional capacity and in accordance with the requirements of the Medicines Act or any regulation made thereunder;
(bb) from a pharmacist in terms of an oral instruction or a prescription in writing of such medical practitioner, veterinarian, dentist or practitioner; or
(cc) from veterinary assistant or veterinary nurse in terms of a prescription in writing of such veterinarian,
with the intent to administer that substance to a patient or animal under the care treatment of the said medical practitioner, veterinarian, dentist or practitioner;
(iii) he is the Director-General: Welfare who has acquired or bought any such substance in accordance with the requirements of the Medicines Act or any regulation made thereunder;
(iv) he, she or it is a patient, medical practitioner, veterinarian, dentist, practitioner, nurse, midwife, nursing assistant, pharmacist, veterinary assistant, veterinary nurse, manufacturer of, or wholesale dealer in, pharmaceutical products, importer or exporter, or any other person contemplated in the Medicines Act or any regulation made thereunder, who or which has acquired, bought, imported, cultivated, collected or manufactured, or uses or is in possession of, or intends to administer, supply, sell, transmit or export any such substance in accordance with the requirements or conditions of the said Act or regulation, or any permit issued to him, her or it under the said Act or regulation;
(v) he is an employee of a pharmacist, manufacturer of, or wholesale dealer in, pharmaceutical products, importer or exporter who has acquired, bought, imported, cultivated, collected or manufactured, or uses or is in possession of, or intends to supply, sell, transmit or export any such substance in the course of his employment and in accordance with the requirements or conditions of the Medicines Act or any regulation made thereunder, or any permit issued to such pharmacist, manufacturer of, or wholesale dealer in, pharmaceutical products, importer or exporter under the said Act or regulation; or

exceptions apply, whereas Section 5(b)[6] prohibits dealing in the same substances as those mentioned in Section 4(b).

Section 22A(10) of the Medicines Act[7] in essence prohibits the sale or administration of any "scheduled substance or medicine" for any purposes

---

(vi) he has otherwise come into possession of any such substance in a lawful manner.".

6 "No person shall deal in— …

(b) any dangerous dependence-producing substance or any undesirable dependence producing substance, unless—
  (i) he has acquired or bought any such substance for medical purposes—
    (aa) from a medical practitioner, veterinarian, dentist or practitioner acting in his professional capacity and in accordance with the requirements of the Medicines Act or any regulation made thereunder;
    (bb) from a pharmacist in terms of an oral instruction or a prescription in writing of such medical practitioner, veterinarian, dentist or practitioner; or
    (cc) from a veterinary assistant or veterinary nurse in terms of a prescription in writing of such veterinarian, and administers that substance to a patient or animal under the care or treatment of the said medical practitioner, veterinarian, dentist or practitioner;
  (ii) he is the Director-General: Welfare who acquires, buys or sells any such substance in accordance with the requirements of the Medicines Act or any regulation made thereunder;
  (iii) he, she or it is a medical practitioner, veterinarian, dentists, practitioner, nurse, midwife, nursing assistant, pharmacist, veterinary nurse, manufacturer or, or wholesale dealer in, pharmaceutical products, importer or exporter, or any other person contemplated in the Medicines Act or any regulation made thereunder, who or which prescribes, administers, acquires, buys, transships, imports, cultivates, collects, manufactures, supplies, sells, transmits or exports any such substance in accordance with the requirements or conditions of the said Act or regulations, or any permit issued to him, her or it under the said Act or regulation; or
  (iv) he is an employee of a pharmacists, manufacturer of, or wholesale dealer in, pharmaceutical products, importer or exporter who acquires, buys, transships, imports, cultivates, collects, manufacturers, supplies, sells, transmits or exports any such substance in the course of his employment and in accordance with the requirements or conditions of the Medicines Act or any regulation made thereunder, or any permit issued to such pharmacist, manufacturer of, or wholesale dealer in, pharmaceutical products, importer or exporter under the said Act or regulation.".

7 Section 22A(10) of the Medicines Act reads as follows: "Notwithstanding anything to the contrary contained in this Section, no person shall sell or administer any Scheduled substance or medicine for [any purpose] other than medicinal purposes: Provided that the Minister may, subject to the conditions or requirements stated in such authority, authorize the administration outside any hospital of any Scheduled

outside of medical purposes, whereas Section 22A(9)(a)(i), when read with Schedule 7 of GN R509 of 2003, amounts to a prohibition of the acquisition, use, possession, manufacture or supply of cannabis (amongst other substances).[8]

III. In the High Court[9]

The crux of the application in the High Court was that the court was required to determine whether the infringement of the right to privacy, as enshrined in Section 14 of the Constitution,[10] by the impugned provisions, was justifiable in terms of Section 36 of the Constitution. Section 14 reads as follows:

> "14. Privacy — Everyone has the right to privacy which includes the right not to have —
>
> (a) their person or home searched;
> (b) their property searched;
> (c) their possessions seized; or
> (d) the privacy of their communications infringed."

The writer will consider relevant case law in respect of the overall reach of the right to privacy generally, and the workplace specifically, more extensively at a later stage.

Returning to the questions the High Court sought to answer in this matter: as is required by the Constitution, the Court focused on whether or not the impugned provisions violated the right to privacy in a manner

---

substance or medicine for the satisfaction or relief of a habit or craving to the person referred to in such authority.".

8 Section 22A(9)(a)(i) of the Medicines Act reads as follows: "No person shall— (i) acquire, use, possess, manufacture or supply any Schedule 7 or Schedule 8 substance, or manufacture any specified Schedule 5 or Schedule 6 substance unless he or she has been issued with a permit by the Director-General for such acquisition, use, possession, manufacture, or supply: Provided that the Director-General may, subject to such conditions as he or she may determine, acquire or authorise the use of any Schedule 7 or Schedule 8 substance in order to provide a medical practitioner, analyst, researcher or veterinarian therewith on the prescribed conditions for the treatment or prevention of a medical condition in a particular patient, or for the purposes of education, analysis or research."

9 *Prince v Minister of Justice* [2017] ZAWCHC 30; 2017 4 SA 299 (WCC).

10 Constitution of the Republic of South Africa Act No. 108 of 1996 (hereafter referred to as the Constitution).

that was justifiable in terms of Section 36 of the Constitution. Before this, it had to determine whether the impugned provisions violated the right to privacy. It came to this very conclusion, stating in essence that the breach or violation was only “tepidly” contested by the opposing parties and the court ought to accept that a breach in fact exists.[11]

The rights outlined in the Bill of Rights may only be limited by a law of general application to the extent that the limitation is reasonable and justifiable in an open and democratic society based on human dignity, equality and freedom.[12] In undertaking this analysis a court must consider the nature of the right,[13] the importance of the purpose of the limitation,[14] the nature and extent of the limitation,[15] the relationship between the limitation and its purpose,[16] and whether there are any less restrictive means to achieve the said purpose.[17]

The perspective of the state rested on the importance and purpose of the limitation as well as the relation between the limitation and its purpose. The state argued that it advanced the purpose of the limitation relating to issues surrounding the reduction and prevention of crime, the prevention of the negative effects on driving ability of users and the detrimental neurological, cardiovascular and respiratory effects on users. The court did not accept these justifications stating, in essence, that the state had not shown reasons why less restrictive means to achieve these purposes could not be instituted. Specifically, the court stated:

> “In other words, even if the Court finds that the evidence cited in their report, including the views of the Central Drug Authority of South Africa, does not carry sufficient evidential weight, if the respondents wish to restrict so important a right as a private act of consuming cannabis in the intimacy of a home, they should attempt to employ means of doing so which are the least restrictive of the rights being infringed. The limitation should in other words be narrowly tailored to achieve its purpose, should be carefully focused, and should not be overbroad.”[18]

---

11 See the *Prince* case (n. 9) para. 7.
12 Section 36(1) of the Constitution.
13 Section 36(1)(a) of the Constitution.
14 Section 36(1)(b) of the Constitution.
15 Section 36(1)(c) of the Constitution.
16 Section 36 (1)(d) of the Constitution.
17 Section 36(1)(e) of the Constitution.
18 See the *Prince* case (n. 9) para. 104.

The High Court went on to explain that there are a multitude of options available to the state which fall short of the "blunt use" of the criminal justice system and that the state must rather utilise these less restrictive means.[19] In its useful analysis, the court also considered the Convention against Illicit Traffic in Narcotic Drugs and Psychotropic Substances of 1998. This Convention notably distinguishes between the possession, purchase or cultivation of narcotic substances for personal consumption (in Article 3(2)), and trafficking and dealing conduct as set out in Article 3(1) which is described as "serious". Similarly, the South African Drugs Act also recognises a difference between unlawfulness related to possession and unlawfulness in relation to dealing. The Act creates a presumption in Section 21(1)(a)(i) that a person possessing more than 115 grams of cannabis is dealing, and is not merely in possession for personal use. However, this provision in relation to specifically the presumption of dealing has been declared unconstitutional.[20] The prescribed quantity currently remains in force.

In the end, based on the above reasoning, the High Court held that the state respondents had failed in discharging their onus to demonstrate that the limitation was reasonable and justifiable in terms of Section 36. Therefore, it held that the impugned provisions were constitutionally invalid.

The matter then went to the Constitutional Court for the required confirmatory proceedings.[21]

IV. In the Constitutional Court[22]

The Constitutional Court spent a considerable part of its judgment considering relevant case law in relation to the extent and scope of the right to privacy. I will consider case law specifically related to employment law at a later stage in this discussion, but at this stage will consider case law that outlines the nature of this right more broadly.

---

19 The *Prince* case (n. 9) para. 107.

20 *S v Bhulwana, S v Gwadiso* 1996 1 SA 388 (CC).

21 As per Section 172(2)(a) of the Constitution, the High Court may make an order concerning the constitutional validity of an Act of Parliament but such an order bears no force until confirmed by the Constitutional Court.

22 *Minister of Justice and Constitutional Development and Others v Prince (Clarke and Others Intervening), National Director of Public Prosecutions and Others v Rubin, National Director of Public Prosecutions and Others v Acton* 2018 6 SA 393 (CC).

The judge in *Bernstein* considered the right to privacy as defined by the Consultative Assembly of the Council of Europe:

> "The right to privacy consists essentially in the right to live one's own life with a minimum of interference. It concerns private, family and home life, physical and moral integrity, honour and reputation, avoidance of being placed in a false light, non-revelation of irrelevant and embarrassing facts, unauthorized publication of private photographs, protection from disclosure of information given or received by the individual confidentially."[23]

A useful point for our purposes, which emanated from *Bernstein* reads as follows:

> "A very high level of protection is given to the individual's intimate sphere of life and the maintenance of its basic preconditions and there is a final untouchable sphere of human freedom that is beyond interference from any public authority… [I]n regard to this most intimate core of privacy, no justifiable limitation thereof can take place… [T]his inviolable core is left behind once an individual enters into relationships with persons outside this closest intimate sphere; the individual's activities then acquire a social dimension and the right of privacy in this context becomes subject to limitation."[24]

This consideration is most significant when it comes to our discussion specifically in relation to the workplace, and the details and practicalities of regulating the use of cannabis in a space that is, in fact, not private.

As a start, Zondo ACJ concluded that the right to privacy was in fact infringed by the impugned provisions and proceeded to consider whether the limitation was justifiable in terms of Section 36. Particularly in respect of the importance of the limitation, the Court considered the submissions of the State that the basis of the prohibition was the "protection of the health, safety and psychological well-being of persons affected by the use of cannabis". The State further submitted that the prohibition served an important function in the "war against drugs". The Court also took note of the discussion by Ngcobo J in this regard in *Prince II*[25] where the majority

23 *Bernstein v Bester* [1996] ZACC 2, 1996 2 SA 751 (CC), 1996 4 BCLR 449 (CC) para. 73.

24 The *Bernstein* case (n. 23) para. 77.

25 *Prince v President of the Law Society of the Cape of Good Hope* [2002] ZACC 1; 2002 2 SA 794 (CC); 2002 3 BCLR 231 (CC).

noted that the prohibition seeks to address the harm caused by the drug problem by not only prohibiting use but also possession.[26]

Zondo ACJ also considered the overall extent of the limitation to be quite invasive because of the fact that it criminalises possession.[27] When considering the relationship between the limitation and its purpose, the Court considered the evidence of Dr Gous, a pharmacist relied upon by the State. Dr Gous made various points that related to, amongst other things, the negative psychoactive effects of cannabis, unpleasant side effects such as anxiety, increased symptoms of chronic bronchitis, fluctuation of blood pressure, and the possibility of miscarriage when used during pregnancy.[28]

The Court turned to the minority judgment in *Prince II,* which interestingly noted that

> "[26] The harmful effect of cannabis which the prohibition seeks to prevent is the psychological dependence that it has the potential to produce. On the medical evidence on record, there is no indication of the amount of cannabis that must be consumed in order to produce such harm.
>
> ….
>
> [61]…. [H]owever, on the medical evidence on record it is equally clear that there is a level of consumption that is safe in that it is unlikely to pose any risk of harm…."[29]

Zondo ACJ also noted a report by the World Health Organization on the health and social consequences of non-medical cannabis use. The WHO report noted that the health and social consequences of people seeking treatment for dependence on cannabis appear to be less severe than those seeking treatment for dependence on alcohol or opioids.[30] The same report also noted a small impact of cannabis on traffic injuries compared to the effects of alcohol.[31] Lastly, Zondo ACJ noted that South Africa's own Drug Authority stated in 2016 that possession of small amounts of cannabis for personal consumption in one's home should be decriminalised.[32]

---

26 The *Prince* case (n. 25) para. 116.
27 See the *Minister of Justice* case (n. 22) para. 66.
28 The *Minister of Justice* case (n. 22) para. 67.
29 See the *Prince* case (n. 25) paras. 26 and 61.
30 See the WHO Report (n. 1), 24, para. 3.1.3.
31 The WHO Report (n. 1), 23, para. 5.1.6.
32 See *Minister of Justice* case (n. 22) para. 78. See also *Stein,* 106 SAMJ 2016, 569, 570.

In considering these factors, Zondo ACJ took the view, which was supported by the majority, that the prohibition of possession for private use as well as the cultivation for private use of cannabis in one's own home, is inconsistent with the right to privacy in the Constitution, and is, thus, constitutionally invalid. Interestingly Zondo ACJ went one step further in his judgment than the High Court and included in its judgment a much broader consideration of "privacy of the person". The High Court focused its declaration of invalidity to possession, use and cultivation within a private dwelling. The judgment of the Constitutional Court, however, states that

> "there was no persuasive reason why the High Court confined its declaration of invalidity to the use or possession or cultivation of cannabis at a home or in a private dwelling. In my view, as long as the use or possession of cannabis is in private and not in public and the use or possession of cannabis is for the personal consumption of an adult, it is protected."

Conceivably, this widens the locality of private use to, for example, one's own vehicle or the dwelling of a friend or family member. I do not assert that the "private consumption" extends to a workplace. However, my view is that the implications of said private use may very easily extend to the workplace, a terrain the Constitutional Court simply did not enter.

V. The right of an employer in terms of Section 7 of the Employment Equity Act

Section 7 of the Employment Equity Act[33] permits employers to perform medical testing of employees under certain circumstances, and it is quite common practice for employers to test employees for substances to ensure that they are not under the influence of any harmful substances such as drugs or alcohol. Where the effects of alcohol use may be considerably clear, this is not the case for cannabis.

Crean, Crane and Mason considered a broad spectrum of cognitive functions and noted that attention, concentration, decision-making, impulsivity, reaction time, verbal fluency and working memory were impaired by the use of cannabis. However, these effects are all dose-dependent.[34]

---

33 Act No. 5 of 1998.

34 See the WHO Report (n. 1), 19.

Moreover, other commentators note certain benefits of the use of marijuana for employees specifically, and that, generally speaking, it affects different people in different ways. Sarah Sullivan, a risk-control services coordinator at an insurance broker and professional services firm, notes that "less than one third of studies found a correlation between marijuana use and decreased functioning" and that "[o]ne study even showed a statistically significant increase in output per hour for marijuana users".[35]

In relation to alcohol, an employer cannot control its private use by an employee. It is only where the employee's alcohol use or abuse enters the workplace that an employer may intervene.

The duration of the urinary cannabis detection window is a question that is unsettled in science. However, research indicates that the window is anywhere between 1–5 days for infrequent users, and up to 32 days for frequent users.[36] This, in my view, is where the challenge arises in the employment context.

Suppose an employee were to smoke cannabis over the weekend in his home. The same employee wakes up on Monday morning without smoking any cannabis and goes to work. Conceivably, this employee, should he be tested by the employer, may be found to be under the influence of cannabis despite not actually being intoxicated, and could accordingly be disciplined in terms of the employer's substance abuse policy.

If we are to compare this concern to the use of alcohol in the workplace, we have two useful judgments that emanate from the Labour Court and Labour Appeal Court respectively. In *Tanker Services*, it was held that an employee would only be "under the influence of alcohol" if he were not able to perform the tasks entrusted to him.[37] Similarly, the Labour Court upheld a CCMA award in another matter in relation to an employee who had been dismissed for being under the influence of alcohol. The employee tested positive after a breathalyser test, but the employer failed to prove that the employee was actually under the influence because the employee was still able to perform work tasks assigned to him without incident.

35 *Alsop*, "The hazy issue of weed and work" (2017), http://www.bbc.com/capital/story/20170725-the-hazy-issue-of-weed-and-work (last visited 13 Nov 2019).

36 *Cary*, The marijuana detection window: Determining the length of time cannabinoids will remain detectable in urine following smoking, National Drug Court Institute, 4 Drug Court Practitioner Fact Sheet 2006, issue 2, https://www.ndci.org/sites/default/files/ndci/THC_Detection_Window_0.pdf (last visited 18 Nov 2019).

37 *Tanker Services (Pty) Ltd v Magudulela* [1997] 12 BLLR 1552 (LAC).

The commissioner held that the dismissal was substantively unfair and the Labour Court upheld this decision.[38]

In my view, it stands to reason that similar logic must be applied to cases where an employee prohibits the use of cannabis at work, which it is entitled to do. This approach also resolves the concerns around when exactly an employee consumes cannabis in his or her private time. Nevertheless, we already have an award emanating from the CCMA that presents us with a vastly different perspective despite the precedents set particularly by the Labour Appeal Court.

In *Mthembu and Others v NCT Durban Wood Chips*[39] three employees were dismissed after testing positive for cannabis during a test conducted during working hours. The employees maintained that they had not consumed cannabis during working hours. The employer had a zero tolerance approach to working under the influence of drugs or alcohol due to the dangerous work in which the company is involved. The employees were aware of the policy.

In 2017, the applicants were suspected of being under the influence of cannabis and accordingly their urine was tested. What is not clear from the award is why the employees were suspected and subsequently tested. Witnesses indicated that the employees all appeared to be sober and none of them caused accidents at work. The employees primarily gave evidence to the effect that they smoked cannabis outside of working hours. None of the employees disputed that they were aware that they were not allowed to use cannabis at work.

In his reasoning, the commissioner focused primarily on the danger posed by the jobs of each employee. It is also not clear why the commissioner did not consider relevant precedent set in this matter or engage in any way with the questions or research surrounding how long cannabis may remain in one's blood stream. My primary view is that the award stands to be reviewed, if only for want of engagement and subsequent deviation from relevant precedent. However, at the time of writing, the award had not yet been taken on review.

Other commentators disagree to an extent and note that the award may be useful in the context of employers in significantly dangerous workplaces who may need to take a zero tolerance approach.[40] It is, however,

38 *Tosca Labs v CCMA and others* [2012] 5 BLLR 529 (529) LC.

39 [2019] 4 BALR 369 (CCMA).

40 *Mather* and *Gerson*, "Taking your high from home to work – Considering the impact of cannabis on the workplace" (2019), https://www.labourguide.co.za/unilateral-changes/50-new/most-recent-publications/2674-taking-your-high-from-ho

noted that this same approach may not be reasonable in relation to employees who, for example, perform desk jobs. In essence, employers, when considering disciplinary sanctions, will have to demonstrate that the work of the employee concerned was impaired or that the employee was actually under the influence. It is reiterated that an employee may test positive for cannabis whilst not actually being under the influence of cannabis.

It is suggested that a more nuanced approach be taken when considering cannabis use. Further, because cannabis may remain in the bloodstream longer than substances like alcohol, a zero-tolerance approach may result in an infringement on employees' right to privacy because they will be unable to use the substance in their private time. Alsop notes that cannabis may be detectable for weeks or even months after a person has stopped using. He adds:

> "Because of the potential for error and the fact that a positive test result isn't indicative of either impairment or recent drug ingestion, the National Organisation for the Reform of Marijuana Law finds urine, blood and oral fluid tests discriminatory and a violation of an individual's rights. It recommends performance impairment testing rather than bodily fluid screens. For example NORML says, an app called My Canary can detect performance changes by assessing a person's memory, reaction time and balance."[41]

In the same vein, it is pertinent to consider employees' right to privacy in relation to drug testing, particularly because the judgment of the Constitutional Court seeks to protect the right to privacy.

Drug tests are able to detect the presence of drugs such as "opiates, phencyclidine (PCP), cocaine, methamphetamine, amphetamine, Phenobarbital and marijuana".[42]

Urinalysis is the most common and preferred method used in employment spaces, because urine samples can be easily obtained and urine retains the presence of drugs for longer periods of time than, for example, blood.[43] However, it is clear that this method has privacy implications.

In a judgment of the United States, *National Treasury Employees Union v Von Raab,* the court observed that "[t]here are few activities in our society more personal or private than the passing of urine. Most people describe

---

me-to-work-considering-the-impact-of-cannabis-on-the-workplace (last visited 13 Nov 2019).

41 See *Alsop* (n. 35).

42 *Hebert,* Employee Privacy Law (2009), § 2:5.

43 Ibid.

it by euphemisms if they talk about it at all. It is a function traditionally performed without public observation; indeed, its performance in public is generally prohibited by law as well as social custom." Secondly, urinalysis can reveal more than the presence of illegal drugs, it can also reveal "a host of medical facts including whether or not [an employee] is epileptic, pregnant or diabetic".[44] Thirdly, the manner in which urine samples are collected may intrude on the privacy of employees, particularly where the samples are provided under direct observation. Fourthly, the results of a drug test are not always treated as confidential medical records given that they are often shared with third parties such as supervisors, prospective employers, health insurers, management, and if a dispute arises in this respect, the results may even become a matter of public record in the courts.

Blood samples can also be tested for the presence of drugs and are better indicators of recent drug use than urine samples. That being said, blood samples are not often used to detect drugs, since the drawing of a blood sample is a complex procedure not often done on site at workplaces because it requires trained professionals.

Another method of drug testing is hair sample analysis. Hair retains the presence of drugs for longer periods than urine or blood.[45] However, the collection of hair samples for drug analysis comes with its own set of problems.[46] For example, an individual's hair sample may test positive for marijuana because of exposure to marijuana smoke that has become embedded in the hair. In other words, a positive drug test based on hair sample analysis is not always an indication of the personal use of drugs.[47]

The collection of saliva samples for drug analysis is one of the less invasive and intrusive methods of drug testing. The method is also a good indicator of present drug usage and intoxication.[48]

Broadly speaking, all of the aforementioned forms of testing raise privacy concerns about the way in which samples are obtained, not to mention the information gathered by the testing.

Importantly for the purposes of this discussion, the information obtained through drug tests, even though at first glance not private, may further concern the off-duty conduct of employees in the privacy of their homes. In other words, drug tests are able to expose and reveal aspects

44 *Skinner v Railway Labour Executives Association* 489 US 602 (1989) 617.
45 *Hebert* (n. 42), § 2:4.
46 Ibid.
47 Ibid.
48 Ibid.

of the personal life of employees (including any illegal activities they may wish to engage in) outside of working hours. This means that while employers may be entitled to monitor the conduct of employees while on duty, these tests may well ignore the fact that employees have privacy interests outside the workplace.[49]

In *Beattie v St Petersburg*[50] a US district court recognised that drug tests may deprive employees of their privacy interests in off-duty conduct (in this case fire fighters) and in this regard stated that drug tests "reveal activities of a fire fighter's personal life. The fire fighters have a legitimate interest in keeping their personal life shielded from the government's prying eyes, especially when the activity revealed is frowned upon by a large segment of the community and may constitute a crime. In order to pass constitutional muster, the City must demonstrate a compelling interest that outweighs these privacy concerns".[51] These compelling interests may be based on the identification of users of illicit drugs in the workplace, the deterrence of individuals from using drugs in the workplace, and the interest to reduce the incidence of drug related problems such as accidents and illnesses.[52]

Drug testing in employment typically occurs at various points. For example, random testing can be conducted without prior notice, any number of times, and is not based on a triggering event or a reasonable suspicion. Courts have found random testing more intrusive than other types of drug testing.[53] In the United States, employers have justified this type of testing based on safety concerns and courts have upheld the random testing of employees in safety sensitive positions such as air traffic controllers, physicians and dentists.[54]

Employers may also engage in reasonable-suspicion testing of employees where they suspect an employee had been using drugs or is under the influence of drugs. In the United States, courts uphold reasonable-suspicion testing of employees where an employer can prove that his or her suspicion was based on "the existence of illustrative facts" that would guide a reasonable person to suspect that an employee has been using drugs or is under the influence of drugs. Symptoms of drug use and direct

49 *Hebert* (n. 42), § 2:4.

50 733 F Supp 1455 (MD Fla 1990).

51 *Hebert* (n. 42), § 2:4.

52 Ibid.

53 *Transportation Institute v United States Coast Guard* 727 F Supp 648 (D DC 1989) 10; see also *Hebert* (n. 42), § 3:11.

54 See *Hebert* (n. 42), § 3:11.

observation of drug use or possession have been accepted by courts as facts that can guide an employer to engage in reasonable-suspicion testing.[55]

VI. *Comparative perspectives*

There are a number of jurisdictions that have decriminalised or legalised the use and/or sale and purchase of cannabis and this has had an impact on the way their workplaces are regulated.

In Germany, an employee can be terminated if she is under the influence of cannabis while at work, even when cannabis was consumed outside of the workplace, but a drug screening has demonstrated consumption. An employee consuming cannabis at work without it affecting his or her ability to perform her job duties is usually not sufficient for the purposes of dismissal.[56]

In 2014 Uruguay became the first country to legalise the sale of marijuana. Its law prohibits the use of marijuana before work as it prohibits the use of marijuana before driving. The law also allows an employer to remove an employee from her workstation if she is under the influence. However, interestingly, the law also establishes that the employer cannot sanction the employee for consuming cannabis if he or she did not commit any other misconduct.[57]

In Norway, drug testing in itself is considered a violation of the personal integrity of an employee or job applicant and should be conducted only when it is strictly necessary. Such a need may arise, for example, in an attempt to protect the safety of the worker or others.[58]

---

55 Ibid.

56 *Fiore*, "Weed's worldwide impact on the workplace: The employer's guide to marijuana in the workplace, Part Three" (2016), https://www.keglerbrown.com/publications/weed%E2%80%99s-worldwide-impact-on-the-workplace-the-employer%E2%80%99s-guide-to-marijuana-in-the-workplace-part-three/ (last visited 13 Nov 2019).

57 *Boidi* and *Cruz*, Marijuana legalization in Uruguay and Beyond (2014), https://www.wilsoncenter.org/sites/default/files/Marijuana%20Legalization%20in%20Uruguay%20and%20Beyond_brief%20report_v3%20(2).pdf (last visited 13 Nov 2019).

58 *Nafstad* and *Norge*, Negative Consequences of Control and the Enforcement of Norwegian Law regarding cannabis. A literature review and human rights complaint. (2018), https://rusreformutvalget.no/files/2019/02/Innspill-fra-Normal-Norge-rapport-H%C3%B8ringsm%C3%B8te-13.11.18.pdf (last visited 13 Nov 2019).

VII. Concluding remarks

The award in *Mthembu* demonstrates considerable tensions between workplace policies and the judgment of the Constitutional Court. As per the judgment of the Court, Parliament has 24 months to amend the impugned provisions. In addition to this, it would be prudent for Parliament to spend time delineating clearly the boundaries of private use. Even in the workplace, one wonders whether an employer would be able to discipline an employee for having cannabis on his person if the employee is not under the influence of the cannabis. Another question is whether employers could ban their employees from using cannabis altogether to avoid concerns they may have regarding its use. This may amount to a clear violation of the right to privacy? These questions not only arise in employment law but also in relation to traffic safety, and even use of cannabis in private dwellings that may fall within sectional titles. Shaw and others note that "the question of how best to regulate cannabis must take into account and attempt to balance a range of different harms (and benefits) to different groups in society. The reduction of harms… should be understood as the ultimate goal of drug policy".[59]

From an employment perspective, an employer would need to develop very clear policies to address the use of cannabis that will take into account a wide range of factors. These factors may include the nature of the business, the employee's role and responsibilities, the manner of testing and the extent of impairment of the employee's ability. However, it will be critical to balance the interests of the employer in these respects whilst still upholding employees' rights to privacy.

Bibliography

Ronald Alsop, "The hazy issue of weed and work" (2017), http://www.bbc.com/capital/story/20170725-the-hazy-issue-of-weed-and-work (last visited on 13 Nov 2019).

Paul Cary, The marijuana detection window: Determining the length of time cannabinoids will remain detectable in urine following smoking, National Drug Court Institute, 4 Drug Court Practitioner Fact Sheet 2006, issue 2.

---

59 *Shaw, Howell, Faull* and *Kriegler*, Balancing harms in cannabis policy: Some considerations for the South African context (2016), https://daggacouple.co.za/wp-content/uploads/2017/11/The-Shaw-Report_Balancing-Harms-in-Cannabis-Policy.pdf (last visited 13 Nov 2019).

Tony Fiore, "Weed's worldwide impact on the workplace: The employer's guide to marijuana in the workplace, Part Three" (2016), https://www.keglerbrown.com/publications/weed%E2%80%99s-worldwide-impact-on-the-workplace-the-employer%E2%80%99s-guide-to-marijuana-in-the-workplace-part-three/ (last visited 13 Nov 2019).

Camille Hebert, Employee Privacy Law (Thomson Reuters, Toronto 2009).

Nadine Mather and *Amy Gerson*, "Taking your high from home to work – Considering the impact of cannabis on the workplace" (2019), https://www.labourguide.co.za/unilateral-changes/50-new/most-recent-publications/2674-taking-your-high-from-home-to-work-considering-the-impact-of-cannabis-on-the-workplace (last visited 13 Nov 2019).

Mark Shaw, *Simon Howell*, *Andrew Faull* and *Anine Kriegler*, Balancing harms in cannabis policy: Some considerations for the South African context (2016), https://daggacouple.co.za/wp-content/uploads/2017/11/The-Shaw-Report_Balancing-Harms-in-Cannabis-Policy.pdf (last visited on 13 Nov 2019).

Dan Stein, "Position statement on cannabis", 106 South African Medical Journal (SAMJ) 2016, 569.

World Health Organisation, The health and social effects of nonmedical cannabis use, Report (2016), https://www.who.int/substance_abuse/publications/cannabis_report/en/ (last visited 13 Nov 2019).

Register of cases

Beattie v St Petersburg 733 F Supp 1455 (MD Fla 1990).

Bernstein v Bester [1996] ZACC 2, 1996 2 SA 751 (CC), 1996 4 BCLR 449 (CC).

Minister of Justice and Constitutional Development and Others v Prince (Clarke and Others Intervening), National Director of Public Prosecutions and Others v Rubin, National Director of Public Prosecutions and Others v Acton 2018 6 SA 393 (CC).

Mthembu and others v NCT Durban Wood Chips [2019] 4 BALR 369 (CCMA).

Prince v President of the Law Society of the Cape of Good Hope [2002] ZACC 1; 2002 2 SA 794 (CC); 2002 3 BCLR 231 (CC).

Prince v Minister of Justice [2017] ZAWCHC 30; 2017 4 SA 299 (WCC).

Skinner v Railway Labour Executives Association 489 US 602 (1989) 617.

S v Bhulwana, S v Gwadiso 1996 1 SA 388 (CC).

Transportation Institute v United States Coast Guard 727 F Supp 648 (D DC 1989).

Tanker Services (Pty) Ltd v Magudulela [1997] 12 BLLR 1552 (LAC).

Tosca Labs v CCMA and others [2012] 5 BLLR 529 (529) LC.

Comment: The Legalization of Cannabis in Germany

Johannes Kaspar[*]

---

* Johannes Kaspar, Dr. iur.; Professor, University of Augsburg Faculty of Law. Chair of Criminal Law, Criminal Procedure Law, Criminology and Sanctions Law.

I. The current legal position

1. Criminal liability today

a) The universal problem of criminalizing "soft" drugs

The criminalization of so-called "soft" drugs, like cannabis,[1] which are considered not to be as harmful and addictive as other substances, is a very controversial subject in South Africa. This is also the case in Germany. It was very interesting for me to learn that in South Africa, as in Germany, it was not the legislature, but rather a higher court that laid down (at least certain) limitations on criminal liability.

In 2019, the "Cannabis Decision" of the German Federal Constitutional Court (*Bundesverfassungsgericht* – BVerfG) marked its 25th anniversary. In 1994, the BVerfG determined that the ban on cannabis did not violate the German Constitution (*Grundgesetz* – GG), thereby declaring the German Narcotics Act (*Betäubungsmittelgesetz* – BtMG) constitutional in this regard. However, as I will show, the Court did set restrictions at the procedural level on the basis of constitutional law. This judgment has been in doubt ever since, and discussions regarding the general legalization of cannabis have continued to intensify in recent years. Proponents of legalization argue that the prohibition policy of the German *Bundestag*, the German federal parliament, does not fulfil its purpose.[2] One of these proponents, Prof. Dr. Lorenz Boellinger, addressed a petition to parliament in 2013.[3] In this petition, 122 German criminal-law professors raised their doubts about the prohibition policy and demanded that a commission be established to evaluate the current criminal law on drugs. This petition (which I also signed) emphasized the need for substantial reforms to the BtMG and the prosecution of cannabis offenses. There are also increasing numbers of opposition parties in parliament campaigning for the legalization of cannabis, as I will show towards the end of my contribution.

---

1 For an instructive historic overview of Cannabis prohibition in Germany see *Böllinger*, NK 2018, 281; see also *Heinrich* and *van Bergen*, JA 2019, 321.

2 *Nestler*, 5 StV 2019, I.

3 *Böllinger*, NK 2014, 115.

b) Introducing the BtMG

The BtMG refers to various drugs. This includes both "hard" drugs, such as heroin, cocaine or amphetamines, as well as "soft" drugs, like cannabis. According to Section 1(1) BtMG, a detailed listing of the relevant narcotics can be found in Annexes I to III BtMG. It sets out several criminal offenses, especially Section 29 BtMG.[4]

Interestingly, and contrary to the legal position in South Africa, the use of drugs is not itself punishable under the BtMG. This indicates that the purpose of the act is not primarily the protection of consumer health by criminalizing the self-destructive behaviour of adults.[5] Rather, the main purpose is the general protection of public health, especially with regard to children and young people, who should not be tempted to use cannabis in the first place.

For this reason, amongst other things, not only dealing in, but also (and more importantly for present purposes) the mere possession of cannabis are criminal offenses. The relevant penalties apply equally to all narcotic substances mentioned in the three Annexes to the BtMG and do not distinguish between the danger and the addictive potential of the drug in question. There is deliberately no distinction between "hard" and "soft" drugs[6] with regard to the question of criminalization. However, this distinction becomes relevant to sentencing.

---

4 Section 29 BtMG [Criminal Offenses]:
"A term of imprisonment of up to five years or a fine shall be imposed on any person who
illicitly cultivates, produces and trades in narcotic drugs or, without engaging in their trade, imports, exports, sells, supplies, otherwise places them on the market or acquires or procures them in any other way,
produces an exempt preparation (Section 2 subsection 1 number 3) without a license pursuant to Section 3 subsection 1 number 2,
possesses narcotic drugs without being in possession of a written license for their acquisition,
[...]
The court may refrain from imposing punishment pursuant to subsections 1, 2 and 4 if the offender cultivates, produces, imports, exports, carries in transit, acquires, otherwise procures or possesses narcotic drugs merely in small quantities for his personal use.".

5 *Kaspar*, Grundrechtsschutz und Verhältnismäßigkeit im Präventionsstrafrecht (2014), 500 et seq.

6 *Patzak*, in: Körner, Patzak and Volkmer (eds.), Kommentar zum Betäubungsmittelgesetz (9th ed. 2019), § 29, para. 5.

Even though the possession of cannabis is generally prohibited, a court can refrain from imposing punishment in minor cases with small quantities for personal use, according to Section 29(5) BtMG.

Section 31a BtMG[7] constitutes an extension of Section 29(5) BtMG by waiving the court's approval. The provision shifts the decision to the public prosecutor's office as to whether a case is prosecuted or not. However, the requirements in Section 31a BtMG are stricter than those in Section 29(5) BtMG. In addition to the small quantity of cannabis, there must only be a minor degree of guilt involved. Furthermore, there must be no public interest in pursuing the prosecution.[8]

c) The term "small quantities"

In applying BtMG, the term "small quantities" (which appears in both Sections 29(5) and 31a BtMG) has proven problematic. Since the refusal to prosecute or the judicial abolition of punishment depends on this requirement, a lively debate about its interpretation has developed over the years. To date, the legislature has not further detailed the term. This is unfortunate, as there would be more clarity and legal certainty if it did so. In addition, this would eliminate the different standards applied in the federal states.[9]

"Small quantities" is defined as a small amount needed for occasional use and which the user regularly carries in his or her pocket, without having to create a drug supply at home. As already indicated, the various states handle the term quite differently, although the standards have at least converged over time, as the following overview indicates.

---

7 Section 31a BtMG [Refraining from prosecution]:
"If the subject matter of the proceedings is an offence pursuant to Section 29 subsection 1, 2 or 4, the public prosecutor's office may refrain from prosecution if the offender's guilt could be regarded as minor, if there is no public interest in a criminal prosecution and if the offender cultivates, produces, imports, exports, carries in transit, acquires, otherwise procures or possesses narcotic drugs in small quantities exclusively for his personal use. Prosecution should be refrained from if the offender possesses narcotic drugs in a drug consumption room in small quantities exclusively for his personal use, which may be tolerated pursuant to Section 10a, without being in possession of a written licence for acquisition.".

8 *Patzak*, in: Körner, Patzak and Volkmer (eds.), Kommentar zum Betäubungsmittelgesetz (9th ed. 2019), § 31a, para. 5.

9 *Patzak*, in: Körner, Patzak and Volkmer (eds.), Kommentar zum Betäubungsmittelgesetz (9th ed. 2019), § 31a, para. 4.

This is a summary of the procedural closing limits applicable in the different states as of January 2018[10]:

	Procedural closing limits	Regulation changed on	Previous limits
Baden-Wurttemberg	6g	31.12.2016	6g
Bavaria	6g		
Berlin	10g/15g	26.3.2016	6g/15g
Brandenburg	6g		
Bremen	6g	26.5.2008	8g
Hamburg	6g	28.11.2006	10g
Hesse	6g	6.5.2008	6g/15g
Mecklenburg-West Pomerania	6g		
Lower Saxony	6g	7.12.2012	6g
North Rhine-Westphalia	10g	18.5.2011	6g
Rhineland-Palatinate	10g	15.2.2012	6g
Saarland	6g	25.9.2007	6g/10g
Saxony	6g	15.8.2011	6g
Saxony-Anhalt	6g		
Schleswig-Holstein	6g	25.7.2006	30g
Thuringia	10g	20.12.2016	6g

In a study published in 2006 by *Carsten Schäfer* and *Letizia Paoli,* 2011 individual cases against suspects of narcotic drug offenses in six states and a total of 24 district courts were evaluated.[11] The study showed particularly significant differences between the states in the closing of proceedings in cases against minors and adolescents. In Bavaria, only 20 percent and, in Berlin and Saxony, less than 40 percent of proceedings were closed

10 *Patzak*, in: Körner, Patzak and Volkmer (eds.), Kommentar zum Betäubungsmittelgesetz (9th ed. 2019), § 31a, para. 43.
11 *Schäfer* and *Paoli,* Drogen und Strafverfolgung (2006), 37 et seqq.

without conditions, whereas in Schleswig-Holstein and several Hessian judicial districts, more than 80 percent of proceedings were closed without imposing any penalty.[12]

If one compares the closing of proceedings in accordance with Section 31a (1) BtMG to the total number of criminal offenses committed, the following figures result for the different states in 2017 and 2018[13]:

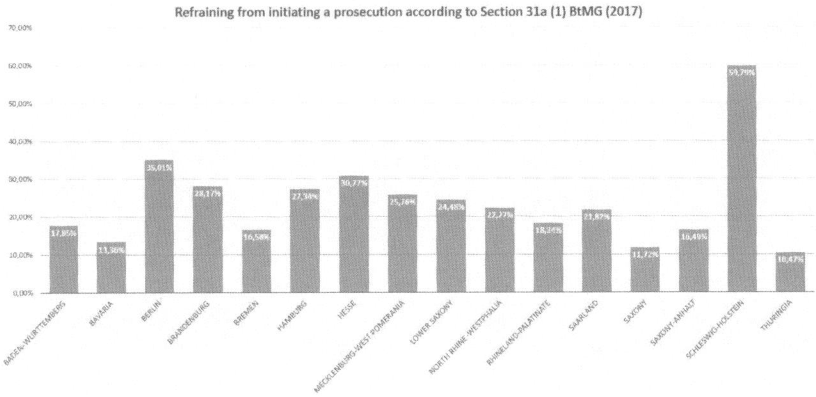

Despite the BVerfG's "Cannabis Decision" in 1994, these significant differences between the states still exist today. At that time, the BVerfG already put forward a different way of handling the concept of small quantities and therefore appealed to the legislature for a uniform structure to eliminate the differences – this has not happened to date. Below, the BVerfG's judgment will be dealt with in more detail.

2. The "Cannabis Decision" of the BVerfG

a) Background

In 1994, the BVerfG addressed the question of whether Section 29 BtMG was unconstitutional. The question was originally submitted by the county court of Stuttgart, and the district courts of Lübeck, Hildesheim

---

12 *Schäfer* and *Paoli*, Drogen und Strafverfolgung (2006), 384.

13 Own calculation using figures from Statistisches Bundesamt, Rechtspflege Staatsanwaltschaften 2017 (2018) and Bundeskriminalamt, Rauschgiftkriminalität – Bundeslagebild 2017 (2018) and Bundeslagebild 2018 (2019).

and Frankfurt, in connection with a constitutional complaint against a previous judgment of the BVerfG.[14] The BVerfG was confronted with the question of whether the BtMG was constitutional and whether punishing minor offenses was proportionate, specifically with reference to the basic rights, namely human dignity (Article 1(I) GG), personal freedom (Article 2(I),(II) GG), equality (Article 3 GG), and due process (Article 20 GG). The BVerfG also considered whether German citizens had a constitutional "right to be intoxicated" that had to be respected by the courts.

b) The judgment of the BVerfG

In its judgment, the BVerfG stated that the purposes of Section 29 BtMG, such as the protection of the population (especially minors) against health hazards arising from drug use, including the risk of addiction, could justify punishment. In addition, it found that punishment should primarily affect the criminal organizations that dominate the drug market. Furthermore, the BVerfG clarified that the GG does not guarantee the "right to be intoxicated".[15] The aspect of human dignity or privacy rights was not considered to be relevant in this regard so, again, there is an important difference in relation to the South African position.

However, the BVerfG also explicitly commented on the term "small quantities": the risk posed by cannabis was not significant if the purchase or possession was limited to small amounts for one's own occasional use only. The public interest in punishment was correspondingly low in such cases. The punishment of these perpetrators could lead to inappropriate and (from the perspective of rehabilitation) rather disadvantageous results, such as an undesirable drift into the drug scene. With regard to Section 29(5) BtMG, the BVerfG held that its application would be strongly advised (if not mandatory) where a casual user procured or owned a small amount of cannabis exclusively for his own use and therefore did not constitute an external danger.[16]

In particular, the BVerfG Senate criticized the differences in the practical application of the term "small quantities" across different states. Different approaches to closing proceedings against perpetrators had already been recognized in the late 1980s. The BVerfG held that the states inter-

---

14 *Ambos*, 78 MschKrim 1995, 47.
15 BVerfG, Judgment of 9 Mar 1994, BVerfGE 90, 145, para. 184.
16 Ibid., para. 189.

preted the term differently in relation to the quantity of the substance, which in turn led to significant differences in applying the provision. Therefore, the Senate appealed to the legislature and the states to ensure a substantially uniform procedure for prosecuting offenders under the BtMG.[17]

c) Criticism

The BVerfG's mere appeal to establish a uniform practice regarding the term "small quantities" can be criticized above all. The Senate did not order the legislature, as many had demanded, to correct or amend the existing provisions of substantive criminal law to counteract the violation of the right to liberty and the principle of proportionality which it had found.[18] In the Senate's opinion, the legislature complied with its duty simply by restricting the obligation to prosecute, while upholding criminalization as such. This so-called "procedural solution", which the BVerfG approved, was described in 1995 as having little effect[19] and is still criticized today. As indicated above, the procedure for the prosecution to drop charges varies significantly from one state to another, especially as regards assessing what constitutes a "small quantity". This has led to the divergent treatment of occasional users depending on whether the offender lives in a rather conservatively-governed, or less-conservatively-governed, state. As a result, the Senate's finding does not meet the requirements of Article 103 GG, which are legal certainty and legality. Given the circumstances, an individual cannot be expected to understand the law sufficiently clearly, so that he or she knows on which conditions he or she will be criminally liable.[20] Prosecution largely depends on law-enforcement authorities – prosecutors and judges. However, the principles of Article 103 GG explicitly require that the legislature decide on the prosecution and punishment of certain conduct. In addition, the BVerfG neglects the relevance of an ongoing threat of punishment to a suspect.[21]

Critics also expected further disputes to come before German courts, as the BVerfG's decision did not provide sufficient clarity regarding the

---

17 Ibid., para. 190.
18 *Ambos*, 78 MschKrim 1995, 47, 48.
19 *Ambos*, 78 MschKrim 1995, 47, 48.
20 Ibid., 48.
21 Ibid., 49.

application of the BtMG.[22] Furthermore, its judgment seems quite contradictory. On the one hand, the BVerfG considered criminal punishment for possessing cannabis appropriate, since this was (in its view) blameworthy and punishable behaviour. On the other hand, it later held that, in certain individual cases, it was not.[23] This contradiction is based on the questionable assumption that punishment can generally be threatened even if its imposition is, in many cases, ultimately impermissible.[24]

Boellinger's criticism is that the Senate's judgment dissolves the *ultima ratio* principle (punishment as a last resort to enforce legal peace)[25] with the result that nothing stands in the way of the unrestrained use of criminal law.[26] Also, in my opinion, the principle of proportionality is violated if minor cases are criminalized. A mere (and relatively vague) procedural solution is not an adequate remedy in this regard.[27]

3. Drug offenses under Section 29 BtMG between 2007 and 2018

In Germany, there has been a steady increase in the number of drug offenses under the BtMG in recent years, as the following overview illustrates[28]:

22 *Kreuzer*, NJW 1994, 2400.

23 *Nelles*, NStZ 1994, 366, 367.

24 Ibid., 367.

25 *Böllinger*, KJ 1994, 405.

26 Ibid., 419.

27 *Kaspar*, Grundrechtsschutz und Verhältnismäßigkeit im Präventionsstrafrecht (2014), 511 et seqq; Recently, another constitutional complaint has been filed against Section 29 BtmG; so far, the BVerfG has not yet decided upon its admissibility, see https://www.lto.de/recht/hintergruende/h/cannabis-normenkontrolle-richtervorlage-ag-bernau-bverfg-entkriminalisierung-zulaessigkeit-legalisierung/ (last visited 07 Oct 2020).

28 Cf. Bundeskriminalamt, Polizeiliche Kriminalstatistik 2007–2018 (available at www.bka.de).

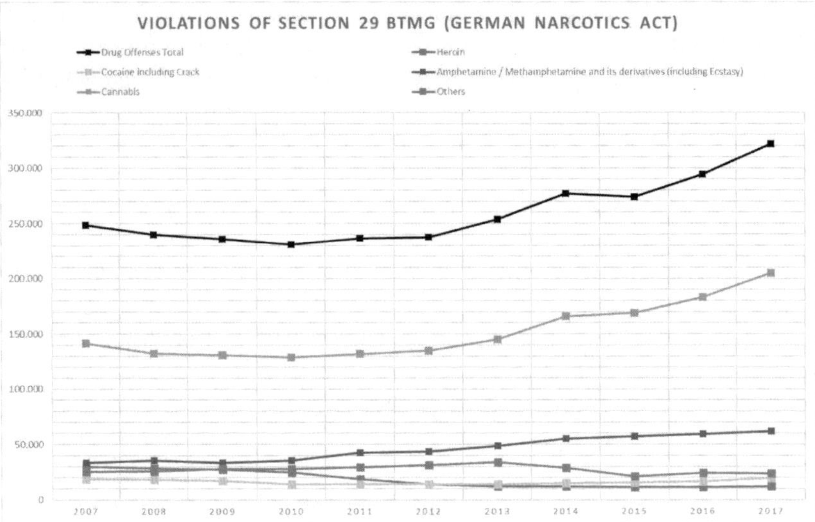

Cannabis clearly stands out (see the second bar from the top). The percentage of cannabis offenses compared to all drug law offenses has always been above 55 percent since 2007, rising to approximately 64 percent in 2018. Cannabis offenses are by far the most common offenses on the German drug scene. While around 128,000 cannabis-related offenses were detected in 2010, their total number was more than 218,000 in 2018. And these are just the official figures: the majority of offenses are very likely to remain unrecorded and therefore unknown.

II. Approaches to legalization

It is no surprise that, under these circumstances, an entirely different approach to cannabis is called for. In the view of several German opposition parties, the leading parties' prohibition policy has failed. Therefore, various approaches have been discussed, which should lead to a complete or partial legalization of cannabis. In addition to these discussions, the German parliament passed a law in 2017, which allows for the partial legalization of cannabis in the medical field.

1. Criticism

The increase in cannabis offenses has been taken as an indication that prohibiting drugs has no effect on their use. Juveniles and young adults in particular are not protected by the current policy, as there has been a steady increase in cannabis use among these two specific groups.[29] Critics observing the current approach to cannabis therefore often raise the following points:

The current approach leads to a stigmatizing and harmful criminalization of occasional users. In addition, the German state incurs costs for prosecutions and criminal proceedings. The amounts spent in the executive and judicial branches are therefore often criticized as a waste of resources, as these are more urgently needed in other areas. Several police entities have shown their support. Quite remarkably, the Confederation of German Criminal Investigators is aiming for a complete decriminalization of cannabis users.[30] The German Police Union has considerable concerns about the legalization of the drug, but also points out that a significant amount of police work in this field is considered to be completely in vain.[31]

Finally, the ban on cannabis also creates a black market that cannot be controlled (for example, in terms of the quality of the drugs), which in turn has an impact on users and also leads to large amounts of illegal proceeds.

2. Cannabis allowed as medicine

In 2017, the German Bundestag adopted an amendment which led to a partial legalization of cannabis in the field of (palliative) medicine. Prior to this decision, exemptions had been granted in a few cases by the Federal Institute for Pharmaceuticals and Medical Products, which permitted the legal cultivation of cannabis at home. However, costs incurred by the

29 See Bundesministerium für Gesundheit, Drogen- und Suchtbericht (2018), 86.

30 See *Keilani*, “Berliner Kripo-Beamte fordern Cannabis-Legalisierung” (6 Feb 2018), https://www.tagesspiegel.de/berlin/drogenpolitik-berliner-kripo-beamte-fordern-cannabis-legalisierung/20929716.html (last visited 7 Oct 2020).

31 See Deutsche Polizeigewerkschaft, “Drogenpolitik/Legalisierung von Drogen”, https://www.dpolg.de/ueber-uns/positionen/drogenpolitik/ (last visited 7 Oct 2020).

patient were not reimbursed. In addition, patients were obligated to document strictly their illness and prior therapy.[32]

Since March 2017, patients with severe illnesses may receive drugs at pharmacies with the active ingredient, THC, in standardized quality. This is however subject to strict prerequisites. First, the cannabis treatment must be diagnosed and prescribed by a doctor. Secondly, it must be determined that there are no alternative therapies available. The purpose of the amendment is to enable patients to access medicines to alleviate their suffering if other methods of medical treatment provided, or any other available medicinal products, do not succeed. The amendment also led to civil-law changes: in narrowly-limited cases, patients with statutory health insurance are entitled to be reimbursed their costs (vgl. BT-Drs. 18/8965). To be reimbursed, patients must meet the following conditions (Section 31(6), Book V of the Social Code (*Sozialgesetzbuch V – SGB V*):

- They have a serious illness.
- There are no other treatments apart from cannabis.
- There is a prospect of a noticeably positive influence on the course of the disease or on serious symptoms.
- The patient participates in anonymized accompanying research.

According to the Federal Ministry of Health, cannabis should be used as an alternative treatment for patients in individual cases of serious disease if it is expected that there will be a noticeably positive effect on the course of the disease or on serious symptoms. This may be the case, for example, in pain therapy, certain chronic diseases, or severe loss of appetite and nausea.[33]

3. Further approaches to legalization

a) The "Cannabis Control Act" – Green Party

In 2017, the Green party in the German Bundestag introduced a bill according to which the cultivation and use of cannabis would be allowed,

---

32 See Die Bundesregierung, "Cannabis für Schwerkranke auf Rezept" (10 Mar 2017), https://www.bundesregierung.de/breg-de/aktuelles/cannabis-fuer-schwerkranke-auf-rezept-485740 (last visited 7 Oct 2020).

33 Bundesministerium für Gesundheit, "Cannabis als Medizin" (19 Jan 2017), https://www.bundesgesundheitsministerium.de/ministerium/meldungen/2017/januar/cannabis-als-medizin.html (last visited 7 Oct 2020).

leading to a decriminalization of the drug. This so-called "Cannabis Control Act" was also supported by the Left Party in parliament. On June 2, 2017, the bill was rejected by the majority in parliament. The bill had already been submitted in the previous legislative period, where it was rejected as well.[34]

The main contents of the bill were as follows:

- The term "small quantities" would be set at 30g. Possession of more than 30g would be punishable. The term allowed the limited stockpiling of acquired cannabis and prevented the unnecessary criminalization of private users.
- The sale of cannabis by specialized shops would be allowed.
- Further points regarding:
  - implementing legalization;
  - provisions on dealing in, cultivating and possessing cannabis; and
  - youth protection.
- A new excise tax would be introduced (the "Cannabis Tax Law").

To justify their bill, the Green Party highlighted the following:

- Cannabis is by far the most used illegal drug despite the ban by the BtMG in Germany.
- There are fewer health risks for adults than for adolescents.
- The ban on cannabis does not prevent adolescents from using cannabis, as several studies show – the policy of deterrence is not effective and the prohibition simultaneously undermines any other protection for minors.
- The threat of punishment constitutes serious interference, without any justification, with the general freedom to act.
- In its decision in 1994, the BVerfG requested the states to ensure a substantially uniform procedure for prosecuting offenders under the BtMG. The states did not comply with this request. The states have indeed issued guidelines. However, these vary from state to state, which ultimately leads to a wide discretionary scope for prosecutors.
- The cannabis market is expanding instead of being curtailed by the current policy.
- Legalization does not automatically lead to an increase in use, according to studies in other countries. In countries where cannabis possession and dealing are legal, use is about the same.

---

34 BT-Drs. 18/4204 and BT-Drs. 19/819.

b) Motions by the Free Democratic Party and the Left Party

The Free Democratic Party (FDP), also known as the liberals, made a motion in 2017 dealing with the legalization of cannabis products. The FDP requested that the government set up and support model projects to investigate the controlled provision of cannabis as a consumable.[35]

The FDP cited the following reasons for this demand:

- The controlled provision of cannabis could contribute to protecting the population's health:
  - By doing this, the quality of cannabis products could be officially adjusted and controlled. Users would not be exposed to the risk of contamination or defective products.
  - Furthermore, by taxing cannabis products, substantial revenues could be generated, which could then be used for addiction prevention and education programs.
- Legalization would relieve the police, prosecutors and the judiciary. This would lead to significant cost savings.

The Left Party also made a formal request to the German Federal Government in this matter.[36] They requested that the government draft a bill to concretize the term "small quantities" in Section 31a BtMG. In addition, there should be no criminal prosecution where the perpetrator carries up to 15g for his or her own use. In general, the Left Party is calling for a review of the possibilities for legal access to cannabis to counteract the black market.

c) The Federal Government's view

In the previous legislative period, the ruling parties had already commented in detail on the Green Party's draft bill and on the use of cannabis in general.[37] The union parties (CDU/CSU) argued that the debate on the legalization of cannabis among the general public, and especially among adolescents, gives the impression that cannabis is harmless, which it is not. Legalization will not ensure the protection of the youth. Also, legalization will not lead to a decline in black-market operations. However, the

35 BT-Drs. 19/515.
36 BT-Drs. 19/832.
37 BT-Drs. 18/12476.

CDU/CSU does acknowledge the growing number of drug-related deaths and drug offenses in the past few years. Therefore, they do intend to refine drugs policy. A specified amount of cannabis for personal use at a low level should be introduced. The German Chancellor, Angela Merkel, does not think much of a general legalization of cannabis. She has said that there is a limited scope of legal application in healthcare, beyond which she does not favour any changes.[38]

The Federal Ministry of Health points out that international studies over the past 10 years have shown that the use and abuse of cannabis could be associated with a number of serious short- and long-term risks, especially among young people. Psychological disorders (for example, schizophrenia), organ-related medical effects (such as cardiovascular complications), and neurocognitive impairments (such as impairments in learning, attention and memory) have been mentioned. Child psychiatrists in Germany and in the Anglo-American area have concluded that cannabis use in childhood should be avoided. Therefore, according to the Ministry, the protection of minors must be given primacy.[39]

The Social Democratic Party of Germany (SPD) has expressed itself to be more open regarding the legalization of cannabis. From its point of view, an explicit orientation towards decriminalization and model projects must be undertaken. First of all, experiences must be derived through the regulated and state-controlled provision of cannabis to defined groups of people. Overall, much more international experience (such as from Uruguay or Switzerland) must be taken into account.[40]

III. Discussion and conclusion

As this short overview has shown, the problem of at least partially decriminalizing "minor cases" of cannabis offenses is a universal one that must

38 See *Ewert* and *Geisenhanslüke*, "Frau Merkel, sehen wir nach der Wahl die Freigabe von Cannabis?" (26 Aug 2017), https://www.noz.de/deutschland-welt/politik/artikel/942392/frau-merkel-sehen-wir-nach-der-wahl-die-freigabe-von-cannabis (last visited 7 Oct 2020).

39 See Bundesministerium für Gesundheit, "Fragen und Antworten zum Gesetz 'Cannabis als Medizin'" (9 Mar 2017), https://www.bundesgesundheitsministerium.de/service/begriffe-von-a-z/c/cannabis/faq-cannabis-als-medizin.html (last visited 7 Oct 2020).

40 See BT-Drs. 18/12476. A lack of empirical knowledge in the ongoing debate is stated by *Duttge* and *Steuer*, MedR 2015, 799. The authors are opposed to a general decriminalization of Cannabis, see *Duttge* and *Steuer* ZRP 2014, 181.

be tackled in several countries,[41] with Germany and South Africa among them. Whereas a complete legalization is not on the political agenda at the moment, Germany has seen partial decriminalization in the past. As in South Africa, a higher-court decision on the basis of constitutional law was influential in this regard. The BVerfG saw the difficulty arising from interfering with citizens' basic rights through the overall criminalization of cannabis, at least in "minor cases", specifically cases of possessing small quantities for personal use. Unlike in South Africa, the BVerfG did not refer to personality rights or the right of privacy, but to general liberty rights. Taken together with the fact that German criminal law prohibits dealing in and possessing, but not consuming cannabis (again unlike the position in South Africa), this is probably why, in the German discussion, the question of location ("private" versus "public" character of the offense) does not play a role. The same is true for the question of work-related use – "minor" cases of possessing small quantities of cannabis for personal use can possibly also arise in a work-related setting. The exemption from criminal liability at the procedural level (Section 29(5) or 31a BtMG) also applies in this case – the worker might breach his duties and face consequences under labour law, but the criminal law would probably react just the same. As has been illustrated, the "solution" to the problem on the procedural level is problematic in several ways.[42] The decisive concept of a "small quantity" is not defined by law, so it is no surprise that we should see remarkable differences in how these provisions are applied from state to state, which is an obvious problem with regard to equality (Article 3 GG) and legal certainty (Article 103(II) GG). Furthermore, the question of avoiding a disproportionate intrusion on the right to liberty should be answered by a provision of substantive criminal law. If particular conduct is not dangerous and blameworthy enough to be punished by criminal law, then the state should decriminalize it and not let the offender rely merely on the (relatively uncertain) possibility that the public prosecutor will close the proceedings. In my eyes, this aspect of the basic right to liberty is the decisive argument here, not saving state resources, which should just be a welcome side-effect. Further steps towards decriminalization should be considered. We must learn from the experience of other countries in this regard – South Africa being one of them.

41 For a Swiss approach making use of administrative sanctions („Ordnungsbussen") see *Albrecht*, NK 2016, 48.

42 See also *Harrendorf*, in: Drenkhahn et al. (eds.), Festschrift für Dünkel (2020), 351, 377.

Bibliography

Peter Albrecht, "Mit Ordnungsbussen gegen den unbefugten Cannabiskonsum", Neue Kriminalpolitik (NK) 2016, 48.

Kai Ambos, "'Recht auf Rausch?' – Anmerkungen zu den Entscheidungen des zweiten Senats des BVerfG vom 9.3.1994 und des kolumbianischen Verfassungsgerichts vom 5.5.1994", 78 Monatsschrift für Kriminologie und Strafrechtsreform (MschKrim) 1995, 47.

Lorenz Böllinger, "Grenzenloses symbolisches Strafrecht – Zum Cannabis-Beschluß des Bundesverfassungsgerichts", Kriminologisches Journal (KJ) 1994, 405.

Lorenz Böllinger, "Strafrechtsprofessoren für eine Reform des Betäubungsmittelstrafrechts: ein Projekt", Neue Kriminalpolitik (NK) 2014, 115.

Lorenz Böllinger, "Aufstieg und Fall des Cannabis-Verbots", Neue Kriminalpolitik (NK) 2018, 281.

Bundeskriminalamt, Polizeiliche Kriminalstatistik 2007–2017 (available at www.bka.de).

Bundeskriminalamt, Rauschgiftkriminalität – Bundeslagebild 2017 (2018), https://www.bka.de/DE/AktuelleInformationen/StatistikenLagebilder/Lagebilder/Rauschgiftkriminalitaet/rauschgiftkriminalitaet_node.html (last visited 7 Oct 2020).

Bundesministerium für Gesundheit, "Cannabis als Medizin" (19 Jan 2017), https://www.bundesgesundheitsministerium.de/ministerium/meldungen/2017/januar/cannabis-als-medizin.html (last visited 7 Oct 2020).

Bundesministerium für Gesundheit, "Fragen und Antworten zum Gesetz 'Cannabis als Medizin'" (9 Mar 2017), https://www.bundesgesundheitsministerium.de/service/begriffe-von-a-z/c/cannabis/faq-cannabis-als-medizin.html (last visited 7 Oct 2020).

Bundesministerium für Gesundheit, Drogen- und Suchtbericht (2018).

Die Bundesregierung, "Cannabis für Schwerkranke auf Rezept" (10 Mar 2017), https://www.bundesregierung.de/breg-de/aktuelles/cannabis-fuer-schwerkranke-auf-rezept-485740 (last visited 7 Oct 2020).

Deutsche Polizeigewerkschaft, "Drogenpolitik/Legalisierung von Drogen", https://www.dpolg.de/ueber-uns/positionen/drogenpolitik/ (last visited 7 Oct 2020).

Gunnar Duttge and *Melanie Steuer*, "Legalisierung von Cannabis: Verkommt Deutschland zu einer berauschten Gesellschaft?", Zeitschrift für Rechtspolitik (ZRP) 2014, 181.

Gunnar Duttge and *Melanie Steuer*, "Zur fehlenden Empirie in der aktuellen Debatte um eine Legalisierung von Cannabis", Medizinrecht (MedR) 2015, 799.

Burkhard Ewert and *Ralf Geisenhanslüke*, "Frau Merkel, sehen wir nach der Wahl die Freigabe von Cannabis?" (26 Aug 2017), https://www.noz.de/deutschland-welt/politik/artikel/942392/frau-merkel-sehen-wir-nach-der-wahl-die-freigabe-von-cannabis (last visited 7 Oct 2020).

Stefan Harrendorf, "Plädoyer für eine umfassende Entkriminalisierung des Umgangs mit Betäubungsmitteln zum Eigenkonsum", in: Kirstin Drenkhahn, Bernd Geng, Joanna Grzywa-Holten, Stefan Harrendorf, Christine Morgenstern, Ineke Pruin (eds.), Kriminologie und Kriminalpolitik im Dienste der Menschenwürde: Festschrift für Frieder Dünkel zum 70. Geburtstag (Forum Verlag Godesberg, Mönchengladbach 2020), 351.

Bernd Heinrich and *Nicolas van Bergen*, "Grundzüge des deutschen Betäubungsmittelstrafrechts und seine Entkriminalisierungstendenzen", Juristische Ausbildung (JA) 2019, 321.

Johannes Kaspar, Grundrechtsschutz und Verhältnismäßigkeit im Präventionsstrafrecht (Nomos, Baden-Baden 2014).

Fatina Keilani, "Berliner Kripo-Beamte fordern Cannabis-Legalisierung" (6 Feb 2018), https://www.tagesspiegel.de/berlin/drogenpolitik-berliner-kripo-beamte-fordern-cannabis-legalisierung/20929716.html (last visited 7 Oct 2020).

Harald Hans Körner, *Jörn Patzak* and *Mathias Volkmer* (eds.), Kommentar zum Betäubungsmittelgesetz (C.H. Beck, 9th ed., Munich 2019).

Arthur Kreuzer, "Die Haschisch-Entscheidung des BVerfG", Neue Juristische Wochenschrift (NJW) 1994, 2400.

Ursula Nelles, "Einstellungsvorschriften als Korrektiv für unverhältnismäßige Strafgesetze?", Neue Zeitschrift für Strafrecht (NStZ) 1994, 366.

Cornelius Nestler, "Cannabis und die verantwortungsbewusste Freiheit", 5 Strafverteidiger (StV) 2019, I.

Carsten Schäfer and *Letizia Paoli*, Drogen und Strafverfolgung (Max-Planck Insitut für ausländisches und internationales Strafrecht, Freiburg 2006).

Statistisches Bundesamt, Rechtspflege Staatsanwaltschaften 2017 (2018), https://www.statistischebibliothek.de/mir/receive/DEHeft_mods_00092135 (last visited 7 Oct 2020).

Register of cases

BVerfG, Judgment of 9 Mar 1994, 2 BvL 43/92 et al., BVerfGE 90, 145.

Sustainable Development, Bureaucratic Implementation and the Need for Jurisprudential Certainty

*Jenny Hall**

Abstract: The concept of sustainable development is widely accepted as the approach that must be followed to address the range of environmental problems which we are facing. This is true in the case of South Africa where sustainable development has been incorporated into the environmental right contained in the Constitution and environmental legislation. The challenge in balancing the three pillars of sustainable development in practice, however, is that this legislation does not generally provide extensive detail regarding how the different facets of sustainable development must be balanced in the implementation of the legislation. The result is that the operationalisation of sustainable development in practice takes place through hundreds of individual decisions by officials on issues such as applications for authorisation and in respect of compliance and enforcement. The courts consequently have a potentially valuable role to play in developing the jurisprudence on sustainable development which can guide officials in the exercise of their decision-making discretion. This Chapter accordingly sets out a preliminary exploration of how the South African courts have engaged with the concept in the government decision-making context and makes some tentative observations about the consistency, or lack thereof, in the development of a body of jurisprudence on sustainable development.

* Jenny Hall, *B.A., LL.B., LL.M., Ph.D.*, Senior lecturer, University of Johannesburg.

I. Introduction

The concept of sustainable development emerged as a response to growing concerns about the impact of human activities on the environment. It is now widely accepted by the international community as being the foremost principle which should be implemented to address the increasing number of environmental problems facing the earth. However, its scope and potential for doing so effectively is contested. Bugge summarises this contestation as follows:

> "The main criticism is the vagueness of the concept, expressed in such terms as 'there really is no substance' or 'everyone can agree because it can be understood in so many ways'. Some see it as a contradiction: If economic growth is the cause of the problems – how can more growth be the cure?"[1]

This Chapter sets out a preliminary exploration of how the South African courts have engaged with the concept of sustainable development in the government decision-making context. It examines the extent to which the courts have been consistent in their approach and have grappled with the contested nature of the content of the term successfully. The discussion below begins with an overview of the evolution of sustainable development in the international arena and the reception of the principle into South African law. That overview is followed by some observations on the nature of environmental decision-making before discussing a selection of cases related to decision-making on applications for authorisation and actions taken to secure compliance. It concludes with some tentative observations about the consistency, or lack thereof, in the development of a body of jurisprudence on sustainable development.

1 *Bugge*, in: Bugge and Voigt (eds.), Sustainable Development in International and National Law (2008), Part I, Chapter I.1., 3–21, as republished in: Freestone (ed.), Sustainable Development and International Environmental Law (2018), 42.

II. The emergence of sustainable development in the international arena

Sustainable development was arguably first introduced to the international agenda by the Club of Rome's report titled *The Limits to Growth* in the 1970s, in which it was argued that existing trends in economic and population growth could harm both the environment and future economic growth.[2] The term was only formally defined and accepted as the future of environmental policy, however, some years later in the Brundtland Report where it was defined as meaning "[d]evelopment that meets the needs of the present without compromising the ability of future generations to meet their own needs."[3]

The understanding of what sustainable development entails is not static. Over the past few decades, it has evolved and adapted to keep up with global trends and developments. In this regard, a number of international initiatives have taken place in order to give further effect to the underlying objectives of sustainable development. In 1992, for example, the United Nations Conference on Environment and Development (the Rio Conference) constituted one of the first attempts to put concrete measures in place to achieve worldwide sustainable development. Apart from opening two important multilateral environmental agreements for signature,[4] the Rio Declaration – one of the outcomes of the Conference – saw the introduction of principles that are considered to be critical for giving effect to sustainable development.[5] Two of the key ones are found in Principles 1 and 4. Principle 1 states that

> "[h]uman beings are at the centre of concerns for sustainable development. They are entitled to a healthy and productive life in harmony with nature."

---

2 *Meadows, Meadows, Randers* and *Behrens*, The Limits to Growth (1972), as cited by *Verschuuren*, in: Fisher (ed.), Research Handbook on Fundamental Concepts of Environmental Law (2016), 277.

3 World Commission on Environment and Development, United Nations Report of the World Commission on Environment and Development: Our Common Future (1987), 41.

4 United Nations Framework Convention on Climate Change (1992) and Convention on Biological Diversity (1992).

5 Rio Declaration on Environment and Development (1992).

Principle 4 on the other hand says that

> "[i]n order to achieve sustainable development, environmental protection shall constitute an integral part of the development process and cannot be considered in isolation from it."

These principles provide much needed guidance and insight regarding the understanding of sustainable development and what it entails. Some of the other more prominent principles that are included in the Rio Declaration include: the precautionary principle (also known as the preventative principle); the principle of public participation (which is closed linked to access to information); the "polluter pays principle"; the principle of intra-generational and inter-generational equity; and the principle of integration.[6]

As a result of the Rio Conference it is generally accepted that realising sustainable development depends on balancing three pillars i.e. the social, economic and environmental. Many of the subsequent conferences that have taken place over the years have built on this foundation. These conferences include the 2002 World Conference on Sustainable Development, Johannesburg; the 2012 United Nations Conference on Sustainable Development, Rio de Janeiro; and the 2015 United Nations Sustainable Development Summit, New York which resulted in the adoption of the outcome-based document titled *Transforming Our World: The 2030 Agenda for Sustainable Development*.[7] The document introduces 17 sustainable development goals and 169 targets[8] and makes a commitment to ensuring "the lasting protection of the planet and its natural resources".

However, notwithstanding the increasing visibility of the term "sustainable development" in both soft and hard law international instruments, its nature is still somewhat obscure and there is debate as to how effective it can be in and of itself in addressing environmental problems. Sands *et al*, for example, state that the factual position of many species not being managed sustainably illustrates the difficulty of turning the concept into a "practical development tool".[9] A detailed discussion of these dynamics and debates is beyond the scope of this Chapter. Nevertheless, bearing the fact

6 Principles 15, 10, 16 and 3 respectively.

7 General Assembly of the United Nations, Transforming our world: the 2030 Agenda for Sustainable Development (25th Sep 2015), https://sustainabledevelopment.un.org/post2015/transformingourworld (last visited 09 Sep 2019).

8 Ibid.

9 *Sands*, *Peel*, *Fabra* and *MacKenzie*, Principles of International Environmental Law (2012), as cited by *Verschuuren* (n. 2), 295.

that they exist in mind is important for understanding the context within which the South African courts must adjudicate environmental disputes.

III. The introduction of sustainable development into South African law

Sustainable development was formally introduced into South African law post democracy when an environmental right was included in the so-called interim Constitution.[10] The same wording was retained in the environmental right that is contained in Section 24 of the "final" Constitution which reads as follows:

> "Everyone has the right –
>
> (a) to an environment that is not harmful to their health or well-being; and
> (b) to have the environment protected, for the benefit of present and future generations, through reasonable legislative and other measures that –
>   (i) prevent pollution and ecological degradation;
>   (ii) promote conservation; and
>   (iii) secure ecologically sustainable development and use of natural resources while promoting justifiable economic and social development."[11]

The provisions on sustainable development that are contained in Section 24(b) are not self-executing. Rather they require government to operationalise it, or to breathe life into the concept, by passing appropriate legislation and by giving effect to it in its decision-making activities. Government responded to this imperative by initiating an environmental law reform process to overhaul drastically the existing environmental legislation that was outdated and which did not encompass sustainable development. As a result of this process, a suite of environmental framework legislation was passed. The National Environmental Management Act, 1998 (NEMA) was the first of these.[12] It introduced the new overarching approach to environmental management that informs approaches to decision-making, not only in terms of NEMA, but also to decisions made in terms of

---

10 Section 23 of the Constitution of the Republic of South Africa, 1993 (Act No. 200 of 1993).

11 Constitution of the Republic of South Africa, 1996.

12 Act No. 107 of 1998.

the related specific environmental management Acts (SEMAs) that deal with different sectoral issues such as air quality, waste management and biodiversity.

Importantly for the purposes of this Chapter, NEMA provides more detail than the Constitution regarding what sustainable development involves. In this regard, "sustainable development" is defined in Section 1 of the Act as meaning "[T]he integration of social, economic and environmental factors into planning, implementation and decision-making to ensure that development serves present and future generations."

In addition to the definition, NEMA contains an extensive set of principles which must, amongst others, guide government decision-making. The first two principles are overarching ones. They require that environmental management must place people and their needs at the forefront of its concern and serve their physical, psychological, development, cultural and social interests equitably; and that development must be socially, environmentally and economically sustainable.[13] These two principles are amplified by an additional 18 subprinciples, some of which are themselves subdivided. These sub-principles essentially "unpack" the different aspects of sustainable development and resonate with many of the Rio Declaration Principles.[14] For example, the precautionary principle is set out in Section 2(4)(a)(vii), and the polluter-pays principle is found in Section 2(4)(p). The principles and sub-principles apply to all decisions which are made by officials – including decisions on licence applications and compliance and enforcement activities – when the decision may significantly affect the environment.[15]

NEMA also has a Chapter dedicated to integrated environmental management.[16] The general objectives of integrated environmental management are listed in Section 23 of Chapter 5 as being to –

"(a) promote the integration of the principles of environmental management set out in section 2 into the making of all decisions which may have a significant effect on the environment;

(b) identify, predict and evaluate the actual and potential impact on the environment, socioeconomic conditions and cultural heritage, the risks and consequences and alternatives and options for mitigation of activities, with a view to minimising negative impacts, maximis-

13 Section 2(1) and (2) respectively.

14 *Kidd*, Environmental Law (2nd ed. 2011), 38.

15 Section 2(1)(b), (c) and (e).

16 Chapter 5.

ing benefits, and promoting compliance with the principles of environmental management set out in section 2;

(c) ensure that the effects of activities on the environment receive adequate consideration before actions are taken in connection with them;

(d) ensure adequate and appropriate opportunity for public participation in decisions that may affect the environment;

(e) ensure the consideration of environmental attributes in management and decision-making which may have a significant effect on the environment; and

(f) identify and employ the modes of environmental management best suited to ensuring that a particular activity is pursued in accordance with the principles of environmental management set out in section 2."[17]

The main tool for achieving these objectives is the environmental impact assessment (EIA) process and the associated requirement to obtain environmental authorisation for certain developmental activities, as well as the power of government to secure compliance with these provisions. In this regard, Chapter 5 is complemented by a set of EIA Regulations which define an EIA as, "a systematic process of identifying, assessing and reporting environmental impacts associated with an activity and includes basic assessment and [Scoping & Environmental Impact Report]."[18] Although this definition may create an impression that the EIA process is limited to environmental issues, this is not the case. This is clear at least from the stipulated requirements of the reports that must be submitted in support of an application. These include a requirement that the impact and risk assessment process contain an assessment of "cumulative impacts which focused on determining the geographical, physical, biological, *social, economic, heritage, and cultural sensitivity* of the sites and locations within sites".[19]

The EIA system has been now in existence for more than 20 years and therefore provides a useful point of departure for considering the extent to which environmental, social, and economic considerations co-exist effectively in decision-making. Comprehensive powers for securing compliance with the EIA regime and other environmental issues regulated by NEMA and the SEMAs are slightly newer (having been officially incorporated into

17 Section 23(1) and (2)(a)–(f).

18 Regulation 1. The current Regulations and Notices are found in GNR 982, 983, 984 and 985, GG 38282, 4 Dec 2014, as amended.

19 Appendix 1(2)(d).

NEMA in 2005), but are also old enough to have stimulated litigation which can provide an insight of the court's approach to sustainable development in that context.

IV. The nature of environmental decision-making and sustainable development – a challenging mandate

The discussion above shows that the position in South African constitutional and environmental legislation is clear at a conceptual level. Sustainable development is part of the law and must be given effect to in the implementation of that legislation. However, the legislation does not generally provide extensive detail regarding how the different facets of sustainable development must be balanced in the implementation of the legislation. In effect it provides a general mandate, or imperative, and a framework for operationalising sustainable development.

The result of this is that the operationalisation of sustainable development in practice takes place through hundreds of individual decisions by officials on issues such as applications for authorisation and in respect of compliance and enforcement. Environmental decisions therefore become extremely complex, and non-routine, because officials are left with the challenge of unpacking how the three pillars of sustainable development – and the detailed principles in NEMA relating to sustainable development – should be juggled in any particular situation. In other words, it is up to an official to determine first, how sustainable development finds application in the context of the facts of a particular decision, and, second, what balancing the three pillars requires in that context. In the absence of detailed guidelines, this position means that the official is responsible for considering both micro and macro issues – a heavy burden indeed.

The fact that in practice the weight of realising sustainable development effectively in South Africa rests on a number of individual officials' shoulders ought to raise questions about the feasibility of the approach and its implications for the sustainable development project. Apart from the obvious risk of a lack of consistency because of the number of decision-makers involved, the ability of the officials to be successful in the endeavour is likely to be influenced by the fact that few will be qualified in all the aspects that are involved, i.e. economics, social studies and environmental management.

Notwithstanding this, the safeguard to overseeing the ability of officials to "get this right" lies in the right of affected parties to challenge official decisions before the courts. Given the complexities of sustainable development in practice, it is hardly surprising that disputes regarding decisions involving sustainable development go to the courts fairly frequently. Where they do, the courts have a potentially valuable role to play, not only in providing a unique insight to government's decision-making practices on sustainable development, but also in the development of a sustainable development jurisprudence which can provide guidance to officials for future decision-making processes.

V. Jurisprudential beginnings – authorisations and adjudication in the early years

The environmental right and new environmental legislation did not spawn a wave of environmental litigation initially, despite the incorporation of various mechanisms in NEMA – such as expanded *locus standi* and the potential for more socially minded costs orders – providing a platform conducive to increased litigation.[20] The first time the Constitutional Court heard an environmental matter was in 2001 in the case of *Minister of Public Works and Others v Kyalami Ridge Environmental Association and Others (Mukhwevho Intervening)*.[21] It was a disappointing start to the development of a jurisprudence on sustainable development and the case has been widely criticised.[22] In this regard, the court was required to decide, amongst other issues, how the principles in NEMA and the EIA requirements applied to government's decision to build a temporary transit camp for flood victims on land which it owned. In considering the dispute, the court indicated that it was "not appropriate" to decide on whether the principles applied to disputes between government and individuals, although it accepted that they did for the purposes of the judgment.[23] In that sense at least, the resulting judgment was a missed opportunity in so far as it relates to developing a platform for a sound sustainable development jurisprudence and its application to disputes between government and the public.

Arguably, the next milestone in the development of jurisprudence on sustainable development began in 2004 when a number of cases involving filling station developments were heard. These cases were based on the

20 Section 32.

21 2001 3 SA 1151 (CC).

22 See, for example, *Kidd*, 9 PER 2006 issue 3, 72, 72 and *Kidd*, 8 SAJELP 2001, 119.

23 The *Kyalami Ridge Environmental Association* case (n. 21) para. 70.

same underlying issues: they were either concerned with filling stations that had applied unsuccessfully for environmental authorisation challenging the government's refusal, or with existing filling station owners, not wanting new competition, challenging government's decisions to grant environmental authorisation to newcomers.

The first two cases – *Sasol Oil (Pty) Ltd and Another v Metcalfe N.O.* (*Sasol*)[24] and *BP Southern Africa v MEC for Agriculture, Conservation, Environment and Land Affairs* (*BP*)[25] – which were handed down by the same High Court, both required the court to consider whether the Gauteng provincial environmental department was entitled to take socio-economic considerations into account in its guideline on filling station applications. The court reached diametrically opposite findings. In the *Sasol* case, the court found that government did not have the power to regulate the commercial aspects of filling stations in terms of the EIA Regulations. In *BP*, however, the court found that the department was obliged to take socio-economic considerations into account.[26] The basis for the court's finding in *BP* was that the environmental right expressly creates a linkage between environmental and socio-economic considerations that is supplemented by NEMA because of the principles in NEMA which require authorities to evaluate the "social, economic and environmental impacts of activities"[27] as well as the provisions in NEMA regarding EIAs.[28]

The conflicting approaches reflected in these judgments were continued in subsequent filling station cases over the next year. In these subsequent judgments the emphasis was not so much on whether socio-economic impacts could be taken into account at all, but on whether government decision-makers are obliged to take the economic impacts of proposed filling stations on existing filling station owners into account. The Transvaal Provincial Division (as it was then) was given the opportunity to consider the issue four times between February and July 2005, one in respect of a decision by the Gauteng provincial environmental department and three in respect of the Mpumalanga provincial environmental department. These cases provided an opportunity for the court to create a consistency in government decision-making as the Mpumalanga department initially

---

24 2004 5 SA 161 (W).

25 2004 5 SA 124 (T). "MEC" is the abbreviation for Member of the Executive Council and refers to a provincial Minister.

26 The *BP* case (n. 25) 150E.

27 The *BP* case (n. 25) Section 2(4)(i).

28 The *BP* case (n. 25) 150–151.

followed a different approach to the Gauteng department in that it did not consider itself obliged to take socio-economic considerations into account.

Unfortunately, clarity was not forthcoming from the judgments because the court's findings were again contradictory. In *All the Best Trading CC t/a Parkville Motors and Others v S N Nyagar Property Development and Construction CC & Others* the judge expressly departed from the *BP* judgment and elected to cite *Sasol* to justify its finding that government's decision-making powers in respect of EIAs is "intrinsically related to the environment as opposed to any consideration of trade".[29] In the other three cases, however, the *BP* reasoning was applied i.e. in *Capital Park Motors CC & Another v Shell South Africa Marketing (Pty) Ltd & Others,*[30] *Turnstone Trading CC v Director-General Environmental Management, Department of Agriculture, Conservation and Development and Others*[31] and *Fuel Retailers Association of Southern Africa (Pty) Ltd v The Director-General Environmental Management, Department of Agriculture, Conservation and Environment for Mpumalanga Province and Others* (*Fuel Retailers*),[32] the court concluded that socio-economic factors must be taken into account and that this included the impact of a proposed development on existing competitors.

In 2006 clarity was provided when the Supreme Court of Appeal handed down its judgment in respect of the *Sasol* appeal.[33] In an approach that supported the *BP* judgment, the court remarked that –

> "Of particular importance is NEMA's injunction that the interpretation of any law concerned with the protection and management of the environment must be guided by its principles.[34] At the heart of these is the principle of 'sustainable development', which requires organs of state to evaluate the 'social, economic and environmental impacts of activities'."[35]

The court also stressed the importance of not unduly compartmentalising aspects of the decision-making process when sustainable development is involved where it stated that –

---

29 2005 3 SA 396 (T) at 300I–J and 400A.

30 (T) Case No. 3016/05 of 18 Mar 2007 (unreported).

31 [2005] ZAGPHC 166 (11 Mar 2005).

32 [2005] ZAGPHC 288 (28 Jul 2005).

33 *MEC for Agriculture, Conservation and Environment v Sasol Oil (Pty) Ltd & Another* 2006 1 SA 66 (SCA).

34 Section 2(1)(e) of NEMA.

35 The *Sasol* case (n. 33) Section 2(3); Section 2(4)(i).

> "To attempt to separate the commercial aspects of a filling station from its essential features is not only impractical but makes little sense from an environmental perspective. It also flies in the face of the principle of sustainable development, which is referred to above. The adoption of such a restricted and literal approach, as contended for by the respondents would defeat the clear purpose of the enactment."[36]

The Supreme Court was consistent in following this *ratio* the following year in the appeal on the *Fuel Retailer* judgment referred to above, where it noted that "it is clear from a number of decisions that socio-economic considerations must be taken into account in making decisions".[37] Absolute confirmation of the approach was provided shortly afterwards in the *Fuel Retailer* appeal from the Supreme Court of Appeal to the Constitutional Court.[38] In its judgment (*Fuel Retailers* Constitutional Court judgment), the Constitutional Court held that –

> "NEMA makes it abundantly clear that the obligations of environmental authorities includes the consideration of socio-economic factors as an integral part of its environmental responsibility."[39]

With regards to the economic impacts on existing competitors, it stated that –

> "The cumulative effect of the proposed development must naturally be assessed in the light of existing developments. A consideration of socio-economic conditions therefore includes the consideration of the impact of the proposed development not only in combination with existing developments, but also its impact on existing ones."[40]

The judgment has been criticised on the basis that the court blurred the distinction between the environmental, social and economic aspects of sustainable development.[41] Nevertheless, what the court did achieve in these judgments is to make it clear to officials that the principle of sustainable development underlies their decisions and that their decisions rest on all

---

36 The *Sasol* case (n. 33) 490 para. 16.

37 *Fuel Retailers Association of SA (Pty) Ltd v Director-General, Environmental Management, Mpumalanga and Others* 2007 2 SA 163 (SCA) para. 14.

38 *Fuel Retailers Association of Southern Africa (Pty) Ltd v Director-General, Environmental Management, Mpumalanga and Others* 2007 6 SA 4 (CC).

39 The *Fuel Retailers* case (n. 38) 27 para. 62.

40 The *Fuel Retailers* case (n. 38) 31 para. 72.

41 See, for example, *Feris*, 1 Constitutional Court Review 2008, 236; *Tladi*, 1 Constitutional Court Review 2008, 255; and *Kidd*, 15 SAJELP 2008, 85.

three pillars of sustainable development. In that sense at least, it provided much needed certainty to bring consistency to decision-making between the different provincial environmental departments as well as the national department.

VI. Building new jurisprudential dimensions on decision-making and sustainable development – more recent developments

If the energy sector was the source of judicial precedent on the integration of economic considerations into environmental decisions, it has also, somewhat ironically – together with disputes involving the mining sector – laid the basis for judicial precedent regarding the extent to which environmental and social factors should be considered in decision-making. Both the energy and mining sectors are significant players in the national economy and accordingly enjoy a high degree of political support and status. Proposed developments in both sectors also attract opposition because of the significant environmental impacts that are associated with their activities. The tension between economic clout and environmental impacts has accordingly become a site of contested terrain and the subject of a relatively high number of legal challenges in recent years.

The 2017 judgment of *Earthlife Africa, Johannesburg v Minister of Environmental Affairs and Others,*[42] for example, is a good illustration of how the court has had to balance the competing interests of broad economic needs i.e. energy security, development, economic growth and social development with environmental considerations. The case involved a decision to grant environmental authorisation for the development of a coal-fired power station, Thabametsi. It is worth noting that the decision to authorise the power station was made at a time when there was pressure from the global community to move away from such technologies because of the environmentally unsustainable nature thereof, but also at a time when South Africa's need to produce additional electricity had become a national priority.[43]

Earthlife Africa (Earthlife) argued that the decision of the Minister to grant environmental authorisation for Thabametsi should be overturned

---

42 *Earthlife Africa Johannesburg v Minister of Environmental Affairs and Others* 2017 2 All SA 519 (GP).

43 Article 3 of the Kyoto Protocol to the United Nations Framework Convention on Climate (1992).

because the climate change impacts associated with the proposed power station had not been considered prior to granting authorisation. Much of the justification for its argument lay in the wording of Section 24O(1) of NEMA which provides a list of relevant factors that decision-makers must take into account when making a decision on an application for environmental authorisation. This list includes factors such as any pollution and environmental impacts, or environmental degradation, that is likely to be caused if the application is approved or refused. Earthlife argued that this wording includes a requirement to consider the climate change impacts of the development.

By contrast, government attempted to deflect Earthlife's argument with a response that "there is no provision in our domestic legislation, regulations or policies that expressly stipulates that a climate change assessment must be conducted before the grant of an environmental authorisation" and that there is similarly no provision in terms of South Africa's obligations under international law.[44] Government also attempted to counter the argument by raising economic considerations. Rather than balancing those with the environmental considerations, it appears to have suggested that economic interests should prevail. In this regard, it pointed to "national mitigation measures and sectoral plans [which] are aimed at balancing South Africa's development needs with its climate change imperatives" as well as the fact that the "country is facing acute energy challenges that hamper economic development".[45] On the basis of these macro-economic considerations, it argued that "Earthlife's submissions lose sight of the broader developmental context". Although part of government's argument is that climate change issues need to be addressed at a macro level before being translated in individual decision-making processes, the underlying suggestion in the government's defence was that in situations where there are national economic considerations at play, economic considerations should triumph over environmental ones.

The court accepted government's argument to the extent that it noted that the Department of Energy's policy documents consider Thabametsi as being a critical project for meeting the country's electricity demand and that it has been registered as a strategic infrastructure project due to its economic and social importance.[46] However, it also emphasised the requirements of the Constitution and NEMA in relation to environmental

---

44 The *Earthlife* case (n. 42) para. 16.

45 The *Earthlife* case (n. 42) para. 18.

46 The *Earthlife* case (n. 42) para. 36.

impacts. In this regard it held, citing the *Fuel Retailer* Constitutional Court judgment with approval, that –

> "NEMA, like all legislation, must be interpreted purposively and in a manner that is consistent with the Constitution, paying due regard to the text and context of the legislation.[47] Section 2 of NEMA sets out binding directive principles that must inform all decisions taken under the Act, including decisions on environmental authorisations. Competent authorities must take into account the directive principles when considering applications for environmental authorisation.[48] The directive principles promote sustainable development and the mitigation principle that environmental harms must be avoided, minimised and remedied. The environmental impact assessment process is a key means of promoting sustainable development, by ensuring that the need for development is sufficiently balanced with full consideration of the environmental impacts of a project with environmental impacts. The directive principles caution decision-makers to adopt a risk-averse and careful approach especially in the face of incomplete information."[49]

The court also noted that the environmental right

> "recognises the interrelationship between the environment and development. Environmental considerations are balanced with socio-economic considerations through the ideal of sustainable development."[50]

These remarks make it clear that the court is not willing to accept the devaluing of the environmental component of sustainable development in instances of prevailing national economic interest. To the contrary, it took note of the significance of the environmental impacts associated with coal-fired power stations, remarking both that Thabemetsi was anticipated to be responsible for between 1.9 and 3.9 per cent of South Africa's total greenhouse gas emissions[51] and that –

> "Climate change poses a substantial risk to sustainable development in South Africa. The effects of climate change, in the form of rising temperatures, greater water scarcity, and the increasing frequency of

---

47 *Cool Ideas 1186 CC v Hubbard and Another* 2014 4 SA 474 (CC) para. 28.
48 Sections 23 and 24 of NEMA.
49 The *Earthlife* case (n. 42) para. 80.
50 The *Earthlife* case (n. 42) para. 82.
51 The *Earthlife* case (n. 42) para. 42.

> natural disasters pose substantial risks. Sustainable development is at the same time integrally linked with the principle of intergenerational justice requiring the state to take reasonable measures protect [sic] the environment 'for the benefit of present and future generations' and hence adequate consideration of climate change. Short-term needs must be evaluated and weighed against long-term consequences."[52]

The court accordingly made a number of important findings. Firstly, it found that the wording of Section 24O is peremptory and that the list of relevant factors to be taken into account is therefore an obligation which decision-makers must discharge.[53] Secondly, it found that the EIA process is an open-ended one which means that the issues and factors that need to be considered will vary depending on the circumstances of the application.[54] Thirdly, it noted that NEMA "must also be interpreted consistently with international law" and that "[s]ection 233 of the Constitution provides that when interpreting any legislation, every court must prefer any reasonable interpretation of the legislation that is consistent with international law over any alternative interpretation that is inconsistent with international law".[55]

In holding that a climate change impact assessment ought to have been done before authorisation was granted, the court also refers to the precautionary approach and intergenerational equity as it refers to both the ecological sensitivity of the area as well as the 40 year lifespan of the power station. Furthermore, the court leaves no room for misinterpretation regarding the fact that economic needs cannot trump environmental ones *per se* when it says that –

> "the respondents' reliance on the IRP and the Determination [the Department of Energy's policies] to excuse the lack of consideration of the specific climate change impacts in relation to the Thabametsi power station basically misconstrues the nature of their duties under Section 24O(1) of NEMA."[56]

The judgment accordingly lays down firm guidance regarding the role of environmental considerations in decision-making and makes it clear that the rules of decision-making cannot be diluted because of political

---

52 The *Earthlife* case (n. 42) para. 82.
53 The *Earthlife* case (n. 42) para. 79.
54 The *Earthlife* case (n. 42) para. 89.
55 The *Earthlife* case (n. 42) para. 83.
56 The *Earthlife* case (n. 42) para. 98.

imperatives. In the face of the environmental right it may appear odd that this issue is litigated on at all. However, ensuring that environmental considerations are adequately taken into account has also been an issue in decision-making processes involving the mining sector where there has often been intimations that the importance of the sector's contribution to the national economy ought to overshadow its inherently unsustainable nature. There have long been policy debates regarding who has the right to regulate the environmental impacts of the sector.[57] Although mining legislation now includes environmental provisions and indicates that sustainable development must be taken into account as a decision-making criterion, many have felt that the department responsible for mining has a conflict of interests as its primary mandate is to promote the sector and that it cannot, or should not, be both referee and player.[58]

This debate arguably first became visible in the courts in 2010 in *City of Cape Town v Maccsand (Pty) Ltd and Others.*[59] The judgment provides an insight to the views of the Department of Minerals and Energy regarding its assumptions about the supremacy of its mandate and the priority of the mining sector's economic contribution to the country. In this regard, the case deals with the relationship between regulatory requirements imposed by mining, environmental and town-planning legislation. The Department had granted Maccsand (Pty) Ltd (Maccsand) certain mining rights and approvals in terms of the Minerals and Petroleum Resources Development Act[60] (MPRDA) to conduct mining activities on land owned by the City of Cape Town. The City had made it clear to both Maccsand and the Department during the application process that it did not support Maccsand's application for the mining rights and approvals. It also pointed out that Maccsand was obliged to comply with the requirements of the Land Use Planning Ordinance[61] (LUPO) before mining activities could commence. At some stage the City also indicated that Maccsand was required to obtain environmental authorisation in terms of NEMA. (It is not clear from the judgment precisely when this point was raised for the first time). When Maccsand disregarded the City's stance and started mining, the City accordingly applied to the Western Cape High Court for an interdict.

57 See, for example, Department of Environmental Affairs and Tourism, Green Paper on an Environmental Policy for South Africa (1996).

58 Ibid.

59 2010 6 SA 63 (WCC).

60 Act No. 28 of 2002.

61 Ordinance No. 15 of 1985.

The Department held the view that once it had authorised mining, no other legislative requirements could veto or trump its decision. In other words, the Department's stance was that the exercise of its powers ousted the jurisdiction of all other departments. It, and Maccsand's, defence was also based on the premises that: NEMA is not applicable to environmental impacts which eventuate from mining activities because the MPRDA trumps environmental legislation; the administration of mining matters provided for in NEMA was in the process of being transferred to the Department; and that the MPRDA incorporates the requirements of NEMA and should be considered as "special statutory measures to deal with the management of the environment in respect of prospecting and mining operations".[62] In other words, in the Department's opinion, the mining sector is required to be treated differently from other economic sectors.

The court rejected the respondents' approach on the basis of its findings regarding the constitutional approach to the powers of the three spheres of government. Following the approach in the *Fuel Retailers* Constitutional Court judgment, it held that it is perfectly permissible for more than one legislative regime to apply to an activity because the focus of the different regimes varied in terms of their underlying objectives.

In respect of the application of NEMA, the court held that although amendments which were made to NEMA, but which had not yet commenced, would transfer the administration of environmental authorisations relating to mining to the Department –

> "mining activity will not be absolved from the requirement that authorizations under NEMA are obtained if mining or related operations will entail activities listed under NEMA. All that will happen is that the power to issue those authorizations will be transferred from the National Environment Minister or the provincial MECs, to the Mining Minister. The authorizations, which he or her successor in that office will issue, will be authorizations in terms of NEMA.
>
> …
>
> Environmental protection is enshrined as a right in the Constitution. Hence, this Court must interpret legislation to give as much tangible protection to this right as the language of the applicable statutes can reasonably bear. That is the effect of the mandate given to this Court by Section 39(2) of the Constitution. In any event, there is no express

62 The *Maccsand* case (n. 59) para. 31.

provision that the provisions of the MPRDA outlined above, render the NEMA provisions redundant."[63]

The City was accordingly granted the interdict and Maccsand was ordered to comply with both town-planning and environmental legislative requirements. Maccsand appealed the decision to the Supreme Court of Appeal.[64] The Supreme Court of Appeal upheld the principle that more than one authorisation may be required for a mining activity and that authorisation under the MPRDA did not exclude the requirement to obtain permissions under other legislation. However, it noted that the relevant provisions in the NEMA Regulations related to mining had been repealed between the case being argued and handed down in the court *a quo* and it therefore set aside the orders in respect of NEMA. It also refused to grant a declaratory order on the subject.

Maccsand then appealed the Constitutional Court.[65] The Constitutional Court declined to give a declaratory order in respect of NEMA because, at the time of the hearing, mining had still not been relisted as an activity requiring environmental authorisation in terms of NEMA, but it upheld the finding of the court *a quo* that LUPO could apply to mining matters and, therefore, that mining legislation does not trump other legislative requirements.

Although *Maccsand* sent an unequivocal message that environmental protection is not to be downplayed in the authorisation of mining activities, a tendency to do so has continued in certain situations as is illustrated by the 2018 decision in *Mining and Environmental Justice Community Network of South Africa and Others v Minister of Environmental Affairs and Others.*[66] In this case a number of nongovernmental organisations challenged the decisions of both the Minister of Environmental Affairs and the Minister of Mineral Resources to grant authorisation for coal mining activities to take place in the Mabola Protected Environment in Mpumalanga – a decision which was made without any public consultation.

From the judgment it appears that the area is protected because it "comprises of wetlands and grasslands which have been largely classified as 'Irreplaceable Critical Biodiversity Areas' and 'Optimal Critical Biodiversity Areas' and numerous organs state [sic] and other stakeholders have

63 The *Maccsand* case (n. 59) para. 33.

64 *Maccsand (Pty) Ltd and Another v City of Cape Town and Others* 2011 6 SA 633 (SCA) para. 8.

65 *Maccsand (Pty) Ltd v City of Cape Town and Others* 2012 4 SA 181 (CC).

66 2019 1 All SA 491 (GP).

previously recognised the fundamental ecological and environmental importance of the area". The case is an interesting one in that it deals with a situation where one might expect that environmental considerations would trump socio-economic ones because of the special status of the area as a protected environment. That this approach ought to be the default decision-making one is also arguably reflected in legislation as, notwithstanding any other authorisations which are required, Section 48 of the National Environmental Management: Protected Areas Act[67] (NEMPAA) provides that no mining may take place in a protected area without the permission of the Ministers of Environmental Affairs and Mineral Resources.

In what may have been an attempt to circumvent the litigation, just before the application was heard, the MEC of the environmental department published a notice in the *Provincial Gazette* indicating his intention to exclude the mining area in question from the protected environment. Since much of the applicants' case was based on the area being a protected area subject to the requirements of NEMPAA, the court initially had to consider whether the case should proceed because the applicants' arguments would be redundant if the MEC finalised his decision. In the event, the court decided to proceed with hearing the matter.

The court begins its reasoning by pointing out the application of the NEMA principles and the fact that NEMPAA makes government the trustee of protected areas in securing the environmental right. It also pointed out that the correct way to interpret Section 48 of NEMPAA is as follows –

> "despite the fact that a person may have obtained all the necessary authorisations required in terms of all other applicable statutory provisions in order to lawfully conduct mining activities on a certain portion of land, should that land fall within a protected environment as contemplated in NEMPAA, then such a person would, in addition, need to obtain the written permission of both the Ministers of Environmental Affairs and Mineral Resources to do so. In considering a request for such permission, the ministers shall act as custodians of such protected environment and with a strict measure of scrutiny take into account the interests of local communities and the environmental principles referred to in Section 2 of NEMA."[68]

---

67 Act No. 57 of 2003.

68 The *Mining and Environmental Justice Community Network* case (n. 66) para. 10.7.

It appears that the Ministers acted with undue haste in making their decision to permit the mining activity. Apart from not allowing for any public participation in respect of their decision – a principle of NEMA – the decision was also taken before internal appeals on *inter alia,* the environmental authorisation and water use licence had run their course. The situation smacked of undue political interference, a probability which the court was alive to when it stated, in response to the Ministers' argument that they were justified in departing from the requirements of public participation, that –

> "Before dealing with the aforesaid justification issue, it needs to be mentioned that there is a disturbing feature in the conduct of the Ministers or their departments which gave rise to one of the complaints of a lack of transparency and it is this: the primary beneficiaries of the mining activity sought to be permitted are based off-shore and their local BEE component is, to an extent, 'politically connected'. There was therefore, apart from the statutory requirements, a compelling need for environmental decision-making to take place openly.
> ...
> It is, to my mind, astounding that in an admitted novel procedure, the Ministers decided (if indeed they had done so) that it would be procedurally fair not to hear the applicants whilst well-knowing that each and every preceding [sic] authorisation had been hotly contested. Whatever the case, it resulted in an unjustifiable and unreasonable departure from the PAJA prescripts and lead [sic] to procedurally unfair administrative action which should be reviewed and set aside on this ground alone."[69]

In a resounding loss for the respondents, the court pointed out that the Ministers had abdicated their decision-making responsibility by relying on input to other authorisation processes; had reached a decision prematurely and before the appeal processes in respect of other authorisations had been concluded; had failed to take important considerations into account; and had failed to take the interests of the community into account properly.

An important feature of the judgment is the court's consideration of the precautionary principle, as one of the sub-principles of sustainable development set out in NEMA. The applicants had argued that the Ministers had failed to take a risk-averse and cautionary approach in respect of

69 The *Mining and Environmental Justice Community Network* case (n. 66) para. 11.2.6.

the sensitivity of the ecosystem and the acid mine drainage which would eventuate from the mining activity. The court responded by stating that –

> "Without raising the 'cautionary approach' to a substantive ground of review beyond its compulsory inclusion in the decision-making process by means of Section 48(4) of NEMPAA, it is clear from the findings and reasons for their decisions and from the conditions imposed by the Ministers, that they simply relied on the mitigation and management of '*acid mine drainage, where applicable, according to the requirements of DWS*' (this is a quotation of one of the conditions and 'DWS' refers to the Department of Water and Sanitation).
> The above constitutes both an impermissible abdication of decision making authority and a non-compliance with Section 48(4) of NEMPAA, rendering the decisions reviewable."[70]

Finally, like the *Thabemetsi* case, the court dealt with South Africa's international obligations. It held that –

> "a failure to take South Africa's international responsibilities relating to the environment into account and a failure to take into account that the use and exploitation of non-renewable natural resources must take place in a responsible and equitable manner would not satisfy the 'higher level of scrutiny' necessary when considering whether mining activities should be permitted in a protected environment or not. Such failures would constitute a failure by the state of its duties as trustees of vulnerable environments, particularly where it has been stated that 'most people would agree, when thinking of the tomorrows of unborn people that it is a present moral duty to avoid causing harm to the environment'."[71]

VII. Jurisprudential development in the compliance and enforcement context – the early years of adjudication

The jurisprudence discussed above which has emanated mainly from decision-making on applications for authorisation to conduct certain activities, focuses on asserting the place of the three pillars of sustainable development in this decision-making process. It shows both that socio-economic

---

70 The *Mining and Environmental Justice Community Network* case (n. 66) para. 11.8.1.
71 The *Mining and Environmental Justice Community Network* case (n. 66) para. 11.11 (with reference to *Du Plessis*, SAJHR 2015, 260).

considerations must be considered as part of environmental decision-making process and that environmental considerations should not be relegated to a "Cinderella status" when there are pressing economic imperatives at play. A strong contribution of the courts in these situations has been their insistence that these disputes be adjudicated within the context of the environmental right and the sustainable development principles contained in NEMA. It is likely that where this occurs, the outcome of the dispute will be more predictable.

The question arises, however, as to how consistent the courts have been when adjudicating disputes in a different context. In this regard, the courts have also been called on to adjudicate disputes regarding government's compliance and enforcement efforts and, particularly for the purposes of this Chapter, disputes involving administrative enforcement notices that have been issued by government inspectors.

Since administrative enforcement notices are instruments which are used to secure compliance with environmental legislation, it can be anticipated that they constitute "other legislative measures" which Section 24(b) of the environmental right requires government to adopt. In view of this, it may seem self-evident that any dispute involving an administrative enforcement notice would be considered to be a constitutional matter and that the dispute would be located within the context of the environmental right.

The courts were given the opportunity to consider this in 2006 in the matter of *HTF Developers (Pty) Ltd v Minister of Environmental Affairs and Tourism and Others.*[72] In this case, the Gauteng provincial environmental department had issued an administrative enforcement notice to HTF in terms of Section 31A of the Environment Conservation Act, the precursor to NEMA, to stop making preparations for the construction of a residential development until it had obtained authorisation.[73] Early in the judgment the court sets out a reasonably detailed explanation of the environmental right, the obligations that are imposed by Section 24(b) of the right, the principle of sustainable development, the requirement of the state to act as custodian for future generations and the role of EIAs in securing the right.[74] The court dismissed the application and held the administrative enforcement notice to be enforceable, not only because the development was held to be one which required authorisation, but also because the

72 [2006] ZAGPHC 132 (28 Mar 2006).
73 Act No. 73 of 1989.
74 The *HTF Developers* case (n. 72) paras. 16–20.

department's policy on ridges (often particularly sensitive environments) – which was not legally binding – could be applied to the situation. The court's reliance on the department's policy shows a willingness to draw on policy tools which are aimed at giving effect to sustainable development in the adjudication of disputes, even if they are not legally binding.

HTF took the matter on appeal.[75] In the Supreme Court of Appeal it raised a new point. It argued that Section 32 of the Act, which contained a provision requiring all directives issued in terms of the Act to be published for comment in the *Government Gazette*, was applicable and that the department's failure to do so invalidated the notice which had been issued. The majority of the court adopted a very literal interpretation and found in favour of HTF. However, when the minority judgment took the spirit of the Constitution into account, it reached a different conclusion.

The MEC then appealed this decision to the Constitutional Court.[76] The Constitutional Court judgment makes it abundantly clear that environmental legislation, including the administrative enforcement provisions contained therein, are aimed at giving effect to the environmental right and must be interpreted in that context. This is evident from wording such as –

> "[m]ore fundamentally, however, the section requires an interpretation that gives effect to the environmental right contained in the Constitution";[77]

and

> "[u]nderlying the relationship between the two provisions (i.e. section 31A and section 32) is section 24 of the Constitution."[78]

It is therefore not surprising that when the court looked at the situation through the lens of the environmental right, it reached the conclusion that an overly literal interpretation of the provisions of Section 32 could defeat the aspirations of the environmental right in many practical situations. The Constitutional Court accordingly found in favour of government and upheld the validity of the directive.

---

75 *HTF Developers (Pty) Ltd v The Minister of Environmental Affairs and Tourism and Others* 2007 (5) SA 438 (SCA).

76 *MEC: Department of Agriculture, Conservation and Environment and Another v HTF Developers (Pty) Ltd* 2008 2 SA 319 (CC).

77 The *HTF Developers* Constitutional Court appeal case (n. 76) para. 19.

78 The *HTF Developers* Constitutional Court appeal case (n. 76) para. 23.

VIII. A step backwards? – Concurrent and recent compliance and enforcement judgments

The HTF Constitutional Court and High Court judgments created a firm platform from which the application of sustainable development in compliance and enforcement cases could be developed. Unfortunately, in parallel to the *HTF* judgments, there were also ones which resulted in different outcomes on appeal. In this regard, the Department of Water Affairs faced a significant environment problem in at least the early 2000s when acid water from mining operations was draining into a highly sensitive underground cave and water system in Gauteng. In response to the situation the Department issued administrative enforcement notices to several mines in the area in terms of Section 21 of the National Water Act.[79] The formalities surrounding the issuing of such notices are almost identical to those that relate to notices which are issued in terms of NEMA.

One of the obligations imposed by the notice required the Stilfontein Gold Mining Company Limited (amongst other mines) to pump out this acid water on an ongoing basis. In 2005 the Department approached the courts for an order compelling the company to comply. The order was granted, but the Department had to approach the courts again in 2006 because Stilfontein Gold mining was not complying with the directive or court order. This time, in the matter of *Minister of Water Affairs and Forestry v Stilfontein Gold Mining Company Limited & Others*, the court found in the Department's favour and granted an order holding the company and four directors guilty of contempt of court for failing to comply with the previous court order, a seemingly appropriate order as the directors had attempted to avoid their compliance obligations by resigning as directors – a situation which could set an unhealthy precedent for environmental liability in other cases.[80]

The directors appealed the decision and in *Kebble v The Minister of Water Affairs and Forestry* the court found in favour of the appellants on the basis that the administrative enforcement notice was held to be unclear in what was required.[81] It is noteworthy that the environmental right and the obligations on government to address situations where gross environmental pollution is taking place were not mentioned. The matter was disposed of

79 Act No. 36 of 1998.

80 2006 5 SA 333 (W).

81 2007 JDR 0872 (SCA).

as if it was an ordinary "non-constitutional" matter. Furthermore, Humby points out that –

> "since April 2000 the remaining mines in the KOSH basin had participated in an inter-mine forum relating to the pumping of underground water and that the directives assumed that they would thus be able to reach agreement amongst themselves. As the respondent pointed out, no mine other than the SGM had trouble in understanding what was required. Secondly, the court's emphasis on SGM only being in non-compliance by a certain date (30 June 2005), failed to take into account the environmental impacts of SGM's daily non-compliance to extract and treat a specified amount of litres of underground water; i.e. the filling of the basin with water, and thus the creation of conditions conducive to the generation of acid mine drainage. Linking due performance to one specific date in these circumstances was thus wholly inappropriate. Thirdly, the court's unwillingness to determine a standard of accountability in regard to the pumping of underground mine water, against which the directors' mass resignation could have been evaluated, is highly disappointing."[82]

Despite this judgment, the precedent that contempt of court proceedings can be used to enforce the environmental right remains intact – provided of course that the underlying obligation is clear.

More recently, there has been another example of the court failing to locate a compliance and enforcement dispute within the context of the Constitution. In this regard, the unreported judgment of *Interwaste (Pty) Ltd v Petlane N.O. and Others*[83] which was handed down in 2018, deals with the Gauteng environmental department's attempts to secure Interwaste's compliance with the provisions of the National Environmental Management: Waste Act[84] in respect of one of its landfill sites. The landfill site in question is in close proximity to approximately 500 000 residents, many of whom live in poverty and, although not discussed in the judgment, the landfill site has been the subject of hundreds of complaints from

82 Centre for Environmental Rights, Mining and Environment Litigation Review (Dec 2011), 12, https://cer.org.za/wp-content/uploads/2011/12/Wits-CER-Mining-Litigation-Review-6-December-2011.pdf (last visited 09 Sep 2019).

83 [2018] ZAGPPHC 28 (13 Feb 2018).

84 Act No. 59 of 2008.

residents over the last few years.[85] These complaints range from nuisance matters such as odour, to allegations of far more significant health impacts, including respiratory ailments.

The essence of the case turned on the fact that Interwaste was granted a waste management licence to operate the site in 2011 that was subject to renewal. The Department contended that the licence had not been renewed within the specified time period and, after some less formal compliance proceedings, it issued an administrative enforcement notice requiring operations at the site to cease until such time as a valid (renewed) licence had been obtained. In finding for the applicant, the reasoning in the judgment reflects a very literal and constrained approach. At no stage was the Constitution, the environmental right or the context of the situation mentioned at all. The former is surprising in view of the precedent created by *HTF* and the latter is equally surprising as the *amica curiae* was a residents' association which had long been involved in and affected by the operation of the landfill site.

Whilst the cases discussed above are clearly not representative of all environmental litigation which has taken place in respect of attempts to enforce the environmental right through securing compliance with environmental legislation passed to give effect to the right, it appears that the binding precedent created by the Constitutional Court in the *HTF* case has had less impact on other judgments than the *Fuel Retailers* CC judgment has had in judgments on decisions regarding environmental authorisations. To this extent, the court has been less emphatic in creating jurisprudence which asserts the role of the environmental right and the need to secure the three pillars of sustainable development and providing certainty and guidance to officials in compliance and enforcement matters.

IX. Conclusion

South Africa has followed international trends by incorporating sustainable development into its Constitution and national legislation. However, it has generally done so by stipulating the requirement to give effect to sustainable development in general terms rather than providing specific guidance to government decision-makers. Operationalising sustainable de-

85 *Hall*, "Taking the Sting out of the (Green) Scorpion's Tail: Latest Developments in the Adjudication of Waste Management Enforcement Disputes", 25 SAJELP 2019, forthcoming publication.

velopment therefore takes place in a myriad of daily decisions by individual government officials who are required to exercise their discretion regarding how the different facets of sustainable development must be balanced and given effect to in a particular situation.

In overseeing the exercise of these decision-making functions, the courts have had to consider what this means in the context of a developing country which faces particular challenges and tensions regarding the need for economic and social development. The discussion of the judgments in this chapter reveals that initial litigation in post-apartheid South Africa resulted in some inconsistency in the courts' approaches in respect of decisions on applications for environmental authorisation. However, a strong body of precedent has now emerged in judgments in respect of these disputes in which much of the courts' energy has focused on asserting the need to consider all three pillars of sustainable development in the decision-making process. This provides potentially valuable certainty, consistency and guidance to officials.

However, there has been less guidance about the nature and role of sustainable development in official decision-making when it comes to the adjudication of compliance and enforcement disputes. A key reason for this is that the courts have not been as systematic about locating the dispute within the context of the environmental right in these instances and that they have adopted a traditional and literal interpretative approach rather than a rights-based one. The potential difference to the sustainable development outcome where the courts adopt an approach such as that set out in *Maccsand* that they "must interpret legislation to give as much tangible protection to this [environmental] right as the language of the applicable statutes can reasonably bear" as opposed to a narrowly literal one is illustrated by the *HTF* judgments where the SCA minority judgment and Constitutional Court appeal judgment reach different conclusions to the majority in the SCA. This is an important disjuncture since it is often in the failure to comply with legislative requirements that the interface between economic activities, negative environmental impacts and social injustice becomes most visible and where the objectives of sustainable development are subverted. There is accordingly more scope for the court to play a role in realising the environmental right by developing a consistent rights-based approach to the application of sustainable development in government officials' attempts to enforce environmental legislation.

Bibliography

Hans Christian Bugge, "1987 – 2007: 'Our Common Future' Revisited" in: Hans Christian Bugge and Christina Voigt (eds.), Sustainable Development in International and National Law (Europa Law Publishing, Groningen 2008), Part I, Chapter I.1., 3 – 21, republished in: David Freestone (ed.), Sustainable Development and International Environmental Law (Edward Elgar Publishing, Cheltenham 2018), 42.

Centre for Environmental Rights, Mining and Environment Litigation Review (Dec 2011), https://cer.org.za/wp-content/uploads/2011/12/Wits-CER-Mining-Litigation-Review-6-December-2011.pdf (last visited 09 Sep 2019).

Loretta Feris, "Sustainable Development in Practice: Fuel Retailers Association of Southern Africa (Pty) Ltd v The Director-General Environmental Management, Department of Agriculture, Conservation and Environment for Mpumalanga Province", 1 Constitutional Court Review 2008, 236.

Jenny Hall, "Taking the Sting out of the (Green) Scorpion's Tail: Latest Developments in the Adjudication of Waste Management Enforcement Disputes", 25 South African Journal of Environmental Law and Policy (SAJELP) 2019, forthcoming publication.

Michael Kidd, Environmental Law (Juta, 2nd ed., Cape Town 2011).

Michael Kidd, "Greening the Judiciary", 9 Potchefstroom Electronic Law Journal (PER) 2006 issue 3, 72.

Michael Kidd, "Removing the Green-tinted Spectacles: The Three Pillars of Sustainable Development in South African Law", 15 South African Journal of Environmental Law and Policy (SAJELP) 2008, 85.

Michael Kidd, "The Constitutional Court's Dilution of NEMA: Minister of Public Works and Others v Kyalami Ridge Environmental Association and Another" 8 South African Journal of Environmental Law and Policy (SAJELP) 2001, 119.

Phillipe Sands, *Jacqueline Peel*, *Adriana Fabra* and *Ruth MacKenzie*, Principles of International Environmental Law (Cambridge University Press, 3rd ed., Cambridge 2012).

General Assembly of the United Nations, Transforming our world: the 2030 Agenda for Sustainable Development (25th Sep 2015), https://sustainabledevelopment.un.org/post2015/transformingourworld (last visited 09 Sep 2019).

Dire Tladi, "Fuel Retailers, Sustainable Development and Integration: A Response to Feris", 1 Constitutional Court Review 2008, 255.

Jonathan Verschuuren, "The Growing Significance of the Principle of Sustainable Development as Legal Norm", in: Douglas Fisher (ed.), Research Handbook on Fundamental Concepts of Environmental Law (Edward Elgar Publishing Limited, United Kingdom 2016), 276.

World Commission on Environment and Development, United Nations Report of the World Commission on Environment and Development: Our Common Future (Oxford University Press, Oxford 1987).

Register of cases

All the Best Trading CC t/a Parkville Motors and Others v S N Nyagar Property Development and Construction CC & Others 2005 3 SA 396 (T).

BP Southern Africa v MEC for Agriculture, Conservation, Environment and Land Affairs 2004 5 SA 124 (T).

Capital Park Motors CC & Another v Shell South Africa Marketing (Pty) Ltd & Others (T) Case No. 3016/05 of 18 Mar 2007 (unreported).

City of Cape Town v Maccsand (Pty) Ltd and Others 2010 6 SA 63 (WCC).

Cool Ideas 1186 CC v Hubbard and Another 2014 4 SA 474 (CC).

Earthlife Africa Johannesburg v Minister of Environmental Affairs and Others 2017 2 All SA 519 (GP).

Fuel Retailers Association of Southern Africa (Pty) Ltd v The Director-General Environmental Management, Department of Agriculture, Conservation and Environment for Mpumalanga Province and Others (35064/02) [2005] ZAGPHC 288 (28 Jul 2005).

Fuel Retailers Association of SA (Pty) Ltd v Director-General, Environmental Management, Mpumalanga and Others 2007 2 SA 163 (SCA).

Fuel Retailers Association of Southern Africa (Pty) Ltd v Director-General: Environmental Management, Mpumalanga and Others 2007 6 SA 4 (CC).

HTF Developers (Pty) Ltd v Minister of Environmental Affairs and Tourism and Others (24371/05) [2006] ZAGPHC 132 (28 Mar 2006).

HTF Developers (Pty) Ltd v The Minister of Environmental Affairs and Tourism and Others 2007 5 SA 438 (SCA).

Interwaste (Pty) Ltd v Petlane N.O. and Others (44773/16) [2018] ZAGPHC 28 (13 Feb 2018).

Kebble v The Minister of Water Affairs and Forestry 2007 JDR 0872 (SCA).

Maccsand (Pty) Ltd and Another v City of Cape Town and Others 2011 6 SA 633 (SCA).

Maccsand (Pty) Ltd v City of Cape Town and Others 2012 4 SA 181 (CC).

MEC for Agriculture, Conservation and Environment v Sasol Oil (Pty) Ltd & Another 2006 1 SA 66 (SCA).

MEC: Department of Agriculture, Conservation and Environment and Another v HTF Developers (Pty) Ltd 2008 2 SA 319 (CC).

Mining and Environmental Justice Community Network of South Africa and Others v Minister of Environmental Affairs and Others 2019 1 All SA 491 (GP).

Minister of Public Works and Others v Kyalami Ridge Environmental Association and Others (Mukhwevho Intervening) 2001 3 SA 1151 (CC).

Minister of Water Affairs and Forestry v Stilfontein Gold Mining Company Limited & Others 2006 5 SA 333 (W).

Sasol Oil (Pty) Ltd and Another v Metcalfe N.O. (Sasol) 2004 5 SA 161 (W).

Turnstone Trading CC v Director-General Environmental Management, Department of Agriculture, Conservation and Development and Others (3104/04) [2005] ZAGPHC 166 (11 Mar 2005).

Comment: Sustainable Legislation

Matthias Rossi[*]

I. Preliminary remarks

Jenny Hall describes in her article[1] the development of the principle of sustainability at the international level, its introduction into South African law and then addresses the question of how the principle of sustainability is "operationalized" in the application of the law. For this purpose, she examined a series of court rulings, which, in turn, were decided on the basis of the National Environmental Management Act (NEMA) in various cases concerning environmental protection. The analysis of this case law

---

* Matthias Rossi, *Dr. iur.*; Professor, University of Augsburg Faculty of Law. Chair for Constitutional Law, Administrative Law, European Union Law and Legislation Theory. I would like to thank my Academic Assistant Aqilah Sandhu for her assistance in translating this paper.

1 The oral presentation was delivered by *Jenny Hall* and *Sikhulile Ngcobo* together. This comment refers to the written contribution of *Jenny Hall* as submitted and published in this book, 257 et seqq.

shows that there is no clear line. Sometimes the ecological component is emphasized, in others the economic component of the sustainability principle is put into the foreground. The principle of sustainability is therefore, as a result, an indeterminate legal concept that does not provide sufficient legal certainty. While the author does not say it explicitly, she gives the reader the impression that the sustainability principle is used by South African courts to justify – ultimately even arbitrarily – political decisions in law.

Whether or not this impression is correct, I cannot assess – for I am neither familiar with South African environmental law nor do I know the specific court decisions. Viewed from a distance, however, I consider it necessary to relativize these findings for three reasons: First, it is in principle difficult to try to understand the "actual legal situation" by means of a casuistic approach studying some court decisions and to expect coherence in this respect. Courts decide on concrete issues of dispute. With regard to the factual circumstances, they are largely dependent on the submissions of the individual parties. Therefore, one should not expect to derive abstract-general legal principles from court rulings that might, beyond the concrete dispute, even clarify or avoid all other future issues of dispute. Secondly, the principle of sustainability must not be equated with the aim to fundamentally enhance environmental protection. As the contribution has correctly pointed out, the principle has, in addition to the ecological element, also a social and an economic element. If in the case law at hand sometimes the one and at times the other element prevails, it is therefore not objectionable in general. Thirdly, the steering effects of general principles simply must not be overestimated. This applies all the more if such principles – as is the case with the principle of sustainability – contain several sub-objectives of government action, which in turn are in a relationship of mutual tension. Neither the embodiment of the sustainability principle in the constitution nor its repetition in a legal statute may lead to the expectation that this will completely and exclusively determine a concrete approval decision in favour of environmental protection. Precisely because the principle has different elements, the only thing that can be derived from it is, at most, the requirement to give proper consideration to the various interests in the decision-making procedure, however not the anticipation of a specific result of the decision. Therefore, the sustainability principle is neither the only nor the decisive legal standard for decisions of the executive and the judiciary.

II. Sustainability in German and European environmental law

Against this background, I will not comment on the individual cases that have been described in the contribution of *Hall*, but rather provide a very brief overview of the situation in Germany and the EU, which is comparable in principle.

1. Sustainability in German environmental law

The principle of sustainability was enshrined in the Basic Law (*Grundgesetz* – GG) in 1994. At that time, Article 20a of the Basic Law introduced the state objective of environmental protection, which obliges the state to "protect the natural basis of life for future generations as well". The term "responsibility for future generations" is also described as an environmental law principle of sustainability. Some laws and ordinances have taken up this principle of sustainability. Surprisingly, however, not all laws on environmental protection make mention of it. For example, while Section 1 of the Federal Water Resources Act elevates the aim of sustainable water management to the central purpose of the entire water law and the Federal Nature Conservation Act refers to the "sustainable usability of natural resources", "sustainable soil fertility" or in general to "sustainable development" in various parts (but aside from that also makes reference to the aim of "sustainable energy supply" and "sustainable tourism" for instance), the Federal Immission Control Act makes no reference to it at all or only in the context of an authorization of the executive to issue a "biofuel sustainability ordinance". The principle of sustainability has instead been concretized further in urban development law and in spatial planning law in particular. In its pure form, the principle of sustainability is still reflected in the Federal Forest Act. This is because the principle of sustainability has been known in German (and Swiss) forestry since the second half of the 18th century. In this field, it is primarily a management principle. Put simply, it requires that only as many trees may be felled in a given period as will grow again in the same period. The English term "sustainable development" in the *Brundlandt*-report of 1987, which *Jenny Hall's* contribution correctly mentions, was therefore a translation of the German term sustainability.

2. Sustainability in EU law

At the level of the European Union, the principle of sustainability has been developed as a legal principle as well. Article 3 para. 3 of the Treaty on European Union (TEU) obliges the EU to work for the "sustainable development of Europe based on balanced economic growth and price stability, a highly competitive social market economy, aiming at full employment and social progress, and a high level of protection and improvement of the quality of the environment." Furthermore, Article 3 para. 5 of the TEU sets the goal of the "sustainable development of the Earth".

Closer focusing on environmental protection, the so-called cross-section clause of Article 11 of the Treaty on the Functioning of the European Union (TFEU) requires that environmental protection requirements must be taken into account when defining and implementing the Union's policies and activities, in particular with a view to promoting sustainable development. This provision is accompanied by Article 37 of the Charter of Fundamental Rights (the Charter): "A high level of environmental protection and the improvement of the quality of the environment must be integrated into the policies of the Union and ensured in accordance with the principle of sustainable development." Despite being enshrined in the Charter, this provision is not understood as a subjective right. Rather, it only legitimizes legal acts which promote environmental protection, even if they restrict fundamental rights. Given its function, Article 37 of the Charter is therefore not a fundamental right but a justification to restrict fundamental rights.

3. From three pillars of sustainability to 38 reference topics

Most importantly, however, I would like to point out that the issue of sustainability has also emancipated itself from environmental protection in Germany (and in the EU). Here, too, the three-pillar concept – aiming at striking a balance between the economic system, the social structure and the environment – has established itself in the political and academic debate.

A closer examination of the legal structure, however, reveals that each of these three objectives first of all stands for itself – there are environmental, economic and social sustainability requirements, each with different normative binding force. The principle of sustainability as such is not legally binding, it may rather be characterized as a political or ethical principle.

Instead, legally binding force is only achieved by concretizing the principle in corresponding laws.

In Germany, in addition to the aforementioned Article 20a of the Basic Law referring to environmental protection, the financial constitution must also be taken into account, which contains a "debt brake" capping public debt in Article 109 para. 3 and Article 115 of the Basic Law since 2009. Sustainability in this context means that future generations will have sufficient financial resources to shape the future in accordance with their respective political requirements. The principle of sustainability, understood as the scope of action of future generations, is thus rooted in the principle of democracy. In order to ensure that each generation has sufficient financial leeway, constitutional limits on national debt have been enshrined both in German law as well as at the level of the European Union. However, in politics as well as in the economic sciences not only the exact limits on public debt, but even their very basic purpose are being debated. In this respect, the fundamental message of the article by *Jenny Hall* is also confirmed by German and European law: The principle of sustainability – at least from a legal perspective – is in danger of degenerating into an empty formula that is filled with content depending on the political objective.

This applies all the more to the third pillar, social sustainability, which is from the very outset only indirectly anchored in the constitution. On the one hand, it is understood as a guarantee for a dignified human material sustenance and in this respect only seems to choose a different label for familiar content. However, it also contains a second component in which the basic idea of sustainability is expressed more strongly: the state social security systems must be designed in a way such as not to benefit the current beneficiaries at the expense of the current or future contributors. Here the principle of sustainability is complemented by the idea of intergenerational justice.

In Germany, these three subgoals are summarized and condensed into a common concept of the sustainability strategy, which was first adopted in 2002, revised in 2016 and again updated in 2018. It aims at making sustainable development the guiding principle of the Federal Government's policy and is therefore primarily a voluntary commitment. The three subgoals are measured by the sustainability strategy against a total of 38 key indicators, including poverty, land management, food security, health, air pollution, education, gender equality, water quality, resource conservation, innovation and distributive justice. This partial enumeration is deliberately not structured in terms of content, as the 38 areas cover almost all policy areas and read more like a promising program of a political party before an election than a concept of a government setting priorities. In addition, the quantification of the objectives in the individual areas is not comprehensible – it is unclear why the contribution to climate financing should be doubled by 2020 compared to the sum of 2014 and not changed by another factor, particularly since it is just as unclear which measures are considered to contribute to climate financing. The same applies to the goal of "affordable housing" – here the goal of reducing the proportion of "overburdened persons" in the population to 13 percent by 2030 is proclaimed.

Overall, therefore, the sustainability strategy must not be overestimated. It can be considered as a management tool that aims at contributing to a holistic, integrative sustainability policy through management rules, the definition of objectives and the allocation and measurement of indicators. From a legal perspective, however, it should be noted that the binding effect of the strategy must be put into perspective in several respects: Firstly, the strategy has not been legally adopted. Secondly, insofar as it is at least a voluntary self-commitment, it misses its actual goal, namely to enable a long-term or at least longer-term planning, because it can at best bind new federal governments politically. Thirdly, its content and, in part, its objectives are to a large extent open to interpretation. What is meant by a "significant reduction" (in carbon dioxide emissions from public-sector vehicles) or what is meant by "innovation", for example, is ultimately left open by the sustainability strategy.

III. Sustainability as a procedural concept

Due to a lack of detailed substantive requirements, sustainability is primarily a procedural concept. Sustainability is a task, not a solution.[2] Sustainability is a permanent balancing process.[3] Such a proceduralisation of the concept of sustainability does justice to the complexity of its task. However, even if understood as a procedural instrument, the capability of the sustainability principle must not be overestimated. Its effectiveness largely depends on how the procedure is designed.

In this respect, the contribution of *Jenny Hall* shall first be taken into consideration again. Referring to the legal rulings on various cases from South Africa, she describes only the very last step in the implementation

---

2 *Meßerschmidt*, in: Kahl (ed.), Nachhaltigkeit durch Organisation und Verfahren (2016), 195, 198.
3 *Lepsius*, in: Kahl (ed.), Nachhaltigkeit als Verbundbegriff (2008), 326, 349.

and enforcement of the constitutional sustainability postulation. The principle of sustainability as a constitutional principle is primarily binding on the legislator. The legislator itself is required to take sustainability into account and to develop it further when drafting laws, especially in the field of environmental protection. However, the constitutional principle of sustainability hardly plays an independent role in the application and interpretation of the laws by the authorities and the courts. This is because they primarily apply the law as enshrined in the statutes. Only where the legislator leaves the authorities and courts room for discretion does the constitutional principle of sustainability gain importance, as an interpretative guideline under certain circumstances, but it is then as open in content as described and – rightly – criticized by *Jenny Hall* in her article. Whether and in how much detail the legislator provides guidelines, namely to the authorities, which after all still have adequate professional competence, or also to the courts, which alone have the competence to judge, is perhaps a question of constitutional law, but above all a question of constitutional culture. However, the lack of coherence in the jurisprudence of South African courts, which the author has criticized, will certainly be achieved sooner and better by further concretizing the legal requirements more precisely.

More important than the question to which extent the three state powers are bound by the constitutional principle of sustainability or can and may concretize it, is the question of the procedure in which the concept of sustainability is operationalized irrespective of its binding nature. A variety of models are conceivable here. The participation of associations and other interest groups[4] or even the entire public[5] is one possibility, the creation of sustainability councils another.[6] Both procedures emphasize above all the democratic component and aim primarily at maintaining public support. If, on the other hand, a scientifically defined objective is the primary objective, expert advice is a good option.[7] And, of course, all

4 On this cf. *Leschke*, in: Kahl (ed.), Nachhaltigkeit durch Organisation und Verfahren (2016), 235 et seqq.

5 *Gärditz*, in: Kahl (ed.), Nachhaltigkeit durch Organisation und Verfahren (2016), 351 et seqq.

6 See *Calliess*, in: Kahl (ed.), Nachhaltigkeit durch Organisation und Verfahren (2016), 275 et seqq.

7 See *Wischmeyer*, in: Kahl (ed.), Nachhaltigkeit durch Organisation und Verfahren (2016), 253 et seqq.

these components can be combined and ideally further developed into a "sustainable governance".[8]

IV. *Sustainability as a general guideline for legislation*

Germany took such a combined approach and in 2000 convened a Council for Sustainability, which in 2002 presented its first sustainability strategy "Perspectives for Germany" that – as already mentioned – was revised in 2016 and updated in 2018.

1. Internal guidelines of the Federal Government

In addition, the Common Rules of Procedure of the Federal Government (*Gemeinsame Geschäftsordnung der Bundesregierung* – GGO) were amended in 2009. In the drafting process of legislative proposals, the Federal Government is since then obliged under Section 44 para. 1 sentence 3 of the GGO to "explain whether the impacts of the project correspond to sustainable development, in particular what long-term effects the project has".

As can already be seen from the systematic placement of this provision within the GGO, the sustainability impact assessment is thus designed in form of an impact assessment of the law.[9] In contrast to the "normal" impact assessment of laws, however, it is longer-term oriented and focuses more strongly than the "normal" impact assessment on the undesirable side effects of a proposed law. Although the "normal" impact assessment of laws must also forecast and evaluate the unintended side effects in addition to the intended effects, the sustainability assessment attaches much greater importance to the – conceivable – side effects.

Moreover, the actual significance of the sustainability principle is well expressed in the wording of Section 44 para. 1 sentence 3 of the GGO. It is less concerned with concrete or even abstract specifications. It is insofar noteworthy that Section 44 para. 1 sentence 3 of the GGO does not provide any further specification of such effects, i.e. it does not refer to the

---

8 See *Reimer*, in: Kahl (ed.), Nachhaltigkeit durch Organisation und Verfahren (2016), 43 et seqq.

9 More detailed on this *Kahl*, in: Kluth and Krings (eds.), Gesetzgebung (2014), § 13, paras. 35 et seqq.

triad of environment, economy and social affairs, but takes into account all (possible) effects. Its specific feature however, lies much more in the time perspective: the "long-term" effects of projects. It certainly is a reasonable demand that explicitly expands the political time horizon, which is usually limited to one legislative period. The aim of Section 44 of the GGO is thus to add fact-oriented rationality to political rationality by means of the Rules of Procedure. The legislator – or more precisely: the government as the initiator of laws – should bear in mind the long-term consequences of the laws it creates and, if possible, should only choose measures that do not unduly narrow the scope of action for future generations.

Nevertheless, it must again be born in mind that the Common Rules of Procedure only bind the Federal Government when drafting bills. Neither the other constitutional bodies nor individual citizens, associations or companies can invoke the GGO. Thus, if the sustainability imperative has not been observed at all or only insufficiently met and if legislative proposals do not sufficiently take into account the long-term effects or if such effects have not been evaluated, this does not prevent the practical effectiveness of the law. As the Federal Government proposes about three-quarters of all enacted laws, the practical significance of the Common Rules of Procedure must certainly not be underestimated. However, even considering this, disregarding the Rules of Procedure does not lead to the unconstitutionality of a law. In addition, the provisions of the Rules of Procedure can be circumvented if legislative proposals are introduced disguised as parliamentary proposals in the German Bundestag or if they are initiated in parallel not by the Government, but by a parliamentary group in the Bundestag.

2. Institutional complementation in the German Bundestag

One special feature of the sustainability assessment according to Section 44 para. 1 sentence 3 of the GGO was the introduction of a Parliamentary Advisory Council for Sustainable Development at the German Bundestag in 2004. This is no regular committee and therefore does not decide on concrete draft laws. However, it is a special body with the task of accompanying strategies for sustainable development and monitoring the Federal Government with regard to sustainable development. In this respect, it is in close, inter-institutional contact with the Federal Government.

V. Conclusion: Disillusion

Despite the embodiment in positive law and the institutional embedding of the sustainability principle, it cannot be said even in Germany that the laws at federal and state level have become more sustainable than before. It is still true that what the respective majority considers to be right, is shaped into law and if the majority changes, what was previously enacted in the name of sustainability is changed or repealed in the very same name again later. The expectations in terms of sustainability seem to foremost increase the efforts made to justify a measure, but less to shape the content of the laws. The legislation follows its own, sometimes very different rationalities.[10] Does the sustainability principle above all create "much ado about nothing"?

The question cannot be answered. It cannot be answered for the reasons that were also the result of *Jenny Hall's* contribution: it is simply unclear what sustainability is meant to imply. The general idea behind sustainability is still clear: every generation must solve its own problems and must not burden them onto future generations. In this sense, the *Brundtland* Commission has already stated: "Sustainable development is development that meets the needs of present generations without compromising the ability of future generations to meet their own needs". But even this basic rule faces the problem of recognizing that it is impossible to define what the needs of future generations will be. While it is important to become aware of the – also long-term – consequences of government action, it would be wrong to label politically desirable action with the seal of sustainability and to exclude politically undesirable action as a violation of the principle of sustainability. Sustainability must not become a meta-argument that prevents the discussion of the concrete factual arguments. If it does, there is a real danger that it is used as a means to enforce goals that would, if pursued as such, not be capable of gaining majority support and enforceability.

Bibliography

Christian Calliess, "Nachhaltigkeitsräte – Stand und Perspektiven", in: Wolfgang Kahl (ed.), Nachhaltigkeit durch Organisation und Verfahren (Mohr Siebeck, Tübingen 2016), 275.

10 On this comprehensively *Steinbach*, Rationale Gesetzgebung (2017), passim.

Klaus F. Gärditz, "Nachhaltigkeit durch Partizipation der Öffentlichkeit", in: Wolfgang Kahl (ed.), Nachhaltigkeit durch Organisation und Verfahren (Mohr Siebeck, Tübingen 2016), 351.

Wolfang Kahl, "§ 13 Gesetzesfolgenabschätzung und Nachhaltigkeitsprüfung", in: Winfried Kluth and Günter Krings (eds.), Gesetzgebung (C.F. Müller, Heidelberg 2014), 309.

Oliver Lepsius, "Nachhaltigkeit und Parlament", in: Wolfgang Kahl (ed.), Nachhaltigkeit als Verbundbegriff (Mohr Siebeck, Tübingen 2008), 326.

Martin Leschke, "Nachhaltige Gesetzgebung und Interessengruppen", in: Wolfgang Kahl (ed.), Nachhaltigkeit durch Organisation und Verfahren (Mohr Siebeck, Tübingen 2016), 235.

Klaus Meßerschmidt, "Nachhaltigkeit im EU-Gesetzgebungsverfahren", in: Wolfgang Kahl (ed.), Nachhaltigkeit durch Organisation und Verfahren (Mohr Siebeck, Tübingen 2016), 195.

Franz Reimer, "Nachhaltigkeit und 'Good Governance'", in: Wolfgang Kahl (ed.), Nachhaltigkeit durch Organisation und Verfahren (Mohr Siebeck, Tübingen 2016), 43.

Armin Steinbach, Rationale Gesetzgebung (Mohr Siebeck, Tübingen 2017).

Thomas Wischmeyer, "Nachhaltige Gesetzgebung und Sachverständigenberatung", in: Wolfgang Kahl (ed.), Nachhaltigkeit durch Organisation und Verfahren (Mohr Siebeck, Tübingen 2016), 253.

Labour Law, Vulnerable Workers and the Human-Rights Paradigm

Elmarie Fourie[*] / *Marius van Staden*[**]

Abstract: This chapter considers how legislative provisions have been interpreted in several instances by the South African judiciary to give life to key human rights. As a result, protection was extended to vulnerable workers in the informal economy. First, the contribution considers the interrelationship between labour law and human rights. Second, the contribution considers the significance of judicial interpretation in the activation of human rights with specific emphasis on the interpretive approach which has been adopted by the South African judiciary after the advent of constitutional democracy. Third, the contribution considers the role of the courts in extending protection to vulnerable informal economy workers with specific emphasis on the role of human dignity. To this end the chapter discusses landmark cases in which protection was extended to vulnerable workers. The chapter concludes that labour legislation must be widely interpreted so as to advance constitutionally-guaranteed human rights. It is further concluded that labour law can no longer function in isolation to other branches of law and that other branches of the law, such as social security law, corporate law, human rights and family law, will increasingly have an impact on the human dignity of workers. A new framework is called for which intrinsically links labour law to concepts such as democracy, social justice, freedom and human rights.

* Elmarie Fourie, *B.Proc., Advanced Diploma in Labour Law, LL.M., LL.D.*, Senior Lecturer, Department of Public Law, University of Johannesburg.

** Marius van Staden, *LL.B., LL.M., LL.D.*, Senior Lecturer, Department of Public Law, University of Johannesburg.

I. Introduction

Constitutional rights impact upon labour law in three distinct ways: First, the validity of labour legislation can be tested against the rights entrenched in the constitution. Second, labour legislation must be interpreted to give life to these rights. Third, the judiciary can interpret these rights to develop the common law.[1] In the context of the interpretation of labour legislation several human rights contained in the Constitution of the Republic of South Africa, 1996 (Constitution) impact upon labour relations:[2] Section 9 (the equality clause); Section 10 (the guarantee of human dignity); Section 13 (the right to be free from slavery, servitude and forced labour); Section 14 (the right to privacy); Section 17 (the right to assembly, demonstration, picket and petition); Section 18 (the right to freedom of association); Section 22 (the right of all citizens to choose their trade, occupation and profession freely); Section 23 (the right to fair labour practices); Section 27 (the right of access to health services and social security, including appropriate social assistance where necessary); Section 32 (the right of access to information); and Section 33 (the right to administrative action that is lawful, reasonable and procedurally fair).[3] In this contribution we highlight the centrality of human rights to the central function of labour law, and argue that labour law should be founded upon and advance fundamental human rights, and empower workers by facilitating their capacities.

The Constitutional Court has firmly established the principle that "[w]here there is legislation giving effect to a right in the Bill of Rights, a claimant is not permitted to rely directly on the Constitution".[4] This means that litigants are prohibited from relying directly on constitutionally-protected human rights. They must either rely on the provisions of the applicable labour legislation or attack the constitutionality thereof.[5] The litigant, therefore, cannot circumvent the statute and rely directly on the Constitution. This does not mean that the Constitution will play no

---

1 *Van Niekerk* and *Smit* (eds.), Law@work (2018), 39.

2 Ibid., 35.

3 Ibid.; *Cooper*, in: Woolman, Roux and Bishop (eds.), Constitutional Law of South Africa (2014), 53–2 note 2.

4 *Sali v National Commissioner of the South African Police Service* 2014 9 BLLR 827 (CC), para. 4; 72 and note 2. See also *S v Mhlungu* 1995 3 SA 867 (CC), para. 59; *MEC for Education KwaZulu-Natal v Pillay* 2008 1 SA 474 (CC); and *South African National Defence Union v Minister of Defence* 2007 5 SA 400 (CC), para. 51.

5 *South African National Defence Union v Minister of Defence* (n. 4), para. 52.

role in the adjudication of labour matters as the legislative provision in the labour context must be interpreted in terms of Section 39(2) of the Constitution so as to "promote the spirit, purport and objects of the Bill of Rights".[6] Human rights will have little influence on ordinary workers if legislative provisions are not interpreted to advance these rights. As a consequence, those who find themselves outside of the employment relationship will ultimately be denied their constitutionally-guaranteed rights and the aspirations of the Constitution will be circumvented.

The contribution will argue that labour legislation must be widely interpreted so as to advance constitutionally-guaranteed human rights. The Constitutional Court explained in *National Education Health and Allied Workers Union v University of Cape Town*[7] that "the courts and the legislature act in partnership to give life to constitutional rights".[8] It is therefore incumbent to interpret statutory provisions in a sufficiently broad and liberal manner and in a way that advances and gives life to key societal values. The chapter will also highlight how legislative provisions have been interpreted in several instances to animate key human rights and as a result of which protection was extended to vulnerable workers in the informal economy. The role of the acknowledgement of the human dignity of vulnerable workers by the judiciary in ensuring enhanced protection for this group will be considered.

II. Labour law and human rights

When one considers the function of labour law and the fact that large numbers of workers are left without protection, it is important to evaluate the relationship between labour law and human rights.[9] Although the development of labour law and fundamental human rights has been distinct, and various role players have adamantly kept them separate, there is growing support for their integration.[10] Human rights are accorded to

6 For criticism of this development, see *Woolman*, SALJ 2007, 262, 263 and *Woolman*, in: Woolman and Bishop (eds.), Constitutional Conversations (2008), 113; and for an opposing view, see *Michelman*, Constitutional Court Review 2008, 1.

7 2003 3 SA 1 (CC).

8 Para. 14.

9 Social and labour rights were recognised in the 1919 Weimar Constitution inspired by Hugo Sinzheimer. See also *Hepple*, in: Davidov and Langille (eds.), The Idea of Labour Law (2011), 32.

10 *Arthurs*, in: Davidov and Langille (n. 9), 23.

all human beings, and these rights are universal.[11] Hepple[12] states that the right to work is as important to people as the right to vote, and Fudge[13] claims that "[a] core component of the project to recast labour standards as international human rights is to elevate their moral appeal".

Labour rights are internationally and regionally seen as human rights, and the concept of human dignity is often mentioned in relation to labour rights and social protection.[14] Support for the universal nature of human rights can also be found in international instruments such as the Universal Declaration of Human Rights, 1948. In this Declaration the right to work, decent work, protection against unemployment, non-discrimination, freedom of association and a right to conditions that ensure human dignity, including social protection, are protected.[15] Other labour rights that can certainly be classified as universal include the prohibition of child labour and prohibitions of forced labour.[16] Regarding the regional acknowledgement of labour rights as human rights, certain national constitutions of countries in the Southern African Development Community (SADC) region contain important fundamental rights for workers in the region and can support vulnerable workers in the informal economy.[17]

The justiciability of these rights and their enforcement can protect the poor and vulnerable in society and provide a life with human dignity. In the *Certification* judgment[18] the Constitutional Court validated the justiciable nature of socio-economic rights even if this does have budgetary implications.[19] All countries should be able to protect civil and political rights; however, as socio-economic rights are often linked to the resources available in countries, the protection and provision of these rights are

11 *Collins*, in: Davidov and Langille (n. 9), 141.

12 *Hepple*, CLLPJ 1995, 634.

13 *Fudge*, DalhLJ 2014, 609.

14 The European Charter of Fundamental Social Rights provides in art. 1 that "human dignity is inviolable" and that it must be protected and respected, and art. 31 links human dignity to the right of workers to working conditions that will support the human dignity of the worker.

15 See art. 23.

16 *Such as the* ILO Minimum Age Convention and ILO Worst Forms of Child Labour Convention.

17 Constitution of the Republic of South Africa, 1996; the Constitution of Angola, 2010; the Constitution of Malawi, 1994; and the Constitution of the Democratic Republic of the Congo, 2006.

18 See *Ex Parte Chairman of the Constitutional Court Assembly: In re Certification of the Constitution of the Republic of South Africa* 1996 4 SA 744 (CC).

19 See paras. 77–78.

more challenging for developing countries.[20] Davies[21] argues that socio-economic rights are universal but that the content of these rights may vary according to each country's level of development. Collins argues that the justification and realisation of labour law through socio-economic rights could remove any justification for labour rights and labour law.[22] He argues:

> "Although it is true that most people are likely to satisfy their basic needs of this kind (food, shelter and clothing) through paid employment, it does not follow that it is necessary for there to be labour rights or that to address those needs the state would have to regulate employment."[23]

The South African Constitution is based on values such as human dignity, freedom and equality (including non-sexism and non-racialism), and these certainly should be recognised as universal values.[24] If one considers the global universal plight of specifically vulnerable workers in the informal economy, these values can certainly play an important role in improving their lives. Section 23 of the South African Constitution reads as follows:

"(1) Everyone has the right to fair labour practices.
(2) Every worker has the right -
  (a) to form and join a trade union;
  (b) to participate in the activities and programmes of a trade union; and
  (c) to strike.
(3) Every employer has the right –
  (a) to form and join an employers' organisation; and
  (b) to participate in the activities and programmes of an employers' organisation.
(4) Every trade union and every employers' organisation has the right –
  (a) to determine its own administration, programmes and activities;
  (b) to organise; and
  (c) to form and join a federation.

---

20 *Davies*, Perspectives on Labour Law (2009), 41.
21 Ibid., 43.
22 *Collins* (n. 11), 153.
23 Ibid.
24 Sec. 1 of the Constitution of the Republic of South Africa, 1996.

(5) Every trade union, employers' organisation and employer has the right to engage in collective bargaining. National legislation may be enacted to regulate collective bargaining. To the extent that the legislation may limit a right in this Chapter, the limitation must comply with Section 36(1).

(6) National legislation may recognise union security arrangements contained in collective agreements. To the extent that the legislation may limit a right in this Chapter, the limitation must comply with Section 36(1)."

Together with other fundamental rights such as those to human dignity[25] and equality,[26] these have already had an impact on the rights of many workers in South Africa. Fundamental rights, including the right to human dignity, the right to fair labour practices, socio-economic rights and the protection of ethnic, religious and linguistic minorities, can play an important role in achieving decent work for all. However, when extending socio-economic rights to vulnerable workers in the informal economy, specifically vulnerable women workers, a substantive approach with reference to equality is required.[27] This will require a restructuring of institutions to address gender inequalities. In other words, when extending these rights to women, their specific circumstances, including socio-economic factors, must be considered.

The notion of substantive equality and vulnerable women workers refers to the fact that equality in this regard does not necessarily encompass identical treatment, but rather the following, as stated by Sen:

> "Equal consideration for all may demand very unequal treatment in favour of the disadvantaged. The demands of substantive equality can be particularly exacting and complex when there is a good deal of antecedent inequality to counter."[28]

---

25 Sec. 10. Constitution of the Republic of South Africa, 1996.

26 Sec. 9.

27 *Fredman*, SAJHR 2009, 417. Women are particularly vulnerable as indicated by the linkages between informality, gender and poverty, namely: more poor women than non-poor women work in the informal economy and that there is a gender gap in earnings in the informal economy as women are earning less than their male counterparts and were less likely to be organised and have social protection. *Chen, Vanek and Carr,* Mainstreaming informal employment and gender poverty in reduction, Commonwealth Secretariat, London 2004.

28 *Sen*, Inequality Re-Examined (1992); *Fredman* (n. 27), 418.

Social justice can thus also be promoted and achieved through the human rights aspect (the law) and enforced through (strategic) litigation.[29]

The protection of the fundamental right to human dignity can play a vital role in respect of labour and social protection for vulnerable workers in the informal economy. The right to human dignity can include the right to social protection and equal treatment, and a life free from violence and harassment to enable these workers to live a life that they value. In the *South African Informal Traders Forum*[30] judgment, the Constitutional Court stated that "[t]he ability of people to earn money and support themselves and their families is a component of the right to human dignity".[31] In this case the right to human dignity[32] was of paramount importance as the outcome of the case was substantially based on this right and value. This is an example where the Court used the concept of human dignity within the realm of labour law, moving into the sphere of human rights. The Court did this by using principles and rights not found specifically in labour law, but instead used more general constitutional values, rights and principles. McCrudden[33] argues that this only happens in extreme circumstances and that the concept of human dignity is more closely linked to "ideas of humiliation" than to labour law. We disagree with McCrudden's view. The human dignity of these precarious workers is infringed when they are denied social and labour protection. The inclusion of justiciable socio-economic rights under the auspices of fundamental rights will also contribute to a life lived with more human dignity for vulnerable workers.[34] Collins[35] even describes "dignity" as a modern-day replacement for the slogan "labour is not a commodity". The concept of decent work is also intrinsically linked to human dignity, as the South African courts have confirmed this in a number of instances.[36] Human dignity is also linked

29 *Fourie* and *Smit*, "Precarious work, gender and non-discrimination: South African and region", unpublished paper, Labour Law Research Network (LLNR) Conference, Vrije Universiteit Amsterdam, June 2015.

30 *South African Informal Traders Forum v City of Johannesburg* 2014 4 SA 371 (CC). See also para IV below.

31 Para. 31.

32 Sec. 10 of the Constitution.

33 *McCrudden*, in: Blog et al (eds.), The Autonomy of Labour Law (2015), 288.

34 See for example secs. 26, 27 and 29 of the South African Constitution.

35 *Collins* (n. 11), 151.

36 See *South African Informal Traders Forum v City of Johannesburg* (n 30), para. 31 and *Makwickana v eThekwini Municipality* 2015 3 SA 165 (KZD), para. 136.

to empowerment, and decent work can empower workers to contribute to their own subsistence and to society.[37]

Women workers as a specific category of vulnerable workers in the informal economy can also benefit from a labour law system entrenched in fundamental human rights.[38] Such a system or discourse will allow workers to align with other universal "right seekers" to ensure adequate labour and social protection.[39] These workers will be able to form alliances and organisations through innovative methods of mobilisation outside the traditional labour law realm that may be more appropriate and perhaps also more effective to address their needs, such as cooperatives and member-based organisations as opposed to the traditional concept of trade unions.

According to Hepple, substantive equality should be seen as a special function of labour law. This would mean something more than just formal equality between employer and employee.[40] Hepple states that equality as an overarching value encompasses the idea that labour is not a commodity.[41] An approach based on the notion of substantive equality will require taking into consideration the special needs of various categories of workers.[42] Diversity of regulated structures, standards and tailor-made statutory provisions such as affirmative action measures support the notion of substantive equality. Labour law must be responsive to the needs of workers in new forms of work, such as workers in the informal economy that represent immense diversity.[43] These workers are vulnerable and will often require tailor-made regulation that offers more protection.[44]

In Malawi, the Human Rights-Based Approach (HRBA) supports the International Labour Organisation (ILO) Agenda for decent work and considers it society's responsibility to respond to the basic rights of human beings.[45] This approach recognises that poverty entails more than merely a lack of income, but also shows up other vulnerabilities, exclusions and the lack of a voice – all factors that characterise the precariousness of

37 *Gilabert*, PhilSocCrit 2016, 183.
38 *Arthurs* (n. 10), 23.
39 Ibid.
40 *Hepple* (n. 9), 647.
41 Ibid.
42 In *MEC for Education Kwazulu-Natal v Pillay* (n. 4), the Court confirmed that people who are not similar should not be treated alike.
43 See also *Weiss*, in: Davidov and Langille (n. 9) 47.
44 Ibid.
45 Ibid., 109.

workers in the informal economy. The objective of this approach supports social justice and highlights the importance of both legal and economic empowerment for the vulnerable and marginalised, and also endeavours to combat structural inequality.[46] The result of an approach such as this to extend labour rights and social protection is an integrated strategy that includes legal, political, economic, cultural and social components.[47]

Although human rights in certain instances can be valuable vehicles for the extension of protection to vulnerable workers, there are constraints when they are used as a basis for the development of labour law. The success of social rights often is dependent on policies that create an environment conducive to realise these rights.[48] Hepple[49] argues that by classifying rights as fundamental and enforceable, disputes are moved from the political and industrial arena to that of the judiciary, and this is perilous as "it is easy for judges to read their own notions of policy into a bill of rights".[50]

Section 9(1) of the Constitution provides that everyone is equal before the law and has the right to equal protection and benefit of the law, while Section 9(2) states that equality includes the full and equal enjoyment of all rights and freedoms. When considering the extension of protection to vulnerable workers, both values and rights are relevant and it is of the utmost importance to acknowledge that the constitutional concept of equality has two dimensions, namely, formal and substantive equality.[51] The notion of formal equality requires that all people must be treated the same, despite their circumstances. Substantive equality focuses on outcomes, and this will require an analysis of the social and economic conditions of groups and individuals.[52] The transformative nature of the South African Constitution is illustrated by its commitment to equality.[53]

---

46 *Chinsinga* and *Kayuni*, in: Banik (ed.), The Legal Empowerment Agenda: Poverty, Labour and the Informal Economy in Africa (2011), 110.

47 Ibid.

48 *Hepple* (n. 9), 634.

49 *Hepple* (n. 9), 644.

50 Ibid.

51 The Constitutional Court has on a number of occasions confirmed the concept of substantive equality and given meaning to the concept; see *President of the Republic of South Africa v Hugo* 1997 4 SA 1 (CC), para. 41; *Minister of Finance v Van Heerden* 2004 12 BLLR 1181 (CC), paras. 23–35; *Brink v Kitshoff* 1996 4 SA 197 (CC), paras. 33, 41–42, 44.

52 *Van Niekerk* and *Smit* (n. 1), 121–123.

53 See also *South African Police Service v Solidarity obo Barnard* 2014 6 SA 123 (CC), para. 29 and *Minister of Finance v Van Heerden* (n. 51), paras. 23–25.

According to Le Roux,[54] transformative constitutionalism means social change through law; thus fundamental social change can be achieved through legal reforms, supported by proper mobilisation and enforced through, *inter alia*, litigation.

Sections 23(1) and (2) of the South African Constitution provide for the following fundamental labour rights:

"(1) Everyone has the right to fair labour practices.
(2) Every worker has the right –
   (a) to form and join a trade union;
   (b) to participate in the activities and programmes of a trade union; and
   (c) to strike."

In *SA National Defence Union v Minister of Defence*,[55] O'Regan J, with reference to the ILO and Article 2 of the Freedom of Association and Protection of the Right to Organise Convention (1948), concluded that "workers" should be interpreted to include members of the armed forces. Her interpretation of the right was generous, thereby providing "workers" (as opposed to "employees") with better protection. This generous approach to the interpretation of the concept "worker" may provide an important tool when extending labour protection to female workers in the informal economy. This is not to say that a full range of protection can be extended in such a way. In the *SA National Defence Union* case, for example, the right to strike was nevertheless not extended to members of the armed forces.

In addition to Section 23 of the Constitution, fundamental rights such as the right to human dignity,[56] socio-economic rights,[57] property rights,[58] the right to administrative action,[59] access to courts,[60] the right of all citizens to choose their trade, occupation or profession freely[61] and the protection of ethnic, religious and linguistic minorities,[62] may play a vital role in the achievement of social justice and the goal of decent work

54 *Le Roux*, in: Du Toit (ed.), Exploited, Undervalued – and Essential: Domestic Workers and the Realisation of their Rights (2013), 39.
55 (N. 4), para. 25.
56 Sec. 10 of the Constitution.
57 Secs. 26 and 27 of the Constitution.
58 Sec. 25 of the Constitution.
59 Sec. 33 of the Constitution.
60 Sec. 34 of the Constitution.
61 Sec. 22 of the Constitution.
62 Sec. 31 of the Constitution.

for all.[63] Social change can be achieved through the law and can be enforced through litigation. If we accept that the South African Constitution supports substantive equality,[64] and our courts view our Constitution as transformative,[65] then the fundamental values of freedom, human dignity, social justice and non-discrimination must be recognised when considering the protection of poor female workers in the informal economy.

Human dignity is a concept found in various legal texts applicable to labour law and is intrinsically linked to the world of work.[66] When one considers the precarious position of workers in the informal economy, without adequate labour and social protection, without a safe working area, stigmatised and harassed, the right to human dignity is of paramount importance as a human right.

The theory of Freedland and Kountouris provides that it is important to optimise the dignity accorded to these workers and to increase their capabilities.[67] The increase of capabilities is closely linked to the legal and economic empowerment of these workers in an attempt to develop a more sustainable approach.

Labour law must also have a constitutional function that broadens its scope from the individual employment relationship to a constitutional task of contributing to a specific economic and social order.[68] Those opposed to a human rights approach to labour law often fear that it will undermine the collective element of labour law, and that individual rights can never trump the power of trade unions in equalising the imbalance inherent to the employment relationship.[69] However, as the right to freedom

---

63 See *South African Informal Traders Forum v City of Johannesburg* (n. 30). The Court stated that the ability of informal traders to earn money and support themselves is an important component of the right to human dignity and without it these workers face humiliation and degradation (para. 32).

64 *South African Police Service v Solidarity obo Barnard* (n. 53); *President of the Republic of South Africa v Hugo* (n. 51), *Minister of Finance v Van Heerden* (n. 51). See also *Brink v Kitshoff* (n. 51); *National Coalition for Gay and Lesbian Equality v Minister of Justice* 1999 1 SA 6 (CC); *Bato Star Fishing (Pty) Ltd v Minister of Environmental Affairs* 2004 7 BCLR 687 (CC).

65 *S v Makwanyane* 1995 3 SA 391 (CC). See *Langa*, Stell LR 2006, 3.

66 See for example Sec. 10 of the South African Constitution, as well as international instruments such as the ILO Declaration of Philadelphia, the Decent Work Agenda, the Universal Declaration of Human Rights and the EU Charter of Fundamental Rights.

67 *Freedland and Kountouris*, The Legal Construction of Personal Work (2011), 49. See also a critical analysis of their theory in *McCrudden* (n. 33), 276.

68 *Dukes*, in: Davidov and Langille (n. 9), 65.

69 *Davies* (n. 20), 48.

of association and the right to form and join trade unions and to engage in collective bargaining are entrenched in the Constitution, such concerns may be overstated.

The constitutionalisation of labour rights and the constitutional promotion of substantive equality in South Africa certainly have contributed to the social order of an open democratic society based on values such as human dignity, equality and freedom and the furtherance of economic and social justice.

III. *Significance of interpretation in the activation of human rights*

Legislation has become an indispensable source of contemporary law, if not the most important source, both generally and in the context of labour law. Consequently, the role of statutory interpretation has grown significantly. Spigelman observed that statutory interpretation has become the most important field of study as no area of the law has escaped legislative intervention.[70] Similarly, Von Savigny regarded the interpretation of laws as "the foundation of legal science".[71] Labour law is no exception to this observation and it is trite that labour law has not escaped such statutory modification. To this end, an enormous number of statutory arrangements, mainly directed towards the protection of employees and the advancement of Section 23 of the Constitution,[72] have been enacted in South Africa.[73] The legislature has responded with the promotion of job security and the setting of minimum standards, as well as the promotion and protection of collective bargaining. The third response was the creation of specialist tribunals and tailor-made procedures to enforce these fundamental principles.[74]

There are many reasons for considering the impact of the interpretive approach of the judiciary. Chief among these is the concern that the ne-

70 *Spigelman*, Australian Bar Review 2001, 224.

71 *Von Savigny*, System des Heutigen Romischen Rechts (1840), para. 32.

72 Sec. 23 of the Constitution affords "everyone" protection from unfair labour practices, and every "worker" the right to form and join a trade union, to participate in the activities and programmes of a trade union and to strike.

73 Legislation such as the Basic Conditions of Employment Act 75 of 1997, the Labour Relations Act 66 of 1995, the Employment Equity Act 55 of 1998 and the Skills Development Act 97 of 1998.

74 *Grogan*, Workplace Law (2014), 4.

glect of such inquiries will impair the predictability of legal dispositions.[75] If citizens and litigants in labour matters, in particular, are incapable of predicting what legislative provisions require of them, then legal certainty, which is a central requirement of the rule of law, is compromised.[76] The purpose of any legislative or constitutional provision is to create a norm to which citizens may conform their conduct.[77] Predictability of outcomes is key to legal certainty and is a central requirement of the rule of law and, as such, scholarship about the interpretation of statutes advances a central constitutional value.[78] Section 1(c) of the Constitution states that the Republic is founded upon the values of "supremacy of the Constitution and the rule of law".

This is not to say, however, that it is possible, through the rules, canons and methodologies of statutory interpretation, to predict with certainty what the interpretive outcomes of each case would be.[79] As Cowen has remarked, "[i]t is not possible to reduce the subject to a system of formulas which will yield solutions with computer-like facility 'a sort of table of juristic logarithms'".[80] However, this also does not mean that outcomes in decision making may be likened to a judicial throw of the dice. As the author has argued, "there is more room for helpful guidance than is often supposed – provided we attend more closely to underlying theory and assumptions".[81]

By studying the methods employed by the judiciary in the interpretation of legislative provisions, we can avoid some of the pitfalls and understand the real difficulties inherent in the interpretation of these provisions.[82] Nevertheless, even though predictability in law may not be entirely possible, it remains the goal towards which legal science must strive. Indeed, "predictability is bound to increase proportionately as the subject becomes more thoroughly and more sensitively understood".[83]

In law, meaning-generation is a function of statutory interpretation, and every application of a text to particular circumstances entails interpre-

75 *Scalia* and *Gardner*, Reading Law: The Interpretation of Legal Texts (2012), xxvii.

76 *Maxeiner*, Hous J Int'l L 2008, 27, 30. See also *President of the Republic of South Africa v Hugo* (n. 51), para. 102.

77 *Endicott*, in: Marmor and Soames (eds.), Philosophical Foundations of Language in the Law (2013), 14, 16.

78 *Maxeiner* (n. 76), 30.

79 *Corocraft v Pan-American Airways* 1968 2 All ER 1059.

80 *Cowen*, TSAR 1976, 131, 133.

81 Ibid.

82 *Von Savigny* (n. 71), para. 32.

83 *Cowen* (n. 80), 133.

tation.[84] As text has no pre-interpretive meaning,[85] this means that every text must be interpreted to attach meaning to provisions, and (labour) legislation is no exception to this observation.[86] Thus, if a person seems to meet a legislative provision that does not have to be interpreted, that is because that person has interpreted it already. Sunstein has stated that interpretive principles are always at work.[87]

A meaning that seems to leap off the page is a meaning that flows from interpretive assumptions that are so deeply entrenched that they have become invisible.[88] This is so because a statute is a legal instrument that, according Endicott, is "a normative text with a technical effect" in that "the law itself has techniques for determining the effect of the normative text".[89] The well-known *dictum "in claris non fit interpretatio"* (clear rules do not require interpretation) has, therefore, been discredited.[90] The Israeli Supreme Court per Barak J has held that all legislative provisions, including those of which language is "clear", require interpretation and that the statute is only "clear" because interpretation has clarified it.[91]

In labour law, statutory interpretation is also of significant importance, not only because all legislative provisions, including labour legislation, must be legally interpreted in order to assign meaning to them, but also because labour legislation often utilises vague terms, concepts and standards to regulate the employment relationship. Consider, for example, the vague concept "unfair labour practice" as contained in Section 23 of the Constitution. When the concept was first introduced in South Africa, it was defined as "any labour practice that in the opinion of the Industrial Court is an unfair labour practice".[92]

In effect, the former Industrial Court was therefore given an extensive discretion to decide for itself what conduct amounted to unfair labour practices and what did not, and this leeway, according to some, "amount-

---

84 *Scalia and Garner* (n. 75), 53.
85 *Sunstein*, Harvard Law Review 1989, 405, 411.
86 *Barak*, Purposive Interpretation in Law (2005), 12.
87 *Sunstein*, The Partial Constitution (1993), 104.
88 *Fish*, Doing What Comes Naturally: Change Rhetoric, and the Practice of Theory in Legal Studies (1989), 358. *Gadamer*, Truth and Method (1979), 147.
89 *Endicott* (n. 77), 15.
90 *Barak* (n. 86), 12.
91 *Air Tour (Israel) Ltd v Chair of the Council for Antitrust Oversight* 39(1) PD 169, 176. See also *Gov Ari Ltd v Netanya Local Planning and Construction Council* 35(4) PD, 764, 769.
92 Sec. 1(f) of the Industrial Conciliation Amendment Act 94 of 1979.

ed to a licence to legislate".[93] Later interventions by the legislature to introduce more specific definitions could also not produce the intended certainty and produced general and open-ended definitions requiring the Court to use its own discretion in interpreting them.[94] In *National Education Health and Allied Workers Union v University of Cape Town*, the Constitutional Court found it "neither necessary nor desirable" to define this concept as it is currently contained in the Constitution.[95] Instead, the Court preferred the concept to be left to gather meaning through judicial interpretation.

In South African labour law there are legislative instruments that can be similarly characterised as vague. Consider, for example, the concept "unfair labour practice" as contained in the Constitution which is not defined,[96] whilst the same concept is precisely defined in labour legislation.[97] Other vague standards such as "rational", "unfair", "arbitrary", and "justifiable" are also utilised in the context of labour discrimination law.[98] It is clear that the legislature had intentionally chosen to introduce these vague concepts, and the question therefore arises why the legislature would choose to employ these terms as legislative devices. In this chapter the focus will be on the similarly vague concept of "employee".[99]

In legal parlance vague language is often viewed as "bad", while precise language is viewed as "good". Vague language is seen to be a product of poor legislative drafting. The concern is understandable. The purpose of any legislative provision is to create a norm to which citizens may conform their conduct. When a norm is vague, it is seemingly incapable of guiding a citizen's conduct (nor does it control the conduct of the officers or

93 *Vettori*, Alternative Means to Regulate the Employment Relationship in the Changing World of Work (2005 thesis University of Pretoria), 301; *Thompson and Benjamin*, South African Labour Law (1997), A-60.

94 The definition was amended by Sec. 1(h) of the Labour Relations Act Amendment Act 95 of 1980; Sec. 1(h) of the Labour Relations Act Amendment Act 83 of 1988; and Sec. 1 of the Labour Relations Act Amendment Act 9 of 1991.

95 Para. 26.

96 Sec. 23 of the Constitution.

97 Sec. 186 of the Labour Relations Act 66 of 1995.

98 Sec. 11 of the Employment Equity Act 55 of 1995, as recently amended by Sec. 6 of the Employment Equity Amendment Act 47 of 2013.

99 Sec. 213 of the Labour Relations Act 66 of 1995 defines an "employee" as "(a) any person, excluding an independent contractor, who works for another person or for the state and who receives, or is entitled to receive, any remuneration; and (b) any other person who in any manner assists in carrying on or conducting the business of an employer".

public officials responsible for applying them). How then is it possible for individuals to conform their conduct to the norm?

In addition, concerns related to the separation of powers and the function of the legislature *vis-à-vis* the judiciary are raised.[100] This is so because the task of giving content to and determining the scope of the application of a vague norm is transferred first to an applying official, but ultimately to the courts. In effect, vague norms open the doors for judicial law making. Our legal system, however, consists of both vague and precise norms, and vague norms are not always "bad", but sometimes even politically desirable. As such, legislatures may consciously choose to frame legislative provisions in a vague manner.[101] The effect would be to create a vague norm so that its application is unclear.

There may be instances where, although the text of a legislative provision is seemingly clear or precise, the technical effect of legal language means that "[l]egal rules of interpretation may give a vague effect to a precise term".[102] This is so because "there is no straightforward, general relation between the language used in a legal instrument to make law, and the law that is made".[103]

To understand why vagueness can be valuable, the starting point must inevitably be to ask why precision is valuable. According to Endicott, precision is valuable for the following reasons: First, precision has "guidance value" because a precise standard makes it clear what people's rights and obligations are. Second, precision has "process value" because it directs officials in a legal system.[104] From here it is easy to formulate the chief points of criticism against the use of vague concepts: The provision does not make it clear what the obligations or rights of affected persons are.

It might be useful for the legislature to leave it to the judiciary to give content to a legislative norm. According to Endicott, this choice has

---

100 *Minister of Health v Treatment Action Campaign (2)* 2002 (10) BCLR 1075, para. 199; and *Doctors for Life International v Speaker of the National Assembly* 2006 6 SA 416 (CC), para. 37.

101 In *Matiso v The Commanding Officer, Port Elizabeth Prison* 1994 (3) SA 592 (SE), 597I-598B it was stated that "[t]he values and principles contained in the Constitution are, and could only be, formulated and expressed in wide and general terms, because they are to be of general application. In terms of the Constitution the courts bear the responsibility of giving specific content to those values and principles in any given situation.".

102 *Endicott* (n. 77), 16.

103 Ibid.

104 *Endicott* (n. 77), 19.

"power allocation value" and "private ordering value".[105] Substantively, the legislature delegates to the courts the power to determine, based on the vague criteria contained therein, whether or not an act amounted to unfair discrimination. The allocation of this power to the judiciary is justifiable as judges possess specialised expertise to develop legislation in light of norms. The doctrine of precedent will then allow the norm to develop incrementally and to revise general principles through the processes of appeal.

The processes of the courts mean that general rules would develop only after taking cognisance of the interests of both employees and employers. Hart similarly adopted the view that it may be inevitable and desirable for there to be a margin of uncertainty as it will leave judges to arrive at sensible results in unforeseen future cases.[106] It may also be valuable to leave the persons affected by a rule (*in casu* the employers and employees) uncertain as to its application as employers will have an incentive to come up with creative ways to avoid accountability.

Similarly, it may be argued that the vagueness and uncertainty around terms such as "employee" may be desirable for employers. Employers will tend to come up with innovative means to avoid the duties imposed on them by labour legislation by excluding them from the ambit of the term "employee". Therefore, it is clear that such vagueness would largely not be to the benefit of the more vulnerable party. The judiciary, however, is capable, through its power of interpretation, to increase the ambit of protection afforded to workers significantly, by interpreting the term "employee" widely.[107]

There is a more pertinent reason why the legal profession should be concerned with matters of interpretation. As Smit has indicated, "[t]he judiciary has through its power of interpretation the potential to contribute to the transformation of South African society".[108] It may be argued that the *only way* the judiciary can contribute to the transformation of society and the achievement of social justice is through its power of interpretation. This is so because the Constitutional Court has firmly established the subsidiary principle in so far as "[w]here there is legislation giving effect to

105 Ibid., 26–28.

106 *Hart,* The Concept of Law (1994), 130, 251–252.

107 *Van Staden*, De Jure 2013, 470, 473.

108 *Smit v Workmen's Compensation Commissioner* 1979 1 SA 51 (A), 11.

a right in the Bill of Rights, a claimant is not permitted to rely directly on the Constitution".[109]

Subsidiarity does not mean that the Constitution will play no role in adjudication as a provision in question must be interpreted in terms of Section 39(2) of the Constitution so as to "promote the spirit, purport and objects of the Bill of Rights". The Constitutional Court has stated that "[a]ll statutes must be interpreted through the prism of the Bill of Rights".[110] The Constitution must inspire the meaning that is attributed to legislative provisions. If this is not done, primarily because of an adherence to out-dated and literalistic modes of statutory interpretation, it may be argued that the provisions of the Constitution will become obsolete (except to the extent that it may be argued that the legislation concerned has been adopted to give effect to a constitutional provision).

In *Van Rooyen v The State* the Constitutional Court explained how human rights may impact upon legislation in general: First, all law must be interpreted ("read down") to avoid inconsistency with the Constitution. Second, if this is not possible, the law (or at least the offending parts thereof) must be declared unconstitutional and invalid. Third, the court may remedy the unconstitutionality by means of severance, reading in, or notional severance. If this is not possible, then the ultimate remedy must be granted in declaring the law (completely) invalid.[111] In addition, the Constitution also empowers the courts to limit the impact of the order of invalidity by suspending or limiting the retrospective effect of the order.[112] The Constitutional Court has also on several occasions allowed an interim remedy of notional or actual severance, or reading in during a period of suspension to diminish the effects of the continued violation of rights.[113]

---

109 *Sali v National Commissioner of the South African Police Service* (n. 4), para. 4, 72 and n. 2. See also *S v Mhlungu* (n. 4), para. 59; *MEC for Education: KwaZulu-Natal v Pillay* (n. 4); and *South African National Defence Union v Minister of Defence* (n. 4), para. 51.

110 *Investigating Directorate: Serious Economic Offences v Hyundai Motor Distributors (Pty) Ltd. In re: Hyundai Motor Distributors (Pty) Ltd v Smit* 2001 1 SA 545 (CC), para. 21.

111 2002 5 SA 246 (CC), para. 88.

112 Sec. 172(1)(b).

113 *Dawood v Minister of Home Affairs* 2000 3 SA 936 (CC); *Janse van Rensburg v Minister of Trade and Industry* 2001 1 SA 29 (CC); *Booysen v Minister of Home Affairs* 2001 4 SA 485 (CC); *Volks v Robinson* 2005 5 BCLR 446 (CC); *Moseneke v The Master of the High Court* 2001 2 SA 18 (CC); *South African Liquor Traders Association v Chairperson, Gauteng Liquor Board* 2006 8 BCLR 901 (CC); *C v Department of Health and Social Development* Case 55/11 (CC) (unreported).

It is clear that the Constitutional Court has endorsed a multiple-step approach in dealing with constitutional challenges to legislation. Indeed, the adoption of such a methodology might easily be explained if one has regard to the traditionally-accepted distinction between reading strategies (exercises of statutory interpretation), on the one hand, and remedies, on the other. Severance and reading-in are constitutional remedies – as opposed to reading strategies – provided for in Section 172(1)(b). Interpretation in conformity with the Constitution is rather seen as a reading strategy which is used in order to prevent it from being struck down because it is unconstitutional. O'Regan has also stated that "[r]eading down a statute does not require any order or remedy, it is something that is done in the text of the judgment itself with no consequential relief to follow".[114] This, however, is not the position in all other jurisdictions.

The judiciary has adopted an approach to the interpretation of statutes that seeks to animate the values and rights in the Constitution.[115] Section 39 of the Constitution can therefore be seen as an instruction to interpreters to look beyond the text in which a statutory provision is couched to give meaning to such provisions. Additionally, the Constitutional Court in *Wary Holdings (Pty) Ltd v Stalwo (Pty) Ltd*[116] found that "[w]here two conflicting interpretations of a statutory provision could both be said to be reflective of the relevant structural provisions of the Constitution as a whole, read with other relevant statutory provisions, the interpretation which *better* reflects those structural provisions should be adopted".[117]

Botha declares that "[t]he fundamental principle of statutory interpretation is that the purpose of the legislation must be determined in the light of the spirit, purport and objects of the Bill of Rights in the Constitution".[118] It is striking that this principle endorses the purposive approach while qualifying it at the same time. Indeed, teleological interpretation may be regarded as a species of purposive interpretation which goes beyond simply ascertaining the purpose of a legislative provision.

---

114 "Fashioning Constitutional Remedies in South Africa: Some Reflections" 2011 *Advocat* http://www.sabar.co.za/law-journals/2011/april/2011-april-vol024-no1-pp41-44.pdf (last visited 23 January 2012).

115 See *Botha*, Waarde-Aktiverende Grondwetuitleg: Vergestalting van die Materiële Regstaat (1996 thesis UNISA).

116 2009 1 SA 337 (CC).

117 Para. 46.

118 *Botha*, Statutory Interpretation: An Introduction for Students (2005), 10, 66, 75. The author does not repeat this supposition in *Botha*, Statutory Interpretation: An Introduction for Students (2012) but does not deny it either.

Du Plessis has indicated that purposive interpretation *simpliciter* "has the potential to turn into a rather unruly horse if three *caveats* are not heeded".[119] First, the processes involved in the interpretation of statutes are too complicated for the purpose of a statutory provision to be described in a simple catchword or catchphrase.[120] Second, merely enquiring what the purpose of a statutory provision is may be restrictive, as the purpose may indeed be restrictive. Merely enquiring into the purpose of a statutory provision without having regard to the broader purpose of a statutory provision can, therefore, be limiting and may ignore the injunction placed upon the courts by Section 39 of the Constitution to "promote the spirit, purport and objects of the Bill of Rights" when interpreting legislation. Third, Du Plessis warns that purpose can also only be determined through processes of interpretation and that "the purpose of a provision can simply not be known prior to interpretation".[121] The author warns that such a narrow approach "too easily seduces an interpreter to read a purpose or object into a provision prematurely, and therefore in an arbitrary manner, shedding the responsibility to justify or, at least, explain his or her preference".[122]

The method of statutory interpretation which goes beyond merely asking what the purpose of a statutory provision is, is generally referred to as "teleological interpretation",[123] a "value-activating strategy",[124] or the "value-coherent theory" of statutory interpretation.[125] It has become commonplace for this principle to guide the interpretation of legislation and this has been endorsed by the Constitutional Court.[126] The approach was best described (although not explicitly endorsed) in *African Christian Democratic Party v Electoral Commission*:

> "[I]n approaching the interpretation of provisions of ... legislation, courts ... must understand those provisions in the light of their legislative purpose within the overall ... [legislative] framework. That

119 *Du Plessis*, in Woolman, Roux and Bishop (n. 3), 32–54.
120 Ibid.
121 Ibid., 32–55.
122 Ibid.
123 *Botha* (n. 118) (2005), 59.
124 *Devenish*, Interpretation of Statutes (1992), 40.
125 Ibid., 39.
126 *African Christian Democratic Party v Electoral Commission* 2006 3 SA 305 (CC); and *Department of Land Affairs v Goedgelegen Tropical Fruits Pty Ltd* 2007 6 SA 199 (CC).

framework must be understood in the light of the important constitutional rights and values that are relevant."[127]

According to Le Roux, this "[b]roader approach" favoured by the Court has four distinct steps: First, the purpose of the provision must be established. Second, it should be asked whether "that purpose would be obstructed by a literal interpretation of the provision". If that is the case, thirdly, "an alternative interpretation of the provision that 'understands' its central purpose" must be adopted. Fourthly, it must be ensured "that the purposive reading of the legislative provision also promotes the object, purport and spirit of the Bill of Rights".[128] The Constitutional Court has also expressly endorsed this approach with regard to labour matters in *National Education Health and Allied Workers Union v University of Cape Town.*[129]

IV. The role of the courts in extending protection to vulnerable workers

In South Africa the constitutionalising of labour rights has on several occasions been to the advantage of workers, and the policy notions read in by the Constitutional Court judges have been in line with those of an open democratic society based on the values of human dignity, equality and freedom. It is also important to note that in a number of cases constitutional jurisprudence has extended protection to workers that are particularly vulnerable. This is indicative of the fact that the constitutionalising of labour rights may be used effectively to extend protection and develop labour law. However, this will be dependent on the specific history and social economic framework of each country.[130] Thus, social justice can also be promoted and achieved through human rights (the law) and enforced through (strategic) litigation.[131]

---

127 (N. 126), para. 34.

128 *Le Roux*, SA Public Law 2006, 382, 386.

129 2003 (3) SA 1 (CC).

130 The infringements of the labour rights of vulnerable workers in the informal economy can in certain instances also be seen as infringements of human rights.

131 *Fourie* and *Smit* (n. 29). For a discussion of the advantages and disadvantages of the constitutionalising labour law, see *Beatty*, ILJ 1993, 1. Dukes stated that considering labour law in terms of its constitutional function allows for a wider focus on the imbalance of power in employment relations. According to her, this also allows labour law to contribute to a constitutional task of creating a specific economic and social order. *Dukes* (n. 68), 65.

A landmark decision was obtained regarding the rights of street traders from the High Court (KZD) in July 2015.[132] The Legal Resources Centre assisted a 65 year-old informal trader, whose goods had been confiscated by a police officer when the applicant allegedly failed to produce a trading permit. The applicant in this matter was also a member and leader of various street traders' organisations[133] and brought the application in his personal capacity and in terms of Sections 38(c) and (e) of the Constitution.[134] He also acted in the public interest in terms of Section 38(d) of the Constitution. The Court recognised the right of street traders as "a group in a poverty-stricken socio-economic class to challenge the validity of laws and practices prevailing in the informal trade sector".[135]

The applicant challenged the constitutionality of Section 6A(1)(d) of the Business Act and the eThekwini Municipality By-Law, and specifically the fact that the Act does not provide for a limit in respect of a fine.[136] The applicant also claimed compensation in an amount of R775 for the impounded goods.

Local authorities have an unrestricted discretion in respect of the amount of the fine imposed, and this often is not proportional to the seriousness of the infringement.[137]

The informal traders in this area are mostly indigent black Africans who are constantly harassed and intimidated by authorities.[138] The applicant also challenged Section 6(A)(1)(d)(ii) of the Act as it is vaguely defined and does not provide for adequate procedure in respect of the removal and consequent impoundment of goods.[139] Both these sections provide

---

132 *Makwickana v eThekwini Municipality* 2015 3 SA 165 (KZD).

133 The applicant was the Chairperson of the Traders against Crime Association and the Deputy President of the Masibambasane Traders' Association (*Makwickana* (n. 132), para. 1).

134 The application was brought in terms of the applicant acting as a member of, or in interests of, a group or class of persons and as anyone acting in the public interest.

135 Para. 2.

136 Sec. 6(A)(1)(d).

137 Para. 35(a).

138 Para. 121.

139 This subsection provides as follows: "A by-law made under this subsection – (ii) may provide for the removal and impoundment by an officer of any goods, receptacle, vehicle or movable structure (aa) which he reasonably suspects is being used or intended to be used or has been used in or in connection with the carrying on of the business of street vendor, peddler or hawker; and (bb) which he finds at a place where in terms of a by-law under subsection (1)(a)(ii) or (iii), the carrying on of such business is restricted or prohibited and which, in

authorities with unfettered powers to exercise the above rights, and this unfair discretion negatively affects the ability of the informal traders to earn a livelihood.[140]

The Court recognised that the provisions of the Businesses Act[141] can be remedied by subordinate legislation, such as by-laws. The Court had to decide whether Section 35 of the current by-laws,[142] which provides for the removal and impoundment of goods, meets the constitutional challenge and specifically the challenges with references to Sections 9 (equality), 25 (property) and 34 (access to courts).

Section 35 of the By-law allows for the removal of the trader's goods "upon the mere suspicion, reasonably held, that the informal trader has contravened a provision in the by-law", without access to a hearing, and the goods are then sold without any notification to the trader. In this regard the Court stated:

> "Although s 35(1) confers a power to impound only, the first respondent's officials effectively confiscate the impounded goods. The right to a refund and the return of the goods remains merely theoretical for as long as the court proceedings are not finalised before the goods are disposed of. Even though the applicant was entitled to return of his goods after the magistrates' court had directed the first respondent to release them to him and such release became impossible once the first respondent had disposed of them, the first respondent tendered no compensation for the goods to the applicant. Only as a result of access to court via this application did the applicant eventually elicit from the first respondent at the hearing a possible tender for compensation. The luxury of litigation is not an option for every street trader whose property is impounded."[143]

---

his opinion, constitutes an infringement of such law, whether or not such goods, receptacle, vehicle or movable structure is in the possession or under the control of any person at the time of such removal or impoundment.".

140 Para. 35(b).

141 71 of 1991.

142 eThekwini Municipality: Informal Trading By-Law, 2014. Sec. 35(1) of the by-law states: "An authorised official may remove and impound any goods of an informal trader which he or she reasonably suspects is being used, has been used or is intended to be used for or in connection with informal trading which is in contravention of this By-law or any other applicable law." See also *Makwickana* (n. 132), para. 80.

143 Para. 84.

Access to courts is specifically problematic for traders as they do not have the necessary financial resources and, in addition, being in court and away from their stalls may result in a loss of income. The Court found that Section 35 of the By-law limited the constitutional right of access to courts in respect of the impoundment as well as the subsequent disposal of the property for alleged contraventions, without the supervision of a judicial officer or any applicable tribunal or forum.[144]

In respect of Section 25 of the Constitution, the Court stated that "[t]o deprive street traders of their property permanently, s 35 of the By-laws has to overcome additional hurdles of fair procedure, rationality and proportionality".[145] African women are even more disadvantaged and the By-laws contributed to the prejudice of these poor and vulnerable traders with Section 35 directly and indirectly discriminating against poor black people.[146]

The Court also found that Section 39 of the By-law that indemnifies the municipality against any damages or compensation for anything done *bona fide* is unconstitutional.[147] This means that traders now at least can be compensated for lost goods. This would require that the informal traders are informed of the infringement of the law before the removal, impoundment and disposal of the goods.[148] The By-law clearly lacks procedural fairness in the removal, impoundment and disposal of the goods of these traders. Section 35 infringes on the constitutional right of access to property as the impoundment and disposal are found to be "irrational" and "arbitrary".[149] The irrational and arbitrary impoundment of goods also infringes on the right of these traders to trade.[150]

The Court in its judgment with reference to the *Zondi* case[151] stated that "[s]treet traders are similarly situated to the African owners of livestock and all other Africans whose systematic impoverishment and powerlessness are traceable to their loss of land before and after 1913".[152] The judgment illustrates that by-laws must be in line with the Constitution;

144 Para. 91.

145 Para. 96.

146 Paras. 122 and 124. Sec. 35 of the By-law discriminates against the traders in respect of Sec. 9(3) of the Constitution. The court highlights that women and specifically African women are particularly vulnerable category.

147 Para. 124. This provision infringes secs. 9, 12, 22 and 25.

148 Para. 96.

149 Para. 99.

150 Para. 102. See also Sec. 22 of the Constitution.

151 *Zondi v MEC for Traditional Local Government Affairs* 2008 3 SA 589 (CC).

152 Para. 88.

if they are not, they exceed their mandates and will be declared unconstitutional.[153]

Section 33 of the Constitution provides everyone with the right to administrative action that is lawful, reasonable and procedurally fair. Just administrative action is also applicable to informal traders, in respect of decisions taken by local authorities that are not procedurally fair and adversely affect the rights of these traders. Actions by local authorities include decisions by municipalities to close trading areas without any consultation with the traders and without any reasonable justification to deny them the opportunity to earn a living.[154]

It is thus submitted that informal traders have a right to just administrative action, meaning that it must be lawful,[155] reasonable[156] and procedurally fair.[157] Before *Makwickana*,[158] cases dealt mainly with the infringement of fundamental rights and the constitutionality of laws, including by-laws. The notion of just administrative action in the context of informal vendors can provide a remedy. This can be applicable where decisions have been made with reference to the issuing, suspension or revocation of licences;[159] the use of public spaces and the allocation of trading areas; the confiscation and impounding of goods;[160] and the imposing of fines and other penalties.[161] The Promotion of Administrative Justice Act (PAJA)[162] applies to administrative action[163] which "materially and adversely" affects the rights of any person, and provides that it must be procedurally fair.[164] Informal traders can thus institute a claim in this regard based on PAJA.

153 See also Sec. 153(3) of the Constitution. According to this Section a by-law that is in conflict with national or provincial legislation is invalid.

154 *Harvey* et al, Compendium of WIEGO and SEWA Case Studies (2016), 4.

155 This will include that the authority act within the scope of given powers (*Kohn*, Using Administrative Law to Secure Informal Livelihoods (2017), 10).

156 This will include rationality and proportionality, where rationality refers to a legitimate purpose to be achieved by the provisions.

157 In Sec. 33 administrative justice is entrenched as a fundamental right.

158 *Makwickana* (n. 132).

159 According to Hoexter, these issues surrounding licensing can qualify as administrative action (*Hoexter*, Administrative Law in South Africa (2012), 184).

160 The Court in *Makwickana* (n. 132), paras. 68 and 75, clearly stated that the impoundment of goods of a street trader falls within the scope of administrative action.

161 *Dawood v Minister of Home Affairs* (n. 113), para. 4.

162 Act 3 of 2000.

163 Sec. 1.

164 Sec. 3.

Within the framework of judicial review,[165] Section 8 of the Act provides for an order that is "just and equitable". This wide discretion with reference to remedies includes directing the decision maker to provide reasons, the setting aside of the administrative action, compensation and even an order substituting or varying the administrative action. In instances where workers in the informal economy are adversely affected by decisions or the exercise of public power that fall outside the ambit of administrative action, it can be construed as a direct constitutional challenge, as was the case in *Makwickana*.[166]

The Court in *Makwickana*[167] stated that legislation must clearly state the extent and conditions of powers to enable the public to assess whether the act committed was within the scope of the powers.[168] The Court, with reference to the *Zondi* case, stated that the impoundment of the property of informal traders was an administrative act and a challenge of this act must follow the procedure described in Section 7 of PAJA.[169] The right to just administrative action will also include the right to be heard before the impoundment of the property of street vendors.[170] With reference to informal vendors, the following statement in *Zondi*[171] is important: "It is a fundamental element of fairness that adverse decisions should not be made without affording the person to be affected by the decision a reasonable opportunity to make representations". The format of such opportunity should preferably be determined by all role players and this includes the nature thereof, for instance whether a mere interaction on the street would suffice as an opportunity to make representations.[172] The Court[173] found that impounding the goods without a hearing and authorisation was *ultra vires* as it violated Section 6(2)(a)(i)[174] and Section 6(2)(c)[175] of PAJA, as well as the concept of legality in Section 1(c) of the Constitution.

---

165 The procedure for judicial review is prescribed in Sec. 7 of PAJA.

166 *Kohn*, (n. 156), 21.

167 *Makwickana* (n. 132).

168 Para. 39.

169 In *Makwickana* the Court dispensed with the procedure because all the information relevant to the powers of the respondents were pleaded and common cause (para. 68).

170 *Makwickana* (n. 132), para. 71.

171 Para. 112.

172 *Makwickana* (n. 132), para. 72.

173 Ibid., para. 74.

174 This Section allows for judicial review in instances where the administrator took action for which he was not authorised by an empowering provision.

175 This provides for judicial review when the action was procedurally unfair.

Informal traders and their associations are often unaware of their remedies within an administrative framework. Empowerment programmes must be designed to inform these traders and their organisations of their legal rights under administrative law. Very few informal traders will be able to afford legal action with reference to every administrative action that affects their livelihood; however, the by-laws should provide adequate dispute resolution mechanisms in this regard. This judgment set a precedent and can now be used by informal traders to challenge discriminatory and unconstitutional provisions by authorities. It also marks a shift from the criminalisation of these activities to emphasising the importance of fair and just administrative action.[176] As informal traders fall outside the scope of labour legislation, the court in this instance extended protection to workers on the basis of administrative law remedies and did not consider concepts such as unfair labour practices or the narrow conceptual framework of employee. This is so because there is no employment relationship and therefore these concepts could not be utilised.

In *South African Informal Traders Forum v City of Johannesburg*[177] the Court highlighted the importance of the ability to earn money and to support oneself, in that this is an important component of the right to human dignity and that without it the traders face "humiliation and degradation".

In this case the applicants represented 1210 informal traders trading in the City of Johannesburg. The traders were removed from their trading locations and had their goods impounded by city officials. During these evictions, referred to as "the Mayoral Clean Sweep" (Operation Clean Sweep), the City did not distinguish between legal traders and those who were trading illegally. The applicants unsuccessfully sought urgent relief in the High Court. However, the Constitutional Court granted leave to appeal on the grounds that it was in the interests of justice to do so and a refusal would cause the traders irreparable harm.[178] The applicants showed that the traders and their families' livelihoods depended on their trading

---

176 *Harvey* et al, (n. 155), 5.

177 (N. 30), para. 31. See also *Minister of Home Affairs v Watchenuka* 2004 1 All SA 21 (SCA) where the Supreme Court of Appeal found that "[t]he freedom to engage in productive work – even where that is not required in order to survive – is indeed an important component of human dignity, as submitted by the respondents' counsel, for mankind is pre-eminently a social species with an instinct for meaningful association. Self-esteem and the sense of self-worth – the fulfilment of what it is to be human – is most often bound up with being accepted as socially useful".

178 Sec. 167(6) of the Constitution.

in the City. After their removal from the trading areas, they had been rendered destitute and unable to provide for their families. The City's conduct impaired the dignity of the traders and their families and had a direct and ongoing adverse effect on their rights to trade, basic nutrition, shelter and basic healthcare services. The Court reasoned that, if allowing the traders to continue trading during the verification process were to cause prejudice to the residents of the City, the prejudice would have been temporary. The Court stated that the immediate and irreversible harm that the traders were facing rendered their application urgent and justified the interim relief, which the Constitutional Court granted. Moseneke ACJ stated the following in paragraph 3: "When women and men in government disregard the law, their conduct may very well cause much hardship, particularly for the vulnerable amongst us." It is therefore important that government should strive to create an enabling framework at national and local level to support the informal economy. The Court held:

> "It must be added that the eviction of traders involved constitutional issues of considerable significance. The ability of people to earn money and support themselves and their families is an important part of human dignity. Without it they faced 'humiliation and degradation'."[179]

This highlights the interrelationship between the fundamental rights and the fact that they are mutually reinforcing and interdependent, including the right to human dignity, the right to freedom of trade and the socio-economic rights of children.[180]

The actions of the City were declared illegal, and the legal traders had an undisputed right under Section 4 of the By-laws to trade in their locations.[181] However, this case dealt specifically with the contraventions of the Business Act and the relevant by-laws. Constitutional protection for street traders under the scope of Section 22 of the Constitution may be more limited.[182] The Court recognised that the regulation of street traders did have a legitimate government purpose when lawful, and stated that "[i]t is open to the City to use all *lawful* means to combat illegal trading

179 Para. 31.

180 *Pieterse*, PER 2017, 7.

181 Paras. 25, 28.

182 See *Affordable Medicines Trust v Minister of Health* 2006 3 SA 247 (CC) and *Union of Refugee Women v Director: Private Security Industry Regulatory Authority* 2007 4 SA 395 (CC).

and criminal conduct. But it has no entitlement to cause harm to lawful, if not vulnerable traders".[183]

Judgments by progressive courts throughout the world have an impact far beyond the particular parties that bring the cases to court.[184] They allow us to declare that the poorest and most disadvantaged among us have rights. They affirm human dignity and encourage people to stand up and claim their rights. They promote transparency and public accountability. As lawyers and judges engage with these rights, they affect the lives of millions.

This judgment should serve as a warning to policy makers and those responsible for the implementation thereof, as it is clear that the courts will not hesitate to intervene to ensure compliance with the Bill of Rights. State organs, including municipalities, must promote transparency and accountability in adherence to the Constitution. The judgment has also created an awareness of the plights of informal traders in South Africa and of the fact that state parties cannot merely disregard the law.

It is interesting to note that in a similar Supreme Court case in India, where the goods of informal traders were destroyed by government officials, the Court also equated the actions of the public authorities with an impairment of the constitutional provision of dignity.[185] The Court held that earning a living as a street trader provided those affected with a life lived with dignity.

It should be noted that when courts consider the advancement of socio-economic rights and other fundamental rights, as in the above case, an integrated approach is necessary. In South Africa disadvantages suffered by these vulnerable workers include numerous causes, such as inequality with reference to social class; race and gender; a lack of opportunities for education and work; inadequate housing; limited access to water and sanitation services; and a lack of adequate health care.[186]

---

183 Para. 33 (emphasis added).

184 In *Somali Association of South Africa v Limpopo Department of Economic Development Environment and Tourism* 2015 1 SA 151 (SCA) the position of vulnerable asylum seekers and refugees were considered. The Court also confirmed that in instances where persons will be left destitute and have no other means to support themselves, the right to dignity will be impaired (para. 43).

185 *Maharashtra Ekta Hawkers Union Municipal Corpn. Greater Mumbai* (2014) 1 SCC 490, para. 4.

186 *Hepple*, SALJ 2012, 253.

V. Concluding remarks

The important function of labour law to protect and promote the human dignity of workers will often result in a crossover of various subsystems of the law. In the cases highlighted above, various other legal instruments, such as those found in administrative law, were utilised to come to the aid of and to protect vulnerable workers. The aims of labour law were therefore achieved not by traditional labour law instruments. Labour law should be reimagined to include other legal regimes such as administrative law so as to protect and promote the human dignity of workers. If one considers human dignity as an important component of labour law, one needs to consider an interdisciplinary approach and the promotion of such an approach. This approach will mean that labour law can no longer function in isolation and that other branches of the law, such as social security law, corporate law, human rights and family law, will increasingly have an impact on the human dignity of workers.

When considering the future of labour law, and specifically in relation to the labour and social protection of workers in the informal economy, it is vital that the new framework is intrinsically linked to concepts such as democracy, social justice, freedom and human rights. This can primarily be achieved by testing existing legislation against these rights, by developing the common law so as to accord with these rights and by interpreting existing legislation in furtherance of these rights. As the employment relationship is primarily regulated by legislation and because litigants are prohibited from relying directly on constitutionally-guaranteed human rights where legislation has been adopted to give effect to these rights, the courts will have to act in partnership with the legislature to give effect to these rights through their powers of interpretation.

The stated aim of the Constitution, as well as the Labour Relations Act and the Basic Conditions of Employment Act, is the achievement of social justice. Courts in their interpretive task must advance interpretations that enhance and ensure justice, even if this means that legal instruments outside of the traditionally accepted labour law field. This does not mean that the judiciary will always be asked to consider complex legal-philosophical questions about the requirements of justice, but rather that the courts must follow interpretations that advance the Constitution's vision of a just society. The ultimate aim of the Constitution is a society that reflects the fundamental values of equality, human dignity and freedom. As such, it is possible to argue that a society reflective of these values will be a society where social justice prevails.

Bibliography

Mortimer Adler and *Charles van Doren*, How to Read a Book (Simon and Schuster, New York 1972).

Aaron Barak, Purposive Interpretation in Law (Princeton University Press, New Jersey 2005).

David Beatty, "Constitutional Labour Rights: Pros and Cons", ILJ 1993, 1.

Christo Botha, Statutory Interpretation: An Introduction for Students (Juta, Cape Town 2005).

Christo Botha, Statutory Interpretation: An Introduction for Students (Juta, Cape Town 2012).

Blessing Chinsinga and *Happy Kayuni*, "The Complexities and Paradoxes of Governing the Informal Sector in Malawi: The Case of Street Vending in Zomba and Blantyre", in: Dan Banik (ed.), The Legal Empowerment Agenda: Poverty, Labour and the Informal Economy in Africa (Ashgate, Farnham 2011) 107.

Hugh Collins, "Theories of Rights as Justification for Labour Law", in: Guy Davidov and Brian Langille, (eds.), The Idea of Labour Law (Oxford University Press, Oxford 2011) 137.

Carole Cooper, "Labour Relations" Revision Service 6 2nd ed. 2014 (loose-leaf edition), in: Stew Woolman and Michael Bishop, (eds.), Constitutional Law of South Africa (Juta, Cape Town 2008) 1.

Denis Cowen, "Prolegomenon to a Restatement of the Principles of Statutory Interpretation", TSAR 1976, 131.

Anne Davies, Perspectives on Labour Law (Cambridge University Press, 2nd ed., Cambridge 2009).

George Devenish, Interpretation of Statutes (Juta, Cape Town 1992).

Ruth Dukes, "Hugo Sinzheimer and the Constitutional Function of Labour Law", in: Guy Davidov and Brian Langille (eds.), The Idea of Labour Law (Oxford University Press, Oxford 2011) 57.

Timothy Endicott, "The Value of Vagueness", in: Andrei Marmor and Scott Soames (eds.), Philosophical Foundations of Language in the Law (Oxford University Press, USA 2011) 14.

Stanley Fish, Doing What Comes Naturally: Change Rhetoric, and the Practice of Theory in Legal Studies (Duke University Press, Durham 1989).

Sandra Fredman, "Engendering Socio-Economic Rights", SAJHR 2009, 410.

Mark Freedland and *Nicola Kountouris*, The Legal Construction of Personal Work Relations (Oxford University Press, Oxford 2011).

Pablo Gilabert, "Labour, Human Rights and Human Dignity", PhilSocCrit 2016, 171.

Beth Goldblatt and *Kirsty McLean*, "Introduction: Women and Social and Economic Rights", SAJHR 2009, 407.

John Grogan, Workplace Law (Juta, Cape Town 2014).

Herbert Lionel Adolphus Hart, The Concept of Law (Oxford University Press, New York 1961).

Jenna Harvey et al, Compendium of Wiego and Sewa Case Studies (WIEGO and SEWA, Cambridge (MA) 2016).

Bob Hepple, "Factors Influencing the Making and Transformation of Labour Law in Europe", in: Guy Davidov and Brian Langille, (eds.), The Idea of Labour Law (Oxford University Press, Oxford 2011) 30.

Bob Hepple, "Equality and Empowerment for Decent Work", ILR 2001, 5.

Bob Hepple, "The Future of Labour Law", CLLPJ 1995, 303.

Cora Hoexter, Administrative Law in South Africa (Juta, Cape Town 2012).

Lauren Kohn, Using Administrative Law to Secure Informal Livelihoods: Lessons from South Africa, WIEGO Technical Brief (Law) (WIEGO, Cambridge (MA) 2017).

Pius Langa, "Transformative Constitutionalism", Stell LR 2006, 351.

Wessel le Roux, "Advancing Domestic Workers' Rights in a Context of Transformative Constitutionalism", in: Darcy Du Toit, (ed.), Exploited, Undervalued – and Essential: Domestic Workers and the Realisation of Their Rights (PULP, Pretoria 2013) 31.

Wessel le Roux, "Directory Provisions, Section 39(2) of the Constitution and the Ontology of Statutory Law *African Christian Democratic Party v Electoral Commission*", SA Public Law 2006, 382.

James Maxeiner, "Some Realism about Legal Certainty in the Globalization of the Rule of Law", 31 Houston Journal of International Law 2008, 27.

Christopher McCrudden, "Labour Law as Human Rights Law: A Critique of the Use of 'Dignity' by Freedland and Kountouris", in: Alan Bogg, et al (eds.), The Autonomy of Labour Law (Hart Publishing, Oxford 2015) 275.

Frank Michelman, "On the Uses of Interpretive Charity: Some Notes From Abroad on Application, Avoidance, Equality and Objective Unconstitutionality", Constitutional Court Review 2008, 1.

Kgomotso Mokoena, "Are Uber Drivers Employees? A Look at Emerging Business Models and Whether They Can Be Accommodated by South African Labour Law", ILJ 2016, 1574.

Marius Pieterse, "Rights Regulation and Bureaucratic Impact: The Impact of Human Rights Litigation on the Regulation of Informal Trade in Johannesburg", PER 2017, 1.

Kamala Sankaran, "Protecting the Worker in the Informal Economy: The Role of Labour Law", in: Guy Davidov and Brian Langille (eds.), Boundaries and the Frontiers of Labour Law: Goals and Means in the Regulation of Work (Hart Publishing, Oxford 2006) 205.

Antonin Scalia and *Bryan Gardner*, Reading Law: The Interpretation of Legal Texts (Thomson West, St Paul 2012).

Amartya Sen, Development as Freedom (Oxford University Press, New York 1999).

Amartya Sen, Inequality Re-Examined (Oxford University Press, Oxford 1992).

James Spigelman, "The Poet's Rich Resource: Issues in Statutory Interpretation", Australian Bar Review 2001, 224.

Cass Sunstein, "Interpreting Statutes in the Regulatory State", Harvard Law Review 1989, 405.

Clive Thompson and *Paul Benjamin*, South African Labour Law (Juta, Cape Town 1997)

Andre van Niekerk, et al (eds.), Law@work (LexisNexis, 4th ed., Durban 2018).

Marius van Staden "The Role of the Judiciary in Balancing Flexibility and Security", De Jure 2013, 470.

Stew Woolman, "The Amazing, Vanishing Bill of Rights", SALJ 2007, 262.

Stew Woolman "True in Theory, True in Practice: Why Direct Application Still Matters", in: Stew Woolman, and Michael Bishop (eds.), Constitutional Conversations (Pretoria University Law Press, Pretoria 2008) 113.

Register of cases

Affordable Medicines Trust v Minister of Health 2006 3 SA 247 (CC).

African Christian Democratic Party v Electoral Commission 2006 3 SA 305 (CC).

Air Tour (Israel) Ltd v Chair of the Council for Antitrust Oversight 39(1) PD 169.

Bato Star Fishing (Pty) Ltd v Minister of Environmental Affairs 2004 7 BCLR 687 (CC).

Booysen v Minister of Home Affairs 2001 4 SA 485 (CC).

Brink v Kitshoff 1996 4 SA 197 (CC).

C v Department of Health and Social Development Case 55/11 (CC) (unreported).

Corocraft v Pan-American Airways 1968 2 All ER 1059.

Dawood v Minister of Home Affairs 2000 3 SA 936 (CC).

Democratic Alliance v eThekwini Municipality 2012 2 SA 151 (SCA).

Department of Land Affairs v Goedgelegen Tropical Fruits Pty Ltd 2007 6 SA 199 (CC).

Doctors for Life International v Speaker of the National Assembly 2006 6 SA 416 (CC).

Ex Parte Chairman of the Constitutional Court Assembly: In re Certification of the Constitution of the Republic of South Africa 1996 4 SA 744 (CC).

Gov Ari Ltd v Netanya Local Planning and Construction Council 35(4) PD, 764.

Government of the Republic of South Africa v Grootboom 2000 11 BCLR 1169 (CC).

Investigating Directorate: Serious Economic Offences v Hyundai Motor Distributors (Pty) Ltd. In re: Hyundai Motor Distributors (Pty) Ltd v Smit 2001 1 SA 545 (CC).

J v Director General, Department of Home Affairs 2003 5 SA 621 (CC).

Janse van Rensburg v Minister of Trade and Industry 2001 1 SA 29 (CC).

Maharashtra Ekta Hawkers Union Municipal Corpn Greater Mumbai (2014) 1 SCC 490.

Makwickana v eThekwini Municipality 2015 3 SA 165 (KZD).

Makwickana v eThekwini Municipality 2015 3 SA 165 (KZD).

Matiso v The Commanding Officer, Port Elizabeth Prison 1994 3 SA 592 (SE).

MEC for Education KwaZulu-Natal v Pillay 2008 1 SA 474 (CC).

Minister of Finance v Van Heerden 2004 12 BLLR 1181 (CC).

Minister of Health v Treatment Action Campaign (2) 2002 (10) BCLR 1075.

Minister of Home Affairs v Watchenuka 2004 1 All SA 21 (SCA).

Moseneke v The Master of the High Court 2001 2 SA 18 (CC).

National Coalition for Gay and Lesbian Equality v Minister of Justice 1999 1 SA 6 (CC).

National Education Health and Allied Workers Union v University of Cape Town 2003 3 SA 1 (CC).

President of the Republic of South Africa v Hugo 1997 4 SA 1 (CC).

S v Makwanyane 1995 3 SA 391 (CC).

S v Mhlungu 1995 3 SA 867 (CC).

Sali v National Commissioner of the South African Police Service 2014 9 BLLR 827 (CC).

Smit v Workmen's Compensation Commissioner 1979 1 SA 51 (A).

Somali Association of South Africa v Limpopo Department of Economic Development Environment and Tourism 2015 1 SA 151 (SCA).

Soobramoney v Minister of Health (Kwa-Zulu Natal) 1998 1 SA 765 (CC).

South African Informal Traders Forum v City of Johannesburg 2014 4 SA 371 (CC).

South African Liquor Traders Association v Chairperson, Gauteng Liquor Board 2006 8 BCLR 901 (CC).

South African National Defence Union v Minister of Defence 2007 5 SA 400 (CC).

South African Police Service v Solidarity obo Barnard 2014 6 SA 123 (CC).

Uber South Africa Technological Services (Pty) Ltd and NUPSAW and SATAWU Case WECT12537–16 (CCMA) (unreported).

Uber South Africa Technology Services (Pty) Ltd v National Union of Public Service and Allied Workers Case c449/17 (LC) (unreported).

Union of Refugee Women v Director: Private Security Industry Regulatory Authority 2007 4 SA 395 (CC).

Van Rooyen v The State 2002 5 SA 246 (CC).

Venter v R 1907 TS 910.

Volks v Robinsion 2005 5 BCLR 446 (CC).

Wary Holdings (Pty) Ltd v Stalwo (Pty) Ltd 2009 1 SA 337 (CC).

Zondi v MEC for Traditional Local Government Affairs 2008 3 SA 589 (CC).

Comment: Discrimination in Working Life and Anti-Discrimination Law – Experiments and Experiences in Germany and Europe

Martina Benecke[*]

---

* Martina Benecke, *Dr. iur.*; Professor, University of Augsburg Faculty of Law. Chair for Civil Law, Commercial Law, Labor Law and Economic Law.

I. Introduction: an era of experiments and experiences in legislation against discrimination

Ten years ago, the European directives against discrimination were implemented into national law. The directives ended a long period of a passionate and emotional discussion about discrimination in working life, and were accompanied by hopes on one side and fears on the other. Ten years later, the issues are quite different from the original hopes and fears. This comment will summarise the experiences and the focus in practice and legislation.

In the 1990s, legislation against discrimination had come into the focus of the EU.[1] As a result, the EU passed four new or revised directives around the year 2000:

- Council Directive 2000/43/EC of 29 June 2000 implementing the principle of equal treatment between persons irrespective of racial or ethnic origin,
- Council Directive 2000/78/EC of 27 November 2000 establishing a general framework for equal treatment in employment and occupation,
- Directive 2002/73/EC of the European Parliament and of the Council of 23 September 2002 amending Council Directive 76/207/EEC on the implementation of the principle of equal treatment for men and women as regards access to employment, vocational training and promotion, and working conditions, and
- Council Directive 2004/113/EC of 13 December 2004 implementing the principle of equal treatment between men and women in the access to and supply of goods and services.

With a small delay, Germany implemented these directives into national law by adopting the General Equal Treatment Act (*Allgemeines Gleichbehandlungsgesetz* – AGG).[2] Note that the term "discrimination" does not appear in the name of the Act. This name is the result of a long discussion, which is typical for this era. For Germany and most of the other Member States of the EU, anti-discrimination legislation was a new, special and

---

1 Comparison of European equality law in 2003: *Bell* and *Waddington*, 28 E.L.R. 2003, 349.

2 Official citation manner: Allgemeines Gleichbehandlungsgesetz of 14 Aug 2006 (Federal Law Gazette [BGBl.] of 17 Aug 2006, part I, 1897), last amended by Article 8 of the law dated 3 Apr 2013 (BGBl. of 8 Apr 2013, part I, 610). For an English version, see https://www.gesetze-im-internet.de/englisch_agg/englisch_agg.html (last visited 13 Aug 2019).

quite sensitive subject. Of course, there had been legislation against gender discrimination and disabilities acts, but hardly anyone had cared about age discrimination. Ten years ago, in the European Year of Equal Opportunities for All (2007)[3], most Member States implemented the directives into their domestic law.

So, whilst some advocated as much protection against discrimination as possible, others worried about fraud and feared innumerable claims.[4] More than ten years later, most experiences show that neither approach was entirely reasonable. There had been some legal proceedings, but not an extraordinary number of them, and some instances of fraud, but the main problems were unexpected ones.

Nearly all legal proceedings focus on the fields of employment law and social law. This correlates with the subject matter of the directives, especially Directive 2000/78/EC and Directive 2002/73/EC. Apart from that, discrimination is more likely to be found in the processes of working life than in the process of buying an apple. Furthermore, most legal proceedings were filed in Germany, for the obvious reason is that Germany is the most populous country of the EU. Apart from that, Germans have a reputation for knowing their rights and being willing to go to court, and perhaps for being particularly sensitive to discrimination.[5]

In the following paper, I will discuss the main legislation in Germany and the other Member States – the implementation of which into domestic law has resulted in some intriguing experiments. Because of this, courts faced new challenges. Over the last ten years, several legal proceedings and important judgments have led to some interesting experiences. Based on these experiences, my aim is to evaluate some European, and especially German, anti-discrimination legislation.

---

3 Decision No. 771/2006/EC of the European Parliament and of the Council of 17 May 2006 establishing the European Year of Equal Opportunities for All (2007) – towards a just society, OJ L 146 of 31 May 2006. See also Communication from the Commission to the Council, the European Parliament, the European Economic and Social Committee and the Committee of the Regions – Implementation, results and overall assessment of the 2007 European Year of Equal Opportunities for All, SEC(2009) 781, COM(2009) 269.

4 Summary of the discussion: *Lock*, 38 E.L.R. 2013, 655, 659.

5 In Eastern Europe, the society seems to be more reluctant concerning anti-discrimination law, see *Havelková*, 17 GLJ 2016, 627.

II. Prosecution of discrimination and available sanctions

The first matter, comprising three independent issues, concerns the legal consequences of a discriminating act, its sanctioning and the method of prosecution. First, the legislature has to decide whether an act of discrimination is to be considered as a crime, an offence or a civil wrong. This correlates with the question of the persons authorised to prosecute such discrimination. It may be the law enforcement agency of the Member State, some kind of NGO, or the discriminated person as the injured party. The third inter-dependent matter concerns the sanctions for the discrimination which, due to its importance, merits a section of its own.

Some Member States of the EU opted for a solution in the field of criminal law or in the law of offences. Others – including Germany – opted for solutions in the field of civil law. Some chose a combination of both solutions – for example, racial discrimination is treated as a crime[6], but age discrimination leads only to a civil claim. The most common solution is a solution in civil law, but this leads to a second option: Is there a possibility of collective action, or must the discriminated person assert his or her rights and claims individually?

During the legislative process, I voted for a solution in offence law[7] and I am still not convinced that the current law is the best solution. If a certain act is a legal criminal offence, this legal implementation clarifies the immediate concerns of the state that the law is designed to address. Furthermore, prosecution of discrimination is not the responsibility of the discriminated person but the responsibility of the state. Therefore, there is less danger of fraud. On the other hand, the discriminated person may be too shy or intimidated to take legal action against the discrimination.

On the other hand, the responsibility of the discriminated person has several benefits. It ensures a prosecution even if the discrimination may seem rather trivial. In particular, the sanction of prosecution immediately benefits the discriminated person und may restore his or her dignity. Over the last ten years, there have been several instances of civil proceedings against discrimination, and very few criminal proceedings. It may be that experience has shown that the civil compensation for victims by means of civil action against the offender is the more effective path. However,

6 On the subjects of racial justice in Germany and the current law see *Bechtel*, in: Elósegui and Hermida (eds.), Policies and Courts' Legal Reasoning in Europe (2017), 157.

7 *Benecke* and *Kern*, 16 EuZW 2005, 360.

one must add that there are some cases of fraud and abuse of rights – and they will be addressed below. Also discussed below will be the issue of collective action, because of its connection with the question of institutions extending the protection against discrimination.

III. Persons protected and persons responsible in cases of discrimination

When considering the question of possible claimants and defendants under anti-discrimination laws, one must differentiate between employment law legislation and discrimination under civil law, Sections 19–21 AGG. The latter pools certain listed legal relations under civil law – especially bulk business, private insurance and housing rental (see Section 19 AGG). Of course, both the claimant and opponent may be subject to private law. This part of the AGG has turned to be of little practical importance, with the exception of very few cases concerning private insurance.[8]

In practice, the AGG is a part of the employment laws, and most of its rules deal with employment law – especially the protection of employees against discrimination (Sections 6–18 AGG). Pursuant to the anti-discrimination directives,[9] Section 6 AGG lists the persons covered. The term "employee" as a possible claimant refers not only to persons in dependent employment and persons employed for the purposes of their vocational training, but also to persons of similar status on account of their dependent economic status. Section 6(3) AGG points out that insofar as the conditions for access to gainful employment and promotion are affected, the provisions apply, mutatis mutandis, to the self-employed and to members of an organ of an enterprise, in particular directors and board members. In most cases, the defendant is the employer who, of course, may be a natural or a legal person or an unincorporated firm with the legal capacity to employ persons.

Pursuant to Section 18 AGG, the provisions set out in Part 2 concerning employment law apply, mutatis mutandis, to membership of or involvement in a party to a collective bargaining agreement and similar organisations. This regulation may give an entitlement when the rejection of

8 Cases in Germany summed up by *Heese*, NJW 2012, 572.
9 See above I.

a membership in the listed organisation turns out to be discriminatory. Fortunately, this is hardly ever the case.[10]

IV. *Prohibited grounds of discrimination*

1. Legal situation in Germany

The name of the German Anti-discrimination act – *Allgemeines Gleichbehandlungsgesetz* (General Equal Treatment Act) – is misleading. It suggests that the purpose of the law is to ensure equal treatment of all the possible claimants addressed above. On the contrary – not every discrimination, unequal treatment or harassment will lead to legal consequences and sanctions. It is characteristic for each anti-discrimination legislation – directives as well as their national implementations – to refer to certain prohibited grounds of discrimination.

In the German act, these are set out in Section 1 AGG.[11] The translated wording is the following: "The purpose of this Act is to prevent or to stop discrimination on the grounds of race or ethnic origin, gender, religion or belief, disability, age or sexual orientation." The discrimination grounds have not only been established to protect minorities. As a result, "sexual orientation" not only protects homosexual people, but in the same way heterosexual and religion covers not only the religions or minorities but also the mainstream one or ones. Age means old, young and middle-aged and gender means each gender.[12] On the other hand, only disabled persons are protected against discrimination – a discrimination as a result of not being disabled is hardly imaginable – and "race" does not suggest the existence of human races but takes a stand against racism and racial discrimination.[13]

---

10 *Schlachter*, in: Müller-Glöge, Preis and Schmidt (eds.), Erfurter Kommentar zum Arbeitsrecht (17th ed. 2017), § 18 AGG, para. 2.

11 Wording of the Section: *§ 1 Ziel des Gesetzes: Ziel des Gesetzes ist, Benachteiligungen aus Gründen der Rasse oder wegen der ethnischen Herkunft, des Geschlechts, der Religion oder Weltanschauung, einer Behinderung, des Alters oder der sexuellen Identität zu verhindern oder zu beseitigen.*

12 *Schlachter*, in: Müller-Glöge, Preis and Schmidt (eds.), Erfurter Kommentar zum Arbeitsrecht (17th ed. 2017), § 1 AGG, paras. 12 et seqq.

13 *McInerney*, 56 International and Comparative Law 2008, 211.

Pursuant to Section 3 AGG, the protection against discrimination includes the following acts: direct discrimination,[14] indirect discrimination,[15] harassment, sexual harassment and instructions to discriminate against a person. As mentioned above, these acts have to be motivated by one of grounds referred to under Section 1 AGG. Furthermore, the law provides some possible reasons of justification, so a different treatment on the prohibited grounds does not necessarily always have to be discriminatory. For example, pursuant to Section 8 AGG, differences of treatment may be permissible on grounds of occupational requirements.

2. Legal comparison in Europe: more or less prohibited grounds?

The prohibited grounds are the main item of each anti-discrimination act. Comparison of the different laws shows that several Member States have installed further prohibited grounds into their acts – such as marital or family status, financial status or membership in a party or trade union. Some Member States even regard their list of the prohibited ground as a non-exhaustive list.[16]

It must be asked whether this is a better concept. At first glance, because the struggle against discrimination is a most important issue, it may appear that the scope of an anti-discrimination act cannot be wide enough. In Germany, there is a slogan – *viel hilft viel* – which may be translated as "much helps much". Quoting it leads to some reservations, because in legislation much is not the same as best or optimal. This already emerges from the fact that the wider the scope of a law is, the greater also the risk of legal uncertainty.

Legislation against discrimination has two aims: the prohibition and sanctioning of certain discriminatory acts, and also the political aim of increasing sensitivity and awareness against discrimination on both sides.

---

14 A case of direct discrimination is to be assumed where one person has been treated less favourably than another has been or would be treated in a comparable situation on any of the grounds referred to under Section 1.

15 Indirect discrimination occurs where an apparently neutral provision, criterion or practice would put persons at a particular disadvantage compared with other persons on any of the grounds referred to under Section 1, unless that provision, criterion or practice is objectively justified by a legitimate aim and the means of achieving that aim are appropriate and necessary.

16 See *Benecke*, Rechtsvergleich der europäischen Systeme zum Antidiskriminierungsrecht (2010), 19 et seqq., paras. 68 et seqq.

So, the European directives and the current German law point out the precise concerns of the legislature and, moreover, of society. In contrast, a non-exhaustive list is necessarily vague and difficult to apply. It relativises the concern of the legislature, and the act gives the impression of an obscure and unrealistic entity.

A very long and extensive list of prohibited ground raises similar concerns. For example, the anti-discrimination act of Hungary lists 19 prohibited grounds. I cannot fault a critic who says this is a foolish law. Experience has shown that the anti-discrimination acts with an exhaustive list of prohibited grounds going no further than the areas of discrimination set out in directives have demonstrated the greatest practical importance. If there are legal gaps, there are usually also ways to close them. For example, there has been a discussion, about whether discrimination on grounds of an individual's weight should be incorporated into anti-discrimination law.[17] In 2014, the European Court of Justice (ECJ) ruled that obesity of a worker constitutes a "disability" within the meaning of Directive 2000/78/EC of 27 November 2000.[18]

3. Practical significance of the listed grounds

The question of the practical significance of the particular prohibited grounds leads to some surprising answers. The situation at the turn of the century was the following: There were two prohibited grounds, which were familiar and generally accepted – gender and the protection of disabled persons. In most countries, including Germany, laws concerning these matters had existed for more than twenty years. The other prohibited grounds were less familiar as subjects of civil law. Some hypothesised that the prohibition of racial discrimination might become the most important item. Hardly anyone considered the importance of protection against discrimination because of age – especially of young age. For example, most collective agreements provided more vacation days for older workers than

17 International comparison between U.S. and France: *Huggins*, 38 Fordham Int'l L.J. 2015, 889.

18 This is the case where it entails a limitation resulting in particular from long-term physical, mental or psychological impairments which in interaction with various barriers may hinder the full and effective participation of the person concerned in professional life on an equal basis with other workers; ECJ, Judgment of 18 Dec 2014, C-354/13, ECLI:EU:C:2014:2463 – Fag og Arbejde.

for younger workers, and payment in public services was essentially age-dependent.

Ten years later, most legal proceedings under the anti-discrimination law seem to concern age discrimination.[19] Apart from that, gender discrimination and claims of disabled people have not become less important than ten years ago. Claims on the grounds of racial discrimination mostly concern religion and dress codes, especially the Islamic headscarf. The attitude of employers and customers towards Islamic women wearing headscarves seems to be one of the most controversial issues at the moment,[20] although overall more legal proceedings relate to age discrimination.

V. Legal consequences of discrimination, and sanctions against discrimination

1. Challenges for the legislature

One of the challenges of anti-discrimination acts for legislatures is defining the sanctions that the law provides in cases of discrimination. The directives require that Member States to lay down sanctions rules applicable to infringements of the national provisions adopted pursuant to each directive, and to take all measures necessary to ensure that they are applied. The sanctions – which may comprise the payment of compensation to the victim – must be effective, proportionate and dissuasive.[21]

---

19 See only ECJ, Judgment of 22 Nov 2005, C-144/04, ECLI:EU:C:2005:709 – Mangold; ECJ, Judgment of 16 Oct 2007, C-411/05, ECLI:EU:C:2007:604 – Palacios; ECJ, Judgment of 5 Mar 2009, C-388/07, ECLI:EU:C:2009:128 – Age Concern England; ECJ, Judgment of 19 Jan 2010, C-555/07, ECLI:EU:C:2010:21 – Kücükdeveci; ECJ, Judgment of 12 Oct 2010, C-45/09, ECLI:EU:C:2010:601 – Rosenbladt; ECJ, Judgment of 20 Oct 2010, C-499/08, ECLI:EU:C:2010:600 – Ingeniørforeningen i Danmark v. Region Syddanmark; ECJ, Judgment of 8 Sep 2011, C-297/10, ECLI:EU:C:2011:560 – Hennings; ECJ, Judgment of 19 Jun 2014, C-501/12, ECLI:EU:C:2014:2005 – Specht; international comparison see *Lahey*, 32 Res Aging 2010, 679. On the issue of demographic chance as a possible reason *Hack*, 3 EuZA 2010, 347.

20 See from a comparative legal perspective concerning German and UK law *Lock*, 38 E.L.R. 2013, 655; relating to Germany *Mushaben*, 14 GLJ 2013, 1757; the German problem is even discussed in Canada, see *Mirzazadeh* 28 Pacific McGeorge Global Business & Development Law Journal 2015, 411.

21 Article 15 of Council Directive No. 2000/43/EC of 29 Jun 2000; Article 17 of Council Directive No. 2000/78/EC of 27 Nov 2000; Article 25 of Council Directive No. 2006/54/EC of 5 Jul 2006.

With this wording, the directives point towards the possibility of a solution in the form of civil claims – in particular, the payment of compensation to the victim. As mentioned above, most Member States (including Germany) voted for this option. The result is a quite exceptional legal regulation. Because of the provisions of the directives, the law has to take into account both the prevention of discrimination and compensation for damages.

This leads to three peculiarities of damages in German anti-discrimination law.[22] Firstly, the directives demand liability without fault, although traditional German indemnity law and tort law are based on the principle of fault. Secondly, the required sanctioning and dissuasive effect may be inconsistent with the proportionality of the damages. Thirdly, the directives demand a sanction even in cases without an actual victim.[23]

2. Current German law

Current German law – especially Section 15 AGG – is a complex compromise between these demands. It distinguishes between material and non-material damages, damages and compensation. Pursuant to Section 15(1) AGG, the employer is under an obligation to compensate the damage arising from a violation of the prohibition of discrimination. It is important that this does not apply where the employer is not responsible for the breach of duty.

By contrast, no responsibility is necessary if the damage arising does not constitute economic loss. In this case, the employee may demand appropriate monetary compensation. This compensation is limited: In the event of non-recruitment, it may not exceed three monthly salaries if the employee would not have been recruited if the selection had been made without unequal treatment. Apart from that, pursuant to Section 15(6) AGG, any violation of the prohibition of discrimination on the part of the

---

22 See *Benecke*, in: Gsell, Krüger, Lorenz and Mayer (eds.), BeckOGK (ed. of 1 Aug 2019), § 15 AGG, para. 1.

23 Such a case is the origin of ECJ, Judgment of 10 Jul 2008, C-54/07, ECLI:EU:C:2008:397 – Feryn; the director of the company Feryn had given a public statement that his undertaking was looking to recruit fitters but that it could not employ "immigrants" because its customers were reluctant to give them access to their private residences. There is little doubt about the racial discrimination, but because of the public statement, one cannot identify a certain violated person.

employer will not justify a claim to the establishment of an employment relationship, a vocational training relationship or to promotion, unless such a relationship or promotion results from another legal ground. So in employment law there is generally no obligation to contract.[24]

3. Experiences and evaluation

Since the AGG entered into force, critics have raised doubts that the current legislation meets the demands of the directives – which, as has already been stated, require "effective, proportionate and dissuasive" sanctions. Apart from that, the claim for damages is fault-based, whereas the directives demand otherwise. Only the claim for non-material damages fulfils this requirement: Section 15 AGG has to be seen in conjunction with Section 22 AGG. This legal regulation lessens the burden of proof of the claimant, and it may even shift when the person claiming to be the victim of discrimination can establish a presumption of discrimination. In this circumstances, it is for the respondent to prove that there has been no discrimination.[25]

Evaluating the law, one has to consider the most frequent application in practice – the application procedure. Most cases concern job advertisement with discriminatory wording – such as "young applicants wanted". Many other mistakes occur in the staffing procedure concerning disabled applicants. In these cases, it should be considered that it is almost impossible to prove that there has been no discrimination. It may be that the prevention of legal abuse is an argument in favour of the current law. There have been several cases of fraud that will be discussed below. An overview of the anti-discrimination law shows a great variety of legal consequences, but also quite similar monetary amounts. The amount of financial sanctions – penalty or damages – lies between a few hundred euros or even €10,000–30,000. Nobody in Europe has become rich (or impoverished!) as a result of a discrimination claim.

---

24 Concerning the obligation to contract in general civil law, see *Ebert* and *Pinkel*, 10 GLJ 2009, 1417; *Wiemann*, 11 GLJ 2010, 1131.

25 Communication from the Commission, the European Parliament, the European Economic and Social Committee and the Committee of the Regions about the application of Council Directive (EC) No. 2000/78 of 27 Nov 2000 establishing a general framework for equal treatment in employment and occupation, COM(2008) 225, 8.

VI. *Institutions against discrimination*

The greatest differences between the national implementations of the directives may concern legal institutions against discrimination. Of course, there are courts applying the law – in some countries civil law, in others criminal law. Apart from that, Article 13 of the Racial Equality Council Directive 2000/43/EC demands that the Member States designate a body or bodies for the promotion of equal treatment of all persons without discrimination on the grounds of racial or ethnic origin. In accordance with the Directive, these bodies may form part of agencies charged at the national level with the defence of human rights or the safeguarding of individuals' rights.

Some Member States designated an existing body to be the Article 13 body, while others set up a new body. In several Member States, including Germany, the competences of their independent, specialised body include not only racial discrimination but also the other discrimination grounds. Furthermore, there is a wide variety of the competences allocated to such bodies.

Apart from that, all implementations of the anti-discrimination directives share the commonality that the prosecution of discrimination is never the sole responsibility of the independent body. In some Member States, the specialised body has been given the authority to impose fines and/or to support discriminated claimants during legal proceedings. All specialised bodies offer consulting services concerning legal and other options to fight against discrimination.

Another fundamental legislative decision was the question of popular actions. Some Member States – except Germany – provide for collective actions against discriminatory acts. The complaining party may be the specialised body, a public institution and/or a NGO. Usually, the collective action depends on the consent of the discriminated person, but some Member States provide for the possibility of collective action even without consent. One can debate for hours the question of whether legal proceedings against discrimination without the consent of the victim are sensible. Of course, the dissuasive effect is greater, because attempts to intimidate the victim are useless. Nevertheless, it is a questionable matter to start legal proceedings without the consent of the most affected person. Germany does not provide for the possibility of collective actions in such a case.

In Germany, Sections 25–30 AGG regulate the formation, legal status and competences of the specialised body. It is called the Federal Anti-Discrimination Agency.[26] The agency is attached to the Federal Ministry for Family Affairs, Senior Citizens, Women and Youth (*Bundesministerium für Familie, Senioren, Frauen und Jugend* – BMFSFJ), but is independent in its decisions and is not subject to instructions or directives of the minister. The agency works under the control of its head, whose legal status is regulated in Section 26 AGG.

Section 27 AGG sets out the tasks of the Anti-Discrimination Agency, and Section 28 AGG its competences. Concerning the tasks, it differentiates between tasks to the benefit of individuals and tasks concerning society as a whole. Accordingly, any person who believes he or she has been discriminated against on any of the prohibited grounds may take their case to the Federal Anti-Discrimination Agency, which will give independent assistance. Pursuant to Section 27(3)–(5) AGG, the general tasks of the Agency concerning society are publicity work, measures to prevent discrimination, and academic studies into such discrimination. Compared with other specialised bodies in Europe, its position is relatively weak.[27] The competences of the Agency comprise requests to the involved parties to make submissions, requests to supply necessary information, and co-operation with NGOs.

The Federal Anti-Discrimination Agency is not in an ideal position, and suffers from two chronic problems. Although its financial resources seem to be considerable, it is understaffed,[28] and its employees have little legal expertise. But the main problem of the Federal Anti-Discrimination Agency is its natural ideological orientation. Of course, its direction is as much a fight against discrimination as possible whereas I think a sensible fight against discrimination is the better solution.

---

26 In German: *Antidiskriminierungsstelle des Bundes*, http://www.antidiskriminierungsstelle.de (last visited 13 Aug 2019).

27 *Hack*, 3 EuZA 2010, 347, 352 et seqq.

28 *Bechtel*, in: Elósegui and Hermida (eds.), Policies and Courts' Legal Reasoning in Europe (2017), 157, 162.

VII. *The problem of abuse of the law and fraud: major problem or a trivial matter?*

1. Problems in law and society

One of the main problems of any legislation against discrimination is the possibility of abuse and fraud. The main problem itself is to blame for it. In principle, there is a broad consensus in society that discrimination is to blame, to proceed against and to fight. This leads to two other consensuses: first, that the victim of a discrimination is in need of legal help, and secondly that there have to be noticeable sanctions against the perpetrator.

If someone abuses anti-discrimination law or misuses it to commit fraud, this consensus is perverted and so is the legal system against discrimination. The abuser pretends to be a victim, though a sense of justice raises reluctance to allow this person to benefit and to penalise the act of the perpetrator. This leads to the main legal problem: The greater the benefits for the (apparent) victim, the stronger the incentive for abuse. In addition, legal help for real victims – such as a statutory easing of the burden of proof – facilitates abuse. On the other hand, sanctions for discrimination are the wrong legal consequence and the (apparent) perpetrator is the real victim.

Apart from the legal dilemma, the misuse of anti-discrimination law is a problem of society. Firstly, it jeopardises the consensus against discrimination. Secondly, it jeopardises the legal help for real victims of discrimination. As pointed out, naivety endangers discrimination and the real aim is a sensible fight against discrimination – but this is cheap criticism.

The real legal problems can be summed up in two questions. The first is the definition of abuse or fraud: Which conduct will lead to application of the legal rules, and which has to be excluded for reasons of abuse? One questions whether intent is essential and where the borderline between over-sensitive persons and real victims is located. Linked to this is the second question: do claims of over-sensitive individuals have to be accepted in order not to endanger the claims of the true victims of a mischievous discrimination?

2. Experiences in practice

Before the AGG was adopted, and in the first few years after its adoption, critics had feared an "industry of claimants" and what they called (in a typical mixture of English and German) "AGG-hopping".[29] Ten years later, there is no evidence of an industry. Nevertheless, there are a considerable number of cases that lead to a discussion about the abuse of anti-discrimination law. They have in common claimants who brought a noticeable number of court proceedings, and nearly all of them relate to the processes concerning job applications. Some of these cases deal with disabled claimants. German law provides quite a complex procedure to ensure the protection of disabled applicants, and some applicants seem to apply for a lot of advertised positions, look for mistakes and consequently claim for compensation.[30]

The most discussed anti-discrimination claimant in Germany, and maybe even in Europe, is a Munich lawyer called Nils Kratzer.[31] He is middle-aged and passed his exams with an average grade. Usually his claims concern a job advertisement saying that the potential employer is looking for young applicants, e.g. "young professionals", "you will fit into our young and dynamic team", "we are looking for job starters". His applications may be described as made without love, and in many cases he is not qualified for the position.

The German Federal Labour Court (*Bundesarbeitsgericht* – BAG) is rather reluctant to assume a case of abuse of the law. In a 2016 judgment,[32] the Court stressed that the term *Bewerber für ein Beschäftigungsverhältnis* (applicant for an employment relationship) is a formal one, so the seriousness of the application is no necessary condition for the protection through the Act. Furthermore, the qualification for the position is not necessary, so it did not matter whether the potential employer was looking for applicants who passed their exams with outstanding marks. Neither is the quality of the application or the number of them of any relevance.

In contrast, in another case the ECJ refused Mr. Kratzer the protection of the Anti-discrimination Directives.[33] The First Chamber has ruled that a situation in which a person who in making an application for a post does not seek to obtain that post, but only seeks the formal status as an applicant with the sole purpose of seeking compensation, does not fall

---

29 *Rolfs*, NZA 2016, 586; *Krieger*, 27 EuZW 2016, 696 with an English summary.

30 *Diller*, NZA 2007, 1321.

31 See for example: *Spanner*, "Erst die Absage, dann der Prozess" (13 Nov 2015), http://www.spiegel.de/karriere/diskriminierung-bei-der-bewerbung-anwalt-aus-muenchen-gilt-als-agg-hopper-a-1062076.html (last visited 13 Aug 2019).

32 BAG, Judgment of 19 May 2016, 8 AZR 470/14, BAGE 155, 149.

33 ECJ, Judgment of 28 Jul 2016, C-423/15, ECLI:EU:C:2016:604 – Nils-Johannes Kratzer.

within the definition of "access to employment, to self-employment or to occupation", within the meaning of those provisions. If the requisite conditions under EU law are met, this may be considered to be an abuse of rights. To summarise the judgments, the ECJ is less reluctant than the Federal Labour Court of Germany.

In conclusion: these cases may be annoying, though they are entertaining. Although the abuse of the law is not the greatest problem of anti-discrimination law in Europe. As pointed out above, damages, compensation and penalties are moderate. If there are few opportunities to become rich, but many to become unpopular, working as an Anti-discrimination Act claimant is not the most attractive proposition.

VIII. Conclusion

Over ten years ago, the AGG was an experiment. Although Germany has considerable experience and tradition in fundamental rights review, there was no anti-discrimination act in civil law, and the few legal regulations concerning gender discrimination and protection of disabled persons were fragmentary. Even then, their main application field was employment law and working life. The same can be said of the AGG, which does not have any practical relevance in other fields of law.[34] I recall a 2006 conversation with a judge at the Federal Labour Court, who told me: "We – the judges – have had a first look at the AGG, and have no idea at all how to deal with this piece of law!"

Ten years, and some experiences later, the AGG has ceased to be an experiment and has – surprisingly – become quite a normal and ordinary act. Courts in Europe and its Member States had second and third looks at the acts, developing reasonable ideas about how to deal with anti-discrimination law. There is considerable legal certainty about the interpretation of the prohibited grounds, the illegal acts of discrimination and their legal consequences. The problem of abuse of the law is annoying, but the AGG has this problem in common with other protective legislation, such as consumer protection legislation. At least the law had some consequences, and it may have changed social attitudes in some way. Nevertheless, it cannot be said that private autonomy and freedom in business decision-making

34 Very few cases concern private insurance law, e.g. age or sex discrimination in insurance conditions.

have been seriously jeopardised. In summary, I would like to appeal for a collective cool-down.

Bibliography

Wolfram Bechtel, "The State of Racial Justice in Germany", in: María Elósegui and Cristina Hermida (eds.), Policies and Courts' Legal Reasoning in Europe (Springer International Publishing, Cham 2017), 157.

Mark Bell and *Lisa Waddington*, "Reflecting on equalities in European equality law", 28 European Law Review (E.L.R.) 2013, 349.

Martina Benecke and *Gisela Kern*, "Sanktionen im Antidiskriminierungsrecht – Möglichkeiten und Grenzen der Umsetzung der europäischen Richtlinien im deutschen Recht", 16 Europäische Zeitschrift für Wirtschaftsrecht (EuZW) 2005, 360.

Martina Benecke, Rechtsvergleich der europäischen Systeme zum Antidiskriminierungsrecht – Expertise im Auftrag der Antidiskriminierungsstelle des Bundes (2010), http://www.antidiskriminierungsstelle.de/SharedDocs/Downloads/DE/publikationen/Expertisen/Expertise_Rechtsvergleich_europ_Systeme_zum_AntidiskrRecht.pdf?__blob=publicationFile (last visited 13 Aug 2018).

Franz Christian Ebert and *Tobias Pinkel*, "Restricting freedom of contract through non-discrimination provisions: a comparison of the Draft Common Frame of Reference (DCFR) and the German 'General Equality Law'", 10 German Law Journal (GLJ) 2009, 1417.

Martin Diller, "AGG-Hopping durch Schwerbehinderte", Neue Zeitschrift für Arbeitsrecht (NZA) 2007, 1321.

Erfurter Kommentar zum Arbeitsrecht, *Rudi Müller-Glöge*, *Ulrich Preis* and *Ingrid Schmidt* (eds.) (C.H. Beck, 17th ed., Munich 2017).

Beate Gsell, *Wolfgang Krüger*, *Stephan Lorenz* and *Jörg Mayer* (eds.), beck-online.GROSSKOMMENTAR (BeckOGK) (C.H. Beck, ed. of 1 Apr 2017, Munich 2017).

Melanie Regine Hack, "Impact or potential of anti-discrimination legislation in light of the demographic change – Comparisons between Norway and Germany", 3 Europäische Zeitschrift für Arbeitsrecht (EuZA) 2010, 347.

Barbara Havelková, "Resistance to anti-discrimination law in Central and Eastern Europe: a post-communist legacy?", 17 German Law Journal (GLJ) 2016, 627.

Michael Heese, "Offene Preisdiskriminierung und zivilrechtliches Benachteiligungsverbot", Neue Juristische Wochenschrift (NJW) 2012, 572.

Michael Huggins, "Not 'fit' for hire: the United States and France on weight discrimination in employment", 38 Fordham International Law Journal (Fordham Int'l L.J.) 2015, 889.

Steffen Krieger, "Rechtsmissbrauch durch 'AGG-Hopping'", 27 Europäische Zeitschrift für Wirtschaftsrecht (EuZW) 2016, 696.

Joanna N. Lahey, “International Comparison of Age Discrimination Laws”, 32 Research on Aging (Res Aging) 2010, 679.

Tobias Lock, “Religious freedom and belief discrimination in Germany and the United Kingdom: towards a common European standard?”, 38 European Law Review (E.L.R.) 2013, 655.

Siobhan McInerney, “The Development of Legal Instruments to Combat Racism in a Diverse Europe”, 56 International & Comparative Law 2007, 211.

Tina Mirzazadeh, “Discrimination in the name of secularism: a ban of religious symbols in Québec”, 28 Pacific McGeorge Global Business & Development Law Journal 2015, 411.

Joyce Marie Mushaben, “Women between a rock and a hard place: state neutrality vs. EU antidiscrimination mandates in the German headscarf debate”, 14 German Law Journal (GLJ) 2013, 1757.

Christian Rolfs, “AGG-Hopping”, Neue Zeitschrift für Arbeitsrecht (NZA) 2016, 586.

Elke Spanner, “Erst die Absage, dann der Prozess” (13 Nov 2015), http://www.spiegel.de/karriere/diskriminierung-bei-der-bewerbung-anwalt-aus-muenchen-gilt-als-agg-hopper-a-1062076.html (last visited 13 Aug 2019).

Joachim Wiemann, “Obligation to contract and the German general act of equal treatment (Allgemeines Gleichbehandlungsgesetz)”, 11 German Law Journal (GLJ) 2010, 1131.

Register of cases

BAG, Judgment of 19 May 2016, 8 AZR 470/14, BAGE 155, 149.

ECJ, Judgment of 22 Nov 2005, C-144/04, ECLI:EU:C:2005:709 – Mangold.

ECJ, Judgment of 16 Oct 2007, C-411/05, ECLI:EU:C:2007:604 – Palacios.

ECJ, Judgment of 10 Jul 2008, C-54/07, ECLI:EU:C:2008:397 – Feryn.

ECJ, Judgment of 5 Mar 2009, C-388/07, ECLI:EU:C:2009:128 – Age Concern England.

ECJ, Judgment of 19 Jan 2010, C-555/07, ECLI:EU:C:2010:21 – Kücükdeveci.

ECJ, Judgment of 12 Oct 2010, C-45/09, ECLI:EU:C:2010:601 – Rosenbladt.

ECJ, Judgment of 20 Oct 2010, C-499/08, ECLI:EU:C:2010:600 – Ingeniørforeningen i Danmark/Andersen.

ECJ, Judgment of 08 Sep 2011, C-297/10, ECLI:EU:C:2011:560 – Hennings.

ECJ, Judgment of 19 Jun 2014, C-501/12, ECLI:EU:C:2014:2005 – Specht.

ECJ, Judgment of 18 Dec 2014, C-354/13, ECLI:EU:C:2014:2463 – Fag og Arbejde.

ECJ, Judgment of 28 Jul 2016, C-423/15, ECLI:EU:C:2016:604 – Nils-Johannes Kratzer.

Equality, Legal Certainty and Insolvency

Kathleen van der Linde[*] / *Juanitta Calitz* [**]

Abstract: The contribution considers the continued role and significance of equality of creditors (par condicio creditorum) and the link, if any, between the fundamental/constitutional right to equality and equal treatment of creditors in insolvency law. It argues that the paritas creditorum principle as applied to the distribution of the estate among creditors does not contribute significantly to substantive equality as a fundamental right. This can be attributed to the fact that the paritas creditorum principle represents formal equality whilst the Constitution guarantees substantive or transformative equality. The chapter concludes that there is only a superficial correlation between the right to equality and the equal treatment of creditors in insolvency. It is submitted that the Constitutional Court's tendency to focus on anti-discrimination and inclusion has been too limited to introduce the structural legal changes also required by substantive equality. In addition, the chapter recognises that the courts need a change of approach if the principle of equality is to develop with coherence and purpose.

* Kathleen van der Linde, *B. Iuris*, *LL.B.*, *Hons B.A. (Latin)*, *LL.M.*, *LL.D.*, Professor, Department of Mercantile Law, University of Johannesburg.

** Juanitta Calitz, *B. Iuris*, *LL.B.*, *LL.M.*, *LL.D.*, Associate Professor, Department of Mercantile Law, University of Johannesburg.

I. Introduction

This paper considers the continued role and significance of equality of creditors (*par condicio creditorum*) which is often asserted to be a basic tenet of insolvency law.[1] It reflects on the link, if any, between the fundamental/constitutional right to equality and equal treatment of creditors in insolvency law.

It argues that the *paritas creditorum* principle as applied to the distribution of the estate among creditors does not contribute significantly to substantive equality as a fundamental right. Identical treatment might even entrench inequality and prevent vulnerable persons from progressively realizing their socio-economic rights.[2]

It concludes that the Constitutional Court's tendency to focus on anti-discrimination and inclusion has been too limited to introduce the structural legal changes also required by substantive equality. Equality as applied by this court might even become a stumbling block if it obscures the need for incisive statutory reform. While it may seem that piecemeal minimally invasive development avoids legal uncertainty, a conservative approach focusing on extending the scope of preferential treatment to address vulnerability will in the long run not only impair legal certainty but also the achievement of equality.

II. Legal certainty

It is often mentioned that commercial ventures and transactions are facilitated by legal certainty.[3] In turn, insolvency laws play a vital role through promoting predictability for both creditors and entrepreneurs as they create the rules for the worst possible outcome.[4] It is clear that

---

1 *CSARS v Stand Two Nine Nought Wynberg (Pty) Ltd* 2005 5 SA 583 (SCA).

2 In the *Ex parte Kroese* 2015 1 SA 405 (NWM) judgment Landman J also ultimately criticised South African insolvency law policy, which pays limited attention to the dilemma of certain classes of debtor. See *Evans*, De Jure 2018, 298, 316.

3 *MacNeil*, Edinburgh Law Review 2009, 68, 69.

4 See ibid., 69. In this sense, legal certainty is not directly concerned with the substance of the law, a point made by Lord Mansfield in *Vallejo v Wheeler* (1774) 1 Cowp 143, 153: "In all mercantile transactions the great object should be certainty:

an important factor for investors and potential creditors interested in a particular jurisdiction is an effective insolvency framework that guarantees an orderly proceeding with fair, transparent, and predictable treatment of the stakeholders.[5] The absence of predictability does not only escalate the costs of credit, it even threatens the general availability of credit as lenders will also mandate risk premiums "to compensate for systemic uncertainty in making, managing, and collecting investments in emerging markets"[6].

According to Finch part of the drama surrounding insolvency flows from having to dismantle and then reassemble what were apparently concrete and distinct legal rights and values.[7] Insolvency law thus takes spheres of the law that are certain and trite, desconstructs them, and then uses its own principles to put the pieces back together again. Therein lies the challenge of creating so called legal certainty within the context of insolvency. The international standards and guidelines on best practice recognise that although approaches in different insolvency regimes may vary, effective insolvency systems have a number of generic aims and objectives. The *World Bank Principles* also mention that these systems should aspire "to recognise existing creditor rights and respect the priority of claims with a predictable and established process".[8]

Although the South African Insolvency Act was enacted in 1936[9] and as such most of the policy development was done in a pre-Constitutional era, the Act must not only be consistent with the Constitution but the competing interests raised by insolvency proceedings should also be balanced within the context of the Constitution.[10] This was emphasised in *SARIPA v The Minister*:

---

and therefore, it is of more consequence that a rule be certain, than whether the rule is established one way or the other. Because speculators in trade then know what ground to go upon".

5 The United Nations Commission on International Trade Law (UNCITRAL), Legislative Guide on Insolvency Law (2005), https://www.uncitral.org/pdf/english/texts/insolven/05-80722_Ebook.pdf (last visited 15 Nov 2019).

6 *Falke*, Insolvency Law Reform in Transition Economies (LL.D. thesis Humboldt University, 2005), 55. See also World Bank, "Principles for Effective Insolvency and Creditor/Debtor Rights Regime" (2016), http://pubdocs.worldbank.org/en/919511468425523509/ICR-Principles-Insolvency-Creditor-Debtor-Regimes-2016.pdf (last visited 28 March 2020).

7 *Finch* and *Milman*, Corporate Insolvency Law (3rd ed. 2017), 9.

8 World Bank Principles (n. 6), principle C1.

9 Insolvency Act No. 24 of 1936.

10 *Mabe*, 19 PER/PELJ 2016, DOI https://doi.org/10.17159/1727-3781/2016/v19i0a577 (last visited 27 Nov 2019).

> "However, insolvency, necessarily and appropriately, is shifting from being a creditor-driven regime to focusing on the interests of other stakeholders involved in and affected by the insolvency proceedings. Moreover, it is necessary that insolvency law and its implementation, like all South African law, be constitutionally compliant."[11]

It is precisely this constant assessment as to whether principles such as the equality of creditors enshrined in South African insolvency law are consistent with the values of an open and democratic society based on fundamental human rights, such as the right to equality, that impacts on legal certainty.[12] Exclusion of unpredictability, along with equality and the protection of fundamental rights, counts among the basic tenets of the rule of law.[13]

III. Equality and insolvency law

The equal treatment of creditors is often regarded as a fundamental principle or value of insolvency law.[14] It has been called the "notion at the heart of collective insolvency procedures",[15] the "meme" pervading bankruptcy

11 *South African Restructuring and Insolvency Practitioners Association v Minister of Justice and Constitutional Development and Others, In Re: Concerned Insolvency Practitioners Association NPC and Others v Minister of Justice and Constitutional Development* 2015 2 SA 430 (WCC), para. 24.

12 Refer to *Henrico*, TSAR 2014, 742 for a detailed discussion on the rule of law in the context of the South African constitutional framework.

13 *Van der Walt v Metcash Trading Ltd* 2002 4 SA 317 (CC), paras. 65, 66, 68 and 76. *Venter*, South Africa Introductory Notes, on file with the authors.

14 The ideal is that everyone affected must be treated as equals, and the internal coherence and consistency of principles should be measured against this ideal. See Report of the Review Committee, Cork Report on Insolvency Law and Practice (Her Majesty's Stationery Office, London 1982), 347; *Mokal*, Corporate Insolvency Law (2005), 1–2.

15 *Keay* and *Walton*, Insolvency Law: Corporate and Personal (1st ed. 2003), 423: Most insolvency textbooks confirm the centrality of this principle and assure their readers that the practitioner in a bankruptcy case "stands for the proposition that equity is equality". As the authors explain, the principle "means that unless a creditor can clearly demonstrate that it deserves some priority in the bankruptcy payout, the trustee will assume all creditors are equal and try to maximise the pot for that collective". See also *Skeel*, University of Pennsylvania Law Review 2018, 699, 700.

law,[16] and the "polestar in the bankruptcy firmament".[17] Keay and Walton, for example, write that the first purpose of insolvency law is "to provide an equal, fair and orderly procedure in handling the affairs of insolvents, ensuring that creditors receive an equal and equitable distribution of the assets of the insolvent".[18] In insolvency, an equal and equitable distribution of the estate inevitably entails the allocation of loss[19] or "social costs".[20]

Assertions about the centrality of equality in insolvency law are routinely qualified. Keay and Walton state that the principle has been heavily eroded to the extent that it is only a theoretical doctrine[21] that functions as a default rule.[22] Mokal, referring to *pari passu* as a "myth", observes that it is a rule of non-distribution rather than of distribution.[23] Boraine and Van Wyk assert that it "only exists on paper".[24] It has even been called a "costly distraction".[25]

Scholars differ on the ambit and relevance of the *pari passu* rule. Some adopt a wide approach regarding the rules pertaining to distribution, treatment of executory contracts and the avoidance of antecedent transactions as embedded in the principle of equality while others question the link between equality and the fundamental purposes of insolvency law, arguing instead that the underlying mischief targeted by insolvency principles is not unequal division but rather anti-deprivation and contracting out of insolvency or jumping the queue, so that *pari passu* is simply an approach to the distribution of an insolvent estate.[26] Some of the most prominent law and economics scholars argue that the distributional question is not the core foundation of bankruptcy. Jackson maintains repeatedly that the aim of insolvency proceedings is not to attain a certain distribution of

16 *Skeel* (n. 15), 714.
17 Ibid.
18 *Keay* and *Walton* (n. 15), 21 and 423.
19 *Keay* and *Walton* (n. 15), 20, 22; see also *Warren*, The University of Chicago Law Review 1987, 777–778.
20 *Mokal* (n. 14), 2–4.
21 *Keay* and *Walton* (n. 15), 396.
22 *Keay* and *Walton* (n. 15), 22; *Murray* and *Harris*, Keay's Insolvency (8th ed. 2014), paras. 1.40 (13) and 2.25 (33); *Mokal* (n. 14), 137.
23 *Mokal*, The Cambridge Law Journal 2001, 581.
24 *Boraine* and *Van Wyk*, Journal of Contemporary Roman-Dutch Law 2011, 347, 354.
25 *Skeel* (n. 15), 744.
26 Mokal explains the confusion in literature and cases on exactly what pari passu implies and argues that the rule is less important than it is made out to be and does not always constitute an accurate description of how assets are in fact distributed. See *Mokal* (n. 23), 581–583.

assets, but rather to enforce co-operation among creditors, in order to maximise their aggregate returns.[27]

Even when *paritas creditorum* is seen as a distribution rule only, there are different views as to whether *pari passu* distribution is intended to be a rule for all creditors regardless of their pre-insolvency status as secured or unsecured, or only for unsecured creditors or, even narrower, only for unsecured concurrent creditors.[28] One's view on the ambit of the rule influences one's conception of exceptions to or deviations from the *pari passu* point of departure. Some even see *pari passu* as itself containing an embedded hierarchy, proposing it as the ratio for the absolute priority rule,[29] and hence preferential treatment of certain classes, while others regard such preferential treatment as out of step with equality. Some view it as a base-line rule in the sense that deviations from it must be justified while others regard it as an efficient, low-cost default or fallback rule, or a solution resorted to when the stakes are so low that alternative arrangements are no longer efficient.[30]

As a principle of positive law, equal distribution to creditors is concerned with formal equality and with a very basic classification of similarity based on the pre-insolvency status of the claim (whether it is secured or not) and the presence or absence of statutory priority being conferred on policy grounds.[31]

South African courts recognise a link between equal treatment and the principles governing executory contracts[32] as well as between equal

---

27 *Garrido*, International Insolvency Review 1995, 25–26.

28 Finch seems to claim that there is a normal rule that all creditors, no matter what type, are to be treated equally which according to Mokal is too broad. Mokal is of opinion that there never has been any such "normal rule". See *Finch*, Modern Law Review 1999, 633, 634 and *Mokal* (n. 23), 581.

29 The absolute priority rule is the organizing principle in modern insolvency law and describes the basic order of payment. If one creditor has priority over another, this creditor needs to be paid in full before the other is entitled to receive anything. See *Baird*, University of Pennsylvania Law Review 2017, 785–786.

30 *Finch* and *Milman* (n. 7), 33.

31 Note that the concept developed over time and as such did not include a cohesive policy development process.

32 *Ellerine Brothers (Pty) Ltd v McCarthy Limited* 2014 4 SA 22 (SCA), paras. 1, 11. The main aim of the concursus, according to the SCA in the *Ellerine* case "is to give equal protection to all the creditors without undue preference and to preserve and distribute the estate to the benefit of all of them". The court links this with the principle that the insolvency practitioner cannot be forced to perform.

treatment and the rules on the setting aside of antecedent transactions.[33] It is important to note, however, that in South Africa the equal treatment rule applies only to sequestration and liquidation and not also to business rescue proceedings.[34]

Insolvency legislation often departs from equal treatment of creditors. The ways in which this can be achieved include exempting specific types of contracts from the general rules on executory contracts, allowing post-commencement set-off, disapplying the moratorium in relation to certain claims and exempting transactions from avoidance provisions.[35] In addition, provision is often made for certain claims to enjoy a prior right to distribution compared to concurrent creditors.[36]

33 *Jackson v Louw NO* 2019 2 All SA 145 (ECG). See also *Hosking NO v Coetzee NO* 2005 ZASCA 110 (25 Nov 2005), para. 1: "A central feature of Anglo-American bankruptcy law for almost three centuries has been the principle of equitable distribution amongst concurrent creditors of the assets of the insolvent debtor. And following in the footsteps of that principle has been a perennial debate concerning the validity of dispositions that are made by an insolvent debtor before the axe of bankruptcy falls. For once an insolvent debtor disposes of property to one creditor the risk of loss to the others increases proportionately unless the debtor regains his solvency".

34 Business rescue in terms of chapter 6 of Companies Act No. 71 of 2008, does not envisage equal treatment on any substantive level (only procedural). It expressly allows a plan to set its own ranking of pre-commencement creditors (Section 150(2)(b)(v)). It does prescribe the ranking of post-commencement financing and administration costs (Sections 135 and 143).

35 In South Africa, for example, transactions on licensed exchanges or in terms of master agreements are regulated by Sections 35A and 35B of the Insolvency Act. These provisions contain special rules for unperformed obligations due under such transactions at commencement and allow netting despite a party's insolvency. They also exempt pre-commencement disposals under such transactions from avoidance or claw-back provisions.

36 Examples in the South African context include employee salaries up to specified limits (Section 98A), several statutory obligations of employers in respect of social security contributions and withholding taxes (Section 99), as well as taxes on income (Section 101).

1. The fundamental right to equality

Equality is both a foundational value[37] of and a justiciable right[38] under the Constitution of the Republic of South Africa, 1996.[39] The Constitution provides that "everyone is equal before the law and has the right to equal protection and benefit of the law".[40] It envisages full and equal enjoyment of rights and freedoms and expressly recognises the validity of affirmative measures to protect and advance those disadvantaged by past unfair discrimination.[41]

The meaning of equality is far from settled.[42] A distinction is often drawn between, on the one hand, the Aristotlean concept of formal equality that prescribes similar treatment of those similarly situated and proscribes different treatment based on arbitrary characteristics[43] and the notion of substantive equality on the other. Smith describes substantive equality as involving the dismantling of entrenched inequalities or as

37 Section 1(a) of the Constitution of the Republic of South Africa, 1996 refers to the "achievement of equality". Equal protection of the law is also mentioned in the preamble and again in Section 7(1) as one of the democratic values, the others being human dignity and freedom.

38 Section 9.

39 As mentioned in *Sarrahwitz v Maritz NO* 2015 4 SA 491 (CC), para. 51: "Core business of the State is equal treatment of its citizens and the pursuit of what redounds to the common good of all". See also *Prinsloo v Van der Linde and Another* 1997 6 BCLR 759 (CC), paras. 24–28.

40 Section 9(1).

41 Section 9(2). Section 9(3) and (4) prohibits unfair discrimination by respectively the state and any person. There is a rebuttable presumption in Section 9(5) that discrimination on any of the specific grounds set out in Section 9(3) is unfair.

42 According to Smith, equality has mystified legal authors and thinkers for well over two millennia. To this day, there is no consensus on the exact meaning of equality. As Fredman states: "We all have an intuitive grasp of the meaning of equality and what it entails, yet the more closely we examine it, the more its meaning shifts". See *Smith*, African Human Rights Law Journal 2014, 609, 611.

43 "Likes should be treated alike" – *Aristotle*, in: Barnes (ed.), The Complete Works of Aristotle, The Revised Oxford Translation, vol. 2 (1984). Westen argues that "equality is an idea that should be banished from moral and legal discourse as an explanatory norm" as mentioned in *Fredman*, International Journal of Constitutional Law 2016, 712. Smith comments that the preferred concept of equality is substantive equality which adjusts the right to equality from a negatively oriented right of non-discrimination to a positively-oriented right to substantive equality. See *Smith* (n. 42), 612.

addressing indirect discrimination.[44] Fredman[45] states that the content of substantive equality is "elusive".[46] She explains that scholars and courts tend to refer to it in terms of equality of rights, equality of opportunity, and dignity, while legal formulae such as "unfair discrimination, disparate impact or indirect discrimination, reasonable accommodation and harassment" are employed. She proposes four dimensions of substantive equality: "to redress disadvantage; to address stigma, stereotyping, prejudice and violence; to enhance voice and participation; and to accommodate difference and achieve structural change".[47] These dimensions place the right to equality in the social context where it can respond to disadvantage and marginalisation.[48] MacKinnon[49] maintains, however, that the single underlying principle is social hierarchy.

Albertyn distinguishes between inclusionary and transformative equality. The former can be achieved either by formal equality or a restricted approach to substantive equality that uses a comparator that "intentionally or inadvertently reinforces dominant norms and standards", thus reproducing inequalities.[50] What sets transformative equality apart is that it resorts to "practical and normative solutions that begin to dismantle these [systemic] inequalities" and start developing new norms and conditions, at least by articulating them.[51] This seems to correspond with the fourth dimension identified by Fredman.

The Constitutional Court has referred to "remedial, restitutionary or substantive equality".[52] While it can be accepted that the Constitution

44 *Smith* (n. 42), 613 states that "laws treat individuals as substantive equals, recognising and accommodating peoples' differences. Analysing the effects of laws, policies and practices on a disadvantaged individual or group, substantive equality is concerned with eliminating barriers which exclude certain groups from participation...".

45 *Fredman*, International Journal of Constitutional Law 2016, 712.

46 *Albertyn*, South African Journal on Human Rights 2007, 253, 258.

47 *Fredman* (n. 45), 712.

48 Ibid.

49 *MacKinnon*, International Journal of Constitutional Law 2016, 739, 740: "The 'single principle' underlying the 'substantive conception' of inequality can be recognised in developing substantive equality jurisprudence as it may not be recognizable as a principle in the philosophical sense, because it is not an abstraction but the social content specific to each 'pre-existing disadvantage' based on concrete grounds.".

50 *Albertyn* (n. 46), 253, 259.

51 Ibid.

52 Madlanga J, in *Minister of Constitutional Development and Another v South African Restructuring and Insolvency Practitioners Association and Others* [2018] ZACC, para.

embodies a substantive notion of equality,[53] its jurisprudence has been criticised as inconsistent.[54] Albertyn shows that while the Constitutional Court has on occasion embraced transformative equality by taking into account social context and vulnerability starting to articulate new paradigms, it mostly does not move beyond simple inclusionary equality. The emphasis on inclusion might be explained by the anti-discrimination focus of litigation before the Constitutional Court, often asserting claims of under-inclusivity of protective legislative provisions.[55]

Fredman explains that substantive equality is "expressly asymmetric".[56] The Constitutional Court has also explained that substantive equality

---

61. In *Minister of Constitutional Development and Another v South African Restructuring and Insolvency Practitioners Association and Others* [2018] ZACC 20, para. 1, the court also declared that restitutionary measures are a vital element of our transformative constitutional regime. The drafters of our Constitution concurred that to only abolish discriminatory laws and guarantee equal rights alone would not lead to a just and democratic society envisaged in the Constitution. In *Minister of Finance and Others v Van Heerden* 2004 6 SA 121 (CC), para. 41, Moseneke J nonetheless stressed that if the remedial measures were not likely to achieve the intended outcome through benefiting those who have been disadvantaged by unfair discrimination, they would not constitute measures as envisaged by Section 9(2).

53 In *National Coalition for Gay and Lesbian Equality v Minister of Justice* 1999 1 SA 6 (CC), para. 60, the court referred to the term substantive equality as a "contested expression" which is not found in either Constitution. *Smith* also criticises the Constitutional Court's judgments in *Jordan & Others v S* 2002 6 SA 642 (CC) and *Prince v President, Cape Law Society* 2002 2 SA 794 (CC) where the courts adopted a focus which guaranteed a formal rather than a substantive approach to equality as they failed to address the impact of the legislation in question. See *Smith* (n. 42), 613.

54 *Albertyn* (n. 46), 253.

55 Ibid.

56 *Fredman* (n. 45), 712, 728.

might require unequal treatment.[57] Measures aimed at furthering equality for certain groups do not amount to unfair discrimination against others.[58]

The right to equality is relevant in different contexts of insolvency law, including access to formal insolvency procedures,[59] appointment of insolvency practitioners,[60] consequences of the commencement of proceedings for the debtor[61] and his or her associates,[62] the scope of the insolvent

---

57 *Langa J*, in *MEC for Education: KwaZulu-Natal & Others v Pillay* CCT 51/06 [2007] ZACC 21, para. 15 states that failure to treat the respondent's daughter differently from her peers amounted to withholding from her "the benefit, opportunity and advantage of enjoying fully [her] culture and/or of practising [her] religion" and therefore constituted indirect discrimination. See also *O' Regan J*: "to determine whether the discrimination is unfair it is necessary to recognise that although the long-term goal of our constitutional order is equal treatment, insisting upon equal treatment in circumstances of established inequality may well result in the entrenchment of that inequality" in *President of the Republic of South Africa v Hugo* 1997 4 SA 1 (CC), para. 112.

58 *President of the Republic of South Africa v Hugo* (n. 57), para. 32.

59 *Coetzee*, A comparative reappraisal of debt relief measures for natural person debtors in South Africa (LL.D. thesis University of Pretoria, 2015), 19: It has been alleged, relying on the right to equality, that "the broader insolvency system would fail a constitutional challenge". This statement was made in the context of access to proceedings and the unequal treatment not of creditors, but of debtors. Although the advantage-to-creditors requirement envisages formal equality of debtors whose estates are sequestrated under the Insolvency Act, on a substantive level the requirement of advantage to creditors operates to exclude poor debtors from the prospect of formal insolvency and subsequent discharge upon rehabilitation. Evans points out that this also results in unequal treatment of creditors as the creditors of debtors unable to access proceedings have to forego the possibility of an orderly distribution of the estate in a *concursus creditorum*. *Evans* (n. 2), 298. One might also argue that since companies and close corporations can enter liquidation proceedings without having to show advantage to creditors (it is merely one of the factors a court considers in the exercise of its discretion to order liquidation) there is unfair discrimination between individual and corporate debtors. Moreover, while companies have access to business rescue proceedings, there is no rescue procedure for unincorporated businesses.

60 In *Minister of Constitutional Development and Another v South African Restructuring and Insolvency Practitioners Association and Others* (n. 52) 20 the court held that the policy for the appointment of provisional trustees was irrational as it failed to show that it was reasonably capable of achieving equality.

61 See Section 23(3) of the Insolvency Act that restricts the right of an insolvent to be involved in the business of a general dealer or manufacturer.

62 See *Harksen v Lane NO* 1998 1 SA 300 (CC), para. 40 with regard to Section 21 of the Insolvency Act which provides for the vesting of the assets of a solvent spouse in the insolvent estate of his or her spouse. The Court held that the

estate,[63] and, of course, for creditors. However, we limit our enquiry to the equal treatment of creditors.

2. Equality in *Sarrahwitz*

It might seem ironic that the fundamental right to equality was used in *Sarrahwitz v Maritz NO* 2015 4 SA 491 (CC) to achieve a departure from creditor equality,[64] but this reveals clear tension between formally equal treatment of (unsecured) insolvency creditors and the constitutional notion of substantive equality.

a) The judgment

Sarrahwitz had bought a house and paid the purchase price but the seller's estate was sequestrated before ownership was transferred.[65] Under the general principles governing executory contracts she could not force the insolvency practitioner to transfer the property to her. She would only have a concurrent claim for contractual damages. She relied on an exception under the Alienation of Land Act 68 of 1981 that affords purchasers of residential land in certain instalment transactions the right to claim transfer of the property in the event of the seller's insolvency.[66]

---

differential treatment of spouses did not violate the right to equality because the differentiation served a legitimate purpose.

63 *Brink v Kitshoff NO* 1996 4 SA 197 (CC) – still decided under the transitional constitution of 1993. A provision of the Insurance Act was struck down for violating the right to equality. Although it was enacted to protect certain funds in the hands of a married woman when her husband's estate was sequestrated, following the abolition of a rule invalidating donations between spouses, it had in effect become discriminatory against married women. It excluded from an insolvent estate only a portion of the proceeds of certain life policies ceded in favour of a solvent wife while married men did not forfeit the benefits of insurance policies ceded to them or made in their favour by their wives.

64 *Sarrahwitz v Maritz* NO 2015 4 SA 491 (CC) mentioned the principle of "advantage to creditors" in para. 64. In our opinion the court fumbles on the formulation of the concept of "advantage to creditors".

65 South Africa follows an abstract system of property transfer, and ownership of fixed property is passed through registration.

66 Section 36. The purchaser is obliged to pay the outstanding consideration.

The Constitutional Court found that the relevant provisions were unconstitutional because they differentiated based on the method of payment[67] and thus left vulnerable cash purchasers unprotected in comparable situations. It resorted to the remedies of severance and reading-in to correct the under-inclusive exception. Considerable emphasis was placed on dignity as an underlying value of the Constitution and on the right to adequate housing,[68] one of the socio-economic rights guaranteed by the Bill of Rights. This concern found expression in the definition of "vulnerable purchaser" which the court read into the legislation as "a purchaser who runs the risk of being rendered homeless by a seller's insolvency".[69] Sarrahwitz was in effect granted immunity from the ordinary consequences of executory contracts and obtained full satisfaction.[70]

The minority judgment found there was no unfair discrimination and envisaged protection of Sarrahwitz's possession of the property through existing legislative measures against eviction and cautioned that the majority's approach ultimately constrains Parliament in what it can achieve through protective legislation targeting specific beneficiaries.[71] The minority also warned of the potential for further differentiation and discrimination.[72]

---

67 See *Heyns* and *Mmusinyane*, 20 PER/PELJ 2017, DOI http://dx.doi.org/10.17159/1727-3781/2017/v20i0a1540 (last visited 27 Nov 2019) for criticism in this regard. They argue that the differentiation was based on the rules pertaining to transfer of ownership.

68 See paras. 16–17 in which the court stated that both the concepts of homelessness and vulnerability are central to the determination of the issues at hand.

69 See para. 5 of the court's order. The court fails to deal with the situation where "sales in execution" take place which also figures in the original legislation.

70 See para. 4 of the court's order in *Sarrahwitz* (n. 39).

71 See para. 83: "The Legislature constantly extends statutory protections to vulnerable groups. That is its almost daily work. Who needs statutory protection? How should the group be defined? What are the boundaries of the protection? Making these distinctions in determining the boundaries of beneficial consumer protection legislation is what Parliament is called to do. Is this Court at liberty, every time Parliament makes a differentiation, to find that the protection it has created is irrational because it is under-inclusive?"

72 Para. 83 and para. 86. In this regard see also *Van der Linde* and *Van Staden*, TSAR 2017, 414, who spell out a number of inconsistencies introduced by the majority judgment.

b) Implications and criticism

The *Sarrahwitz* approach depends on:

- the existence of a legislative measure benefiting a specific group of persons in insolvency;
- construing the purpose of that measure as assisting vulnerable persons;[73]
- establishing vulnerability of the excluded group with reference to one or more socio-economic rights in danger of being lost by insolvency;[74] and
- extending the provision to the equally vulnerable category of persons on the basis of the right to equality.

The existing beneficiaries of the special arrangement in the Alienation of Land Act, namely the purchasers of residential land on instalments, were clearly not vulnerable in the same way as members of the excluded group to which protection was extended through the reading-in exercise undertaken in *Sarrahwitz*. Instalment purchasers of residential land do not have to risk becoming homeless in order to enjoy protection. They also need not have paid the full purchase price prior to the seller's insolvency, as long as they could offer to pay the remaining consideration and certain specified costs. The extended provision will only assist previously excluded purchasers if they stand to become homeless and have also paid the full price within a year. If Sarrahwitz had been homeless already, or had paid in full but had not been in occupation of the property, she would not be a vulnerable purchaser according to the definition that was read into the legislation. While the majority remarked that the existing measure was over-inclusive, it abdicated responsibility to the legislature to attend to that aspect. We regard the judicial extension itself as under-inclusive, even as far as purchasers of residential land is concerned. This extension, proposed on behalf of the responsible Minister, was of course tailored to include Sarrahwitz but there was little concern for others who might find themselves in almost the same situation. This might include persons who had purchased other types of property related to the realisation of other guaranteed socio-economic rights, as well as persons whose homelessness

73 In *Sarrahwitz* (n. 39) the court deals with the concept in a rather strained way and in turn creates a problem of over-broadness.

74 Linking vulnerability to the notion of losing an existing enjoyment of certain rights considerably narrows the concept and implies unequal treatment of those who have not even begun to enjoy those rights.

might arise from the way in which other types of executory contracts, such as contracts of lease, are treated in insolvency.[75] The implications of the *Sarrahwitz* judgment remind us that hard cases make bad law.[76]

Another obstacle to achieving greater equality through relying on curing under-inclusive protections is of course that there is a limited supply of protective statutory provisions. Let us consider one such a protective measure that deviates from the *pari passu* principle: the priority afforded to employees in respect of arrear pre-commencement remuneration.[77] The preferent part of the employees' claims[78] rank immediately below administration costs and costs of execution. Preferential treatment of employees is typically justified on policy grounds with reference to their inability to diversify and their impaired ability to absorb the loss of their main source of income. It would be fair to conclude that they are protected because they are vulnerable.[79] But small suppliers and independent contractors might be equally undiversified and equally dependent on payment for their basic subsistence. They might also be at risk of losing their enjoyment of socio-economic rights, including access to adequate housing, food, education or health. Should protection not also be extended to them? And how long would they have to wait their turn in the Constitutional Court?

Even if each possible under-inclusive exception is ultimately subjected to constitutional scrutiny with a view to curing any under-inclusivity, the judiciary is constrained by the particular situation being adjudicated.[80]

---

75 See *Van der Linde* and *Van Staden*, TSAR 2017, 414 for three scenarios illustrating some of the anomalies introduced.

76 A statement that goes back to the early English case *Winterbottom v Wright* (1842) 152 ER 402 in which Rolf J stated: "This is one of those unfortunate cases...in which, it is, no doubt, a hardship upon the plaintiff to be without a remedy but by that consideration we ought not to be influenced. Hard cases, it has frequently been observed, are apt to introduce bad law.".

77 Section 98A of the Insolvency Act. There is no state funding for such pre-commencement claims. Employees who become unemployed through the employer's insolvency will have a claim against the Unemployment Insurance Fund. See Section 16(1)(a)(iii) of the Unemployment Insurance Act No. 63 of 2001.

78 Limited to a maximum period of 3 months' salary and a maximum total of R12 000 per employee. There are also separate priorities in respect of leave pay, retrenchment pay and certain contributions to pension and other funds. See Section 98A(1)(a)(i)-(iv) of the Insolvency Act.

79 Obviously, some employees would be less vulnerable than others and the limits imposed will result in lower-paid employees recovering a higher percentage of what is due to them.

80 For instance, if an independent contractor succeeds in having the employee preference extended a further case may be necessary for vulnerable suppliers of goods.

Of course, the Constitutional Court in *Sarrahwitz* might have designed a better reading in solution for the specific situation or achieved a better result through development of the common law.[81] Still, a once-off judicial development of more general scope would in our view be more conducive to legal certainty than many small adjustments spread over an extensive period. But there are limits to what a judicial band-aid can do to improve an insolvency system that is systemically ill-equipped to deal with vulnerable creditors. An enhanced policy dialogue may assist in evaluating whether a legislative solution may be better suited to the socio-economic context in South Africa.

3. The right to equality and the ranking of claims in insolvency

We have alluded to the differing views of scholars on the content and ambit of the *paritas creditorum* principle.[82] Scholars also differ on the normative merit of *pari passu* distribution.[83] Some defend it as a ground rule that is justified on grounds of fairness or efficiency.[84] They argue that any deviations from it should be justifiable on policy grounds such as the protection of vulnerable creditors.[85] Deviations from it should also be clear and predictable.[86] Before any further exceptions are introduced, their

81 Van der Linde and Van Staden argue that the rule allowing the insolvency practitioner to elect whether or not the company will perform could have been developed in a manner capable of addressing a wider range of situations involving vulnerable creditors. "Anomalies will be avoided if any deviation from the right to equal treatment in the *concursus* is based on the conflicting fundamental rights of the hypothetical vulnerable contract parties…." See *Van der Linde* and *Van Staden* (n. 72), 414.

82 Bridge also mentions the inherent tension between "the two fundamental principles of credit and insolvency law, that of freedom of contract which allows one to bargain for priority, and the mandatory pari passu principle". See *Bridge,* Oxford Journal of Legal Studies 1992, 333, 340.

83 The principle may be traced back to at least the bankruptcy statute of 1542 which stated that: "... for true satisfaction and payment of the said creditors: That is to say, to every of the said creditors, a Portion Rate and Rate alike, according to the Quantity of their Debts". See *Keay*, Northern Ireland Legal Quarterly 2000, 515.

84 Finch regards it as fair on procedural and substantive levels. See *Finch*, Corporate Insolvency Law (2nd ed. 2009), 513.

85 *Finch* (n. 84), 570.

86 Ibid., 569.

impact on distributions to others, who may also not have much capacity to absorb losses, must be considered.[87]

Other scholars do not see value in equal distribution. Skeel claims that equality is an empty concept that has no virtue in insolvency because it is difficult to identify any coherent or consistent groups that would be advantaged or harmed by unequal treatment.[88] Mokal argues that creditors would not choose *pari passu* distribution if they had to reach consensus on a system.[89] Instead, they would agree to a fair distribution based on the effect of the debtor's insufficiency of funds on each type of creditor. Even when the fairness value of equality is denied, *pari passu* may be accepted as an option of last resort – an efficient solution to the division of the usually insignificant residual value.[90]

For purposes of the present discussion we now consider the interaction between the right to equality and different types of claims, namely secured, preferent and concurrent claims. We thus consider whether the special treatment accorded to secured claims and preferent unsecured claims respectively is compatible with the fundamental right to equality. This is followed by an evaluation of alternatives to the *pari passu* ranking of the remaining claims.

4. Equality and the existence of secured claims

Whether or not pre-insolvency private bargains should be respected in insolvency or should be adjusted in the public interest depends on whether the purpose of insolvency law is seen as maximising the overall return to creditors or as also serving a redistributive role.[91]

---

87 Ibid., 569.

88 *Skeel* (n. 15), 699, 742. The same person can be a debtor or a creditor and a creditor can have different claims in the same or different estates.

89 *Mokal* proposes an authentic consent model. The model entails that "all those affected by insolvency law are to be regarded as equals, with the consequence that their interests must be accorded equal care and concern in the choice of insolvency law principles". The relevant parties would be given the chance to bargain with each other under the appropriate conditions. See *Mokal* (n. 14), 61.

90 See *Mokal* (n. 14), 137; *Skeel* (n. 15), 739.

91 In *Salomon v Salomon & Co. Ltd.* [1897] AC 22, 53 the court held that "[e]verybody knows that where there is a winding-up debenture-holders generally step in and sweep off everything; and a great scandal it is". According Olivares-Caminal "[s]ecured transactions result from the legal system allowing a bilateral contractual convention reflecting a pre-established policy interest to alter the equal ranking

Regardless of whether the preferential distribution to secured creditors is seen as an exception to the equal distribution principle[92] or as not subject to it in the first place,[93] the fairness of secured credit has been questioned.[94] While security is typically defended on the basis that it reduces the cost of credit, Bebchuck and Fried have argued that the subordination of unsecured creditors through consensual arrangements to which they are not parties is particularly unfair towards involuntary creditors. Unlike voluntary unsecured creditors who can adjust the terms upon which they engage with the debtor, involuntary creditors cannot be said to have impliedly consented to security arrangements.[95] They proposed that secured creditors should not be entitled to the entire proceeds of their security. Non-adjusting creditors should either be prioritised over secured creditors,[96] or a fixed percentage should be carved out from the proceeds of security and applied towards unsecured claims.

As early as 1982 the Cork Committee in the UK suggested a carve-out in favour of unsecured creditors.[97] Twenty years later, provision was made for a prescribed part of the proceeds of assets subject to a floating charge[98] to be set aside for the satisfaction of unsecured creditors.[99] It must be noted

of creditors. The rationale for allowing this bilateral agreement to undermine the equal right of other parties lies in the ulterior motive of facilitating liquidity, which will most likely result in economic growth". See *Olivares-Caminal*, Law and Contemporary Problems 2018, 89.

92 *Keay* and *Walton* (n. 15), 424, submit that creditors holding security will almost always be guaranteed payment and even though the *pari passu* principle is fundamental it is often undermined by different types of creditors' security rights. See also *McCormack*, JBL 2003, 389.

93 Either because the assets are not regarded as falling in the insolvent estate or because the rule is limited to unsecured creditors. *Goode*, Principles of Corporate Insolvency Law (2nd ed. 1997), 152.

94 See *Bebchuk* and *Fried*, 105 Yale Law Journal 1995/1996, 857; *McCormack* (n. 92), 389, 401; *LoPucki*, Cornell Law Review 1997, 29, 34.

95 *Bebchuk* and *Fried* (n. 94), 857.

96 The adjustable priority rule.

97 Cork Report Insolvency Law and Practice (n. 14), 347.

98 A prescribed part is the part of the proceeds from realising the assets covered by a floating charge, that is set aside and kept available, so it can satisfy any unsecured debts. See Section 176A of the Insolvency Act 1986 and the Insolvency Act 1986 (Prescribed Part) Order 2003.

99 Section 176A, introduced by the Enterprise Act of 2002. It was inserted at the same time that Crown priority (which ranked before the floating-charge claim) was abolished and the idea was that the windfall that would accrue to the floating charge holder as a result of this would make up for the new arrangement. The claim of a floating charge holder is treated differently from other secured claims

though, that the floating charge of English law is distinguished from other forms of security.[100] In essence, the prescribed part arrangement boils down to having a not-so-preferent preferential claim because it is partially subordinated to the claims of unsecured creditors.[101]

Boraine and Van Wyk consider whether a case could be made out for carving out a percentage of the value of secured assets to satisfy the claims of unsecured debtors.[102] Their concern is with certain categories of unsecured creditors, specifically involuntary creditors and they conclude that it might be justifiable to carve out a portion of security for them. If a portion of all security is carved out, secured creditors would be incentivised to take too much security. However, a carve-out should have no influence on the extent of a floating charge as it is over all the residual assets in any case.

We now consider whether the priority afforded to secured creditors might be unconstitutional for violating the right to equality. In order to determine whether it discriminates unfairly, the test developed in *Harksen v Lane* will be applied.[103] This established staged test applies in matters where the right to equality is at stake.[104]

The first step is to determine whether there is indeed differentiation between secured and unsecured creditors in insolvency. There clearly is. Does the differentiation serve a legitimate government purpose? In the absence of a legitimate government purpose, it will be unfair discrimination and the enquiry would end. Respecting security does, in our view, serve legitimate purposes. It facilitates access to credit and reduces the cost of credit and as a result also stimulates economic growth. It also respects

---

and ranks on the free residue behind preferential claims. The reason for targeting floating charges is that they extend over a changing fund of all movables of the debtor and there is thus less publicity compared to other forms of security. *Mokal* (n. 15), 13 criticises the fact that all unsecured creditors, including the Crown, share in the prescribed part on an equal basis. The general notarial bond over movables in South Africa is in some ways similar to the floating charge and its ranking is also comparable, viz after other preferential claims and immediately before concurrent creditors – see Section 102 of the Insolvency Act. See further *Locke*, Comparative and International Law Journal of Southern Africa (2008), 140.

100 Boraine and van Wyk appear to have overlooked the essential distinction between floating charges and other forms of security in the UK. The South African equivalent is a general notarial bond over movables.

101 It is a fixed-fraction partial-priority rule, as Bebchuck and Fried would describe it; see *Bebchuk* and *Fried* (n. 93), 1323.

102 *Boraine* and *Van Wyk* (n. 24), 365.

103 *Harksen v Lane* (n. 62), para. 53.

104 *Kruger*, South African Law Journal 2011, 497.

the right to property, protects freedom of contract and promotes legal certainty.[105]

The next question is whether the discrimination is fair. We can assume it is fair towards secured creditors as well as unsecured creditors who are capable of assessing the associated risk of entering into insolvency proceedings, because the risk will be calculated into a lower or higher price for credit.[106] However, involuntary creditors as well as unsophisticated creditors are incapable of altering the terms of their transactions to reflect the risk they are assuming. We will therefore assume that the discrimination is not fair towards such non-adjusting unsecured creditors as the priority system tends to load the risk disproportionately onto their shoulders which cannot be justified on the grounds of either efficiency or fairness.[107]

The final step in the analysis is whether the discriminatory impact on non-adjusting creditors can be justified under the limitation clause in Section 36 of the Constitution. The limitation is sanctioned by law of general application: in addition to the general principles of contract and property law, the Insolvency Act 24 of 1936 protects security rights.[108] But the limitation will also have to be reasonable and justifiable in an open and democratic society based on human dignity, equality and freedom, taking into account all relevant factors, including the nature of the right, the importance of the purpose of the limitation, the nature and extent of the limitation, the relation between the limitation and its purpose, and the existence of less restrictive means to achieve the purpose.[109] The limitation analysis thus involves a "proportionality exercise, in which the purpose and effects of the infringing provisions are weighed against the nature and extent of the infringement caused".[110]

In employing the previous factors, the impact of the discrimination on non-adjusting creditors is apparent. However, dishonouring the rights of secured creditors may have a damaging effect on the entire economy as it could discourage creditors from extending credit and result in higher pricing of credit. While the aim of any insolvency framework should be to accommodate the broader macro-economic policies within the insolvency

105 *Bebchuk* and *Fried* (n. 93), 1331.
106 *Finch* (n. 92), 633.
107 *Virgos* and *Garcimartin*, The European Insolvency Regulation (2004), 13.
108 See Section 83, for example.
109 Section 36 of the Constitution.
110 *Brink v Kitshoff* (n. 63), para. 46.

system, it would be unrealistic to disregard the wider global context in which trade and commerce operate.[111]

An analysis of the general international principles regarding the treatment of stakeholder rights and priorities yields the conclusion that the priority of secured creditors in their security or "collateral" should be maintained and not subordinated to other creditors.[112] According to the World Bank Principles, one of the pillars of a modern credit-based economy is to facilitate the ability to own and freely transfer ownership interests in property, and to award security rights to lenders in order to gain access to credit at more affordable prices. The Principles also declare that: "[l] aws governing secured credit mitigate lenders' risks of default and thereby increase the flow of capital and facilitate low-cost financing. Discrepancies and uncertainties in the legal framework governing security rights are the main reasons for the high costs and unavailability of credit, especially in developing countries."[113] Interestingly the Principles also declare that public interests generally should not be given precedence over private rights.[114]

Section 36(1) of the Constitution permits the limitations of rights, provided that these limitations are authorised by law and that they are reasonable and justifiable. When applying the limitation clause as well as the test of proportionality, it is thus our opinion that the rights of the secured creditors outweigh the competing interests of the non-adjusting creditors.

5. Equality and the recognition of statutory priorities

The existence of priority distribution rights explains why the pari passu idea is routinely qualified. While preferential rights to distribution differ across jurisdictions, some trends are discernible, such as preferences for employees and for taxes and other government claims. In the South African context, priority distribution rights should also be aligned with the Constitution and the doctrine of legality, which entails that any law should be rationally connected to the legitimate purpose for which it is passed.[115] Employee claims are often prioritised on the basis that they

111 *Ramsay*, Theoretical Inquiries in Law 2006, 625.
112 World Bank Principles (n. 6), principle A3.
113 Ibid.
114 Ibid.
115 *Courtis*, Constitutional Court Review 2011, 32.

cannot adjust and are undiversified.[116] While there is certainly merit in prioritising employees, we have raised the question[117] whether this is fair towards independent contractors and certain trade creditors with similar low capacities to absorb loss. Clearly, some employees might be better able to deal with loss than others. Nevertheless, as the maximum pay-out to any employee is capped (on a fairly low amount) lower paid employees will enjoy priority for a higher percentage of their claims.

The desirability of preferences in favour of the State is often debated.[118] There has been a trend of abolishing such preferences.[119] However, the South African Insolvency Act still grants preferences to various social security agencies and to the revenue authority.[120] These rank lower than

116 *Finch* and *Milman* (n. 7), 569–570. See *Murray* and *Harris* (n. 22), 207.

117 See the text at n. 78 above.

118 See, for example, South African Law Commission, Project 63 Report on Insolvency/Review of the Law of Insolvency, vol. 1 (Feb 2000). The introduction of preferences may respond to the prevalent economic climate. Following an increase in retail insolvencies, the extension of priority to consumers in respect of prepayments was considered in the UK. See Law Commission, Report on Consumer Prepayments on Retailer Insolvency (2015), https://assets.publishing.service.gov.uk/government/uploads/system/uploads/attachment_data/file/767922/law-commission-report-government-response.pdf (last visited 27 Nov 2019), followed by the Report Consumer Prepayments on Retailer Insolvency (2016), https://www.gov.uk/government/publications/consumer-prepayments-on-retailer-insolvency (last visited 27 Nov 2019). On 11 July 2019, the UK government published draft legislation which contains important changes to insolvency law through the reintroduction of Crown preference for certain taxes in insolvencies from April 2020. See Draft Finance Bill 2020 – HMRC debts: priority on insolvency https://assets.publishing.service.gov.uk/government/uploads/system/uploads/attachment_data/file/816182/Changes_to_protect_tax_in_insolvency_cases_-_Draft_legislation.pdf (last visited 27 Nov 2019).

119 For example, in 2003 the Crown preference in the UK was abolished by the Enterprise Act 2002, ch. 40. However, the UK Government has published draft legislation according to which the UK tax authorities (Her Majesty's Revenue and Customs ("HMRC")) will be prioritised in insolvency proceedings in respect of certain employee taxes and value-added tax. See n. 118.

120 See Section 99. Over the years, the South African Law Commission published various research reports and working articles, including certain work concerned with statutory preferences. See South African Law Commission Working Paper 1, Preferences on Insolvency (1982), and subsequent Report on Preferences on Insolvency (1984). In the Preferences Report of 1984, the South African Law Commission recommended that the only claims to be paid out of the free residue with preference over other creditors had to be the costs of liquidation and administration of the estate; claims by employees; and claims for arrears of maintenance in terms of a court order. It was further recommended that all

employee claims, but the preferences are not limited with reference to time period or amount.[121]

IV. Alternatives to the pari passu ranking of remaining claims

If we accept that the *pari passu* principle is flawed within the South African insolvency law context it becomes necessary to consider whether there is a possible alternative which could represent a more suitable method of distribution. Shuchman suggests that insolvency law should be steered away from its current arbitrary classification that can be "attributed to historical accident and political leverage". He suggests that alternative systems might be based on the need of the creditor and the merit of the underlying transaction.[122] He does admit, though, that it would be uncertain, inefficient and even unfair to base a ranking on individual position. On the other hand, using classes raises problems of classification and justification.

While Mokal discounts the relevance of the pre-insolvency form of claims (*i.e.* whether they are secured or unsecured), he regards both the pre- and post-insolvency interests and obligations of the parties as equally relevant to the question of distribution. Thus, in his authentic consent model, creditors might all agree that the recognition of a security interest is justified because it reduces the risk that the debtor will go insolvent in the first place.[123] However, it would not be allowed if the arrangement is exploitative.[124]

Finch considers several alternative default rules for distribution of the free residue to unsecured non-preferent creditors:[125]

other preferences provided for in the Insolvency Act including preferences for taxes had to be abolished. In the 1984 Report, the Commission mentioned that justified preferences should have the consideration of fairness as foundation. It should be accepted as a general premise that the unsecured creditors should be dealt with on an equal footing except for preferences that can be justified in a modern society. In 1989 Cabinet, however, resolved that the abolition of preferences could not be supported as the abolition of preferences for taxes would have undesirable cost implications for the State. See *Keay, Boraine* and *Burdette*, International Insolvency Review 2001, 190.

121 Section 99 of Insolvency Act.

122 *Shuchman*, UCLA Law Review 1973, 403, 445–446.

123 *Mokal* (n. 14), 121.

124 Ibid., 122–123.

125 *Finch* and *Milman* (n. 7), 569 et seq.

a) debts ranked chronologically – first-come-first-served: Ranking debts in accordance with the order in which they were incurred would reflect the fact that later creditors can assess the risk of default based on the debtor's pre-existing exposure while earlier creditors cannot adjust.[126] As Finch points out, creditors would be reluctant to extend financing as the debtor comes closer to insolvency. Such a system would also require appropriate record-keeping and disclosure mechanisms. Curiously, South Africa – at least in theory – applies such a system in respect of certain post-commencement financing claims.[127]
b) debts ranked ethically: This is a utilitarian approach aligning distribution with the needs of unsecured creditors or other societal needs in order to maximise the sum of human happiness. While it might be an option on a group basis to protect specific classes of creditors, Finch notes that it would be unpredictable and inefficient on an individualised basis.[128] A class approach is, however, less targeted.
c) debts ranked on size: On the assumption that smaller creditors are more vulnerable, such a system might distribute a higher percentage dividend on claims below a certain amount.[129] However, it is not accurate to assume a correlation between debt size and vulnerability, and smaller creditors may even be more diversified than larger ones.
d) debts paid on policy grounds: Such a system would also have different rates for different types of creditors. Consumer creditors, for example, might be paid more because it is not their business to extend credit. However, some argue that consumers are not necessarily less diversified and more vulnerable to loss than certain trade creditors.

In our opinion, the most appropriate solution for South Africa would be an ethical ranking of debts aimed to pay unsecured creditors according to the creditors' needs. The standard criticism against such proposal would be with respect to creditor uncertainty because predicting positions in the payment hierarchy would be nearly impossible. This in turn may lead to

126 The problem with this option is that earlier creditors are not incentivised to monitor the risk of default and enforce timeously.

127 Section 135(3)(b), read with Section 135(2) of the Companies Act of 2008: During its business rescue proceedings the company may obtain financing and such post commencement finance (except employee payments) will be paid in the order of preference in the order in which claims were incurred over all unsecured claims against the company. See Section 135(1) and n. 34.

128 *Shuchman* (n. 122), 445–446.

129 According to Shuchman the Talmud provides for such a system. *Shuchman* (n. 122), 446.

higher cost of credit due to inability of creditors to assess present and future risks. Instead, attention should be given to the disparate effect of insolvency on vulnerable creditors. Scholars have identified two relevant factors with which we agree: the ability to adjust for the risk of insolvency through negotiating the terms of credit or priority for repayment and the capacity to absorb losses arising from insolvency, which is influenced by the ability to diversify.[130] We propose that concerns about the realisation of socio-economic and other fundamental rights and values would be accommodated within these factors.

V. Conclusion: To equality and beyond?

There is only a superficial correlation between the right to equality and the equal treatment of creditors in insolvency. This can be attributed to the fact that the *paritas creditorum* principle represents formal equality whilst the Constitution guarantees substantive or transformative equality which envisages the ultimate achievement of equality through unequal measures that address vulnerability.

Insolvency law can, and often does, contribute to substantive equality through measures that deviate from the equal treatment of creditors. However, ill-designed deviations can introduce fresh distinctions that may have to be eradicated through future development.

In the absence of principled legislative reform, the courts, particularly the Constitutional Court, plays a crucial role in promoting the achievement of substantive equality. Equal protection of the law and full and equal enjoyment of all rights and freedoms does not necessarily have to be achieved through direct application of the justiciable right to equality. In fact, the Constitutional Court's tendency to focus on anti-discrimination and inclusion has been too limited to introduce the structural (legal) changes also required by substantive equality. It implies that equality is advanced only when someone else happens to be "more equal". Equality as narrowly applied in the *Sarrahwitz* case represents a missed opportunity that will delay and even impede the achievement of equality. Legal certainty, and equality, would be better served by broader, more assertive solutions that address vulnerability on a principled basis.

Despite our criticism of the Constitutional Court's approach, its reading in of a definition of "vulnerable purchaser" holds promise if extended

130 *Finch*, Insolvency Lawyer 2000, 194, 206–210.

to the broader concept of vulnerable creditor in insolvency. It should be possible, through legislative intervention, to design a set of general rules – covering at least the approach to executory contracts and priority of distribution – based on the disparate effect of insolvency on vulnerable creditors.

A constant theme throughout the discussion is to evaluate whether our present insolvency system reflects the foundational values of our own society. Moseneke very appropriately pronounced this principle when he stated:

> "I am not overstating the character of our democratic transition when I say it is a constitutional revolution. It is the outcome of a collective, but solemn pact to transform our society in a fundamental way. Our aspirations of a good and socially just society stand proudly in our highest law. As our nightmarish past gave way to our idyllic future, the very process of the transition was carefully scripted. Law sanctioned every step of the revolution. The bad and the ugly were to be jettisoned and the good to be kept and nourished with the new found rules and foundational values of the Constitution."[131]

Looking to the future, we argue that the courts need to change their approach if insolvency law is to develop with coherence and purpose. Further research is needed in order to develop a framework for such an approach. It is high time that policy- and lawmakers embark on a holistic review of insolvency law as opposed to applying band-aid solutions that could result in an unequal system short on legal certainty and focus.

Bibliography

Catherine Albertyn, "Substantive equality and transformation in South Africa", South African Journal on Human Rights 2007, 253.

Aristotle, "Nicomachean Ethics", in: Jonathan Barnes (ed.), The Complete Works of Aristotle, The Revised Oxford Translation, vol. 2 (Princeton University Press, Princeton 1984).

Douglas Baird, "Priority matters: absolute priority, relative priority, and the costs of bankruptcy", University of Pennsylvania Law Review 2017, 785.

Lucian Bebchuk and *Jesse Fried*, "The uneasy case for the priority of secured claims in bankruptcy", 105 Yale Law Journal 1995/1996, 857.

131 *Moseneke*, Speculum Juris 2007, 2.

Andre Boraine and *Jani Van Wyk*, "Reconsidering the plight of the five foolish maidens: Should the unsecured creditor stake a claim in real security?", Journal of Contemporary Roman-Dutch Law 2011, 347.

Michael Bridge, "The Quistclose Trust in a World of Secured Transactions", Oxford Journal of Legal Studies 1992, 333.

Hermie Coetzee, A comparative reappraisal of debt relief measures for natural person debtors in South Africa (LL.D. thesis University of Pretoria, 2015).

Christian Courtis, "Rationality, reasonableness, proportionality: Testing the use of standards of scrutiny in the constitutional review of legislation", Constitutional Court Review 2011, 32.

Roger Evans, "Waiving of rights to property in insolvent estates and advantage to creditors in sequestration proceedings in South Africa", De Jure 2018, 298.

Mike Falke, Insolvency Law Reform in Transition Economies (LL.D. thesis Humboldt University, 2005).

Vanessa Finch, Corporate insolvency law: perspectives and principles (Cambridge University Press, 2nd ed., Cambridge 2009).

Vanessa Finch, "The pari passu passé", Insolvency Lawyer 2000, 194.

Vanessa Finch, "Security, insolvency and risk", Modern Law Review 1999, 633.

Vanessa Finch and *David Milman*, Corporate Insolvency Law: Perspectives and Principles (Cambridge University Press, 3rd ed., Cambridge 2017).

Sandra Fredman, "Substantive Equality Revisited", International Journal of Constitutional Law 2016, 712.

José Garrido, "The Distributional Question in Insolvency: Comparative Aspects", International Insolvency Review 1995, 25.

Roy Goode, Principles of Corporate Insolvency Law (Sweet & Maxwell, 2nd ed., London 1997).

Radley Henrico, "Re-visiting the rule of law and principle of legality: Judicial nuisance or licence?", TSAR 2014, 742.

Anri Heyns and *Boitumelo Mmusinyane*, "Should the Alienation of Land Act 68 of 1981 be amended to address homelessness? Sarrahwitz v Maritz 2015 8 BCLR 925 (CC)", 20 PER/PELJ 2017, DOI http://dx.doi.org/10.17159/1727-3781/2017/v20i0a1540 (last visited 27 Nov 2019).

Andrew Keay, "In Pursuit of the Rationale behind the Avoidance of Pre-Liquidation Transactions", Sydney Law Review 1996, 70.

Andrew Keay, "Insolvency law: a matter of public interest?", Northern Ireland Legal Quarterly 2000, 515.

Andrew Keay, *Andre Boraine* and *David Burdette*, "Preferential debts in corporate insolvency: a comparative study", International Insolvency Review 2001, 190.

Andrew Keay and *Peter Walton*, Insolvency Law: Corporate and Personal (Pearson, 1st ed., Harlow 2003).

Rosaan Kruger, "Equality and unfair discrimination: refining the Harksen test", South African Law Journal 2011, 497.

Natania Locke, "Security granted by a company over its movable property: the floating charge and the general notarial bond compared", Comparative and International Law Journal of Southern Africa, 2008, 136.

Lynn LoPucki, "Should the secured credit carve out apply only in bankruptcy? A systems/strategic analysis", Cornell Law Review 1997, 29.

Zingapi Mabe, "Section 27 of the Insolvency Act 24 of 1936 as a Violation of the Equality Clause of the Constitution of South Africa: A Critical Analysis", 19 PER/PELJ 2016, DOI https://doi.org/10.17159/1727-3781/2016/v19i0a577 (last visited 27 Nov 2019).

Gerard McCormack, "The Priority of Secured Credit: An Anglo-American Perspective", JBL 2003, 389.

Catharine MacKinnon, "Substantive Equality Revisited: A reply to Sandra Fredman" International Journal of Constitutional Law 2016, 739.

Iain MacNeil, "Uncertainty in Commercial Law", Edinburgh Law Review 2009, 68.

Rizwaan Mokal, Corporate Insolvency Law (Oxford University Press, 1st ed., Oxford 2005).

Rizwaan Mokal, "Priority as pathology: The Pari Passu myth", The Cambridge Law Journal 2001, 581.

Dikgang Moseneke, "Transformative Adjudication in Post-Apartheid South Africa – Taking Stock after a Decade", Speculum Juris 2007, 2.

Michael Murray and *Jason Harris*, Keay's Insolvency: Personal and Corporate Law and Practice (Thomson Reuters, 8th ed., Sydney 2014).

Rodrigo Olivares-Caminal, "Creditor equality, secured transactions, and systemic risk: a complex trilemma", Law and Contemporary Problems 2018, 87.

Ian Ramsay, "Functionalism and Political Economy in the Comparative Study of Consumer Insolvency: An Unfinished Story from England and Wales", Theoretical Inquiries in Law 2006, 625.

Review Committee, Cork Report on Insolvency Law and Practice (Her Majesty's Stationery Office, London 1982).

Philip Shuchman, "An Attempt at a 'Philosophy of Bankruptcy'", UCLA Law Review 1973, 403.

David Skeel, "The Empty Idea of 'Equality of Creditors'", University of Pennsylvania Law Review 2018, 699.

Anne Smith, "Equality constitutional adjudication in South Africa", African Human Rights Law Journal 2014, 609.

South African Law Commission, Project 63 Report on Insolvency/Review of the Law of Insolvency, vol. 1 (Feb 2000).

Kathleen van der Linde and *Marius van Staden*, "Judicial development (and activism) in insolvency law", TSAR 2017, 414.

Miguel Virgos and *Francisco Garcimartin*, The European Insolvency Regulation: Law and Practice (Kluwer Law International, The Hague 2004).

Elizabeth Warren, "Bankruptcy Policy", The University of Chicago Law Review 1987, 777.

World Bank, "Principles for Effective Insolvency and Creditor/Debtor Rights System" (2015), https://www.worldbank.org/en/topic/financialsector/brief/the-world-bank-principles-for-effective-insolvency-and-creditor-rights (last visited 15 Nov 2019).

Register of cases

Brink v Kitshoff NO 1996 4 SA 197 (CC).

CSARS v Stand Two Nine Nought Wynberg (Pty) Ltd 2005 5 SA 583 (SCA).

Diener NO v Minister of Justice and Others 2019 4 SA 374 (CC) (29 Nov 2018).

Ellerine Brothers (Pty) Limited (Ellerine) v McCarthy Limited 2014 4 SA 22 (SCA).

Ex parte Kroese 2015 1 SA 405 (NWM).

Harksen v Lane NO 1998 1 SA 300 (CC).

Hosking NO v Coetzee NO 2005 ZASCA 110 (25 Nov 2005).

Jackson v Louw NO 2019 2 All SA 145 (ECG).

Jordan & Others v S 2002 6 SA 642 (CC).

Minister of Finance and Others v Van Heerden 2004 6 SA 121 (CC).

National Coalition for Gay and Lesbian Equality v Minister of Justice 1999 1 SA 6 (CC).

MEC for Education: KwaZulu-Natal & Others v Pillay CCT 51/06 [2007] ZACC 21.

Minister of Constitutional Development v South African Restructuring and Insolvency Practitioners Association (CCT13/17) [2018] ZACC 20.

National Coalition for Gay and Lesbian Equality v Minister of Justice 1999 1 SA 6 (CC).

President of the Republic of South Africa and Another v Hugo 1997 4 SA 1 (CC).

Prince v President, Cape Law Society 2002 2 SA 794 (CC).

Prinsloo v Van der Linde and Another 1997 6 BCLR 759 (CC).

Sarrahwitz v Maritz NO 2015 4 SA 491 (CC).

Salomon v Salomon & Co. Ltd. [1897] AC 22.

South African Restructuring and Insolvency Practitioners Association v Minister of Justice and Constitutional Development and Others, In Re: Concerned Insolvency Practitioners Association NPC and Others v Minister of Justice And Constitutional Development 2015 2 SA 430 (WCC).

Vallejo v Wheeler (1774) 1 Cowp 143.

Van der Walt v Metcash Trading Ltd 2002 4 SA 317 (CC).

Comment: The Principle of Equal Treatment of Creditors and its Limits Under German Law, Illustrated on the Basis of the Law on Limited Liability Companies

*Michael Kort**

* Michael Kort, Dr. iur.; Professor, University of Augsburg Faculty of Law. Chair for Civil Law, Economic Law, Intellectual Property Law and Labour Law.

I. The relationship between private autonomy and equal treatment of creditors under German law

Concerning the question of equal treatment of creditors (*par conditio creditorum*), German law is characterised by a conflict between equality and freedom.[1]

1. Civil law and commercial law

Owing to the far-reaching principle of freedom of private contractual autonomy and the principle of economic (and legal) free trade, under German civil law and German commercial law there is no general principle that debtors must treat their creditors equally – i.e. must satisfy their claims equally.

2. Insolvency law

However, under German insolvency law the principle of equal treatment of creditors applies (*par conditio creditorum*).[2] This principle has been closely linked to the safeguarding of social peace since the beginnings of insolvency law in Europe, i.e. long before a statutory regulation of insolvency law in Germany. This goal of securing social peace can already be found in the rules of ancient Roman law on insolvency issues.[3]

The principle of equal treatment of creditors under insolvency law as applied in ancient Roman law – and also still applied in German law today – should preclude individual creditors of a debtor from having select access to the debtor's assets after the opening of insolvency proceedings, and thus starting a "race for the assets".

From the point of view of the debtor and the insolvency administrator, the equal treatment of creditors is required to compensate for this prohibition of individual access to the debtor's assets in insolvency proceedings.

The prohibition of unequal treatment in insolvency proceedings, which already existed in Roman law, was later supplemented by a prohibition on

---

1 *Paulus*, in: Beuthien, Fuchs, Roth, Schiemann and Wacke (eds.), FS Medicus (2009), 281.

2 *Rattunde*, in: Rattunde, Smid and Zeuner (eds.), InsO (4th ed. 2019), § 226, para. 1.

3 *Häsemeyer*, Insolvenzrecht (4th ed. 2007), 66.

individual creditors having access to the debtor's assets in the run-up to insolvency proceedings, i.e. during a certain period prior to the opening of insolvency proceedings. German law, for example, provides for the possibility of *Anfechtung* (contesting of debtor's transactions) in insolvency proceedings (Sections 129 ff. of the Insolvency Act (*Insolvenzordnung* – InsO)). Access by individual creditors to the debtor's assets during a certain period prior to the opening of insolvency proceedings that contravenes the principle of equal treatment is to be reversed in favour of the entire group of creditors.[4]

Outside the period of the insolvency proceedings and outside the critical phase prior to the opening of insolvency proceedings, a debtor does not have to satisfy its creditors equally.

II. No general principle of equal treatment of creditors (par conditio creditorum)

From a historical perspective, there has never been a general principle in European legal systems that creditors of a debtor should be treated equally with regard to satisfaction of debts.

On the contrary, the development of insolvency law shows that even in insolvency proceedings the principle of equal treatment of creditors was not and is not strictly adhered to. Since the former Bankruptcy Code (*Konkursordnung*) of 1877 – which was the predecessor of the modern German Insolvency Act – German insolvency law has instead been shaped by the principle that creditors are to be divided into different groups. Some of these groups are privileged over other groups. This division of creditors into groups therefore means that the principle of equal treatment of creditors applies only within a group ("rank") and not in respect of all of the debtor's creditors.

III. Insolvency law for legal entities, such as limited liability companies (GmbH)

The limits of the principle of equal treatment of creditors in insolvency proceedings and outside insolvency proceedings apply in principle in German law even if the debtor is not a natural person but a legal entity – such as a German limited liability company (*Gesellschaft mit beschränkter*

4 *Häsemeyer*, Insolvenzrecht (4th ed. 2007), 66 et seqq.

Haftung – GmbH). According to German limited liability company law, a GmbH is only liable to the creditors of the GmbH with respect to its own assets. The shareholders of the GmbH are not personally liable for the debts of the GmbH. Therefore, in the event of an insolvency of the GmbH and in the period before the insolvency of the GmbH, the question of equal treatment of the creditors of the GmbH arises.

IV. Duty to file for insolvency

Under German law, the managing directors of a GmbH who are responsible both for the internal management of the GmbH and for the external representation of the GmbH have a duty to file for insolvency: if the GmbH is either insolvent or overindebted, the managing directors must file for insolvency.

V. (Restricted) equal treatment of creditors upon insolvency of the GmbH

If insolvency proceedings are opened over the assets of the GmbH, the creditor satisfaction in the insolvency proceedings takes place according to the limited principle of equal treatment of creditors described above. There may be different groups (ranks) of creditors; within these groups (ranks) the principle of uniform satisfaction of creditors applies in insolvency proceedings.

VI. Refusal to open insolvency proceedings for insufficiency of assets

Problems arise if the insolvency court refuses to open insolvency proceedings due to an insufficiency of assets. This is the case if there are so few assets of the GmbH as debtor that a proper implementation of the insolvency proceedings is not possible.

In the event of a refusal to open insolvency proceedings against the assets of the GmbH for insufficiency of assets, proceedings will then be initiated under company law. These proceedings are not governed by the rules of insolvency law, but by (general) company law provisions on the winding up (liquidation) of the GmbH (Sections 60 ff. of the Limited Liability Companies Act (*Gesetz betreffend die Gesellschaften mit beschränkter Haftung* – GmbHG)).

The objective of any liquidation of a GmbH is to wind up the GmbH. The liquidation of the GmbH begins with its dissolution according to Section 60 GmbHG. Pursuant to Section 60(1) no. 5 GmbHG, one of several reasons for the dissolution and thus for the liquidation of a GmbH is the legal force of the decision by which the opening of insolvency proceedings was rejected for insufficiency of assets.

VII. Objectives of the liquidation of a GmbH

Irrespective of which of the grounds for dissolution under Section 60 GmbHG exists – i.e. whether, as here, the reason for the winding up of the GmbH is the refusal to open insolvency proceedings for insufficiency of assets or whether there is a completely different reason for the dissolution – the liquidation of the GmbH aims to terminate ongoing contractual relationships, collect receivables, settle liabilities and then convert any remaining assets of the GmbH into cash and – insofar as assets still exist – distribute these funds among the shareholders of the GmbH.

Satisfying the creditors of the GmbH is thus one of several objectives of the winding up (liquidation) of the GmbH.

VIII. No general principle of equal treatment of creditors in the winding up (liquidation) of a GmbH

There is agreement under German law that creditors do not have to be treated equally during the winding up of the GmbH, since the liquidation of the GmbH takes place in accordance with company law and not insolvency law.

The liquidators have to complete the tasks set out above in order to wind up the GmbH. The liquidators are either the managing directors of the GmbH or other persons appointed as liquidators. According to prevailing opinion, the liquidators must be guided by the welfare of the company when carrying out their tasks. However, the actions of the liquidators are not aimed at the continuation of the GmbH through active participation in commercial transactions, but at winding up the GmbH.

The liquidators do not act in the public interest, but in the interest of the GmbH. Their legal status can therefore be compared with the legal status of the managing directors of a GmbH, but not with the legal status of an insolvency administrator of a GmbH. Therefore, the principle of equal treatment of creditors of the GmbH does not generally apply during the liquidation (winding up) period.

During the winding up period, the liquidators must meet the company's due obligations. Liabilities that are not yet due and liabilities in dispute must be secured.[5] The liquidators determine at their own discretion the order in which liabilities are discharged.[6] The Federal Court of Justice (*Bundesgerichtshof* – BGH)[7] and the prevailing opinion in academic legal literature[8] take the view that, in principle, the liquidators are not obliged to ensure equal satisfaction of creditors (*par conditio creditorum*).

IX. Winding up of a GmbH with no assets

However, in the special situation of refusal to open insolvency proceedings for insufficiency of assets, there is much controversy as to whether the liquidators are nevertheless obliged to ensure uniform satisfaction of company creditors in the interest of all creditors.[9]

According to some part of the literature, the principle of equal treatment of creditors (*par conditio creditorum*) does apply to the winding up of a GmbH on the basis of a refusal to open insolvency proceedings for insufficiency of assets.[10] The argument for this view is that, in such cases the liquidation of the GmbH takes the place of the insolvency proceedings. Therefore, in the case of a GmbH being liquidated without assets, certain principles of insolvency proceedings must be taken into account – in particular the principle of equal treatment of creditors (*par conditio creditorum*).

However, the fact that the liquidation of a GmbH and the conduct of insolvency proceedings serve different purposes, and therefore an application of the principle of *par creditio creditorum* is ruled out in the case

5 *Haas*, in: Baumbach and Hueck (eds.), GmbHG (22nd ed. 2019), § 70, para. 5.

6 OLG Stuttgart, Judgment of 24 Jun 2009, 14 U 5/09, GmbHR 2010, 46; *Haas*, in: Baumbach and Hueck (eds.), GmbHG (22nd ed. 2019), § 70, para. 5.

7 BGH, Judgment of 18 Nov 1969, II ZR 83/68, BGHZ 53, 71, 74.

8 *Haas*, in: Baumbach and Hueck (eds.), GmbHG (22nd ed. 2019), § 70, para. 5; *Gesell*, in: Schmidt-Leithoff (ed.), GmbHG (6th ed. 2017), § 70, para. 11.

9 *Paura*, in: Ulmer, Habersack and Löbbe (eds.), GmbHG (2nd ed. 2016), § 70, para. 11; *Haas*, in: Baumbach and Hueck (eds.), GmbHG (22nd ed. 2019), § 70, para. 5; *Nerlich*, in: Heidinger, Leible and Schmidt (eds.), GmbHG (3rd ed. 2017), § 70, para. 23.

10 *Brünkmans* and *Hofmann*, in: Gehrlein, Born and Simon (eds.), GmbHG (4th ed. 2019), § 70, para. 16.

of liquidation, speaks against an obligation to satisfy company creditors equally.[11]

It is sometimes argued that although the *par conditio creditorum* of insolvency law does not apply in company liquidations, the liquidators must take account of the interests of known creditors and must not favour any of them.[12]

What speaks against this view, however, is that this would result in a "back door" *par conditio creditorum* that would be very similar to the insolvency law *par conditio creditorum* – namely through an indirect requirement of equal treatment of creditors in liquidation.

A further argument against applying the principle of equal treatment of creditors during the winding up period (even in the case of insolvency with insufficient assets) is that individual foreclosure by the creditors is possible, i.e. in the liquidation period there is no suspension of enforcement and enforcement acts can therefore thwart the rights of the individual creditors anyway.[13]

A comprehensive requirement for equal treatment of creditors in liquidation where there are insufficient assets cannot be justified by the argument that insufficiency of assets is a case of insolvency, and that liquidation where there are insufficient assets should logically be carried out taking into account the insolvency situation.[14] Rather, the interplay between company law and insolvency law shows that the legislature has opted for company law to be applied in the event of the GmbH having insufficient assets and that general principles of company law thus apply. A kind of spillover effect of insolvency law onto company law could only be justified if the legislature acted accordingly, i.e. *de lege ferenda* (by future law), but not on the basis of *lex lata*.

Therefore, there is no general (company law) requirement of equal treatment of creditors in the event of liquidation of the GmbH after a refusal to open insolvency proceedings for insufficiency of assets.

However, there are certain limits to the unequal treatment of creditors in the event of liquidation of the GmbH where there are insufficient assets. For example, the liquidators are prohibited from priority satisfaction of their own claims or claims of persons close to them to the detriment

---

11 *Kleindiek*, in: Lutter and Hommelhoff (eds.), GmbHG (20th ed. 2020), § 70, para. 9.

12 *Kleindiek*, in: Lutter and Hommelhoff (eds.), GmbHG (20th ed. 2020), § 73, para. 8; *Servatius*, in: Bork and Schäfer (eds.), GmbHG (4th ed. 2019), § 70, para. 9.

13 *Müller*, in: MünchKomm-GmbHG (3rd ed. 2018), § 70, para. 23.

14 *Schmidt* and *Bitter*, in: Scholz (ed.), GmbHG (11th ed. 2015), § 70, para. 10.

of other company creditors in the case of liquidation where there are insufficient assets.[15]

X. Legal policy considerations de lege ferenda

For some time now, there has been a discussion in Germany as to whether the legislature is obliged *de lege ferenda* to ensure equal treatment of creditors in the event of the liquidation of a company without assets.[16] The consequence of this would be that in the event of insufficiency of assets, the insolvency law principle of equal treatment of creditors would be applied under company law.

The German legislature did not take up these considerations in the reform of insolvency law which took place about two decades ago.[17]

XI. Summary

Under German company law, liquidators must focus[18] solely on the purpose of the winding up, even in the case of a liquidation where there is an insufficiency of assets, but not (additionally) on a requirement of treating creditors equally.

Bibliography

Adolf Baumbach and *Alfred Hueck* (eds.), Kommentar zum GmbHG (C.H. BECK, 22nd ed., Munich 2019).

Reinhard Bork and *Carsten Schäfer* (eds.), Kommentar zum GmbHG (RWS, 4th ed., Cologne 2019).

---

15 *Kleindiek*, in: Lutter and Hommelhoff (eds.), GmbHG (20th ed. 2020), § 73, para. 8.

16 *Schulz*, Die masselose Liquidation der GmbH (1986), 106 et seqq., 160 et seqq., 167 et seqq.; *Konzen*, in: Habersack, Hommelhoff, Hüffer and Schmidt (eds.), FS Ulmer (2003), 323, 346 et seqq.

17 *Altmeppen*, in: Roth and Altmeppen (eds.), GmbHG (9th ed. 2019), § 70, para. 15.

18 *Müller*, in: MünchKomm-GmbHG (3rd ed. 2018), § 70, para. 23; *Brünkmans and Hofmann*, in: Gehrlein, Born and Simon (eds.), GmbHG (4th ed. 2019), § 70, para. 14.

Markus Gehrlein, *Manfred Born* and *Stefan Simon* (eds.), Kommentar zum GmbHG (Carl Heymanns, 4th ed., Cologne 2019).

Ludwig Häsemeyer, Insolvenzrecht (Carl Heymanns, 4th ed., Cologne 2007).

Andreas Heidinger, *Stefan Leible* and *Jessica Schmidt* (eds.), Kommentar zum GmbHG (C.H. BECK, 3rd ed., Munich 2017).

Peter Hommelhoff and *Marcus Lutter* (eds.), Kommentar zum GmbHG (Dr. Otto Schmidt, 20th ed., Cologne 2020).

Horst Konzen, "Der Gläubigerschutz bei Liquidation der masselosen GmbH", in: Mathias Habersack, Peter Hommelhoff, Uwe Hüffer and Karsten Schmidt (eds.), Festschrift für Peter Ulmer zum 70. Geburtstag am 2. Januar 2003 (De Gruyter, Berlin 2003), 323.

Münchener Kommentar zum Gesetz betreffend die Gesellschaften mit beschränkter Haftung (MünchKomm-GmbHG), *Holger Fleischer* and *Goette Wulf* (eds.), vol. 3 (C.H. BECK, 4th ed., Munich 2019).

Christoph G. Paulus, "Freiheit und Gleichheit als Grenzmarkierung zwischen Zivilrecht und Insolvenzrecht", in: Volker Beuthien, Maximilian Fuchs, Herbert Roth, Gottfried Schiemann and Andreas Wacke (eds.), Perspektiven des Privatrechts am Anfang des 21. Jahrhunderts, Festschrift für Dieter Medicus zum 80. Geburtstag am 9. Mai 2009 (Carl Heymanns, Cologne 2009), 281.

Rolf Rattunde, *Stefan Schmid* and *Mark Zeuner* (eds.), Kommentar zur Insolvenzordnung, (Kohlhammer, 4th ed., Stuttgart 2018).

Günter H. Roth and *Holger Altmeppen* (eds.), Kommentar zum GmbHG (C.H. Beck, 9th ed., Munich 2019).

Christian Schmidt-Leithoff and *Heinz Rowedder* (eds.), Kommentar zum GmbHG (Franz Vahlen, 6th ed., Munich 2017).

Franz Scholz (ed.), Kommentar zum GmbHG, vol. 3 (Dr. Otto Schmidt, 11th ed., Cologne 2015).

Wolf Schulz, Die masselose Liquidation der GmbH (Decker & Müller, Heidelberg 1986).

Peter Ulmer, *Mathias Habersack* and *Marc Löbbe* (eds.), Kommentar zum GmbHG (Mohr Siebeck, 2nd ed., Tübingen 2016).

Register of cases

BGH, Judgment of 18 Nov 1969, II ZR 83/68, BGHZ 53, 71.

OLG Stuttgart, Judgment of 24 Jun 2009, 14 U 5/09, GmbHR 2010, 46.

Market Conduct Regulation in Perspective: Triumphs and Tribulations post Twin Peaks

Daleen Millard[*] / *Choene Jacqueline Maholo*[**]

Abstract: Market conduct regulation aims to ensure fair outcomes for consumers. As such, the main aim of any such regulation should always be to place the needs of a specific group of consumers first and to interrogate these needs very carefully before new regulation is put into place. This contribution evaluates the so-called "Twin Peaks" model of regulation that divides oversight over the financial markets into prudential regulation under the Prudential Authority, and market conduct under the Financial Sector Conduct Authority, and provides an overview of the key statutes that constitute the Twin Peaks system. In addition to providing an evaluation of the Financial Services Regulation Act, the Insurance Act and the 2017 Policyholder Protection Rules, the contribution briefly canvasses the Conduct of Financial Institutions Bill and concludes that although the new regulatory dispensation is comprehensive and inclusive, it brings about an expensive bureaucracy that will in all likelihood not promote financial inclusion.

[*] B Iur, LLB, LLM, LLD, Professor in Private Law, University of Johannesburg.
[**] LLB, LLM, Assistant lecturer in Mercantile Law, University of Johannesburg.

I. Introduction

The aim with the Financial Sector Regulation Act (FSRA)[1] is to establish a so-called "Twin Peaks" model of regulation that divides oversight over the financial markets into prudential regulation under the Prudential Authority (PA), and market conduct under the Financial Sector Conduct Authority (FSCA). Market conduct regulation encompasses *all* financial products and services, and to date, the best examples of market conduct regulation and financial inclusion is found in the insurance industry. This contribution provides an overview of the key statutes that constitute the Twin Peaks system and evaluates the role of these instruments in creating a safer financial environment in which consumers are better protected. It provides an overview of the supervisory framework, followed by an evaluation of the FSRA, the Insurance Act,[2] and the 2017 Policyholder Protection Rules that came into force on 1 January 2018 (2018 PPRs) as the key legislative instruments that aim to realise the objectives of the Twin Peaks system.

II. Supervisory framework: Overview

In 2011, South Africa embarked on a complete regulatory overhaul which resulted in the formation of the PA[3] and FSCA[4] as the two main regulatory authorities, with the PA being responsible for supervising the safety and soundness of financial institutions and the FSCA as the authority that supervises how financial services firms conduct their business and treat customers.[5] These two regulatory authorities underpin the so-called "Twin

1 Financial Sector Regulation Act No. 9 of 2017.

2 Insurance Act No. 18 of 2017.

3 Established in terms of chapter 3, part 1, Sec. 32 FSRA.

4 Established in terms of chapter 4, part 1, Sec. 56 FSRA.

5 National Treasury, "New Twin Peaks Regulators Established" (29 Mar 2018), 1, https://bit.ly/2UBiKKt (last visited 20 Aug 2019) (henceforth referred to as NT

Peaks regulatory system" and signal a complete shift away from South Africa's former fragmented and complex regulatory approach that regulated financial sector components in silos.[6] Prompted by the momentous global financial crisis in 2008, recommendations of the International Monetary Fund (IMF) and the World Bank's 2008 Financial Sector Assessment Programme (FSAP), South Africa deemed it befitting to implement a Twin Peaks system of regulation, thereby recognising that the two objectives of strengthening financial stability and ensuring consumer protection are better spearheaded by two separate regulators.[7] In addition to establishing two separate regulators, the regulatory and supervisory framework of the Twin Peaks system is intended to minimise the scope of "regulatory arbitrage or forum shopping and close gaps in the regulatory system". Furthermore, the reformed financial regulatory framework aims to make the financial sector safer and make it work more effectively in the interests of all South Africans, by reducing potential threats to financial stability and better protecting customers by ensuring that financial institutions treat their customers fairly.[8]

For market conduct regulation, the FSCA prioritises market conduct regulation and supervision throughout the entire financial services sector.[9] The need for such supervision stems from deep-rooted ills, such as the unequal bargaining position that is omnipresent between customers and

---

Media Statement 2018). Sec. 33 of the FSRA sets out the objectives of the PA and the objectives of the FSCA are found in Sec. 57.

6 Before the implementation of the Twin Peaks regulatory system, South Africa's regulatory system remained functional and partially integrated. See *Rajendaran*, "Approaches to financial regulation and the case of South Africa" (6 Mar 2012), https://www.dvara.com/blog/2012/03/06/approaches-to-financial-regulation-and-the-case-of-south-africa/ (last visited 20 Aug 2019). On jurisdictions that have embarked on the Twin Peaks movement, see further *Schmulow*, 25 Afr. J. Int'l & Comp. L. 2017, 393. The Reserve Bank as central bank also functions prominently in this model with an expanded mandate for financial stability. See Sec. 11 of the FSRA (Responsibility of the Reserve Bank for financial stability), Sec. 12 (Monitoring of risks by the Reserve Bank) and Sec. 13 (Financial stability).

7 *Van Niekerk* and *Van Heerden*, 80 THRHR 2017, 636, 642. See also *Godwin* and *Schmulow*, 132 SALJ 2015, 756. See also *Godwin, Howse* and *Ramsay*, 134 SALJ 2017, 665.

8 NT Media Statement 2018 (n. 5).

9 National Treasury, Twin Peaks in South Africa: Response and Explanatory Document (Dec 2014), 10, https://juta.co.za/media/filestore/2015/03/2014_12_12_Response_document.pdf (last visited 20 Aug 2019) (henceforth referred to as NT response and explanatory document). This document was published as an accompaniment to the second draft of the Financial Sector Regulation Bill.

providers of financial products and services and which exposes vulnerable customers to exploitation. Rigorous scrutiny of financial institutions' activities are required, which is why the primary task of the FSCA is to ensure the realisation of its objectives as set out in Section 57 of the FSRA, namely to:

> "(a) enhance and support the efficiency and integrity of financial markets; and (b) protect financial customers by— (i) promoting fair treatment of financial customers by financial institutions; and (ii) providing financial customers and potential financial customers with financial education programs, and otherwise promoting financial literacy and the ability of financial customers and potential financial customers to make sound financial decisions; and (c) assist in maintaining financial stability."

These objectives illustrate that the FSCA must equally avert misconduct and the abuse of consumers by financial institutions, *and* empower customers to protect themselves by strengthening their ability to make informed financial decisions. To achieve these objectives, the FSCA will have to adhere to the myriad of functions stipulated in Section 58 of the FSRA.[10]

---

10 Chapter 4, part 1, Sec. 58 FSRA sets out the functions of the FSCA as follows: "(1) In order to achieve its objective, the Financial Sector Conduct Authority must— *(a)* regulate and supervise, in accordance with the financial sector laws, the conduct of financial institutions; *(b)* co-operate with, and assist, the Reserve Bank, the Financial Stability Oversight Committee, the Prudential Authority, the National Credit Regulator, and the Financial Intelligence Centre, as required in terms of this Act; *(c)* co-operate with the Council for Medical Schemes in the handling of matters of mutual interest; *(d)* promote, to the extent consistent with achieving the objective of the Financial Sector Conduct Authority, sustainable competition in the provision of financial products and financial services, including through co-operating and collaborating with the Competition Commission; *(e)* promote financial inclusion; *(f)* regularly review the perimeter and scope of financial sector regulation, and take steps to mitigate risks identified to the achievement of its objective or the effective performance of its functions; *(g)* administer the collection of levies and the distribution of amounts received in respect of levies; *(h)* conduct and publish research relevant to its objective; *(i)* monitor the extent to which the financial system is delivering fair outcomes for financial customers, with a focus on the fairness and appropriateness of financial products and financial services and the extent to which they meet the needs and reasonable expectations of financial customers; and *(j)* formulate and implement strategies and programs for financial education for the general public.".

Section 60 of the FSRA provides for the establishment of an Executive Committee, whose task is to generally oversee the management and administration of the FSCA to ensure that it is efficient and effective, and, furthermore, to act for the FSCA in an array of matters such as licensing, supervision, enforcement and the adoption of a regulatory strategy to enable the FSCA to achieve its statutory objective and policy goals.[11] It is rather the six strategic initiatives that may be noted apart from the operational objectives. In no particular order, the FSCA is required to promote financial inclusion by ensuring previously excluded South Africans are embraced in the economic mainstream by giving them timely and fair access to affordable financial products and services,[12] and must promote transformation by extending financial services and products to all demographics of South Africa in furtherance of the constitutional ideology of achieving an equitable society.[13] The FSCA must further provide a robust legal framework ensuring the fair treatment of customers throughout the typical financial product lifecycle.[14] Given the asymmetry of information between customers and financial institutions, the FSCA is required to empower customers, through financial education programmes and by promoting financial literacy, to make sound business decisions.[15] It is submitted that these objectives signal the true change that is needed in the financial services industry and that, if properly executed, has the power to transform the financial services industry for the better.

While the FSCA is primarily tasked with market-conduct regulation, one should not lose sight of the functions of the PA. This juristic entity is housed within the South African Reserve Bank (SARB) and operates "within the administration of the Reserve Bank".[16] The objectives of the PA are to promote and enhance the safety and soundness of financial institutions that provide financial products and securities services; promote and enhance the safety and soundness of market infrastructures; protect financial customers against the risk that those financial institutions may

11 Sec. 60(1) and (2) FSRA. Note that matters such as licensing, supervision, enforcement and the ombud system are harmonised between the PA and the FSCA under the FSRA.

12 FSCA, Regulatory Strategy of the Financial Sector Conduct Authority (Oct 2018), 26, https://www.fsca.co.za/Documents/FSCA_Strategy_2018.pdf (last visited 20 Aug 2019). The FSCA plans to fulfil its regulatory and supervisory priorities in the next three years – October 2018 to September 2021.

13 Ibid. 31–36.

14 Ibid. 37–43.

15 Ibid. 44–45.

16 Chapter 3, part 1, Sec. 32(2) FSRA.

fail to meet their obligations; and assist in maintaining financial stability.[17] In order to achieve its objectives, the PA is mandated to fulfil its functions as embodied in the FSRA.[18]

It would be uncanny to ignore the dire repercussions suffered by many financial systems around the globe following the Global Financial Crisis. This is one of the many reasons why the regulatory design of the prudential regulator goes a step further by expressly conferring a mandate of financial stability to the SARB. The SARB has a comprehensive overall financial stability mandate and is the apex guardian of financial stability in the South African Twin Peaks model. Both the FSCA and PA are required, as part of their objectives, to assist in maintaining financial stability. Godwin and Schmulow warned against a possible conflict of interest which may arise between the SARB and the PA given the similarly competing priorities between these two regulators.[19] The authors also considered the debate in respect of housing the PA within the SARB and how it could compromise the PA's autonomy and operational independence.[20] According to Godwin and Schmulow, it was recommended that "it will be necessary to ensure that the Prudential Authority achieves an appropriate

17 Chapter 3, part 1, Sec. 33(1) FSRA.

18 Chapter 3, part 1, Sec. 34 FSRA stipulates as follows: "**Functions** (1) In order to achieve its objective, the Prudential Authority must— *(a)* regulate and supervise, in accordance with the financial sector laws— (i) financial institutions that provide financial products or securities services; and (ii) market infrastructures; *(b)* co-operate with and assist the Reserve Bank, the Financial Stability Oversight Committee, the Financial Sector Conduct Authority, the National Credit Regulator and the Financial Intelligence Centre, as required in terms of this Act; *(c)* co-operate with the Council for Medical Schemes in the handling of matters of mutual interest; *(d)* support sustainable competition in the provision of financial products and financial services, including through co-operating and collaborating with the Competition Commission;*(e)* support financial inclusion; *(f)* regularly review the perimeter and scope of financial sector regulation, and take steps to mitigate risks identified to the achievement of its objective or the effective performance of its functions; and (g) conduct and publish research relevant to its objective." One noteworthy function is that the PA is responsible for the prudential regulation and supervision of an array of regulated financial institutions, such as banks, cooperative banks and insurers, and will assist the SARB in maintaining overall financial stability and prevent systemic events that may arise from systemically important financial institutions. See Financial Regulatory Reform Steering Committee, Implementing a Twin Peaks Model of Financial Regulation in South Africa (1 Feb 2013), 43–44, https://bit.ly/2XyMOp1 (last visited 20 Aug 2019) (henceforth referred to as FRRSC Document).

19 *Godwin* and *Schmulow*, 132 SALJ 2015, 756, 759.

20 Ibid.

level of operational independence in practice, and that the risks of conflicts of interest and competing priorities…are appropriately managed".[21] While the PA and the SARB meander through this prudential regulatory journey, the impact of their efforts will undoubtedly also contribute, albeit indirectly, towards improved market conduct regulation. It is suggested that priorities of the PA and SARB are not in fact all that similar – the SARB has the mandate for financial stability whilst the PA has the mandate for safety and soundness of financial institutions. In fact it is possible that in some instances these priorities may conflict, for example where the SARB is of the opinion that a failing financial institution should be bailed out in the interest of financial stability whereas the PA is of the opinion that such institution should be allowed to fail and exit the financial system as it lacks prudential safety and soundness.

It is evident that there are many elements that underlie the effectiveness of the Twin Peaks system. It is important to ensure that the regulatory and supervisory approaches of the PA and FSCA are harmonised across the various types of regulated financial institutions to avoid ambiguity and confusion and the FSRA does provide for an alignment of these approaches.[22] This is a positive development as harmonisation is key to financial stability.

III. Legislative instruments

1. The Financial Services Regulation Act

It is already apparent from the previous paragraph that the FSRA forms the cornerstone of Twin Peaks. As such, it provides an overarching, robust legal framework that enables strict oversight on all facets of the financial

---

21 Ibid.

22 The entire chapter 5 of the FSRA provides for co-operation and collaboration between the two financial sector regulators and the Reserve bank, as well as collaboration with other organs of state. Sec. 79 also provides for a Financial System Council of Regulators. Sec. 79(2) provides as follows: "The objective of the Financial System Council of Regulators is to facilitate co-operation and collaboration, and, where appropriate, consistency of action, between the institutions represented on the Financial System Council of Regulators by providing a forum for senior representatives of those institutions to discuss, and inform themselves about, matters of common interest.".

sector. As a point of departure, the object of the Act is set out in Section 7(1) and best quoted *verbatim*:

> "The object of this Act is to achieve a stable financial system that works in interests of financial customers and that supports balanced and sustainable economic growth in the Republic, by establishing, in conjunction with the specific financial sector laws, a regulatory and supervisory framework that promotes—
> *(a)* financial stability;
> *(b)* the safety and soundness of financial institutions;
> *(c)* the fair treatment and protection of financial customers;
> *(d)* the efficiency and integrity of the financial system;
> *(e)* the prevention of financial crime;
> *(f)* financial inclusion;
> *(g)* transformation of the financial sector; and
> *(h)* confidence in the financial system."

In addition to separating prudential and market conduct regulation, the FSRA, as alluded to above, expressly confers onto the SARB the primary responsibility of protecting and enhancing financial stability. Consider, for example, the calamitous impact an imminent bank failure or corporate scandal could have on a country's financial stability – the risks that could arise from such an impact could lead to the provision of financial products or services being curtailed, customers losing their funds, or even worse, the financial sector could succumb to severe adverse effects due to failure in customer confidence and trust. The FSRA characterises these risks as "systemic events" and should they adversely affect financial stability, the SARB will have to assume its responsibility under Section 26 (b) of the FSRA to restore and maintain financial stability.[23] The Financial Stability Oversight Committee (FSOC) supports the SARB's mandate by coordinating financial stability issues and mitigating systemic risks.[24] A Financial Sector Contingency Forum (FSCF) furthers supports the SARB in managing systemic risks, including cooperation and coordination with representatives from the financial sector industry.[25] Furthermore, the PA and the FSCA, together with other additional financial sector regulators such as

23 The term "systemic events" is defined in chapter 1, part 1, Sec. 1 FSRA.
24 The FSOC is established in terms of chapter 2, part 3, Sec. 20 FSRA.
25 The FSCF is established in terms of chapter 2, part 4, Sec. 25 FSRA.

the National Credit Regulator, are required to co-ordinate, co-operate and collaborate with the SARB to maintain financial stability.[26]

The most valuable stipulations in the FSRA relates to the manner in which the Twin Peaks system endeavours to harmonise the financial sector's regulatory and supervisory framework. See, for instance, the stipulations pertaining to prudential and market-conduct standards,[27] the fair treatment of customers by financial institutions and representatives,[28] and the issuing of joint standards.[29] Issues pertaining to governance are not new (for instance, licensing[30] and enforcement[31]).

From a consumer protection perspective, it is more important to note that the FSCA introduces an Ombud Council. The Financial Services Ombud Schemes Act (FSOS Act)[32] seeks to prioritise consumer protection by making provision for the recognition of financial services ombud schemes. A number of successful statutory and voluntary ombud systems already exist for the purposes of maintaining an unwavering stance against any unfair treatment to customers. Despite the fact that voluntary ombud systems have in the past been successful in assisting financial consumers, certain gaps and weaknesses were identified.[33] In order to improve the ombud system's effectiveness and efficiency, the Ombud Council was created in terms of Chapter 14 of the FSRA.[34] The objective of the Ombud Council is "to assist in ensuring that financial customers have access to, and are able to use, affordable, effective, independent and fair alternative dispute resolution processes for complaints about financial institutions in relation

26 Chapter 2, part 5, Sec. 26(1) FSRA.

27 Chapter 7, part 2 of the FSRA empowers the PA and the FSCA to issue standards governing specific conduct in connection with a financial product or a financial service falling within the realm of their respective authorities. The standards must be aimed at achieving their various objectives – for instance, prudential standards need to further the objective of ensuring the safety and soundness to financial institution and assisting in maintaining financial stability. See in particular chapter 2, part 2, Sec.105(2)(b) FSRA.

28 Chapter 2, part 2, Sec. 106 FSRA.

29 Chapter 2, part 2, Sec. 107 FSRA.

30 Chapter 8 FSRA.

31 Chapter 9 FSRA.

32 Financial Services Ombud Schemes Act No. 37 of 2004.

33 Gaps and weaknesses identified in the FRRSC Document (n. 18) include, among many others, consumer confusion, administrative inefficiencies, governance challenges, and inconsistencies in approach.

34 NT Media Statement 2018 (n. 5), 3.

to financial products, financial services, and services provided by market infrastructures".[35]

Although the Ombud Council will fulfil important functions such as encouraging co-operation between, and co-ordination of, the activities of ombuds, striving to protect the independence and impartiality of ombuds, taking steps to facilitate access by financial customers to appropriate ombuds, and, most importantly, monitoring the performance of ombud schemes,[36] there is the fear that the FSRA merely added another layer of bureaucracy to an already expensive system. It is, however, too soon to evaluate this development as "good" or "bad" as it might increase the effectiveness of dispute resolution.

It is evident from the discussion of key stipulations of the FSRA that it is a revolutionary legislative instrument for the financial services sector. It is all-encompassing in its nature – manifestly appreciative of the varying complexities and challenges inherent within the sector. The question one ought not to ask is whether the government has accomplished its mandate by implementing the Twin Peaks system through the FSRA to address the challenges brought about by the Global Financial Crisis. Since South Africa remained relatively unscathed by the Global Financial Crisis, it can be argued that South Africa's challenges were not brought about by the Global Financial Crisis. However, it was necessary to rethink the approach to financial regulation whilst also being mindful of the general lessons revealed by the Global Financial Crisis, such as the need for improved macroprudential supervision and the need for prudential and market conduct regulation to operate in tandem. In light of this, the question is rather whether the FSRA will weather the storm in the advent of another financial crisis. The statute does provide the armour. It is decidedly up to the troops to use it.

2. The Insurance Act

a) Aim of the Act

The Insurance Act (IA) came into effect on 1 July 2018, with the exception of a number of Sections.[37] The IA repealed quite a number of Sections of

35 Chapter 14, part 1, Sec. 176 FSRA.
36 Chapter 14, part 1, Sec. 177 FSRA.
37 See Government Gazette No. 41388 of 18 Jan 2018.

the Long Term Insurance Act (LTIA)[38] and the Short Term Insurance Act (STIA)[39] but it is important from a market-conduct regulatory perspective to note that Section 55 of the STIA and Section 62 of the LTIA were not repealed. These Sections enable the legislature to promulgate the PPRs, and, as will be discussed below, these rules form the core of the current market-conduct regulatory rules.

The main purpose of the IA is to give effect to the Twin Peaks method of financial regulation and as such, is mostly concerned with prudential matters. It is fitting to remark at the outset that the objectives of the IA are "to provide for a legal framework for the prudential regulation and supervision of insurance business in the Republic that is consistent with the Constitution of the Republic of South Africa, 1996". In addition, it promotes the maintenance of a fair, safe and stable insurance market; introduces a legal framework for microinsurance to promote financial inclusion and replaces certain parts of the Long-term Insurance Act, 1998, and the Short-term Insurance Act, 1998.[40]

At best, the stipulations in the IA may be described as prudential in nature and as such, do not have any *direct* bearing on consumer protection. This is perhaps the very heart of the matter, namely that the IA represents an important milestone on the way to complete implementation of the Twin Peaks system, illustrating that prudential matters are closely related to market conduct. It is submitted that by constituting a proper framework for insurance and by ensuring that all registered insurers are properly run, consumers are in fact protected, albeit in an indirect way. Good governance and product standards do ensure safe and stable markets.[41]

---

38 Long Term Insurance Act No. 52 of 1998.

39 Short Term Insurance Act No. 53 of 1998.

40 At present, the IA is divided into 9 chapters which deal with the interpretation and objective of the act (chapter 1), conducting insurance business and insurance group business (chapter 2), key persons and significant owners (chapter 3), licensing, suspension and withdrawal of licence (chapter 4), governance (chapter 5), financial soundness (chapter 6), reporting and public disclosures (chapter 7), transfers of business and other significant transactions (chapter 8) and resolution (chapter 9).

41 *Millard*, 21 Juta's Insurance L Bul 2018, 35, 52.

b) Classification of insurance business

Conceptually, the IA distinguishes between non-life insurance (formerly: short-term insurance) and life insurance (formerly: long-term insurance). While this new distinction is no doubt on par with international standards, the PPRs still refer to long-term insurance and short-term insurance and this dual system will remain until the PPRs are incorporated into the IA.[42] Insurance business in South Africa will henceforth be classified into life and non-life insurance as the two broad categories and for each of these categories, product classes and sub-classes have been identified.[43] These product types may further be categorised as personal and commercial insurance. The most important remark on the re-categorising of insurance in this manner is that the IA attempts to classify current insurance offerings in South Africa in a sufficiently detailed manner.[44] Save for microinsurance, none of these products are new. Classifications do not only assist in standardising product features but also relate directly to licensing requirements. Better classification of products and appropriate licensing therefore have the potential to create a compliance structure that is better able to address mis-buying and mis-selling.[45]

c) Financial inclusion and microinsurance

The objectives of financial inclusion and the introduction of microinsurance are in line with the overall objectives of the financial services industry

42 *Reinecke, Van Niekerk* and *Nienaber*, South African Insurance Law (2013), 10 remarked on the distinction in the LTIA and STIA between long-term insurance and short-term insurance: "[E]ven more anachronistic and curious is the (probably uniquely South African) division of insurance chosen by the legislature, that between long-term insurance and short-term insurance. Not only is there generally no difference in the principles applicable to long-term insurance contracts and to short-term insurance contracts, but the distinction is also not clearly based on the actual duration of the respective types of insurances.".

43 Table 1 of the IA (Life Insurance) classifies life insurance as risk, fund risk, credit life, funeral, life annuities, individual investment, fund investment, income drawdown and reinsurance. Table 2 of the IA (Non-life Insurance) classifies non-life insurance as motor, property, agriculture, engineering, marine, aviation, transport, legal expense, liability, consumer credit, trade credit, guarantee, accident and health, travel, "miscellaneous" and reinsurance.

44 *Millard* (n. 41), 53–59.

45 *Millard* (n. 41), 59.

of facilitating access to affordable financial services.[46] One of the triumphs in market-conduct regulation that speaks to the transformative power of the IA lies in the rules pertaining to microinsurance. The IA defines microinsurance business as insurance business conducted in respect of life insurance[47] and non-life insurance[48] for certain classes and limited to maximum amounts prescribed.

Although the remainder of the IA is tacit about microinsurance, the 2017 PPRs, that came into effect on 1 January 2018, were amended on 1 October 2018 to include market-conduct regulation on microinsurance.[49] Before microinsurance is discussed any further, these Rules will first be considered.

3. The Policyholder Protection Rules

a) Introduction

The current PPRs were published on 15 December 2017.[50] It is important to understand that the insurance industry has for some time made use of PPRs and that the first rules were promulgated in terms of the both the STIA and LTIA in 2001,[51] updated in 2004[52] and further amended in 2010.[53]

---

46 Ibid.

47 Classes 1 (risk), 3 (credit life), 4 (funeral) or 9 (reinsurance).

48 Classes 1 (motor), 2 (property), 3 (agriculture), 9 (legal expense), 11 (consumer credit), 14 (accident and health) and 17 (reinsurance); and class 10 (liability). In the instance of liability insurance, microinsurance policies may only be sold if those liabilities relate directly to one of the other classes mentioned.

49 *Millard* (n. 41), 60.

50 GN 1433 in Government Gazette No. 41329 of 15 Dec 2017 (in terms of Section 55 of the Short-term Insurance Act) and under GN 1407 in Government Gazette No. 41321 of 15 Dec 2017 (in terms of Section 62 of the Long-term Insurance Act).

51 GN R164 in Government Gazette No. 22084 of 23 Feb 2001 (in terms of Section 55 of the Short-term Insurance Act).

52 GN R1128 in Government Gazette No. 26853 of 30 Sept 2004 (in terms of Section 55 of the Short-term Insurance Act) and GN R1129 in Government Gazette No. 26854 of 30 Sept 2004 (in terms of Section 62 of the Long-term Insurance Act).

53 GN R1213 in Government Gazette No. 33881 of 17 Dec 2010 (in terms of Section 55 of the Short-term Insurance Act) and GN R1214 in Government Gazette No. 33881 of 17 Dec 2010 (in terms of Section 62 of the Long-term Insurance Act).

Market-conduct rules are therefore not new for insurance and have always played a role in protecting consumers[54] but the true "game-changer" in the 2018 PPRs is the inclusion of the so-called "Treating Customers Fairly" or TCF principles. Rule 1.4 of both sets of PPRs stipulate that an insurer must have appropriate policies in place to achieve fair treatment of policyholders and that such fair treatment should accomplish at least the following, well-known principles, namely:

> "*(a)*policyholders can be confident that they are dealing with an insurer where the fair treatment of policyholders is central to the insurer's culture;
> *(b)*products are designed to meet the needs of identified types, kinds or categories of policyholders and are targeted accordingly;
> *(c)*policyholders are given clear information and are kept appropriately informed before, during and after the time of entering into a policy;
> *(d)*where policyholders receive advice, the advice is suitable and takes account of their circumstances;
> *(e)*policyholders are provided with products that perform as insurers or their representatives have lead them to expect, and the associated service is both of an acceptable standard and what they have been led to expect; and
> *(f)*policyholders do not face unreasonable post-sale barriers to change or replace a policy, submit a claim or make a complaint."

54 From the outset, aspects such as arbitration, time bar clauses, days of grace and aspects of the claims process have been part of the PPRs. On the PPRs and the claims process, *Reinecke*, *Van Niekerk* and *Nienaber* (n. 42), 366 state as follows: "These rules in the main impose a range of duties on insurers as far as the claims process is concerned, duties that they either did not bear at common law or, not surprisingly, did not impose upon themselves by the terms of their insurance contracts. An insurer must accept, reject or dispute a claim or the *quantum* of a claim for a benefit under a policy within a reasonable period after receipt of 'a' (presumably 'that' and not 'any') claim. This is only fair, given that the insured is ordinarily under a duty to submit his claim to the insurer within a specified or determinable period of time after the occurrence of the event giving rise to it. What is a reasonable period will naturally depend on the circumstances of every case and, for instance, on matters such as the nature of the loss and the complexity of the claim. The insurer should be given a reasonable time, in the circumstances, to investigate the claim before coming to a decision. The insurer's obligation to decide, it seems, arises not only when it accepts the claim or rejects it outright, but also when it accepts the claim but disputes merely an aspect of it, for instance the *quantum*.".

On this basis, all market conduct regulation in fact relates to one of these outcomes and pertains to one or more of the stages of the product-life cycle.[55] For insurance, as for many financial products, a typical cycle is divided into six stages, namely: product service and design; promotion and marketing; advice; point of sale; information after point of sale; and complaints and claims handling. These will now be discussed.

b) Product service and design

Rule 2 in both sets of PPRs stipulate that insurers must, in developing products, make use of adequate information on the "needs of identified types, kinds or categories of policyholders or members". Insurers have an obligation to assess the main characteristics of a new product, the distribution methods intended to be used in relation to the product, and the disclosure documents related thereto.[56] The rule further stipulates that before an insurer may market a new product, a managing executive of the insurer must in writing approve the product and confirm that it meets the needs of those principles set out in the rule. One of the objectives of this requirement is clearly to ensure that there is a strategy behind the way in which the insurer conducts its business and that all aspects pertaining to the product are in harmony with its target market. The new categories of insurance policies as set out above, coupled with the obligations contained in the PPRs, have the potential to force insurers to put more thought into product design and this may be the impetus to combat mis-buying and mis-selling.

c) Promotion and marketing

The promotion and marketing of insurance products give rise to practices such as cold calling,[57] and in a competitive market direct marketers sell

55 *Millard* (n. 41), 38.

56 *Millard* (n. 41), 40.

57 See the enforcement action in *The Registrar of Financial Services Providers v Catsicadellis and Botha (now Greyvenstein)*, Enforcement Committee Case No. 6 of 2012, where the cold calling practices of the respondents were said to bring the financial services industry into disrepute. For a discussion of the case, see *Millard*, 76 THRHR 2013, 604–622. See also *The Registrar of Financial Services Providers v Talksure Trading (Pty) Ltd*, Enforcement Committee Case No. 20 of 2014.

insurance products telephonically, and, more often than not, chase the sale for commercial gain and not with a view to offer clients the best product to suit their needs.[58] Before the enactment of the 2018 PPRs, the Financial Advisory and Intermediary Services Act[59] prescribed standards on fairness in the promotion and marketing of insurance products.[60] In addition, the General Code of Conduct (GCC) determines that FSPs may not place advertisements that are fraudulent, untrue or misleading.[61]

Industry-specific, detailed rules on advertising in the 2018 PPRs repeat certain aspects pertaining to advertising that have formed part of the FAIS Act for quite some time, for instance the stipulations that advertising must be factually correct, provide a balanced presentation of key information and must not be misleading.[62] What is new is the definition of "advertisement" and the detailed rules of those internal processes that need to be followed before an advertisement may be placed. What is no doubt useful is a stipulation in the PPRs that advertisements should be in plain language[63] and terms used must be defined or explained if "the average targeted poli-

---

58 See e.g. *Mahadeo v Direct Insurance Ltd* 2008 4 SA 80 (W).

59 Financial Advisory and Intermediary Services Act No. 37 of 2002.

60 To this end, chapter VII, Sec. 8(8)*(b)*, FAIS Act stipulates that a provider must, in all its business documentation, advertisements and other promotional material, include a reference to the fact that it holds a licence. The insertion of "an authorised Financial Services Provider" in all documentation and advertisements ensures compliance with this requirement. See para. 14 of BN 80 of 2003. For instance, where performance data is included, the source and date of the source must be provided (para. 14 of BN 80 of 2003); where it uses illustrations, forecasts or hypothetical data, it must include the assumptions, clarify that they are not guaranteed and only used for illustrative purposes and indicate whether the returns are dependent on underlying assets or variable market factors. There must also be a warning of the risk involved in relying on the illustrations, forecasts or hypothetical data and a statement that past performance is not an indication of future performance (para. 14(1)(*b*)(ii) of BN 80 of 2003). Where investment values are not guaranteed, there should also be a statement to that effect (para. 14(1)(*c*) of BN 80 of 2003). See *Millard* and *Hattingh*, The FAIS Act Explained: A Guide to Understanding the Financial Advisory and Intermediaries Act 37 of 2002 (2016), 114; *The Registrar of Short-term Insurance v Discovery Insurance Limited*, Enforcement Committee Case No. 28 of 2015, available at www.fsca.co.za, as discussed in *Millard*, 18 Juta's Insurance L Bul 2015, 81, 82. The Enforcement Committee is the FSCA's (previously, FSB's) watchdog that ensures compliance with all the statutes that fall within its jurisdiction.

61 Para. 14 of BN 80 of 2003.

62 Rules 10.4.2 to 10.4.12.

63 Rule 10.7.1.

cyholder could not reasonably be expected to understand them".[64] Unfortunately it is extremely difficult to determine the level of understanding of the average, targeted policyholder. Hence, although the principles of plain language can be lauded in the context of financial services, it will be difficult to judge whether any particular advertisement did comply with this rule. This is an excellent example of a well-intended rule the execution of which is likely to give rise to difficulties in practice.[65]

d) Advice and point of sale

Although advice and point of sale are two distinct stages in the product-life cycle, it often happens that advice pertaining to, and the sale of insurance products, take place at the same time. As with advertising, detailed rules on how advice is to be provided in relation to financial products have to date been part of the FAIS Act. The fact that new rules have been incorporated into the PPRs is evidence of the fact that these rules have now been tailor-made for the insurance industry, and that product-specific advice has been written into the PPRs. This argument is supported by rule 3.1 in the short-term PPRs ("Credit life and consumer credit insurance") which stipulates that an insurer "must not provide a mandatory credit life insurance policy to a policyholder, unless that policy and the costs associated with that policy comply with any relevant credit life insurance regulations made by the Minister of Trade and Industry under Section 171 of the National Credit Act".[66] Another example is found in rule 4 on cooling-off rights. This rule stipulates that a policyholder may cancel a policy within 14 days, provided that no claim has been made.[67] Further examples abound, for instance negative option selection of policy terms and conditions,[68] determining premiums and excesses,[69] void provisions,[70] waiver of rights[71] and

64 Rule 10.7.2.

65 The remainder of the rules on advertising cover aspects such as record keeping of advertisements (rule 10.8), negative option marketing (rule 10.8), unwanted direct advertising (rule 10.10), comparative marketing (rule 10.11), puffery (rule 10.12), endorsements (rule 10.13), loyalty benefits or bonuses (rule 10.14), and prominence (rule 10.15).

66 *Millard* (n. 41), 42.

67 *Millard* (n. 41), 42.

68 Rule 5.

69 Rule 6.

70 Rule 7.

71 Rule 8.

signing of blank and uncompleted forms.[72] These rules no doubt set the minimum standards for market conduct and it is submitted that while some of these aspects have in the past formed part of common law, they have now been codified.

One of the most important market-conduct aspects that form part of advice and point of sale pertains to disclosure duties. As with other aspects, the GCC in terms of the FAIS Act has also made provision for disclosure duties on insurers but the PPRs now contain several rules on disclosures, which may be categorised as disclosure duties on insurers in general,[73] du-

---

72 Rule 9.

73 Rule 11. To illustrate the point, for purposes of clarity, rule 11.3.1 is quoted *verbatim*: "Language and format 11.3.1 Any communication by an insurer to a policyholder in relation to a policy must— *(a)* be in plain language; *(b)* not be misleading; *(c)* be provided using an appropriate medium, taking into account the complexity of the information being provided; *(d)* where applicable, be in clear and readable print size, spacing and format; and *(e)* in respect of any amount, sum, premium, value, charge, fee, remuneration or monetary obligation mentioned or referred to therein, be stated in actual monetary terms, provided that where any such amount, sum, premium, value, charge, fee, remuneration or monetary obligation is not reasonably pre-determinable, its basis of calculation must be clearly and appropriately described." Rule 11.3.2 is entitled "Timing of the provision of information to policyholders" and provides as follows: "Subject to any specific provision in this rule relating to the timing of the provision of information, an insurer must take reasonable steps to ensure that a policyholder is given appropriate information about a policy in good time so that the policyholder can make an informed decision about the policy prior to inception and throughout the duration of the policy." 11.3.3 provides as follows: "In determining what is 'in good time', an insurer must consider the importance of the information to the policyholder's decision-making process and the point at which the information may be most useful." Furthermore, on the "content of the provision of information to policyholders" rule 11.3.4 provides as follows: "Information provided must enable a policyholder to understand the features of the policy and help the policyholder understand whether it meets the policyholder's requirements. In determining the level of information to be disclosed the insurer must consider— *(a)* the factually established or reasonably assumed knowledge and experience of the policyholder or average targeted policyholder at whom the communication is targeted; *(b)* the policy terms and conditions, including its main benefits, exclusions, limitations, conditions and its duration; *(c)* the policy's overall complexity, including whether it is entered into together with other goods and services; and *(d)* whether the same information has been provided to the policyholder previously and, if so, when." Rule 11.3.5 further complicates matters by stating that "An insurer must take particular care to provide adequate information in respect of more complex or bundled features which are likely to be difficult for a policyholder to understand, particularly regarding the costs and

ties before a policy is entered into,[74] duties after the inception of the policy[75] and ongoing disclosure.[76] Again, although these stipulations no doubt to bring about better protection for consumers through the provision of information, it is another example of ambitious and detailed regulation that "sounds right" but may be a nightmare to implement. It is, however, too soon to judge whether these disclosure requirements may be evaluated as triumphs of consumer rights. This is equally true of ongoing disclosures.[77]

---

risks involved, including defining or explaining terms that could not reasonably be expected to be understood."

74 Rule 11.4.

75 Rule 11.5.

76 Rule 11.6.

77 Rule 11.6 provides that insurers must, on an ongoing basis, disclose information on terms and conditions and changes thereto. Rule 11.6.1 stipulates that an insurer must in writing disclose to the policyholder information on any contractual changes during the duration of the policy and, on an ongoing basis, disclose to the policyholder relevant information depending on the type of policy. In addition, rule 11.6.2, dealing with ongoing information on terms and conditions, stipulates as follows: "Information that must be provided on an ongoing basis, and at least annually, includes any changes to information referred to in rules 11.4 and 11.5 to the extent that the policyholder can reasonably be expected to require such information in order to make an informed decision as to whether the policy continues to meet the policyholder's requirements." Furthermore, rule 11.6.3 dealing with information on changes to terms and conditions, stipulates: "An insurer must provide the following to a policyholder in writing— (a) notification of any change to the premium payable under a policy; (b) appropriate details of the reasons for any change to the premium payable under a policy; (c) appropriate details of the reasons for any change to the provisions, terms or conditions of the policy, together with an explanation of the implications of that change; (d) appropriate details of any change to or addition to the information referred to in rules 11.4 and 11.5 arising from any change referred to in paragraphs (a) to (c); and (e) an explanation of the policyholder's rights and obligations regarding such changes, including what cooling-off rights are offered and procedures for the exercise thereof." Further disclosures are required where the policy is renewed. Rule 11.6.5 dealing with information on renewal of the policy stipulates as follows: "An insurer must, at least 31 days before the renewal date of a policy, where applicable, provide the following to a policyholder in writing— *(a)* the premium to be paid by the policyholder on renewal of the policy; *(b)* the premium last paid by the policyholder under the policy to enable the policyholder to compare the premium to the premium referred to in paragraph *(a); (c)* any change to the terms or conditions on renewal of the policy, together with an explanation of the implications of that change; *(d)* any change to or addition to the information referred to in rules 11.4 and 11.5 arising from the renewal; *(e)* the policyholder's rights and obligations regarding the renewal, including what cooling-off rights

e) Information after point of sale

Rule 11.6 dealing with ongoing disclosures was discussed above. Further stipulations on information after point of sale are contained in rule 13 on data management, rule 15 on periods of grace and rule 17 on claims management. As with the other stages, the rules promote fairness as the underlying value. It is submitted that insurance products differ from banking and credit as financial instruments. In the case of insurance, in the absence of any claims, there is relatively little contact between the insurer and policyholder during the currency of the policy. The policyholder pays the premium and the insurer carries the risk and "no news is good news". Hence, unless there are premium increases or other policy stipuations that change and must be communicated, there is relatively little need for the insurer to do anything. In the banking and credit environment, however, there are numerous transactions between the provider and the customer and fairness takes on an entirely different dimension as a great variety of daily transactions may potentially lead to the unfair treatment of customers. In this sense, insurers may find it easier to comply with fairness requirements.

f) Complaints and claims handling

Apart from the internal claims management process that an insurer must henceforth have in place (which is essentially a compliance aspect), rule 17.8 on communications with claimants drives home the important point that much is expected from insurers when handling claims. The rule stipulates that an insurer must ensure that claims processes and proce-

---

are offered and procedures for the exercise thereof; and *(f)* a statement indicating that the policyholder should consider whether the level of cover to be offered on the renewal is appropriate for the policyholder's needs.".

Rule 11.6.6 stipulates that an insurer must provide the policyholder with a written notification in the event that it did not receive the premium payable under a policy and rule 11.6.7 further states that the notification referred to in rule 11.6.6 must be sent to the policyholder in good time, but no later than 15 days after the insurer became aware of the non-payment of the premium. In instances of non-payment, rule 11.6.6 stipulates that an insurer must provide the policyholder with a written notification in the event that it did not receive the premium payable under a policy and rule 11.6.7 further states that the notification referred to in rule 11.6.6 must be sent to the policyholder in good time, but no later than 15 days after the insurer became aware of the non-payment of the premium.

dures are transparent, visible and "accessible through channels that are appropriate to the insurer's policyholders and claimants".[78] Furthermore, all communications must be in plain language[79] and an insurer must disclose to a claimant the type of information required from the claimant;[80] where, how and to whom a claim and related information must be submitted;[81] any time limits on submitting claims;[82] any excesses payable by the claimant;[83] details of any administrative fee payable in relation to management of the claim;[84] and any other relevant responsibilities of the claimant.[85] Further stipulations require insurers only to require from a claimant information or documentation which is essential to the assessment of the claim[86] and to keep claimants informed of the progress of their claims, reasons for any delays, and, most importantly, the insurer's decision in response to the claim.[87] These rules are aimed at being fair to the policyholder and every single aspect of the claims procedure is now subject to rules. Where this article has commented that the detailed rules for the other stages in the product-life cycle may constitute an "overkill", this is not true of claims, as unfairness has always been particularly evident from the way in which insurance companies handled claims.[88]

Rule 18 also provides for the establishment of a complaints management framework to ensure that insurers treat claimants fairly. Fair treatment must be proportionate to the nature, scale and complexity of the

---

78 Rule 17.8.1.
79 Rule 17.8.2.
80 Rule 17.8.3*(a)*.
81 Rule 17.8.3*(b)*.
82 Rule 17.8.3*(c)*.
83 Rule 17.8.3*(d)*.
84 Rule 17.8.3*(e)*.
85 Rule 17.8.3*(f)*. In addition, rule 17.8.4 stipulates as follows: "A claim is deemed to have been received on the day the insurer or its representative or an independent intermediary, binder holder or any other service provider that has been mandated by the insurer to manage claims on its behalf, receives notification thereof and an insurer or such independent intermediary, binder holder, service provider or representative must within a reasonable time after receipt of a claim acknowledge receipt thereof and inform a claimant of the process to be followed in processing the claim, including *(a)* contact details of the person or department that will be processing the claim; *(b)* indicative timelines for finalising the claim; and *(c)* details of any outstanding requirements.".
86 Rule 17.8.5.
87 Rule 17.8.6.
88 See e.g. *Barkhuizen v Napier* 2007 5 SA 323 (CC).

insurer's business and risks[89] must be appropriate to the business model, policies, services, policyholders and beneficiaries,[90] and must not impose unreasonable barriers on complainants.[91] The detail contained in rule 18 is quite staggering. It is submitted that the portion on communication with claimants again evidences the way in which fairness is part and parcel of market conduct regulation.[92]

Overall, it is evident that the new PPRs cover matters that have not previously formed part of insurance legislation and focus very sharply on fairness and transparency. This is undoubtedly heralded as one of the triumphs of market-conduct regulation and is expected to provide consumers with real, enforceable remedies.

4. The COFI Bill

In what signals the next step towards the Twin Peaks system, the Conduct of Financial Institutions Bill (COFI) was published on 11 December 2018, inviting comments before 1 April 2019. While the FSRA describes the

89 Rule 18.2.1*(a)*.

90 Rule 18.2.1*(b)*.

91 Rule 18.2.1*(d)*.

92 Rule 18.9 entitled "Communication with complainants" stipulates as follows: "18.9.1 An insurer must ensure that its complaint processes and procedures are transparent, visible and accessible through channels that are appropriate to the insurer's policyholders and beneficiaries. 18.9.2 An insurer may not impose any charge for a complainant to make use of complaint processes and procedures. 18.9.3 All communications with a complainant must be in plain language. 18.9.4 An insurer must, wherever feasible, provide policyholders with a single point of contact for submitting complaints. 18.9.5 An insurer must disclose to a complainant— *(a)* the type of information required from a complainant; *(b)* where, how and to whom a complaint and related information must be submitted; *(c)* expected turnaround times in relation to complaints; and *(d)* any other relevant responsibilities of a complainant. 18.9.6 An insurer must within a reasonable time after receipt of a complaint acknowledge receipt thereof and promptly inform a complainant of the process to be followed in handling the complaint, including— *(a)* contact details of the person or department that will be handling the complaint; *(b)* indicative timelines for addressing the complaint; *(c)* details of the internal complaints escalation and review process if the complainant is not satisfied with the outcome of a complaint; and *(d)* details of escalation of complaints to the office of a relevant Ombud where applicable. 18.9. Complainants must be kept adequately informed of— *(a)* the progress of their complaint; *(b)* causes of any delay in the finalisation of a complaint and revised timelines; and *(c)* the insurer's decision in response to the complaint.".

duties of financial institutions towards the financial sector regulators, the COFI Bill provides the draft regulatory framework that outlines the relationship between financial consumers and industry players. According to the National Treasury, the Bill "aims to significantly streamline the legal framework for the regulation of the conduct of the financial institutions, and to give legislative effect to the market conduct policy approach, including implementation of the Treating Customers Fairly (TCF) principles".[93] The COFI Bill is envisaged to be a more principles-based than rules-based regulatory framework.

The regulatory framework of the COFI Bill is designed to replace the conduct provisions of most existing financial sector laws.[94] In the same way that the Financial Services Board (FSB) regulated financial institutions under the Financial Services Board Act,[95] the FSCA currently has jurisdiction over the market conduct of all financial institutions in South Africa in terms of the FSRA. This statute defines a financial institution as any entity that provides a financial product or financial service, and while some financial institutions will require a direct conduct licence from the FSCA in terms of the COFI Bill[96] licensing process, other institutions will be licensed and supervised through other laws and subject to requirements of the COFI Bill.[97] In this respect, there are similarities between the FAIS Act and the COFI Bill. Another similarity is the Bill's focus on requirements set for persons performing critical functions. These key individuals are, for instance, the chief executive officer, director, actuary or compliance officer who fulfil a "critical governance function".[98]

The Bill has been published for comment and will no doubt be amended before finally becoming law, which is why it is prudent to provide an overview of the prominent features of the Bill only, starting with its (rather ambitious) objectives. Clause 3 states that the object of the COFI Act is to "establish a consolidated, comprehensive and consistent regulatory framework for the conduct of financial institutions". The clause further

93 National Treasury, "Media Statement: Invitation for Public Comments on the Draft Conduct of Financial Institutions Bill 2018" (11 Dec 2018), https://bit.ly/2UHBoAq (last visited on 20 Aug 2019).

94 National Treasury, Explanatory Policy Paper Accompanying the Conduct of Financial Institutions Bill – Paper accompanying the first draft of the COFI Bill (2018), 20, https://bit.ly/2IiouCo (last visited on 20 Aug 2019) (henceforth referred to as NT Explanatory Policy Paper).

95 Financial Services Board Act No. 97 of 1990.

96 Seeing that it still is only a Bill, the word "Bill" will be used throughout.

97 NT Explanatory Policy Paper (n. 94), 20.

98 Ibid.

stipulates that the act should protect financial customers, promote the fair treatment and protection of financial customers by financial institutions, support fair, transparent and efficient financial markets, promote innovation and the development of and investment in innovative technologies, processes and practices, promote trust and confidence in the financial sector, promote sustainable competition in the provision of financial products and financial services, promote financial inclusion, promote transformation of the financial sector and assist the South African Reserve Bank in maintaining financial stability.

The FSCA will be able to regulate smaller providers which pose low conduct risk and should therefore not be subject to onerous compliance structures. This means that as the regulator, the FSCA will be mandated to devise a proportionate supervisory approach that takes into account the "nature, size, scale and complexity of the risks associated with a type of activity or financial institution".[99] This is in fact an innovation that can be welcomed, seeing that one of the most important objectives of Twin Peaks is to promote access to financial products and to open the markets to previously disadvantaged consumers. If the regulatory framework supports financial inclusion by supervising according to the size of any particular business, financial inclusion is not an overly ambitious ideal.

Whether the COFI Bill, once enacted, will be a triumph in its entirety is an open question. A tentative opinion is that, while the FAIS Act was the correct statute for its time, the COFI Bill has the advantage of moving away from one-size-fits-all compliance without compromising on clear, strict rules pertaining to the conduct of financial institutions. Therefore, the fundamental understanding that COFI should be principles-based signals a much-needed shift away from an overly rules-based approach. As the final piece in the Twin Peaks puzzle, the COFI Bill will bring together all the loose strands that will see the two peaks settle into their rightful place in the South African financial landscape. A detailed discussion of this Bill is not only premature but also falls outside of the scope of this discussion due to the Bill comprising some 118 clauses, all of which are rather complex.

99 NT Explanatory Policy Paper (n. 94), 16; see clause 7 of the COFI Bill.

IV. Critical evaluation

The Twin Peaks system is aimed at streamlining the regulatory environment by integrating all financial institutions. This means that there will be broad generic rules with which financial institutions will have to comply (for example in relation to market practices) by virtue of being financial institutions but this does not mean sector specific laws are going to fall away.

The rational underpinning of this approach is that all institutions providing financial services should be recognised as "financial institutions" and authority needs to be conferred onto the PA and the FSCA to fulfil their defined mandates relating to market conduct and financial soundness respectively. Both bodies will have broad jurisdiction over the financial sector.[100] By including all financial institutions under Twin Peaks, holistic systemwide surveillance will be better accomodated and the system will be able to respond better to risks and curb them before they morph into disasters that affect the entire financial services industry and lead to financial ruin for consumers. As a concept, the system comprises all the checks and balances to ensure that errant role players are taken to task and the FSCA is duty-bound to take administrative action by undertaking appropriate remedial and enforcement action for such misconduct.[101] This public power is characteristic of a strong and effective market conduct authority and it recognises the fact that market failure in one business or area (such as investments) has a knock-on effect in the highly interconnected financial system that can destabilise the entire economy. Conversely, such power must be counterbalanced by robust measures to ensure that it is exercised responsibly, fairly and consistently with the law.[102]

As far as market conduct regulation is concerned, it is submitted that the FSRA, IA, PPRs and COFI Bill form a strong foundation upon which market conduct regulation in South Africa will rest. It is also evident from this contribution that the mandate of the FSCA is not a "copy and paste"

100 NT response and explanatory document (n. 9), 10.

101 Sec. 92 and 93 of the FSRA.

102 Notably, administrative action should be taken fairly and in accordance with Sec. 33 of the Constitution of the Republic of South Africa, 1996 which guarantees the right to administrative justice. In addition, administrative action should be taken in accordance with the Promotion of Administrative Justice Act No. 3 of 2000, and this means, inter alia, that any person who is subject to administrative action should be given the opportunity to be heard.

of its predecessor, the FSB.[103] Rather, the scope of the FSCA's activities has been widened extensively so as to extend consumer protection to as many consumers as possible. The mandate of the FSCA even includes taking enforcement action against unregistered business that does not meet the definition of a financial product. In serious cases, the FSCA can refer the matter to, and work in collaboration with, the National Prosecuting Authority (NPA) to enable criminal prosecution. Brandon Topham, the FSCA's new Divisional Executive for Investigations and Enforcement, revealed in a recent article that "[t]here are a number of cases where the regulator has investigated and identified potential criminal activity, but the matters either take many years to get to court or no criminal conviction is obtained".[104] It is therefore hoped that the FSCA's Investigations and Enforcement team will dedicate themselves to ensuring a safer financial services industry by effectively prosecuting transgressors. This requires close cooperation between the FSCA and the NPA.[105]

Other triumphs include a memorandum of understanding between the FSCA and the National Credit Regulator to ensure that regulatory gaps are closed and that no single financial service, product or instrument falls through the cracks. This is long overdue as services such as medical schemes have for years been treated differently from other financial services.

A more cynical perspective on Twin Peaks is that it was in fact possible to regulate market conduct effectively throughout the financial services industry by bringing about changes to the existing FAIS Act, most notably the definition Section that stipulates what should be regarded as a financial product. Furthermore, although "advice" and "intermediary services" were central to the FAIS Act and the statute perhaps over-emphasised these aspects and did not place as much emphasis on other aspects pertaining to financial services and products (such as product design and complaints handling), it is submitted that the General Code of Conduct ("GCC") in terms of the FAIS Act already addressed several aspects pertaining to all the

---

103 It should be noted that the FSCA is not just the "old FSB". It is, however, true that the FSB was the institution that was tasked with market-conduct regulation before the Twin Peaks system was introduced.

104 *Geldenhuys*, "FSCA investigations and enforcement" (14 Mar 2019), https://www.moonstone.co.za/fsca-investigations-and-enforcement/ (last visited 20 Aug 2019).

105 Ibid.

stages in the financial product life cycle.[106] It is debatable whether it was in fact necessary to draft a brand new statute on market conduct. The rules contained in the GCC could have been scaled to the size of the business in question and that would have dispensed of the criticism that the FAIS Act follows a "one size fits all" approach.

In addition, it is submitted that the new bureaucracy will be expensive and the costs of compliance and governance will be just as high, if not higher, than it has been. This simply means that financial services and products will remain expensive and this will further discourage South Africans from using formal financial products to manage their finances properly. The rather complicated, espensive new regulatory framework will also deter new role players from setting up shop and the effect could be the opposite of what is intended by the COFI Bill, namely to encourage black-owned enterprises to participate in the financial services industry.

A further point of criticism against the IA is that the setting of product standards by the PA will have the effect of limiting insurance companies to certain categories of products and services only, thereby depriving insurers of the opportunity to market and sell products to consumers that provide them with a competitive edge. Although minimum standards enable consumers to compare products with each other, the profit motive in insurance should not be under-estimated: it is precisely this feature that supports the sustainable growth and solvency of insurance companies. A "cookie cutter" approach is dangerous, especially since regulators are not well-positioned to predict what the market needs and wants.

V. *Conclusion*

The Twin Peaks ideal is no doubt evident from these legislative instruments and the mammoth task of establishing a sound basis for consumer protection has now been accomplished. As has been indicated throughout the text, several statutory provisions aim at regulating market conduct. In this respect it should be noted that although the idea may have been to move towards principles-based financial regulation, the detailed rules that have seen the light so far, we submit, indicate that the system remains very

106 The GCC contains stipulations on the specific duties of an FSP when rendering financial services (the entire clause 3), avoidance of a conflict of interest (clause 3A), confidentiality (clause 3(3), contact with clients (clause 6(*a*)), duties when rendering financial services (clause 4(3), disclosure requirements (clause 4(1) and reporting to clients where ongoing financial services are rendered (s 7(4)).

much rules-based. This is somewhat disappointing but not unexpected. It is further suggested that more bureaucrats will be needed to manage financial oversight successfully in accordance with this legislation, and, no doubt, the new structures will increase the cost of compliance.

It is submitted that the long and winding road to Twin Peaks is now nearly at its end seeing that COFI has yet to be enacted. While it is too soon to evaluate the success of this model, it is clearly evident that market conduct has been placed on a sound footing. The legislative framework shines a light into every dark corner and leaves absolutely no doubt as to the fact that the legislature has accomplished what it has set out to do. The twin regulatory model is in place. Whether role players will one day herald this as the best route to establish fair and safe markets, is an open question.

Bibliography

Financial Regulatory Reform Steering Committee, Implementing a Twin Peaks Model of Financial Regulation in South Africa (1 Feb 2013), https://bit.ly/2XyMOp1 (last visited 20 Aug 2019).

FSCA, Regulatory Strategy of the Financial Sector Conduct Authority (Oct 2018), https://www.fsca.co.za/Documents/FSCA_Strategy_2018.pdf (last visited 20 Aug 2019).

Janine Geldenhuys, "FSCA investigations and enforcement" (14 Mar 2019), https://www.moonstone.co.za/fsca-investigations-and-enforcement/ (last visited 20 Aug 2019).

Andrew Godwin, *Timothy Howse* and *Ian Ramsay*, "Twin Peaks: South Africa's Financial Sector Regulatory Framework", 134 SALJ 2017, 665.

Andrew Godwin and *Andrew Schmulow*, "The Financial Sector Regulation Bill in South Africa, Second Draft: Lessons from Australia", 132 SALJ 2015, 756.

Daleen Millard, "Hello, POPI: On Cold Calling, Financial Intermediaries and Advisors and the Protection of Personal Information Bill", 76 THRHR 2013, 604.

Daleen Millard, 18 Juta's Insurance L Bul 2015, 81.

Daleen Millard, 21 Juta's Insurance L Bul 2018, 35.

Daleen Millard and *Wendy Hattingh*, The FAIS Act Explained : A Guide to Understanding the Financial Advisory and Intermediaries Act 37 of 2002 (LexisNexis, Durban 2016).

National Treasury, Explanatory Policy Paper Accompanying the Conduct of Financial Institutions Bill – Paper accompanying the first draft of the COFI Bill (2018), https://bit.ly/2IiouCo (last visited on 20 Aug 2019).

National Treasury, "Media Statement: Invitation for Public Comments on the Draft Conduct of Financial Institutions Bill 2018" (11 Dec 2018), https://bit.ly/2UHBoAq (last visited on 20 Aug 2019).

National Treasury, "New Twin Peaks Regulators Established" (29 Mar 2018), https://bit.ly/2UBiKKt (last visited 20 Aug 2019).

National Treasury, Twin Peaks in South Africa: Response and Explanatory Document (Dec 2014), https://juta.co.za/media/filestore/2015/03/2014_12_12_Response_document.pdf (last visited 20 Aug 2019).

Gerda van Niekerk and *Corlia van Heerden*, "Twin Peaks: The Role of the South African Central Bank in Promoting and Maintaining Financial Stability", 80 THRHR 2017, 636.

Darshana Rajendaran, "Approaches to financial regulation and the case of South Africa" (6 Mar 2012), https://www.dvara.com/blog/2012/03/06/approaches-to-financial-regulation-and-the-case-of-south-africa/ (last visited 20 Aug 2019).

Machiel Fredrick Briedenhann Reinecke, *Johan Petrus van Niekerk* and *Petrus Millar Nienaber*, South African Insurance Law (LexisNexis South Africa, Durban 2013).

Andrew Schmulow, "Financial Regulatory Governance in South Africa: The Move Towards Twin Peaks", 25 Afr. J. Int'l & Comp. L. 2017, 393.

Register of cases

Barkhuizen v Napier 2007 5 SA 323 (CC).

Mahadeo v Direct Insurance Ltd 2008 4 SA 80 (W).

The Registrar of Financial Services Providers v Catsicadellis and Botha (now Greyvenstein), Enforcement Committee Case No. 6 of 2012.

The Registrar of Financial Services Providers v Talksure Trading (Pty) Ltd, Enforcement Committee Case No. 20 of 2014.

The Registrar of Short-term Insurance v Discovery Insurance Limited, Enforcement Committee Case No. 28 of 2015.

Comment: Market-Conduct Regulation in Germany and Europe

Thomas M.J. Möllers[*]

* Thomas M.J. Möllers, *Dr. iur.*; Professor, University of Augsburg Faculty of Law. Managing Director of the Center for European Legal Studies. Chair for Civil Law, Economic Law, European Law, Private International Law and Comparative Law.

I. Introduction

The following notes reflect on the supervisory systems of Germany and Europe in the field of capital markets law. The developments over the last 10 years will not only be outlined, but also critically examined. The balance sheet scandal and insolvency of Wirecard in Summer 2020 demonstrates very well, that the German and European Capital Market Law still contain a lot of loopholes.[1]

II. The supervisory system in German capital markets law

1. The current position – a critical analysis

a) The BaFin

On 1 May 2002, the former supervisory institutions for banks, insurance companies and securities were merged into one authority, the Federal Financial Supervisory Authority (*Bundesanstalt für Finanzdienstleistungsaufsicht* – the BaFin).[2] Due to its wide-ranging responsibilities, it is sometimes referred to as a universal financial supervisory body (*Allfinanzaufsicht*). The rationale for this merger was that insurance companies offered financial services as well, so joint supervision was more sensible than allocating responsibilities to several different authorities.[3] However, there is no such universal financial supervisory authority at the European level.[4] The six stock markets in Germany are supervised by private trade-monitoring offices.[5] In addition, the public prosecutor's office has jurisdiction over cases

---

1 For further reading cf. *Bundesministerium der Finanzen*, Sachstandbericht und Chronologie Wirecard v. 16.7.2020, https://www.bundesfinanzministerium.de/Content/DE/Standardartikel/Themen/Internationales_Finanzmarkt/Finanzmarktpolitik/2020-07-17-Sachstandsbericht-Wirecard.pdf?__blob=publicationFile&v=3 (last visited 7 Oct 2020).

2 In the past, there were the Federal Banking Supervisory Office (*Bundesaufsichtsamt für Kreditwesen* – BAKred), the Federal Securities Trading Supervisory Office (*Bundesaufsichtsamt für den Wertpapierhandel* – BAWe) and the Federal Insurance Office (*Bundesaufsichtsamt für das Versicherungswesen* – BAV).

3 *Buck-Heeb*, Kapitalmarktrecht (10th ed. 2018), para. 1192.

4 See below III.

5 See Section 7 Stock Exchange Act (*Börsengesetz* – BörsG). In Germany, there are six stock exchanges in Düsseldorf, Frankfurt am Main, Hamburg, Munich, Stuttgart and Berlin.

involving potential criminal offences. While the BaFin monitors compliance with market regulations, the Federal Bank of Germany is responsible for banking supervision, for example ensuring that the bank has sufficient capital.[6]

In accordance with the Freedom of Information Act (*Informationsfreiheitsgesetz* – IFG), any citizen can generally ask to inspect the BaFin's files. The BaFin has opposed this for a long time, as they regard the confidentiality of their cooperation with the investment service providers as being at risk.[7] However, professional secrecy can mitigate this claim. The European Court of Justice (ECJ) recently emphasised that professional secrecy can only be invoked as a restriction on the right to information if the interests of the person disclosing, or of a third person, are at risk.[8] Furthermore, a citizen cannot file a claim for damages if the BaFin breaches its supervisory duties. This is clear from Section 4(4) of the Act Establishing the Federal Financial Supervisory Authority (*Gesetz über die Bundesanstalt für Finanzdienstleistungsaufsicht* – FinDAG), which stipulates that the BaFin only works in the public interest. The ECJ considered this to be compliant with European law.[9]

b) The relationship between supervisory authorities and the public prosecutor's office

European capital markets law has significantly tightened sanctions over the last couple of years, for example for the offence of market abuse.[10] Notably, market manipulation proceedings at the BaFin have been increasing for years. The number of proceedings handed over to the public prosecu-

---

6 Cf. Section 5 Banking Act (*Kreditwesengesetz* – KWG); BVerfG, Judgment of 24 Jul 1962, 2 BvF 4/61 et al., BVerfGE 14, 197, 218.

7 To the previous legal situation see *Möllers* and *Wenninger*, 170 ZHR 2006, 455; BVerwG, Judgment of 24 May 2011, 7 C 6/10, ZIP 2011, 1313 – Auskunftsanspruch gegenüber BaFin; with comments *Möllers* and *Niedorf*, EWiR 2011, 569; ECJ, Judgment of 12 Nov 2014, C-140/13, ECLI:EU:C:2014:2362, para. 42 – Altmann et al. v. BaFin.

8 ECJ, Judgment of 19 Jun 2018, C-15/16, ECLI:EU:C:2018:464, para. 46 – BaFin v. Baumeister; to this *Herz*, NJW 2018, 2601 et seqq.; *Holzborn* and *Israel*, WM 2004, 1948, 1950.

9 ECJ, Judgment of 12 Oct 2004, C-222/02, ECLI:EU:C:2004:606, para. 30 – Paul et al.; BGH, Judgment of 20 Jan 2005, III ZR 48/01, BGHZ 162, 49 – Staatshaftung bei fehlerhafter Bankenaufsicht.

10 Council Directive 2014/57/EU of 16 Apr 2014 (market abuse directive).

tor's office have also increased significantly: from 22 proceedings in 2007 to 291 proceedings in 2015, and then to 300 proceedings in 2016.[11] However, in 2015 and 2016, more than 300 proceedings were closed, but only 6 and 10 respectively led to post-trial convictions. This is equivalent to only 2 to 3 % of proceedings.[12] In Germany, the public prosecutor's office is responsible for the crime scene according to Section 143 of the Courts Constitutional Act (*Gerichtsverfassungsgesetz* – GVG) read with Sections 7 et seq. of the Code of Criminal Procedure (*Strafprozessordnung* – StPO). This can be the crime scene itself, a place of residence, or the location or place of capture.[13] While greater expertise is available in larger cities and federal states, this does not apply to every public prosecutor's office in every federal state. Even in the larger public prosecutor's offices, it is openly acknowledged that know-how in the area of market manipulation is only partially available, and that reliance has to be placed on the BaFin's expertise. After all, criminal law only contemplates natural persons as offenders. There is no corporate criminal liability in Germany.[14] As long as it is not possible to attribute the conduct in question to an individual perpetrator, no conviction will follow.

11 The BaFin annual reports are instructive here; for older figures see *Fleischer,* in: Fuchs (ed.), Wertpapierhandelsgesetz (2nd ed. 2016), vor § 20a, para. 38 et seqq.; *Mock*, in: Hirte and Möllers (eds.), Kölner Kommentar zum WpHG (2nd ed. 2014), § 20a, para. 73; *Maume*, 180 ZHR 2016, 358, 373 et seqq.

12 BaFin, Jahresbericht der Bundesanstalt für Finanzdienstleistungsaufsicht 2015 (2016), 232; BaFin, Jahresbericht der Bundesanstalt für Finanzdienstleistungsaufsicht 2016 (2017), 177 et seqq.

13 Critically already *Maume*, 180 ZHR 2016, 358, 392.

14 Regarding this discussion: legislation proposal of the state North Rhine-Westphalia – Gesetz zur Einführung der strafrechtlichen Verantwortlichkeit von Unternehmen und sonstigen Verbänden, https://www.landtag.nrw.de/Dokumentenservice/portal/WWW/dokumentenarchiv/Dokument/MMI16-127.pdf;jsessionid=650FA1EF38D5AB386263C E7DD 6723AAA.ifxworker (last visited 7 Oct 2020); *Kempf* et al., Unternehmensstrafrecht (2012); *Pieth* and *Ivory*, Corporate Criminal Liability (2011); *Schmitt-Leonardy*, Unternehmenskriminalität ohne Strafrecht? (2013); *Tschierschke*, Die Sanktionierung des Unternehmensverbundes (2013); *Bosch*, Organisationsverschulden in Unternehmen (2002); *Kubiciel*, Kölner Papiere zur Kriminalpolitik 2/2014 (Feb 2014), https://assets.uni-augsburg.de/media/filer_public/59/a2/59a244cd-0ebf-43e7-a8a8-dc872607ebcd/02_2014_verbandsstrafe.pdf (last visited 7 Oct 2020).

2. Legal proposals

a) Establishing a Germany-wide public prosecutor's office for capital markets crimes

It is certainly not optimal that the supervision of stock-exchange members in Germany is divided between the BaFin, the local stock markets' trade-monitoring offices and the local public prosecutor's offices.[15] If the authorities require years to investigate before the proceedings are closed, punishable acts will not be sanctioned as they should. In concrete terms, only the company concerned can assess the extent to which the allegations made in a research report are accurate or not. In this respect, the supervisory authorities are also dependent on the know-how of the company concerned. Ideally, the BaFin, the trade-monitoring office and the company concerned would cooperate quickly so that trading on the stock exchange could also be suspended rapidly.

In addition, a more effective public prosecutor's office should be called for. It is unrealistic to expect 20 or 30 public prosecutor's offices throughout Germany to build up know-how in the area of market manipulation. It also makes less sense for the relevant public prosecutor's office to keep this know-how up to date if such an offence is prosecuted only once every few years. Several Higher Regional Courts in a federal state can already set up an Attorney General's Office pursuant to Section 143(4) GVG. It would be even more preferable if there were only one public prosecutor's office at the largest German stock exchange in Frankfurt, Germany.[16] Political endeavours in this direction have not yet been successful. However, when it comes to achieving parity of power in relation to organised crime, appropriate expertise will be needed. Alternatively, the Federal Prosecutor (who may even now assume responsibility) could take charge of such violations as state security offences or certain serious offences involving a foreign terrorist group (Sections 142a and 120 GVG).

15 However, the coordination among each other is described as good.

16 For the competent public prosecutor's office in Frankfurt am Main, see *Waßmer*, in: Fuchs (ed.), Wertpapierhandelsgesetz (2nd ed. 2016), vor §§ 38–40b, para. 63.

b) The right to implement regulatory sanctions

Another option would be to strengthen the BaFin's powers.[17] Specifically, the supervisory authority could be given the right to implement regulatory sanctions rather than handing the process over to the public prosecutor's office. In this way, the powers of intervention that the BaFin already has could also be used more efficiently.[18] Since the implementation of the Market Abuse Directive (*Marktmissbrauchsrichtlinie* – MAR), the Securities Trading Act (*Wertpapierhandelsgesetz* – WpHG) has provided for heavy fines for market manipulation: up to EUR 15 million and 15 % of total sales.[19] If large fines were imposed on companies in accordance with Sections 30 and 130 of the Administrative Offences Act (*Ordnungswidrigkeitengesetz* – OWiG), the short-selling industry could be contained.

III. The supervisory system in European capital markets law

1. Harmonisation efforts over the past few decades

a) The Lamfalussy process

Since 1985, the European Commission (the Commission) has committed itself to the concept of minimum harmonisation.[20] Capital markets law was characterised by this general approach, and many legislative areas featured so-called minimum clauses that expressly allowed for stricter national law.[21] Thus, no level playing field could be established across Europe. Under the direction of Baron Alexander Lamfalussy, the Commission set up a Committee of Wise Men in July 2000, which investigated how the efficient and dynamic functioning of the securities market could

---

17 This is also the result of *Maume*, 180 ZHR 2016, 385, 394.

18 See Section 6 WpHG.

19 See Section 120(15) number 2 and (18) number 1 WpHG.

20 *Köndgen*, in: Basedow et al. (eds.), Economic Regulation and Competition of Services in the EU, Germany and Japan (2002), 27, 47 et seqq.; *Köndgen*, in: Everling and Roth (eds.), Mindestharmonisierung im Europäischen Binnenmarkt (1997), 111.

21 See Article 6 Council Directive 89/592/EEC of 13 Nov 1989 (no longer in force); recital 5 Council Directive 79/279/EEC of 5 Mar 1979; recital 3 and Article 11(1) of Council Directive 93/22/EEC of 10 May 1993. Further examples in *Möllers*, The Role of Law in European Integration (2003), 11 et seq.

be guaranteed by EU regulation.[22] This was first effected with the release of the four framework directives of the so-called Lamfalussy process: the Market Abuse Directive,[23] the Prospectus Directive,[24] the Misuse of Financial Instruments Directive (MiFID)[25] and the Transparency Directive.[26] To overcome the existing problems, the Committee suggested a four-stage process for creating European law in the area of financial services, which was ultimately based on the Comitology Decision of the Council of the European Union.[27] Two committees were set up: the European Securities Committee and the Committee of European Securities Regulators (the CESR).

At the third stage, the CESR had to specify the norms created at the first and second stages of the Lamfalussy process.[28] Its goal was to ensure that the Member States' national supervisory bodies transposed and implemented the norms, created during the first two stages of the process, in a harmonised way.[29] This took place by means of supposedly non-binding standards, guidelines and recommendations.[30] Guidelines tended to be oriented towards supervisory authorities and recommendations directly towards market participants.[31] In contrast to the WpHG, no duties were allocated to the CESR in any European framework directive. The directives only delegated to the CESR the interpretive authority regarding the norms created in the first two stages. The CESR was not permitted to undertake any activity that went beyond the objects of the framework and implementing directives. The work of the CESR at the third stage of the

---

22 Final Report of the Committee of Wise Men on the Regulation of European Securities Markets (7 Oct 2020), https://www.esma.europa.eu/sites/default/files/library/2015/11/lamfalussy_report.pdf (last visited 7 Oct 2020).

23 Council Directive 2003/6/EC of 28 Jan 2003 (market abuse).

24 Council Directive 2003/71/EC of 4 Nov 2003.

25 Council Directive 2004/39/EC of 21 Apr 2004.

26 Council Directive 2004/109/EC of 15 Dec 2004.

27 Council Decision 1999/468/EC of 28 Jun 1999 (no longer in force); on this topic see *Karpf* et al., 3 Zeitschrift für Finanzmarktrecht 2007, 1, 6; *Schmolke*, 22 NZG 2005, 912.

28 CESR, The Role of CESR at 'Level 3' under the Lamfalussy process (Apr 2004), CESR/04–104b.

29 See Final Report of the Committee of Wise Men on the Regulation of European Securities Markets (15 Feb 2001), 46, https://www.esma.europa.eu/sites/default/files/library/2015/11/lamfalussy_report.pdf (last visited 7 Oct 2020).

30 *Ferran*, Building an EU Securities Market (2004), 104.

31 CESR, Publication and Consolidation of MiFID Market Transparency Data (Feb 2007), CESR/07–043, para. 1.14.

Lamfalussy process was, as such, already characterised as non-binding in the final report of the Committee of Wise Men.[32] This was also consistent with the the CESR's perception of itself, according to which recommendations did not constitute acts creating law and therefore did not require any national transposition.[33] The Lamfalussy process has since been extended from securities to banking,[34] insurance and pension funds,[35] and has seen committees created to improve the supervision of finance groups that offer services in banking, insurance and securities.[36]

b) *Larosière*: from the CESR to the ESMA

Following the Larosière Report[37], the European Commission proposed a supervisory scheme built around three European supervisory authorities.[38]

---

32 Final Report of the Committee of Wise Men on the Regulation of European Securities Markets (15 Feb 2001), 38: "The outcome of this work would be non-binding although clearly it would carry considerable authority.".

33 CESR, The Role of CESR at 'Level 3' under the Lamfalussy process – Action Plan for 2005 (Oct 2004), CESR/04–527b, para. 2.3.9; CESR, Publication and Consolidation of MiFID Transparency Data (Feb 2007), CESR/07–043, para. 1.12: "The outcome of CESR's work is reflected in common guidelines and recommendations *which do not constitute European Union legislation and will not require national legislative action*" [emphasis added]. See also CESR's recommendations for the consistent implementation of the European Commission's Regulation on Prospectuses No. 809/2004 (Jan 2005), CESR/05–054b, para. I.9.

34 For this purpose, the European Banking Committee (EBC) – Commission Decision 2004/10/EC of 5 Nov 2003 – and the Committee of European Banking Supervisors (CEBS) – Commission Decision 2004/5/EC of 5 Nov 2003 – were established.

35 A European Insurance and Occupational Pensions Committee (EIOPC) – Commission Decision 2004/9/EC of 5 Nov 2003 – and a Committee of European Insurance and Occupational Pensions Supervisors (*CEIOPS*) – Commission Decision 2004/6/EC of 5 Nov 2003 – were established.

36 The European Finance Conglomerate Committee (EFCC) based on Council Directive 2002/87/EC of 16 Dec 2002 was established.

37 Larosière Group, Report of the High-Level Group on Financial Supervision in the EU (25 Feb 2009), para. 67 and recommendation 3: "[...] within the EU, a strengthened CESR should be in charge of registering and supervising CRAs.", http://ec.europa.eu/economy_finance/publications/pages/publication14527_en.pdf (last visited 7 Oct 2020).

38 To the following see *Möllers*, 10 EBOR 2010, 379 et seqq.; *Ohler*, in: Derleder, Knops and Bamberger (eds.), Deutsches- und Europäisches Kapitalmarktrecht, (3rd ed. 2017), § 90, para. 23 et seqq.

The European system of supervision is based on two pillars: the macro- and micro-levels.[39] The macro-level supervises systemic risk through the European Systemic Risk Board (the ESRB).[40] The micro-level manages financial-market activities through the European System of Financial Supervision (the ESFS). The ESFS comprises national supervisory authorities in the Member States as well as three new European Supervisory Authorities (the ESAs). The ESAs are: a European Banking Authority (the EBA),[41] a European Insurance and Occupational Pensions Authority (the EIOPA),[42] and a European Securities and Markets Authority (the ESMA).[43] The ESMA cooperates with the ESRB.[44] The regulation expressly mentions Article 114 of the Treaty on the Functioning of the European Union (TFEU) as the source of the European legislature's authority.[45] In addition, there is the European Central Bank (ECB). The ECB has exclusive jurisdiction over the accreditation of all credit institutions. Furthermore, it supervises significant credit institutions.[46]

As the CESR has done in the past, the ESMA is to develop technical standards, guidelines and recommendations to facilitate the interpretation of harmonised EU legislation. So too, the ESMA is to create dispute resolution mechanisms and to ensure the consistent application of harmonised law through a peer-review procedure. The real innovations have remained rather hidden. They do, however, carry tremendous potential for debate as they significantly expand powers at the European level. To ensure the consistent application of EU rules, the proposal for a regulation establishing the ESMA also significantly expands supervisory powers over national authorities compared to the regulation on credit-rating agencies. It introduces a three-step mechanism.[47] First, the ESMA adopts a recommendation for action addressed to the national authority considered to be

---

39 *Kalss*, in: Riesenhuber (ed.), European Legal Methodology (2017), § 19, para. 5.

40 Council Regulation (EU) No. 1092/2010 of 24 Nov 2010.

41 Council Regulation (EU) No. 1093/2010 of 24 Nov 2010.

42 Council Regulation (EU) No. 1094/2010 of 24 Nov 2010.

43 Council Regulation (EU) No. 1095/2010 of 24 Nov 2010.

44 Ibid., Article 36.

45 Ibid., para. 17; reference is made to ECJ, Judgment of 2 May 2006, C-341/04, ECLI:EU:C:2006:281, para. 44 – United Kingdom of Great Britain and Northern Ireland v. European Parliament and Council of the European Union. Prior to this already European Commission, Communication from the European Commission on European financial supervision of 27 May 2009, COM(2009) 252, 8.

46 Articles 4 and 6(4) Council Regulation (EU) No. 1024/2013 of 15 Oct 2013.

47 Recital 28 and Article 39 Council Regulation (EU) No. 1095/2010 of 24 Nov 2010.

deviating from existing EU legislation. Secondly, if the recommendation is not complied with, the Commission may require the national supervisory authority to either take specific action or refrain from acting. Thirdly, the ESMA may, as a last resort, make a decision directed at financial institutions. To ensure healthy market competition, or to guarantee the functioning and integrity of the financial system, the ESMA must be able to intervene as quickly as possible.[48] However, the prerequisites for such an intervention are difficult to satisfy. The following diagram depicts the relationship between the relevant bodies:

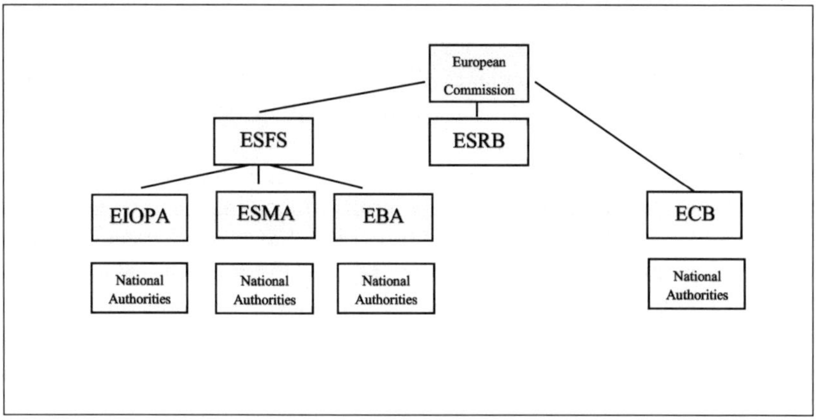

2. Proposals with a view to future regulation

The European supervisory regime is not yet perfect. On the one hand, it is too weak and on the other it is exaggerated, and thus violates the principle of subsidiarity twice.

a) In favour of more: A European task force

It was correct to transfer to the ESMA authority for the areas immediately concerning the internal market. The ESMA had already been responsible

48 Recitals 29 et seq. and Article 17(3), (4) and (6) Council Regulation (EU) No. 1095/2010 of 24 Nov 2010.

for monitoring rating agencies,[49] especially in the areas of short-selling[50] and benchmarks.[51] Like the regulations for competition law, the responsibility of a European supervisory body for capital markets law should always be for *cross-border* cases, as these affect the internal market. The restructuring of European capital markets law has, at the very least, led to an upgrade in the powers of European authorities. In the past, Member States had had exclusive jurisdiction over capital markets law. The reformed Lamfalussy process changed this.

Even if Germany were to become more effective by way of an intervention force and a central public prosecutor's office, this would only be an important first step. With 28 Member States, however, short-sellers would still have an easy time avoiding stock exchanges in other Member States. Therefore, European action is required. Cooperation between national supervisory authorities and the ESMA was indeed contemplated in Articles 22–29 MAR.[52] The BaFin reports that it cooperates with 24 foreign supervisory authorities.[53] Nevertheless, requests for mutual assistance are time-consuming, cumbersome and rarely successful. However, the question is whether this is sufficient and thus establishes the necessary parity of power between the perpetrator and the enforcer.

The requirements of the subsidiarity test in Article 5(3) of the Treaty on the European Union (TEU) are clearly available: negatively speaking, the national authority cannot take sufficient action against these forms of market manipulation. If market manipulation is rightly penalised, then a sanction must also be possible. The inaction or ineffectiveness of the previous legislation damages confidence in capital markets. Ultimately, Article 12 MAR (formerly Section 20a WpHG) and the previous Section 88 of the Stock Exchange Act (*Börsengesetz* – BörsG) remain largely ineffective with regard to misleading research reports in cross-border situations.

European antitrust law has demonstrated its own effectiveness. Over the last 60 years, it has proved to be extremely effective against foreign com-

---

49 Article 5b Council Regulation (EU) No. 1060/2009 of 19 Sept 2009.

50 Article 28 Council Regulation (EU) No. 236/2012 of 14 Mar 2012.

51 Article 37 et seqq. Council Regulation (EU) No. 2016/1011 of 8 Jun 2016; See *Brosig*, Benchmark-Manipulation – Eine Ökonomische und Regulatorische Analyse des Libor Manipulationsskandals (2018).

52 See *Thiele*, Finanzaufsicht (2014), 531 et seq.; *Grundmann*, in: Staub (fdr.), HGB, vol. 10 Bankvertragsrecht Teil 1 (5th ed. 2016), para. 297; *Zollner*, in: Ventoruzzo and Mock (eds.), Market Abuse Regulation (2017), B.24.01 et seqq.

53 BaFin, Jahresbericht der Bundesanstalt für Finanzdienstleistungsaufsicht 2016 (2017), 177.

panies illegally operating on the European market. Landmark claims have been filed against Microsoft, Google and, most recently, Qualcomm.[54] As in competition law, legislative power should always exist for cross-border cases[55] because these affect the internal market. Specifically, market participants enrich themselves at the expense of others through unlawful conduct when the stock price falls. A company is damaged by a lower stock price, but also by numerous – and possibly also professional – market participants if, for example, stop-loss prices are triggered. The reliability and truth of pricing is negatively affected, and confidence in integrity impaired.[56]

If European law is to be finally regulated through European regulations, appropriate powers of intervention are also required, at least in cross-border cases, to achieve the necessary parity of power in relation to this form of organised crime. As a first step, the ESMA's authority would have to be expanded significantly. The US Securities and Exchange Commission (SEC), which takes effective action against market manipulation, illustrates that things could be different.[57] Effective supervision was also demonstrated by the VW diesel scandal in the US. The US Department of Justice ordered the companies Bilfinger, Daimler, Siemens and Volkswagen to have a monitor supervising the companies and reporting back to the Department.[58]

An intervention force like this would require the further expansion of authority at the European level for such serious cases. There is already a Directorate-General (DG) for Financial Stability, Financial Services and Capital Markets Union.[59] Not least the Wirecard scandal has fuelled the political demand for a superordinate European supervisory authority based on the model of the US Securities and Exchange Commission.[60]

---

54 European Commission, "Antitrust: Commission fines Qualcomm €997 million for abuse of dominant market position" (24 Jan 2018), http://europa.eu/rapid/press-release_IP-18-421_int.htm (last visited 7 Oct 2020).

55 See Articles 101(1), 102(1) TFEU.

56 See Council Regulation (EU) No. 596/2014 of 16 Apr 2014, recital.

57 See *Möllers*, 53 International Lawyer 2020 (in printing).

58 See *Zwiebel* and *Lohmeier*, Compliance-Berater 2016, 250 et seqq.; *Schneider*, Compliance-Berater 2017, 441 et seqq.; *Freytag*, FAZ of 10 Feb 2018, 19.

59 For their responsibilities see European Commission, "Financial Stability, Financial Services and Capital Markets Union", https://ec.europa.eu/info/departments/financial-stability-financial-services-and-capital-markets-union_de#responsibilities (last visited 7 Oct 2020). About ESMA competencies, see Articles 8 et seq. Council Regulation (EU) No. 1095/2010 of 24 Nov 2010.

60 Cf. https://boerse.ard.de/aktien/bafin-chef-weist-vorwuerfe-zurueck100.html.

In addition, for reasons of general prevention, consideration should be given to extending authority, and specifically to how the DG Competition could be given the means to intervene. A European ministry of justice would probably be more effective than a local public prosecutor's office. Furthermore, the involvement of the judicial branch could be extended by setting up of a court of first instance for competition matters and one for capital markets.

b) In favour of less: devolving authority on the basis of irrelevance to the internal market

aa) The principles of conferral of powers and subsidiarity derived from Article 5 TEU oppose the automatic urge to regulate through the European institutions. Furthermore, the obligation to justify legislative acts according to Article 296(2) TFEU must additionally secure and provide a basis for this. Apart from this, a regulatory reasoning burden can be demonstrated as the legislative body is obliged to prove the need for the regulation.[61] Fortunately, despite the abovementioned flood of regulations, the EU has withdrawn harmonising regulations over the past few years and therefore devolved authority over these areas to the Member States. Initially, a quarterly-information obligation should also support alignment with US regulations, as they have been demanding these reports since 1946.[62] The introduction of this quarterly-reporting duty was quite controversial because of the significant costs and the influence of special seasonal factors.[63] The requirement for interim reports, in which companies had to disclose certain financial information for the first and third quarters of the financial year (Article 6(1) 2004/109/EEC old version), was again limited by the Transparency Harmonisation Directive (Directive 2013/50/EU). The aim was to reduce the administrative burden on small- and medium-sized businesses, to encourage long-term thinking on the part of the companies

61 Hereto *Montesquieu*, De l'esprit de lois (1748), vol. 2, book 29, chapter 16, translated from French: "When there is no necessity for exceptions and limitations in a law, it is much better to omit them"; cf. *Fleischer*, 37 ZGR 2008, 185, 190.

62 Explanatory Memorandum of the Commission of the European Communities for a Directive on the harmonization of transparency, COM(2003) 138, 16, 20; see also *Merkt* and *Göthel*, RIW 2003, 23 et seqq.

63 The Porsche AG, for example, had left the M-DAX, see for example *Scherff*, FAZ of 8 Aug 2001, 23.

obliged to report, and to condemn the flood of information to investors.[64] The stock markets' private standards can still demand quarterly reports for certain market segments – every Member State can define these for itself.[65] Initially, the EU wanted all publications under corporate and capital markets law (for example, *ad hoc* announcements, directors' dealing announcements, annual financial statements, and interim reports) to be listed in one annual report at the end of a business year. The legislature introduced a disclosure obligation for listed stock corporations through the Securities Prospectus Act (*Wertpapierprospektgesetz* – WpPG), which came into effect on 1 July 2005. However, this information was already available to the capital markets after being published, which meant that, apart from giving rise to additional costs, the annual report did not add any value. This is a perfect example of information overload.[66] Justifiably, the European legislature repealed this act.[67]

bb) It does not serve the purpose of helping the consumer if transactional costs rise to such a degree that banks stop counselling investors. In my opinion, the principles of Article 11 of the directive on investment services in the securities field (Council Directive 93/22/EEC) were sufficient to enable a European standard to be developed. Apart from this, the German courts have developed comprehensive obligations in the area of counselling by banks.[68] The legislative history of MiFiD II, in which Great Britain's fee-based advice and Germany's commission-based advice clashed, demonstrates that harmonisation is often impossible.[69] Instead of favouring one over the other, each Member State should experiment for itself if it would like to delight its banking clients with a consultation protocol, a product-information sheet, extensive requirements for commission

64 *Seibt* and *Wollenschläger*, ZIP 2014, 545, 546; in England and France, the obligation to report quarterly had already been lifted again previously, *Buchheim*, *Hossfeld* and *Schmidt*, WPg 2016, 1347, 1350, 1352.

65 On the Frankfurt Stock Exchange, for example, Section 53 Stock Exchange regulations for the Frankfurt Stock Exchange (*Börsenordnung der Frankfurter Wertpapierbörse* – BörsO FWB) requires a so-called "quarterly report" for companies in the "Prime Standard". This is an abbreviated form of the previous quarterly report. Companies in the "General Standard" are exempt from this requirement.

66 *Möllers*, Juristische Methodenlehre (2nd ed. 2019), § 5, para. 148 et seq.

67 Section 10 WpHG has been deleted by the Act Implementing Directive 2010/73/EU and Amending the Stock Exchange Act of 26 Jun 2012, Federal Law Gazette (BGBl.) of 29 Jun 2012, part I, 1375.

68 Hereto *Möllers* and *Leisch*, in: Gerke and Steiner (eds.), Handwörterbuch des Bank- und Finanzwesens, (3rd ed. 2001), 311 et seqq.

69 In detail *Möllers*, ZEuP 2016, 325, 341 et seqq.

reimbursements (kick-backs) or a complaint register. These requirements are not relevant to the internal market.

c) Realising European legal principles and regulatory objectives under capital markets law

Such a horizontal division of labour relevant to the internal market would also take the principle of subsidiarity under Article 5(3) TEU seriously. Market manipulation meets the requirements of the subsidiarity test in favour of the EU. If the test is viewed negatively, it concludes that the Member State cannot resolve the problem sufficiently, which is why the EU (as a more effective entity) is required to take action against cross-border market manipulation. Ultimately, Article 12 MAR will have no effect in cross-border cases involving misleading Research Reports, just as the previous Sections 20a WpHG and 88 BörsG did not. However, the ineffectiveness of capital markets law also damages trust in capital markets, which is why European enforcement of the law is necessary.

This also applies in the opposite case: if the famous "Lieschen Müller of the Raiffeisenbank Buxtehude"[70] purchases a bond for EUR 1,000, this is neither system-relevant nor does one need a European regulation or directive. But the principle of subsidiarity demands that authority must remain on the lower level if this level can better resolve the problem. This gives rise to a comparison with the ECJ's *Keck* case. The fact that English pubs still serve beer after 10 p.m., or German shops are closed on Sundays, does not affect the internal market and these are only sales-related measures, and as such not protected by the free movement of goods.[71] This is why, in the field of investment-counselling, every Member State should be able to determine itself under which conditions such counselling is permissible.

In addition, the positive and negative sides of the subsidiarity principle would increase efficiency on two fronts: On the one hand, European intervention would assist in those cases in which national authorities are overwhelmed. On the other hand, resources and transactional expenses

70 "Lieschen Müller" is a German placeholder name, referring to the everyman citizen and is often portrayed as being naïve.

71 Essentially ECJ, Judgment of 24 Nov 1993, C-267/91 et al., ECLI:EU:C:1993:905, para. 16 – Criminal proceedings against Keck and Mithouard. See *W. Schroeder* in: Streinz (ed.), EUV/AEUV (3rd ed. 2018), Article 34 TFEU, paras. 41 et seqq., 45; *Kingreen*, in: Callies and Ruffert (eds.), EUV/AEUV (5th ed. 2016), Articles 34–36 TFEU, paras. 49 et seqq.

could be saved if national or local action is sufficient. The European legislature would not weaken the competitiveness of companies and banks in relation to US and Chinese competitors, but strengthen it through clever deregulation.[72] At the same time, with Brexit on the doorstep, it would be possible to demonstrate what a future-oriented Europe might look like.

Bibliography

Bundesanstalt für Finanzdienstleistungsaufsicht, Jahresbericht der Bundesanstalt für Finanzdienstleistungsaufsicht 2016 (2017).

Petra Buck-Heeb, Kapitalmarktrecht (C.F. Müller, 10th ed., Heidelberg 2018).

Nikolaus Bosch, Organisationsverschulden in Unternehmen (Nomos, Baden-Baden 2002).

Isabella Brosig, Benchmark-Manipulation – Eine Ökonomische und Regulatorische Analyse des Libor Manipulationsskandals (Nomos, Baden-Baden 2018).

Regine Buchheim, *Christopher Hossfeld* and *Martin Schmidt*, “Quartalsberichterstattung in Europa”, Die Wirtschaftsprüfung (WPg) 2016, 1347.

Christian Calliess and *Matthias Ruffert* (eds.), EUV/AEUV (C.H. Beck, 5th ed., Munich 2016).

CESR, The Role of CESR at ‘Level 3’ under the Lamfalussy process – Action Plan for 2005 (Oct 2004), CESR/04–527b.

CESR, Publication and Consolidation of MiFID Transparency Data (Feb 2007), CESR/07–043.

CESR, CESR’s recommendations for the consistent implementation of the European Commission’s Regulation on Prospectuses No. 809/ 2004 (Jan 2005), CESR/05–054b.

European Commission, “Antitrust: Commission fines Qualcomm €997 million for abuse of dominant market position” (24 Jan 2018), http://europa.eu/rapid/press-release_IP-18-421_int.htm (last visited 7 Oct 2020).

European Commission, “Financial Stability, Financial Services and Capital Markets Union”, https://ec.europa.eu/info/departments/financial-stability-financial-services-and-capital-markets-union_de#responsibilities (last visited 7 Oct 2020).

European Commission, Explanatory Memorandum of the Commission of the European Communities for a Directive on the harmonization of transparency, COM(2003) 138.

72 To the level playing field see *Hopt* and *Voigt*, in: Hopt and Voigt (eds.), Prospekt- und Kapitalmarktinformationshaftung (2004), 1, 2 et seqq.; rapporteur *Edgardo Maria Iozia* in his opinion of the European Economic and Social Committee, Proposal for a regulation of the European Parliament and the Council on key information documents for investment products, COM(2012) 352, para. 3.4.

European Commission, Communication from the European Commission on European financial supervision, COM(2009) 252.

Ellis Ferran, Building an EU Securities Market (Cambridge University Press, Cambridge 2004).

Holger Fleischer, "Finanzinvestoren im ordnungspolitischen Gesamtgefüge von Aktien-, Bankaufsichts- und Kapitalmarktrecht", 37 Zeitschrift für Unternehmens- und Gesellschaftsrecht (ZGR) 2008, 185.

Bernd Freytag, "Gefährliche Bilanzkosmetik", Frankfurter Allgemeine Zeitung (FAZ) of 10 Feb 2018, 19.

Andreas Fuchs (ed.), Wertpapierhandelsgesetz (WpHG) (C.H. Beck, 2nd ed., Munich 2016).

Benjamin Herz, "Neue Rechtsprechung zum Zugang zu Informationen von Finanzaufsichtsbehörden", Neue Juristische Wochenschrift (NJW) 2018, 2601.

Heribert Hirte and *Thomas M.J. Möllers* (eds.), Kölner Kommentar zum WpHG (Carl Heymanns, 2nd ed., Köln 2014).

Timo Holzborn and *Alexander Israel*, "Das Anlegerschutzverbesserungsgesetz – Die Veränderungen im WpHG, VerkProspG und BörsG und ihre Auswirkungen in der Praxis –", Wertpapiermitteilungen (WM) 2004, 1948.

Klaus J. Hopt and *Hans Christoph Voigt*, „Empfehlungen", in: Klaus J. Hopt and Hans Christoph Voigt (eds.), Prospekt- und Kapitalmarktinformationshaftung (Mohr Siebeck, Tübingen 2004), 1.

Edgardo Maria Iozia, Proposal for a regulation of the European Parliament and the Council on key information documents for investment products, COM(2012) 352.

Susanne Kalss, "European Capital Market Law", in: Karl Riesenhuber (ed.), European Legal Methodology (Intersentia, Cambridge/Antwerp/Portland 2017), 489.

Alexander Karpf, *Corina Weidinger-Sosedan* and *Karin Zartl*, "Die Integration der Finanzmärkte der EU – Die Rolle der CESR und CEIOPS im Lamfallusy-Prozess", 3 Zeitschrift für Finanzmarktrecht (ZFR) 2007, 1.

Eberhard Kempf, *Klaus Lüderssen* and *Klaus Volk*, Unternehmensstrafrecht (De Gruyter, Berlin/Boston 2012).

Johannes Köndgen, "Mindestharmonisierung im Bankrecht", in: Ulrich Everling and Wulf-Henning Roth (eds.), Mindestharmonisierung im Europäischen Binnenmarkt (Nomos, Baden-Baden 1997), 111.

Johannes Köndgen, "Regulation of Banking Services in the European Union: A Comparative View", in: Jürgen Basedow, Harald Baum, Klaus J. Hopt, Hideki Kanda and Toshiyuki Kono (eds.), Economic Regulation and Competition: Regulation of Services in the EU, Germany and Japan (Kluwer Law International, Zuidpoolsingel 2002), 27.

Michael Kubiciel, Die Verbandsstrafe – Verfassungskonformmität, Systemkompatibilität. Folgen, Kölner Papiere zur Kriminalpolitik 2/2014 (Feb 2014), https://assets.uni-augsburg.de/media/filer_public/59/a2/59a244cd-0ebf-43e7-a8a8-dc872607ebcd/02_2014_verbandsstrafe.pdf (last visited 7 Oct 2020).

Larosière Group, Report of the High-Level Group on Financial Supervision in the EU (25 Feb 2009), http://ec.europa.eu/economy_finance/publications/pages/publication14527_en.pdf (last visited 7 Oct 2020).

Philipp Maume, "Staatliche Rechtsdurchsetzung im deutschen Kapitalmarktrecht: eine kritische Bestandsaufnahme", 180 Zeitschrift für das gesamte Handels- und Wirtschaftsrecht (ZHR) 2016, 358.

Hanno Merkt and *R. Stephan Göthel*, "Vorschriften und Ansätze der Quartalsberichterstattung: Vergleich USA – Deutschland", Recht der internationalen Wirtschaft (RIW) 2003, 23.

Charles de Montesquieu, De l'esprit des lois, vol. 2 (Barillot & Fils, Geneva 1748).

Thomas M.J. Möllers and *Charis Niedorf*, "BVerwG, 24.5.2011 – BVerwG 7 C 6.10: Auskunftspflicht der BaFin hinsichtlich der Überschreitung meldepflichtiger Beteiligungen an Drittstaatemittenten", Entscheidungen zum Wirtschaftsrecht (EWiR) 2011, 569.

Thomas M.J. Möllers and *Franz Clemens Leisch*, "Prospekthaftung", in: Wolfgang Gerke and Manfred Steiner (eds.), Handwörterbuch des Bank- und Finanzwesens (Schäffer-Poeschel, 3rd ed., Stuttgart 2001).

Thomas M.J. Möllers and *Thomas Wenninger*, "Informationsansprüche gegen die BaFin im Lichte des neuen Informationsfreiheitsgesetzes (IFG)", 170 Zeitschrift für das gesamte Handels- und Wirtschaftsrecht (ZHR) 2006, 455.

Thomas M.J. Möllers, "Europäische Gesetzgebungslehre 2.0: Die dynamische Rechtsharmonisierung im Kapitalmarktrecht am Beispiel von MiFID II und PRIIP", Zeitschrift für Europäisches Privatrecht (ZEuP) 2016, 325.

Thomas M.J. Möllers, Juristische Methodenlehre (C.H. Beck, 2nd ed., Munich 2019).

Thomas M.J. Möllers, "Market Manipulation trough Short-Selling and misleading financial analyses", 53 International Lawyer 2020 (in printing).

Thomas M.J. Möllers, "Sources of Law in European Securities Regulation – Effective Regulation, Soft Law and Legal Taxonomy from Lamfalussy to Larosière", 10 European Business Organization Law Review (EBOR) 2010, 379.

Thomas M.J. Möllers, The Role of Law in European Integration (Nova Science Publishers, Hauppauge 2003).

Christoph Ohler, "§ 90 Europäisches Bankenaufsichtsrecht", in: Peter Derleder, Kai-Oliver Knops and Heinz Georg Bamberger (eds.), Deutsches und europäisches Bank- und Kapitalmarktrecht (Springer, 3rd ed., Berlin/Heidelberg 2017).

Mark Pieth and *Radha Ivory*, Corporate Criminal Liability (Springer, Dordrecht/Heidelberg/London/New York 2011).

Dyrk Scherff, "Börse verbannt Porsche aus dem M-Dax", Frankfurter Allgemeine Zeitung (FAZ) of 8 Aug 2001, 23.

Olaf Schneider, "Step-by-step: Das neue Compliance-System bei Bilfinger", Compliance Berater (CB) 2017, 441.

Klaus Ulrich Schmolke, "Der Lamfalussy-Prozess im Europäischen Kapitalmarktrecht – eine Zwischenbilanz" 22 Neue Zeitschrift für Gesellschaftsrecht (NZG) 2005, 912.

Christoph H. Seibt and *Bernward Wollenschläger*, "Revision des Europäischen Transparenzregimes: Regelungsinhalte der TRL 2013 und Umsetzungsbedarf", Zeitschrift für Wirtschaftsrecht (ZIP) 2014, 545.

Hermann Staub (fdr.), *Claus-Wilhelm Canaris*, *Mathias Habersack* and *Carsten Schäfer* (eds.), Handelsgesetzbuch (HGB), vol. 10 Bankenvertragsrecht Teil 1 (De Gruyter, 5th ed., Berlin 2016).

Rudolf Streinz (ed.), EUV/AEUV (C.H. Beck, 3rd ed., Munich 2018).

Anja Tschierke, Die Sanktionierung des Unternehmensverbundes: Bestandsaufnahme, Perspektiven und Europäisierung (Nomos, Baden-Baden 2013).

Marco Ventoruzzo and *Sebastian Mock* (eds.), Market Abuse Regulation (Oxford University Press, Oxford 2017).

The Committee of Wise Men, Final Report of the Committee of Wise Men on the Regulation of European Securities Markets (15 Feb 2001), https://www.esma.europa.eu/sites/default/files/library/2015/11/lamfalussy_report.pdf (last visited 7 Oct 2020).

Alexander Thiele, Finanzaufsicht (Mohr Siebeck, Tübingen 2014).

Sebastian Zwiebel and *Markus Lohmeier*, "Corporate Monitoring: Eine Chance für Deutschland?", Compliance Berater (CB) 2016, 250.

Register of cases

European Court of Justice (ECJ)

ECJ, Judgment of 12 Nov 2014, C-140/13, ECLI:EU:C:2014:2362 – Altmann et al. v. BaFin.

ECJ, Judgment of 19 Jun 2018, C-15/16, ECLI:EU:C:2018:464 – BaFin v. Baumeister.

ECJ, Judgment of 12 Oct 2004, C-222/02, ECLI:EU:C:2004:606 – Paul et al.

ECJ, Judgment of 2 May 2006, ECLI:EU:C:2006:281 – United Kingdom of Great Britain and Northern Ireland v. European Parliament and Council of the European Union.

ECJ, Judgment of 24 Nov 1993, C-267/91 et al., ECLI:EU:C:1993:905 – Criminal proceedings against Keck and Mithouard.

German Federal Constitutional Court (BVerfG)

BVerfG, Judgment of 24 Jul 1962, 2 BvF 4/61, BVerfGE 14, 197.

German Federal Court of Justice (BGH)

BGH, Judgment of 20 Jan 2005, III ZR 48/01, BGHZ 162, 49 – State liability in the event of incorrect banking supervision.

Federal Administrative Court (BVerwG)

BVerwG, Judgment of 24 May 2011, 7 C 6/10, ZIP 2011, 1331.